BUDGET EUROPE ACCESS®

Orientation	2
Amsterdam/*The Netherlands*	6
Barcelona/*Spain*	24
Berlin/*Germany*	42
Florence/*Italy*	62
London/*England*	82
Paris/*France*	104
Prague/*Czech Republic*	132
Rome/*Italy*	150
Venice/*Italy*	172
Zurich/*Switzerland*	192
Index	207

Second Edition ©1996 by **ACCESS**®PRESS. All rights reserved. No portion of this publication may be reproduced or transmitted in any form or manner by any means, including, but not limited to, graphic, electronic, and mechanical methods, photocopying, recording, taping, or any informational storage and retrieval systems without explicit permission from the publisher. **ACCESS**® is a registered trademark of HarperCollins Publishers Inc.

Orientation

Time was, you could tame that spirit of wanderlust by traipsing through Europe's great cities on as little as five bucks a day. Granted, it was a budget trek, and you didn't slumber under goose-feather comforters or dine on caviar and Dom Pérignon, but it was possible to sleep, eat, and see spectacular sights for a reasonable price. Today that allowance wouldn't let you wet your whistle at a sidewalk cafe on the **Champs-Elysées**, let alone pay for a bedroom at an Italian pensione. Still, that doesn't mean frugal globe-trotters should put away their passports and toss out their backpacks. Despite the sobering impact the weak dollar, high inflation, and other fiscal woes have had on many countries' economies (not to mention the effect they've had on travelers' disposable incomes), you can still see Europe on a budget—though the minimum expenditure is more likely to be $50 a day, *if* you manage your money right.

How can you visit Europe's premier attractions and get the most bang for your buck? *Budget Europe ACCESS* tells you where to see the best for less in 10 top European travel destinations: **Amsterdam, Barcelona, Berlin, Florence, London, Paris, Prague, Rome, Venice,** and **Zurich.**

Sure, there are less costly cities to explore on the Continent, but most travelers aren't planning their trip around Europe's cheapest beds and burgers. They're usually more interested in a first-hand perspective of some of the most memorable European venues. Each chapter in this guide includes a city introduction that pinpoints the destination's appeal, followed by coverage of the city, neighborhood by neighborhood. So whether you opt to visit all 10 of these urban hot spots in one fell swoop or simply hopscotch from the canals of Amsterdam to the mountains of Zurich, this guide provides you with a pennywise selection of lodgings, restaurants, and each city's most intriguing attractions.

Begin with an amble through Amsterdam's lively university district, **Spui.** You'll find that the convivial "brown cafes" (Dutch beer halls) are the perfect spot to hoist a cold Heineken or sample a potent *jenever* (gin). Wander over to the blossom-laden barges at the floating flower market on the **Singel Canal.** In Barcelona, exuberant Modernista architecture holds center stage. The city is filled with buildings designed by **Antoni Gaudí i Cornet**, from the 1906 private home, **Casa Batlló**, to his final and unfinished masterpiece, the **Templo Expiatorio de la Sagrada Família** (Church of the Holy Family). An evening of Baroque music under the sweeping roof of Berlin's **Philharmonie**, followed by a fiery nightcap of schnapps and a plate of *weisswurst* (veal sausage), is an indulgence that won't decimate your budget. Although little remains of the **Berlin Wall**, readers of spy fiction will want to visit the storehouse of Cold War memories at the **Checkpoint Charlie Museum.**

There is little in the Western World that can rouse the passions of culture buffs like the incomparable Renaissance arts of Florence, the hometown of Michelangelo and Leonardo da Vinci. No matter how tight the budget, a visit to the **Galleria degli Uffizi** (Uffizi Gallery) is worth every penny. Visitors to London with an interest in architecture will find the artistry of **Christopher Wren** irresistible: His masterpiece, **St. Paul's Cathedral**, stands proudly amid modern office buildings in the heart of the city. Those of a literary bent can browse to their hearts' content at the specialized bookstalls in **Bloomsbury**, north of **Covent Garden** near the **British**

Museum, or pay homage to English literary giants such as Chaucer and Spenser in the **Poet's Corner** of **Westminster Abbey.** In Paris, just a walk along the banks of the **Seine** affords views of formal gardens, Baroque bridges, the **Tour Eiffel** (Eiffel Tower), and **Notre-Dame.** The price of admission to the **Musée du Louvre** enables you to view the priceless *Venus de Milo, Mona Lisa,* and 400,000 other treasures housed there.

The cobblestoned streets and arched bridges of Prague's **Staré Město** (Old Town) are among the loveliest anywhere in Europe. In this city, such Old World charm exists side by side with a wide variety of avant-garde art and music. Discover Prague's young spirit on a late-night visit to the **Rock Club Bunkr.** The ultimate day in Rome might include exploring the archaeological sites of the **Foro Romano** (Roman Forum), stopping off at **Basilica San Pietro** (St. Peter's Basilica) to see Renaissance piety at its grandest, and a truly romantic dinner at a homey trattoria. But, if it's romance you want, nothing compares to Venice. The **Canal Grande** (Grand Canal) meanders past monuments to Europe's mercantile history and architectural triumphs, offering views of ornate, orderly Renaissance palazzi, churches and towers, the romance of gliding gondolas, and the original essence of cosmopolitanism.

Zurich, an enclave of Alpine hospitality with its friendly residents and orderly streets, is predictably Swiss—immaculate. Art and architecture meet across the ages at the **Fraumünster,** a venerable church whose stained-glass windows by Marc Chagall and Alberto Giacometti add a 20th-century flourish to the 13th-century architecture.

What you won't find in this book are pointers for procuring a park bench for the night or where to wash dishes in exchange for a bed and a breakfast; you'll have to ferret out those kinds of bargains on your own. But we offer the insider's scoop on out-of-the-way cafes that allow you to dine like a prince on a pauper's per diem, buy wine that's cheaper (and more palate-pleasing) than Evian, and locate low-budget lodgings with flushable toilets, electricity, and other essentials all for a price that won't bankrupt you for the coming year.

Thriftiness—whether forced or voluntary—has its intangible rewards as well. Visitors who bypass the beaten path wind up in spots where they meet locals and are privy to an authentic taste of the city's culture, whether it's in a neighborhood pub sharing pints of bitters between rounds of darts or jostling among residents to buy bread, fruit, and wine at a weekend bazaar. These are the unpredictable experiences that are truly priceless—and those that will linger long after the memory of a room with a view has faded.

Serendipity, of course, adds to the excitement of navigating through Europe. As any veteran traveler will point out, many of the highlights of an overseas sojourn are unexpected events and encounters: finding, for instance, the perfect trattoria straight out of Fellini at the epicenter of an old piazza when searching for a hostel, or stepping into one of Prague's solemn, ancient synagogues amid the 20th-century din of democracy and discotheques. You may have to stop and count your pennies, *lire, centimes,* or *pfennig* from time to time and regretfully pass up a few luxe hotels, but don't let it dampen your spirits. After all, while funds may be limited, adventures are still free for the taking.

Orientation

How To Read This Guide

BUDGET EUROPE ACCESS® is arranged so you can see at a glance where you are and what is around you. The numbers next to the entries in the following chapters correspond to the numbers on the maps. The text is color-coded according to the kind of place described:

Restaurants/Clubs: Red   **Hotels:** Blue
Shops/ 🌳 Outdoors: Green   **Sights/Culture:** Black

Rating the Restaurants and Hotels

The restaurant star ratings take into account the quality, service, atmosphere, and uniqueness of the establishment. A pricier restaurant doesn't necessarily ensure an enjoyable evening; however, a small, relatively unknown spot could have good food, professional service, and a lovely atmosphere. Therefore, on a purely subjective basis, stars are used to judge the overall dining value (see the star ratings at right). Keep in mind that chefs and owners often change, which sometimes drastically affects the quality of a restaurant. The ratings in this guidebook are based on information available at press time.

The price ratings, as categorized at right, apply to restaurants and lodging. These figures describe general price-range relationships among other restaurants and hotels in the same city. The restaurant price ratings are based on the average cost of an entrée for one person, excluding tax and tip. Hotel price ratings reflect the base price of a standard room for two people for one night during the peak season.

Restaurants

★ Good
★★ Very Good
★★★ Excellent
★★★★ An Extraordinary Experience
$ On a Shoestring Budget
$$ The Price is Right

Hotels

$ On a Shoestring Budget
$$ The Price is Right

Map Key

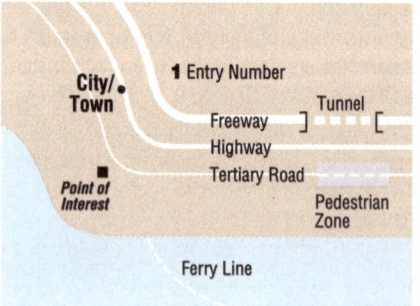

City/Town
1 Entry Number
Freeway
Tunnel
Highway
Tertiary Road
Point of Interest
Pedestrian Zone
Ferry Line

Trains, Buses, & Automobiles

When exploring your travel options, you may want to consider renting a car for one leg of the trip or longer. Having a car at your disposal allows you go where you want to, when you want to—not just when the train schedule says so. The countryside suddenly becomes accessible, for instance, when you're not confined to the larger cities and towns

along train routes. Car travel can also make economic sense for a small group: Four people can usually travel more cheaply by automobile than by paying individual train or bus fares, despite the outrageous cost of gasoline in Europe.

There are, however, numerous downsides to car travel that you should take into account, not the least of which is that you stand to miss the chance encounters with other train and bus travelers that often make for spontaneous changes in plans. Europeans also tend to be aggressive motorists and they can become understandably peeved (to put it mildly) with foreigners who don't grasp the local rules of the road. Driving through big cities like Paris and Rome is to be avoided if you desire a favorable impression of those places. And what if you're traveling alone or with only one other equally frugal person?

Happily, there are various rail passes to choose from, as alternatives to the individual train and bus fares. The multitude of different rail passes (international, regional, and national) are designed for either extended treks or

4

Orientation

intermittent travel throughout the continent. The longer the pass, the cheaper it is per day. The *Eurailpass* offers the widest range of consecutive rail travel destinations—17 countries in all, for durations ranging from 15 days to three months—making it possible to do anything from the Grand Tour to a single country. The *Eurailpass* is most economical for travel in countries whose rail systems are expensive (like Germany, Ireland, and Switzerland), or on itineraries that cover hundreds of miles a day. However, although passes are convenient, individual tickets in countries such as the Czech Republic, Portugal, and Italy may in fact be cheaper than multiple-day passes.

Adult passes (age 26 or older) are sold only on a first-class basis, whereas youth passes land you in perfectly comfy—and 50 percent cheaper—second-class. Upgrades are possible, as are refunds, though only for up to 85 percent of the remaining value. Special "partner" passes allow a traveling companion (assuming they continue to travel in tandem) to pay half-fare.

The little brother of the *Eurailpass*, the *Europass*, offers many overnight accommodations (berths, sleeperettes, etc.), as well as seat reservations and other perks, at an even lower price. The *Europass* is available in combinations of three, four, or five contiguous countries; you can buy a pass for the Benelux and Scandinavian countries, or a *European East Pass*, which covers Austria, the Czech Republic, Hungary, Poland, and Slovakia.

Outside the **Eurail** system, Great Britain has its own comprehensive rail system called **BritRail**. Partly because of the advent of the Channel Tunnel (or "Chunnel"), **BritRail** passes can now be combined with several other **Eurail** national railways—the *BritIreland*, *BritFrance*, and *BritGermany Railpasses*. The fare for the Chunnel *Eurostar* is not included in the **BritRail** or **Eurail** mainland passes because its prices fluctuate by season and demand. *Flexipasses* provide even more permutations for travelers with less stringent itineraries; they're available for five, 10, or 15 days of travel within a two-month period.

Europe's overnight rail accommodations are often good deals. The *couchettes*, in particular, allow safe and uninterrupted slumber. With an extra cost of about $15 in Europe (around $24 through a US agent), these compartments are monitored by attendants who handle your tickets and customs needs for you while you sleep. Book in advance.

Buses often can be the superior mode of long-distance travel in individual countries. Spain and Portugal, for example, have much cheaper public bus systems, and Spain's *Flexipass* is inordinately expensive. Greece, too, has a slow and frustrating train system but a good bus network (although the island-hopping ferries, the choice of most Argonauts these days, are competitively priced). A new network of buses throughout Europe, created with student-age travelers in mind, is **Eurobus**. Youth can travel on this one-way, figure-eight route (Munich is the crossroads) for three months for $325 and two months for $250 ($75 more apiece for adult fare). Call **Eurobus** (c/o Eurotrips) at 800/517.7778 or ask your local travel agent. Also new to the budget bus market is **Cityzap**. At press time, it operated twice daily out of London, Paris, and Amsterdam. The fare is $49 one way between any two cities, $86 round-trip. Contact **Cityzap** (c/o Thomas McFerran Inc.) at 800/430.9070.

Finally, there's also the option of various a la carte combos for car and other add-ons, for those who wish to explore farther into the hinterland than can be done by train. **Rail Europe**, the outfit that sells **Eurail** passes, has devised a way for you to enjoy the best of both travel options in one package deal through its *Euraildrive* pass. Call **Rail Europe** at 800/438.7245 for reservations and information, or ask your local travel agent. The pass must be purchased before leaving the US. For added savings, inquire about rail pass supplements—discounted fares on affiliated hotels, commuter rail lines, buses, and ferries—even ships in the Norwegian fjords and mountain lifts in the Swiss Alps!

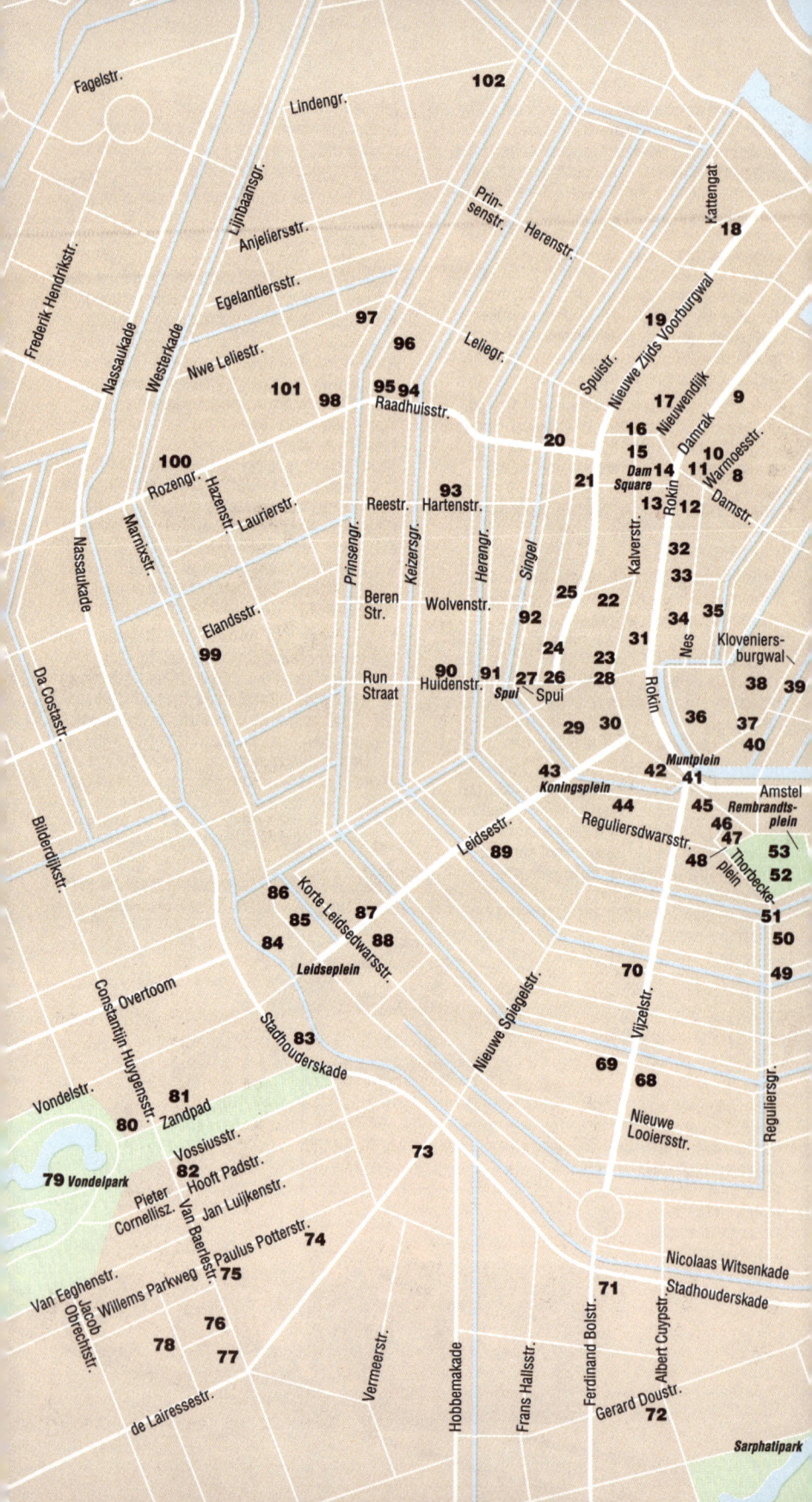

Amsterdam

One either hates Amsterdam for its funkiness or adores it for its offbeat, quirky charm—there's no middle ground. Fortunately, most visitors fall in love with this compact, cosmopolitan city of canals and gabled houses and get in step with the congenial, open-minded, and open-hearted Dutch.

For a wonderful first day in the Dutch capital, dally along the canals in early morning and then delight in the sights, smells, and sounds of one of the daily markets: Best choices are the **Waterlooplein** flea market, the canal-side **Bloemenmarkt** (flower market) on the **Singel** canal, or the **Albert Cuyp Markt**, the city's largest street market.

Near **Waterlooplein** is **Rembrandthuis**, the home of 17th-century Dutch artist Rembrandt van Rijn. Or plant yourself for an afternoon in the **Amsterdam Historisch Museum** (Amsterdam Historical Museum) to learn more about the wealthy merchants who inhabited all those canal houses in the 17th century and the global trading empire that financed them. Nearby, don't miss the quiet courtyard, the **Begijnhof**, with its tiny houses and quiet **Engelsekerk** (English Church).

You'll need at least one full day to do justice to Amsterdam's art museums. The **Rijksmuseum** offers the world's finest collection of Northern European paintings, including Rembrandt's famous *The Night Watch;* the **Van Gogh Museum** displays nearly every work ever created by that artist; plus, on the same block, the **Stedelijk Museum** is a premier museum of contemporary art. A delightful end to a day of art is a concert at the nearby **Concertgebouw**, an acoustically perfect auditorium favored by many of the great classical music performers of the world, or a performance of ballet, modern dance, or opera at the city's large and glittering **Muziektheater** overlooking the **Amstel River.**

Finally, be sure to visit the **Anne Frankhuis** (Anne Frank House) and, if possible, save time, too, for the **Joods Historisch Museum** (Jewish Historical Museum), which documents the impact of World War II on the Jewish community of Amsterdam. Also worth visiting is the **Tropenmuseum** (Tropical Museum), which is devoted to the cultures of Holland's former colonies in the East and West Indies. For a change of pace, shoppers can follow a seemingly endless path of streets that twist and turn through the city from **Dam Square** to the **Concertgebouw**, offering non-stop opportunities to buy all sorts of goods—fine and shoddy, costly or not.

Night is a time of special charm along the lamplit canals; it's also a spirited time in Amsterdam, particularly on weekends. There are countless "brown cafes," the Dutch equivalent of cozy neighborhood bars, throughout the city. The principal discotheques, clubs, and cafes are centered near **Rembrandtplein** and **Koningsplein;** and there is a small cluster of night spots on **Nes**, a back street in the student quarter. At **Leidseplein**, restaurants and fast-food outlets are mixed among the small clubs that feature live music. The **Holland Casino Amsterdam** is here too, and the well-known **Bimhuis** jazz mecca is nearby. And all the world knows about **Walletjes** (Red Light District)—a roadside attraction for tourists in the evening hours and a center of hard-core (but legal) prostitution later at night.

However you decide to discover Amsterdam—on foot or by canal—take your time and explore at will. The city spent centuries building its intriguing network of alleys and waterways and the fascinating array of attractions and amusements here—it can wait a few days longer while you fully admire its many attributes.

To call from the US, dial 011 (international access code), 31 (country code), 20 (city code), and the local number. When calling from inside the Netherlands, dial 020 and the local number. City codes appearing within the text are for areas outside Amsterdam.

Getting to Amsterdam
Airports
Located about 24 kilometers (15 miles) from downtown Amsterdam, **Schiphol Airport** (06/35034050) is one of the largest and most efficient airports in the world. In addition to tourist information desks, currency-exchange facilities, and car-rental agencies, there are five wings of flight gates and a 45-store duty-free shopping center offering more than 120,000 items. All are open daily.

The cheapest way into town is offered by the national train company, **Nederlandse Spoonwager NS** (06/9292). Trains to and from **Centraal Station** depart every 20 minutes, from 5:30AM to midnight daily, and the trip takes about 16 minutes.

A **KLM Shuttle** (6491393) operates a bus service to and from the airport, using several central hotels as pickup and drop-off points. Buses run daily; every 30 minutes between 6:30AM and 3PM, once an hour from 3 to 8PM.

Avis (6836062), **Budget** (6216066), and **Europcar** (6832123) all maintain counters for rental cars at the airport.

Train Station (Long-Distance)
Debarking at busy **Centraal Station** (domestic information 06/9292, international information 6202266) could hardly be more convenient for the first-time visitor. (It could be safer, though, so guard your bags carefully.) Positioned at the hub of Amsterdam's concentric semicircles of canals and streets, the terminal not only is served by international trains, but also is a starting point for most of the bus and tram routes through the city and suburbs.

Getting around Amsterdam
Bicycles Amsterdammers really do ride bicycles for transportation, and in the crowded city center they favor them over every other means of transit. To join the action, try **Holland Rent-A-Bike** (Damrak 247, near Beursplein, 6223207) or **Take-A-Bike** (Stationsplein 33 at Centraal Station, 6248391).

Buses Buses leave from in front of **Centraal Station** (06/9292) and are best for taking trips to the countryside and the suburbs. (For inner-city transportation see "Trams," below.)

Canal Boats A leisurely way to appreciate the city's fine canal-side houses is to take a trip on a canal boat. **Canal Bus** (6239886) follows two routes through the canals between **Centraal Station** and the **Rijksmuseum,** making six stops for access to major attractions; day tickets (which include reduced admission fees to two museums) allow you to get on and off at will. **Amsterdam Museumboot** (6222181) makes a seven-stop circuit throughout the city and entitles day-ticket holders to a 50-percent discount on museum entrance fees. Both companies also offer hourlong tours. Boats operate daily, leaving from the piers opposite **Centraal Station.**

Driving This compact, water-laced city is *not* driver-friendly. There's a shortage of parking spaces coupled with well-enforced parking restrictions, madly careening trams and cyclists to be mindful of, and hopelessly snarled traffic. It's best to stash the car for the duration in one of the secured parking lots or garages around town: **Parking Plus** (Prins Hendrikkade, near Centraal Station, 6854061) or **Parking Byzantium** (Tesselschadestraat, near the Leidseplein, 6166416).

Subway Amsterdam's single-line underground transit system is very fast, but is primarily for commuters living in the outlying areas. Call 06/9292 for more information.

Taxis Cabs generally don't troll the streets in search of fares. Taxi stands are scattered throughout downtown—at Leidseplein, Rembrandtplein, **Museumplein, Spui, Westerkerk,** and **Centraal Station.** For 24-hour pick-up call the central taxi number (6777777). For a change of pace, try a water taxi (6222181).

Tours The **Yellow Bike Tour Company** (6206940) offers group bike excursions around the city and surrounding countryside. **NZH Travel** (6250772) schedules city tours by both bus and canal boat, and special excursions to nearby fishing villages and windmills and day trips to Delft and Rotterdam. **Mee in Mokum** (6251390) offers 2.5-hour walking tours of Amsterdam's historical and cultural sites. Bonus tip: A free ferry crosses the **IJ**-harbor just behind **Centraal Station** and offers terrific views of the harbor and downtown Amsterdam; it runs 24 hours daily.

Trams These brightly painted cars—rolling advertisements for everything from orange juice to **MTV**—are the ideal transport for city exploring. They operate from 5:45AM to midnight, Monday through Friday. Weekends, service begins at 6:30AM on Saturday, 7:30AM on Sunday, and the last trams return to **Centraal Station** at 12:30AM. Day tickets and discounted, multiple-ride *stripkaarten* (strip tickets) can be used on trams, buses, and the subway; purchase them at the ticket office at **Stationsplein** opposite **Centraal Station,** and at most tobacco shops and post offices. Stamp your *stripkaarten* at the yellow machine on board (one strip per zone traveled, including the zone you travel from, which means stamping two strips per trip for most central destinations). For tram schedules and information, call 06/9292.

Walking Amsterdam is a big city on the scale of a small town, and walking is the best way to see it. It's also the fastest, easiest way to get from place to place and often incorporates an additional feature of your visit: the shortest route from **Dam Square** to the **Rijksmuseum,** for example, takes you along a non-stop string of shopping streets.

Amsterdam

FYI

Accommodations Reservations are always advisable in Amsterdam—and essential during tulip season (April and May). The **NRC/Netherlands Reservations Centre** (PO Box 404, 2260 AK Leidschendam, 070/3202500; fax 070/3202611) offers a free advance hotel booking service for Amsterdam and the rest of the country. If you arrive without a reservation, the **VVV Amsterdam Tourist Office** information centers at **Stationsplein** and **Leidseplein** charge a nominal fee for their lodging location services. Also worth considering if you expect to be in Amsterdam a week or more is short-term apartment or houseboat rental; rates per person for two people compare with budget hotel accommodations, and the savings is considerable if several people are traveling together. To book in advance, contact **Villas International** (800/2212260, fax 415/2810919). An important note if you decide to stay in a canal house or town house–style hotel: Dutch staircases are very steep and elevators are nonexistent in such places; keep the luggage light.

Business Hours Banks are open Monday through Friday from 9AM until 4 or 5PM. Most museums are open daily; a few close on Monday. It's the store hours that get confusing. Traditionally, shopping hours in the Netherlands have been tightly regulated (and fairly limiting), although the matter is currently a hot topic in the government and Amsterdam is experimenting with such innovations as Sunday shopping and supermarkets open later than 6PM. Until the matter is sorted out, however, stores are permitted to be open on Monday from 11AM until 6PM; Tuesday, Wednesday, Friday, and Saturday from 9AM until 6PM; and on Thursday from 9AM until 9PM.

Climate Amsterdam is similar to Seattle: inclined to be foggy and have light rain. But if you don't like the weather, just wait a few minutes and it'll change. Summer temperatures rarely exceed 75 degrees and you can expect gray skies and showers from May through August and from November through January. Winters are damp and chilly—but it hardly ever snows (although the canals sometimes freeze over).

Consulates and Embassies

Canada ....Sophialaan 7, Den Haag (The Hague),
....070/3614111
UK ....Koningslaan 44 (at Emmalaan), 6764343
US...........Museumplein 19 (at Gabriel Metsustraat),
....6645661

Discount Tickets The *Amsterdam Pass*, sold by the **VVV Amsterdam Tourist Office** (see "Visitors' Information," below), is a coupon book that includes more than two dozen vouchers and entitles the bearer to such goodies as free or discounted admission to major museums (including the **Rijksmuseum, Vincent van Gogh Museum, and Madame Tussaud's Scenerama**) and the **Holland Casino Amsterdam**, as well as discounts and free offerings for tours, restaurants, cafes, and trams.

Drinking/Drugs Alcoholic beverages are available only to those 18 years or older. All drugs are officially illegal here, but Amsterdam is more tolerant of their use than most European cities and police tend to ignore users of small quantities of marijuana. They come down hard on the dealing and possession of hard drugs, however. Play it safe and pass up the invitations of all street dealers. There are two important telephone help lines: **Crisis Line** (6161666) and **Drug and Alcohol Information** (5702355).

Emergencies Dial 06/11 to reach a 24-hour switchboard that deals with ambulance, fire, and police emergencies. The **Central Doctors Service** (06/35032042) will help you find an English-speaking doctor, dentist, or pharmacy. For legal help, call your country's embassy or consulate.

Gambling Amsterdam is one of the few cities in the world to have a casino right in the heart of town. One of the largest gambling venues in Europe, **Holland Casino Amsterdam,** is just off **Leidseplein**.

Laundry When your wardrobe reaches the point of offending passersby, stop at a self-service laundromat. **Oosterpark** (1er Oosterparkstraat 118, at Camperstraat) is open daily, and **Dorst en Koelma** (Kastanjeplein 4-6, at Kastanjeweg) is open Monday through Friday and on Saturday mornings.

Money The guilder is the standard monetary unit of the Netherlands; it's variously abbreviated as Dfl, fl, and f. **GWK Bank** operates exchange services at six travel-related locations in the city including **Schiphol Airport** and **Centraal Station** (both open 24 hours a day), and at the streetside office of the **VVV Amsterdam Tourist Office** (Leidseplein 1, facing Leidsestraat, 06/34034066), which is open daily until midnight. **American Express** (Damrak 66, at C&A Passage, 5207777) exchanges their travelers checks commission-free and provides cash advances for cardholders. The office is open from Monday through Friday, and on Saturday mornings; there also is a 24-hour cash machine for cardholders.

Personal Safety Amsterdam is like any other urban jungle: You need to watch out for pickpockets. During the summer, packs of youths prey on the trains to and from **Schiphol Airport**, where neglected baggage can be easily whisked away. **Centraal Station** is another lodestone for petty thieves. Avoid deserted streets at night, especially in the Walletjes.

Postal Services Big, red public mailboxes can be spotted around town by the **PTT Post** white-on-red logo. The main post office (Singel 250, near Raadhuisstraat, 5563311) is open Monday through Friday, and until 3PM on Saturday. Another branch (Oosterdokskade 3-5, next to Centraal Station) is open until 7PM Monday through Friday, and on Saturday mornings.

Publications Two good English-language publications for visitors are *What's On* and *Time Out Amsterdam*. Both are published weekly and provide excellent calendars of events. *Uitkrant* is a monthly Dutch-language newspaper that offers comprehensive cultural and nightlife event listings that are easy to decipher.

Amsterdam

Public Holidays New Year's Day, Good Friday, Easter Sunday and Monday, Ascension Day, Queen's Birthday (30 April), Liberation Day (5 May), Whitmonday/Pentecost, Sinterklass (December 5), Christmas, and Boxing Day (December 26).

Public Rest Rooms These are in short supply, and the few existing public *urinoirs* are for men only. In a pinch, seek out a cafe or hotel (and be prepared to leave a small tip).

Restaurants Most hostels and hotels include a typical Dutch breakfast—yogurt, bread, cheese, cold cuts, coffee—in the cost of a room, so most restaurants don't open for breakfast. Lunch is generally served from noon to 2PM. Dinner hour begins around 7PM and extends until 10 or 11PM. Most budget-priced restaurants don't take reservations.

Shopping The shopping streets (some of them pedestrian only) run from **Dam Square** to **Leidseplein**. The biggies are **Kalverstraat** (including its side alleys), **Heiligeweg, Koningsplein,** and **Leidsestraat** for general shopping (especially clothing and shoes). Near the museums, **P.C. Hooftstraat** and **Van Baerlestraat** are the venues for high fashion, and **Utrechtsestraat** is the place for funky clothing as well as general shopping.

Smoking The Dutch, like the French, pursue a notorious smoking habit. In this country, where cigars are not only manufactured with pride but smoked with gusto, you'll want to think twice before asking anyone to stop polluting the air.

Street Plan Canals dominate Amsterdam and course through the city in a series of semicircles that begin and end at the harbor (looking at the map; the pattern is like a multistranded necklace). In the center of it all is **Dam Square**, and cutting through the pattern from the southeast is the Amstel River. Crossing the canals and cutting between them throughout the city are streets and alleys of varying sizes and degrees of activity that carry traffic—and trams—out from the center (like spokes of a wheel). In practice, finding your way in Amsterdam is simple if you recognize that with a slight mental adjustment for the curving of the waterways, the lay of the land here is, basically, a grid.

Taxes In the Netherlands, all taxes and service charges are included in the prices you pay for goods and services.

Telephones Here, as in most places in Europe, coin-operated phone boxes are becoming obsolete. Buy a telephone card (with a fixed amount of money on it) at newstands throughout the city. **PTT Telecom Telehouse** (Raadhuisstraat 46-50, 6743654) provides 24-hour telephone and fax services.

Tickets Information about tickets, and the tickets themselves, for more than 12,000 annual performances of music (all kinds), dance, theater, and opera are available at the **VVV Amsterdam Tourist Offices** (see below) or at the large and ever-busy ticket center of the **AUB/Amsterdam Uit Buro** (Amsterdam Out Bureau), adjacent to the **Stadsschouwburg** theater (Leidseplein 26, at Marnixstraat, 6211211); open Monday through Saturday.

Tipping Although a service charge is included (along with tax) at bars, cafes, and restaurants, a small tip is always appreciated ("rounding up" the tab is the general practice); for an exceptional meal, it is not uncommon to leave 5 to 10 percent extra. Taxi fares also include service, but here, too, rounding up is customary.

Visas There are no visa requirements for the Netherlands; all you need is a valid passport.

Visitors' Information There are two **VVV Amsterdam Tourist Offices** in the heart of the city: at Stationsplein 10, across from **Centraal Station,** and at Leidseplein 1, facing Leidsestraat. Both are open daily, but their hours vary throughout the year. Information is available by phone (06/34034066) during business hours Monday through Friday.

---

1 Centraal Station One of Europe's most impressive train stations, it was embroiled in controversy when it was built in the late 1880s. The station's location—atop three specially constructed islands in the IJsselmeer River—incensed the townspeople because it robbed Amsterdam of views of the harbor. The station was designed by architect **P.J.H. Cuypers,** who also designed the **Rijksmuseum** and would one day be known as "the grandfather of modern Dutch architecture." As in decades past, the area outside the station's main entrance is generally filled with itinerant musicians, ice-cream and flower vendors, and colorful characters. If you stop to watch the passing human parade, keep a tight grasp on your belongings. ♦ Ticket offices: daily; M-F until 8PM. Stationspl (at Damrak). Domestic information 06/9292; international information 6202266

2 Schrierstoren (Tower of Tears) Little remains of the medieval fortifications that once defended this city from approaches along the former Zuider Zee (now the IJsselmeer). According to legend, this tower (dating to 1569) is where sailors' wives tearfully saw their husbands off on their journeys. (The open sea was much closer in those days.) As a bronze memorial plaque tells, this also was the point from which New World explorer Henry Hudson set sail in 1609. Unfortunately, it's not open to the public. ♦ Prins Hendrikkade (at Gelderskade)

Amsterdam is a city of bridges. Although no one has come up with a definitive count, there are supposed to be more than 1,200 of them—more than any other city in the world.

11

Amsterdam

3 Langedoksbrug (Long Dock's Bridge) This new, decorative silver bridge lies between **Centraal Station** and the **Nederlands Scheepvaart Museum** (Maritime Museum; see below). This old section of Amsterdam's port runs along a dock that's lined with classic sailing ships. ♦ East of Centraal Station along the Oosterdokskade

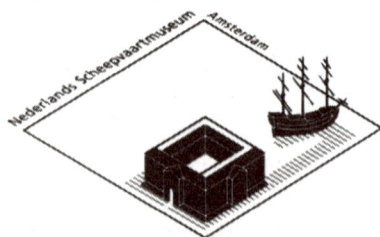

4 Nederlands Scheepvaartmuseum (Maritime Museum) One of the richest maritime collections in the world presents a vivid re-creation of the Netherlands' long and lucrative sailing heritage. More than 500 authentic ship models, charts, instruments, and paintings are on display. The gold-trimmed royal sloop is quartered here; also at dockside is a replica of the *Amsterdam*, an 18th-century East India Company trading vessel. In the multi-media theater, visitors embark on a simulated Golden Age voyage to Indonesia. ♦ Admission. Tu-Sa; Su afternoons. Kattenburgerpl 1 (between Prins Hendrikkade and Kattenburgerstr). 5232222

5 Walletjes The city's oldest neighborhood was named for the medieval walls that once surrounded it. Tree-draped canals and lovely 16th- and 18th-century residences give the area a picturesque quality, but it is known primarily as Amsterdam's notorious Red Light District. Many of the prostitutes, lured here from Third World countries, ply their trade in shifts from behind windows identified by a strip of red neon light, continuing a tradition that began when sailors, from nearby Zeedijk (the former Sailors' Quarter) were the chief source of income. Although not every resident and business in the neighborhood has a stake in the bawdy trade, the area is rather dicey by day and actually a bit dangerous at night. Watch out for drug dealers and muggers. ♦ Oude Zijds Voorburgwal (between Zeedijk and Damstr), Oudekerkspl, and side streets

5 Amstelkring Museum (Our Lord in the Attic) During the Reformation, Amsterdam Catholics were forbidden to practice their religion. In the attic of this small canal house is a tiny chapel where they worshiped in secret. ♦ Admission. M-Sa; Su afternoons. Oude Zijds Voorburgwal 40 (at Heintje Hoekstr). 6246604

6 De Waag (Weigh House) Dating to 1488, this squat, turreted structure (not open to the public) was part of an old gate and a fragment of the old city walls. Over the centuries, it was converted into a public weigh station and a guild house for bricklayers and surgeons. In one of the rooms on an upper floor, Rembrandt painted *The Anatomy Lesson* (1656), which now hangs in the **Rijksmuseum**. ♦ Nieuwmarkt (at Kloveniersburgwal)

7 The Shelter $ This Christian youth hostel offers 166 clean and relatively tidy accommodations in a central location. There are separate dorms and bathrooms for women and men. The price is rock-bottom and still includes breakfast; attendance at prayer meetings is optional. ♦ No credit cards accepted. Barndesteeg 21 (off Nieuwmarkt). 6253230; fax 6232282

7 Jacob Hooy & Co. Since 1743 this shop has dispensed teas, herbs, and medicinals to Amsterdammers from barrels, jars, and wooden drawers. Today's stock includes modern medications and vitamins. ♦ M-Sa. Kloveniersburgwal 10 (at Koestr). 6243041

8 Condomerie Het Gulden Vlies This condom boutique (whose name means "The Golden Fleece") and erotic art gallery offers a colorful and amusing array of functional—and fun—items in its inventory. ♦ Tu-Sa afternoons. Warmoesstr 141 (at Papenbrugsteeg). 6274174

9 Outmayer ★$ Here's a quick and convenient place in the center of town to take a break and enjoy sandwiches, sweets, and coffee or cappuccino. ♦ Cafe ♦ M-Sa breakfast and lunch. Damrak 59 (at Onze Lieve Vrouwesteeg). 6224674. Also at: Reguliersbreestr 24 (near Rembrandtpl). 6241496

9 Beurs van Berlage (Berlage's Stock Exchange) The world's first stock exchange started in Amsterdam in 1611. This handsome building (next door to the original) was the site of Amsterdam's second stock exchange, designed in 1896 by **Hendrik Petrus Berlage**. The trading rooms have been moved and most of the building is now given over to two elegant concert halls, which serve as the official residence of the **Het Nederlands Phylharmanesh Orkest** (Netherlands Philharmonic Orchestra). It's also a venue for occasional art and architecture exhibitions. ♦ Damrak 219-241 (near Beurspl). 6270466

9 Holland Rent-A-Bike While it might be insanity to try biking in other world cities, Amsterdam is geared to cyclists, with special lanes on most major streets and bike racks at convenient parking locations throughout town. ♦ Daily 7AM-7PM. Damrak 247 (near Beurspl). 6223207

Amsterdam

10 Magizijn de Bijenkorf Offering everything from kitchenware and furniture to cosmetics and clothes, Amsterdam's main department store is usually called just **de Bijenkorf** (The Beehive). And it does buzz with activity. Hungry shoppers regularly make a beeline for the main level cafe or the buffet restaurant on the fourth floor. ♦ M-Sa; Th until 9PM. Dam 1 (at Damrak). 6218080

11 China Corner ★$$ For centuries, nearby Walletjes has been home to a large contingent of Chinese residents—and restaurants. This place, located just off **Dam Square,** is slightly more civilized, and decidedly more accessible, than most. It's large by Amsterdam standards and offers a multicolumn menu of classic Chinese favorites, from fried rice to Peking Duck; there's a reasonably priced seven-course prix-fixe menu as well. ♦ Chinese ♦ Daily lunch and dinner. Damstr 1 (at Dam Sq). 6228816

12 Amsterdam Diamond Center The diamond trade developed a strong presence in Amsterdam in the 16th century. When these precious stones were discovered in Dutch-controlled parts of South Africa in 1867, Amsterdam quickly established its prominence in the diamond-cutting industry; it was rivaled only by neighboring Antwerp, Belgium. Two of the stones that make up the British Crown Jewels, the Koh-i-Noor (Mountain of Light) and the Cullinan Diamond, were cut by Amsterdammers. The Center is primarily a sales showroom, but visitors also can stop in at several factories in the city to see how diamonds are polished: Try **Coster Diamonds B.V.** (Paulus Potterstraat 2-4, at Hobbemastraat, 6762222) or **Van Moppes Diamonds B.V.** (Albert Cuypstraat 2-6, at Vizelstraat, 6761242). ♦ Daily; Th until 8:30PM. Rokin 1 (at Dam Sq). 6245787

13 Madame Tussaud's Scenerama This is the only branch of the famous wax museum on the continent. With a few exceptions, the celebrity mannequins (among them, Michael Jackson, Tina Turner, Charlie Chaplin, and Joan Collins) are not very impressive. What attracts the crowds is *Amsterdam Man,* a huge, looming figure with a Rembrandt face, who is arrayed in a montage of windmills, buccaneers, and tulips. He's the doorway to a series of unique multimedia tableaux depicting the 17th-century Golden Age of the city. ♦ Admission. Daily. Dam 20 (between Rokin and Kalverstr). 6229239

14 Dam Square Site of the original dam that crossed the Amstel River and gave this town its first moniker, **Amstelledamme,** this is the most famous plaza in the Netherlands. Because of the illustrious buildings that surround it—**Koninklijk Paleis** and **De Nieuwe Kerk** (see below, for both)—the square has a long tradition of pomp and pageantry. But since 1956, when the **Nationale Monument** was constructed here in honor of World War II dead, it has become the site of Liberation Day celebrations, when Amsterdammers remember the end of the Nazi occupation. On 5 May at 8PM, the square fills with people who pay their respects with two minutes of silence. ♦ Bounded by Damrak and Nieuwe Zijds Voorburgwal, and by Paleisstr and Mozes en Aaronstr

15 Koninklijk Paleis (Royal Palace) This stately Palladian-style marble building was built between 1648 and 1655, from plans by architect **Jacob van Campen,** as the city hall. During the French occupation of the Netherlands (beginning in 1808), it served as a palace for Louis Napoleon, brother of the French emperor. When the Dutch House of Orange regained the throne in 1815, the palace became the family's official residence (although it has never been used as a domicile, but only for official functions). It's open for visitors during limited time periods and is often closed for special functions. ♦ Admission. Daily afternoons June-Aug; W afternoons Sept-May. Dam Sq (at Paleisstr). 6248698

16 De Nieuwe Kerk (New Church) Constructed around 1500, this distinguished church earned its name simply because it was built later than other churches in the city center. Often referred to as the "Dutch Westminster Abbey," this is where the present queen, Beatrix, was crowned. Many national heroes are buried here. Art exhibitions and concerts played on the antique (1655) organ are scheduled throughout the year and, in summer, the church runs a little cafe with a popular terrace. ♦ Admission. Dam Sq (at Mozes en Aaronstr). 6386909

17 „De Drie Fleschjes" "The Three Bottles," as it translates, is just the place to sample this country's unusual range of liqueurs and *jenever* (Dutch gin). Operated by the Bootz Company, maker of exotic liqueurs, this old-fashioned tasting room has been here since 1650 (notice the wall of wooden vats and the traditional sand on the floor). Nuts, cheese, and *bitterbollen* (meatball croquettes with hot mustard) are served as an accompaniment to the drinks. ♦ M-Sa noon-8:30 PM; Su 3-7PM. Gravenstr 18 (between Nieuwendijk and Nieuwe Zijds Voorburgwal). 6248443

18 De Keuken van 1870 ★$ This is traditionally the cheapest place to eat in Amsterdam. The price of the daily special

13

Amsterdam

is comparable to the cost of an appetizer at most other restaurants in town. Expect simple food (meat and potatoes) and not much atmosphere; but you can pay with a credit card. ♦ Dutch ♦ Daily lunch and dinner. Spuistr 4 (near Kattengat). 6248965

19 **Bob's Youth Hostel** $ This two-story, 180-bed hostel not far from **Centraal Station** has long been a home away from home for adventurous backpackers who favor the ultra–laid-back, "dorm from hell" atmosphere. Men and women lounge about playing chess, getting stoned, or sitting on the sidewalk watching the trams go by. It's fairly clean, and breakfast is included in the low price. ♦ No credit cards accepted. Nieuwe Zijds Voorburgwal 92 (at Korte Kolksteeg). 6230063; fax 6756446

20 **Meneer Pannekoek** ★$$ What the French call crepes, the Dutch know as *pannekoeken*, or pancakes. Served flat on the plate, they are heaped with sweet or savory accompaniments. Filled with smoked salmon or cheese and hot dill sauce, they make a solid meal. Dessert options include ice-cream–sundae *pannekoeken* and simple sugared crepes. Omelettes, burgers, and reasonably priced steak or chops entrées are also available here. ♦ Dutch ♦ Daily lunch and dinner. Raadhuisstr 6 (at the Singel). 6278500

21 **Magna Plaza** This shopping center is located behind the **Koninklijk Paleis** (see page 13) in a four-story monument that was designed as a post office nearly a century ago. As you ride the modern escalators to reach the chichi shops that purvey everything from lingerie to riding gear, you'll get a good vantage point of the building's glass dome, Gothic/Moorish interior, and fine English fixtures and detail work. The entire basement level is home to the Amsterdam branch of **Virgin Records** (6228929). ♦ M-Sa; Th until 9PM. Nieuwe Zijds Voorburgwal 182 (at Raadhuisstr).

22 **Amsterdam Historisch (Historical) Museum** This complex of elegant 17th- and 18th-century buildings and courtyards once served as a convent and later as an orphanage. The museum offers an extensive overview of Amsterdam's history, focusing especially on its Golden Age. The famous **Schuttersgalerij** (Civic Guard Gallery) of portraits of the city's prestigious early militia is located in a narrow street outside the museum's walls, protected by a glass ceiling and two guards. ♦ Admission. Daily. Entrances at Kalverstr 92 (at Wijde Kapelsteeg) and Nieuwe Zijds Voorburgwal 357 (at St. Luciensteeg). 5231822

Within the Amsterdam Historisch Museum:
David & Goliath Cafe ★$$ A life-size sculpture of the legendary Philistine champion greets you at the door of this cafe, which makes a good lunch or afternoon Dutch-apple-cake-and-coffee break for shoppers and museum goers. ♦ Cafe ♦ Daily lunch. 6236736

23 **Begijnhof** Walk out the historical museum's back entrance and you'll find yourself at the gateway to this tranquil garden, or *hofjes*. Around the secluded courtyard a group of small houses was established in the 14th century as a convent for the Beguine sisters, a religious order of unmarried women who lived communally and took vows of chastity. The last of these sisters died in 1974. The building at **No. 34** is the oldest preserved "wooden" house in Amsterdam, dating to 1475; the **Engelsekerk** (English Church) at **No. 30** offers Sunday services and occasional chamber music concerts. ♦ Gedempte Begijnensloot (at Begijnsteeg). Concert information 6249665

24 **Haesje Claes** ★★$$ While Amsterdam has its fair share of trendy, Deco-decorated cafes, this restaurant stays true to its Old Dutch decor (complete with fringed lampshades), traditional menu, and reasonable prices. Large tables and a series of dining rooms make it popular with groups. There's a moderately priced prix-fixe menu that could include chicken with madeira sauce, salmon béarnaise, or, in the winter months, rabbit with red cabbage. ♦ Dutch ♦ Daily lunch and dinner. Nieuwe Zijds Voorburgwal 320 (near Spui). 6249998

25 **Gollem** This tiny bar is big on character, and claims a large inventory of potent bottled beers from around the world. At last count, there were 100 varieties, mostly from Belgium. There's food served here, too. ♦ Daily 4PM-2AM. Raamsteeg 4 (at Spuistr). 6266645

26 **Athenaeum News Centrum** Located on the historic **Spui**, an old, intimate square next to **Amsterdam University** that is a prime spot for protest demonstrations, this is the place to stock up on international periodicals, postcards, and guidebooks. There are also shelves and shelves full of Dutch books and textbooks. ♦ M-Sa until 10PM; Su. Spui 14-16 (between Spuistr and Nieuwe Zijds Voorburgwal). 6233933

26 **Friday Book Market/Sunday Art Market on the Spui** At the weekly Friday gatherings here, vendors peddle everything from coffee-table art books to first editions of Chekhov to turn-of-the-century French cookbooks and special editions of Shakespeare's sonnets. On Sunday from April through December, local artists show and sell their work here. Don't be

14

Amsterdam

afraid to bargain. ♦ Book market: F 10AM-6PM. Art market: Su 10AM-6PM Apr-Dec. Spui (between Nieuwe Zijds Voorburgwal and Gedempte Begijnensloot)

27 Broodje van Kootje ★$ The basic lunchtime *broodjes* (sandwich rolls) on sale here contain meat, cheese, and maybe tuna or chicken salad. The kitchen is open until 1:30AM (every night except Sunday), so you can grab a bite after an evening sipping *jenever*. ♦ Fast food ♦ Daily lunch, dinner, and late-night meals. No credit cards accepted. Spui 28 (at Spuistr). 6269620. Also at: Leidsepl 20-22 (at Korte Leidsedwarsstr). 6269620

CAFFE ESPRIT

28 Caffè Esprit ★$$ Attached to the local branch of **Esprit**, the California casual-clothing store, this is a great spot to eat chic on the cheap. It's especially good in warm weather, when outdoor seating is available and the young and the stylish reign. Salads, sandwiches, and pasta dishes are among the tasty offerings, as are juices and yogurt concoctions. ♦ California ♦ M-Sa lunch and dinner. Spui 10a (at Gedempte Begijnensloot). 6278281

29 Dansen bij Jansen Amsterdam has its share of warehouse-size discos, but this is a more intimate venue, primarily favored by students. ♦ Cover. Daily 11:30PM-5AM. Handboogstr 11 (at Heiligeweg). 6201779

30 American Book Center Holding forth in the heart of the city's busiest shopping street, this is the place to pick up maps and guidebooks, as well as books and periodicals from the US and UK. More than 40 categories are stocked and they have CD-ROM capability for title searches; if you're going to be in town for a while, they'll order books for you. ♦ Daily; Th until 10PM. Kalverstr 185 (near Heiligeweg). 6255537

P.G.C. HAJENIUS

31 P.G.C. Hajenius This elegant tobacco shop has been selling its wares since 1826. With its air-controlled humidor room and assorted accoutrements, it could easily be mistaken for a cigar museum. ♦ M-Sa. Rokin 92 (at Watersteeg). 6237494

32 Rokin Hotel $$ Three dozen rooms, all clean and pleasant with modern furniture, some with canal views, and 23 with private baths, are scattered throughout five different buildings in the neighborhood. There is no restaurant, but breakfast (included in the price) is served in a comfortable breakfast room. ♦ Rokin 73 (near Wijde Lombardsteeg). 6267456; fax 6256453

33 Frascati Cafe ★★$$ On Amsterdam's principal theater street is a cafe adjacent to and sharing a name with one of the city's principal legitimate theaters (Dutch and English plays). This spirited mahoghany-lined cafe is practically a local canteen for actors and low-key financiers from the nearby stock exchange. Steak and spareribs are on the menu, but the real attraction is the fresh-baked apple cake. ♦ Bistro ♦ M-Sa dinner. Nes 59 (at Sint Barberenstr). 6241324

34 The String This cozy little music club provides a pleasant time warp with its bluegrass and folk music format. Sunday is open mike night for local wannabes. ♦ Daily 10PM-2AM. Music begins at 10:30PM. Nes 98 (at Kuipersteeg). 6259015

34 Sisters ★★$$ One of the specialties of this vegetarian restaurant is falafel, but the kitchen also dishes up large portions of other wholesome veggie fare. There's no liquor license, so try one of the fresh fruit juices. ♦ Vegetarian ♦ Daily dinner. Nes 102 (at Kuipersteeg). 6263970

35 Muziekcafe Kapitein Zeppo's ★$$ A lively crowd gravitates to this cafe for its music and inexpensive daily specials. The live music program varies widely in style, but it's guaranteed to be unusual. ♦ Cafe ♦ Daily dinner. Gebed Zonder End 5 (at Grimburgwal). 6242057

36 Allard Pierson Museum Everybody comes to see the Egyptian mummies, but this museum also has extensive archaeological displays of clay tablets, ceramics, and sculptures from ancient Rome and Greece. Sadly, though, while the collection is exceptional, most of the exhibits lack imagination, and explanatory texts in English are difficult to find. ♦ Tu-F; Sa-Su afternoons. Oude Turfmarkt 127 (at Nieuwe Doelenstr). 5252556

37 The Atrium ★$ One of the best-kept secrets in town is the **University of Amsterdam's** cafeteria. The public eats at a slightly higher price than the groggy-eyed men and women who look as if they've been cramming a term's worth of biology in two days. But it's still a deal. The menu is diverse—including vegetarian dishes—and though it's not gourmet, it's a cut above standard dorm fare. ♦ Cafeteria ♦ M-F lunch and dinner. No credit cards accepted. Oudezijds Achterburgwal 237 (at Oudemanhuispoort). No phone

15

Amsterdam

38 Oudemanhuispoort (Old Men's House Gate) Bookmarket This covered passageway in the **University of Amsterdam** complex was once the doorway to the city "poorhouse." Today it is lined with stalls selling secondhand books (most in Dutch, some in English), postcards, prints, and other memorabilia. The location is less than salubrious (this part of town is heavy with drug use), so only true book hounds will want to check it out. ♦ M-Sa. Oudemanhuispoort (between Kloveniersburgwal and Oudezijds Achterburgwal).

39 Stadsdoelen Youth Hostel $ Its central location on a picturesque canal means this place is almost always booked to capacity with students and postgraduates. There are separate-sex floors and some mixed rooms (186 beds total) with six showers for every 40 guests. Oversize lockers for backpacks are included in the price, as is breakfast. ♦ No credit cards accepted. Kloveniersburgwal 97 (at Raamgr). 6246832; fax 6391035

40 De Jaren ★★$$ Trendsetters have taken over this modern two-story cafe, even arriving at the dockside terrace by boat. But there's still plenty of room inside for students, tourists, and blasé locals who just want to hang out at the reading table. A variety of eye-pleasing cheese and meat sandwiches are available, along with desserts such as tiramisù and apple pie. ♦ Bistro ♦ Daily lunch and dinner. No credit cards accepted. Nieuwe Doelenstr 20 (at Binnengasthuisstr). 6255771

41 Muntplein (Mint Square) This square connects seven main streets, including the popular Kalverstraat shopping street, and acts as a bridge between the Singel canal and the Amstel River. Coins were once minted in the former guardroom next to the **Munttoren** (Mint Tower), a 15th-century structure left over from one of the old city-wall gates. This tower was given its distinctive spire by renowned Renaissance architect **Hendryk de Keyser** in 1620. If you happen to walk underneath the tower's arch on Friday between noon and 1PM, you can see (and hear) the tower's carillon bells chiming away. ♦ Junction of Rokin and Vijzelstr

---

There is no natural stone whatsoever to be found on damp Dutch soil and building has always been a matter of mounting brick upon wood piles. The Koninklijk Paleis (Royal Palace) was built upon 13,659 piles. In the 16th century Erasmus likened the Dutch in their homes to crows perched on the tops of trees.

Restaurants/Clubs: Red   **Hotels:** Blue
Shops/ 🌴 Outdoors: Green   **Sights/Culture:** Black

42 Roxy A former movie house has been converted into one of the city's more outrageous and trendy discos. Wednesday is gay night, while the mix for straights is best on Friday and Saturday. If you want to grab a late-night snack before you boogie, don't worry; this place doesn't heat up until about 1AM. ♦ Cover. W-Su 11PM-4AM; F-Sa until 5AM. Singel 465 (off Muntpl). 6200354

43 Albert Heijn This Dutch supermarket that is part of the nation's largest chain is a good pit stop for munchies and bottled water, fresh fruit, or forgotten toothpaste. ♦ M-Sa; Th until 9PM. Koningspl 6 (at Singel). 6245721

43 Odeon Young and old(er) students and others congregate here five nights a week—either hanging out at the convivial bar or dancing to their choice of music. Downstairs it's jazz, pop, and funk; on the main floor, acid rock; and upstairs it's music of the 1970s. ♦ Cover. Tu-Sa 11PM-5AM. Singel 460 (near Koningspl). 6249711

43 Agora $$ This hotel enjoys one of the most central locations in Amsterdam. It's a traditional canal house hotel (that means the staircase is steep) with a comfortable non-traditional mix-and-match decor in its 15 rooms, 12 of which have private baths. No credit cards accepted. ♦ Singel 462 (at Koningspl). 6272200; fax 6272200

44 Bloemenmarkt (Flower Market) Like an open-air mall for flowers and plants, this floating market began about 200 years ago and is a favorite of Amsterdammers, who buy low-priced plants, flowers, and gardening supplies (including clogs to keep your feet dry in the mud) year-round from barges permanently moored canal-side. In December, even Christmas trees are sold here. ♦ M-Sa. Singel (between Koningspl and Muntpl)

45 Hema A large low-price store stocked with clothes, film, batteries, sundries, and a food department where European essentials—bread, cheese, and wine—prevail. ♦ M-Sa; Th until 9PM. Reguliersbreestr 10 (between Muntpl and Rembrandtpl). 6246506. Also at: Nieuwedijk 174 (near C&A Passage). 6234176

46 Tuschinski Theater Built in 1921 by a Polish cinema buff, this theater has one of the most beautiful interiors in the world, with an extravagant Art Deco design and a red-and-gold color scheme. It's a six-plex for first-run features (mostly American) with an ever-crowded bar in the lobby. For the complete movie-palace experience, catch whatever is playing in the main theater. Arrive early, as lines can get long; this is one of the most popular movie houses in the city. ♦ Daily. Tours: M, Su from 10:30AM. Reguliersbreestr 26-28 (between Rembrandtpl and Muntpl). 6262633

Amsterdam

47 Kwekkeboom ★$ This pastry shop/snack bar is the place to try *kroketten* (beef-paste croquettes) topped with mustard. The less adventuresome can stick with the excellent cheese croissants or delicious pastries.
♦ Snack bar ♦ M-Sa lunch and snacks. Reguliersbreestr 36 (at Rembrandtpl). 6231205. Also at: 20 Damstr (between Dam Sq and Oude Zijds Voorburgwal). 6248365

48 Eetsalon Van Dobben B.V. ★$ This popular sandwich shop attracts a loyal following among the daytime business and late-night party crowd from nearby **Rembrandtsplein** for—what else—*broodjes* (meat or cheese sandwiches on soft rolls).
♦ Fast food ♦ M-Sa lunch, dinner, and late-night snacks. Korte Reguliersdwarsstr 5 (at Reguliersdwarsstr). 6244200

49 Hotel Seven Bridges $$ The decor is a trompe l'oeil of marble and murals, with long antique runners to carry the eye along the narrow hallway and up the steep stairs to the 11 cheery, brightly decorated rooms, six of which have private baths. The rooms with private baths bump up the budget price, but they're worth every guilder. ♦ Reguliersgr 31 (at Keizersgr). 6231329

50 Hotel de la Poste $$ Located just minutes from the **Rembrandtplein** and convenient to the cafes and shops along the Utrechtsestraat, this canal house contains 14 rooms, 10 with private bathrooms. A Dutch breakfast is included in the price. ♦ Reguliersgr 5 (at Herengr). 6237105

51 Bridge of the 15 Bridges With all the canals, is it any wonder that Amsterdam is a city of bridges? To get a good perspective of just how many there are, walk south from **Rembrandtplein** and **Thorbeckeplein** to the intersection of the Reguliersgracht and Herengracht canals. Looking south down the Reguliersgracht, you'll see six bridges, and to the east, down the Herengracht, six more. Another pair of bridges will be to the west, which means you are standing on the 15th bridge. When the bridge lights are on, this is truly a sight to behold. ♦ Reguliersgr and Herengr

52 Mister Coco's ★$ Amidst the bars, cafes, and clubs of the **Rembrandtplein** is this English publike oasis for American and British expatriates and college students. Chalk up its appeal to the Happy Hour, when drinks are served two-for-the-price-of-one. When you're ready to eat, go for the spareribs or burgers.
♦ Daily lunch and dinner. Happy Hour: daily 5-6PM. Thorbeckepl 8 (at Reguliersdwarsstr). 6272423

53 Escape By day, the **Rembrandtplein** neighborhood is quiet, but night lends more intrigue and activity, from peep shows and striptease houses to trendy cafes all peppering this district tucked into a bend of the Amstel River. Among the clubs in this after-hours neighborhood is Amsterdam's largest disco. Video screens, special lighting effects, and the house-mix of music keep things lively. A multiroom layout accommodates the crowds. ♦ Cover. Th-Su 11PM-4AM; F-Sa until 5AM. Rembrandtpl 11 (at Halvemaansteeg). 6221111

54 iT If you really want to experience Amsterdam's outrageous side, drop in at this largely gay discotheque with the most diverse crowd and the wildest scene in town. Saturday is for gays only, but relentless house music brings in a colorful and eclectic crowd on Thursday, Friday, and Sunday. ♦ Cover. Th-Su 11PM-4AM. Amstelstr 24 (between the Amstel and Rembrandtpl). 6250111

55 Het Muziektheater (Music Theater) Commanding a splendid open space overlooking the bending Amstel River, and sharing a vast complex with Amsterdam's city hall, this impressive theater building is the Lincoln Center of the Netherlands. Home to the **Nederlands Dans Theatre** (Netherlands Dance Theater), **Het Nationale Ballet** (The National Ballet), and **De Nederlandse Opera** (Netherlands Opera), it offers a full calendar of music and dance. There are free lunchtime concerts on Tuesdays. ♦ Box office: M-Sa from 1PM; Su from 11:30AM. Amstel 3 (at Waterloopl). 6255455

17

Amsterdam

Within Het Muziektheater:

Cafe Dantzig ★★$$ In warm weather, the cafe's large terrace facing the Amstel River is *the* place to be. The menu changes with every new theater premiere, but tends to feature French, Italian, and Dutch specialties. Dinner can be expensive, but there are less expensive options: Go for lunch, or have a drink and appetizer on the terrace at sunset. ♦ Continental ♦ Daily lunch and dinner. Reservations recommended for dinner. Zwanenburgwal 15 (at the Amstel). 6209039

56 Waterlooplein This famous open air flea market for goods of every kind and description is found in the heart of what was Amsterdam's pre-World War II Jewish sector of the same name. Located adjacent to the town hall, stalls also stretch along the canalside. Search for genuine antiques among the attic detritus, but beware of ripoffs. ♦ M-Sa. Waterloopl (between Mr. Visserpl and Zwanenburgwal)

57 Rembrandthuis (Rembrandt House) Prolific 17th-century painter Rembrandt van Rijn paid a pretty price for this stately, three-story merchant's home in 1639—at the height of his fame as a portraitist. When he refused to compromise his artistic talents, his fortunes declined, and Rembrandt was forced to file for bankruptcy in 1656. Two years later he sold the house to meet rising debts. The furnishings still reflect the family life of Amsterdam's most famous painter. More than 250 Rembrandt etchings are on view inside. ♦ Admission. M-Sa; Su afternoons. Jodenbreestr 4-6 (at Zwanenburgwal). 6249486

58 Bimhuis Modern jazz aficionados hang out here to catch the famous and the wannabes of the local and international scene. Musicians such as jazzmen James Moody and Franky Price and trumpet master Nat Adderley are among the luminaries who have performed at this hip venue. Aside from the concerts, workshops and jam sessions are often on the bill. ♦ Cover. Th-Sa 8PM-5AM. Box office: M-F noon-4PM. Reservations required. Oude Schans 73-77 (at Houtkopersburgwal). 6277310

The Netherlands grows at least 650 varieties of tulips, and exports about 780 billion flowers and bulbs each year. Tulips arrived in Holland from Turkey in 1550 and flourished in the damp lowland soil. The sale of this national symbol has become a million-dollar-a-year industry.

The large hooks that you see just under the tops of gables are there to hoist furniture that cannot fit up the narrow stairways into the houses.

59 Joods Historisch Museum (Jewish Historical Museum) Housed in four former synagogues, all dating to the 17th and 18th centuries and now linked by a modern glass-and-steel construction, this is a touching monument to the past and present. The permanent exhibition illustrates the history of Jews in the Netherlands, and, in particular, the Holocaust's impact on them (over 140,000 Dutch Jews were deported to concentration camps). There is a collection of ceremonial objects, including antiques and modern pieces. Guided tours are available by special arrangement. ♦ Admission. Daily. Jonas Daniel Meijerpl 2-4 (at Nieuwe Amstelstr). 6269945, 6254229

60 Portuguese Israeli Synagogue When it was built in 1675, this stately building was the largest synagogue in the world. The 17th-century interior is still intact, and private, weekly services are still conducted by candlelight, as they were more than 300 years ago. The gift shop sells a unique collection of Judaica. ♦ Admission. M-F; Su 10AM-3PM. Mr. Visserpl 3 (at Muiderstr). 6245351

61 Hortus Botanicus This green haven offers plants from around the world, a state-of-the-art greenhouse, a palm exhibit, and an herb garden. Drop in when you need a break from sight-seeing. ♦ Admission. Daily. Plantage Middenlaan 2 (at Plantage Parklaan). 6258411

62 Wertheim Park In this small park, located in a former Jewish neighborhood, Dutch writer and artist Jan Wolkers installed his *Holocaust Memorial* in 1993. The work is a simple but moving construction of plate-glass squares arranged on the ground. ♦ Plantage Middenlaan (at Plantage Parklaan)

63 Hollandsche Schouwburg This former theater, built in 1892, was renamed the **Joodsche Schouwburg** (Jewish Theater) during the Nazi occupation of 1941, and was restricted to Jewish artists and audiences. A year later, the Nazis turned the building into an assembly point for Dutch Jews being sent to concentration camps. After the war, it reopened briefly as a theater, but public outcry that the building would again be used for entertainment purposes made it a short-lived run. In 1993, the renovated structure was turned into a historical monument and

Amsterdam

memorial. A permanent exhibit examines the persecution of Dutch Jews. ♦ Admission. Daily. Plantage Middenlaan 24 (at Plantage Kerklaan). 6269945

64 Artis More than 6,000 animals call this place home. Founded in 1838, Amsterdam's zoo is the oldest in Europe. Also on the property are an aquarium, a planetarium, and zoological and geological museums. The gardens are an ideal place to recharge your batteries. ♦ Admission. Daily. Plantage Kerklaan 38-40 (at Plantage Middenlaan). 5233400

65 Tropenmuseum (Tropical Museum) When it originally opened in the 1920s, this was supposed to be a tribute to the Dutch colonial past; now its focus has shifted to the people and cultures of Third World countries. Replicas of Indian and Indonesian villages, combined with displays of Oceanic art and traditional musical instruments, make for a fascinating you-are-there experience. Offbeat concerts are often scheduled during the week and there's also a special children's museum. ♦ Admission. M-F; Sa-Su afternoons. Linnaeusstr 2 (at Mauritskade). 5688215

66 ARENA Sleep In $ This "mother of all youth hostels" has a total of 506 beds: some in double rooms (with private showers) and some traditional in dormitories. Besides being a budget hotel/youth hostel catering to a range of age groups, the large complex (a former girls' home) also serves as a youth cultural center, with live music, exhibitions, and dances. A bar and a basic restaurant are among the plusses. Bring sheets. ♦ No credit cards accepted. S-Gravesandestr 51 (at Mauritskade). 6947444

67 Hotel Prinsenhof $$ This canal house hotel sits between the Amstel River and the Utrechtsestraat shopping street and offers 10 guest rooms (named for 1930s movie stars). None of the rooms has a private bath, but breakfast is included in the price. ♦ Prinsengr 810 (at Utrechtsestr). 6231772

68 Cafe Panini ★★$$ During afternoon hours, enjoy crisp Italian sandwiches on panini bread, stuffed with mozzarella and tomato, Parma ham, and other delectables. At dinner, macaroni fans can feast on pasta with pesto sauce or lasagna of the day. Leafy choices include the salad *appaninica* (with smoked chicken, avocado, and walnuts) and spinach *salvatici* (a variation of spinach salad with pine nuts and garlic dressing). ♦ Italian ♦ Daily lunch and dinner. Vijzelstr 3 (at Prinsengr). 6264939

69 Cafe Descartes ★★$$ Located *within* the French consulate building (second entrance from the canal), this restaurant depends on its charming owner/chef from the south of France for ambience and allure. Ariane Ghirardi creates her menus according to whim and market bounty. A daily quiche special and homemade pâté are dependable, but the real standouts are the desserts. Save room for the *tarte du jour* or crème caramel, two house specialties. ♦ French ♦ M-F lunch and dinner; closed in August. Vijzelstr 2a (at Prinsengr). 6221913

70 Hotel Keizershof $$ There are only six guest rooms (with shared bathrooms) in this charming 17th-century canal house run by the DeVries family. The spiral staircase is worth the climb, and a grand piano in the parlor is perfect for a Chopin interlude. The price includes a typical Dutch breakfast. ♦ Keizersgr 618 (at Vijzelstr). 6222855

71 Heineken Brewery Although beer hasn't been produced here since the late 1980s, the public still adores this original site of the family-operated, 400-year-old **Haystack Brewery** too much to shutter its doors entirely. Tours and tastings are now offered on a first-come, first-served basis for those 18 years and older. ♦ Admission. Tours: M-F until 2:30PM May-Sept. Stadhouderskade 78 (at Ferdinand Bolstr). 5239239

72 Albert Cuyp Markt This open-air market is one of Europe's best and biggest, selling everything from shellfish and fresh herbs to shirts and fabrics. But watch for pickpockets in the crowds. ♦ M-Sa. Albert Cuypstr (between Van Woustr and Ferdinand Bolstr)

73 Rijksmuseum If you blink twice when you see this museum, yes, it does bear a striking resemblance to **Centraal Station.** Both neo-Renaissance masterpieces were the work of architect **P.J.H. Cuypers.** World-renowned for its collection of Dutch masters, this museum attracts more visitors each year than any institution in the Netherlands. After

Amsterdam

seeing major works by the big guns—Rembrandt, Frans Hals, Jan Steen, and Vermeer—there are also Dutch still lifes, domestic scenes, medieval religious paintings, sculpture, and even ship models to keep you busy. Give yourself at least a day to negotiate this magnificent 150-room museum. A first-floor shop sells English-language guidebooks—you'll need one to figure out where you're going. At press time, the Asiatic art and 18th- and 19th-century painting collections were closed for renovations. ♦ Admission. Tu-Sa; Su afternoons. Stadhouderskade 42 (between Hobbemakade and Jan Luijkenstr). 6732121

74 Van Gogh Museum This surprisingly modern building, the creation of Dutch architect **Gerrit Rietveld,** opened in 1972 and was enlarged in 1990 for a major van Gogh retrospective. The permanent collection (nearly the entire lifework) includes 200 paintings, 400 drawings, and 700 letters by the post-Impressionist, who achieved critical acclaim only after committing suicide in 1890 at the age of 37. Changing exhibits reflect on van Gogh's development as a painter and the times in which he lived; occasional exhibitions of other artists are also held here. ♦ Admission. Daily. Paulus Potterstr 7 (at Van Der Veldestr). 5705200

75 Stedelijk (Municipal) Museum Amsterdam's fine modern art museum is housed in most unmodern quarters: a neo-Renaissance structure designed in 1895 by **A.W. Weissmann.** In addition to the changing exhibitions of contemporary artists (including Andy Warhol, Frank Stella, and Dutch-born Willem de Kooning), there is also a permanent collection of classic Dutch and French paintings dating back to the mid-19th century. Turn your head and you'll also spot works by Monet, Cezanne, and Chagall. Don't miss the sculpture garden; it faces the **Museumplein** and has a separate entrance (no charge). ♦ Admission. Daily. Paulus Potterstr 13 (at Van Baerlestr). 5732911

76 Intertaal More than 100 mother tongues can flap after a visit to this comprehensive multi-language bookstore offering learning texts and cassettes and books about languages (but no foreign-language literature). They also sell videos, and computer software. ♦ M-Sa. Van Baerlestr 76 (at J.W. Brouwersstr). 6715353

76 Muziekhandel Broekmans & Van Poppel Appropriate to its illustrious neighbor, the **Concertgebouw,** this music store offers a very comprehensive array of sheet music, compact discs, and books about music. ♦ M-Sa. Van Baerlestr 92-94 (at J.W. Brouwersstr). Compact discs 6751653, sheet music and books 6628084, 6796575

77 Concertgebouw (Concert Building) This venerable concert hall celebrated its centennial in 1988 with the addition of a new glass-walled main entrance. The large hall's flawless acoustics are said to rival the sound quality at only two other halls in the world: Boston and Vienna. More than 500 concerts are given here annually by the **Concertgebouw**'s orchestra and dozens of recitalists. Free lunchtime concerts are scheduled every Wednesday at 12:30PM (except during the summer). ♦ Box office: daily. Performances: daily. Concertgebouwpl 2 (at de Lairessestr). 6754411

78 Hotel Verdi $$ Just around the corner from the **Concertgebouw,** this comfortable family-run hotel offers 12 rooms (five with private bathrooms). There's no restaurant or snack bar, but it's not unusual to find musicians rehearsing in the parlor. ♦ Wanningstr 9 (at J.W. Brouwersstr). 6760073; fax 6739070

79 Vondelpark Named in honor of Amsterdam's most famous poet, Joost van den Vondel (whose statue can be found near the open-air theater in the middle of the park), this 120-acre refuge was originally private, for the use of residents of the posh surrounding neighborhood only. Since the 1960s, it has been a meeting place for young people. Anything goes here, so brace yourself for an array of dancers, jugglers, lovers, drummers, and uninhibited sunbathers expressing themselves freely. In the summer look for free open-air concerts (classical, rock, jazz) and two outdoor cafes. At twilight the park empties, and it is best to avoid it after dark. ♦ Stadhouderskade (between Vossiusstr and Zandpad)

80 Nederlands Filmmuseum (Netherlands Film Museum) Housed in a grand 19th-century teahouse, this local mecca for serious celluloid lovers holds at least two daily showings of classic international films (silent films receive wonderful live piano

20

Amsterdam

accompaniment). The two theaters are in beautifully restored auditoriums (one with an 1890's decorative ceiling, the other in Art Deco style), and the museum has an inventory of 20,000-plus Dutch and European films to draw upon for programming. ♦ Admission. M-Sa; Su afternoons. Vondelpark 3 (at Roemer Visserstr; entrance is from inside the park). 5891400

Within the Nederlands Filmmuseum:

Cafe Vertigo ★★$$ In summer, the cafe terrace is packed with assorted film aficionados who come to see and be seen. The menu choices are lively and varied. ♦ Cafe ♦ Daily lunch and dinner. 5891400

81 NJHC Vondelpark $ Close to the party-hearty environs of **Leidseplein**, yet with an idyllic view of the **Vondelpark**, this hostel includes nonsmoking areas, a cook-it-yourself kitchen, and lockers. The 300 accommodations are in single-sex dorms, bathrooms are communal, and curfew is at 2AM. No credit cards accepted. ♦ Zandpad 5 (at Stadhouderskade). 6831744; fax 6166591

82 Hotel Piet Hein $$ The decor of this chic, small residential hotel overlooking the **Vondelpark** would do a chain hotel proud; so would the friendliness of the owner. The prices push the high end of the budget scale, but all 36 rooms have private baths, breakfast is included, and there's an elevator. ♦ Vossiusstr 52-53 (at Constantijn Huygensstr). 6627205; fax 6621526

83 Paradiso A former church, this theater has long been the venue of choice for a wide range of pop and rock musicians. Van Morrison, Los Lobos, and Joan Baez have all played here. ♦ Box office from 8PM. Weteringschans 6 (at Leidsekruisstr). 6264521

83 Holland Casino Amsterdam Just off **Leidseplein** is one of the largest casinos in Europe. Games range from roulette and blackjack to electronic bingo and slot machines. The casino complex includes a restaurant, brasserie, and dinner theater. ♦ Cover. Daily 1:30PM-3AM. Identification is compulsory (passport preferred). Must be 18 or older to enter. Max Euwepl 62 (off Leidsepl). 6201006.

84 Cafe Americain $$ Okay, there is no way that this is a budget operation, but if you're going to splurge once in Amsterdam, this is the place to do it. A stately oasis in the **American Hotel** features an elegant *jugendstil* (Art Nouveau) ambience and a century-old reputation as Amsterdam's "living room." Dinner is really expensive, but go for the dessert buffet (famous for its apple strudel) or high tea, which includes scones, petit fours, bonbons, canapes, and cake. ♦ Continental ♦ Daily lunch, dinner, and afternoon tea. Leidsepl 28 (at Leidsekade). 6245322

85 De Stadsschouwburg Built in 1894, this municipal theater, with its redbrick turrets, showcases international dance, music, and theater productions. The portraits on the staircase are of prominent patrons of the arts—reflecting a time when they arrived here grandly by horse and carriage. ♦ Box office: daily. Check newspapers for scheduled events. Leidsepl 26 (at Marnixstr). 6242311

86 De Melkweg (The Milky Way) Stoned soul-seekers have made this place a stop on their circuit since the 1960s. In addition to an eclectic schedule of stage acts—everything from ethnic works to gay theater to stand-up comedy—there's also a dance floor, concert hall, cinema, gallery, and cafe in this multimedia center. ♦ Box office: daily. Lijnbaansgr 234a (at Spiegelgr). 6241777

87 Gary's Muffins ★$ Gary Feingold, a Los Angeles transplant and former dancer with a Rotterdam dance troupe, is the local muffin maven. The daily changing selection features at least eight kinds of muffins, along with bagels (plus cream cheese and lox, if you like), brownies, and giant cookies. ♦ Bakery ♦ Daily. Prinsengr 454 (at Leidsestr). 4201452

88 Bojo ★$ When you've danced—or gambled—the night away at the nearby clubs and casino, this rambling Indonesian restaurant will still be open to take care of your hunger, and at a price that will keep your budget intact. The kitchen serves until 2AM during the week and until 5AM on weekends. ♦ Indonesian ♦ Daily lunch, dinner, and late-night dinner. Lange Leidsedwarsstr 51 (at Leidsekruisstr). 6227434

"What other place in the world could you choose where all of life's comforts and all the novelties are so easy to obtain as here, and where you can enjoy such a feeling of freedom?"

René Descartes, 1631

Restaurants/Clubs: Red **Hotels:** Blue
Shops/ ♛ Outdoors: Green **Sights/Culture:** Black

Amsterdam

88 Alto Jazz is the mainstay at this tiny pub/club near **Leidseplein**. Beer is served in the traditional Dutch way with a thick head (it's a sign the beer's fresh) and the music is live seven nights a week. No credit cards accepted. ♦ M-Th 9PM-2AM; F-Sa 10PM-2AM. Korte Leidsedwarsstr 115 (at Leidsekruisstr). 6263249

89 Medieval Torture Museum How low can human beings sink in their treatment of one another? Consider the guillotine, or ponder the pain of an Inquisition-era chair of nails. This museum is definitely not for the squeamish: More than 60 instruments of abuse are on display here, along with explanations of how each device was used to its most gruesome effect. ♦ Admission. Daily. Leidsestr 27 (at Keizersgr). 6204070

90 Pompadour ★★$$ This tiny Old-World tearoom/patisserie specializes in chocolate treats. Bonbons, truffles, and pastries abound—forget that diet and indulge. ♦ Tearoom ♦ Tu-Sa. Huidenstr 12 (at Herengr). 6239554

91 Casa di David ★$$ This cozy, two-story Italian restaurant near Spui serves pizzas hot from the oven and a selection of traditional Italian entrées. Bonus: They serve until midnight. ♦ Italian ♦ Daily dinner. Singel 426 (at Wijde Heisteeg). 6245093

92 Hotel Hoksbergen $$ For a room with a view, try this small canal house. There are 14 guest rooms, all with private baths. An ample Dutch breakfast is included in the bill. ♦ Singel 301 (at Raamsteeg). 6266043; fax 6383479

93 Hotel Belga $$ Located on a charming shopping street between canals, this is a no-frills hotel with 10 guest rooms and shared baths. No restaurant, but breakfast is included. ♦ Hartenstr 8 (at Herengr). 6249080; fax 6236862

94 Homomonument A large triangle of pink granite, containing three smaller triangles, is artist Karin Daan's tribute to the homosexual victims of World War II. The main structure rests on the water, then extends to the **Westermarkt**, adjacent to the **Westerkerk**. World AIDS Day (1 December) is observed here, as is Coming Out Day (5 September). ♦ Westermarkt (at Keizersgr)

95 Westerkerk After a seven-year restoration, this stunning church, created by **Hendryk de Keyser**, remains one of Amsterdam's architectural showpieces. Built between 1620 and 1631, the church's tower—at 276 feet, the tallest in the city—is literally topped with a golden crown. A nominal admission charge lets you climb the tower to the first level; you must be accompanied by a guide. This is the church where Dutch Queen Beatrix married Prince Claus in 1966, and Rembrandt is buried (sorry, his grave is not on view). The restored 17th-century organ can be heard during Monday evening concerts. ♦ Church: free. Tower: admission. M-Sa; Su for church services only. Westerkerkpl (at Prinsengr). 6247766

96 Anne Frankhuis (Anne Frank House) Since it opened to the public in 1960, the house immortalized in *The Diary of Anne Frank* has left a powerful impact on millions of visitors. This building dates back to 1635, but the topmost annex (where the Frank family lived with four other people) was added in the 18th century. You can still see the bookcase and the spare room behind it, well known to *Diary* readers as the place where Anne and the seven others hid for two long years before they were found and taken to concentration camps toward the end of World War II. In addition, there's a fine exhibition about the Frank family and anti-Semitism. ♦ Admission. M-Sa, Su afternoons Sept-May; M-Su until 7PM June-Aug. Prinsengr 263 (at Leliegr). 6264533

97 De Prins ★★$ This cafe has been around forever—like most of Amsterdam's brown cafes—and gives meaning to the Dutch term, *gezelligheid*, or coziness. There's more of a menu here than at most such places, with burgers, tacos, and satays during the day; kebabs and filet of beef at night. Save room for tiramisù for dessert. ♦ Cafe ♦ Daily lunch and dinner; bar open until 1AM. Prinsengr 124 (at Bloemgr). 6249382

98 Koophandel This wood-beamed old warehouse of a brown cafe is another popular after-hours hangout. ♦ Daily 10PM-5AM. Bloemgr 49 (near Bloemdwarsstr). 6239843

99 Kunst & Antiekcentrum De Looier (De Looier Art and Antique Center) Housed in an old warehouse in the Jordaan section (just beyond the Prinsengracht canal) is the largest permanent "art" and "antiques" center in the Netherlands. The selection includes dolls, silver items, porcelain, paintings, glassware, memorabilia, old clothes, jewelry, and more. And for bridge players, there are games going on here every evening. ♦ M-Sa; Th until 9PM. Elandsgr 109 (at Marnixstr). 6249038

100 Eben Haezer (Christian Youth Hostel) $ The atmosphere here is fairly laid-back, which means that Bible discussion is optional, but you may have to work off your party-animal inclinations elsewhere. During the week, a midnight curfew is the rule, but you get to stay out an extra hour on Friday and Saturday. There are separate dorms for men and women (114 beds in all), and cleanliness is closer to godliness here than at other hostels. No credit cards accepted. ♦ Bloemstr 179 (at Lijnbaansgr). 6244717; fax 6232282

Amsterdam

Hotel van Onna

101 Van Onna Hotel $$ This Jordaan hideaway in a 17th-century canal house is operated by the friendly Loek van Onna, who has 39 guest rooms, all with private baths, in three adjacent buildings. Over breakfast (included in the bill), he often regales guests with stories of the hotel's history. ♦ Bloemstr 120 (at 1e Leliedwarstr). 6265801

102 Noordermarkt An open-air market has been thriving on this square since the 17th century, when Amsterdammers came to buy and sell cattle as well as textiles. The cows have long moved on to greener pastures, but on Saturdays look for a traditional bird market, as well as a popular farmers' market where bread, cheeses, organic fruits and vegetables, and flowers are for sale. Minstrels sometimes perform here. On one side of this square is the **Noorderkerk** (North Church), which was erected in 1620. ♦ Sa. At Prinsengr

During the housing shortage that followed World War II, inventive people bought boats to live in and moored them in the city. Today there are more than 2,400 floating houseboat homes in Amsterdam.

Bests

Odette Taminiau
Public Relations and Protocol, City Hall

One of my favorite pastimes is sitting with a good glass of cool Heineken on one of the many sidewalk terraces in the center of town, watching the crowd go by: Amsterdammers running to the floating flower market to buy bundles of colorful tulips or on their way to the international **Albert Cuyp Markt** to buy the ingredients for a good *rijsttafel* (Indonesian rice-table) dinner. A true beehive, particularly on Saturdays.

A favorite area for people watching and for eating is the **Spui** and the **Spuistraat**, a stone's throw away from the floating flower market on **Singel** and **Kalverstraat**, Amsterdam's main pedestrian shopping area. The Spui is an area with typical brown cafes, good and moderately priced restaurants filled with Amsterdammers and tourists alike. Great fun. Spui is a good place to meet friendly, English speaking, locals.

When I am in the mood for good Dutch food, I love to go to **Haesje Claes** restaurant. It serves wonderful dishes "from canapes to caviar" in a traditional Dutch atmosphere for very, very reasonable prices. Do not miss it.

The best (and fun!) museum is the **Stedelijk**, the modern art museum. It has an outstanding permanent collection and very interesting international exhibits. It's located right next to the **Van Gogh Museum** and the **Rijksmuseum**, with Rembrandt's famous *Nightwatch*.

Tip: Walk in the city or take public transport. Trams and buses take you anywhere. Or do as the Amsterdammers do: Take a bike!

Els Wamsteeker
Public Relations Manager, VVV Amsterdam Tourist Office

Amsterdam, city of 1,281 bridges, 160 canals, 550,000 bicycles, and friendly people with a knowledge of many foreign languages.

The city is great for markets: flower markets, flea markets, food markets, book markets.

Take a walk in the **Jordaan**, a former working class area, with mixed people, great atmosphere, narrow streets, courtyards, second-hand boutiques, and small restaurants with international cuisine.

There are outdoor cafes and brown pubs all over the city. My favorite restaurant for Dutch food: **Haesje Claes.**

Visit the **Rijksmuseum** with Rembrandt's paintings, the **Van Gogh Museum,** and many other surprising small museums in beautiful Golden Age 17th-century canal houses or mansions.

Concerts at the **Concertgebouw** have the best acoustics in the world.

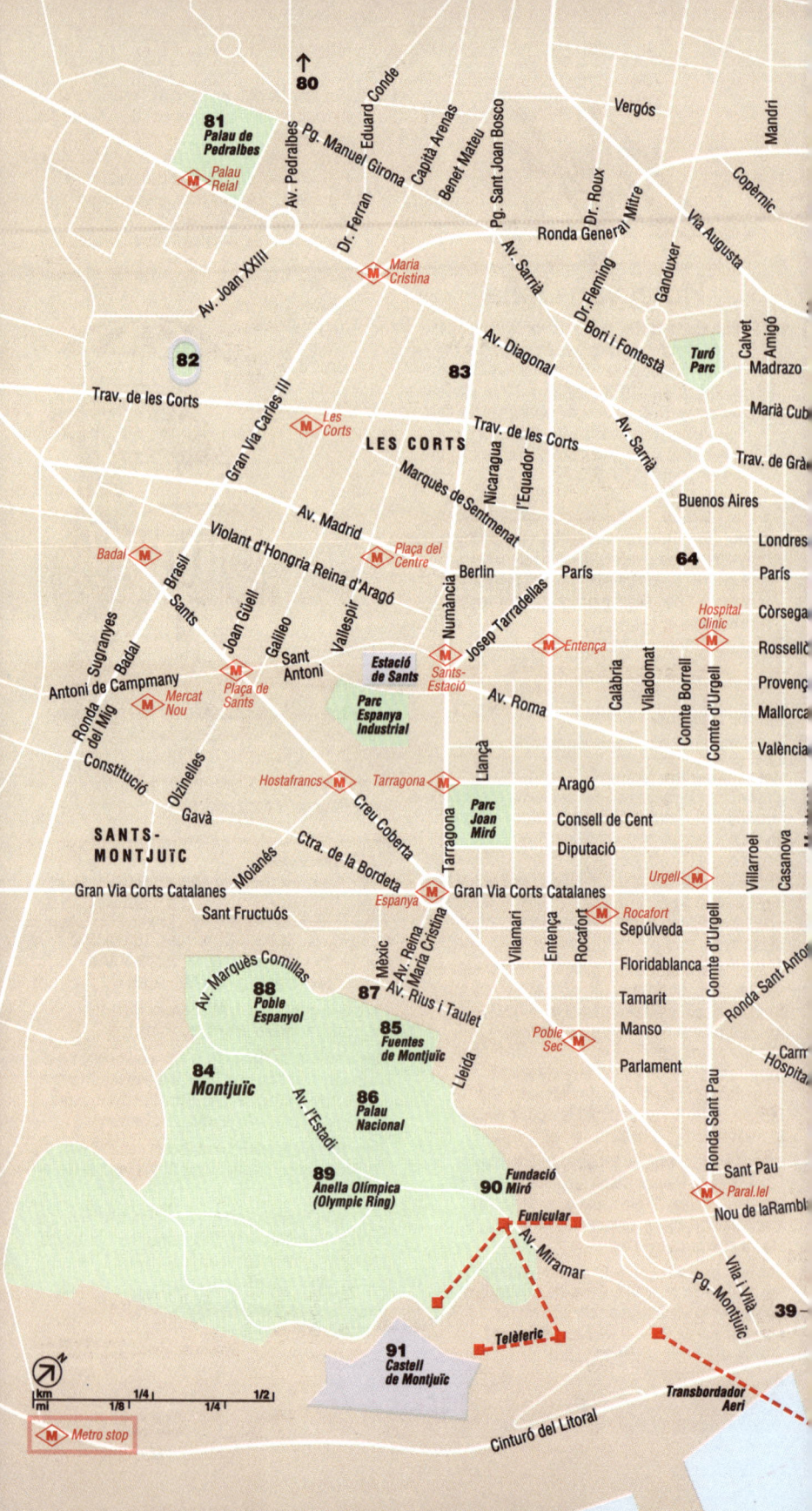

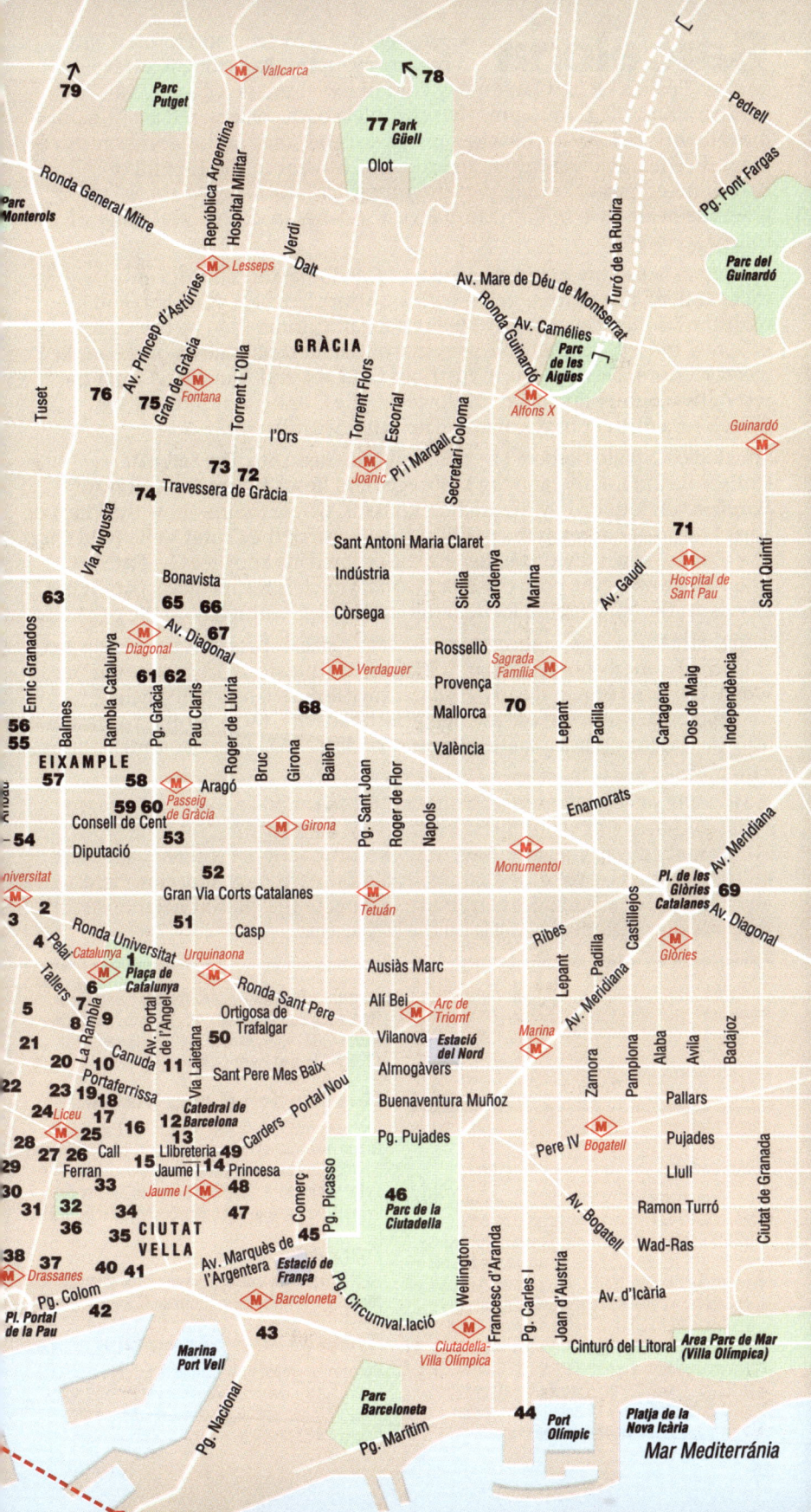

Barcelona

Cosmopolitan, efficient, and infused with a progressive spirit, Barcelona is a traveler's fantasy. Spain's second-largest city contains well-preserved medieval barrios; a host of art museums that chronicle both ancient and avant-garde movements; welcoming beaches and parks; and some of the world's most magnificent and adventurous architecture. Moreover, the 1.6 million Barceloneses, proud of their city and mindful of the lucrative tourist trade, greet the nearly two million annual visitors with an exceptional range of tourist services.

Barcelona is also the maritime capital of Catalonia, for centuries an independent, prosperous region with a distinct language (Catalan) and traditions influenced more by Mediterranean cultures than by the legacy of Spain. Indeed, the palpable presence of Catalan regionalism occasionally creates tension between the industrious Catalans and "outsiders" from the rest of the country and beyond. However, the Catalonian culture gives Barcelona a distinct flavor; it is like no other Spanish city.

Situated on a plain bordered by the **Mediterranean Sea**, the **Serra de Collserola** mountains, and the **Llobregat** and **Besòs Rivers**, the colony of **Barcino** was founded by the ancient Romans, whose forum—now the **Plaça de Sant Jaume**—endures as the political focal point of the **Ciutat Vella (Old City)**. The Ciutat Vella is divided in two by the promenade known as **La Rambla**. As one walks toward the port, the **Barri Gòtic**, which is the medieval part of the city, is on the left, and the **Raval**, built in the 18th century, is on the right.

Above the **Plaça de Catalunya**, an ancient maze of passageways gives way to the broad, orderly boulevards of **L'Eixample** (literally "The Expansion"), where the late 19th- and early 20th-century industrialists built their mansions. To the north are the neighborhoods of **Gràcia**, **Sants**, **Pedralbes**, and **Sarrià**, formerly separate villages now absorbed into the municipality.

The Ciutat Vella is Barcelona's least expensive barrio, with numerous reasonably priced accommodations centered around La Rambla. Its many restaurants offer an economical *menú del día* at lunchtime, and the tapas bars are good for cheap eats in the evening. An international student card banishes cultural hunger by yielding significant discounts at most museums and attractions. For affordable merrymaking, look to the vibrant neighborhood festivals that periodically dress up the city streets.

To call from the US, dial 011 (international access code), 34 (country code), 3 (city code), and the local number. When calling from inside Spain, dial 03 and the local number. City codes appearing within text are for areas outside Barcelona.

Getting to Barcelona

Airports

Both international and national flights land at **El Prat Airport** (3792454), located about 10 kilometers (6 miles) southwest of the city. Tourist information and currency-exchange facilities are located in the **International Arrival Hall**; both are open daily. To get into Barcelona travelers can take either the regular, inexpensive **RENFE** trains or the **Aerobús** to the city center. With service every 30 minutes, the railway leaves passengers at either **Estació de Sants** (Plaça Joan Peiro, 4900202) or **Plaça de Catalunya;** the **Aerobús** operates every 15 minutes and makes several stops in the city, the last at Plaça de Catalunya. Both take approximately half an hour. Rental car operators with offices at the airport are: **Atesa** (3022832), **Avis** (3794026), **Europcar** (3799051), and **Hertz** (4908662).

Bus Station (Long-Distance)

Most international buses arrive in the **Estació de Sants** (see above), where you can hop on the metro. Domestic buses drop passengers either at the **Estació del Nord** (2657845), next to the **Arc de Triomf** metro stop, or somewhere in the center city.

Ferries

Ferries from the Balearic Islands dock at the **Estació Marítima** (4432532), at the end of La Rambla.

Train Station (Long-Distance)

Barcelona's main train station is **Estació de Sants** (see above). Some international trains and some long-distance Spanish trains pull into the elegant **Estació de França** (Av Marquez del La' Argentera and Paseo Picasso, 4900202), a few blocks from the **Barceloneta** metro stop. Both stations have tourist information offices, banks, and luggage storage facilities.

Getting around Barcelona

Bicycles People do ride bicycles, but Barcelona is not really a bike-friendly city. Dedicated cyclists, however, can rent bicycles from the following businesses: **Bicitram** (Av Marquès de l'Argentera 15, at C Comerç, 7922841); **Grup de Treball Bici-Clot** (C Sant Joan de Malta 1, at C Verneda, 3077475); and **Sun Bike** (C Navata 6, at C Onofre, 4340824). All are open during general business hours, Monday through Saturday.

Buses Barcelona's bus routes are a bit complicated, but there's usually a detailed map at each stop. Regular service generally runs from 6:30AM to 10PM, with late-night service from 10PM to 4AM. Buy a ticket from the driver or have the machine up front punch your multitrip bus/metro ticket, purchased only at metro stations (see below).

Driving Traffic is heavy, there are many one-way streets, and pedestrians and motor scooters are likely to dart out without warning, so plenty of caution is in order. On the broader streets, the far right-hand lane is reserved for buses and cabs, and woe unto the driver who uses it, except to make a right-hand turn. The worst problem is finding a place to park—there are a lot of public garages throughout the city, but they are very expensive.

Funiculars and Telèferics The **Montjuïc** funicular runs between the **Paral.lel** metro stop and the top of **Montjuïc**. It operates on Saturday and Sunday throughout the year, with daily service during the summer months and at Christmas and Holy Week holiday times. The funicular deposits passengers at the top of the mountain, near the amusement park and near a *telèferic* (or cable car) station which connects to the **Castell de Montjuïc**; call 4430859 for information. Another way up the mountain is via the **Transbordador Aéreo del Puerto** *telèferic* (4430859), which runs from Barceloneta to Montjuïc daily from noon until 6PM, with extended evening hours in spring and summer. It doesn't stop near any attractions, though: The ride is merely a scenic one. To reach **Mont Tibidabo**, site of Barcelona's other mountaintop amusement park, take the *Tramvia Blau* (blue tram) from the **Ferrocarrils de la Generalitat de Catalunya (FF.CC)** station at Avinguda Tibidabo to connect with the funicular (2117942) at the base of the mountain. The tram runs daily in the summer months, and on Saturday, Sunday, and holidays during the rest of the year.

Metro Barcelona's clean, efficient subway (4120000) operates Monday through Thursday from 5AM to 11PM, with service until 1AM Friday, Saturday, and nights before holidays. Metro tickets are sold singly or in packages: the T1 is valid for 10 trips on the metro, bus (except for certain night buses), and the **FF.CC** trains; the T2 allows 10 trips on the metro and **FF.CC** trains only. There are also one-, three-, and five-day passes, good for unlimited travel on both the metro and buses. All metro stations sell the T1, T2, and one-day passes; the three- and five-day passes are sold only at the **Sants-Estació, Universitat,** and **Sagrada Família** stations.

Taxis The city's black-and-yellow taxis are plentiful and not too expensive. Hail one from any street corner, wait at the nearest taxi stand (marked by a "T" sign), or call 3577755, 3581111, 3922222, or 4431020.

Tours For the best deal in town take local bus *100*, which makes a continuous loop stopping at the city's 15 most-frequented sights. The bus departs from **Plaça de Catalunya** every 20 minutes between 9AM and 7:30PM daily, from 12 June through 12 October. Organized bus tours of the city are offered by **Julia Tours** (3176454) and **Pullmantur** (3171297).

Trains There are two local rail lines: one originates at **Plaça de Catalunya**, the other at **Plaça d'Espanya**. Call the **FF.CC** offices (2051515) for schedules and information.

Walking Barcelona is one of the world's greatest cities for walking. Whether on a wide boulevard or a narrow back street with laundry hanging from the balconies, there is always a lovely building to see. A walk through the old city, or down La Rambla, punctuated with stops at cafes along the way, is the very best way to savor this city.

FYI

Accommodations Whether for hotels or hostels, advance reservations are strongly advised. Visitors who arrive without them may have to spend a long time searching for a room because the tourist offices don't book accommodations. For a list of bed-and-breakfast establishments contact the **Barcelona Tourist Bureau** at 4231800.

Business Hours The midday break is firmly established in Barcelona. Most retail stores and businesses are open Monday through Saturday from 10AM to 1:30PM, and then again from from 4 or 5PM until 8PM. Banking hours are 8:30AM to 2PM Monday through Friday, and 8:30AM to 1PM on Saturday; in summer, many switch to an 8AM-3PM schedule, with no Saturday service. Most museums are closed on Monday and on Sunday afternoons; the remaining days have a long midday break (usually between 1:30 and 4PM), but most reopen and stay open until well into the evening.

Restaurants serve lunch between 1:30 and 3PM, with dinner beginning after 9PM. Trendy bars and discos don't get rolling until after midnight, and there are some that don't close until 8AM—allowing just enough time to go home, shower, and return to work.

Climate Barcelona's climate is moderate. By May it is warm enough to hit the beach; the ensuing summer months can be quite hot (up to 95 degrees), and most places are not air-conditioned. Although winter temperatures rarely drop below freezing, even 45 degrees can feel cold and damp since many older buildings don't have upgraded heating systems.

Consulates and Embassies

Canada Trav les Cortes 265, between C Numancia ....and C Vallespir, 4106699

UK Av Diagonal 477, between C Calvet and C Urgell, ...4199044; fax 4052411

US Paseo Reina Elisenda 23, between Pl Sarria and ....Pl Pedralbes, 280222; fax 2055206

Barcelona

Discount Tickets Most museums offer student discounts (with I.D.); inquire at the admissions desk. Most movie theaters have a weekly "day of the viewer," which offers tickets at a reduced price; these are listed in the newspaper each day. The **Barcelona Youth Council** (C Calabria 147, near C Consell de Cent, 4838378) provides information about discounted tickets and travel.

Drinking Eighteen is the legal drinking age in Spain. While Barcelonese rarely drink to excess, they do like to drink; in addition to bars and clubs, almost all cafes and restaurants serve alcohol.

Emergencies Dial 061 for an ambulance or to locate a doctor in an emergency situation. The hospital for emergencies is the **Hospital Clinico** (C Villaroel and C Provença). If time permits, call your country's consulate for a list of English-speaking physicians. Daily newspapers list local all-night pharmacies, and closed pharmacies post a notice identifying the nearest open pharmacy. For a police emergency, call the **Guardia Urbana** (3019060). For legal help, contact your country's consulate.

Language Barcelona is the capital of autonomous Catalonia, and thus Catalan is the city's principal written and spoken language. Street signs and menus are usually in Catalan, but nearly every tourist brochure will have a Spanish or English version, and locals will converse in Spanish if necessary.

Laundry There are plenty of laundromats around town where you can wash your own or leave it to be done at a reasonable price. Just one block from the **Plaça Reial** is the **Lavanderia Tigre** (C Rauic 20, between C Ferran and C Tres Llits, no phone). It's open Monday through Saturday.

Money The *peseta* (abbreviated as Pta) is the unit of currency. There are scores of banks and money-exchange offices at **Plaça de Catalunya** and south along La Rambla, in the **Estació de Sants, Estació de França,** and at the airport. Several exchange offices keep extended hours, often staying open daily until 11PM. Many banks now have cash machines that are accessible 24 hours a day. The **American Express** office (Pg de Gràcia 101, at C Rossello, 2170070) is open Monday through Friday and on Saturday mornings.

Personal Safety Take the usual precautions to foil pickpockets and purse snatchers. Avoid displaying large sums of money in public, carry your wallet in a front pocket or a waist-pack, keep a hand on your belongings at all times, and stay off the deserted streets of the **Barrio Chino** and **Barri Gòtic** at night.

Walls built by the Romans in the fourth century protected Barcelona until the 13th century, when a new enclosure was erected by King Jaume I. There is evidence that Roman Barcino was larger than the boundaries indicate; fortifications stand on the remains of even older Roman buildings, and Roman artifacts have been found as far outside the walls as the Sants district.

Postal Services The main post office, **Correus i Telègrafs** (Plaça d'Antóni López, 3183831) is open Monday through Saturday from 8AM until 10PM, and on Sunday from 9AM until 2PM.

Publications The daily newspapers *(La Vanguardia, El Pais, El Periodico)* all have extensive entertainment sections each day, listing films, music, galleries, theater, and other events. For the most comprehensive information about upcoming happenings—museums, music, restaurants, and bars—buy *Guia de Ocio;* it's published weekly and sold at newsstands.

Public Holidays New Year's Day, Day of the Kings (6 January), Holy Thursday, Good Friday, Easter Sunday and Monday, Labor Day (1 May), Feast of the Assumption (15 August), National Day of Catalunya (11 September), Day of Our Lady of Mercy (24 September), Feast of the Virgin of Pilar (12 October), All Saints Day (1 November), Constitution Day (6 December), Feast of the Immaculate Conception (8 December), Christmas, and St. Stephen's Day (26 December).

Public Rest Rooms Most parts of the city do not have any free public rest rooms. There are public lavatories behind **La Boqueria** market, but the attendant at the door collects a small fee. There are rest rooms on most floors of the department store **El Corte Ingles** in the **Plaça Catalunya**.

Restaurants The Spanish are famous for their late hours, and Barcelona is no exception. Supper is often put on the table as late as 10PM, and no one goes to a restaurant for dinner before 9PM. Lunch usually begins sometime between 1:30PM and 3PM. There is no general rule about reservations; some places require them, some won't take them.

Shopping This is the equivalent of a national pastime in Barcelona, with options (and prices) ranging from the swank shops along La Rambla Catalunya and Passeig de Gràcia, to the **Els Encants** flea market on the **Plaça de les Glòries Catalanes** and the huge used-book market held every Sunday at the **Mercat San Antoni**.

Smoking It's permitted everywhere (except **Metro** stations, where the no-smoking rule is frequently ignored); cigarette smoke is a fact of life here.

Street Plan In the **Ciutat Viella,** or old city, a hopeless labyrinth of narrow streets branches off from the spine of La Rambla, all the way from **Plaça Catalunya** to the sea. But above the **Plaça Catalunya** a modern street plan takes hold, and everything is orderly (even alternating one-way streets) in the 585-block grid of the **Eixample**.

Taxes Generally, the price posted for an item or service already includes the tax; a notable exception is the seven percent hotel tax that is added to the price of accommodations.

Telephones Public *locutorios* (phone centers) are the most economical way to place direct and collect international calls, but be prepared for long lines. *Locutorios* can be found at **Estació de Sants, Estació de Nord,** and at the airport. The **Estació de Sants** office is open daily from 8AM until 10:30PM; the other two are open Monday through Friday.

Barcelona

Tipping Restaurants include a 15-percent service charge in the bill, so additional tipping is not required. Taxi drivers expect 10 to 15 percent on the meter.

Visas No visas are required. Visitors to Barcelona need only a valid passport.

Visitors' Information Travelers with questions can call the 24-hour **Information Hotline** at 010. There are tourism offices at **Estació de Sants** (Plaça Paisos Catalans); **Estació de França** (Av Marquès l'Argentera); and, from 1 June to 31 August, **Ajuntament de Barcelona** (Plaça Sant Jaume).

Besides offering indispensable city, metro, and bus maps, these offices have excellent informational brochures. In summer, the city sets up temporary aid stations in prime tourist zones and employs roving uniformed guides to answer travelers' questions. For cultural information stop in at the **Centre d'Informació** in the **Palau de la Virreina** (La Rambla 99, between C Carme and C Petxina, 3017775).

A few records set during the 1992 Summer Olympic Games in Barcelona: Number of postcards received—45,000 (by the American basketball Dream Team). Number of faxes received—8,900 (Japanese delegation). Number of condoms dispensed in the Olympic Village—7,751.

---

1 Plaça de Catalunya Separating the Ciutat Vella, or old city, and the Eixample, this grand plaza is Barcelona's civic, if not geographic, hub. A fine place to settle on a bench and watch the locals pass, it's graced by two fountains and various sculptures, including *Le Deessa* ("The Goddess") by Josep Clarà. ♦ Bounded by Rambla Catalunya, Ronda Universitat, Pg Gràcia, and C Fontanella

2 Australia Residencial $ The friendly, English-speaking owners lived in New South Wales for 18 years—hence the name of this clean and comfortable little pensione. Some of the eight guest rooms have private baths; one double connects with an adjoining room, ideal for families. It's often booked a month in advance. ♦ Closed in August. Ronda Universitat 11 (between C Balmes and Pl Universitat). 3174177

3 Pension L'Isard $ This bright, inexpensive pensione offers a number of pleasant, money-saving triples. The 14 quiet guest rooms have comfortable beds, but only two rooms have private baths. ♦ C Tallers 82 (between C Gravina and Pl Universitat). 3025183

4 Pelayo 14 This music store has great bargains on CDs, records, and tapes of everyone from Paco de Lucia to Guns 'N Roses to Grace Jones. ♦ M-Sa. C Pelai 14 (at C Gravina). 3187776

5 Museu d'Art Contemporani Barcelona's newest museum is still under construction, but it's open and exhibiting about 1,000 works of art. The museum's permanent collection will showcase works from the second half of the 20th century by artists from all over the world. ♦ Admission. Tu-Su. Plaça dels Angels 1 (between C Elisabets and C Valldonzella). 4120810

6 La Rambla With bird-sellers and buskers, flower vendors and palm readers, this broad boulevard is Barcelona's most entertaining urban attraction. Stretching from the gracious **Plaça de Catalunya** to the seedy edge of the Barrio Chino (the name means Chinatown, but there is nothing even vaguely Oriental about it) and the harbor beyond, the street was once a stream that ran along the city's 13th-century walls. These days everybody—businesspeople, artists, transvestites, tourists—comes here to browse at the news kiosks or to sip beer at the outdoor cafes. Don't miss the **Font de Canaletes** at the top of the promenade; whoever drinks from this 19th-century iron fountain, so the legend goes, will return to Barcelona. The boulevard's midpoint, **Plaça de la Boqueria,** is marked by a circular mosaic by Joan Miró; at the waterfront end of La Rambla is Gaietà Buïgas's towering *Monumento a Cristobal Colón*. ♦ Between Plaça Portal de la Pau and Plaça de Catalunya

7 Hotel Lloret $$ The full-frills rooms will blow a hole in most strict budgets, but the management maintains some doubles without private baths or air-conditioning whose rates are within means. The staff of the 52-room establishment is multilingual, and with La Rambla right below, the location is ideal. There is no restaurant. ♦ La Rambla 125 (at C Tallers). 3173366

8 L'Ovella Negra Locals and tourists alike flock to this enormous, boisterous tavern where the food and drink are proletarian-priced. Loud music and pool tables create a frat-party feel. ♦ Daily 9AM-2:30AM. C Sitjàs 5 (between C Bon Succés and C Tallers). 3171087

9 Hotel Capitol $$ The least expensive option in a multihotel building at the top of La Rambla exudes old-fashioned charm while

29

Barcelona

supplying modern conveniences. Some baths are private and some shared, but there are televisions and telephones in all 11 rooms. There is no restaurant. ♦ La Rambla 138 (between C Santa Anna and Pl Catalunya). 3010872; fax 4123142

10 Govinda ★★$$ A healthful salad bar and generous daily specials draw lunchtime crowds to this excellent vegetarian Indian restaurant. Travel companions should be sure to share a *thali* (a tray of various delicacies); the fruit and yogurt concoctions are likewise delicious. ♦ Vegetarian/Indian ♦ M-Sa lunch and dinner; closed in August. Pl Vila de Madrid 4-5 (between C Duc Victoria and C d'En Bot). 3187729

11 Casa Martí Els Quatro Gats Between 1897 and 1903, the ground floor of this four-story structure was the celebrated cafe hangout of the group of modern masters known as *Els Quatro Gats* ("The Four Cats"), founded by Ramón Casas, Santiago Rusiñol, Miguel Utrillo, and Pere Romen. Eventually Pablo Picasso joined this dynamic circle, which organized poetry readings and art exhibits (Picasso's first public show was held here in 1900), and produced a magazine (still in publication) bearing the group's name. ♦ C Montsio 3 (at Ptge Patriarca)

Within Casa Martí Els Quatro Gats:

4CATS

Quatro Gats ★★$$ Unless you're ready to splurge, skip the Art Noveau dining room and head straight for the cafe to sample a tasty tapa or two and soak up the arty ambience at a fraction of the cost. ♦ Catalan ♦ M-Sa lunch and dinner; Su dinner; closed in August. 3024140

12 Catedral de Barcelona A Romanesque church stood on this site as early as 1046, but work on the current Gothic basilica began in 1298, with the bulk of it completed between 1365 and 1388. By the time the facade and dome were finished in 1913, the building had been six centuries in the making. Of special note are the high altar, created in the 14th century; the decorative choir stalls, completed in 1459; and the crypt of Santa Eulàlia (one of the city's two patron saints), with its alabaster sepulcher by Jaume Fabre. The cloisters, replete with palm trees and geese, house the **Museu de la Catedral** and its prized possession, *La Pietat* by Bartolomé Bermejo, which dates from the late 15th century. Visitors to the cathedral on Saturday or Sunday (except in August) can catch the 6:30PM performance of *sardanas*, a Catalan folk dance; the building is then illuminated at 7PM—an inspiring sight. ♦ Museum: daily 11AM-1PM. Pl Seu (between C Comtes and C Bisbe). 3151554

13 Plaça del Rei Located in the heart of the Barri Gòtic, this square is one of the Ciutat Vella's premier plazas. Here you can see the former home of the Catalan royal family, the **Palau Reial Major** (Great Royal Palace). This complex owes much of its current appearance to Guillem Carbonell, who transformed a 10th-century salon into the spacious **Saló del Tinell** in 1370; it's widely held that King Ferdinand and Queen Isabella received Columbus in this wide-arched hall after he discovered the New World. The Gothic **Capella Reial de Santa Agueda** (Royal Chapel of Saint Agueda) contains the **Retaule del Condestable**, a remarkable 1465 altarpiece by Jaume Huguet.

For a rooftop view of the palace, visitors can climb the **Torre del Rei Martí** (Tower of King Martin) where a multilingual history student is usually posted to answer questions. Across the plaza, the lovely 16th-century **Casa Clariana-Padellàs** houses the **Museu d'Història de la Ciutat** (Museum of City History), whose highlights include in-site excavations from the city's Roman past and the oldest known inscription of the ancient colony's complete name: **Colonia Iulia Augusta Faventia Paterna Barcino**. ♦ Admission to museum includes access to all of the above. Tu-Sa, Su 10AM-2PM Oct-June; Tu-Sa 10AM-8PM, Su 10AM-2PM July-Sept. Plaça del Veguer 2 (between C Tapineria and C Comtes). 3151111

GELATERIA ITALIANA PAGLIOTTA

14 Gelateria Italiana Pagliotta The gregarious Italian owner of this ice cream parlor dishes up Barcelona's creamiest gelato. In addition to the caloric concoctions, he makes a sugarless version. ♦ M-Th, Sa-Su until 11:30PM Mar-June, daily until 11:30PM July and Aug; closed 16 October-1 March. C Jaume I 15 (between Pl l'Angel and C Trompetes). 3105324

14 Hotel Rey Don Jaime I $$ This centrally located, exceptional budget hotel rents 30 spacious rooms, each with a private bath, phone, and small balcony. About half of the rooms are doubles that can be converted to triples. There is no restaurant. ♦ C Jaume I 11 (at C Freneria). 3154161; fax 3154161

15 Plaça de Sant Jaume Note the impressive facades of the **Palau de la Generalitat**, the seat of Catalonia's government, and **Casa de la Ciutat** (City Hall). The pure Renaissance styling of the **Palau**'s 1596 front facade is a rarity in Barcelona, and its Gothic elevation facing

Barcelona

Carrer Bisbe features a magnificent 15th-century medallion of Sant Jordi, Catalonia's patron saint. The Carrer Ciutat side of the **Casa de la Ciutat** is a striking example of Flamboyant Gothic architecture, and the mid–19th-century Neo-Classical facade facing the plaza is the work of architect **Josep Mas i Vila.** On summer mornings, visitors are allowed into the ground-level tourist information office to sneak a peak at Albert Ràfaiks Casamada's marvelous frescoes. ♦ Bounded by C Ciutat and C Sant Honorat, and Pl Sant Miguel and C Bisbe

16 Churreria San Ramon For years, this bakery has been producing its own delectable version of *churros*—sugary strips of fried dough. Buy a bagful and then take them to the *granja* (milk bar/cafe) a few doors down and dunk them in coffee. ♦ M, W-Su 8AM-8:30PM. C Banys Nous 8 (between C Ferran and C Ave Maria). 3187691

17 Plaça de Sant Josep Oriol The convivial cafes and weekend art market at this square draw young people from Barcelona and beyond. ♦ Bounded by C Pi, C Ave Maria, and C Cecs de la Boqueria

17 El Pi Antic ★★$$ Italian-style pizza and pasta (try the seafood lasagna) are served here, along with more typical Catalan entrées and pastries. Have a seat at the wrought-iron tables for an afternoon beer; perhaps you'll be tempted to linger until evening, when live piano music makes it a romantic place to dine. Unlike many of the surrounding restaurants, this one stays open in August. ♦ Italian/ Catalan ♦ Daily breakfast, lunch, and dinner. Plaça de Sant Josep Oriol 4 (at Plaça del Pi). 3017191

18 Plaça del Pi Christened for its lone pine tree, this plaza is the site of the **Esglesia de Santa Maria del Pi,** an exquisite example of the Catalan Gothic style of architecture. ♦ Bounded by C del Cardenal Casañas and C Petritxol

Within Plaça del Pi:

Ganiveteria Roca, S.A. Although this shop dates from 1911, it's literally on the cutting edge of technology, and boasts an impressive selection of Swiss Army knives, menacing daggers, and some truly monstrous cook's cleavers. ♦ M-Sa. Pl del Pi 3 (at C Petritxol). 3021241

19 Huespedes Colmenero $$ Located on one of the most charming streets in the Ciutat Vella, this nearly 30-year-old hotel is often booked a month or two in advance. Its seven guest rooms (one with private bath) are by no means spacious, but they're spotless and serene. ♦ C Petritxol 12 (between Pl del Pi and C Portaferrissa). 3026624

19 La Pallaresa ★★$ Come early evening; it's never easy to find a table at this *xocolateria.* You'll understand why after one sip of the creamy hot chocolate or sweet *horchata* (a cold, milklike drink made from *chufa,* or tiger nuts). ♦ Daily. C Petritxol 11 (between Pl del Pi and C Portaferrissa). 3022036

20 Los Toreros ★$ Plastered with pictures of current and retired bullfighters, this inexpensive restaurant offers an extensive selection of Spanish specialties, including paella and a piquant gazpacho. ♦ Spanish ♦ M-F lunch and dinner; Su lunch. C Xuclà 3-5 (between C Carme and C Pintor Fortuny). 3182325

21 Biocenter ★★$ Loyal patrons of this vegetarian restaurant were delighted when it relocated from its former cramped quarters to this large, airy space across the street. Check out the ample salad bar and creative entrées. ♦ Vegetarian ♦ M-Sa lunch and dinner. C Pintor Fortuny 25 (between C Xuclà and C Doctor Joaquim Dou). 3014583

22 Antic Hospital de la Santa Creu This medieval-era hospital served Barcelona's sick and injured from 1410 until 1926. The elegant Gothic structure now houses special-interest libraries: **Biblioteca de Catalunya,** the **Institut d'Estudis Catalans,** and the **Acadèmia de Medicina.** Peek into see the vestibule's 17th-century tiles painted with scenes from the life of Sant Pau, as well as the cloisters beyond and the extravagant lecture hall. ♦ M-F. Bounded by C Hospital and C Carme, and C Floristes Rambla and C Egipcíaques

23 Palau de la Virreina Built in 1778 by **Josep Ausich** at the command of the viceroy of Peru, this Rococo building typifies residences of Barcelona's upper crust from that era. Today the palace, named for the viceroy's wife, hosts art exhibitions and houses **Casa Beethoven** (3014826), a music store that sells every kind of sheet music from Bach to the Beatles. The palace also contains the **Centre d'Informació,** the city's cultural information office. ♦ Exhibit Hall: Tu-Sa 11AM-9PM; Su 11AM-3PM. Casa Beethoven: M-Sa. La Rambla 99 (between C Petxina and C Carme). 3017775

23 Mercat de Sant Josep (La Boqueria) The bustling stalls of this food market, located here since 1840, contain every foodstuff imaginable and some, such as *criadillas de toro* (bull's testicles), you might rather not imagine. ♦ M-Sa 6:30AM-7PM. La Rambla 85-89 (between C Petxina and C Carme)

Contemporary Catalan opera stars include Monserrat Caballé, Victoria de los Angeles, and José Carreras.

31

Barcelona

24 Restaurant Egipte ★$$ This inviting wood-paneled restaurant, tucked behind **La Boqueria**, is known for quick service and reasonably priced fare. ♦ Catalan/Spanish ♦ M-Sa lunch and dinner. C Jerusalem 3 (between C Hospital and Pl Gardunya). 3177480. Also at: La Rambla 79 (at C Hospital). 3179545

25 Hotel Inglés $$ In spite of its name, this commendable hotel is frequented more by Europeans than by Anglos. The staff is hospitable, and the 30 guest rooms with private baths are ample and neat. There's a convenient on-site laundry service and a full board option, with meals served in the hotel's restaurant. ♦ C Boqueria 17 (at La Rambla). 3173770; fax 3027870

26 Cafè de L'Opera ★★$ At the turn of the century, this was *the* posh place for coffee and conversation. In the 1990s, it is decidedly less fancy but no less popular. ♦ Cafe ♦ Daily 9AM-2AM. La Rambla 74 (between C Ferrand and C Boqueria). 3177585

27 Gran Teatro del Liceu Barcelona's famed opera house made its debut with a performance of Donizetti's *Ana Bolen* in 1847; since then, Pavlova, Callas, and other luminaries have tread these venerable boards. In a feat of architectural innovation, the auditorium was constructed without a single interior supporting column. Much to the dismay of music-lovers, the theater is now closed due to a fire. It is undergoing renovations and is scheduled to reopen sometime in 1997 to celebrate its 150th anniversary. ♦ La Rambla 61 (between C Unió and C Sant Pau). 4123532

Only the French can designate their sparkling wine as *champagne*, so Spanish vintners call their version *cava*, stemming from the Catalan word for "wine cellar."

28 Hotel Peninsular $ Popular with students of architecture and art history, this Modernista building boasts a colorful past that includes a brief stint as a bordello. Centered around an enormous courtyard overflowing with hanging plants, its 80 rooms (70 with private baths) are simple and comfortable. The effusive staffers know all the trendy and vibrant parts of the city. There is no restaurant. ♦ C Sant Pau 34 (between C Arc de Sant Agustí and C Junta de Comerç). 3023138; fax 3023138

28 Els Tres Bots ★★$ The chalkboard menu outside this large, down-home restaurant lists only a fraction of the affordable dishes, especially fish and seafood, prepared by the capable kitchen. Generous portions compensate for what the restaurant lacks in atmosphere. ♦ Catalan/Spanish ♦ Daily lunch and dinner. C Sant Pau 42 (between C Arc de Sant Agustí and C Junta de Comerç). 3171042

29 Pollo Rico ★$ The specialty of the house is revealed by the rows of featherless fowls roasting in the front window. This one-note restaurant is fast, and easy on the *pesetas*. ♦ Chicken ♦ M-Tu, Th-Su lunch and dinner. C Sant Pau 31 (at C Junta de Comerç). 4413184

30 London Bar Since its debut on a midsummer's eve in 1910, this Modernista bar has been the watering hole favored by actors, artists, musicians, and, more recently, *guiris* (foreigners). There's live music almost every night; some acts are of dubious abilities, but then again, there's no cover charge. ♦ W-Sa 7PM-3AM. C Nou de la Rambla 34 (between C Penedides and C Sant Ramon). 3185261

31 Palau Güel Now a performing arts library and archives, this palace was designed by the architect **Antoni Gaudí i Cornet** at the height of his creative powers. The 1888 structure, built for the architect's patron, combines Gothic elements with Arabic flourishes, resulting in a fantastic, castlelike visage. The cylindrical stone grille carries the eagle-capped Catalonian coat of arms. Don't miss the ceramic and stone mosaics (known as *trencadís*) on the 18 chimneys. ♦ Admission. M-Sa. C Nou de la Rambla 3-5 (between La Rambla and C Lancaster). 3173974

32 Plaça Reial A graceful square inspired by the French plazas of the Napoleonic era brims with outdoor cafes, bars, hostels, and discos. The plaza is a hip (and slightly seamy) gathering spot for the young and restless. (The once-booming nocturnal drug trade, however, has been seriously curtailed by the ever-present police.) In the square's center, a fountain, the **Fuente de las Tres Gracias**, flows; the lampposts are attributed to a young **Gaudí**. ♦ East of La Rambla (between C Escudellers and C Ferran)

Restaurants/Clubs: Red   **Hotels:** Blue
Shops/♦ Outdoors: Green   **Sights/Culture:** Black

Barcelona

32 Barcelona Pipa Club A great spot to relax and listen to some cool music, this jazz club features a small stage with good acoustics, comfortable couches and chairs, and a classy wooden bar serving reasonably priced drinks. Though it's officially a members-only club, anyone can ring the doorbell and pay a small, one-time cover charge. ♦ Cover. M-Tu, Th-Su 10PM-3AM. Pl Reial 3. 3024732

32 Albergue Juvenil Kabul $ A "great party atmosphere" boasts the brochure, which successfully attracts punkers, tie-dye types, and other youthful revelers to this independent hostel. Music blares in the game room, which is equipped with a bar, pool tables, and satellite TV. The dormitories, with space for 150 people, are packed and the communal bathrooms less than sparkling clean. ♦ Pl Reial 17. 3185190; fax 3014034

32 Hostal de Joves Internacional Colon III $ This 100-bed private youth hostel offers doubles, triples, and quads, in addition to crowded dormitory-style rooms. All baths are shared. Bonuses include laundry service and the lack of a curfew, but the atmosphere is frenetic. If it overwhelms you, ask about its nearby sister hostel **Hostal Palermo** (C Boqueria 21, near La Rambla, 3024002), which is a little more tranquil. ♦ C Colom 3 (between Pl Reial and La Rambla). 3180631

33 Itaca The most appealing and most affordable collection of glasswork and pottery in the Barri Gòtic includes handblown candlesticks from Majorca and ceramic coffee mugs from Seville. Shipping pieces home is prohibitively expensive, but the owners are expert at wrapping purchases to withstand travel. ♦ M-Sa. C Ferran 26 (between C Avinyó and C Rauric). 3013044

33 La Manual Alpargatera Watch espadrilles being stitched by hand at the rear of this shoe store. ♦ M-Sa. C Avinyó 7 (between Bda Sant Miquel and C Ferran). 3010172

33 Hostal Levante $ Don't let the dilapidated 19th-century facade put you off: hidden within is an excellent budget hotel, with 27 clean, airy guest rooms and comfortable beds. Eight rooms have private baths. ♦ Bda Sant Miquel 2 (at C Avinyó). 3179565

34 Casa Huéspedes Mari-Luz $ Owner Mari-Luz and her husband, Fernando, keep their pensione sparkling clean. There are 15 rooms, two of which have private baths. Guests consistently rave about the firm beds and the solicitous proprietors. ♦ C Palau 4 (between Comtessa de Sobradiel and C Cervantes). 3173463

34 Alberg Juvenil Palau $ Housed in a mid-19th century building, this 40-bed hostel outshines its center-city counterparts. The refurbished facilities feature tile floors, modern bath and kitchen facilities to share, and spacious guest rooms. One room has two beds, while the others have four. Rates include breakfast; sheets are extra. There's a midnight curfew, but the doors reopen briefly at 3AM for night owls. ♦ C Palau 6 (between C Comtessa de Sobradiel and C Cervantes). 4125080

35 Harlem Jazz Club Considered by many to be the city's best venue for jazz, this club books international as well as local acts. Even if no performers are scheduled, there's still music in the air: from the club's outstanding collection of jazz recordings. ♦ Tu-Su 8PM-4AM; closed in August. C Comtessa de Sobradiel 8 (between C Ataülf and C Avinyó). 3100755

35 El Gallo Kiriko ★★$ This Pakistani restaurant deep in the heart of the old city offers excellent couscous, served with meat or vegetables, at rock-bottom prices. The front room has eight tables that are usually filled by a budget-conscious international crowd. Walk on through to the back room to see if there is a seat at one of the four tables set in a cave, the walls of which are said to be the old Roman walls of the city. ♦ Pakistani ♦ M-Sa lunch and dinner; Su lunch. C Avinyó 19 (between Comtessa de Sobradiel and C Cervantes). No phone

---

Architect Antonio Gaudí i Cornet worked on the Sagrada Família cathedral for 43 years; the project consumed his professional life in the last 15 years before his death, and he lived in a workshop on the construction site. When he was run over by a tram in 1926, he had become so reclusive that he went unrecognized in the hospital.

Barcelona

36 La Fonda ★★$$ Heaping platters of fabulous food and surprisingly low prices have Barceloneses queuing up around the block for a table at this attractive eatery. Specialties include cod in a savory tomato sauce, monkfish with potatoes, and black rice. Don't pass up the luscious dessert sampler. ♦ Catalan ♦ Tu-Su lunch and dinner. C Escudellers 10 (at Ptge Escudellers). 3017515

37 Hostal Marítima $ Vittorio Rosellini, an exuberant Italian, is meticulous about keeping his 12-room, no-frills refuge clean. There is laundry service, but guests must journey through the reception area for a bath. ♦ La Rambla 4 (at Ptge Banca). 3023152

38 Pastís In recorded song and dusty art, the memory of Edith Piaf pervades this Barcelona landmark. The crowd covers a broad spectrum of humanity, and prospective patrons should be aware that transvestite prostitutes regularly parade past its tiny windows. ♦ M-F 12:30PM-3AM; Sa-Su 7:30PM-3AM. C Santa Mònica 4 (between La Rambla and Ptge Lluís Cutchet). 3187980

39 Drassanes Reials (Royal Shipyards) Built in the 14th century, this is the most complete extant example of a medieval shipyard. Within the fascinating Gothic complex is the **Museu Marítim** (Maritime Museum), where exhibits include a full-scale replica of *La Galera Real,* the ship John of Austria rode to victory at the 1571 Battle of Lepanto; a model of the world's first submarine; and centuries-old charts and maps. ♦ Admission; half price on Wednesdays; free first Sunday of the month. Tu, Sa; Su mornings. Av Drassanes (at Pg Colom). 3183245

40 Zebra The funky fashions in this tiny store range from retro to au courant, and most items are one-of-a-kind. ♦ M-Sa. C Avinyó 50 (between C Gignàs and C Comtessa de Sobradiel). 3015842

40 Pitarra Restaurant ★★$$ Located in the former home of beloved 19th-century Catalan poet and playwright Federico Soler Hubert (a.k.a. Serafí Pitarra), this elegant restaurant has been pleasing patrons for more than 100 years. The fish is always fresh, and in the autumn look for game and wild mushrooms among the daily specials. The proprietors have restored the building's original decor, and diners may visit the upstairs room where Pitarra composed his scripts and verses. ♦ Catalan ♦ M-Sa lunch and dinner; closed in August. C Avinyó 56 (at C Gignàs). 3011647

41 Tasca El Corral ★★$ One of many stops along *la ruta de las tapas* (the string of tapas bars lining Carrer Mercè), this place specializes in spicy sausage bits set aflame tableside. Also on hand are a head-spinning sangria and a pungent goat cheese appetizer, which may (or may not) explain the presence of pealing goat bells hanging above the bar. ♦ Tapas ♦ Daily 5PM-2AM. C Mercè 17 (between C Marquet and C Plata). 3152059

42 Moll de la Fusta Until 1982, this wooden pier was a depository for timber—today it's a promenade lined with palm trees and chichi bars, a symbol of the city's determined effort to revitalize its waterfront. To the east of the **Moll de la Fusta** is **Maremagnum,** Barcelona's newest seaside development, with an aquarium, a shopping mall, an Imax theater and stylish night spots. To the west is **Barceloneta** (see below). ♦ Along Pg Colom (between Via Laietana and Pl Portal de la pau)

43 Barceloneta In 1749, the residents of this wedge-shaped spit of land were summarily displaced by Philip V's troops. French military architect **Prospère Verboom**'s plan to provide a new, respectable neighborhood for the citizenry called for a grid of narrow streets and uniform apartment houses, each of the same height and design. The area is still mostly nautical in nature with shops selling marine equipment, and copious, colorful seafood restaurants, especially along Passeig Don Juan de Borbò Conte le Barcelona. Passeig Marítim leads to the **Olympic Village** and the municipal beaches (see below). ♦ Pg Nacional (off Pg Colom)

43 Vaso de Oro ★★$ The tapas selection is admittedly limited at this narrow, boisterous bar, but the few items served are of the highest quality. To induce gastronomic rapture, taste the spicy tuna, the roasted potatoes with aioli, and the calamari. ♦ Tapas ♦ Daily lunch and dinner; closed in September. C Balboa 6 (at Pg Nacional). 3193098

44 Platja de la Nova Icària With the **1992 Summer Olympics** for a rationale, the city reclaimed its seashore from a dingy jumble of warehouses and railroad tracks, and the resulting 1.5 mile of beach is a favorite gathering spot on sunny weekends. There are numerous cafes serving aperitifs and tapas, and a number of excellent (but fairly pricey) restaurants. Sun worshipers abound, and the athletically inclined can rent sailboats and Windsurfers. ♦ Between Barceloneta and Port Olímpic

45 Hostal Nuevo Colón $ Despite the sprucing up it received before the **1992 Summer Olympics,** this part of the city remains somewhat tawdry. The best of the neighborhood's budget hotels has 26 slightly noisy but clean guest rooms. Seven of them

34

Barcelona

have private baths. There is no restaurant. The hotel is conveniently located across from the **Estació de França** train station. ♦ Av Marquès de l'Argentera 19 (between Pg Picasso and C Comerç). 3195077

46 Parc de la Ciutadella In the 1880s, a much-loved municipal sanctuary replaced a much-hated military citadel constructed on this site in the 18th century by Philip V's troops. This urban oasis contains acres of fragrant gardens; an artificial lake; an ornate waterfall and fountain designed by **Treball de Fontserè**, with help from an apprentice named **Gaudí**; the **Parlament de Catalunya**; and several museums, including the **Museu de Geologia** and the **Museu de Zoologia**.
♦ Bounded by Pg Circumval.lació and Pg Pujades, and C Wellington and Pg Picasso

Within Parc de la Ciutadella:

Museu d'Art Modern Located in the **Arsenal de la Ciutadella**, the modern art museum chronicles Catalonia's artistic accomplishments of the 19th and early 20th centuries with works by Casas, Gaudí, Nonnell, Rusiñol, Manolo, Nogues, and Sunyer. ♦ Admission. M, W-Su 9AM-9PM. Pl d'Armes. 3195728

46 Museu de Zoologia (Zoo) The stars here are the world's only captive albino gorilla, *Copito de Nieve* (Snowflake), and the performing whales and dolphins—all great for kids.
♦ Admission. Daily. Near C de Wellington. 2212506

47 El Xampanyet ★★$ When this tavern opened in 1929, the proprietor chose not to give it a name, believing that bars are best remembered for a distinctive house drink. To this day, no identifying sign is to be seen, but natives know where to find a taste of sparkling Xampanyet wine and a plate of seafood tapas.
♦ Tapas ♦ Tu-Sa lunch and dinner; Su dinner; closed in August. C Montcada 22 (between C Sombrerers and C Barra de Ferro). 3197003

47 Església de Santa Maria del Mar (Church of St. Mary of the Sea) Constructed between 1329 and 1384, when Catalonia's commercial dominance of the Mediterranean extended as far south as Greece, this gem honors the local seafarers' patron saint; in fact, to many Barceloneses it has greater historical and sentimental significance than does the official city cathedral. The vast, unadorned surfaces, elegant proportions, and octagonal, flat-topped towers are characteristic of Gothic Catalan construction. Equally impressive is the church's stained glass; note the rose window facing Plaça de Santa Maria. ♦ Pg Born 1 (at C Montcada). 3102390

48 Pensión-Residencia Lourdes $ There are no laundry facilities or phones at this bare-bones hostelry, whose rates are on a par with many youth hostels. There are 36 guest rooms, none of which have private baths. The rooms facing Carrer Princesa, while brighter and bigger than those on the alley, are also infinitely noisier. ♦ No credit cards accepted. C Princesa 14 (between C Montcada and Via Laietana). 3193372

48 Museu Picasso Occupying a trio of 15th century Gothic palaces in the carefully preserved medieval barrio of La Ribera, the city's most popular museum possesses a collection of 3,000 works that span Pablo Picasso's long, fruitful, and multifaceted career, from childhood sketches to the Blue Period to his final years. This is a must-see. The bookstore has an exhaustive supply of postcards, posters, and texts. ♦ Admission. Tu-Sa 10AM-8PM; Su. C Montcada 15-19 (at C Cremat Gran). 3196310

49 Lluna Plena ★★$$ This charming, brick-and-beam Catalan eatery offers a nourishing, three-course *menú del día* that, *peseta* for *peseta*, is one of the city's epicurean bargains.
♦ Catalan ♦ Tu-Sa lunch and dinner; Su lunch; closed in August. C Montcada 2 (at Pl Marcús). 3105429

50 Palau de la Música Catalana (Catalan Concert Hall) With its explosion of domes, striking mosaics, and stained-glass flights of fancy, this concert hall, an exuberant Art Nouveau work with a Catalan twist, was completed in 1908 and is arguably **Lluís Domènech i Montaner's** most imaginative creation. Contemporary architects **Oscar Tusquets** and **Carlos Diaz** (both Barceloneses) have contributed some new touches to the interior. The **Orfeó Català** (Catalan Choir) and other musical groups perform here throughout the year; if you can't attend a concert, call and make a reservation for an escorted tour. ♦ Free; charge for escorted tour and for concerts. M-F. Sant Fransesc de Paula 2 (at C Sant Pere Més Alt). 2681000

In Catalonia, 23 April is three holidays in one: the feast of Sant Jordi, the region's patron saint; the festival of the rose (custom dictates giving friends and family members a rose and a book); and the anniversary of the writer Saavedra Cervantes's death.

35

Barcelona

51 Laie ★$$ Providing food for both stomach and mind, this cafe/bookstore is named for the pre-Iberian settlement that allegedly existed on Montjuïc. The food is basic and the meal prices are inflated (but they do include access to several international daily newspapers). A good selection of English-language literature makes up part of the stock of predominantly Catalan selections. ♦ Catalan ♦ M-Sa breakfast, lunch, and dinner. C Pau Claris 85 (at C Casp). Cafe: 3027310; bookstore: 3181739

52 Hostal Palacios $$ The mismatched furniture and funky carpets may remind students of their digs back home, but the accommodations are neat, clean, and not nearly as noisy as one might assume given their location on a busy street. Thirteen of the 25 guest rooms have private baths. ♦ Gran Via Corts Catalanes 629 (between C Roger de Llúria and C Pau Claris). 3013792

53 Hostal Oliva $$ The ascent in the turn-of-the-century glass-and-wood elevator may be the high point of a stay here. All 16 rooms are well scrubbed, eight of them have private baths, and some contain lovely wooden furniture. ♦ Pg Gràcia 32 (at C Diputació). 4880162

54 Satanassa Antro Bar "Antro" is a difficult word to translate, but "dive" is pretty close. A mostly gay crowd rollicks to the beat of this outlandish bar/disco, one of the Eixample's steamiest nightclubs. ♦ Daily 10PM-5AM. C Aribau 27 (at C Consell de Cent). 4510052

55 Gran Bodega ★★$$ A real find for budgeteers, this bar has served a menu of over 80 tapas and dozens of Spanish wines for more than 40 years. Besides the superb *raciones* of fish, sausage, and cheese, they prepare perhaps the tastiest *pa amb tomàquet* (bread with tomato) in town. ♦ Tapas ♦ Daily lunch and dinner. C València 193 (between C Enric Granados and C Aribau). 4531053

56 La Palmera ★★$$ With its clean design and comfortable ambience, this small restaurant is popular among students and young professionals. Offerings include a wide selection of salads and cold cuts, as well as specialties prepared with salt cod; the stuffed peppers are especially good. ♦ Catalan ♦ Tu-Sa lunch and dinner; Su dinner. Reservations recommended. C Enric Granados 57 (at C Mallorca). 4532338

ALTAÏR

57 Altaïr Packed with maps and guides in a variety of languages, Barcelona's best travel bookstore is bound to fan the flames of anyone's wanderlust. ♦ M-Sa. C Balmes 69 (between C Aragó and C València). 4542966

FUNDACIÓ ANTONI TÀPIES

58 Fundació Antoni Tàpies (Antoni Tàpies Foundation) Designed in 1886 by **Lluís Domènech i Montaner,** this building vies with **Casa Vicens** (a private residence in the Gràcia neighborhood) for the honor of being the first Modernista structure in Catalonia. Now the building houses a museum founded in 1984 by acclaimed Catalan artist Antoni Tàpies. Holdings include a fine collection of Tàpies's work, as well as exhibits by other contemporary artists. ♦ Admission. Tu-Su 11AM-8PM. C Aragó 255 (between Pg Gràcia and Rambla Catalunya). 4870315

59 Forn de Sant Jaume Fine chocolates, pastries, and homemade ice cream tempt at this 19th-century shop. Modern additions include an adjoining cafeteria, with an outdoor terrace, which is an excellent setting for breakfast or a midday break. ♦ Daily 9AM-9:30PM. Rambla Catalunya 50 (between C Consell de Cent and C Aragó). 2160229

60 Casa Batlló Commissioned by the Batlló family, leading textile manufacturers of the day, **Gaudí** tackled every detail of this 1906 house. It's closed to the public, but passersby can still take in the details: the undulating facade, the cast-iron balconies, and the colorful garret. The house is located on the so-called Mançana de la Discòrdia ("block of discord"), named because of the eclectic styles of its buildings. Nearby Modernista masterpieces that merit a stare are: **Casa Lleó Morera** (No. 35) by **Domènech i Montaner, Casa Ramon Mulleras** (No. 37) by **Enric Sagnier,** and **Casa Amatller** (No. 41) by **Josep Puig i Cadafalch.** To see a splendid interior of the genre, visit the **Patronat de Turisme** (by **Domènech i Montaner**) in **Casa Lleó Morera;** this isn't a public tourist office, but you can still stick your head in and look around. ♦ Pg Gràcia 43 (between C Consell de Cent and C Aragó)

"It would be a betrayal to even think of finishing the Sagrada Família. . . . Let it remain there, like a huge rotting tooth."

Salvador Dalí

Barcelona

61 Llibreria Francesa By no means limited to French, the texts in this well-stocked bookstore come in many tongues. There's plenty of good material on Barcelona here. ♦ M-Sa 10AM-8PM. Pg Gràcia 91 (at C Provença). 2151417

62 Casa Milà (La Pedrera) This 1910 structure elicited scoffs in its youth, but observers now marvel at **Gaudí**'s magnificent use of the curve. By supporting this apartment house with stone and brick columns and an ingenious metallic web, the architect seemed to escape the laws of physics. Visit the roof to see the fantastical chimneys and surrealistic ventilation towers. Take advantage of the free 30-minute-long guided tours (offered on the hour) in several languages. ♦ Tu-Sa. Reservations required. Pg Gràcia 92 (at C Provença). 4873613

63 Velvet Vanguard designer **Alfredo Arribas** created the interior of this fashionable club. Park yourself on one of the buttocks-shaped bar stools and try to blend with the upscale crowd. The music will take you back a few decades. ♦ Daily 7:30PM-4AM. C Balmes 161 (between C Còrsega and C París). 2176714

64 Tijuana ★$ If you're tired of tapas, this neighborhood cantina, full of small wooden tables and Mexican bric-a-brac, provides a welcome change. The food could be more spicy and generously portioned, but the guacamole and margaritas are fine. ♦ Mexican ♦ M-Sa lunch and dinner; Su lunch. C Comte Borrell 296 (between C París and C Londres). 4391109

65 Residencia Montserrat $$ A trio of rooms with terraces are the prize accommodations in this attractive hotel, although the other 30-odd rooms are equally tidy and inviting. Firm mattresses, adjoining bathrooms, and phones are standard. There is no restaurant. ♦ Pg Gràcia 114 (at C Còrsega). 2172700

66 Barcelona Brewing Company The **BBC**, opened in 1992 by a half-dozen Englishmen and one Catalan, ferments its heady, all-natural brew in steel vats right on the premises. A large foreign contingent can always be found downing pint after delicious pint. ♦ Daily 1-4PM, 8PM-2AM. C Sant Agustí 14 (between C Còrsega and C Bonavista). 2372132

67 Indigo Barcelona teems with stores selling batik clothes and silver jewelry from Indonesia and India, but this spacious, artfully decorated boutique stands above the rest. Its stylish clothes and stunning textiles, pottery, and furniture have slightly higher prices commensurate with their higher quality. ♦ M-Sa. Av Diagonal 432 (between C Roger de Llúria and C Pau Claris). 4161980

68 Hostal Felipe II $$ Religious paintings and icons adorn this homey, 11-room pensione whose bright, well-tended rooms come with fans and with or without bath. It's wise to reserve ahead of time. ♦ C Mallorca 329 (at Av Diagonal). 4587758

69 El Encants This Barcelona flea market, out a bit from the city but conveniently located near a subway stop, is well worth a visit. All kinds of new and used goods are for sale—furniture, clothes, and knickknacks. Bargaining is expected and part of the fun. When you've had enough, head for one of the many nearby inexpensive cafes which offer tasty lunch specials. ♦ M, W, F, Sa dawn to dusk. Plaça de les Glòries Catalanes (between Av Diagonal and Av Meridiana)

70 Templo Expiatorio de la Sagrada Família (Church of the Holy Family) An extraordinary emblem and celebrated symbol of Barcelona, this cathedral (illustrated below) is perhaps the boldest expression of **Gaudí**'s genius, although after more than a century it remains a work-in-progress, overlaid with scaffolding and besieged by chisels. In 1891, when the architect took over the project in midstream, he devised an intricate plan around a whopping five naves. His design called for three monumental facades representing the Nativity, the Passion, and the Resurrection, as well as 18 spiraling towers to symbolize the 12 Apostles, the four Evangelists, the Virgin Mary, and Christ. Only the **Nativity Facade** was completed before his death in 1926.

Templo Expiatorio de la Sagrada Família

Barcelona

Construction proceeded until 1936, when a fire destroyed the crypt and **Gaudí's** study; using the few drawings that survived, the job resumed in 1952. Since then, the **Passion Facade** and its spires have been finished.

As the work continues, so does the polemic, with many critical of the current aesthetic. But some believe that **Gaudí** realized he would never finish and he anticipated that future architects would carry on in their own styles. Climb the towers for a dizzying view, or, for a small charge, ride an elevator to the top and then walk down. A small museum documents the building process and looks at **Gaudí's** singular career. ♦ Pl Sagrada Família (at C Sardenya). 4550247

71 Hospital de la Santa Creu i Sant Pau Many consider **Domènech i Montaner's** hospital to be the consummate Modernista complex. While wandering through the pavilions, observe the brick vaulting overhead, the superlative ornamentation—mosaics, tiles, stained glass—and the sculptures by renowned artists. The information booth inside the door has plans of the hospital in several languages. ♦ Daily 24 hours. C Sant Antoni Maria Claret 167-171 (at C Cartagena)

72 El Tastavins ★★$$ Neighborhood families pile into this affordable restaurant, which specializes in cheeses and pâtés paired with wines. Among the entrées, the chicken with prunes and peppers with anchovies are delectable, but steer clear of the Hungarian goulash. ♦ Catalan ♦ M-Sa breakfast, lunch, and dinner. C Ramon i Cajal 12 (between Pl Revolució and C Torrent L'Olla). 2136031

73 Plaça del Sol Gràcia was a village known for its independent spirit long before it was incorporated into Barcelona in 1898. Now a friendly, mostly middle-class barrio, it is composed of narrow streets and secret plazas, containing some of the liveliest bars and restaurants in the city. Start your exploration of Gràcia's charms from this square, which has several bars, a disco, and, in the southwestern corner, a well-stocked health-food store. ♦ Bounded by C Torrent L'Olla and C Valls, and C Maspons and C Planeta

74 Jugolandia ★★$$ Stop here for a fresh, frothy, fruit *batido* (shake). They're available in spiked or nonalcoholic versions. ♦ Cafe ♦ Daily 5PM-2AM. Trav de Gràcia 114 (at Gran de Gràcia). 2188082

75 Pension San Medín $$ The best bet in Gràcia, these 14 chambers are pleasantly decorated and comfortable. The smallish rooms are sparkling clean, and all have private baths. The noise level can be high; request a quiet room. There is no restaurant. ♦ Gran de Gràcia 125 (between C Sant Marc and Rambla Prat). 2173068

76 Otto Zutz Party people should make this sleek club their last stop of the night. If the strobe-lights of the dance floor don't keep your eyes open, there are couches upstairs to accommodate temporary crashing. ♦ Cover for live music. Tu-Sa 11PM-4:30AM. C Lincoln 15 (between C Laforja and C Madrazo). 2380722

77 Park Güell Only two of the proposed 60 houses and a few of the public spaces commissioned by Eusebi Güell were completed by **Gaudí** before Barcelona's administrators turned it into a park in 1922. The remaining structures are quintessential **Gaudí**: two whimsical pavilions (shown below) flanking the entrance gate; the grand stairway embellished with a lizard of many hues; the 96 columns of the hall (intended as the city's marketplace); and the serpentine balustrade/bench in the plaza, which boasts magnificent vistas of the city. The park also contains the house **Gaudí** occupied from 1906 until his death: Designed by his disciple **Francesc Berenguer**, it's now the **Casa-Museu Gaudí**. ♦ Free. Park: daily; until 8PM April, September; until 9PM May-August. Museum: M-F. C Olot

Park Güell

Barcelona

(at Av Santuari de Sant Josep de la Muntanya). Park 4243809; museum 2846446

78 Alberg Mare Déu de Montserrat $ Travelers on tight budgets should consider making the long haul out to this impressive 182-bed hostel. Reasons include an enormous cafeteria that serves three squares daily, roomy lounges, and a terrace with a panoramic view of Barcelona. Rooms have four to six beds each, spotless adjacent baths, and facilities for people with disabilities. Reservations are necessary, and there's a three-day maximum stay; those who don't have the required hostel card can buy one at the reception desk. Bus *28* from **Plaça de Catalunya** stops in front. ♦ Pg Mare de Déu del Coll 41-51 (between C Castellterçol and Ptge Tona). 2105151

79 Mont Tibidabo The highest peak of the Serra de Collserola range that marks Barcelona's northern border lures innumerable visitors with its breathtaking views and assorted attractions, from the Neo-Gothic **Temple Expiatori del Sagrat Cor** (Temple of the Sacred Heart) church, to an amusement park (2117942), to architect **Norman Foster**'s 800-foot-tall **Torre de Collserola**, built but never used as the telecommunications station for the **1992 Olympic Games**. To reach Tibidabo, take the **FF.CC. de la Generalitat** to the *tramvia blau* (whose slow pace gives riders time to gape at the stately mansions lining Avinguda Tibidabo) and then ride the funicular up the mountain. ♦ End of the Tramvia Blau Line

On Mont Tibidabo:

Bar Mirablau Most establishments would charge sky-high prices for the privilege of enjoying this spectacular view, but this place doesn't. So sip and enjoy. ♦ Daily noon-5AM. Pl Funicular, at the end of Av Tibidabo. 4185879

80 Monestir de Pedralbes This monastery was founded in 1326 by Elisenda de Montcada, Queen of Aragon and fourth wife of Jaume II el Just, who lived her last 37 years of life here after the king's death. In addition to the outstanding 14th-century murals by Ferrer Bassa in the small chapel dedicated to Sant Miquel, there's the three-storied Gothic cloisters, a medieval herbal apothecary, several monks' cells, a working kitchen, and a 16th-century sickroom. Part of the **Thyssen-Bornemisza** collection of paintings and sculptures (most of which is at the Prado in Madrid) is installed here. ♦ Admission. Tu-Su. Bda Monestir 9 (at Pl Monestir). 2039282

81 Palau de Pedralbes Once a royal residence and guesthouse for visiting dignitaries, this 1929 Italianate palace now houses the terrific **Museu de Ceràmica** (Ceramic Museum) which includes what is arguably the most important collection of medieval ceramics in Europe. Contemporary pieces by Abella, Miró, Picasso, and others are showcased as well. Lovely gardens, featuring a small drinking fountain by **Gaudí**, surround the palace. ♦ Admission. Museum: Tu-Su. Gardens: daily. Av Diagonal 686 (between C Fernando Primo de Rivera and C Tinent Coronel Valenzuela). 2801621

82 Nou Camp F.C. Barcelona Home to Barcelona's soccer heroes, the stadium seats 120,000 roaring, rabid fans, making it one of the largest of such arenas in Europe. ♦ Stadium ticket office: M-F; Sa-Su mornings. Phone orders M-F 8AM-8PM, 4044191. C Arístides Maillol (between Trav les Corts and Av Joan XXIII). 3309411

83 Alberg Pere Tarrés $ Travelers praise the quiet setting of this 100-bed hostel, which is a 15-minute walk from **Estació de Sants** train station, but they sometimes complain about its crowded dormitories and small showers with insufficient hot water. However, it does have a pleasant common room with a TV, as well as a dining room, laundry facilities, a rooftop terrace, and parking, and hostel cards are not required. Curfew is at midnight, but the doors open for 10 minutes at 2AM—a reprieve for late-night revelers. ♦ C Numància 149-151 (between Trav les Corts and Av Diagonal). 4102309

84 Montjuïc Site of the **1992 Summer Olympic Games**, this area actually owes much of its development to an earlier international extravaganza, the **1929 World's Fair**, which prompted the whirlwind construction of palaces, pavilions, exhibition halls, and gardens here. Indeed, this former Jewish cemetery (its name translates as "hill of the Jews") has six museums, an open-air theater, a five-acre model village, and an amusement park. There's a whole day's worth of sight-seeing here: Take the funicular or cable car to the top and walk back down, or hop on and off bus **No. 61**, which starts from the **Plaça d'Espanya** and then makes a circuit around the slopes. Another option is to take the moving stairway from **Plaça d'Espanya**; this route combines walking with a series of outdoor escalators. ♦ Av Marquès Comillas and Av Reina María Cristina

---

Modernism, the Catalan cousin of Art Nouveau, flourished from the 1880s through the first two decades of this century. While artists of all media embraced the movement, its strongest proponents were the Catalan architects, who integrated contemporary technology with traditional decorative crafts—such as metalwork, stained glass, mosaics, and sgraffiti—to create some wondrous structures.

Restaurants/Clubs: Red   **Hotels:** Blue
Shops/ ♦ Outdoors: Green   **Sights/Culture:** Black

39

Barcelona

Poble Espanyol

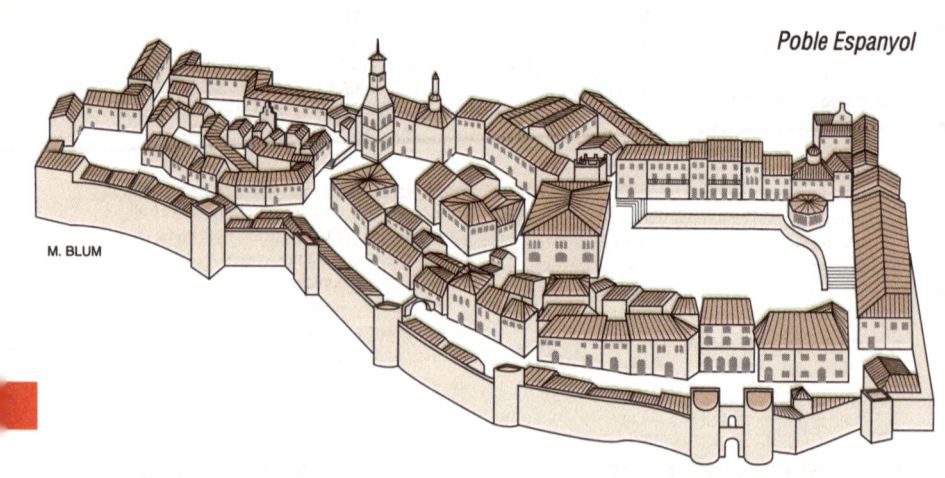

M. BLUM

85 Fuentes de Montjuïc The illuminated fountains designed by **Carles Buigas** for the **1929 World's Fair** are closed. They've been replaced by a high-tech laser show. ♦ Free. Shows: Th-Su 10PM, 10:45PM, 11:30PM June-Sept. Pl Carles Buïgas (between Pl Marquès Foronda and Av Marquès Comillas)

86 Palau Nacional This enormous, diversely styled palace (pictured below) contains the **Museu Nacional d'Art de Catalunya (National Art Museum of Catalonia)**, with its unparalleled collection of 10th- to 12th-century Catalonian paintings, statues, frescoes, and murals. The palace, however, is undergoing a thorough restoration (which will transform it into one of the largest art complexes in Europe) and thus exhibits only a small part of its permanent collection. ♦ Admission. M, W-Su 9AM-9PM. Mirador del Palau Nacional (at Pg Cascades). 4237199

87 Pavelló Mies van der Rohe Designed by **Ludwig Mies van der Rohe,** this pavilion was Germany's entry in the **1929 World's Fair.** Reconstructed 56 years later, its stark planes of glossy green marble and onyx, glass walls, and pebble-bottomed decorative pools are a pinnacle of modern architecture. ♦ Av Marquès Comillas (at C Méxic). 4234016

88 Poble Espanyol (Spanish Village) The buildings in this five-acre model village (shown above), which were created for the **1929 World's Fair,** illustrate 104 indigenous architectural styles, ranging from 11th-century plazas to 20th-century houses. Visitors can shop in the myriad high-end crafts shops that line the streets, and eat, drink, and dance in the popular—and pricey—restaurants and nightclubs. The village's **Barcelona Experience** is an audiovisual spectacular about the city's storied past. ♦ Admission. M 9AM-8PM; Tu-Th 9AM-2AM; F-Sa 9AM-4AM; Su 9AM-10PM. Av Marquès Comillas (at Pg Simon Bolivar). 3257866

89 Anella Olímpica (Olympic Ring) More than 9,400 athletes from 160 delegations competed in this state-of-the-art sports complex, which today is used for all manner of cultural and athletic events. Within is the **Olympic Stadium,** constructed for the **1929 World's Fair** and refurbished to accommodate up to 70,000 spectators for the **1992 Summer Olympic Games.** At the far side of the stadium, the **Galeria Olímpica** features an impressive multimedia exhibit meant to evoke "the emotion of those 16 days of glory." The **Palau D'Esports Sant Jordi** (St. George Sports Palace) is a feat of engineering technology; its 525-foot-long, 360-foot-wide metallic mesh roof was raised in one piece by means of 12 hydraulic pistons. ♦ Stadium: daily Oct-Mar; until 8PM Apr-Sept.

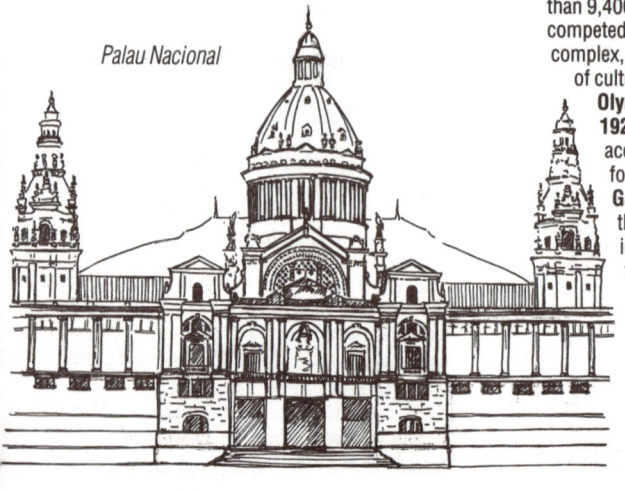

Palau Nacional

Barcelona

Esplanade: Daily M-Th until 8PM, F-Su until 11PM July-August; Sa-Su September-June. Galería Olímpica: Tu-Su. Av l'Estadi (at Pg Olímpic). 4262089; Galeria Olímpica 4260660

90 Fundació Miró This innovative museum pays homage to the 20th-century abstractionist Joan Miró. More than 200 paintings, 150 sculptures, nine textile pieces, the artist's complete graphic works, and almost 5,000 drawings—including his earliest childhood sketches—are housed here, along with an extensive contemporary art library and bookshop. ♦ Admission. Tu-Su; Th until 9:30PM. Pl Neptú (at Av Miramar). 3291908

91 Castell de Montjuïc Built in 1751 on the remains of a 17th-century castle, this star-shaped fortress was the scene of countless battles and executions; it also served for some years as a military prison. The museum here exhibits antique cannon and weaponry, but perhaps more riveting are the sensational views of the city and port from the castle's walls. ♦ Admission. Tu-Su. Montaña de Montjuïc (between Av Castell and Ctra Montjuïc). 3298613

> Santa Eulàlia was Barcelona's sole patron saint until the Convento de la Mercè monks managed to get their Virgen de la Mercè declared a municipal intercessor as well. Since then, it almost always rains on the festivities of 24 September, the feast day of the newcomer. Some believe the drizzle is an expression of Eulàlia's unsaintly lingering.

Bests

Carmen Martinez
Assistant Professor, Universidad Autónoma de Barcelona

Barcelona is a great city to walk. I would recommend spending a few hours walking through the **Barri Gòtic** and **La Ribera** districts. Take a look at the magnificent patios inside the buildings (many of them now converted into museums). Particularly enchanting places are the **Plaça del Rei, Plaça de Sant Filip Neri,** and the **Museu d'Art de Catalunya**.

Another beautiful area to get lost in is the district called **Eixample** or **El Ensanche**. It has plenty of beautiful Art Nouveau buildings. You just have to walk and look up from time to time to discover anonymous buildings that are jewels.

At night, if you like to eat fish, there are small restaurants, very casual in the **Port Olimpic** area. This is also the area of the Barcelona beaches. It's a nice place to spend summer nights.

Maria Jesus Morte Ortega
Student, Jean D'Estrées Center of Aesthetics

The **Plaça de Catalunya** is where people generally meet on weekend nights when it's time to go out (between midnight and 7AM).

To walk down **La Rambla de les Flors** is a pleasure, seeing the painters, jugglers, and actors practice their arts in the middle of the street while a large group of people watches.

The **Passeig de Gràcia** is beautiful—it's unique in the world—and its facades, cinemas, stores, and original Modernista street lamps fascinate everyone who walks down it.

Toward the mountains, near the **Gràcia** neighborhood, is the **Park Güell**. It is divine and enchanting—you have to see it. The **Templo Expiatorio de la Sagrada Família,** another **Gaudí** work, is very representative for Barceloneses.

At night, have a drink at **Velvet** or **L'Ovella Negra**. All you have to do is walk along **Carrer de Balmes, de Valencia, d'Aragó, de Provença,** or **del Roselló**, and you'll find a ton of bars where you don't have to pay to get in and if you don't buy a drink, you're not hassled.

Joan Marc Queralt
Student, Center of Tourism Studies

First, to orient yourself, take the elevator up the **Torre de Collserola** on **Tibidabo** or go to the top of **Montjuïc,** and you'll discover Barcelona.

Take some time to see the work of **Gaudí,** the greatest exponent of Modernism, although the least typical of the Modernistas. See **Park Güell,** the **Sagrada Família, La Pedrera,** and **Casa Batlló**.

For more Modernism, walk along the **Passeig de Gràcia** and **Rambla de Catalunya**. Go to the **Patronat de Turisme,** a work by **Domènech i Montaner**. When you visit the **Fundació Tàpies,** another building by **Montaner,** you'll find one of the best examples of Modernista architecture.

In the **Barri Gòtic,** there's of course the **Cathedral, Plaça de Sant Jaume,** and **Plaça de Sant Felip Neri,** with its church, fountain, and trees that will make you feel like you're not in a city.

When you leave the **Museu Picasso,** walk down **Carrer Montcada** and try to see the interior gardens of the old palaces. Visit the old market on **Passeig del Born** and the Gothic church of **Santa Maria del Mar**.

For coffee, I recommend **Cafè de l'Opera** and **Cafè del Pi**. Good inexpensive restaurants: Try **Pollo Rico** (for chicken), or **Egipte,** a very pretty restaurant, which offers a varied and delicious *menú del día*. **La Fonda** is the trendiest place to eat—the spot to see and be seen.

After dinner, have a drink at **Torres de Avila** in **Poble Espanyol,** perhaps the most beautiful bar in the city. If you like French songs, visit **Pastís,** a small bar full of history. To dance, go to **Satanassa,** the craziest place in the city.

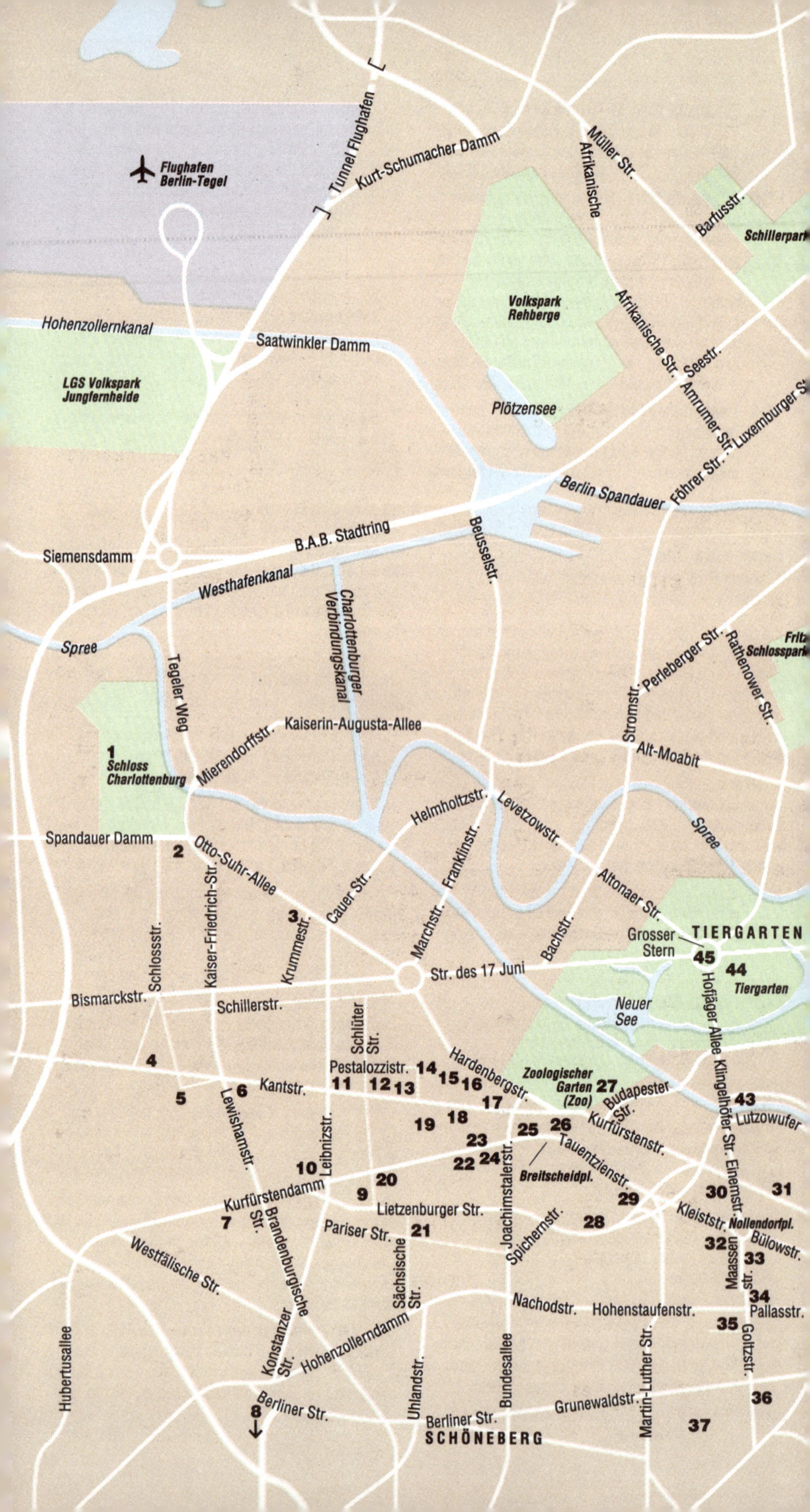

Flughafen Berlin-Tegel
Tunnel Flughafen
Kurt-Schumacher Damm
Müller Str.
Afrikanische
Barfusstr.
Schillerpark
Volkspark Rehberge
Hohenzollernkanal
Saatwinkler Damm
LGS Volkspark Jungfernheide
Afrikanische Str.
Seestr.
Amrumer Str.
Luxemburger S
Plötzensee
Föhrer Str.
Berlin Spandauer
B.A.B. Stadtring
Siemensdamm
Beusselstr.
Westhafenkanal
Charlottenburger Verbindungskanal
Spree
Tegeler Weg
Fritz Schlosspark
Perleberger Str.
Rathenower Str.
Stromstr.
Kaiserin-Augusta-Allee
Mierendorffstr.
Alt-Moabit
1 Schloss Charlottenburg
Helmholtzstr.
Levetzowstr.
Spree
Spandauer Damm
2
Otto-Suhr-Allee
Kaiser-Friedrich-Str.
Franklinstr.
Cauer Str.
Altonaer Str.
3
Krummestr.
Marchstr.
Bachstr.
Grosser Stern
TIERGARTEN
45
44
Tiergarten
Schlossstr.
Str. des 17 Juni
Bismarckstr.
Schillerstr.
Hofjäger Allee
Neuer See
Schlüter Str.
4
Pestalozzistr.
14
15
16
Hardenbergstr.
Zoologischer Garten (Zoo)
27
5
6
Kantstr.
11
12
13
17
Budapester Str.
43
Klingelhöfer Str.
Lutzowufer
Lewishamstr.
19
18
25
26
Kurfürstenstr.
23
Tauentzienstr.
10
Leibnizstr.
22
24
Breitscheidpl.
Joachimstalerstr.
20
Einemstr.
30
31
Kurfürstendamm
9
29
Lietzenburger Str.
7
Str.
Brandenburgische
21
Spichernstr.
28
Kleiststr.
Nollendorfpl.
Pariser Str.
Westfälische Str.
32
Bülowstr.
33
Maassen str.
Sächsische Str.
34
Nachodstr.
Hohenstaufenstr.
Pallasstr.
35
Goltzstr.
Konstanzer Str.
Hohenzollerndamm
Hubertusallee
Uhlandstr.
Bundesallee
Martin-Luther Str.
36
Grunewaldstr.
8
Berliner Str.
Berliner Str.
37
SCHÖNEBERG

Berlin Map

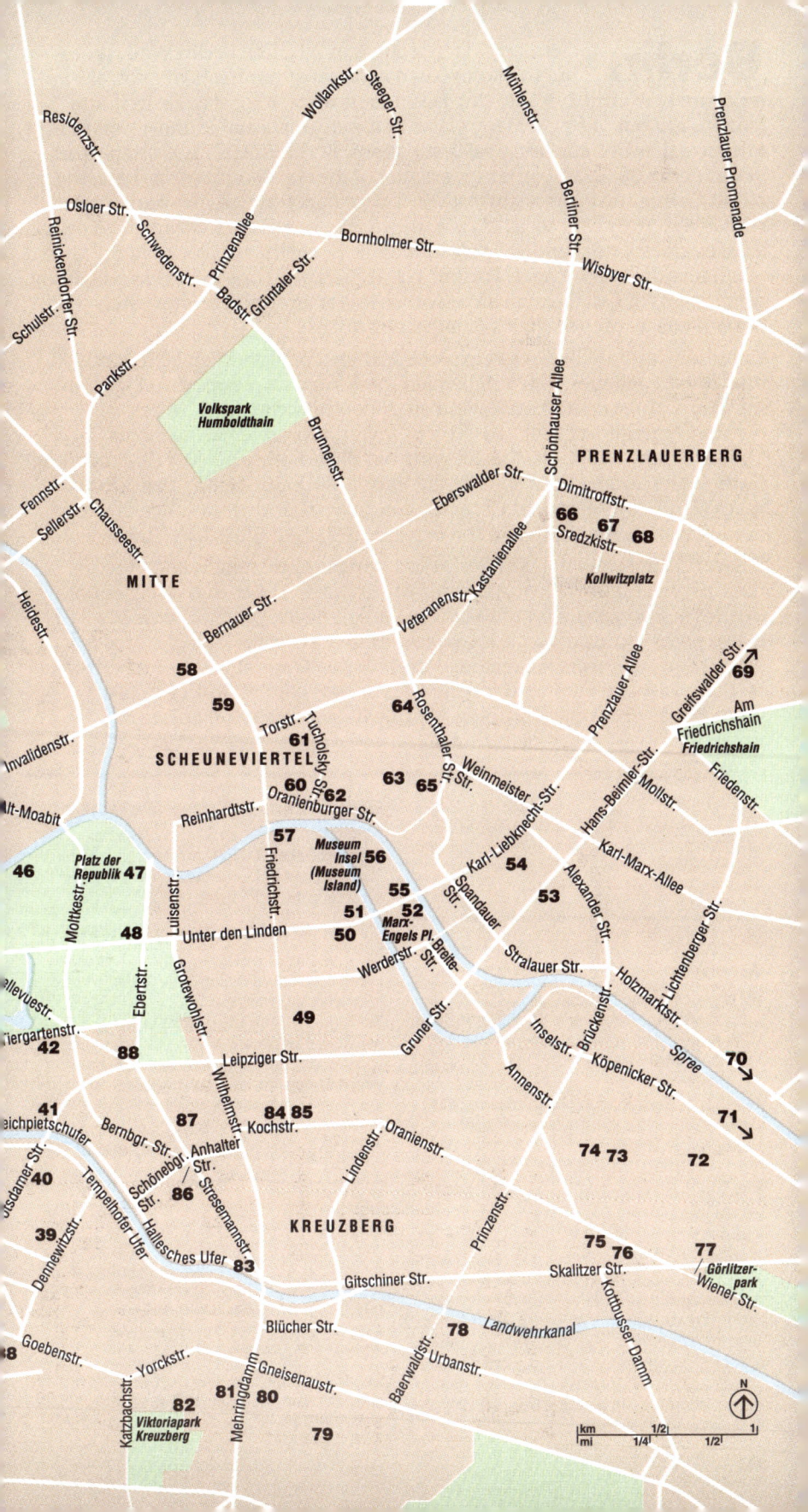

Districts
- **MITTE**
- **PRENZLAUERBERG**
- **SCHEUNEVIERTEL**
- **KREUZBERG**

Parks
- Volkspark Humboldthain
- Platz der Republik
- Viktoriapark Kreuzberg
- Friedrichshain / Am Friedrichshain
- Görlitzer park
- Tiergartenstr.

Streets (north to south, roughly)

- Residenzstr.
- Osloer Str.
- Reinickendorfer Str.
- Schulstr.
- Wollankstr.
- Steeger Str.
- Prinzenallee
- Schwedenstr.
- Mühlenstr.
- Prenzlauer Promenade
- Bornholmer Str.
- Berliner Str.
- Wisbyer Str.
- Badstr.
- Grüntaler Str.
- Pankstr.
- Brunnenstr.
- Schönhauser Allee
- Dimitroffstr.
- Fennstr.
- Sellerstr.
- Chausseestr.
- Eberswalder Str.
- Sredzkistr.
- Kollwitzplatz
- Bernauer Str.
- Veteranenstr.
- Kastanienallee
- Heidestr.
- Invalidenstr.
- Alt-Moabit
- Torstr.
- Tucholsky Str.
- Rosenthaler Str.
- Weinmeister Str.
- Prenzlauer Allee
- Greifswalder Str.
- Reinhardtstr.
- Oranienburger Str.
- Karl-Liebknecht-Str.
- Hans-Beimler-Mollstr.
- Friedenstr.
- Luisenstr.
- Friedrichstr.
- Museum Insel (Museum Island)
- Spandauer Str.
- Karl-Marx-Allee
- Moltkestr.
- Unter den Linden
- Marx-Engels Pl.
- Breite Str.
- Alexander Str.
- Lichtenberger Str.
- Ebertstr.
- Grotewohlstr.
- Werderstr.
- Stralauer Str.
- Holzmarktstr.
- Hallevuestr.
- Leipziger Str.
- Gruner Str.
- Inselstr.
- Brückenstr.
- Köpenicker Str.
- Spree
- Wilhelmstr.
- Kochstr.
- Annenstr.
- Reichpietschufer
- Bernbgr. Str.
- Anhalter Str.
- Lindenstr.
- Oranienstr.
- Prinzenstr.
- Potsdamer Str.
- Schönebgr. Str.
- Stresemannstr.
- Tempelhofer Ufer
- Hallesches Ufer
- Skalitzer Str.
- Kottbusser Damm
- Wiener Str.
- Dennewitzstr.
- Gitschiner Str.
- Blücher Str.
- Baerwaldstr.
- Landwehrkanal
- Urbanstr.
- Goebenstr.
- Katzbachstr.
- Yorckstr.
- Mehringdamm
- Gneisenaustr.

Numbered locations
38, 39, 40, 41, 42, 46, 47, 48, 49, 50, 51, 52, 53, 54, 55, 56, 57, 58, 59, 60, 61, 62, 63, 64, 65, 66, 67, 68, 69, 70, 71, 72, 73, 74, 75, 76, 77, 78, 79, 80, 81, 82, 83, 84, 85, 86, 87, 88

Scale
km: 1/2 · 1
mi: 1/4 · 1/2

N ↑

Berlin

Germany's largest city is in flux. The **Berlin Wall** is gone but the Bonn-based national government will not take up residence here until 1999, leaving Berlin to shrug off its past while its future remains just out of reach. Many places that were unreachable under Communist rule have now become principal destinations. **Berlin Mitte**, once a sterile part of east Berlin, for example, is now a center of the city's youth scene. Here, the recent Communist past is still evident. Take a walk through **Alexanderplatz**, built as a showcase for socialist modernism. The huge **Fernsehturm** (TV Tower) soars overhead, surrounded by gigantic Stalinist apartment blocks. At the far end you'll find the **Marx-Engels Forum**, a large plaza with one of the few remaining monuments of East German days. The Cold War atmosphere is palpable—but hurry if you want to see it; it's disappearing quickly.

Culturally, unified Berlin has exploded. There are more than 80 museums, plus 200 art galleries, 400 independent performance groups, two Egyptian museums, three opera houses, and an underground club scene that's constantly renewing itself. For history lovers, monuments and "great buildings" abound, from the 200-year-old **Brandenburger Tor** (Brandenburg Gate) to the bombed-out spire of the **Kaiser-Wilhelm-Gedächtniskirche** (Kaiser Wilhelm Memorial Church), reminders that this was once the heart of the Prussian Kingdom and the nerve center of Adolf Hitler's Third Reich.

You can almost feel the new Berlin springing into existence, and you can certainly hear it. A walker in downtown east or west Berlin is rarely out of earshot of a construction project. The pace of development is dazzling, but it also poses some problems for visitors as sites are occasionally closed for renovations or streets are renamed to eliminate Communist nomenclature. Merging East and West and sorting out the new combination will take years. But as the process unfolds, Berlin will be a fascinating place to watch history—again—being made.

To call from the US, dial 011 (international access code), 49 (country code), 30 (city code), and the local number. When calling from Germany, dial 030 and the local number. City codes appearing within the text are for areas outside Berlin.

Getting to Berlin

Airports

The city's main airport, **Berlin-Tegel** (41012306), which services most commercial flights to and from North America and Western Europe, is located 15 kilometers (nine miles) northwest of central Berlin. The terminal has visitor-information and currency-exchange facilities. **Berlin Transit Authority (BVG)** bus *No. 109* will take you to city center in about 30 minutes; buses run daily with departures about every 15 minutes. Rental cars are available from **Avis** (2611881), **Europcar** (2137097), and **Hertz** (2611053).

Berlin-Schönefeld Airport (67870), in the former east Berlin, is situated in the city's southeast corner, about 25 kilometers (16 miles) from downtown. But unless you're on a charter flight or heading for Eastern Europe, you probably won't get to see this newly renovated facility, complete with information desks and money-exchange kiosks. The **S-Bahn** subway (*S9* and *S45* trains) connects the airport with downtown Berlin; service is daily, with trains departing every 15 minutes.

Bus Station (Long-Distance)

Long-distance buses arrive at the **Zentralen Omnibus-Bahnhof (ZOB)**, or central bus station, on **Masurenallee** (at Messedamm). For bus schedules and information, call 19449.

Train Station (Long-Distance)

Berlin has three main railway stations. The central terminal is **Bahnhof Zoologischer Garten,** (Hardenbergstr, at Joachimsthaler Str) commonly called **Zoo Station,** a wonderful glass-roofed edifice overlooking the wooded **Tiergarten.** Most trains coming from European and German destinations also stop at **Hauptbahnhof** (Am Hauptbahnhof, at Str der Pariser Kommune) and **Berlin-Lichtenberg** (Frankfurter Allee, at Einbecker Str) in the eastern part of the city. Call 19419 for all train information and schedules.

Getting around Berlin

Bicycles Two-wheeling in Berlin has become something of a contact sport. For all the dangers, though, this is a cyclist's city, with a broad network of bicycle lanes. To rent a bike, try **Berlin by Bike** (Möckernstr 92, between Kreuzbergstr and Hagelbergerstr, 2169197) or **Räderwerk** (Körterstrasse 14, at Südstern, 6918590).

Buses There are more than 150 bus routes that run every day from 4AM until 1AM. An additional 45 night-owl lines—designated with an "N" in front of the route number—operate from 1 to 4AM. See "Public Transportation," below.

Driving On most city streets the speed limit is 50 kilometers (30 miles) per hour, but watch for specially marked 30kph (20mph) zones. The speed limit for city expressways is 80 kph (50 mph). When driving through the eastern part of Berlin, watch for cavernous potholes and plan carefully so that you don't run out of gas (there are few filling stations).

Public Transportation Public transit tickets are interchangeable between bus, subway, and trams. One ticket is valid for up to two hours in any direction. Buy single tickets from booths and vending machines in **U-** and **S-Bahn** stations, or from bus drivers. *Sammelkarte* (multiple-trip tickets), short-hop, *kurzstrecke* (one-way), and all-day passes are also available at discounted prices. For transit information, call 19449.

Subways The reunification of Berlin also brought together the city's extensive **U-Bahn** (underground) and **S-Bahn** (inner-city) rail systems. Stations are well marked at street level with a large "U" or "S." Trains operate daily between 4AM and 1AM; on Friday and Saturday, lines *U1* and *U9* run all night long.

Taxis You can hail a cream-colored cab from the street, pick up one at a taxi stand (generally located on strategic street corners), or call one of three numbers for assistance: 241026, 6902, or 240024.

Tours Several companies offer bus tours, which depart from various locations along **Kufürstendamm** (between Kankestr and Uhlandstr). The best idea is to walk along the street and compare their offerings; all provide English translators. **BBS Tours** (2148790) is a reputable company with several bus tours each day. Walking tours in English are given from April through October by **Berlin Walks** (2116663). And hourlong boat tours along the **River Spree** are offered by **Stern & Kreisschiffahrt** (6173900). The double-decker boats depart from their dock near the **Palast der Republik** five times a day from April through October.

Trams Speedy they're not, but east Berlin's 30-plus pre-war tram lines start to look good when your sightseeing feet have given out. They run daily, from 4AM until 1AM.

Walking Berlin is a large city and it's not possible to walk through all of it. Nevertheless, walking around its several livelier sections is a great way to see the city and feel its pulse. Spend an afternoon window-shopping in the upscale Kurfürstendamm area. A 30-minute walk along **Unter den Linden** from the **Brandenburger Tor** to **Alexanderplatz** is filled with historic buildings and sites.

FYI

Accommodations Berlin has a number of inexpensive lodging choices. In addition to the traditional youth hostels are small hotel/pensiones, which are often converted private residences and offer private bedrooms with mostly shared baths. If you arrive in town without room reservations, go to any of the **Berlin Tourist Information** offices (see "Visitors' Information," below) for help in booking a bed.

Business Hours Most banks, shops, and other businesses are open from 9AM until 5PM on weekdays, and until 2PM on Saturday. Some museums close on Monday, some on Tuesday.

Climate The average summer temperature is 70 degrees, and skies are often overcast. Be prepared for *everything:* Don't be surprised if you need a sweater in summer, or encounter winter days that include everything from blizzards to sunshine to sleet and fog, all within a 12-hour period.

Consulates and Embassies

Canada Friedrichstr 95 (between Georgenstr and ....Clara-Zetkin-Str); 2611161

UK Unter den Linden 32-34 (between Friedrichstr ....and Glinkastr); 2202431

US Clayallee 170 (between Saargemünder Str and ....Hüttenweg); 8197465

Discount Tickets Students with valid identification are generally charged a reduced rate for entry into museums, and admission to many theaters. Near the **Bahnhof Alexanderplatz** is **Hektticket** (Rathausstr and Goutardstr, 2426709), which is open daily and sells discounted theater tickets for same-day performances.

Drinking The legal drinking age is 18. Don't drink and drive, as there are frequent spot checks, and getting caught will land you in big trouble—the least of which is the loss of your license.

Drugs Foreigners caught with illegal drugs are subject to prison or deportation.

Emergencies The emergency number for Berlin police is 110. For an ambulance, call 112. For other emergency medical service, dial 310031; ask for an English-speaking operator if you cannot speak German. In a legal emergency, the best course of action is to call your country's embassy.

Laundry *Wasch salons* (laundromats) do exist, but they're not easy to find and most don't have phones. **WaschCenter** is a chain with a number of locations: (Leibnizstr 72, Charlottenburg); (Bergmannstr 109, Kreuzberg); and (Oderbergerstr 1, Prenzlauer Berg). **WaschCenters** are open daily from 6AM unitl 10PM.

Money The official paper currency is the *Deutschmark* (DM), and coins come in several *pfennig* denominations. Most establishments do not accept credit cards, and are even less likely to accept traveler's checks, so be prepared to pay cash. Banks will exchange foreign money and traveler's checks, and give cash advances on credit cards. But better exchange rates (without hefty processing fees) can be had at *wechselstuben* (currency exchange offices). **Deutsche Verkehrsbank** has two *wechselstuben* branches: **Bahnhof Zoologischer Garten** and **Bahnhof Friedrichstrasse,** both of which are open daily. In the eastern part of the city, go to **Alex Exchange** in the **Bahnhof Alexanderplatz;** it's open Monday through Saturday.

Personal Safety Compared to most big American cities, Berlin remains fairly safe. Pickpockets, however, have begun to work the sidewalks; pay especially close attention to your wallet or bag on the **Kurfürstendamm** (Ku'damm to locals) bus routes and at principal tourist sites. At night, don't ride the **S-Bahn** to outlying areas, loiter around railroad

Berlin

stations, or wander around shadowy side streets in and far-off eastern **Kreuzberg** neighborhood. The threat posed by skinheads and neo-Nazis is an unfortunate fact of life in post-Wall Berlin, but they seem to have confined themselves to the poorer and more remote sections of town, such as **Lichtenberg** and **Marzahn,** leaving the central area safe.

Postal Services Most post offices are open from Monday through Friday from 8AM until 6PM, and on Saturday mornings. Two notable exceptions are branches at train stations: the centrally located **Bahnhof Zoologischer Garten,** open until midnight on weekdays, and **Hauptbahnhof** (Am Hauptbahnhof, at Str der Pariser Kommune 8-12) in the eastern part of the city, open until 9PM weekdays.

Publications *TIP* and *Zitty,* Berlin's two magazines of events listings, are published on alternate Wednesdays. *Checkpoint,* a monthly program guide available at the international press stands in the **Europa Center** (Budapester Str 1, at the foot of Ku'damm), contains information about English-language events.

Public Holidays New Year's Day, Good Friday, Easter Sunday and Monday, Labor Day (1 May), Ascension Day (12 May), Whitmonday (23 May), Feast of Corpus Christi (2 June), Feast of the Assumption (15 August), German Unity Day (3 October), Day of Prayer and Repentance (18 November), Christmas, and Boxing Day (26 December).

Public Rest Rooms These are few and far between, although new toilet cubicles have sprouted up along some of Berlin's main drags. Rest rooms can be found in subway stations and department stores. Restaurants are required to let you use their facilities, but they're not always gracious about it.

Restaurants The restaurant scene has improved greatly over the past few years as the once-isolated city has sharpened its palate. There's a good selection of foreign cuisines and even the much-maligned German cuisine has improved with the rise of *neue deutsche* cooking, the equivalent of nouvelle cuisine. Breakfast—usually a plate of cheese, cold cuts, fruit, and whole-grain bread—is very popular, and often takes the place of lunch since it is served well into the afternoon. Berliners tend to eat dinner early and the busiest time for restaurants is between 6:30 and 8PM. Reservations are not generally required. Few restaurants have a host or hostess—just walk in and grab a table. A service charge of 15 percent is included in the price of a meal.

Shopping This is not really a bargain-hunter's town. Typical German souvenirs—cuckoo clocks, porcelain steins, and well-designed electronic gadgets—are expensive. The best buys are to be had on funky former East German memorabilia: Take a stroll down **Bergmannstrasse,** where at least six *trödel* (junk shops) line the street between **Mehringdamm** and **Zossenerstrasse.**

Smoking Berlin is a hard-smoking town. No smoking signs and people willing to obey them are relatively new phenomena. Lighting up is allowed in restaurants, and it's unheard of to ask people to put out their cigarettes.

Street Plan The central area of Berlin lies along a main thoroughfare that, under several different names, stretches in a long straight line fron east to west. It starts in the east at **Schloss Brücke** (Palace Bridge) as **Unter den Linden.** On the other side of the **Brandenburger Tor** (in another country, of course, until 1990), it becomes **Strasse des 17 Juni.** Stretching westward it progressively becomes **Bismarckstrasse, Kaisersdamm,** and then **Heerstrasse.** At the eastern end, radiating in a wide area around **Schloss Brücke,** is the Mitte district, the downtown area of pre-World War II Berlin. At the western end of Strasse des 17 Juni is the downtown area that grew up after the division of the city. Between the two lies the **Tiergarten,** Berlin's beautiful city park.

Taxes Listed prices already include the appropriate tax: hotel (14 percent), restaurants (15 percent), retail merchandise (15 percent).

Telephones Most public phones now function only with pre-paid telephone cards, available at post offices. Calls from phones in bars or cafes are more expensive than from booths in public areas, and the cheapest place to make international calls is from booths in post offices.

Tipping Service is already included in hotel and restaurant bills. However, Berliners tend to add a bit extra for waiters, rounding up the tab to the whole *deutsche mark.* Hand the tip to your server, don't leave it on the table. One *deutsche mark* is the average tip for taxi drivers and the per-bag norm for porters.

Visas Travelers need only a valid passport to enter Berlin.

Visitors' Information There are four **Berlin Tourist Information** offices: **Europa Center** (Budapester Str 1; 2626031), open Monday through Saturday from 8AM until 10:30PM and on Sunday from 9AM until 9PM; **Bahnhof Zoologischer Garten** (3139063), open Monday through Saturday from 8AM until 11PM; **Hauptbahnhof** (2795209) in what was formerly East Berlin, open daily from 8AM until 10PM; and at the main hall in **Tegel Airport** (41013145), which operates daily from 8AM until 11PM.

"To be in Berlin meant a constant thrill in itself. My enthusiasm transformed the bleak squares and avenues into a labyrinth swarming with mysteries and adventures. What fun!—to stroll along those fabulous streets whose very names were charged with risky allurements: Friedrichstrasse, Unter den Linden, Tauentzienstrasse, Kurfürstendamm."

Klaus Mann (author of *Mephisto*)

"Berlin's destiny is to be in a constant state of becoming and never to be."

Karl Scheffler (German author)

Berlin

Schloss Charlottenburg

1 Schloss Charlottenburg When all of Berlin's so-called grand buildings were on the other side of the Wall, this one (illustrated above) was West Berlin's main claim to palatial fame. What began in the 1690s as an intimate summer residence for Queen Sophie Charlotte was successively added to and improved upon for the next 100 years to become a sprawling, rococo palace par excellence. The only way to view the opulent royal apartments (a must for antique-furniture lovers) is to take a guided tour, which can seem interminable even if you understand German. Americans are advised to invest in the detailed English-language guidebook available on site, or to head straight for the exquisite **Knobelsdorff-Flügel Wing**, restored to better than its pre-war condition and filled with paintings, including some by French master Antoine Watteau. Visitors can purchase a combination ticket to all attractions on the castle's grounds, or buy tickets for individual attractions. ♦ Admission. Tu-Su. Spandauer Damm (at Schlossstr). 320911

Within Schloss Charlottenburg:

Galerie der Romantik Look for masterworks from the German Romantic period, including 25 paintings by Caspar David Friedrich (1774-1840), all housed in the **Knobelsdorff-Flügel Wing**. ♦ Admission. Tu-Su. 320911

Karl Friedrich Schinkel Pavilion A delightful contrast to the grandeur of the **Schloss**, this tiny, Italian villa-style summer house, located at the eastern end of the palace, was added to the grounds in 1824 by **Karl Schinkel**. The decorated rooms are filled with beautifully executed drawings and paintings by this prolific architect who transformed 19th-century Berlin into a model of Neo-Classicism. ♦ Admission. Tu-Su

Belvedere This lovely 1788 building, at the far end of the park, is an earlier work by **Carl Gotthard Langhans**, the designer of the famed **Brandenburger Tor.** This former teahouse now houses a collection of KPM porcelain, products of the Berlin company founded by Friedrich the Great and still in operation today. ♦ Admission. Tu-Su

Schloss Park One of Berlin's best-loved public gardens, this greensward behind **Schloss Charlottenburg** was originally laid out in the French style in 1697, but was turned into an English garden in the 19th century. Only after the ravages of World War II was it restored to its Baroque form. It's a lovely spot to stroll, especially at twilight. A mausoleum on the western side of the gardens contains the remains of King Friedrich Wilhelm III and Kaiser Wilhelm I. ♦ Bounded by the River Spree, Sophie-Charlotten-Str, and Spandauer Damm

2 Ägyptisches Museum (Egyptian Museum) Berlin's most adored artistic treasure, a bust of the mysteriously beautiful Nefertiti, has a room of its own at this former barracks of the royal bodyguards. Dating back to about 1350 BC, the bust was supposedly created as a model for other representations of the ancient queen. It was discovered at Akhetaten in 1912, during one of many German excavations in Egypt, and brought to Berlin. As World War II was winding down, Nefertiti was evacuated from the Soviet half of the city, and hasn't been back since. The museum, located just across the street from **Schloss Charlottenburg,** contains other Egyptian relics of merit as well, though the mummies are better at eastern Berlin's **Bodemuseum** (see page 56). ♦ Admission. Daily. Schlossstr 70 (at Spandauer Damm). 32091261

3 Stadtbad Charlottenburg (Charlottenburg Public Pool) Ornate majolica columns and blue-and-white enameled bricks (circa 1896-98) make this the prettiest public pool in the city. It's even warm—85 degrees. Serious swimmers,

47

Berlin

however, may prefer the more modern Olympic-size pool in the new hall next door. Swimming here is cheap; for a real splurge pay the extra charge to use the sauna and steam room upstairs. ♦ Admission. Pools: M-Sa. Sauna: daily until 11PM (M and Th, reserved for women only). Krummestr 8-10 (between Bismarckstr and Otto-Suhr-Allee). Old hall: 34303214, new hall: 34303241, sauna: 3423078

4 TY BREIZh ★$$ Gregarious chef/owner Patrick Mattei has been serving hearty country cuisine from Brittany for more than 10 years in this funky bistro. Try the fish soup with Pernod or the *boeuf bourguignonne,* and definitely save room for the profiteroles. ♦ French ♦ Daily dinner. No credit cards accepted. Kantstr 75 (between Windscheidstr and Suarezstr). 3239932

Restaurant GÖRS

5 Görs $$ Intellectuals, students, and everyday folk are the mix at this popular cafe and *kneipe* (no-frills bar), one of many joints on and around Stuttgarter Platz. What sets it apart from the pack are its culinary innovations, such as adding chutney to the grilled chicken breast salad. Berliners love their breakfasts, so like many cafes in town this one serves it until 4PM. ♦ German/Continental ♦ Daily breakfast, lunch, and dinner. Stuttgarter Platz 21 (off Windscheidstr). 8249948

6 Harry Lehmann On the Berlin scene since 1926, this just might be the smallest perfume factory in the world. The liquid wares are sold by the gram, and customers can choose from more than 50 scents, including pure floral perfumes and eau de colognes. ♦ M-Sa. Kantstr 106 (between Wilmersdorferstr and Kaiser-Friedrich-Str). 3243582

SCHAUBÜHNE AM LEHNINER PLATZ

7 Schaubühne am Lehniner Platz An important and much loved example of 1920s architecture, **Erich Mendelsohn**'s theater complex, with its bowed facade, definitely warrants a short detour up the Ku'damm. ♦ Kurfürstendamm 153-163 (on Lehniner Platz)

8 Dahlem Museums When the Wall went up, the East may have won the architectural sweepstakes, but the West came out miles ahead in the art department. This seven-museum complex is located in Dahlem, a well-heeled and easy-to-reach suburb, just to the southwest of central Berlin, that's also home to the **Free University (FU).** ♦ Take the U-Bahn line 1 to Dahlem-Dorf station and follow the signs

Within the Dahlem Museums complex:

Gemäldegalerie (Picture Gallery) The star of **Dahlem,** with a roster of 13th- to 18th-century painters and other first-rate works, is a veritable who's who of art history. Look for pieces by Van Eyck, Holbein, Breugel, Rubens, Rembrandt, Vermeer, Giotto, Botticelli, Raphael, Titian, Caravaggio, Watteau, Gainsborough, and many others. ♦ Admission; free on Sunday. Tu-Su. Arnimallee 23/27 (off Fabeckstr). 8301216

Museum für Indische Kunst (Museum of Indian Art) Four thousand years of art from India, Thailand, Indonesia, Tibet, and Burma are displayed here, along with a world-famous collection of Buddhist monastery cave paintings. ♦ Admission; free on Sundays. Tu-Su. Lansstr 8 (between Fabeckstr and Takustr). 8301361

Museum für Islamische Kunst (Museum of Islamic Art) Exquisite Persian rugs, a 16th-century Koran, and Turkish tiles are featured among the Islamic art treasures exhibited here. ♦ Admission; free on Sundays. Tu-Su. Lansstr 8 (between Takustr and Fabeckstr). 8301362

Museum für Volksrkunde (Ethnological Museum) Don't expect to cover the entire collection—a half-million tools, costumes, and pieces of furniture collected from around the world—in one visit. But you can certainly have fun trying. ♦ Admission; free on Sunday. Tu-Su. Lansstr 8 (between Takustr and Fabeckstr). 8301226

8 Luise ★$ The beer garden here is one of Berlin's prettiest, and indoor dining at this popular student hangout can also be pleasant. ♦ German/Continental ♦ Daily breakfast, lunch, and dinner. Königin-Luise-Str 40 (between Takustr and Iltisstr). 8328487

8 Brücke Museum Somewhat over the river and through the woods, it takes some work to find this museum, but the effort is amply rewarded. Showcasing works by members of the German Expressionist movement *Die Brücke* ("The Bridge"), the museum includes pieces by Ludwig Kirchner, Karl Schmidt-Rottluff, Emil Nolde, and Erich Heckel. ♦ Admission. M, W-Su. Bussardsteig 9 (off Clay-allee, between Fohlenweg and Käuzchensteig). 8312029.

"Berlin is a city where one can still see the stars."

Wim Wenders, film director

Berlin

8 Botanischer Garten und Botanisches Museum (Botanical Garden and Museum Berlin-Dahlem) This haven for horticulture fans covers 104 acres and 16 greenhouses, and boasts 18,000 plant species. The museum is less inspiring. ♦ Museum: Tu-Su; W until 7PM; garden open daily. König-Luise-Str 6-8 (at König-Luise-Platz). 830060

9 Hotel Pension Modena $$ Located right off Ku'damm, the Art Deco lobby and stairwell of this building are lovely, the rooms are in order, and Peter Trabandt is far more personable than most pension owners. There are 22 guest rooms, five of which have private baths. The hotel does not have a restaurant. ♦ Wielandstr 26 (between Olivaer Platz and Kurfürstendamm). 8857010; fax 8815294

10 Hotel Pension Majesty $$ This tastefully decorated pension does business in a typical Berlin turn-of-the-century apartment house, complete with a beautiful wood-paneled lobby. There are 25 guest rooms; 13 have a private bath or shower, but none have private WCs. Not only is this place quiet, but it's convenient to Savignyplatz and Ku'damm. ♦ Mommsenstr 55 (between Leibnizstr and Wilmersdorferstr). 3232061

11 Condomi A fun and decidedly unsleazy shop specializing in every color, shape, style, and even flavor of condom known to man—and woman. ♦ M-Sa. Kantstr 38 (between Leibnizstr and Weimarer Str). 3135051

12 Dralle's ★$ This attractive and surprisingly price-conscious cafe, surrounded by boutiques and secondhand bookshops, is one of the few places in town to get a decent BLT. ♦ Cafe ♦ Daily lunch, dinner, and late-night supper. Schlüter Str 69 (at Pestalozzistr). 3135038

13 A Trane What a find: a smart-looking jazz club in a swanky part of town, with a low cover charge—this spot is downright democratic. ♦ Cover. Daily 9PM-4AM. Bleibtreustr 1 (at Pestalozzistr). 3132550

14 Ashoka $ This *imbiss* (snack bar), specializing in Indian dishes, serves everything from *dal* (lentils) to chicken *saag* (with spinach) at excellent prices. Another bonus: Outdoor seating is available. ♦ Indian ♦ Daily lunch and dinner. No credit cards accepted. Grolmanstr 51 (off Savignyplatz). 3132066

15 Cafe Bar Tiago ★★$$ Without a doubt, some of the best salads in town can be had here. Try the corn salad with ham, cheese, red pepper, and a yogurt dressing. In typical fashion, the breakfast menu is served until 3PM. ♦ German/Cafe ♦ Daily breakfast, lunch, and dinner. No credit cards accepted. Knesebeckstr 15 (between Savignyplatz and Goethestr). 3129042

15 Pension Knesebeck $$ At this well-located pension, the quality of your breakfast, according to the manager, depends on how polite you are. The nine guest rooms in this former residence, all with shared bathroom facilities, are charming and comfortable. ♦ Knesebeckstr 86 (between Savignyplatz and Goethestr). 317255

15 Berlin Zinnfiguren Kabinet The specialty of this hobby shop is tiny, hand-painted tin figurines—just the thing for well-behaved children and discriminating adults. Don't miss the dinosaur series. ♦ M-Sa. Knesebeckstr 88 (between Savignyplatz and Goethestr). 310802

16 Restaurant Filmbühne am Steinplatz $ This spacious cafe/restaurant is usually filled with students and film fans grabbing a bite to eat before or after a movie (sometimes with English subtitles) at the renowned arts cinema (3129012) of the same name, and in the same building. ♦ Cafe ♦ Daily breakfast, lunch, and dinner. No credit cards accepted. Hardenbergstr 12 (at Steinplatz). 3129013

16 Cafe Hardenberg ★$ Students congregate en masse to talk, eat, sip more than 20 varieties of tea, and relax in a space that, during the Nazi era, contained a high-class brothel and, later, a cabaret. ♦ Cafe ♦ Daily breakfast, lunch, and dinner. No credit cards accepted. Hardenbergstr 10 (at Steinplatz). 3122644

16 Jugendgästehaus am Zoo $ What it lacks in atmosphere, Berlin's most centrally located youth hostel makes up for in cost (cheap) and flexibility (no midnight curfew). The age limit of 27 is not enforced when vacancies remain. The 17-room guest house has single, double, and four- to eight-person dorm rooms. Reservations are accepted for dorm rooms only. ♦ Hardenbergstr 9A (between Fasanenstr and Uhlandstr). 3129410

17 Quasimodo The oldest and best-known jazz venue in Berlin and then some—this small, smoky club often surprises with its musical mix. ♦ Cover. Daily 9PM-4AM. Kantstr 12A (at Fasanenstr). 3128086

49

Berlin

18 Schwarzes Cafe $$ Here is the place to go for breakfast at 5AM—or any other time, as the kitchen stays open 24 hours. Try the "Love on the Run" special, which includes cheese, sausage, and rolls. Tofu-veggie kabobs and tortellini are other good choices. ♦ German/Continental ♦ Daily breakfast, lunch, and dinner. Kantstr 148 (between Fasanenstr and Uhlandstr). 3138038

19 Cafe Aedes ★$$ Welcome to a prime haunt of the beautiful people, nestled under the S-Bahn tracks at Savignyplatz. The cafe adjoins the **Aedes Galerie and Architecktur Forum,** which exhibits plans and photos of contemporary architectural projects. ♦ Continental ♦ Daily breakfast and snacks. S-Bahn-Bogen 599/600 (between Knesebeckstr and Bleibtreustr). 3125504

20 Hotel Bogota $$ This big, old, rambling hotel, unfortunately redecorated in hideous 1970s style, is centrally located and an affordable alternative to pension living. It's got 127 rooms; 60 have complete private bathrooms, 12 have their own showers, 55 have nothing private but a sink. There is no restaurant, but there is a dining room where complimentary breakfast is served. ♦ Schlüterstr 45 (between Lietzenburger Str and Kurfürstendamm). 8815001; fax 8835887

21 Hotel-Pension Pariser-Eck $$ This small, friendly pension, situated on a block studded with boutiques, bars, and cafes, is only five minutes from the Ku'damm bustle. It's got 12 basic, yet comfortable, rooms; six have their own showers but all WCs are communal. ♦ Pariser Str 19 (at Sächsische Str). 8812145; fax 8836335

22 Villa Grisebach This fanciful turn-of-the-century villa harkens back in style to the Italian Renaissance. Fully restored during the 1987 celebration of Berlin's 750th anniversary, the building now houses an auction house and art gallery. It's a gem, inside and out. ♦ M-Sa. Fasanenstr 25 (between Lietzenburger Str and Kürfurstendamm). 8826811

22 Käthe Kollwitz Museum Housed in a stately four-story mansion, this private museum is filled with woodcuts, paintings, and sculptures from the Berlin artist whose pacifist and feminist ideals can be clearly seen in her work. ♦ Admission. M, W-Su. Fasanenstr 24 (between Lietzenburger Str and Küfurstendamm). 8825210

22 Hotel Pension Funk $$ Among all the mid-priced pensions on Berlin's fanciest shopping block, one stands out, for it was once the home of the great 1920s German actress Asta Nielsen. Don't miss the art nouveau stained glass in the hall bathroom (which would be hard to do, since only one of 50 guest rooms claims a private bathroom). Complimentary breakfast is served in the dining room; there is no restaurant. ♦ Fasanenstr 69 (between Lietzenburger Str and Kürfurstendamm). 8827193; fax 8827193

23 Zille Hof In another example of Berlin odd juxtapositions, this junk shop is next door to the four-star **Bristol Hotel Kempinski.** Patience, a good eye, and a weakness for kitsch get rewarded here. ♦ M-F; Sa mornings. Fasanenstr 14 (between Kürfurstendamm and Kantstr). 8819509

24 Leysieffer ★★★$$$ Anyone who's watching their weight or possesses a sweet tooth has to tread carefully here. Hazards include the chocolate temptations in the shop downstairs and cakes in the cafe above. ♦ German/Continental ♦ Daily breakfast, lunch, and dinner. Kurfürstendamm 218 (between Joachimstalerstr and Meinekestr). 8857480

24 Hotel-Pension Imperator $$ Here is the prettiest pension of its price-range in the city. There are 11 huge guest rooms, all beautifully furnished and all with private baths. Across the street is Berlin's outpost of the **Hard Rock Cafe.** ♦ Meinekestr 5 (between Lietzenburger Str and Kürfurstendamm). 8814181; fax 8851919

25 Restaurant Marché ★★$ A self-service restaurant that belongs to the Swiss **Mövenpick** chain, this eatery offers great value and taste for the money. Veggie dishes and salads dominate the menu, and credit cards are even accepted. ♦ German/Continental ♦ Daily breakfast, lunch, and dinner. Kurfürstendamm 14-15 (off Breitscheidplatz). 8827579

26 Kaiser-Wilhelm-Gedächtniskirche (Kaiser Wilhelm Memorial Church) In November 1943, British bombers reduced this pompous 19th-century, Neo-Gothic church to a skeletal ruin, and it's remained that way ever since—a visual testament to the horrors of war. Unfortunately, the more modern churches surrounding this crumbling survivor testify only to the architectural poverty of the early Cold War period. ♦ Tu-Su. Breitscheidplatz (on Kurfürstendamm). 2185023

27 Zoologischer Garten (Zoo) Berlin's oldest and largest animal compound, found on the southwestern edge of the lovely **Tiergarten** (see page 52). Even if you don't venture in to

Berlin

see Berlin's much-loved panda bear, Baobao, don't miss the carved elephant gateway on Hardenbergstrasse, or the pastel dinosaur bas-reliefs at the **Aquarium** next door. ♦ Admission. Daily. Budapester Str (between Nürnberger Str and Breitscheidplatz). 254010

NÜRNBERGER ECK

28 Hotel-Pension Nürnberger Eck $$ Artists swear by this pension, which on occasion stages exhibits and installations, and where even the decor strives to be artistic, or at least interesting. There are only eight guest rooms here (none with private baths) and no restaurant, although a complimentary breakfast is served. ♦ Nürnberger Str 24a (between Lietzenburger Str and Tauentzienstr). 2185371; fax 2141540

29 KaDeWe The city's largest department store boasts the most extensive food department in Europe, taking up the entire sixth floor. Work up an appetite or satisfy one by starting at the extravagant sausage and ham assortment, then wind your way to the breads that numbered over 400 at last count. ♦ M-Sa; Th until 8PM. Tauentzienstr 21-24 (at Wittenbergplatz). 21210

30 Garage A great place to get a last-minute, I-need-a-new-look ensemble, this joint has a unique system—it charges by the kilo for its stock of vintage and used clothing. ♦ M-Sa. Ahornstr 2 (off Einemstr). 2112760

EINSTEIN

31 Cafe Einstein ★★$$ No place in Berlin is closer to being a real Viennese coffeehouse than this place, located in the former town villa of German silent-screen star Hennie Porten. The waiters are appropriately dour and tuxedoed, the interior is charming, and there's a lovely garden in the back for warm-weather dining. One can eat well here, but not as cheaply as in the past. Nevertheless, go ahead and splurge on a serving of warm apple strudel with vanilla sauce and a full-bodied cup of coffee. ♦ Viennese/Continental ♦ Daily breakfast, lunch, dinner, and afternoon cake and coffee. Kurfürstenstr 58 (at Genthiner Str). 2615096

32 Metropol A fraction of its original 1906 size, this theater still towers over Nollendorfplatz and is a majestic sight when lit up at night. Home to playwright Erwin Piscator's theatrical experiments of the 1920s, it has served as a popular grand-scale disco for years now. ♦ Cover. F-Sa 9PM-closing. Nollendorfplatz 5 (Einemstr and Kleiststr). 2164122, 2162787

Within Metropol:

32 The Loft This small venue features concerts of contemporary music. Check the papers for concert schedules. ♦ Box office: M-Sa. 2161020

33 Cafe Berio ★$$ Wouldn't you know it? The quintessential Berlin coffeehouse is owned by an American. The interior, a slightly ratty mishmash, has a decent selection of newspapers and magazines for patrons' reading pleasure, better-than-average cakes, and totally inefficient service (you gotta love it). Breakfast is served until 2PM. ♦ Cafe ♦ Daily breakfast, lunch, and dinner. Maassenstr 7 (between Winterfeldtstr and Nollendorfstr). 2161946

34 Winterfeldt Markt Berliners from all walks of life frequent this bustling street market, especially on Saturdays. (The market operates on Wednesdays, too, but on a smaller scale.) Buy or browse among stands laden with everything from fruit and flowers to Turkish delicacies, homemade pickles, and antique buttons. ♦ W, Sa 8AM-2PM. Winterfeldtstr (between Gleditschstr and Goltzstr)

Habibi

34 Habibi ★$ It was a red-letter day when falafel was introduced to Berlin. Those crispy deep-fried chickpea balls, and other Middle Eastern specialties, satisfy cravings into the wee hours at this place. Wash it all down with fresh carrot juice. ♦ Middle Eastern ♦ No credit cards accepted. Goltzstr 24 (at Winterfeldtplatz). 2153332

35 Cafe M $ Okay, it certainly doesn't look like much, but it's always packed with the city's rising population of young, multicultural trendoids. Breakfast (served until 3PM) is especially popular. ♦ German/Cafe ♦ Daily breakfast, lunch, and snacks. Goltzstr 33 (between Frankenstr and Hohenstaufenstr). 2167092

36 Bayou ★$$ This brightly colored, lively Cajun restaurant serves up generous portions of jambalaya, gumbo, and other New Orleans goodies. Finish off your meal with Key lime pie. ♦ Cajun ♦ Daily dinner. Vorbergstr 10 (beween Gleditschstr and Akazienstr). 7846735

> "The Potsdamer Platz is so big, and so conspicuously bombed out, that it is an easy symbol, but in a way all Berlin is a symbol. It wears its history like scars."
>
> Jane Kramer, *The New Yorker*

Restaurants/Clubs: Red **Hotels:** Blue
Shops/ ♦ Outdoors: Green **Sights/Culture:** Black

51

Berlin

37 Pinguin Club The decor is all rock 'n' roll kitsch in an adorable 1950s redux. The British bartender will serve you any of the over 150 spirits stocked. ♦ Daily 9PM-4AM. Wartburgstr 54 (between Merseburger Str and Eisenacher Str). 7813005

38 Savarin ★$ Vegetable and savory tortes, all at least six inches high, share the bill with sweet dessert tarts, ice cream, and shakes at this cozy and quiet cafe. ♦ Cafe ♦ Daily lunch, dinner, and afternoon cake and coffee. Kulmer Str 17 (between Gross-Görschenstr and Goebenstr). 2163864

39 Neunzig Grad The name means **Ninety Degrees** but this is a cool (yet friendly) dance club. The fun decor is always changing, and the music mix runs the contemporary gamut. It's managed by an "Ami," as Americans are known in these parts. ♦ Cover. Th-Su 11PM-6AM. Dennewitzstr 37 (at Kürfurstenstr). 2628984

40 Kumpelnest 3000 It's divinely tasteless and extremely loud. People either love this jam-packed, everything-goes bar or hate it with a passion. ♦ Daily 5PM-5AM. Lützowstr 23 (between Körnerstr and Potsdamer Str). 2616918

41 Neue Nationalgalerie (New National Gallery) German architect **Ludwig Mies van der Rohe,** a former president of the **Bauhaus** design school who went on to international renown, built only one edifice in Germany after his 1938 emigration to the US. This black-rimmed glass box, designed by **Mies van der Rohe** in 1965, seems to float above the ground. It houses a collection of late 19th- and early 20th-century works by German and international artists. Changing contemporary exhibits keep the museum lively. ♦ Admission for temporary exhibits. Tu-Su; special exhibits until 8PM. Potsdamer Str 50 (at Reichpietschufer). 2662651

"Standing now in the crowded underground car, she looked every inch the chic west Berliner: razored red hair, black leather boots, a white-faced woman with a fuck-you gaze calculated to repel the predatory eyes that swarmed in the U-Bahn."

Ian Walker, *Zoo Station: Adventures in East and West Berlin*

42 Philharmonie This gold-roofed concert hall, built in the early 1960s, has been labeled "one of the most original works of modern architecture." Other critics, however, have shared a less generous view of designer **Hans Scharoun**'s work, calling it one of the ugliest structures on the planet. But there's no faulting the hall's acoustics—just ask the musicians of the resident **Berliner Philharmonisches Orchester.** Concerts are frequently sold out, but try the box office the night of the performance. Or catch a chamber music concert next door at the **Kammermusiksaal** (254880). ♦ Box office: daily. Matthäikirchstr 1 (at Matthäikirchplatz). Box office: 2614383

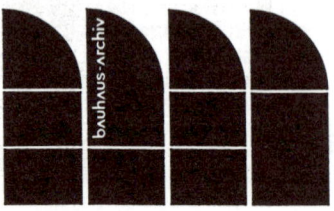

43 Bauhaus-Archiv Erected in 1970 according to plans by the late **Bauhaus** founder and architect, **Walter Gropius,** these archives feature a permanent collection of artifacts, models, and drawings by teachers and students from Germany's most influential design school. Temporary exhibits further reflect the mid-20th century influence of the **Bauhaus** movement, both in Europe and America. You may not be bowled over by the quality of objects on display, as many of the best examples of **Bauhaus** design found their way to America when their creators fled the Nazis. But you certainly won't be bored. ♦ Admission. M, W-Su. Klingelhöferstr 13-14 (between Herkulesufer and Von-der-Heydt-Str). 2540020

44 Tiergarten Berlin's counterpart to New York City's Central Park was originally laid out as a hunting ground by 19th-century master landscaper Josef Lenné, only to be turned into a black smudge during the 1945 Battle of Berlin. Extensive replanting has brought the large, irregularly shaped greensward back to life, and back into the hearts of Berliners. Today, the park is a popular place for leisurely strolls, bike rides, picnics, rowboat rides, and sunbathing (usually nude—Berliners take their clothes off at the drop of a ray). The **Tiergarten** never closes but, as most urban parks, it's best avoided at night, and camping is illegal. ♦ Bounded by Tiergartenstr and the River Spree, and Eberstr and Landwehrkanal. Entrance off Str des 17 Juni

45 Siegessäule (Victory Column) Berlin's best-known woman, Victoria (or "Golden Elsie," as she's more derisively called), holds court atop a 220-foot-tall column

Berlin

commemorating Prussian military victories in the Franco-Prussian War, as well as in earlier Danish and Austrian campaigns. Her original home was at the northeastern corner of the **Tiergarten** in the **Platz der Republik,** but Adolf Hitler—ever the lover of monumental symbolism—had her moved here in 1938. Victoria now rises from the center of a star-shaped roundabout but, even with the traffic ceaselessly circling her skirts, she's a stunning sight. Panorama fiends can climb up this column's 285 steps for a good view east over Berlin toward the **Brandenburger Tor** (see below). ♦ Grosser Stern (on Str des 17 Juni in Tiergarten)

46 Haus der Kulturen der Welt (House of World Cultures) Architect **Hugh A. Stubbin**'s futuristic **Kongresshalle** (congress hall) was built in 1957 as the American contribution to Berlin's first international building exhibition. Nicknamed the "pregnant oyster" by Berliners, the edifice has a new cultural purpose: to showcase displays, performances, and readings by artists from Third World countries. ♦ Admission. Tu-Su. John-Foster-Dulles-Allee 10 (at In den Zelten). 397870

47 Reichstag Ominous in both appearance and history, this building was completed in 1894 by architect **Paul Wallot** as home to the government offices of Chancellor Otto von Bismark's newly unified Germany. Now, stripped by war of its dome and original ornamentation, it is scheduled to once again house the government of a unified Germany—when and if lawmakers move out of Bonn.

Most Berliners will be only too happy to relinquish control over this troubled edifice. It was here in 1918 that a new German Republic (later the Weimar Republic) was declared. Fifteen years later, a mysterious fire roared through the building (possibly started by the SA, precursors to the notorious SS police). The Nazi government retaliated by arresting Communists and other enemies and suspending civil rights.

The monumental structure is currently closed while undergoing renovations in preparation for the arrival of the federal government in Berlin. Still, it's worth a trip to soak up the sight of this history-drenched building. And from behind it, you can still make out the course of the demolished **Berlin Wall** and find plaques commemorating spots where would-be defectors tried to swim across the River Spree. ♦ Platz der Republik (between Scheidemannstr and Paul-Löbe-Str). 39770

48 Brandenburger Tor (Brandenburg Gate) An aura of celebration can still be felt at this poignant symbol of German division and reunification. With almost all of the **Berlin Wall** gone now, this gate (pictured below) remains as one of the most familiar images from the 28 years when West Berlin and East Berlin were separated. The gate was built in 1791 and modeled (by designer **Carl Gotthard Langhans**) after the Propylaea entrance to the Acropolis in Athens. It is the only one of

Brandenburger Tor

Berlin

Berlin's original 18 city gates still standing. Although conceived as a monument to peace, it acquired a triumphal air with the addition of Johann Gottfried Schadow's *Quadriga* statue, which depicts the Goddess of Victory in her horse-drawn chariot. The arch marks the western end of Unter den Linden, the wide avenue which served as the center of East Berlin. Once a popular rallying point for Nazi marchers, it now serves as a starting point for tours of Berlin's historical center. ♦ Pariser Platz (between Unter den Linden and Str des 17 Juni)

49 Gendarmenmarkt (Gendarmes Market) One of the most beautiful and seemingly untouched squares in Berlin came under heavy bombardment during World War II. Restoration didn't begin until the 1970s, and is still underway. In the center of the square is architect **Karl Friedrich Schinkel**'s grandiose, Neo-Classical theater, the **Konzert Haus Berlin** (20902157). Built between 1818 and 1821 and gutted during the war, the concert hall's exterior has been superbly restored, and its interior completely redesigned to serve as a concert hall. Flanking it are two historic churches. The impressive **Deutscher Dom** (German Cathedral), on the southern side of the square, was severely damaged during World War II and is still getting a face-lift; it remains closed to the public. On the northern side of the plaza, the **Französischer Dom** (French Cathedral) reopened in 1987, but not as a place of worship: It now houses the **Huguenot Museum** (221760) in its Baroque tower. Right behind it, a luxury shopping passage, the **Friedrichstadt**, is under construction. ♦ Between Markgrafenstr and Charlottenstr

50 Staatsoper (State Opera) The musical director of the **Chicago Symphony**, Daniel Barenboim, is also the artistic and general musical director of this elegant opera house. Prussia's first, the opera house was built for Frederick the Great in 1741-43 by court architect **Georg Wenzeslaus von Knobelsdorff**.

The building is next to **Bebelplatz**, the infamous site of Nazi propaganda minister Joseph Goebbels's book burning in 1933. This square, in turn, is flanked by the **Alte Bibliothek**, a former royal library that, thanks to its Baroque facade, is known as the Kommode ("chest of drawers"). **St. Hedwigs-Kathedrale (St. Hedwig's Cathedral)**, a rounded edifice that serves as the seat of the Catholic Bishop in Berlin, is just to the opera's south. ♦ Box office: M-Sa. Unter den Linden 7 (at Bebelplatz). 20354494

Europe's only Buddhist temple is in Berlin. Paul Dahlke, a physician, built it on Edelhofdamm 54 in 1924.

50 Operncafe ★$$ The most affordable of four restaurants situated in the stately **Opernpalais** (formerly the **Prinzessinnenpalais** or **Princesses' Palace**), this otherwise run-of-the-mill cafe offers diners a truly mouthwatering selection of cakes and tortes. ♦ German ♦ Daily breakfast, lunch, dinner, and afternoon cake and coffee. Unter den Linden 5 (at Oberwallstr). 2082192

51 Neue Wache (New Guardhouse) If you think you see a Roman temple as you stroll down **Unter den Linden,** don't doubt your eyes. Built by **Karl Friedrich Schinkel** between 1816 and 1818 as a guardhouse for the royal watch, the building was turned into a war memorial in 1931. During East German times, tourists would gather here to photograph the silent, goose-stepping guards. After reunification, the Communist-designed eternal flame inside, dedicated to the victims of militarism and fascism, was replaced by a pietà sculpture by Käthe Kollwitz. ♦ Unter den Linden 4 (at Hinter dem Giesshaus)

51 Zeughaus (Arsenal) This imposing Baroque armory, complete with designer **Andreas Schlüter's** 22 sculptures of dying warriors, is the oldest building on Unter den Linden. It's now home to the **Deutsches Historisches Museum** (German Historical Museum), an unstuffy place that stages some of the most creative exhibits to be seen anywhere in Berlin. ♦ Admission. M-Tu, Th-Su. Unter den Linden 2 (at Am Zeughaus). 215020.

Within the Zeughaus:

CAFÉ · BISTRO
ZEUGHAUS

Café · Bistro Zeughaus ★★$$ Hurrah! Finally, the heart of Mitte has a decent restaurant—in terms of cuisine, service, and atmosphere. Come here for lunch or just for a killer dessert of *Germknödel*, a sweet yeast dumpling that resembles a cannonball and will wreak havoc with any diet. ♦ German ♦ Daily breakfast, lunch, and dinner. 21502130

52 Palast der Republik (Palace of the Republic) For this they blew up the **Stadt Schloss** (the 15th-century Imperial Palace)? East German leader Erich Honecker's idea of state-of-the-art architecture, this multifunctional complex, complete with a populist bowling alley and an assembly room for the parliament, is now closed and threatened with demolition because of its asbestos insulation. A citizens' group is lobbying to have the original palace rebuilt, but public opinion remains divided. ♦ Marx-Engels Platz (at Karl-Liebknecht-Str)

Podewil

53 Podewil An 18th-century palace that served as the **Haus der Jungen Talent** (House of Young Talent) in GDR days still serves as a venue for youthful entertainers, especially those involved in the avant-garde music scene. The program of concerts and performances is culturally diverse, and if you're lucky, you'll catch a truly memorable production. ♦ Admission. Call for individual program hours. Reservations recommended. Klosterstr 68-70 (between Parochialstr and Grunerstr). 247496

54 Alexanderplatz During the East German interregnum, this windswept plaza was meant to symbolize the majesty of socialist Berlin. All it does now is remind people of how much was lost during World War II. Aside from surviving landmarks such as the 19th-century **Rotes Rathaus (Red Town Hall)**, a beautiful structure at the south end that was named for its brick color rather than for political reasons, bombing toppled much of the architecture that once surrounded this square. Novelist Alfred Döblin (who wrote his famous *Berlin Alexanderplatz* in 1929) probably wouldn't even recognize the place today. ♦ Spandauer Str (between Rathausstr and Karl-Liebknecht-Str)

Within the Alexanderplatz:

Fernsehturm (TV Tower) Once there was talk of tearing down what is possibly Berlin's most visible landmark. But this 1,197-foot television tower, which took most of the 1960s to build, seems here to stay. And a good thing, too. The view from the top is unbeatable, and there's a revolving cafe (serving synthetic food, unfortunately) for those who prefer to sit while Berlin goes by. ♦ Admission. Daily 9AM-midnight; closes at 1PM on the second and fourth Tuesdays of every month. 2133333

Marx-Engels Forum West of the **Fernsehturm** is a plaza dedicated to the two radical philosophers, and probably one of the best surviving examples of socialist public art. The centerpiece is a surprisingly modest statue of the pair (not a furrowed brow or clenched fist in sight). The walls surrounding the statue are decorated with pictures and texts of workers' history and independence movements. As the chain stores and neon signs around **Alexanderplatz** proliferate, this plaza becomes ever more anachronistic and interesting.

55 Berliner Dom (Berlin Cathedral) For years, the pomp and ceremony of this Hohenzollern-era (1701-1918) court cathedral (illustrated below) could only be appreciated from the outside as its incredibly ornate interior was in the hands of restorers. Now, however, the whole gaudy spectacle is open for viewing. There are excellent organ concerts held some Sundays, and don't miss the crypt, where 99 Hohenzollern sarcophagi have been laid to rest. ♦ Admission to some areas. Lustgarten (off Karl-Liebknecht-Str)

56 Museum Insel (Museum Island) Commissioned by King Friedrich Wilhelm III in 1820, but not completed until 1930, this famous complex of museums stands on an artificial isle in the middle of the River Spree. Like much else in what was East Berlin, the buildings here are in various stages of restoration or reconstruction. Empty and even a little romantically desolate at night, the island is packed with tour buses during the day. A small flea market operates on the weekends, and the surrounding area is starting to bustle with new restaurants, bars, and shops. The most

Berliner Dom

Berlin

economical—and, alas, eye-straining—deal is to buy a day-pass to all the museums here.
♦ Bounded by Lustgarten, Bodestr, Monbijoustr, and Kupfergraben

At Museum Insel:

Altes Museum (Old Museum) Facing the **Lustgarten** plaza, this gracious museum was built in the 1800s to plans by **Karl Friedrich Schinkel.** Primarily a showcase for special exhibits, the museum's exquisite rotunda is a show in itself, with its Corinthian columns, neo-classical sculptures, and painted walls.
♦ Admission. Tu-Su. Lustgarten (off Karl-Liebknecht-Str). 203550

Neues Museum (New Museum) Designed by noted local architect, **Friedrich August Stüler,** and built in the 1850s as an arts and sciences museum, the structure took a beating during World War II. Restoration work has been going on only since 1990, and hopes are that the building will reopen before the year 2000. ♦ Bodestr (at Kupfergraben)

Alte Nationalgalerie (Old National Gallery) Often overlooked in the rush to get to the more famous **Pergamonmuseum** (see below), this Corinthian-style edifice contains an interesting collection of paintings and sculpture from 19th-century German masters.
♦ Admission. Tu-Su. Bodestr 1-3 (at Friedrichs Brücke). 20355257

Pergamonmuseum Beginning in the 1840s, German treasure hunters descended upon Asia Minor and Egypt like locusts. Later in that century, archaeologist Heinrich Schliemann brought riches back from Turkey—the start of this museum's collection. On the outside, it looks appropriately like a Babylonian temple. Inside are the wonders of the ancient world, including the breathtaking **Pergamon Altar,** dating from 180 to 160 BC, and discovered by German archaeologists in 1876; the **Gate of Ishtar,** a relic from the Babylonian reign of Nebuchadnezzar II; and the relief-decorated facade of a Jordanian prince's palace from 743 AD. Expect to hear a steady stream of oohs and aahs—just walking through this place is an extraordinary experience.
♦ Admission. Tu-Su. Kupfergraben (at Pergamonsteg). 20355504

Bodemuseum Named after Wilhelm von Bode, the museum director who was responsible for bringing key art treasures to Berlin, this charcoal-blackened neo-Baroque building was the original keystone of **Museum Insel.** It now houses a fascinating collection of third-rate Old Masters (the *real stuff* ended up in west Berlin's **Dahlem Museums,** see page 48, after World War II), many religious artifacts from the pre-medieval eastern Mediterranean, an important and extensive coin collection, and some terrific mummies.
♦ Admission. Tu-Su. Monbijoubrücke (at Kupfergraben). 20355503

57 Bahnhof Friedrichstrasse (Friedrichstrasse Rail Station) Sometimes at night, one can almost sense the danger this elevated station inspired when it was a major crossover point during the Cold War. But those days are gone, and the station, as well as the buildings surrounding it, are adapting nicely to the new world order. The nearby **Tränen Palast** (Palace of Tears) was given its name because it was here in 1961 that East Germans bid tearful farewells to departing West German family and friends; today it's a discotheque, film house, and performance club. And the row of S-Bahn arches linking the station and **Museum Insel** has become the site of Berlin's only indoor flea market, a Tex-Mex cantina, bookstores, and **Lucky Strike**—a Cajun restaurant and blues club. ♦ Friedrichstr (between Georgenstr and Weidendamm)

Museum of Natural History Berlin
Museum für Naturkunde

58 Museum für Naturkunde (Museum of Natural History) How can you resist this musty old science museum, evoking the Victorian romance of world exploration? The dinos are stupendous, as are the meteor chunks and the slightly moth-eaten stuffed specimens. Don't miss the gorgeous staircase in the back. ♦ Admission. Tu-Su. Invalidenstr 34 (between Chausseestr and Schwarzer Weg). 28972540

59 Keller-Restaurant ★$$ This pleasant eatery is located in the basement of **Brecht Haus,** the last home of playwright Bertolt Brecht (whose plays include *Mother Courage* and *The Good Woman of Szechuan*). Brecht lived here with his wife, Helene Weigel, after their return to Berlin in 1949 from a self-imposed exile in the United States. The house itself is a must for Brechtophiles, although the half-hourly guided tours can be rather boring

Berlin

if you're not familiar with the playwright's work. More Brecht memorabilia and stage set models adorn the restaurant walls, and an Austrian menu reflects the cooking traditions of his wife. Both Brecht and Weigel are buried in the **Dorotheenstadt Cemetery** next door. ♦ Austrian/German ♦ Daily dinner. Reservations recommended. Chausseestr 125 (between Torstr and Invalidenstr). 2823843

60 Tacheles Located in Berlin's old Jewish section of Scheunenviertel (literally, the Barn Quarter, named for the barns that still operated here in the early 20th century), this is the cultural flagship of Oranienburger Strasse, east Berlin's hippest street. It also happens to be a ruin. In 1990, squatters took over what remained of a bombed-out shopping passage and turned it into an alternative arts center—and the cafes and tourists followed. While locals say the collective has lost its edge, something wild is generally going on in one of its cinemas, theaters, or concert spaces. ♦ Admission. Oranienburger Str 53-56 (between Tucholskystr and Friedrichstr). 2826185

60 VEB Oz A small and humorous Trabi automobile theme bar, literally built from East German Trabi parts, this place is at its prime during the week. ♦ Daily 9AM-4AM. Auguststr 92 (at Oranienburger Str). No phone

61 Cafe Beth ★$ Jewish food with an Israeli accent (sorry, no corned beef) is the fare at this intimate cafe. There's outdoor dining in a secluded back courtyard. ♦ Israeli ♦ M-F, Su breakfast, lunch, and dinner; closes two hours before sundown on Fridays. Tucholskystr 40 (between Auguststr and Linienstr). 2818135

62 Cafe Orange ★$$ Attractive peach walls and white stuccoed ceilings make this the most civilized eating environment in the Scheunenviertel. And the food's not bad either. The menu changes, but try the lasagna when it's offered, as well as the salad of warm potatoes and herring. The breakfast menu is served until 2PM. ♦ Continental ♦ Daily breakfast, lunch, and dinner. Oranienburger Str 32 (between Krausnickstr and Tucholskystr). 2820028

62 Neue Synagoge (New Synagogue) The 1930s violence of *Kristallnacht* and the rain of Allied bombs wreaked severe damage on this majestic house of Jewish worship, which was completed in 1866 and designed by two of the city's leading architects, **Eduard Knoblauch** and **Friedrich August Stüler**. The glistening golden domes were regilded in the last years of the German Democratic Republic (GDR), and the facade was restored as well. Work is now going on in the interior. The anchor of this multifaceted neighborhood, the synagogue is incongruously flanked by cafes and a red-light street. ♦ Oranienburger Str 30 (between Krausnickstr and Tucholskystr)

62 Café Oren & Restaurant ★★$$ Serving fish and vegetarian dishes, this Israeli restaurant was an instant hit with young and old, locals and visitors. The vegetable torte is huge, and the hummus and falafel plates are a garlic lover's delight. It's always crowded at night, but tables are easier to come by at lunchtime. ♦ Middle Eastern ♦ Daily breakfast, lunch, and dinner. Oranienburger Str 28 (between Krausnickstr and Tucholskystr). 2828228

62 Cafe Silberstein ★$ A popular spot in spite of its potentially lethal sculpted metal chairs, in summer this bar's street-side tables are great for watching the parade go by. ♦ M-F 4PM-4AM; Sa-Su noon-4AM. Oranienburger Str 27 (between Krausnickstr and Tucholskystr). No phone

63 Sophienclub No doorman hassles, just an easygoing dance club full of students, scenemakers, and heavy alternative types (who look much meaner than they are). It's located on a prettily restored block. ♦ Daily 9PM-4AM. Sophienstr 6 (between Rosenthaler Str and Hamburger Str). 2824551

64 Hackbarth's ★$$ This handsome cafe and bar fills an old bakery space on the Scheunenviertel's main art gallery block. An assortment of intellectual types, most of them ready to party rather than pose, bellies up to the huge rectangular bar for a variety of liquid refreshments. For sustenance, try the quiche. Or order breakfast until 2PM. ♦ Cafe ♦ Daily breakfast and snacks. No credit cards accepted. Auguststr 49a (at Joachimstr). No phone

65 Chamäleon Variete The continental version of vaudeville features acrobats, jugglers, magicians, slapstick, and nonsense of all forms. It's enjoying a renaissance in Berlin right now, and nowhere with more fun and gusto than here. This club, housed in a former art nouveau ballroom, is part of the **Hackescher Hof**, one of the largest commercial, residential, and cultural courtyard complexes in Europe. A knowledge of German is not required to enjoy the exuberant goings-on. ♦ Admission. Shows: W, Th, Su 8:30PM;

Berlin

F-Sa 8:30 PM, midnight. Rosenthaler Str 40-41 (between Oranienburger Str and Sophienstr). 2827118

FRANZ

66 Franz Club Blues, rock, jazz, and various sorts of world music peal out nightly at one of the oldest music venues in Prenzlauer Berg, a mixed working-class and bohemian neighborhood known for its alternative lifestyles. This club, on the former site of an 1880s brewery, also sports a decent cafe and pool table. ♦ Cover. F-Su. Box office daily from 9PM. Schönhauser Allee 36-39 (at Sredzkistr). 4485567

67 Husemannstrasse Short but showy, this 19th-century tenement block was niftily refurbished by the East German regime, just in time for Berlin's 750th birthday in 1987. The locals have since taken over, turning the street into a popular cafe and bar strip. ♦ Between Kollwitzplatz and Dimitroffstr

On Husemannstrasse:

Museum Berliner Arbeiterleben um 1900 (Museum of Berlin Working-Class Life Around 1900) The name allows for no misinterpretation: A re-created worker's apartment from the turn of the century, complete with daily household articles, is the museum's centerpiece. Temporary exhibits elaborate on working-class life in Berlin. ♦ Admission. Tu-Su. Husemannstr 12 (between Kollwitzplatz and Dimitroffstr). 4485675

The Original Times ★$$ The interior of this airy bistro-style restaurant jibes with the attractive 19th-century architecture of the outside street. The food is good, but pricey. ♦ Cafe ♦ Daily lunch and dinner. No credit cards accepted. Husemannstr 10 (between Kollwitzplatz and Dimitroffstr). No phone

Restauration 1900 ★★$$ One of east Berlin's trendiest restaurants, even in the days of the divide, this place serves traditional German dishes with some flair. But it gets demerits for being snobby and expensive. ♦ German ♦ Daily lunch and dinner. Husemannstr 1 (at Kollwitzplatz). 4422494

68 Krähe ★$$ Blessedly free from Prenzl'berg's rapidly spreading plastic furniture virus, this cafe (whose name means "the Crow") has deliberately retained its rundown charm, as well as its agreeable atmosphere and food. ♦ German/Continental ♦ Daily breakfast, lunch, and dinner. No credit cards accepted. Kollwitzstr 84 (between Wörther Str and Sredzkistr). 4428291

69 Jüdischer Friedhof in Weissensee (Jewish Cemetery in Weissensee) The largest Jewish cemetery in Europe, dating from 1880, is also considered to be the most beautiful. A peaceful melancholy suffuses the large, shaded park. Rambling avenues provide access to 115,000 gravestones and mausoleums, many of them grown over with wild ivy. Thoughts of the Holocaust haunt this ground, yet pre-war memories are even more vivid. Male visitors must wear a hat or borrow a yarmulke from the custodian. ♦ M-F, Su. Herbert-Baum-Str 45 (at Puccinistr). No phone

70 East Side Gallerie Since the **Berlin Wall** tumbled down in 1989 this three-quarter milelong stretch of concrete—the last significant stretch—has been painted, sprayed, and otherwise totally transfigured into what is considered the world's largest open-air gallery. ♦ Mühlenstr (from Oberbaumbrücke to Berlin Hauptbahnhof)

71 Sowjetisches Ehrenmal (Soviet War Memorial) Designed in formal Stalinist style, this gigantic monument in **Treptower Park** honors thousands of Soviet soldiers who fell during the 1945 Battle of Berlin. Twin avenues of carved bas-reliefs lead to a hill upon which a giant soldier strides atop a mausoleum, as he clutches a child in one arm and a huge sword in the other. Symbolically, the Soviets built all this with marble taken from Hitler's destroyed **Chancellery,** a building that had been designed by monumentalist architect **Albert Speer** in 1938 and once sat just south of the **Brandenburger Tor** (see page 53). ♦ Treptower Park (off Puschkinallee)

72 Künstlerhaus Bethanien (Bethanien Artists' House) This lovely 19th-century hospital in Kreuzberg was once abandoned and slated for demolition. But in 1974 it earned a second lease on life as a contemporary arts center, housing studios for international visiting artists, an exhibition space, and a library. ♦ Tu-Su noon-7PM. Mariannenplatz 2 (bounded by Mariannenstr and Adalbertstr, and Waldemarstr and Bethaniendamm). 25884152

73 Henne Alt-Berliner Wirtshaus ★★★$ Come prepared to wait up to two hours for a table if you haven't reserved one, and then a

Berlin

minimum of another 30 minutes after you place your order for what is indisputably Berlin's best crunchy-right-down-to-the-bones chicken. The *kraut salat* (cabbage slaw) is an ideal accompaniment. ♦ German ♦ W-Su dinner. Reservations recommended. Leuschnerdamm 25 (at Waldemarstr). 6147730

74 Zur kleinen Markthalle ★★$ Don't despair if you get shut out of **Henne** (see above). Its competitor, right across the way, serves the second-best chicken in town, plus other hands-on German delicacies such as *schweinehaxe* (gargantuan roast joints of pork). A shaded beer garden in front is ideal for warm-weather dining. ♦ German ♦ Tu-Sa dinner. No credit cards accepted.

Legiendamm 32 (between Dresdener Str and Waldemarstr). 6142356

75 Diyar ★★$$ The young crowd flocks here for well-prepared Turkish food in a contemporary atmosphere. The mixed appetizer plates are delicious and big enough for a meal. ♦ Turkish ♦ Daily lunch and dinner. Dresdener Str 9 (off Oranienstr). 6152708

76 Bierhimmel Here is a truly nice bar on a street that prides itself on downright nastiness. Up front are bronze-green stenciled walls, ornate gold-framed mirrors, and candlelit tables. The back room is a cocktail lounge right out of the 1950s, complete with padded doors. ♦ Daily 3PM-3AM. Oranienstr 183 (between Mariannenstr and Adalbertstr). 6153122

Your Student ID: Don't Leave Home Without It

Rich in intellect, curiosity, and spirit, but cash poor, students merit special status—according to the Europeans. But to reap all the potential benefits, such as discounts on museums, theater tickets, and local transportation, you must first be certified as a student. That's where the International Student Identity Card (ISIC) comes in. Sponsored by the International Student Travel Confederation, which consists of student travel organizations in 70 countries, the ISIC is the most widely accepted student identification card. At under $20, it's a good investment, too; your school ID won't get you nearly as far.

In addition to discounts (which are listed in a 64-page directory that comes with the card), card-holders are automatically entitled to basic sickness and accident insurance, including emergency medical travel and access to a 24-hour travelers' assistance hotline in English.

To be eligible for the card, you must be enrolled in a degree or diploma program at an accredited institution in the current year or in the previous fall term. The card is valid for 16 months—from 1 September of the year in which you apply, through 31 December of the following year.

Student ID cards can be obtained from the main office of the **Council on International Educational Exchange (CIEE)** at 205 East 42nd Street, New York, New York 10017, 212/661.1414; or at **CIEE**-affiliated **Council Travel,** which has 41 offices throughout the US. For information and an application, call or write **CIEE** for a free copy of the magazine *Student Travels,* or visit a **Council Travel** office, where you can also buy youth hostel cards, **Eurail passes**, and discounted airline tickets.

Even if you're not a student, you can apply for **CIEE**'s International Youth Card if you are 26 years or younger. The council also issues an International Teacher Identity Card. Both cards provide benefits similar to, though not as extensive as, those provided by the ISIC.

To apply for an ISIC, you'll need to complete an application and return it with a passport-size photo with your name printed on the back in pencil; a check or money order for the card, plus postage and handling; and proof of student status. The latter can include one of the following: a photocopy of your transcripts, a bursar's receipt, the school's seal stamped on the application, or a letter from the registrar or dean (on official stationery) stating that you are enrolled for the academic year and working toward a degree or diploma. For a youth card, a photocopy of the personal data page from your passport is needed, along with the passport-size photo. Teachers must submit a letter from the department chair, principal, or other school official on school letterhead, verifying that they are full-time faculty members.

Berlin

77 Cafe Bar Morena ★★$$ Before the Wall fell, Wienerstrasse was the center of the alternative club and bar action. This particular cafe still draws big crowds, because of its great breakfast menu (available until 5PM) and drinks, served in a spacious environment where you can almost hear yourself think—which is quite the trick for a Kreuzberg bar or cafe. ♦ German/Cafe ♦ Daily breakfast and snacks. No credit cards accepted. Wiener Str 60 (at Spreewaldplatz). 6114716

78 van Loon ★★★$$ An idyllic cafe in a most unusual setting: a Dutch houseboat built in 1914 and moored on Berlin's Landwehrkanal since 1988. Eat on the sundeck in good weather, or try the cozy cabin, which seats 35 (tightly). The small evening menu reflects the boat's Dutch origins, with dishes such as Matjes herring with pan-fried potatoes. ♦ Dutch/German ♦ Daily breakfast, afternoon cake and coffee, and dinner. Reservations recommended. Carl-Herz-Ufer 5 (at Krankenhaus am Urban). 6926293

79 Cafe Restaurant Milagro ★$$ A friendly atmosphere, an interesting menu that changes daily, and generous portions have made this one of the best places to chow down on Bergmannsstrasse, a Kreuzberg street lined with junk shops, boutiques, and other cafes. Almost unique in this cigarette-loving town, there's a room set aside for nonsmokers. ♦ German/Continental ♦ Daily breakfast, lunch, and dinner. No credit cards accepted. Bergmannstr (between Schenkendorfstr and Nostitzstr). 6922303

80 Checkpoint Residents of this neighborhood thrive on cast-offs and grunge, and this shop gives visitors an opportunity to do likewise. There are racks and racks of cotton dresses and flannel shirts, and a nearly limitless supply of leather jackets. It's hip, but still cheap. ♦ M-Sa. Mehringdamm 57 (between Bergmannstr and Gneisenaustr). 6944344

81 Hotel Transit $ This loft hotel for young people is contained in an old tobacco factory (without the pungent odors). Clean, simple, and tastefully furnished, it provides the added bonuses of washing machines, a complimentary breakfast buffet, an all-hours cafe, and a comfy TV corner. The 39 guest rooms have from one to six beds, individual showers, and—amazing!—both credit cards and traveler's checks are accepted. ♦ Hagelberger Str 53-54 (between Mehringdamm and Grossbeerenstr). 7855051; fax 7859619

82 Osteria No. 1 ★★$$ Things have been known to go awry in the kitchen, but when the cook's in top form (which seems to be most of the time, actually), the large, thin-crust pizzas and steaming plates of pasta *are* number one. Always lively, it attracts a trendy but not obnoxious crowd. ♦ Italian ♦ Daily lunch and dinner. Reservations recommended. No credit cards accepted. Kreuzbergstr 71 (at Grossbeerenstr). 7869162

83 Grossbeerenkeller ★★$$$ If you wonder what draws people into the dark alleyway behind the **Hebbel Theatre,** it's this traditional and much-loved *kneipe*. The prices at this cellar establishment, serving hearty German fare, have skyrocketed like everything else in Berlin, but a plate of Nurenberger bratwursts with perfectly browned pan-fried potatoes is still within the reach of everyone's pocketbook. ♦ German ♦ M-Sa dinner. Reservations recommended. Grossbeerenstr 90 (at Stresemannstr). 2513064

84 Café Adler ★$$ Journalists working in this publishing district, tourists visiting the nearby **Checkpoint Charlie Museum** (see below), and nostalgic Berliners all come here for the popular breakfast menu, which is available until 5PM, as well as the other entrées and salads. ♦ German ♦ Daily breakfast, lunch, and dinner. Friedrichstr 206 (at Zimmerstr). 2518965

85 Checkpoint Charlie Museum Readers of spy fiction will be disappointed to find that little remains of this famous Allied crossing point of the Cold War era. At least the museum is still here, a storehouse of memories that documents human experiences engendered by the **Berlin Wall** through films, photos, and homemade aircraft used by desperate escapees from East Germany. ♦ Admission. Daily until 10PM. Friedrichstr 44 (between Kochstr and Zimmerstr. 2511031

86 Bahnhof Anhalter (Anhalter Rail Station) Or what's left of it, anyway. The remaining fragment of this 1870 landmark is sadly moving: It was once considered, after the Gare de l'Est in Paris, to be the finest train

---

Restaurants/Clubs: Red   **Hotels:** Blue
Shops/ ♥ Outdoors: Green   **Sights/Culture:** Black

Berlin

terminal in Europe. ♦ Askanischer Platz (Anhalter Str, at Stresemannstr)

87 Martin Gropius Bau A stately rectangular building—designed in 1877 by **Martin Gropius**, one of **Karl Friedrich Schinkel**'s pupils and uncle to architect **Walter Gropius**—this was originally the city's ethnology museum. It now plays host to large-scale exhibitions of art and history, and also contains the **Jewish Department of the Berlin Museum**, which chronicles Jewish life in the city. The building's interior is stunning, highlighted by a beautiful glass cupola, mosaic floors, and majolica bas-reliefs. ♦ Admission. Tu-Su until 8PM. Stresemannstr 110 (between Anhalter Str and Niederkirchnerstr). 254860

Behind Martin Gropius Bau:

Topography of Terror More evil sprang from this corner of Berlin than anywhere else. This was the site of **Prince Albrecht Palace**, home to the Nazi Gestapo, before it—along with most of the surrounding Reich Security buildings—was bombed to rubble by Allied forces in World War II. The museum documents the history of the Third Reich security forces and their victims, with access to dug-out cellars where SS prisoners were tortured and often murdered. Most of the display information is in German, but an English synopsis is available at the desk. ♦ Free. Tu-Su. 25486703

88 Potsdamer Platz This was once the busiest square in all of Europe. Today, it's an expansive wasteland, awaiting renewal. Daimler-Benz and Sony have both snapped up parcels of surrounding land, and there's talk of turning the square into a grand piazza surrounded by office blocks, shopping facilities, and restaurants. So far, the most excitement is provided by daredevils who periodically bungee jump from a crane. ♦ Intersection of Leipziger Str, Potsdamer Str, and Bellevuestr

Bests

Ed Ward
Associate Editor, *Checkpoint*/Contributor, National Public Radio's *Fresh Air*

Walking the wide streets of the **Prenzlauer Berg** around **Kollwitzplatz** on a summer afternoon.

A night at **Pinguin** when everybody's in a good mood and there aren't too many gawkers hanging around.

A well-chosen night of blues or jazz at the **Franz Club**, one of the few places in town that makes it a point to present live music every night of the year.

A cold Berlin pilsner: Now that the Wall's down, we realize that Berlin *did* have good beer after all!

Finding one of the rare blocks where the bullet- and mortar-holes are still in the walls of the houses. The absolute silence just reinforces the fury of the conflict that happened 50 years ago on this spot.

Cobblestone streets and gaslights.

Raul Sterk
Freelance Journalist

Here are some of my favorite places which have the *esprit* that makes Berlin the most unique city in Germany.

Savignyplatz. Around this place you'll find bookstores, galleries, fashion shops, and nice cafes with international news magazines. In the **Savigny Passage** there is a small "art cafe" called **Aedes** that has a *savoir vivre* atmosphere and very handsome customers. Around the **Savignyplatz** are lots of small restaurants with decent prices. There are about eight Indian restaurants with very cheap menus.

Kreuzberg. This part of the city is connected with squatters and riots in the early 1980s. After the reunification of East and West Berlin it became the center of the city and business investors have certainly changed the structure of Kreuzberg. However, it is still a place where one is sure to find independent galleries, fringe theater, and strange bars. There are also many restaurants.

Rosenthalerplatz. This area, formerly East Berlin, is the most quickly developing part of Berlin. In only five years this historical, Jewish section of the city became the new spot for nightlife. There's a touristy section around the rebuilt synagogue on **Oranienburgerstrasse** and a lot to explore on the way to Rosenthalerplatz. Have a drink in **Hackbarth's** in Auguststrasse where former East and West Germans sit together as if reunification had happened years ago.

Martin Courtney
Distribution and Sales, *Checkpoint*

S-Bahn Trip: The older trains date from before the war, have wooden interiors, and shake pleasantly. Start at **Alexanderplatz** where you can witness the heart of old East Berlin before it is rebuilt. You won't necessarily fall in love with it, but it's history. Go up the tower. Eat at the revolving restaurant. Now take the **S-Bahn** to **Zoologischer Garten Station.** This trip takes you around the **Tiergarten** and ends up at the center of what used to be West Berlin. Next you cross the **Museum Insel,** an island with a colony of Greek-style buildings, including the **Pergamonmuseum** and other important museums. Next sight, to the left is the **Reichstag**, without dome, rear view. A golden winged figure is in view above the trees. It's "Golden Elsie," on her victory column. *Wings of Desire* fans will recognize her immediately. Among half a dozen towers and other landmarks you now see the inevitable Mercedes-Benz sign on a high-rise. To the right of it is the broken-tooth profile of the **Kaiser-Wilhelm-Gedächtniskirche** (Memorial Church), which marks the center of west Berlin. The **Zoo** is on your left and you've arrived.

61

Map of Florence

Major landmarks:
- Fortezza da Basso
- Stazione Centrale di S. Maria Novella
- Piazza della Stazione
- Piazza dell' Unità Italiane
- Piazza Santa Maria Novella
- Piazza San Lorenzo
- Piazza della Repubblica
- Piazza della Indipendenza
- Chiesa di Ognissanti
- Piazza di Ognissanti
- Ponte Amerigo Vespucci
- Ponte alla Carraia
- Ponte S. Trinita
- Ponte Vecchio
- Piazza del Carmine
- Piazza Santo Spirito
- Piazza de' Pitti
- Palazzo Pitti
- Giardino di Boboli
- Giardino Torrigiani
- Forte di Belvedere
- Fiume Arno

Streets (selected):
- V. Belfiore
- V. Cittadella
- V. d. Ghiacciaie
- V. Guido Monaco
- V. Filippo Strozzi
- V. Jacopo da Diacceto
- V. Luigi Alamanni
- Vle. Fratelli Rosselli
- V. d. Scala
- Vle. Filippo Strozzi
- V. Valfonda
- V. Bernardo Cennini
- V. d. Fiume
- V. d. Pratello
- V. d. Fortezza
- V. d. Barbano
- V. C. Ridolfi
- V. E. Poggi
- V. G. Dolfi
- V. S. Caterina d'Alessandria
- V. XXVII Aprile
- V. S. Zanobi
- V. S. Reparata
- V. Faenza
- V. Guelfa
- V. Nazionale
- V. Chiara
- V. Taddea
- V. Panicale
- V. d. Ariento
- Borgo La Noce
- V. d. Stufa
- V. d. Ginori
- V. S. Antonino
- V. Canto d. Nelli Gori
- B. S. Lorenzo
- V. d. Martelli
- V. Rucellai
- V. d. Orti Oricellari
- V. Palazzuolo
- V. d. Albero
- V. Panzani
- V. d. Conti V.F. Zannetti
- V. Giglio Alloro
- V. d. Cerretani
- V. Il Prato
- V. Palestro
- V. Curtatone
- Borgo Ognissanti
- V. Montebello
- V. d. Maso Finiguerra
- V. Meleg...
- V. Benedetta
- V. d. Avelli
- V. Rondinelli
- V. d. Pecori
- V. d. Tosighi
- V. d. Oc...
- V. Corso Italia
- V. Porcellana
- V. d. Porcellana
- V. d. Scala
- V. d. Belle Donne
- V. d. Corsi
- V. d. Pescioni
- V. d. Vecchietti
- Calimala
- V. d. Speziali Corso
- V. d. Calzaiuoli
- V. d. Fossi
- V. d. Moro
- V. d. Sole
- V. d. Spada
- V. d. Tornabuoni
- V. d. Strozzi
- V. Pellicceria
- V. d. Vigna Nuova
- V. d. Anselmi
- V. d. Parione
- Lung. Amerigo Vespucci
- Lung. Corsini
- V. Porta Rossa
- V. d. Cimatori
- Condotta
- Lung. Soderini
- V. L. S. Onofrio
- V. d. Piggione
- V. d. Terme
- Borgo SS. Apostoli
- V. P. S. Maria
- V. Calimaruzza
- V. d. Signa...
- Bartolini
- Borgo San Frediano
- Lung. Guicciardini
- Lung. Acciaioli
- P. d. Uffizi
- Lung. Archibusieri
- Lung. Torrigia...
- V. d. Orto
- Borgo Stella
- Lung. Santo Spirito
- V. Coverelli
- Lung. Torrigiani
- V. d. Bardi
- Costa di San Giorgio
- V. d. Magnoli
- Costa Scarpucc...
- V. Santa Monaca
- V. d. Leone
- V. d. Maffia
- Borgo San Jacopo
- V. d. Sprone
- Costa di San...
- V. d. Ardiglione
- V. Sant' Agostino
- V. d. Presto di S. Martino
- V. d. Velluti
- V. Toscanella
- V. d. Chiesa
- V. d. Serragli
- V. d. Caldaie
- Borgo Tegolato
- V. Mazzetta
- V. Maggio
- V. Guicciardini
- V. d. Campuccio
- V. Romana
- V. d. Cava

Scale: km 1/16 – 1/8 – 1/4 mi

N ↑

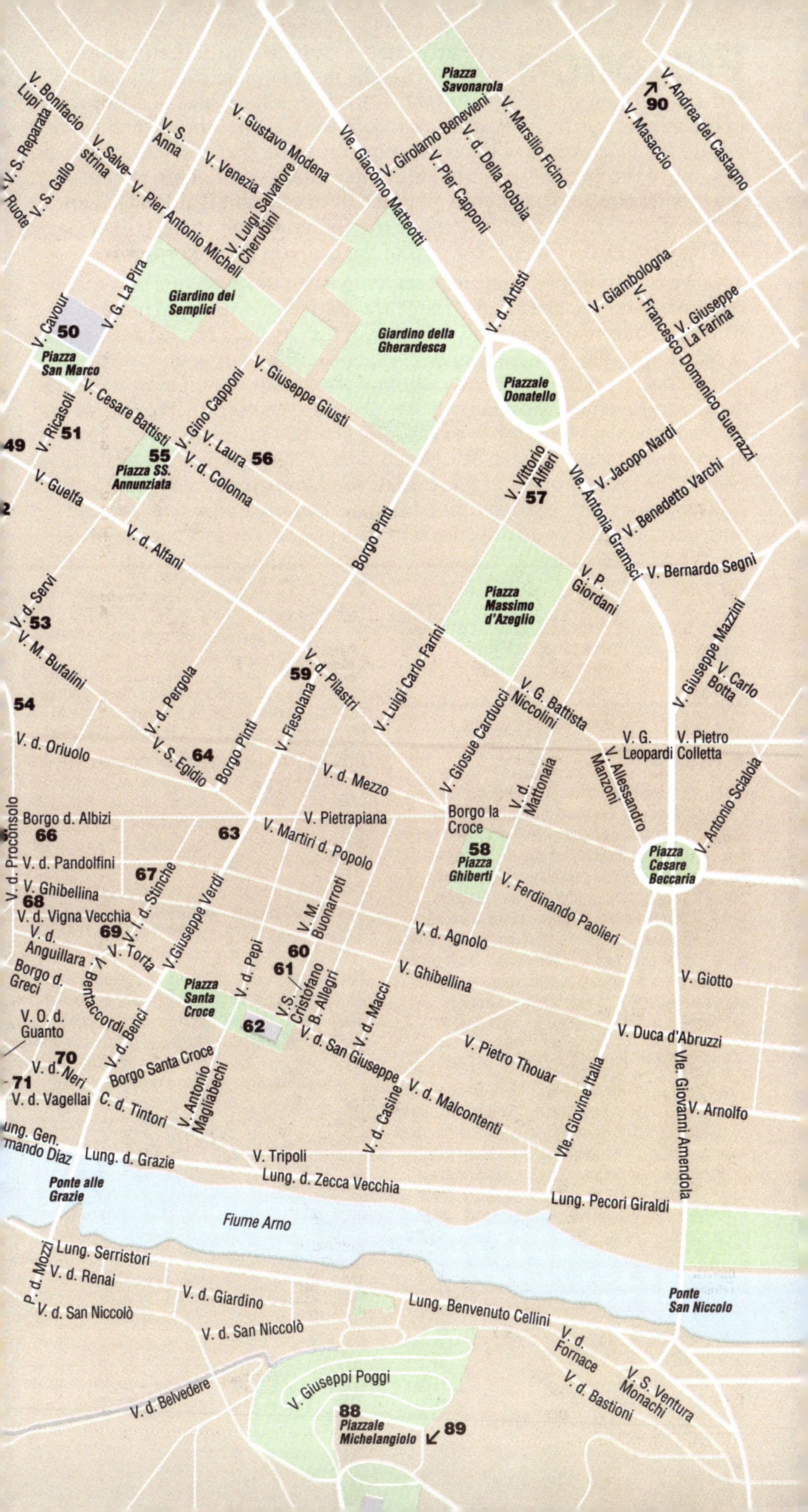
Piazza Savonarola
V. Andrea del Castagno
90
V. Masaccio
V. Marsilio Ficino
V. Girolamo Benevieni
V. d. Della Robbia
V. Pier Capponi
Vle. Giacomo Matteotti
V. Gustavo Modena
V. Bonifacio Lupi
V. S. Reparata
V. S. Gallo
Ruote
V. Salvestrina
V. S. Anna
V. Venezia
V. Luigi Salvatore Cherubini
V. Pier Antonio Micheli
V. d. Artisti
V. Giambologna
V. Francesco Domenico Guerrazzi
V. Giuseppe La Farina
V. G. La Pira
Giardino dei Semplici
Giardino della Gherardesca
Piazzale Donatello
V. Cavour
50
Piazza San Marco
V. Cesare Battisti
V. Giuseppe Giusti
V. Gino Capponi
V. Ricasoli
51
49
55
Piazza SS. Annunziata
V. Laura
56
V. d. Colonna
V. Vittorio Alfieri
57
V. Jacopo Nardi
V. Benedetto Varchi
Vle. Antonia Gramsci
V. Bernardo Segni
V. Guelfa
V. d. Alfani
Borgo Pinti
Piazza Massimo d'Azeglio
V. P. Giordani
V. d. Servi
53
V. M. Bufalini
V. Giuseppe Mazzini
V. Carlo Botta
54
V. d. Pergola
59
V. d. Pilastri
V. Luigi Carlo Farini
V. G. Battista Niccolini
V. Fiesolana
V. Giosue Carducci
V. G. Leopardi
V. Pietro Colletta
V. d. Oriuolo
V. S. Egidio
64
Borgo Pinti
V. d. Mezzo
V. d. Mattonaia
V. Allessandro Manzoni
V. Antonio Scialoia
V. d. Proconsolo
Borgo d. Albizi
66
63
V. Pietrapiana
Borgo la Croce
V. Martiri d. Popolo
58
Piazza Ghiberti
Piazza Cesare Beccaria
V. d. Pandolfini
67
V. I. d. Stinche
V. Ghibellina
68
V. d. Vigna Vecchia
69
V. Giuseppe Verdi
V. M. Buonarroti
V. Ferdinando Paolieri
V. d. Agnolo
V. d. Anguillara
V. Torta
V. Bentaccordi
60
V. d. Pepi
61
Borgo d. Greci
Piazza Santa Croce
V. S. Cristofano
B. Allegri
V. Ghibellina
V. Giotto
V. d. Macci
V. O. d. Guanto
V. d. Benci
62
V. d. San Giuseppe
V. Duca d'Abruzzi
V. Pietro Thouar
70
V. d. Neri
71
Borgo Santa Croce
V. Antonio Magliabechi
V. d. Malcontenti
Vle. Giovanni Amendola
V. Arnolfo
V. d. Vagellai
C. d. Tintori
V. d. Casine
Vle. Giovine Italia
Lung. Gen. ...mando Diaz
Lung. d. Grazie
V. Tripoli
Lung. d. Zecca Vecchia
Lung. Pecori Giraldi
Ponte alle Grazie
Fiume Arno
P. d. Mozzi
Lung. Serristori
V. d. Renai
V. d. Giardino
V. d. San Niccolò
Lung. Benvenuto Cellini
Ponte San Niccolo
V. d. San Niccolò
V. d. Fornace
V. S. Ventura Monachi
V. d. Bastioni
V. d. Belvedere
V. Giuseppi Poggi
88
Piazzale Michelangiolo
89

Florence

Of all of Italy's glorious tourist destinations, Florence is the most popular stop. The birthplace of the Renaissance, the city's primary attraction is its wealth of artistic and architectural treasures from that period. In the **Centro Storico** (Old City), behind the harsh stone of the city's numerous churches and patrician palazzi lie some of the greatest works of art in the western world. This, after all, is the city of Michelangelo, Leonardo da Vinci, Botticelli, and Ghirlandaio, and their works are here in profusion—in the **Galleria degli Uffizi** (Uffizi Gallery) and **Palazzo Pitti** (Pitti Palace), and in the **Galleria dell'Accademia**.

Florence can't hide her sophistication, even when her guests are on a budget. The university, situated around the **Piazza San Marco** area, and more than 30 foreign-university programs throughout the city have created a large student population, so Florence has plenty of experience in catering to those on tight budgets. Comfortable and charming *pensioni* are within most travelers' means, and even the most inexpensive places to eat—wine bars (*enoteche* and *fiaschetterie*), neighborhood bar/cafes, and *pizzerie*—maintain a traditional pride in ambience and good food. The Florentines' infallible sense of style is evident even in the touristy open-air **Mercato di San Lorenzo** where, bypassing the Taiwan-made dross, the determined shopper can still find accessories and souvenirs of excellent quality, made in Italy and for sale at moderate prices.

To call from the US, dial 011 (international access code), 39 (country code), 55 (city code), and the local number. When calling from inside Italy, dial 055 and the local number. City codes appearing within the text are for areas outside of Florence.

Getting to Florence

Airports

Just 5 kilometers (2.5 miles) from downtown Florence, **Amerigo Vespucci Airport** (373498) handles flights to and from other European cities. Bus service operates daily, at about 30-minute intervals, and deposits passengers at the **Santa Maria Novella** station in the center of Florence. But it's **Galileo Galilei Airport**, in Pisa, a distant 85 kilometers (53 miles) from Florence, that services most transatlantic flights. There is daily train service (the ride takes about an hour) to Florence's **Santa Maria Novella**. Both airports have currency-exchange kiosks and visitor-information desks.

Train Station (Long-Distance)

Rail travel has improved in recent years, and second class is no longer a drudgery, but theft is a hazard on overnight trips. The *EuroCity (EC)* is an international train; its domestic equivalent, the *InterCity (IC)*, operates between major cities; the *diritto* stops at most stations; and the *locale* makes all the stops. Florence's train station is the **Santa Maria Novella** (Piazza della Stazione; 288785), right smack in the center of town.

Getting around Florence

Bicycles and Mopeds To rent a bicycle or moped contact **Alinari** (Via Guelfa 85r, at Via Nazionale, 280500); **Motorent** (Via San Zanobi 9r, at Via Guelfa, 490113); or **Vesparent** (Via Pisana 103r, between Via Chiesino and Via Monticelli, 715691).

Buses The orange city buses, called ATAF, run frequently and efficiently. Tickets, good for an hour, are available at most newsstands, tobacconists, and bars/cafes. A special seven-day Carta Arancio permits unlimited travel on all city buses, as well as other buses and trains throughout the province of Florence. This pass can be purchased at the **ATAF** office (open daily) in the **Piazza della Stazione**.

Driving The pedestrian area of the Centro Storico grows every year. If you arrive by car, leave it in a garage and spend your stay in Florence getting around on foot or by taxi. Taxis and buses are allowed to make their way through the pedestrian zones; private vehicles are not.

Taxis There are plenty of taxis waiting at the major piazzas around town; they may also be called by dialing 4390, 4798, and 4242. Ask about additional charges for evening, Sunday, and holiday service, and for luggage.

Tours Unlike larger cities such as Rome or Milan, Florence is rather small and quite self-contained. Much of the Centro Storico is closed to noncommercial traffic (although taxis and limited bus service are allowed) and with the help of a city map, most principal sites of interest are within walking distance. Half- and full-day tours of the city and nearby Tuscan towns are arranged through **American Express** (see "Money" below) and **SITA** (15r Via Santa Caterina da Siena, across from the main train station, 483651). Private guides are expensive, but a luxurious way to splurge for history or art buffs; the **Informazione Turistica** booths (see "Visitors' Information," below) have lists of qualified guides.

Walking Florence is a large city, but most of the sight-seeing is in or near the Centro Storico, which is easily navigable on foot. In fact, much of it is a *zona blu* (pedestrian zone).

D.H. Lawrence described Renaissance Florence as "the perfect center of man's universe."

FYI

Accommodations The best bet for budget travelers are the small, family-run hotels (formerly called *pensioni*). These offer clean and safe accommodations, often with shared bathrooms and rarely with breakfast included in the price. Travelers who arrive without reservations should inquire at the **Informazione Turistica** (see "Visitors' Information," below).

Addresses Residences are distinguished by black numerals on the buildings; commercial addresses are posted in red numerals followed by the letter "r." The two sequences of numbers don't always correspond; for example, don't be surprised if a bar at No. 55r is located next to a residential building at No. 4.

Business Hours The lengthy midday break is a fact of life in Italy. Banks are open Monday through Friday from about 8:30AM to 1:30PM, and reopen for an hour or so (usually 3:30 to 4:30PM) in the afternoon. In winter, stores and businesses are generally open Monday from 3:30 until 7:30PM; and on Tuesday through Saturday from 9AM to 1PM, and again from 3:30 to 7:30PM. In summer, stores and businesses are open Monday through Friday from 9AM until 7:30PM (with a midday break from 1 to 3:30PM), and on Saturday from 9AM until 1PM. Certain tourist-oriented stores in the Centro Storico eschew the midday break in high season, and some are even open on Sunday. Food markets keep roughly the same hours, but are closed on Wednesday afternoons. Most churches are open for viewing Monday through Friday and on Saturday mornings; Sunday visits are discouraged. Most museums are open Tuesday through Saturday and on Sunday mornings.

Climate Located in a valley on the banks of the **Arno River**, Florence is hot and humid in the summertime; in July and August it can reach 95 degrees. Late October and November can be rainy, and winters are cold and damp. The most ideal weather is likely to be encountered in May and June or September and October.

Consulates and Embassies

UK ....Lungarno Corsini 2, between Ponte S
            ....Trinita and Ponte alla Carraia, 284133

The nearest American and Canadian embassies are in Rome.

Discount Tickets Members of **CTS (Centro Turistico Studentesco e Giovanile)** are entitled to discounts for domestic and international travel; their Florence office is located at Via dei Ginori 25r, between Piazza San Lorenzo and Via del Canto dei Nelli; 289721. For **STS Youth & Student Travel** (Via Zannetti 18r, between Via dei Cerretani and Piazza Madonna d'Aldobrandini, at the corner of Via dei Conti; 284183 or 287252), you need be neither young nor a student to qualify for discounts on domestic and international travel. **Baiana** (Via Piazzetta Calamandrei 2, between Via delle Seggiole and Borgo degli Albizi; 264040) offers somewhat lesser discounts on national and international air and train travel, as well as discounts on car rentals, tickets for cultural events, and some hotels. There's a nominal annual fee; no age restrictions.

Hitchhiking is unsafe and discouraged; a good alternative is **Autostop** (Borgo dei Greci 40r, at Piazza San Firenze, 280626), which hooks up drivers and would-be passengers to share costs on long-distance rides.

Drinking There is no such thing as a legal drinking age in Italy. A glass of wine is part of most meals, and there are many wine bars and cafes, but drinking is part of a larger social life and overdrinking is rarely a problem.

Emergencies For medical emergencies call the **Tourist Medical Service** (475411). It's open 24 hours a day and has English-speaking operators to handle incoming calls. In the event of legal problems, contact your country's embassy or consulate.

Laundry Self-service laundromats have only recently entered the Italian lexicon, and so far there's only one: **Wash & Dry** (Via dei Servi 105r; no phone), but it's open daily from 8AM until 10PM and has 20 machines. Traditional service laundries charge by weight, charge extra for ironing, and are open during general business hours. Try **Florentia** (Via Palmieri 5r, between Via dei Pandolfini and Borgo degli Albizi, 2345215) or **Lavanderia** (Via degli Alfani 44r, between Via della Pergola and Via dei Servi, 2479313).

Money The monetary unit of Italy is the *lira;* the plural is *lire,* and it's abbreviated as either "L." or "Lit." Currency exchange facilities at airports and train stations charge high commissions, so try one of the two **American Express** offices (Via Dante Alighieri 22r, at Via Cimatori, 50981; and Via Guicciardini 49r, near Piazza dei Pitti, 288751) or **Universalturismo** (Via degli Speziali 7, off Piazza della Repubblica, 217241). All offices listed are open during general business hours.

Personal Safety Pickpockets operate on crowded buses. Gypsies (often young children) harass natives and visitors alike, usually at busy sites. Keep track of your possessions at any of the open-air markets where crowds and bustle are an integral part of the scene.

Postal Services The main post office, **Poste e Telecommunicazioni (PTT)**, is located at Via Pellicceria 3 (off Piazza della Repubblica). It's open Monday through Friday and on Saturday mornings.

Publications *Firenze Avvenimenti* and *Un Ospite a Firenze (A Guest in Florence),* two Italian-language publications, and *Florence Today* (English language) contain events listings. All can be picked up at tourist offices (see "Visitors' Information," below).

Public Holidays New Year's Day, Epiphany (6 January), Easter Monday, Liberation Day (25 April), Labor Day (1 May), St. John's Day (24 June), Feast of the Assumption (15 August), All Saints' Day (1 November), Immaculate Conception (8 December), Christmas, and St. Stephen's Day (26 December).

Public Rest Rooms There are few public bathrooms in Florence. Try the train station or the **Palazzo Vecchio** in **Piazza della Signoria.** Otherwise, the price of a drink in a cafe will entitle you to ask for the *toletta,* although the hygiene is often poor.

Florence

Restaurants Most restaurants close one or two days a week (the day varies for each establishment), usually a week or so in August (often the entire month), and between Christmas and New Year's Eve. Lunch is served from 12:30 to 2PM. Peak dinner time is 8:30PM; kitchens close around 10:30PM. For the most part, small and inexpensive restaurants don't require reservations.

Shopping Florence has some of the most wonderful—and most expensive—shopping in Europe. Bargain shoppers may have to eschew the gold shops that line the **Ponte Vecchio**, but good buys on leather, woolen goods, and table linens can be found at the **Mercato di San Lorenzo** and the **Mercato Nuovo**.

Smoking It's common everywhere. If you prefer to be away from it, specify *nonfumatore* when making restaurant or train reservations.

Street Plan Florence is divided by the Arno River. Most of the major tourist sites are on the right bank, or north side, of the Arno. From west to east the neighborhoods on the right bank are **Santa Maria Novella, San Lorenzo, Centro Storico,** and **Santa Croce.** The left bank, called **Oltrarno** (meaning "beyond the Arno"), is home to the **Palazzo Pitti** and the **Giardino di Boboli,** but is somewhat less touristy.

Taxes The quoted price for hotel and restaurants tabs already includes a 10- to 15-percent service charge. See "Tipping," below.

Telephones Calls from a hotel room are subject to a hefty surcharge and may cost twice as much as on the outside. Use a public phone booth—operated either with coins or a *scheda* (a pre-paid calling card; available at newsstands). The cheapest way of phoning the US is to call collect and have someone call you back.

Tipping A service charge is usually included in hotel and restaurant bills (look for *servizio incluso* or *servizio compreso*). Diners often add a small, token gratuity on top of that if the service is outstanding. Taxi drivers expect a 15-percent tip.

Visas A valid passport is required for stays of up to 90 days.

Visitors' Information Every visitor's first stop should be at one of the **Informazione Turistica** booths at **Piazza della Stazione** (212245) or **Chiasso Baroncelli** 17/19r, off the **Piazza della Signoria** (2302124). They're open Monday through Saturday from 9AM until 1:30PM.

1 Duomo and Campanile (Cathedral and Bell Tower) Begun in 1296, one of the largest cathedrals in the world can be identified from afar by its red-tiled octagonal cupola (pictured below), a veritable signpost of the Renaissance designed by **Filippo Brunelleschi** in 1436. The Italian tricolor is reflected in the different types of Tuscan marble used in the cathedral's construction—red from the Maremma, white from Carrara, and green from Prato. With an interior that is remarkably spartan, the cathedral stands as a metaphor for the Florentine character—showy on the outside, austere on the inside. A staircase leads down to the **Crypt of Santa Reparata** and vestiges of the cathedral's fifth-century foundation. The campanile, built of the same three marbles, was begun by **Giotto** in 1334; the view from the top, reached by 414 steps, is astounding. ♦ Duomo: free. Campanile, crypt, cupola: admission. M-Sa. Piazza del Duomo

1 Battistero di San Giovanni (Baptistry of St. John) This structure (pictured on page 67), begun in the fifth century, is dedicated to Florence's patron saint and is best known for the gilded bronze doors on three of its eight

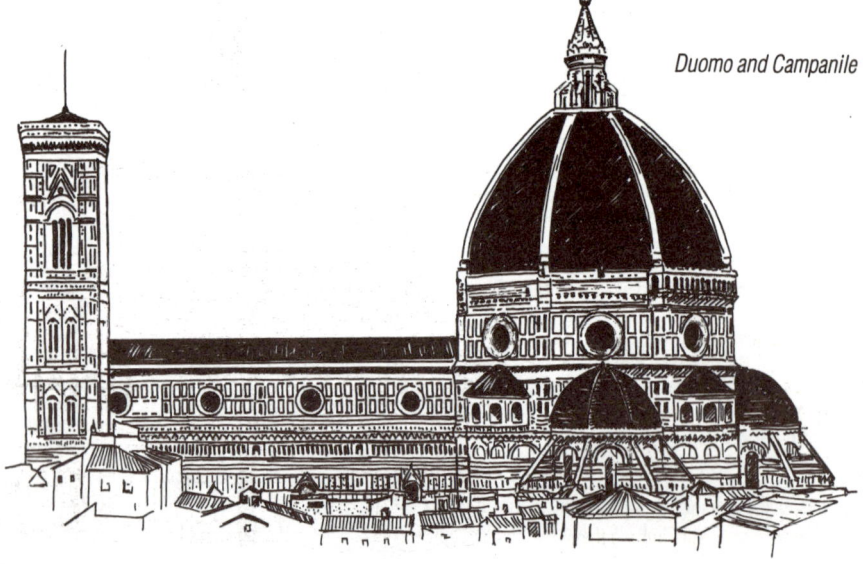

Duomo and Campanile

sides. The original doors, gradually being restored for permanent display in the **Museo dell'Opera del Duomo** (Duomo Museum; see page 75), are replaced here by reproductions. The east and the north portals were designed by **Lorenzo Ghiberti** in the 15th century.
♦ Admission. M-Sa; Su mornings. Piazza del Duomo

2 Aldini $$ It's relatively undiscovered, despite its prime location steps away from the **Duomo,** but this hotel's 15 guest rooms are quickly snapped up by travelers in the know. There's no restaurant, but the private baths, in-room color TVs, air-conditioning, and tasteful decor make this a great bargain, especially on this street. Don't be put off by the slightly shabby entrance. ♦ Via Calzaiuoli 13 (at Piazza del Duomo). 214752; fax 216410

3 Fiaschetteria Torrini ★$ This hole-in-the-wall wine bar is the last of a dying breed and an ideal place for a quick pick-me-up of Chianti and chicken-liver *crostini* (toasts). ♦ Wine bar ♦ M-Sa breakfast and snacks; closed in August. No credit cards accepted. Piazza dell'Olio 15r (off Via dei Cerretani). 2396616

Hotel Pensione Pendini

4 Pendini $$ This 42-room hotel has been in operation for more than 100 years. Currently undergoing refurbishment, it continues to offer Old-World charm and unrivaled value, with its simple but spacious rooms and its ultracentral location on the **Piazza della Repubblica.** On summer nights, the piazza's six outdoor cafes beckon young Florentines, which can make piazza-side rooms too noisy for some. Adults traveling with young children will appreciate guest rooms large enough to accommodate a cot. There is no restaurant.
♦ Via degli Strozzi 2 (on Piazza della Repubblica). 211170; fax 210156

5 Piazza della Repubblica Site of an ancient forum, this later became the **Mercato Vecchio** (Old Market), which bordered the north end of Florence's Jewish ghetto. Florentines still bemoan the 1887 demolition of one of the city's most picturesque piazzas, despite the plaque on the grand arch proclaiming that the restoration eradicated the squalor in the ancient center of the city. Flower shows on Thursdays hark back to the square's commercial roots, but it is better known for the elegant historical cafes that encircle it, most of which move outdoors with the first warm weather. ♦ Between Piazza Davanzati and Piazza del Duomo

5 UPIM Middle-priced merchandise fills this branch of the Italian department store chain. The clothing is unexceptional, with the occasional find; you're more likely to score upstairs among the wide selection of well-designed housewares.
♦ M-Sa. Piazza della Repubblica 1r. 216924

6 Alessi Paride If you're looking for gifts of food or wine, this is one-stop shopping at its best. The ground floor caters to the sweet tooth with seasonal confections, such as the *colomba,* a dove-shaped Easter cake. Downstairs is the real draw, however: It's the best retail wine cellar in town, with a special emphasis on Tuscan varietals. ♦ M-Sa; closed in August. Via delle Oche 27r (off Via Calzaiuoli). 214966

7 COIN The largest Italian department store in Florence provides a change of pace (some deem it welcome, others not) from the local tradition of specialty shops. While not on a par with Bloomingdale's or Harrods, it is a cut above the lower-end **Standa** and **UPIM.**
♦ M-Sa. Via dei Calzaiuoli 56r (near Via del Corso). 280531

8 Albergo Firenze $ Of the small, cheap hotels in the Centro Storico, this is one of the most popular. Not far off the main drag that connects the **Duomo** and the **Piazza della Signoria,** half of its 60 rooms have private baths, many of them recently renovated. The hotel has lately taken to renting rooms on a long-term basis to American students, so book well in advance. There is no restaurant. No credit cards accepted. ♦ Piazza Donati 4 (on Via del Corso). 214203; fax 212370

9 Cantinetta dei Verrazzano ★★$$ A new and notable kid on a heavily trafficked block—it's located midway between the **Duomo** and **Piazza della Signoria**—this handsome spot is always crowded. The wine bar/bread shop (a winning combination) offers simple fare

Battistero di San Giovanni

67

Florence

such as focaccia fresh from a wood-burning oven and an extensive selection of wines by the glass. Owned by an important Chianti wine-producer, most of the *cantinetta*'s specialties come from their estate. ♦ Italian ♦ M-Sa 8AM-8PM. Via dei Tavolini 18/20r (off Via dei Calzaiuoli). 268590

9 Perché No! . . . And why not, indeed, have a morning or midnight ice cream in one of Florence's oldest *gelaterie?* Myriad flavors of creamy gelati and *semi-freddi* (soft ice cream) include *zuppa inglese* (trifle) and *riso* (rice). There are a few stools, but the best bet is to eat it as you stroll through **Piazza della Signoria.** ♦ Daily 11AM-midnight. No credit cards accepted. Via dei Tavolini 19r (off Via dei Calzaiuoli). 2398969

10 I Mascherari The Venetian art of mask-making has its Florentine counterpart in this shop. The masks are all handmade on the premises, and go well beyond the traditional commedia dell'arte characters. There are some imaginative designs derived from the Florentine Renaissance. ♦ M-Sa; closed two weeks in mid-August. Via dei Tavolini 13r (off Via dei Calzaiuoli). 213823

10 Vini del Chianti ★$ A beloved watering hole, this wine bar is run by two brothers whose Chiantis come with a wide selection of cheeses, salami, and various delectable pâtés. It's off the Via de Calzaiuoli on a narrow cobblestoned street lined with shops, bakeries, and produce vendors. ♦ M-Sa breakfast and snacks; closed two weeks in mid-August. No credit cards accepted. Via dei Cimatori 38r (off Via dei Calzaiuoli). 2396096

11 Cravatte & Dintorni This is heaven if you're looking for a fashionable memento for yourself or lightweight gifts to bring home. The emphasis is on ties, but there are also scarves, belts, and umbrellas from such trendsetters as Moschino, Byblos, and Dolce & Gabbana. ♦ M-Sa. Via della Condotta 22r (off Via del Proconsolo). 2396978

Italy has Giorgio Vasari to thank for naming the Renaissance. He first used the word *rinascita* (rebirth) in 1550 to describe local goings-on, but the term had no real context until used by Swiss historian Jacob Burchardt in his classic *Civilization of the Renaissance in Italy* (1860).

Florence's moneylenders were Europe's first financiers. They invented the international letter of credit and established the first stable international currency, the 13th-century florin, which was stamped with the Florentine lily.

Restaurants/Clubs: Red   **Hotels:** Blue
Shops/ ♟ Outdoors: Green   **Sights/Culture:** Black

68

12 Orsanmichele Originally a covered market with a wheat granary upstairs, this odd Renaissance Gothic church was rebuilt in the 14th century. The archways were walled up and used as an oratory for the craftsmen and guilds of Florence. Statues of their patron saints people the niches of the church's facade. The interior houses an elaborate 14th-century tabernacle by Andrea Orcagna and a beautiful Madonna by Bernardo Daddi. ♦ Via dell'Arte della Lana (between Via dei Cimatori and Via dei Tavolini). No phone

13 Mercato Nuovo This "new" covered market was a 16th-century annex to the old one in what is now **Piazza della Repubblica.** It s till functions in the same manner, filled with stalls selling local crafts from leather bags to embroidered tablecloths. Florentines call the market the **Porcellino** (piglet) after their nickname for Pietro Tacca's bronze *Wild Boar* statue at its south end. Tradition dictates that visitors rub the beast's nose to ensure a return to Florence. ♦ M-Sa; no midday closing. Piazza del Mercato Nuovo (at Via Calimala)

14 Piazza della Signoria This piazza has been the center stage for centuries of civic and social life in Florence. A veritable open-air museum, the square and the **Loggia dei Lanzi** (see page 69) on its south side are filled with monumental sculptures; the piazza is unarguably dominated by a replica of Michelangelo's *David.* The original *David* is in the **Galleria dell'Accademia** (Accademia Museum; see below). On the east side of the piazza is the **Palazzo Vecchio** with Amannati's *Neptune* fountain. Unloved by early Florentines and known today as **Il Biancone,** which means "The Great White One," the fountain stands in front of a marble plaque that marks the spot where the fanatic Savonarola was burned to death in 1498. There are also copies of Donatello's *Judith and Holofernes* and his *Marzocco,* the heraldic lion of Florence. If you're inclined to splurge, go to **Cafe Rivoire** (214412) on the west side of the piazza for an alfresco iced tea or, in colder weather, go inside for its famous hot chocolate. The less expensive **Bar Perseo** (2398316) on the piazza's north side offers the same remarkable view at only slightly lower prices. ♦ Between Via Por Santa Maria and Piazza San Firenze

14 Palazzo Vecchio This severe Gothic palazzo and towering campanile (pictured on page 69), where you can enjoy a guard's-eye view of the piazza, was begun in 1299 to house and protect the Signoria, the ministry of the republican government. In 1540, Cosimo I and Eleanor of Toledo set up house here before moving across the river to the **Palazzo Pitti** (see page 80) in 1549, when this place became known as the **Palazzo Vecchio,** meaning "Old Palace." Today, it serves as City Hall. Go through the courtyard past

Florence

Verrochio's bronze *Putto* (the original is upstairs) on your way to the first floor's **Salone del Cinquecento,** a giant room frescoed with Florentine battle scenes and lined with statues, including Michelangelo's *Genius of Victory.* Go to the second floor to visit Eleanor's private apartments. ♦ Admission. M-W; F-Sa; Su morning. Piazza della Signoria. 27681

14 Loggia dei Lanzi On the south side of the **Piazza della Signoria** stands this 14th-century loggia, an arcaded space designed for public ceremonies and last used to receive Queen Elizabeth II. Of interest are a copy of Cellini's *Perseus* and Giambologna's *Rape of the Sabine Women* and *Hercules Slaying the Centaur.* An interminable restoration has kept the loggia encaged in scaffolding for years. ♦ Piazza della Signoria

14 Erboristeria Palazzo Vecchio This *erboristeria* (medicinal herb shop) has one of the widest selections of any in the city. It stocks organic hair-restoring shampoos, conditioners, and more—all good for what ails you. Prettily packaged, the aromatic essences, soaps, candles, tonics, and Tuscan herbs make wonderful gifts. ♦ M-Sa. Via Vacchereccia 9r (off Piazza della Signoria). 2396055

Palazzo Vecchio

15 Galleria degli Uffizi (Uffizi Gallery) In 1560, the Grand Duke Cosimo commissioned **Giorgio Vasari** to build an *ufficio* (office-like structure) befitting the Medici administration; when it was finally completed, the top floor was turned into an art museum with artists' and artisans' studios. Today the most important single museum in Italy, and one of the finest in the world, it came horribly close to total destruction by a terrorist bomb in June 1993. Damage was miraculously limited and none of the Renaissance masterworks was seriously damaged, thanks in part to the protective glass plates shielding most of them. Walking along the top floor's two long galleries, don't overlook the wealth of decorative ceiling frescoes, tapestries, and antique sculptures that offset a collection of paintings bound to make your head swim. Little here is *not* of importance, but don't miss **Rooms X-XIV,** which include a number of works by Botticelli; two masterpieces by Leonardo da Vinci in **Room XV;** and Michelangelo's only painting in Florence, the *Doni Tondi,* in **Room XXV.** ♦ Admission. Tu-Sa; Su mornings. Piazza della Signoria. 23885

16 C.O.I. (Commercio Oreficerie Italiane) There's nothing coy about this gold market boasting the largest selection of wares at the most competitive prices in town. ♦ M-Sa. Via Por Santa Maria 8r (near Piazza della Signoria), Second floor. 283970

17 Gelateria delle Carrozze Silvia, the Italian-Canadian proprietress, claims she knows American tastes, and so far no one has disagreed; she also understands the universal craving for late-night gelato and stays open past midnight. Try a scoop of the natural fruit flavors or the airy *semifreddi.* Seats are available for resting weary feet. ♦ M-Tu; Th-Su; closed three weeks in August. No credit cards accepted. Piazza del Pesce 3-5r (at the Ponte Vecchio). 2396810

17 Archibusieri $$ Sharing the same spectacular location and rooftop breakfast terrace with the more expensive **Hermitage** (see below), this hotel has recently undergone a thorough face-lift. There are seven small, simple rooms, all with private shower, and nice terra-cotta floors. There is no restaurant. ♦ Vicolo Marzio 1 (on Piazza del Pesce). 282480; fax 212208

Above the Archibusieri:

Hermitage $$ Perched in the top three floors of a medieval tower two steps from the **Ponte Vecchio,** its spectacular views of the bridge and the Arno River from its roof garden are all reason enough to stay here. The 22 guest roooms are of average size and tastefully decorated, with private, modernized bathrooms; units in the back are quieter. There is no restaurant. ♦ 287216; fax 212208

69

Florence

Packin' It

The all-too-common approach to packing is to gather everything you think you'll need, then find the one bag large enough to cram it all in. That works if the farthest you have to journey is to the airport and then to a hotel, with a bellhop or two on the horizon. But the reality of traveling in Europe on a shoestring is a lot of do-it-yourself schlepping. Mobility is essential—you'll have narrow train corridors and cobblestone streets to negotiate—so aim for a load that won't weigh you down. Choose a durable, lightweight bag that meets airline carry-on specifications, add a combination lock, and make sure it's clearly tagged with your name, address, and a contact phone number.

As you pack, think like a survivalist: "Do I *really* need this?" The word "no" should echo through your closets. You only need half of what you think you need. Aside from sparing your aching shoulders, a lighter load means less time spent packing and unpacking, and more time to people watch at sidewalk cafes. As a reward for your amazing self-restraint, imagine how good you'll feel breezing by baggage claim with your one carry-on.

Hard as it may be to believe, you really don't need to bring more for a two-month trip than for a two-week one. The list remains the same: a few changes of clothes (plan on a couple of laundry nights in your itinerary), basic toiletries (transfer shampoo and lotions to small, plastic bottles, and leave your hair dryer at home), prescription medicines properly labeled (to avoid potential hassles at customs), and a small first-aid kit.

Mix and match: A few well-chosen pieces of clothing will take you just about anywhere. Add a blazer or light jacket over the T-shirt and jeans you wore during a day trip touring the tulip-dotted Dutch countryside, and you're dressed for dinner in Amsterdam that night; eliminate the jacket and you're ready for an evening in the "brown cafes." Europeans tend to dress casually in the summer, so leave your dressy outfits at home and improvise. Keep in mind that some places, churches in particular, do have spoken and unspoken dress codes when it comes to shorts, tank tops, and the general baring of skin, so plan on something discreet for those visits. And don't bother trying to pack for every change in the weather—you can always buy an umbrella or sweater if necessary. If you can't imagine going a day without your jeans, be warned: They're heavy and slow to dry. Cotton is much more adaptable. As for shoes, go with your sturdy, broken-in favorites—nothing can ruin an otherwise perfect outing like blistered feet. Thongs are welcome accessories in the grungy shower stalls that budget travelers sometimes encounter. Above all, pack with your itinerary, or lack of one, in mind. Think about whether your trip will be heavy on walking, or more geared to lounging on the Lido. Of course, learning about your destination's climate will make packing easier.

A few incidentals such as a Swiss Army knife, a sewing kit, and a small but durable flashlight can prove to be godsends, as can a travel alarm clock (or a wristwatch with a built-in alarm). A knife-fork-spoon set is great for alfresco dining à la grocery store. On the B-list are items like electric converters and adapters; extra prescription medicines or glasses; paper and pens; and guidebooks, phrasebooks, and other reading material. (Warning: Books get heavier as your trip gets longer.) Hostelers need to bring along a bedsheet and a lightweight towel and washcloth. Extras to consider include toilet paper, plastic bags for opened food and wet clothing, and a clothesline and clothespins.

If you'll be toting a lot of film (especially high-speed), it may be worth buying a protective lead-lined bag from a photo shop. While it's true that most airport X-ray machines will not fog lower-speed film, X-rays have a cumulative effect and several trips through the scanning machine can damage film. Otherwise keep the rolls of film in their opaque canisters, and store them in a zip-lock plastic bag that you can hand over to inspectors.

And don't worry too much if you forget something (unless it's your passport); you'll need the extra room for the special souvenirs you'll want to take home.

ART BY ROLANDO CORUJO

70

Florence

18 La Torre Guelfa $$ Housed in a historic 14th-century palazzo on a cobblestone street in the heart of the Centro Storico, this newly renovated hotel has a devoted following. Guests relax in the lobby, discussing where they ate dinner the night before (there's no restaurant in the hotel, but apparently no one minds). The 14 guest rooms are comfortable and have clean, modern, private baths. The *mansarda* (top floor of a palazzo) has its own terrace and a view that rivals the best of them. ♦ Closed in August. Borgo SS Apostoli 8 (off Via Por Santa Maria). 2396338; fax 2398577

19 Museo dell'Antica Casa Fiorentina (Davanzati Museum) A handsome 14th-century palazzo houses displays of everyday objects used in Florence from the Gothic to the Renaissance periods. Numerous Madonnas, textiles, tapestries, chests, and other furniture evoke the domestic life of the palazzo's owners, the Davanzati family, members of Florence's wealthy merchant class. ♦ Admission. Tu-Sa; Su mornings. Piazza Davanzati (on Via Porta Rossa). 2388608

20 Alimentari Orizi ★$ A grocery store/snack bar is a surprise in a neighborhood of lavish shops. Grab one of the barrel seats at the counter and lunch on a made-to-order sandwich and glass of Tuscan wine. Crusty loaves of bread are sliced and generously laden with thick slabs of fresh mozzarella, tomatoes, garlic, aromatic basil, and olive oil. Other offerings include myriad types of hams and salamis, a variety of cheeses, and bologna, in Italy called *mortadella* (and thankfully nothing like the American interpretation). ♦ Italian ♦ M-Tu, Th-Sa lunch. No credit cards accepted. Via del Parione 19r (off Via dei Tornabuoni). 214067

21 Baccus ★$ This gleaming, modern restaurant is perfect for a light dish of pasta (they have 80 kinds) when you're not in the mood—or the price range—for a multicourse meal (although this, too, is available). The clientele is a mixed bag that ranges from the well-heeled (it's down the block from two exclusive hotels) to students. Another bonus: The kitchen is open late. ♦ Italian ♦ Tu-Su lunch and dinner until 12:30AM; closed in August. Borgo Ognissanti 45r (near Piazza Ognissanti). 283714

22 Sostanza ★★$$ If you've decided to splurge, and to try that much-touted regional specialty of *bistecca fiorentina* (juicy grilled steak drizzled with olive oil), this is the place to do it. Reservations are required at the butcher-shop-turned-radical-chic-restaurant, where the tables are communal and the people-watching is as fine as the food. It's a 100 percent Florentine evening. Other offerings include broiled chicken and a tasty artichoke frittata. ♦ Italian ♦ M-F lunch and dinner; closed in August. Reservations required. No credit cards accepted. Via della Porcellana 25r (off Via Palazzuolo). 212691

23 St. James Anglican Church $ If you're homesick for mom's meat loaf, the ladies of this Anglo-American parish cook a down-home American meal on Wednesday nights and charge only a nominal fee for it. Dinner follows a short, consistently worthwhile talk on various topics of interest to Italophiles. Call ahead, as the schedule changes according to the academic calendar. ♦ American ♦ W dinner Sept-June. No credit cards accepted. Via Rucellai 13 (off Via Palazzuolo). 294417

24 Aprile $$ In a palazzo once owned by the Medici, complete with faded traces of frescoes, high vaulted ceilings, and a small breakfast courtyard, this 30-room hotel has a graceful air of antiquity. Rooms are simple (not all have air-conditioning or color TV), but all have private baths. And some have a limited view of the **Piazza Santa Maria Novella.** ♦ Via della Scala 6 (near Piazza Santa Maria Novella). 2162371; fax 280947

24 Officina Profumo-Farmaceutica di Santa Maria Novella Dominican monks first opened this neo-Gothic, temple-like *erboristeria* to the public in 1612, and many of the curing concoctions it sells today are based on the original formulas. Pick out a box of handmade soap or a packet of their trademark potpourri. ♦ M-Sa; closed two weeks in mid-August. Via della Scala 16 (near Piazza Santa Maria Novella). 216276

25 Il Latini ★★$$ This former tavern, bursting with bonhomie, has become a must for visitors in search of the quintessential Tuscan evening. Communal tables are laden with the province's specialties: a variety of soups, grilled and roasted meats, white cannellini beans, and fresh greens sautéed in olive oil, with owner Signor Giovanni Latini overseeing it all. ♦ Italian ♦ W-Su lunch and dinner. Via dei Palchetti 6r (off Via della Vigna Nuova). 210916

26 La Residenza $$ There are only a few top-floor rooms with balconies here (and an elevator!), but all guests can enjoy the view from the roof garden that overlooks the chic

Florence

Via Tornabuoni. The 24 guest rooms of this Renaissance palazzo are bright and have been renovated, and though this isn't for the shoestring budgeteer, the traveler with more to spend won't find better lodging on this street, which is home to **Gucci, Ferragamo,** and **Versace** boutiques. In summer, when you'll want to keep your windows open, ask for a room away from the street. One caveat: The hotel really pushes its "optional" half-board (breakfast plus one meal) during high season. ♦ Via del Tornabuoni 8 (near Via degli Strozzi). 284197; fax 284197

26 Scoti $ Despite its rock-bottom prices and its location on Italy's most elegant shopping street, the lodgings here are not for everyone. The palazzo and its foyer are impressive, but in the rooms, where some see the comfortable patina of age, others see borderline shabby. Everyone, however, seems to agree that it is clean and the owners very friendly. Of the five double and two single rooms, none has a private bath. There is no restaurant. ♦ Via Tornabuoni 7 (near Via degli Strozzi). 292128

27 Belle Donne ★★$$ Named "beautiful women" for this street's earlier tenants, who were practitioners of the world's oldest profession. This small restaurant caters to the neighborhood's current workforce, mostly young professionals who come here for soup-and-salad lunches or the more substantial dinners that include some of the best desserts in town. The brainchild of two young chefs, the cuisine is an innovative blend of the traditional and experimental. Creativity applied to dishes as ordinary as chicken salad, or ingredients as ubiquitous as the chestnut, make dining here a consistent source of unexpected pleasure. The menu changes as often as the offerings at the market, but past delicacies have included chestnut soup, salmon with olive oil mayonnaise, and fava beans with scampi. ♦ Italian ♦ M-F lunch and dinner. Via delle Belle Donne 16 (off Via della Spada). 2382609

28 Ottaviani $ Two of the 19 adequately furnished rooms here have private baths; the rest share facilities that are, if not luxurious, clean and reliable. There's no restaurant and, because of the hotel's proximity to the train station, rooms in the front are noisy even though they're on the second and third floors. Adjacent is the lovely **Piazza Santa Maria Novella.** No credit cards accepted. ♦ Piazza Ottaviani 1, Third floor. 2396223; fax 293355

28 Visconti $ Word is out about this small hotel owned by a local architect and housed in a 14th-century palazzo. Blue, white, and clean is the theme, and the highlight is a lovely plants-filled terrace for outdoor breakfasts. With or without private bath, these 10 rooms need to be booked weeks in advance during high season. There's no restaurant, though an unusual perk is the parking made available to guests. No credit cards accepted. ♦ Piazza Ottaviani 1, Second floor. 213877; fax 213877

29 Universo $ Enjoying the address of one of Italy's great piazze, this hotel is well maintained and pleasant. Of the 41 rooms (31 with bath) try to get **Room 56**: the only room with a terrace facing the piazza and the **Church of Santa Maria Novella.** There is no restaurant. ♦ Piazza Santa Maria Novella 20. 211484; fax 292335

29 Chiesa e Chiostri di Santa Maria Novella (Church and Cloister of Santa Maria Novella) Founded in the 13th century by the Dominicans, this cavernous church (illustrated below) was completed in 1360, except for the colored-marble facade designed by **Leon Battista Alberti** in the 15th century. The vast Gothic interior was richly decorated in the early Renaissance and later refurbished by **Vasari.**

Masterworks are numerous and include the sacristy's 13th-century crucifix by Giotto and a glazed terra-cotta lavabo by Giovanni della Robbia; the **Cappella Strozzi,** whose 14th-century frescoes by Nardo di Cione surround an altarpiece of the same period by Orcagna; the **Cappella Gondi,** designed by Giuliano Sangallo in the early 16th century, and its 15th-century crucifix by Filippo Brunelleschi, his only known work in wood. In the chancel, Domenico Ghirlandaio's well-known 15th-century fresco cycle depicts life in the Renaissance heyday and offsets the high altar that stands before it with a bronze crucifix by Giambologna; the **Cappella Filippo Strozzi** is decorated with 15th-century frescoes by Filippino Lippi. ♦ M-Sa; Su afternoons. Piazza Santa Maria Novella. 282187

Chiesa di Santa Maria Novella

Florence

Next to the Chiesa e Chiostri di Santa Maria Novella:

Chiostro Verde The "Green Cloister" takes its name from the green tint that dominates Paolo Uccello's masterful 15th-century *Universal Deluge* fresco. The adjacent **Chiostro Grande** is closed to the public. ♦ Admission. M-Th mornings; Sa-Su mornings. 282187

30 Standa A grand palazzo has been converted into a *grande magazzino* (department store). This chain does best in the housewares department, which offers insight into how Italians stock their homes and kitchens. Bring home cotton sheets or cheese graters in five sizes to make your own place a little more *italiana*. ♦ M-Sa. Via dei Panzani 31r (at Via del Giglio). 2398963

31 Giotto $ This simple hotel has a great location—a five-minute walk from just about everything. All eight of its high-ceilinged doubles have renovated bathrooms—the thing to look for (but rarely find) when considering Italy's low-end hotels; some have frescoed or coffered ceilings and color TVs. Run by a young couple who enjoy the international exchange with their guests, the hotel is near the **Cappelle Medicee**, midway between the train station and the **Duomo**, and close to the **Mercato di San Lorenzo**. ♦ Via del Giglio 13 (off Via dei Panzani). 289864; fax 214917

HOTEL BELLETTINI

32 Bellettini $ Set in a handsomely restored Renaissance building is a well-kept secret—so hope for an available room and then don't tell a soul about it. Besides its central location (it's quiet despite this), optional air-conditioning, tiled private baths, and frescoed breakfast room (there is no restaurant), some of the 27 rooms even overlook the **Duomo**. And the staff speaks fluent English. ♦ Via dei Conti 7 (between Via dei Cerretani and Via Faenza). 213561; fax 283551

33 Cappelle Medicee (Medici Chapels) This Medici mausoleum has been a must-see for centuries for visitors to Florence. The grandiose 17th-century **Cappella dei Principi**, ornamented with semiprecious stones, contrasts with the earlier **Sagrestia Nuova** (New Sacristy), which contains the tomb of Lorenzo il Magnifico (his brother Giuliano lies opposite the altar in the single tomb topped by Michelangelo's Madonna and Child). Remains of the 16th-century Medicis—Lorenzo, Duke of Urbino, and Giuliano, Duke of Nemours—are housed in tombs crowned with Michelangelo's reclining allegorical statues of Dawn and Dusk, and Night and Day. ♦ Admission. Tu-Su mornings. Piazza Madonna degli Aldobrandini (at Via dei Conti and Via del Canto dei Nelli). 2388602

34 Friggitoria Luisa ★$ Here is one of Florence's last remaining *friggitorie*, hole-in-the-wall eateries featuring fried snacks. Luisa has made-to-order sandwiches inside, but the real draw are the deep-fried eats from the curbside counter. Indulge in the voluptuous *bomboloni* (sugar-dusted custard rolls), *cimballe* (doughnuts), and *crochette di riso* (rice croquettes); for saltier fare try the thin squares of polenta. ♦ Italian ♦ M-Sa snacks. Via Sant'Antonino 50-52r (near Via dell'Ariento). 211630

35 Il Triangolo delle Bermude This splashy *gelateria* is aptly named after the Bermuda Triangle—you'll get lost in the selection of such adventurous flavors as rose, whiskey, peanut, and coffee crunch. ♦ Tu-Su; closed 1-20 January. No credit cards accepted. Via Nazionale 61-63r (near Via Faenza). 287490

36 Anna $ Once you have your first *caffè* and pastry in the geranium-filled courtyard you'll never want to leave. The 20 rooms are simple, with pretty tiled floors; five have private baths, three have private showers. ♦ Via Faenza 56 (near Via Cennini). 2398322; fax 213806

36 Mario $$ This is a good hotel for those who disdain more eccentric quarters; it's slightly more conventional, slightly less casual. Common areas and the 16 guest rooms (with private baths) feature attractive antiques, and everywhere is evidence of Signor Mario's professional hospitality. There is no restaurant. ♦ Via Faenza 89 (at Via Cennini). 216801; fax 212039

37 Mercato Centrale In the middle of the sprawling open-air **Mercato di San Lorenzo** (see page 74) stands this landmark cast-iron market structure, built in 1874. The downstairs explodes with sights, smells, and sounds from the butcher and fishmonger stalls, while fresh produce reigns upstairs. It's well worth a walk-through for a priceless education in Italian gastronomy. ♦ M-Sa mornings. Piazza Mercato Centrale, in the Mercato di San Lorenzo (main entrance on Via dell'Ariento)

Mark Twain, who lived outside Florence while working on *Pudd'nhead Wilson,* was inspired to write more here in four months, he said, than in two years in America.

Florence

Within the Mercato Centrale:

Nerbone ★ $ If you can't find this place on the ground floor of the bustling market, just ask: Everyone knows it as the best spot around for a quick bite and a glass of local wine. Alessandro, the amiable owner, is the son of well-known local restaurateurs. Try the grilled vegetables, daily soup and pasta specials, or the typically-Tuscan *bollito* (beef chunks boiled in broth). Rub elbows with the market merchants and enjoy the high spirits and low prices. ♦ Italian ♦ M-Sa lunch. No credit cards accepted. Mercato Centrale, Ground floor. 219949

38 **Mercato di San Lorenzo (San Lorenzo Market)** This outdoor clothing and souvenir market snakes through the streets behind the church of the same name. Best buys are woolens and leather goods. Everyone speaks English, some of the vendors still bargain (especially if it's off season or you're buying more than one item), and many even take credit cards (there goes your discount). Watch for pickpockets. ♦ M-Sa. Piazza San Lorenzo

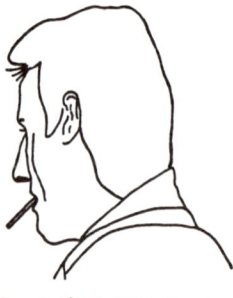

39 **Sergio** $ A neighborhood trattoria, located in the lively **Mercato di San Lorenzo** area, serves delightfully typical Tuscan cuisine (lots of pasta and grilled meats, and a lovely house wine from the Gozzi family's vineyard in Chianti). It's only open for lunch, and caters mostly to market vendors with serious appetites, so don't try to linger. ♦ Italian ♦ M-Sa lunch; closed in August. No credit cards accepted. Piazza San Lorenzo 8r. 281941

40 **Passamaneria Toscana** The most extensive selection of trimmings, cording, braids, and the ubiquitous tassels in every size and color are here, just waiting to be snapped up and tied to the key of your antique armoire or the boughs of your Christmas tree. ♦ M-Sa. Piazza San Lorenzo 12r. 214670. Also at: Via della Vigna Nuova and Via dei Federighi. 2398047

41 **Zà Zà** ★ $$ This popular neighborhood trattoria serves Tuscan classics such as *ribollita* (soup made with white beans, bread, and black cabbage) and grilled slabs of beef and pork drizzled with local olive oil. Sit at butcher-papered communal wooden tables; classic American movie-star posters deck the walls. ♦ Italian ♦ M-Sa lunch and dinner; closed in August. Piazza Mercato Centrale 26r. 215411

42 **Enza** $ The simpatica English-speaking Signora Eugenia has been hosting students for years, and prides herself on a clean, well-kept operation of 15 guest rooms (some spacious enough to accommodate families of four); eight have private baths. To keep costs down, there's no restaurant or breakfast, but there's a bakery across the street. Originally a nunnery in the 14th century, the rooms are as quiet as ever. No credit cards accepted. ♦ Via San Zanobi 45 (near Via XXVII Aprile). 490990; fax 292192

43 **Centro Vegetariano** $ This ever-popular vegetarian eatery is a throwback to the co-op cafeterias of the 1960s: Select from specials written on the blackboard, pay at the cash register, and take your receipt to the kitchen to pick up your food. The veggies are fresh and inventively prepared, but purists beware: They're often combined with eggs and cheese. ♦ Italian ♦ Tu-F lunch and dinner; Sa-Su dinner; closed in August. No credit cards accepted. Via delle Ruote 30r (near Via San Zanobi). 475030

44 **Mensa Universitaria** $ The university cafeteria offers the same reasonably good meal for a few different prices: Show your **International Student Card** and get in at the high end (still a bargain); if you're affiliated with the **University of Florence** and qualify for one of their ID cards, you'll eat for next to nothing. ♦ M-F lunch and dinner; closed in August. No credit cards accepted. Via San Gallo 25 (near Via XXVII Aprile). 4309551

45 **La Ménagère** Approaching its 100th birthday, nothing has changed at this shop—it still resembles an old-fashioned general store with wooden floors, long counters, and a vintage cash register; everything from traditional Tuscan cookware to Richard Ginori china is sold here. Don't miss the selection of Guzzini plastics downstairs. ♦ M-Sa. Via de' Ginori 8r (near Piazza San Lorenzo). 213875

46 **Chiesa e Chiostri di San Lorenzo (Church and Cloisters of San Lorenzo)** Begun in 1419, the interior of the Medici parish church is unusually rich for this period (the facade was never finished). The ubiquitous bluish gray stone, *pietra serena*, provides the backdrop for works by Donatello, Bronzino, Filippo Lippi, and Verrocchio, who designed the 15th-century funerary monument to Piero and Giovanni de' Medici. ♦ Piazza San Lorenzo. 216634

46 **Biblioteca Mediceo-Laurenziana (Medici Library)** To the left of the church are the tranquil 15th-century cloisters that lead, via a magnificent staircase, to the **Laurentian Library.** Designed by

Florence

Michelangelo, the library houses a collection of 10,000 rare manuscripts. ♦ Free. M-Sa mornings. Piazza San Lorenzo. 210760

47 Palazzo Riccardi-Medici In 1444, Cosimo the Elder commissioned the architect **Michelozzo** to build this handsome Renaissance palazzo. It would be the Medici home for 10 years before being passed on to the Riccardi family, who later had the facade lengthened by seven windows on the Via Cavour side. Little remains of the extensive Medici art collection once installed here, but the restored **Cappella dei Magi** and its *Journey of the Magi,* in which various Medicis troop through the Tuscan countryside, is a must-see. The building itself is magnificent. ♦ Chapel: admission. M-Tu, Th-Sa; Su afternoons. Via Cavour 1 (at Via dei Gori). 27601

48 Colomba $ It's a great spot for students, as plain and neat as they come, and sparkling with a fresh coat of paint. The hotel is most memorable, however, for the gracious hospitality of the young English-speaking owners. Of the 17 large, tiled rooms (15 have private baths), some are spacious enough to sleep four, and there's no restaurant to jack up the price. Located near **Piazza San Lorenzo,** the area is a veritable Medici theme park where examples of that family's architectural and artistic legacy abound. ♦ Via Cavour 21 (near Via Guelfa). 289139

48 Casci $ A restoration project has left this former 15th-century convent, with 17th-century ceilings in some of the public rooms, in prime shape, further enhanced by the accommodating Lombardi family who manage it. The 18 guest rooms all have private showers as well as amenities such as color TVs and telephones. It's more than one could hope for in most budget hotels. There's no restaurant. ♦ Via Cavour 13 (near Via Guelfa). 211686; fax 2396461

49 Il Guelfo Bianco $$ A radical refurbishing has left this 29-room hotel in peak condition —it's contemporary, efficiently run, and nicely decorated. Bonuses include location (midway between the **Duomo** and the **Piazza San Marco**), beautiful bathrooms, a helpful staff, and a peaceful courtyard. There are eight more rooms in an adjacent annex. There is no restaurant. ♦ Via Cavour 57 (at Via Guelfa). 288330; fax 295203

50 Museo di San Marco The simple frescoes that Fra Angelico left behind in the tiny monks' cells make this museum of special importance. It was during his stay here as a monk from 1438 to 1445 that Medici architect **Michelozzo** was called in to enlarge the 13th-century monastery. Cross the quiet cloister to visit Ghirlandaio's *Last Supper* and Fra Angelico's *Crucifixion,* and look for his *Annunciation* at the top of the stairs on the way to the dormitory. Savonarola became Prior of San Marco before being dragged off to his death in the **Piazza della Signoria,** and his cell displays the well-known portrait of him by Fra Bartolomeo. ♦ Admission. Tu-Su mornings. Piazza San Marco 3. 2388603

51 Galleria dell'Accademia (Accademia Museum) Michelangelo's *David* is the kingpin of this gallery—best to see it right away to dispel the tension and beat the crowds. Moved here in the 19th century after hundreds of years spent outdoors in the **Piazza della Signoria,** the sculpture occupies the far end of the gallery, perched high above a protective Plexiglas shield installed after a deranged visitor smashed the sculpture's toe with a hammer in 1991. After you catch your breath, turn back to see more works by Michelangelo and others. ♦ Admission. Tu-Sa; Su mornings. Via Ricasoli 60 (between Via degli Alfani and Piazza San Marco). 2388609

52 Viceversa In a city fraught with its Renaissance heritage, here is a sparkling touch of sleek, often witty, Milanese design, where much of the merchandise looks like it belongs in New York's Museum of Modern Art. But it's all for sale, and smaller items of creative design—pens, key rings, travel clocks, tabletop bric-a-brac—fill those suitcase corners. ♦ M-Sa; Su mornings. Via Ricasoli 53r (between Via dei Pucci and Via Guelfa). 2398281

53 Dino Bartolini A vast array of Italian housewares where cookie jars are displayed alongside high-tech Alessi designs. Garlic presses, olive oil dispensers, double-handed *mezzaluna* (chopping or mincing) knives, and a host of other kitchen items make quintessentially Italian gifts. ♦ M-Sa; closed in August. Via dei Servi 30r (at Via M Bufalini). 211895

54 Museo dell'Opera del Duomo Since opening in 1891, works from the **Duomo, Campanile,** and **Battistero di San Giovanni** (see page 67) have been gradually moved here for protection. Two downstairs rooms are devoted to **Brunelleschi** and include his model for the dome; on the mezzanine is a *Pietà* sculpted by Michelangelo shortly before he died; upstairs are two choir stalls by Donatello and Luca della Robbia, as well as Donatello's wooden sculpture of Mary Magdalen. A magnificent 15th-century silver altarpiece and some of Ghiberti's original bronze door panels are from the **Battistero.** ♦ Admission. M-Sa. Piazza del Duomo 9 (between Via dell' Oriuolo and Via dei Servi). 2302885

Florence's Latin name, Florentia, probably refers to the city's florid growth, though historians attribute it to Lo Florinus, the Roman general who besieged the nearby Etruscan hill town of Fiesole in 63 BC.

Restaurants/Clubs: Red   **Hotels:** Blue
Shops/ ♦ Outdoors: Green   **Sights/Culture:** Black

75

Florence

55 Piazza Santissima Annunziata Florence's most perfectly proportioned piazza (illustrated below) is surrounded by loggias on three sides, whose steps serve as a welcome spot for relaxing and recharging your batteries. In the center of the piazza is a pompous statue of *Fernando I de' Medici*, begun by Giambologna and finished by Tacca (whose two rather strange fountains of sea creatures flank it on either side). The Renaissance church of the **Santissima Annunziata** is a first choice for local upper-crust weddings and contains a number of major works, notably Andrea del Sarto's masterpiece, the *Madonna del Sacco*.

On the west side of the square is a 16th-century convent which has been converted into the moderately priced **Loggiata dei Serviti** hotel (289592); and on the east side is the **Ospedale degli Innocenti** (Foundling Hospital), whose 15th-century portico by **Brunelleschi** is decorated with Andrea della Robbia's glazed medallions; the impressive Renaissance picture gallery upstairs is worth a visit as well. ◆ Via dei Servi at Via C. Battisti.

56 Morandi Alla Crocetta $$ The **Villa Laura**, a minute's walk from the **Chiesa della Santissima Annunziata,** was built in 1511 as a convent. It now houses a serene 15-room (all with private baths) hotel that is beautifully furnished with antiques, paintings, icons, and medieval manuscripts. At press time the hotel was in the process of renovating a new wing. The Anglo-Italian owners make guests feel as if they were staying in a private home—albeit one without a restaurant. ◆ Via Laura 50 (near Via della Pergola). 234747; fax 2480954

57 Liana $ Housed in a 19th-century palazzo once occupied by the British embassy, this hotel has 26 peaceful rooms (only three without private baths); some are individually decorated in Art Nouveau style, and many face a garden planted with pines. English-speaking Signor Riccardo hovers over all, attentive and accommodating. The hotel, located in a residential area, is not especially central; it is, however, an oasis of calm. There is no restaurant. ◆ Via Vittorio Alfieri 18 (near Piazza D'Azeglio). 245303; fax 2344596

58 Da Rocco $ Vegetarians and picnickers looking for provisions will fare well here, as will just about anyone else looking for inexpensive homecooking. Choose from a variety of casseroles baked that morning, plus cold cuts, pasta, and roasted or baked vegetables dressed in olive oil. Located within the **Mercato Sant'Ambrogio**, it's a colorful place in which to browse. ◆ Italian ◆ M-Sa lunch. Mercato Sant'Ambrogio, Piazza Ghiberti. No phone

58 Il Cibreino ★★$ This no-frills, no-reservations version of the elegant and pricey **Il Cibreo** restaurant next door offers many of the same exquisitely prepared Tuscan dishes as its elegant big sister, but without the fine china or the high prices. This is Tuscan cuisine reinvented by a young Florentine couple who rely on recipes from centuries ago, reaching back to the very origins of the region's cuisine. No pasta here, but excellent antipasti, soups (especially the one made with yellow peppers), and meat dishes such as rabbit, lamb, or pigeon boned and stuffed with seasonal vegetables. ◆ Italian ◆ Tu-Sa lunch and dinner. Piazza Ghiberti 35r. 2341100

Piazza Santissima Annunziata

Florence

59 Paperback Exchange As its name implies, this is the place to trade your English-language paperback (as well as war stories about your travels) for one of thousands of well-thumbed volumes. Credit for your book is applied to the already discounted price of your next purchase. Half the stock of English-language books is new, with an emphasis on *"Italianistica"*: Florentine and Italian art, culture, and history. If they don't have it, they'll gladly place special orders. ♦ M-Sa. Via Fiesolana 31r (at Via dei Pilastri). 2478154

60 Alle Murate (Vineria) ★$$ A recent and welcome trend has upscale restaurants reserving a more casual dining area where a limited, less expensive menu is offered. Here budget-conscious diners can enjoy the dishes chef Umberto Montano adapts from his native Basilicata, along with *sformato di verdura* (a vegetable timbale) and *anatra all'arancia* (duck stuffed with parsley and Parmesan and served with orange sauce)—a dish, Florentines insist, definitely not invented by the French. ♦ Italian ♦ Tu-Su dinner; closed two weeks in mid-August. Via Ghibellina 52r (near Via M Buonarroti). 240618

61 Dante $$ Book well in advance at this 14-room hotel, off the **Piazza Santa Croce**, that's home away from home for performers at the nearby **Teatro della Pergola**. You needn't be a star to enjoy such amenities as private baths, color TV, air-conditioning, and bedside telephones. Decor is plain and straightforward, and there is no restaurant. ♦ Via San Cristofano 2 (off Via di San Giuseppe). 241772; fax 2345819

62 Chiesa di Santa Croce This church of the Franciscan order, begun in 1294 and completed in the second half of the 14th century, is located in one of Florence's oldest and loveliest piazzas. Within the open, simple space of the church are vast numbers of tombs, cenotaphs, and works of art by Giotto, Agnolo, Taddeo Gaddi, Donatello, and Antonio Canova. The church is a kind of pantheon for some of the city's most illustrious deceased—Galileo is buried here, as are Michelangelo, Machiavelli, and Rossini. ♦ Piazza Santa Croce. 244619

63 I Ghibellini ★$ If you could eat the scenery here, you'd have the meal of a lifetime, but as it is you can enjoy one of Florence's most picturesque little piazzas and choose from the large selection of good and cheap pizzas. Tables are available inside as well. ♦ Italian ♦ M-Tu, Th-Su lunch and dinner; closed one week in mid-August. Piazza San Pier Maggiore 8-10r (off Via G Verdi). 214424

64 Sbigoli Terrecotte Plain and painted terra-cotta is the specialty of this shop, which stocks earthenware from all over Tuscany. Colorful oversize mugs, plates, and ashtrays are easy to carry; reliable shipping can be arranged for items you don't want to schlep, although it usually doubles the cost. ♦ M-Sa. Via Sant' Egidio 4r (at Borgo Pinti). 2479713

65 Brunori $ The only glitch to this perfectly located nine-room hotel (a two-minute walk to the **Bargello**) is that only one room has a private bath. If that's fine with you, you'll like the low rates and the high efficiency of the English-speaking owners as well. Rooms are simple and unadorned, and the only cheaper place in town is the youth hostel. Breakfast is optional and there is no restaurant. No credit cards accepted. ♦ Via del Proconsolo 5 (near Via del Corso). 289648

65 Yellow Bar $ The best testimony to this pub/restaurant with the odd name and Anglo atmosphere is its staying power with both the locals and foreigners, old and young, who have been coming here for years. A full menu includes homemade pasta made daily on the premises, but most of the menu is bypassed in favor of an excellent pizza and beer, served when all the rest of Florence is shutting down. ♦ Italian ♦ M, W-Su dinner until 1:30AM; closed in August. Via del Proconsolo 39r (near Via del Corso). 211766

65 Le Mossacce ★$$ The name means "the rough ones," perhaps referring to the straightforward, rustic cuisine, including lasagna and *spezzatino* (beef or veal stew with tomatoes, potatoes, and herbs), served to a packed house. ♦ Italian ♦ M-F lunch and dinner; closed in August. Via del Proconsolo 55r (near Via del Corso). 294361

66 Guardaroba It's hit-or-miss at this clothing close-out store, one of the largest of four locations, each with men's and women's knitwear, sportswear, separates, and outerwear. Not giveaway fashion, these are high-quality designer clothes at heavy discounts that may or may not strain your budget. ♦ M-Sa; closed three weeks in August. Borgo degli Albizi 85r (near Via del Proconsolo). 2340271

67 Danny Rock $ This "pub," besides gathering a crowd of Florence's gilded youth, is also the only night spot in the neighborhood for late-night crepes, pizza, or hamburgers. There's always a young crowd and good music, then it's off to nearby **Vivoli** (see page 78) for a traditional nightcap gelato. ♦ American/Italian ♦ Tu-Su dinner until 1:30AM; closed two weeks in August. Via dei Pandolfini 13r (at Via M Palmieri). 2340307

The downtown neighborhood of Santa Croce was once an outlying industrial suburb of Florence. The processing of wool and silk was a messy, smelly activity, and fabric mills were relegated to areas far from the elegant core of Florence around the Duomo so as not to offend the genteel classes.

Florence

68 Bargello Once the official residence of the police chief, this fearful 14th-century palazzo was also the site for public hangings. The ground floor's highlights are its arcaded medieval courtyard and the room dedicated to Michelangelo and 16th-century sculpture. This is the most important collection of Renaissance sculpture in the world, with an exhaustive display of works by Donatello, Cellini, Giambologna, Verrocchio, and della Robbia, as well as that period's decorative arts. ♦ Admission. Tu-Su. Via del Proconsolo 4 (at Via Ghibellina). 2388606

69 Acqua al Due ★$ Book in advance for this all-time favorite restaurant that features *assaggi* (tastings). There's a full à la carte menu, but you won't want to miss the pasta *assaggio:* four types of pasta with sauces ranging from mushroom, salmon, and eggplant, to pesto and ragout. ♦ Italian ♦ Tu-Su dinner until 1AM. No credit cards accepted. Via della Vigna Vecchia 40r (at Via dell'Acqua). 284170

69 Il Palottino ★★$$ The menu is *rustico toscano*, the ambience lively and cheerful, and dessert at **Vivoli** next door makes the gastronomic experience complete. If available, the lunchtime *menu turistico*—two courses plus vegetable—is one of the best deals in town. Dinner is considerably more expensive, but it's still affordable. ♦ Italian ♦ Tu-Su lunch and dinner; closed in August. Via Isola delle Stinche 1r (near Via della Vigna Vecchia). 289573

69 Vivoli Florence's world-renowned *gelateria* can be found by following the discarded paper cups to their jam-packed point of origin: a family business that prides itself on fresh ingredients and its ability to make lip-smacking ice cream out of just about anything. ♦ Tu-Su 8AM-1AM; closed in January and August. No credit cards accepted. Via Isola delle Stinche 7r (near Via della Vigna Vecchia). 292334

70 Gelateria dei Neri ★$ Another pretty *gelateria* with friendly service. Their specialty—crunchy chocolate made with nuts—is rightly described as *mitica* (mythical). ♦ Ice cream ♦ M, Tu, Th-Su 1PM-midnight; closed last three weeks of August. No credit cards accepted. Via dei Neri 20-22r (off Via Proconsolo). 210034

71 Fiorino $ The decor is simple, but the 30 rooms are clean; all have private baths and some have air-conditioning. There's no restaurant and no elevator. But what a joy to be so close to the **Uffizi** (see page 69) and the **Piazza della Signoria**. The largely return clientele come for the location and the friendly, attentive staff. ♦ Via Osteria del Guanto 6 (off Via dei Neri). 210579; fax 210579

72 Ponte Vecchio The "Old Bridge," having replaced a 12th-century structure swept away in a flood, dates to the 14th century and spans the Arno at its narrowest point. **Vasari** designed the corridor that runs over the bridge and connects the **Uffizi** museum with **Palazzo Pitti**. (At press time, that corridor was still closed due to damage sustained in a 1993 bombing.) The smelly butcher shops that once lined the bridge were ousted by Ferdinand I de' Medici, who much preferred the genteel craft of the goldsmiths he ordered to take their place, and whose descendants continue the tradition (a bust of goldsmith/sculptor Benvenuto Cellini stands in the middle of the bridge). During the German retreat in World War II, this was the only bridge Hitler's troops did not blow up; they reduced the buildings on either side to rubble, however, which is why much of Via Por Santa Maria looks so modern. These days the bridge is a mecca for Italy's holdout hippies, who gather here on summer evenings to sell crafts and strum guitars. ♦ Between Via Guicciardini and Via Por Santa Maria

73 Chiesa di Santo Spirito Architect **Filippo Brunelleschi**, who died two years after completing his plans for this Renaissance project, would be mighty surprised at the church's 17th-century facade, almost modern in its simplified design. The cool, simple interior houses many works of art; especially notable is Filippo Lippi's 15th-century Nerli altarpiece. The church's tree-shaded piazza hosts a farmers' market in the mornings and is a popular nighttime haunt with its many bars, *gelaterie*, and outdoor seating. ♦ M-Tu, Th-Su. Piazza Santo Spirito (north side of piazza). 2110030

The prized symbol of Florence, referred to since ancient times as *il giglio* (the lily), is, in fact, an iris. The pale blue flower that grows wild throughout Tuscany is frequently mistaken for the French fleur-de-lis, which appears in the Medici family crest. The privilege of displaying the French symbol was granted to Cosimo the Elder, grandfather of Lorenzo il Magnifico, for his role in maintaining a steadfast political alliance between France and Florence.

Florence

74 Sorelle Bandini $ Guests nurse drinks in the terraced bar of this imposing 15th-century building overlooking the **Piazza Santo Spirito** and the nearby Tuscan hills. With such a breathtaking view, you won't really care that only three of the 10 units have private baths, and that there is no restaurant. Rooms are simple, and the whole palazzo is heavy with massive antiques and the spirit of the Renaissance. No credit cards accepted.
♦ Piazza Santo Spirito 9 (at Via Mazzetta). 215308; fax 282761

75 Ostello Santa Monaca $ One of two youth hostels in Florence, this one is in the Oltrarno neighborhood near the picturesque **Piazza Carmine.** The converted 15th-century convent now accommodates more than 100 mostly youngish souls, and does not require student status or Hosteling International membership. It does, however, require a predilection for dormitory sleeping (eight to 20 bunk-beds to each unisex room), shared bathrooms, and a 12:30PM curfew. Economically priced meals can be arranged at a small, nearby restaurant. Fax a reservation request. It doesn't get any cheaper than this! No credit cards accepted. Maximum of seven nights. ♦ Via Santa Monaca 6 (near Piazza del Carmine). 268338, 2396704; fax 280185

76 Chiesa di Santa Maria del Carmine Built for the Carmelite nuns between the 13th and 15th centuries, this church suffered a devastating fire in 1771. Though flames destroyed most of it, the **Cappella Brancacci** was untouched. That chapel contains 15th-century frescoes begun by Masaccio and completed by Filippino Lippi. Masaccio's portion proved a watershed in the history of art: Combining perspective, chiaroscuro, and a rendering of human emotions with unprecedented boldness, it was a seminal work for the painters of the later Renaissance.
♦ Chapel: admission. M, W-Sa; Su afternoons. Piazza del Carmine. 212331, 2382195

77 Carmine ★★$$ Forever popular, this trattoria and its amiable staff serve a number of favorites, including a hefty portion of tagliatelle *a funghi* porcini (pasta ribbons with porcini mushrooms). In warm months, tables edge out onto the piazza. ♦ Italian ♦ M-Sa lunch and dinner; closed in August. Piazza del Carmine 18r (at Borgo San Frediano). 218601

78 Antico Ristoro di' Cambi ★$$ The Cambi family has been running this rustic restaurant in an old wine shop for decades. If you're feeling adventurous, try the *trippa* (tripe) or *lampredotto* (cow intestine). Or stick to the tasty Tuscan soups or excellent *spezzatino*. ♦ Italian ♦ M-Sa lunch and dinner; closed three weeks in August. Via Sant' Onofrio 1r (off Lungarno Soderini). 217134

79 Gould Institute $ The Methodist Waldesian order runs this simple, comfortable hotel with many architectural details redolent of its 17th-century heritage. Almost all of the 26 rooms have private baths, and there's no curfew to hinder night owls. The student-friendly prices attract travelers of all ages. Rooms can be reserved; if you're traveling solo, on arrival request to share a room with another traveler, which is sometimes possible. The office is

Palazzo Pitti

Florence

closed Saturday afternoons and Sundays, so there can be no arrivals or departures at those times. There is no restaurant. No credit cards accepted. ♦ Via degli Serragli 49 (near Via Sant'Agostino). 212576; fax 280274

80 Boboli $ Just beyond the **Palazzo Pitti** and a 10-minute walk to the **Ponte Vecchio,** this lesser-known hotel offers clean if rather plain lodgings. Some of the 30 guest rooms overlook the **Giardino di Boboli** (Boboli Gardens; see below); all have private baths. There's no restaurant, but private parking is available for those with wheels. ♦ Via Romana 63 (near Via del Campuccio). 2298645

81 Annalena $$ Cosimo de' Medici gave this 15th-century palazzo to a pious widow, Annalena, who turned it into a convent. Today it lodges a loyal clientele who appreciate the 20 antiques-furnished rooms (all with private bath), especially those that share a terrace above the gardenlike nursery. There's no restaurant. ♦ Via Romana 34 (near Via del Campuccio). 222402; fax 222403

82 Palazzo Pitti Florence's largest palazzo was commissioned by the wealthy textile merchant Luca Pitti in the mid-15th century. Pitti's impoverished heirs sold the imposing edifice (pictured on page 79) to Cosimo I and Eleanor of Toledo in 1549, making it the official residence of the rulers of Florence. The original palazzo, built with stone quarried from the **Giardino di Boboli** behind it, was enlarged by Medici architect **Amannati,** who made it the most magnificent palace in Europe, a rustic and rambling precursor to Versailles. Now it's home to a number of museums, the most notable being the **Galleria Palatina** where the Pitti's largely Renaissance and Baroque collection is displayed. ♦ Admission. Tu-Sa; Su mornings. Piazza dei Pitti. 213440

83 Giardino di Boboli (Boboli Gardens) Once the private domain of the Medici, this green expanse now provides fresh air, incredible views, and the most pastoral picnic spots in the city. Directly behind the palazzo is an amphitheater modeled on an ancient Roman circus and a path leading to **Neptune's Pond.** From here you can continue onward and upward to the 16th-century star-shaped **Forte Belvedere** and an unrivaled panorama of Florence, or stroll westward down the **Viottolone,** a cypress-studded walk lined with classical statuary. ♦ Admission. Daily. Enter through the Palazzo Pitti. 213440

84 La Scaletta $ Located in a 15th-century palazzo on the street connecting the **Ponte Vecchio** and the **Palazzo Pitti,** this hotel's charm is only enhanced by the presence of owner Barbara Barbieri and her son Manfredo. Each of the 11 rooms is individually decorated, 10 have baths, and some have marble fireplaces; but the pièce de résistance is the view from the verdant roof garden. Dinner is available if requested in advance. ♦ Via Guicciardini 13 (near Piazza dei Pitti). 283028; fax 289562

85 Madova Gloves can be a little cheaper in the **Mercato di San Lorenzo,** but the selection is not always as wide and the quality certainly not up to that of this shop, Florence's premier glove emporium. Gloves in a variety of leathers, linings, and colors—including custom-made sizes—will be shipped anywhere free of charge. ♦ M-Sa. Via Guicciardini 1r (at Via dei Bardi). 2396526

86 Bordino ★$ This small restaurant's super-duper super-cheap *bistecca fiorentina* is a lunch-only deal—dinner costs quite a bit more. For a noontime seat at one of the four outdoor tables or in the cozy interior, you'll have to come early to beat the rush. ♦ Italian ♦ M-Sa lunch and dinner; closed three weeks in August. Via Stracciatella 9r (off Via Guicciardini). 213048

87 Il Torchio This old *torchio,* or printing press, produces lovely marbleized paper and applies it to notebooks, boxes, picture frames, and other items. Being just a tad outside the center of town keeps prices here moderate. ♦ M-F; Sa mornings. Via dei Bardi 17r (off the Lungarno Torrigiani). 23428627

Florence

88 Piazzale Michelangiolo Built in the late 19th century to commemorate the town's most famous son, this hillside piazza offers a postcard-perfect overlook of the city. Much of Florence comes here to escape the summer heat. The **Gelateria Michelangiolo** (2342705) and the watermelon stand are cheap and equally refreshing alternatives to the pretty but pricey **La Loggia** (2342832) bar and restaurant. ♦ Viale Michelangiolo (at Viale Galileo Galilei)

89 San Miniato al Monte Built high on this hill between the 11th and early 13th centuries and visible from the center of town, the geometric green-and-white marble facade of this beloved church is a fine example of Romanesque architecture. Inside is a marble floor inlaid with zodiac signs, a terra-cotta ceiling by Luca della Robbia, Michelozzo's **Cappella del Crocifisso**, and a pulpit crawling with carved animals. At 4:30PM, Benedictine monks sing vespers and say Mass. A stroll around the church cemetery may bring you to the tomb of Carlo Lorenzina, a.k.a. Carlo Collodi, author of *Pinocchio*. ♦ Via del Monte alle Croci (off Piazzale Michelangiolo). 2342768

90 Ostello della Gioventù $ A 15th-century villa near the Fiesole hills is home to Florence's original youth hostel. Distinguished by its rural setting, this hostel accepts written reservations only. To get there, take a 20-minute ride on the *No.17B* bus from the train station or **Piazza San Marco.** You will be required to show a Hosteling International membership card and abide by the 11:30PM curfew. The inn can handle 33 guests, in unisex rooms (without private baths) accommodating from four to eight people. There is no restaurant. No credit cards accepted. ♦ Villa Camerata, Viale Righi 2/4, Fiesole. 601451; fax 610300

Bests

Ilaria Martin
Interpreter and Translator

A trip to Florence without visiting our magnificent **Duomo** and its **Campanile** is like leaving Paris without visiting Notre Dame—but worse. Arrange your day so that you can spend a good part of it in the **Uffizi Gallery**, the greatest collection of Renaissance art in the world.

Rub elbows with the locals in **Torrini**, one of the city's most authentic old fashioned *fiaschetterie* or wine bars. Step up to the bar and for a nominal fee, down a glass of the house wine from the world-class vineyards of Chianti country.

We live with a wealth of medieval and Renaissance history on a daily basis, but overwhelmed tourists may do well to see what everyday life during that period was like by a visit to the **Museo dell'Antica Casa Fiorentina.**

It's expensive and one could do without the attitude, but a beautifully packaged gift from the dramatic **Officina Profumo Farmaceutica di Santa Maria Novella** for centuries has been the quintessentially Florentine memento. Recipes and formulas for soaps, lotions, elixirs and their well-known potpourri may well date back to the 17th century when this *erboristeria* was run by monks.

While the crowds are elsewhere, slip into the cool and serene calm of the **Chiesa di Santa Maria Novella** and head straight for Domenico Ghirlandaio's fresco cycle behind the high altar. It is an exquisite depiction of daily life in the days of 15th-century Florence when Ghirlandaio was one of the local masters.

Enrico Rainero
Photographer

For some exuberant theater, find the 19th-century **Mercato Centrale** amidst the sprawling outdoor **Mercato San Lorenzo**. Every imaginable Italian food product, fresh and packaged, is available here—window shopping at its cheapest and most colorful.

Michelangelo's *David*, one of the symbols long associated with the unrivaled genius of Florence's Renaissance, is the reason to visit the **Galleria dell'Accademia.** Once again, backtrack to the sculptor's *Slaves*, half-finished works that show how Michelangelo "released " his subjects that he believed to be imprisoned in the stone itself.

Yes, it's world famous and always packed with savvy tourists, but for good reason: **Gelateria Vivoli** continues to make the best gelato in town. Grab a cup, then wander the ancient side streets of this neighborhood where Michelangelo lived as a boy, or walk one block over to the **Piazza Santa Croce.** Find a stone bench and watch the kids play soccer in the shadow of one of Florence's most beautiful churches.

Art buffs will know that the recently renovated must-see frescoes by Masaccio (and later completed by Filippino Lippi) in the **Cappella Brancacci** of the **Chiesa del Carmine** will help put the history of Renaissance painting in perspective.

While up at the **Piazzale Michelangiolo** for one of those memorable panoramas that will stay with you for life, stroll to the nearby church of **San Miniato al Monte,** one of the oldest and most interesting churches in Florence. A handful of monks still sing vespers late each afternoon, a lovely experience that will transport you to other worlds and other centuries.

72
Primrose Hill
Camden Town
73
Camden Rd.
St. Pancras Way
College St.
Camden St.
Camden High St.
Parkway
Abbey Rd.
Maida Vale
St. John's Wood
Wellington Rd.
Avenue Rd.
Prince Albert Rd.
Outer Circle
71 London Zoo
Albany St.
Abercorn Pl.
Grove End Rd.
Paddington Recreation Ground
Maida Vale
Elgin Ave.
Mornington Crescent
Pancras Rd.
70 Regent's Park
St. John's Wood Rd.
Park Rd.
Queen Mary's Gardens
Eversholt St.
King's Cross St. Pancras
Shirland Rd.
Lisson Grove
Hampstead Rd.
Euston Square
Euston
Euston Rd.
75
76
Woburn Pl.
Marchmont St.
Warwick Avenue
Baker St.
69
Warren St.
Gower St.
Marylebone
Regent's Park
74
Great Portland St.
Tottenham Court Rd.
Harrow Rd.
A40(M)
Edgware Rd. (Bakerloo)
Marylebone Rd.
Edgware Rd. (Metro & Circle)
Gloucester Pl.
Baker St.
Marylebone High St.
Portland Pl.
Great Portland St.
Russell Square
Royal Oak
Bishop's Bridge Rd.
Goodge St.
Paddington
Praed St.
Sussex Gardens
Edgware Rd.
George St.
Portman Square
68
Manchester Square
Wigmore St.
Cavendish Square
78
79
The British Museum
Queensway
Tottenham Court Rd.
77
New Oxford St.
Seymour St.
49
Oxford St.
Oxford Circus
Bayswater
Lancaster Gate
Bayswater Rd.
48
Marble Arch
Bond St.
47
Queensway
Grosvenor Square
Grosvenor St.
66
67
Regent St.
80
81
82
Shaftesbury Ave.
Long Acre
Broad Walk
45 Kensington Gardens
44 Hyde Park
Berkeley Square
60
Leicester Square
Covent Garden
Round Pond
Park La.
64
65
61
59
58
46 Kensington Palace
63
62
56
57
Strand
The Serpentine
Curzon St.
Piccadilly Circus
55
Charing Cross
Green Park
Pall Mall
Embankment
Hyde Park Corner
50
Piccadilly
54
Hungerford Bridge
Kensington Rd.
51 Green Park
The Mall
42
Knightsbridge
Constitution Hill
Queen Victoria Memorial
53 St. James's Park
Whitehall
Gloucester Rd.
Queen's Gate
Exhibition Rd.
Brompton Rd.
Knightsbridge
Grosvenor Pl.
Buckingham Palace
52
Westminster
43
Birdcage Walk
41
39
40
Belgrave Square
St. James's Park
31
30
Westminster Bridge
Cromwell Rd.
Pont St.
33
32
Westminster Abbey
Gloucester Rd.
South Kensington
Sloane St.
Buckingham Palace Rd.
Victoria St.
Victoria
Rochester Row
Horseferry Rd.
Lambeth Palace
Old Brompton Rd.
Kings Rd.
36
Lambeth Bridge
Sloane Square/Chelsea
37
Sloane Square
35
Millbank
Sydney St.
Kings Rd.
Warwick Way
Vauxhall Bridge Rd.
Tate Gallery
Belgrave Rd.
34
Fulham Rd.
Royal Hospital Rd.
Pimlico
The Chelsea Royal Hospital
Lupus St.
Albert Embankment
Edith Grove
38
Chelsea Embankment
Vauxhall Bridge
Chelsea Bridge
River Thames
Battersea Bridge
Albert Bridge
Vauxhall
Nine Elms La.
Battersea Park
Queenstown Rd.
Fentiman Rd.
Wandsworth Rd.
Prince of Wales Dr.
Lombard Rd.
Battersea Park Rd.
Latchmere Rd.
Queenstown Rd.
Wandsworth Rd.
Stockwell
Clapham Rd.
Stockwell Rd.
York Rd.
N
km
mi
1/2
1
1
2

Highbury & Islington
Balls Pond Rd.
Graham Rd.
Caledonian Rd.
Canonbury Rd.
Barnard Park
Liverpool Rd.
Upper St.
Essex Rd.
Southgate Rd.
London Fields
Mare St.
Angel
Pentonville Rd.
Shepherdess Walk
New North Rd.
Queensbridge Rd.
Haggerston Park
Victoria Park Rd.
Goswell Rd.
St. John St.
City Rd.
East Rd.
Pitfield St.
Kingsland Rd.
Hackney Rd.
Cambridge Heath Rd.
King's Cross Rd.
Gray's Inn Rd.
Rosebery Ave.
Lever St.
Bath St.
Old Street
Curtain Rd.
Bethnal Green Rd.
Bethnal Green
Old St.
Bunhill Row
City Rd.
Theobald's Rd.
Clerkenwell Rd.
Aldersgate St.
Farringdon
Hatton Garden
Chancery Lane
High Holborn
Charterhouse St.
Barbican
Chiswell St.
Bishopsgate
Commercial St.
Brick La.
Shoreditch
Vallance Rd.
87
Moorgate
85
London Wall
Liverpool St.
Whitechapel
Mile End Rd.
Lincoln's Inn Fields
Chancery La.
Holborn Viaduct
18
19
Moorgate
Gresham St.
15
Threadneedle St.
86
Whitechapel Rd.
22
21
20
Fleet St.
Strand
St. Paul's
16
Bank
14
13
Aldgate
Aldgate East
24
Temple
23
Blackfriars
17
Mansion House
12
Leadenhall St.
Cannon Street Rd.
Commercial Rd.
Victoria Embankment
Queen Victoria St.
11
Cannon St.
Fenchurch St.
Minories
25
Waterloo Bridge
Upper Thames St.
Cannon St.
Monument
Tower Hill
Blackfriars Bridge
Southwark Bridge
10
Tower Hill
Cable St.
28
27
9
6 London Bridge
Shadwell
The Highway
Stamford St.
Southwark St.
1 Tower of London
Vaughan St.
Garnet St.
Southwark Bridge Rd.
7
5
London Bridge
2 Tower Bridge
Waterloo
The Cut
Union St.
Borough High St.
St. Thomas St.
8
Wapping
Wapping High St.
Rotherhithe Tunnel
Waterloo Rd.
Blackfriars Rd.
Bermondsey St.
Tooley St.
River Thames
3
Lambeth North
Borough
Tower Bridge Rd.
Druid St.
Rotherhithe
Borough Rd.
Long La.
Brunel Rd.
Salter Rd.
Lambeth Rd.
St. Georges Rd.
Harper Rd.
Great Dover St.
Abbey St.
4
Jamaica Rd.
29
Imperial War Museum
Elephant & Castle
Grange Rd.
Lower Rd.
Kennington Rd.
New Kent Rd.
Southwark Park
Kennington La.
Walworth Rd.
Old Kent Rd.
Southwark Park Rd.
Dunton Rd.
Kennington Park Rd.
Kennington
Rolls Rd.
Rotherhithe New Rd.
Kennington Park
Oval
Albany Rd.
Burgess Park
Trafalgar Ave.
Camberwell New Rd.
Camberwell Rd.
Peckham Park Rd.
Old Kent Rd.
Information
Underground Station
Peckham Hill St.
Myatts Fields
Peckham Rd.
Denmark Hill
Queen's Rd.
Kender St.
New Cross Rd.

London

Samuel Johnson's famous sentiment, "When a man is tired of London, he is tired of life, for there is in London all that life can afford," might lead a cynic to remark, "But who can afford it?" However, those who know where to look usually discover they can sample London's bounty without breaking the bank. Some attractions offer free admission, and others give significant discounts. Treasure troves to explore for free include the antiquities of the **British Museum**, the Pre-Raphaelite paintings of the **Tate Gallery**, and the historic **Westminster Abbey**.

Just walking and looking can be an unforgettable experience. The mighty **River Thames** flows through heart of London, and no visit is complete without a walk along its banks. Behold **Big Ben** on a bright autumn morning, or stroll along the luminous **Embankment** on a warm summer's eve. This is the enchanting London of cinema, teeming with red double-decker buses, chunky black cabs, and umbrella-toting politicians. Pay a visit to the vast greenswards of **Hyde Park** or **Regent's Park**, and observe Londoners at play.

Explore winding streets and narrow alleys to see local London, made up of myriad boroughs that have retained their individual quirks and charms through the centuries. Finance still dominates the **City of London**, politics rules stately **Westminster**, fashion shows off on **Regent Street**, the theaters of the **West End** are legendary, tawdry **Soho** is forever cleaning up its act, the literary legacy of **Bloomsbury** lives on, and the once-derelict **Docklands** has been renovated and is filled with new attractions. After a trip to London, you may agree with another famous British author, H.G. Wells, who said "London is the most interesting, beautiful, and wonderful city in the world to me. . . ."

To call from the US, dial 011 (international access code), 44 (country code), 171 (inner London) or 181 (outer London) and the local number. When calling from inside Great Britain, dial 0171 (or 0181) and the local number. City codes appearing within the text are for areas outside inner London.

Getting to London

Airports

Heathrow (0181/7594321), located about 15 miles (24 km) west of the city center, is the world's busiest airport. There are four terminals, each with its own **Travel Information Centre,** bank, exchange bureau, post office, and hotel booking desk. The quickest and cheapest way to get into central London is via the **Underground** (the subway—also called the "tube"). There are two stations at the airport (both on the *Piccadilly Line*)—one serving **Terminals 1, 2,** and **3**; the other serving **Terminal 4**. Trains leave every four to six minutes during weekday peak hours (7-9:30AM and 4:30-7PM), and approximately every 10 minutes on weekends and other times; trains run from 5AM until 11:30PM Mondays through Saturdays, and from 6AM until 10:45PM on Sundays. The trip takes about 50 minutes; call 2221234 for information. The **London Tourist Board** (daily 8:30AM-6PM) has an office at the station that serves **Terminals 1, 2,** and **3**. Two **Airbus** (2221234) lines service the airport: The *A1* goes to **Victoria Station** via **Hyde Park Corner,** and the *A2* goes to **Russell Square** via **Euston Station.** Buses depart every 15 minutes (every 30 minutes from late afternoon on), but they cost more than the tube and take longer.

Gatwick (1293/535353), some 28 miles (45 km) to the south of the city, is London's second major airport. Charter flights and airlines arrive at either the **North** or **South Terminal** building. Both terminals have 24-hour information desks, as well as banks, exchange bureaus, post offices, and hotel booking desks.

There is a nonstop **Gatwick Express** train to **Victoria Station** from the **South Terminal** train station (a free shuttle connects the **North Terminal**) every 15 minutes (30 minutes late at night); travel time is 30 minutes. **Thameslink** connects the airport with **King's Cross, Blackfriars,** and **London Bridge** rail stations: The train runs every 15 minutes during the day, every half hour at night; the trip takes 35 to 40 minutes.

Car-rental agencies at the airports include **Allied Self Drive** (2242257) and **Eurodollar Rent A Car** (7308773).

Bus Station (Long-Distance)

Long-distance buses from all over Britain arrive at the **Victoria Coach Station** (Buckingham Palace Rd and Elizabeth Bridge, 7300202). The station is a ten-minute walk south of **Victoria Station,** with its subway and rail connections.

Train Station (Long-Distance)

London has many different **British Rail** stations, all of which are accessible by tube or bus; each serves a different part of the country. Call for information about schedules: **Charing Cross** (9285100) for

London

southern England; **Euston** (3877070) for northern Wales, the Midlands, northwestern England, and the west coast of Scotland; **King's Cross** (2782477) for northeastern England and Scotland via the East Coast route; **Liverpool Street** (9285100) for Cambridge and East Anglia; **Paddington** (2626767) for western England and southern Wales; and **Victoria** (9285100) for southern England and trains bound for Paris and Brussels via the Chunnel.

Getting around London

Bicycles This mode of transport is only for those with nerves of steel: There are no special lanes and traffic is heavy and unforgiving. But if you insist, you can rent a bike from **Bikepark** (Stukeley St, Covent Garden, 4300083).

Buses The traditional red double-deckers are fun if not fast, and the views are unbeatable. (By the way, not all buses are red anymore; due to privatization of the industry there are a number of different lines and each has its own color.) Bus routes take a bit of figuring out. Check the front of each bus for its destination/direction. If a bus stop is marked "Request," it means you have to flag down an oncoming bus. Special night buses (marked with an "N") run from central London to the suburbs until around 6AM. **Trafalgar Square** is a main departure point for the night buses.

Driving Unless you absolutely must, don't. Streets are typically congested, drivers are aggressive, and parking is nearly nonexistent. And in the UK, you'll be driving in the left lane. If you still insist on bringing a car into the city, remember to always yield to traffic coming from your right when approaching a roundabout or rotary. To keep from being towed, avoid street parking and head for one of the **National Car Park** lots located throughout central London.

Taxis There are cab stands in front of hotels and major tourist attractions. Elsewhere, flag down any black cab whose yellow "For Hire" sign is lit. If your destination is less than six miles away and within London borders, drivers are obliged to take you. Drivers of the old-fashioned, box-shaped cabs are the most knowledgeable, having passed an arduous exam. If problems arise with a particular driver, contact the **Taxi Drivers' Association** at 2861046.

Tours For a good overview, take a **Hop-on/Hop-off** tour bus, with guide (3570594), which allows you to do just that at a number of major attractions. **Evan Evans** (0181/3322222) offers bus tours of the city with narration by a Blue Badge guide (trained and licensed by the **London Tourist Board**). There are a number of walking tour options—Dickens tours, ghost tours, Beatles tours—check the listings in the weekly *Time Out* magazine or call **Streets of London** (0181/3466931).

Underground "The tube," as it's known, is the quickest, most economical option for getting around London. Service starts at 5AM and ends at midnight Monday through Saturday, and runs from 7AM to 11PM on Sunday. Travel after 9:30AM and save heaps with a one- or seven-day Travelcard, available at any station. The cards are good for unlimited travel (including weekends) on the tube, buses, **Docklands Light Railway,** and **British Rail** in the London area. The **Underground**'s 24-hour travel information number is 2221234.

Walking Although London is much too large for walking to be a viable way to get from one place to another, it's undoubtedly the best way to explore its "villages," or neighborhoods. Take transportation to your destination, but wander around a bit once you're there. **Chelsea** is residential and very pretty once you get off the busy **King's Road**; the City of London is loaded with narrow passageways and atmospheric pubs; and Kensington has many green, leafy squares. Walking is really the only way to explore **Covent Garden** and Soho.

FYI

Accommodations London boasts a variety of shelter options for folks traveling on the cheap. There are numerous hostels for young backpackers, inexpensive bed-and-breakfast accommodations for those past the dormitory age but still willing to share bathrooms, and small no-frills hotels where a bed and bath can be found at a reasonable rate. **Homestead Services** (0181/9494455) can arrange accommodations in private homes in central and suburban London. Those who arrive in London without pre-booked accommodations should head for the **Victoria Station Tourist Information Center** (see "Visitors' Information," below).

Business Hours Banks are open Monday through Friday from 9:30AM until 4:30PM; some are open on Saturday mornings as well. Most stores are open from 9:30AM until 5:30PM Monday through Saturday. Museums keep the same general hours, and most open Sunday afternoons as well.

Climate London's weather is moderate and mild: Summer daily temperatures average 60 degrees; in winter, it tends to stay around 40 degrees. It can be wet at any time of the year, and although the rain is not usually of the downpour variety, it helps to have an umbrella.

Consulates and Embassies

Canada ....Macdonald House, Grosvenor Sq, ...2586600

US ....24 Grosvenor Sq, 4999000

Discount Tickets The **London White Card** is a discount pass to 13 major museums and galleries; buy it at any tourist office. For discount theater tickets, head for the **Leicester Square Ticket Booth** (opposite the **Hampshire Hotel**) to pick up half-price tickets for shows at major West End theaters. It opens at noon for matinees, 2:30PM for evening performances, and accepts only cash or traveler's checks. For information about discounts on local transportation, see "Underground," above.

Drinking The legal drinking age is 18. Pubs are generally open Monday through Saturday from 11AM to 11PM; Sunday from noon until 3PM, and again

London

from 7-10:30PM. Pubs are self-service; order at the bar and pay when served. Tipping is not required.

Emergencies Dial 999 for the police, ambulance, or fire brigade. For legal emergencies, contact your embassy or consulate.

Laundry There are self-service laundromats in every neighborhood of London. Most are open from 8AM until 6 or 7PM, Monday through Saturday. In Bloomsbury, try **Duds 'n' Suds** (Brunswick Shopping Center in Brunswick Square, 8372176); in Westminster, **Launderette and Dry Cleaning Center** (31 Churton St, at Belgrave Rd, 8286039); and in Knightsbridge, **The Launderette Centre** (5 Porchester Rd, at Westbourne Grove, 7277735).

Money The pound sterling (abbreviated £) is the currency of the country. Cash traveler's checks at **American Express** (147 Victoria St, at Palace St, 8284567; open during business hours Monday through Saturday); or at any major bank (**Midland, National Westminster, Lloyds,** and **Barclays**). Round-the-clock cash machines are plentiful. It's also possible to exchange currency at post offices.

Personal Safety Be conscious at all times of your bags and valuables. Many pickpockets operate around the **Underground** system, in the major **British Rail** stations, and on the busiest tourist streets. Use a purse that zips closed and hang onto it. Summer is prime pickpocket season, so be particularly alert in crowds.

Postal Services The **Trafalgar Square Post Office** (24 William IV St, northeast corner of Trafalgar Sq) offers full postal service; it's open Monday through Saturday from 8AM to 8PM. Local post offices are generally open weekdays from 9AM to 5PM, and on Saturday from 9AM to 12PM.

Publications The weekly magazine *Time Out* is the best source for up-to-date information on theater, art shows, movies, concerts, discos, free events, and other miscellaneous happenings.

Public Holidays New Year's Day, Good Friday, May Day Bank Holiday (first Monday of May), Spring Bank Holiday (last Monday of May), Christmas Day, and Boxing Day (26 December).

Public Rest Rooms There are only a few in prime tourist locations, such as opposite the **Houses of Parliament** on **Whitehall.** All public buildings—museums, train stations, department stores—have "loos" and they're fairly accessible. Pub and restaurant facilities are reserved for the establishments' customers.

Tower Bridge

London

Restaurants Going out for breakfast is not a British tradition (most hotels include breakfast in the price of a room), although brasseries and American-style restaurants do serve it. Restaurant dining tends to be expensive but there are plenty of snack bars and inexpensive restaurants in the Covent Garden area, Soho, and near the main train stations. Most of these serve well into the evening. Pubs serve "pub grub"—bread and cheese, shepherd's pie, cold salads—at lunch time. Reservations are not required at most budget eateries.

Shopping London's main shopping area is **Oxford Street**, home to most of the big department stores, including **Selfridges**. Off Oxford is **Regent Street**, which has slightly more upmarket stores like **Burberry's**. That mecca for overseas shoppers, **Harrods**, is located in the posh **Knightsbridge** neighborhood. For boutique shopping, head for **Covent Garden**. For antiques and funky souvenirs, head for the street markets: **Bermondsey Street, Camden Lock,** and **Portobello Road.**

Smoking It's legal to light up most anywhere, except on public transporation or in the train stations themselves. Almost all restaurants have a smoking area.

Street Plan The city is *huge* and sprawling, and not neatly laid out. London grew up around the River Thames, beginning with the Roman settlement near **London Bridge,** an area now called the City of London. Narrow passageways, dating back to medieval times, abound here. Carry a map; they're essential even for Londoners. The "A-Z" (pronounced *zed*) series is the best. Free maps are often available from **London Transport Information Centres,** located at major **Underground** transfer stations.

Taxes VAT (Value Added Tax) is a sales tax of 17.5 percent. Non–European Community visitors can reclaim this sum when leaving the country. Take your passport and ask the store for a VAT form. A miniumum purchase is usually required (often £50 or more).

Telephones Telephone booths, or "boxes," accept a variety of coins or phonecards that are good for a certain amount of calling time (they can be purchased at all post offices and at many newsstands). The most expensive time to make calls is between 8AM-6PM Monday through Friday.

Tipping Service charges of between 10 to 15 percent are usually added to hotel bills, and the tipping standard for restaurants and cabs is also between 10 to 15 percent.

Visas Canadian and US citizens need only a valid passport for stays of up to six months.

Visitors' Information Your first stop should be the **London Tourist Board Information Centre** in the front court of **Victoria Station** (between Buckingham Palace and Vauxhall Bridge Rds, 8280516). Here you will find free information on travel within London and Great Britain; theater, concert and tour bookings; accomodations (with booking fee); as well as maps and guidebooks for sale. Other **LTB** locations are in the basement of **Selfridges** department store on Oxford Street, at **Liverpool Street** underground station, and at **Heathrow** and **Gatwick** airports.

1 Tower of London Over its 900-year history, Britain's "most perfect fortress" has played the role of palace, arsenal, treasury, prison, and even menagerie. Anne Boleyn was executed here; hundreds more died outside the walls. The complex (pictured above) is best known today for stately Beefeaters, who parade around the grounds in blue Tudor uniforms, give entertaining tours, and look after the Tower ravens. Arrive early to avoid the crowds and see the **Crown Jewels**, then explore the **Royal Armories,** the **Traitor's Gate,** and the recently restored **Medieval Palace.**
♦ Admission. Daily. Tower Hill (at Minories) 7090765. Tube: Tower Hill

2 Tower Bridge/Museum Enter via the **North Tower** and climb up to view the 1,000-ton drawbridges, then return to street level through the **South Tower** and the museum. In its heyday, this bridge (illustrated on page 86) opened to allow ships' passage up to 50 times a day; now the event occurs only three or four times a week. A new, high-tech, permanent exhibition in the museum celebrates the bridge's 100th birthday in 1994. The glass-enclosed walkway, 145 feet up, offers wonderful views, including a view of the World War II battle cruiser *HMS Belfast.* ♦ Admission. Daily. Between Tooley St and Tower Hill. 3781928. Tube: Tower Hill

50 Berkeley Square is called "the most haunted house in London." Just touching the outer wall of the psychically charged house, it is claimed, will send a tingle down one's spine.

Restaurants/Clubs: Red   **Hotels:** Blue
Shops/ Outdoors: Green   **Sights/Culture:** Black

London

3 Rotherhithe Youth Hostel $ On the city's outskirts (about a mile from the **Tower of London,** but worth the slight inconvenience), this is the Youth Hostel Association's **(YHA)** newest, most modern London hostel. There are beds for 320 guests. All rooms are dorm-style (including six for disabled guests) with adjoining bathrooms. Like the other six **YHA** lodgings in London, facilities here include a laundry room, *bureau de change,* and an entertainment booking service. There is 24-hour access to the hostel and a nighttime security system, plus a cafeteria that provides breakfast and a three-course evening meal at a good price. Reservations recommended; group rates available. ♦ Island Yard (off Salter Rd), Rotherhithe, East London. 2322114; fax 2372919. Tube: Rotherhithe

4 Bermondsey (New Caledonian) Market This street market is for the serious bargain hunter, who must arrive by 6AM (flashlight in hand) to get the best deals. Antiques, objets d'art, and surprisingly tasteful bric-a-brac abound, in addition to the usual toby jugs and pub mirrors. Professional antiques dealers come here, so adopt a competitive attitude and haggle. ♦ Daily 5AM-2PM. Long La and Bermondsey St. Tube: London Bridge

5 London Dungeon Beneath London Bridge, in the gloomy vaults of the world's first and only medieval horror museum, visitors can learn the finer points of hanging, drawing and quartering, and boiling or pressing people to death. Relive the French Revolution and shiver through the "Jack the Ripper Experience." Frankly, this puts the pricier **Madame Tussaud's** to shame, but it's *not* for the faint of heart—people have passed out in here. ♦ Admission; discount for students. Daily. 28-34 Tooley St (at Joiner St). 4030606. Tube: London Bridge

6 London Bridge You'll need to use your imagination here, since London Bridge has fallen down time and time again. The first wooden bridge to cross the Thames, built during the first century at the behest of Roman emperor Claudius, was located 20 yards or so downstream from today's bridge. A succession of wooden bridges followed until 1176, when a 10-arch stone bridge—embellished with ramshackle wooden houses and traitors' heads on spikes—was constructed for Henry II. The heads were eventually banned, but the bridge remained until John Rennie erected a new one, 20 yards upstream, in 1831. That relic was transported to Lake Havasu City, Arizona, in 1971, and the present cantilevered affair went up in its place. ♦ South Bank: intersection of Borough High St and Duke St Hill. North Bank: intersection of King William St and Upper and Lower Thames Sts. Tube: London Bridge

7 Southwark Cathedral Restoration during the 19th century returned this cathedral, supposedly London's oldest Gothic church, to its former glory. Among those buried here is John Gower, one of the first English poets (like his friend Chaucer, he wrote in English rather than French or Latin). There is a memorial to William Shakespeare, who lived in Southwark from 1599 to 1611; on 23 April every year, a candlelight birthday service is held in his honor. ♦ Montague Close (at Cathedral St). 4073708. Tube: London Bridge

8 The George Inn $ The George dates from 1676 and is London's last timbered galleried inn. In summer, you can catch a Shakespeare play under the same roof where the Bard probably wet his whistle; subsequent customers included Charles Dickens (the inn appears in *Little Dorrit*), Dwight Eisenhower, and Winston Churchill. There's a restaurant menu in addition to standard pub fare, but go for the ambience alone. ♦ British ♦ Pub: daily. Restaurant: M-Sa lunch and dinner; Su dinner. 77 Borough High St (at George Inn Yard). 4072056. Tube: London Bridge

9 The International Shakespeare Globe Centre The part of Southwark known as Bankside was home to Shakespeare, Christopher Marlowe, and a host of Elizabethan actors after they were banished from the City of London in 1574. The area had both brothels and theaters such as the **Globe,** a venue for Shakespeare's plays until it burnt down in 1613. A faithful recreation of the first **Globe** is under construction (scheduled to reopen at press time), using authentic materials of English oak, lime plaster, and thatch; and, in keeping with 16th-century building practices, the structure will be raised without the use of nails. Guided tours take visitors into the building site, and an exhibition explains the development of Tudor theaters. ♦ Admission. M-Sa. 1 New Globe Walk (at Bankside). 9286406. Tube: Mansion House

10 Monument For a good view of the borough known as "The City", climb the 311 steps of this fluted Doric column. It was commissioned by Charles II to "preserve the memory of this dreadful visitation"—the Great Fire of 1666, which burned for four days and nights,

London

destroying nearly three-fourths of London. Its height of 202 feet is equal to the distance between its base and the bakery in Pudding Lane where the fire began on 2 September. ♦ Admission. M-F, Sa-Su 2-6PM May-Sept; daily Oct-Apr. King William St and Monument. Tube: Monument

11 Mansion House Cross Southwark Bridge and walk up Queen Victoria Street to the official residence of the lord mayor, who heads the Corporation of London, better known as "The City." The 18th-century building hosts on average one state banquet a day. It is not open to the general public. Note the frieze on the pediment that depicts London defeating Envy and welcoming Plenty. ♦ Mansion House Pl (at Cornhill St). 6262500. Tube: Bank

12 Royal Exchange At the junction of Threadneedle and Cornhill Streets, this was the first covered meeting place for London traders. The main building is closed to the public, but the smart little shops along the sides will appeal to sophisticated tastes, from antiques to shirts. ♦ Threadneedle and Cornhill Sts. Tube: Bank

13 Stock Exchange Since 1986, computers have replaced the frantic "open-out-cry" method of dealing. Such technology is far removed from its 18th-century coffeehouse origins, where dealing first began, yet "my word is my bond" still exemplifies the business style of the **Exchange**. It's closed to the public but free leaflets on the history of the **Exchange** are available at the entrance. ♦ Old Broad and Threadneedle Sts. Tube: Bank

14 Bank of England/Museum "The Old Lady of Threadneedle Street" (the nickname comes from an 18th-century political cartoon) is the government's banker, regulating the money that flows into the banking system. Established in 1694, the bank moved to Threadneedle Street 40 years later and was rebuilt by architect **Sir John Soane** between 1788 and 1808. **Sir Herbert Baker** gave the Old Lady a controversial face-lift in 1937. Today, the bank prints and destroys five million bank notes daily. Interactive videos and displays of gold bars, coins, and Roman mosaics found beneath the site make this museum more entertaining than you'd think. And it's got a good gift shop. ♦ Free. M-F. Threadneedle St and Bartholomew La. 6015545. Tube: Bank

British Rail recently gave this excuse to passengers on a stationary train: "The train on the platform in front is waiting for a driver stranded on the train behind."

The Economist

CORPORATION OF LONDON

15 Guildhall With 12th-century origins, this is the official center of the City of London's government. The address says Aldermanbury, but the entrance is on Gresham Street. The first lord mayor, Henry Fitz Ailwin, was installed here in 1189, reflecting the merchants' rising power as they slipped out from under the king's thumb (the guilds were early trade unions). The 15th-century crypt is London's largest, and the Gothic porch and medieval walls survived the Great Fire of 1666. Once used for trials such as that of Lady Jane Grey, today the **Guildhall** is a venue for state functions. ♦ Free. Daily May-Sept; M-Sa Oct-Apr; also closes for functions. Gresham St (between Basinghall St and Aldermanbury). 6063030. Tube: Bank, St. Paul's

Within the Guildhall complex:

Guildhall Library Founded by three-time lord mayor Dick Whittington in the 1420s, the library's contents comprehensively cover London history, genealogy, topography, and heraldry. ♦ M-Sa

Worshipful Company of Clockmakers' Guildhall Clock Museum To the left of the **Guildhall Library** entrance is one of the most tranquil museums anywhere, with more than 700 exhibits, many still ticking away. Look for the silver skull-shaped pocket watch, said to have belonged to Mary, Queen of Scots. ♦ Daily

16 St. Paul's Cathedral Once it dominated the London skyline; today, chunky modern office buildings surround it. Yet it remains the most famous monument in the heart of The City. This was the first English cathedral erected under the supervision of one architect, **Sir Christopher Wren**. It is the only one of **Wren's** designs with a dome (the second-largest dome in the world) and the only one built in the Baroque style. Constructed between 1675 and 1708, **Wren's** masterpiece (and his memorial—he's buried here) survived both the Blitz and callous redevelopment plans. Many consider the statue of poet John Donne to be the finest single piece of art in the Cathedral. ♦ Admission (includes crypt); additional charge for galleries. St. Paul's Churchyard and New Change. 2482705. Tube: St. Paul's

89

London

Expand Your Horizons: Work or Study Abroad

Kicking around Europe for a summer with no cares or responsibilities is never a disappointment. But imagine how different the experience would be if you actually joined the culture instead of watching it from the outside as a tourist. If that appeals to you, investigate work or study opportunities in Europe. And don't worry: There'll still be plenty of time left for tramping.

Working in Europe is, of course, particularly attractive to budget travelers: a way to lengthen your stay without depleting your funds. Technically, you must have a permit to work in European countries. You or your employer must apply for the permit, and your employer may have to demonstrate that no nationals are available for the position. The ideal scenario is to line up a job and arrange for a work permit before you leave the US. If you need to enter the country in order to find a job, things get a bit trickier. You may have to leave the country while your permit is being processed (usually a period of several weeks); wait while the papers are sent to your out-of-country address; and then re-enter with permit and passport in hand, ready for the border official's stamp of approval. So goes the drill in Great Britain; regulations vary from country to country. In Germany, for example, you can obtain a work permit from within the country; in France it's more difficult, as current economic problems have forced heavy bureaucratic restrictions on work permits for everyone but students.

ROLANDO CORUJO

Permits are an issue where professional jobs are concerned, but if you're looking for temporary or seasonal positions, you might be able to bypass the permit process altogether; officials are more inclined to look the other way when it comes to unskilled labor. By asking around, you can possibly find work in a restaurant, pub, or hotel, or even as a grape picker in France during the wine harvest. Look in the classified ads for au pair (child care) positions, which are most plentiful in Britain and France. Or consider teaching English. Simply hang out your shingle—in this case, notices on community bulletin boards—and wait for responses. Also keep your eye on the classifieds, as locals often advertise for tutors. For a salaried position, you'll probably need at least a bachelor's degree and certification in teaching English as a second language.

Volunteer jobs are good alternatives in places where paying jobs are hard, if not impossible, to find. Volunteering for a church-restoration project, for instance, or for an archaeological dig is probably more stimulating than washing dishes or making beds. Many volunteer positions offer room and board—so what if the room is a tent and meals are cooked on a camp stove?

Study opportunities in Europe are varied and numerous, from brushing up on the host country's language to earning an MBA. Programs range from credited courses at a university to **Elderhostel** lecture programs for senior citizens.

Listed below are some organizations that can help with work, volunteer, or study arrangements in Europe:

Council on International Educational Exchange (CIEE), 205 East 42nd Street, New York, NY 10017; 212/661.1414. **CIEE** provides a full range of information and services for students who want to travel, work, or study in Europe. Write or call for free copies of the publications *Student Travels, Work Abroad,* and *International Workcamps.* CIEE also publishes and sells *Work, Study, Travel Abroad: The Whole World Handbook,* which describes more than 1,200 work, volunteer, and study programs; and *Smart Vacations: The Traveler's Guide to Learning Adventures Abroad,* which describes more than 200 organizations offering vacations with an educational slant. Ask for a free publications catalog.

Elderhostel, 75 Federal Street, Boston, Massachusetts 02110-1941; 617/426.7788. **Elderhostel** arranges two- to four-week noncredit educational courses, usually at colleges, for people 60 years or older. (Spouses can be any age; significant others, at least 50.) Request a free catalog.

Institute of International Education (IIE), 809 United Nations Plaza, New York, New York 10017-3580; 212/883.8200. **IIE** administers 285 exchange programs throughout the world for governmental agencies, universities, corporations, and nonprofit agencies. They also are a good resource for information regarding study abroad, grants, and scholarships. Call or write for the free booklet *Basic Facts on Study Abroad* and a free publications catalog.

Interhostel, University of New Hampshire, 6 Garrison Avenue, Durham, New Hampshire 03824; 800/733.9753. Similar to **Elderhostel, Interhostel** arranges two-week educational programs for people 50 years or older.

Volunteers for Peace (VFP), 43 Tiffany Road, Belmont, Vermont 05730; 802/259.2759. **VFP** arranges enrollment in work camps in which groups of typically 10 to 20 young adults tackle projects such as environmental restoration and community redevelopment. Nearly all work camps operate from July through September and last two to three weeks. Registration takes place mid-April through mid-May. There is a cost to enroll in a workcamp. Call or write for a free copy of **VFP**'s newsletter, or to order *The International Workcamp Directory,* which describes more than 800 programs in 40-plus countries.

London

17 City of London Youth Hostel $ Though refurbished in 1992, this hostel boasts the same Victorian facade it had when it was the school for St. Paul's choirboys. There are five private guest rooms and two dormitories (one with 10 beds and the other with 15 beds). Bathrooms are communal. Because of parking problems, this hostel is not suitable for groups. ♦ 36 Carter La (at Deans Ct). 2364965; fax 2367681. Tube: Blackfriars, St. Paul's

18 London National Postal Museum From penny blacks to postcards, this vast collection in the **King Edward Building** will make philatelists envious. Postal history fans will appreciate the extensive reference library. ♦ Free. M-F. Angel and King Edward Sts. 239.5420. Tube: St. Paul's

19 Old Bailey You won't meet Rumpole at the **Central Criminal Court,** as it's officially known, but you can watch court cases from the public gallery; check the list of trials posted by the main door. ♦ M-F. Old Bailey and Newgate St. 2483277. Tube: St. Paul's

20 Fleet Street Although most major newspapers have taken up quarters elsewhere, this street was once the hub of journalistic London. In 1500 Wynken de Worde set up a printing press here beside **St. Bride's Church,** and England's first daily newspaper, *The Daily Courant,* was issued from nearby Ludgate Circus around 1702. The pen-and-ink atmosphere remains, as does an informal mixture of architectural styles. At 229 Fleet Street, the timber-framed **Wig and Pen Club** (5837255), dating from 1625, has a restaurant open to the public for lunch Mondays through Fridays. ♦ Between Ludgate Circus and Chancery La. Tube: St. Paul's, Blackfriars, Temple

Ye Olde Cheshire Cheese

21 Ye Olde Cheshire Cheese ★★$$ Also known as "the House," this 17th-century den is famed for its steak-and-kidney pudding as well as for such literary patrons as Charles Dickens, William Makepeace Thackeray, and Mark Twain. Bustling during the week but much quieter on Saturdays, the establishment has no fewer than six bars, all warmly outfitted in traditional dark wood. If you want to say you've visited a true old English pub, splurge on this Fleet Street institution. ♦ English ♦ Pub: Daily. Restaurant: M-Sa lunch and dinner; Su bar food. 145 Fleet St (at Wine Office Ct). 3536170. Tube: St. Paul's, Blackfriars, Temple

22 Public Record Office Museum The 84 miles of records stored here consist mainly of government and legal texts. Located on the site of an old chapel, the museum houses the 11th-century *Domesday Book,* William the Conqueror's survey of England; the wills of William Shakespeare and Jane Austen; and George Washington's letters to George III. ♦ Free. M-F. Chancery La (between Fleet St and High Holborn). 0181/8763444. Tube: Chancery La

23 Temple Bar Monument and The Temple Where **Sir Christopher Wren**'s three-arched gateway once served as a noble monument, today, in its place, is **Horace Jones**'s rendition: a spiky dragon surrounded by figures of Queen Victoria and Edward VIII. The **Temple Bar Monument** marks the boundary between the City of London and the City of Westminster. Down Middle Temple Lane lies the Temple complex, originally home to the monastic (and often murderous) Knights Templar, a 12th-century order. Since the 14th century, however, the buildings have been leased to lawyers; two of England's four **Inns of Court—Middle Temple** and **Inner Temple** —are here now. The peaceful courtyards and warrenlike lanes are delightful for strolling. The **Inner Temple** gateway (dating from 1610-11) is one of the best-preserved half-timbered structures in London. ♦ Inn gates usually close at 8PM, but Middle Temple Lane (by the river) is always open. Middle Temple La (between Embankment and Fleet St). Inner Temple 3531736, Middle Temple 3534355. Tube: Temple

24 Courtauld Institute Galleries/Somerset House Architect **William Chambers** designed this Georgian building to replace the Renaissance palace of the Protector Somerset. London's first palace was home to Elizabeth I, when she was a princess, and various female royals. These days it contains the best collection of Impressionist paintings in Britain. An appointment is required to view drawings by Michelangelo, Rubens, and Rembrandt. ♦ Admission. M-Sa; Su afternoons. Strand (at Lancaster Pl). 8732526. Tube: Temple, Aldwych

25 Victoria Embankment Completed between 1868 and 1874, this attractive riverside walkway stretches from Westminster Bridge to Blackfriars Bridge, but it wasn't originally built for leisurely promenading. In fact, it was an early attempt at pollution control. By the mid–19th century, the Thames was one big sewer; its stench became so bad that 1856 was called "the Year of the Big Stink." Sir Joseph Bazalgette designed London's first sewage system, redirecting the city's waste before it reached the Thames. The Embankment hides one of the sewer pipes. ♦ Between Blackfriars and Westminster Bridges. Tube: Embankment

London

On Victoria Embankment:

Cleopatra's Needle London's oldest outdoor monument is 68 feet high and weighs 186 tons. Cut from Egyptian quarries around 1475 BC, this pink granite obelisk is part of a pair that stood before the Temple of the Sun at Heliopolis. In 1819, it was offered to the British government as a memorial to Nelson and Abercrombie, who defeated the French at the Battle of the Nile. The Needle was towed over in an iron pontoon resembling a giant cigar tube, and was placed here by the river in 1878. ♦ Between Waterloo and Hungerford Bridges. Tube: Embankment

25 Embankment Gardens The 1626 **York House Water Gate** in the gardens marks the original line of the riverbank: it was once the entrance to the Duke of Buckingham's garden from the Thames. Look for a tiny memorial to the Imperial Camel Corps, a statue of Robert Burns by Sir John Steele, and a tree commemorating Queen Elizabeth II's 1953 coronation. ♦ Victoria Embankment (between Horseguards Ave and Savoy Hill). Tube: Embankment

26 South Bank Centre Across the Hungerford Bridge on the South Bank lies the largest arts center in Western Europe. First visit **Royal Festival Hall,** home of the **London Philharmonic Orchestra, Farringdon's** record shop, and the wonderful **Books Etc. Bookshop.** Eat lunch or have a drink at the **Festival Buffet** while listening to free music from the foyer. The smaller **Queen Elizabeth** and **Purcell Room** concert halls are also here, as is the **Voicebox,** used for literary readings. The **Poetry Library** on Level 5 offers free membership and more than 4,500 poetry books. ♦ Daily. Belvedere Rd (between Waterloo and Hungerford Bridges). Information 9280639, recorded information 6330932, box office 9288800. Tube: Waterloo, Embankment

Within South Bank Centre:

Hayward Gallery You'll usually find two art exhibitions here, as well as a cafe and art bookshop. ♦ M, Th-Su; Tu-W until 8PM. 9283144, recorded information 9280127

MUSEUM OF THE MOMI MOVING IMAGE

Museum of the Moving Image (MOMI) This lively museum traces the history of television and cinema from the early days of magic lanterns to today's state-of-the-art computer imaging. Small viewing areas let visitors watch clips of historic films. There are permanent exhibits, including a stellar one on Charlie Chaplin, and changing exhibits on everything from *Dr. Who* to cinema fashions. The museum is staffed by actors dressed in costume who will try to talk you into seeing yourself on TV or in the movies—you can see how you do as a newscaster or watch yourself fly over the Thames in a flight simulation. ♦ Admission. Daily. 4012636

27 National Film Theatre Two thousand films a year are screened in three cinemas. ♦ Box office: daily 11:30AM-8:30PM. South Bank (at Waterloo Bridge). 6330274. Tube: Waterloo, Embankment

27 Royal National Theatre Set up under the direction of Sir Laurence Olivier, the **National** has three stages: the **Olivier,** the **Lyttelton,** and the **Cottesloe.** Forty cheap seats (20 on press nights) for both the **Olivier** and the **Lyttelton** are sold at 10AM on performance days. Also, good standby tickets are usually available. Special matinee "platform" shows are highly discounted for students, senior citizens, and groups. Guided backstage tours can be arranged for a nominal fee; inquire at the **Lyttelton** information desk. ♦ Foyers: M-Sa 10AM-11PM. South Bank (at Waterloo Bridge). 6330880. Tube: Waterloo, Embankment

Houses of Parliament

London

28 South Bank Brasserie ★★★$$ Spruce up your tourist garb so you can dine enjoying a marvelous view of London across the Thames. The decor of the upstairs dining room and downstairs brasserie suggests the 1920s colonial era, while the food is a mixture of European and Oriental dishes. ◆ International ◆ Daily lunch and dinner. 56 Upper Ground (Gabriel's Wharf). 6200596. Tube: Waterloo

Studio Six

28 Studio Six ★★$ The cosmopolitan menu plucks items from the Continent and the US and serves them at bargain prices. Try the vegetarian crepes of the day followed by a slice of homemade cheesecake. Go early or late for lunch to avoid the crowds. ◆ International ◆ Daily lunch and dinner. 56 Upper Ground (Gabriel's Wharf). 9286243. Tube: Waterloo

29 Imperial War Museum Fittingly, the museum of 20th-century warfare was founded (while World War I was still in progress) on the site of a mental hospital popularly known as **Bedlam.** There's a genuine Sopwith Camel (World War I fighter plane) and some 10,000 posters and paintings by Stanley Spencer, Paul Nash, and other war artists. The re-created World War I trench is sobering. The museum is within **Geraldine Mary Harmsworth Park.** ◆ Admission; free after 4:30PM. Daily. Lambeth Rd (at Kennington Rd). 4165000. Tube: Elephant and Castle, Lambeth North

30 Westminster Bridge A stroll over the bridge to the north side of the Thames affords splendid views: To the left is **Big Ben** with the **Houses of Parliament** and **St. Thomas' Hospital** stretching behind; on the right, directly ahead, is **Charing Cross Station.** A statue of Celtic queen Boadicea stands where the bridge joins the Embankment. She burned London to the ground in AD 61 as retribution for the rape of her daughters and persecution of her people by the Romans, who were then in power. ◆ Between York Rd and Victoria Embankment. Tube: Waterloo, Westminster

31 Parliament Square The seat of government surrounds this square in magnificently ornate buildings. Unfortunately, traffic tends to overwhelm both the square and its statues of Churchill and Lincoln. ◆ Whitehall and Victoria Sts. Tube: Westminster

32 Houses of Parliament The parliament complex (illustrated on page 92), officially known as the **Palace of Westminster,** is graced by the 336-foot **Victoria Tower** on one side and **Big Ben** on the other. The clock tower, nicknamed for its 13-ton bell, is also called **St. Stephen's Tower** and is more than 130 years old.

The only original part of the palace is the 240-foot-long **Westminster Hall,** which dates from the 11th century. Its beautiful hammer-beam ceiling has lent grandeur to innumerable ceremonies over the centuries. A fire destroyed the rest of the parliament buildings in 1834, but architect **Augustus Pugin** rebuilt the complex in a meticulous, mock-Gothic style. The **House of Commons** is to the north and the **House of Lords** to the south, the former noted for raucous arguments, the latter for equally raucous snores. Visitors are allowed into the public galleries; try the line for the **Lords**—it's the shorter one. ◆ Commons Sessions: M-Th 2:30PM until late; F 9:30AM-3PM. Prime Minister's Question Time: Tu, Th 3:15PM. 219.4272. Lords: M-W 2:30PM; Th 3PM; some Fridays. Bridge and St. Margaret Sts. 219.3107. Tube: Westminster

33 Westminster Abbey British monarchs have been crowned in this sanctuary (pictured below) since William the Conqueror's coronation in 1066. It is almost certain that a church has been on this site since the sixth century, but the present abbey is largely an 11th-century structure, founded by Edward the Confessor and rebuilt during the 13th and 14th centuries. Later additions include the **Henry VII Chapel,** built in the 1500s. The abbey is replete with memorials, including Winston Churchill's (just inside the west door). Buried in **Poets' Corner** are Geoffrey Chaucer, Ben Jonson, Alfred Lord Tennyson, and many others; Lord Byron was refused permission to be buried here because of his lifestyle. ◆ Nave and cloisters: free. Poets' Corner and Royal Chapels: admission; free Wednesday 6-7:45PM. Daily. South side of Parliament Sq. 2225152. Tube: Westminster

Westminster Abbey

London

34 Tate Gallery One of the foremost art collections in the world, comprising 10,000 works, this is a daunting challenge for even the most dedicated museum enthusiast. Displays are changed annually to allow various components of the collection to be rotated from storage to exhibition. You'll find paintings by Constable and Turner, as well as works by Francis Bacon and Frank Auerbach, in a comprehensive collection that spans the spectrum of mostly British art from the 16th through the 20th centuries. From William Blake to Jasper Johns, Rothko to Rodin, this museum (pictured below) will leave you awestruck. ♦ Free; admission for temporary exhibits. M-Sa; Su afternoons. Millbank (at Atterbury St). 8878000. Tube: Pimlico

Within the Tate Gallery:

Coffee Shop ★★$ Those on a budget can come here for salads and wine, or afternoon tea. ♦ Coffee shop ♦ M-Sa breakfast, lunch, and tea; Su lunch and tea. 8878000

Tate Gallery Shop Its prints, posters, postcards, and excellent art book selection are almost as much fun as the museum itself. ♦ M-Sa; Su afternoons. 8878000

35 Elizabeth Hotel $$ Located on one of the many garden squares in London, this comfortable family-run hotel has a loyal following. It's a no-frills place—no restaurant, no TV in the rooms, and only 28 of the 43 rooms have private baths. But a full English breakfast is included in the price, and the hotel is coveniently located midway between **Victoria Station** and **Victoria Coach Station.** ♦ 37 Eccleston Sq (between Belgrave Rd and St. George's Dr). 6286812; fax 8286814. Tube: Victoria

35 Windermere $$ This is a very attractive, very clean hotel with 23 nicely furnished guest rooms (19 have private baths). The breakfast room, where the traditional complimentary breakfast is served, is also a restaurant. Its niceties include fine china and fresh flowers. ♦ 142-44 Warwick Way (between Vauxhall Bridge and Buckingham Palace Rds). 8345163; fax 9766535. Tube: Victoria

36 Alison House Hotel $$ Near **Victoria Station** in the posh Belgravia district stands "the small hotel with the big welcome." The hype is true. There are 12 guest rooms at this family-run enterprise, where sharing a standard double or triple works out to only a couple of pounds more than staying at many hostels—and the location can't be beat. The least expensive rooms share baths; for a little more money, you get your own. There's no restaurant, but a full English breakfast is included in the room rate. ♦ 82 Ebury St (between Elizabeth and Eccleston Sts). 7309529; fax 7305494. Tube: Victoria

37 Sloane Square/Chelsea One of the wealthiest residential areas in London, Chelsea is a maze of small streets with row upon row of white Georgian frontages. At its heart is **Sloane Square,** surrounded by tony restaurants and shops. Slicing through Chelsea is the slightly less upmarket King's Road, once a private path for Charles II that led to **Hampton Court.** This road found fame in the 1960s (Mary Quant opened her first boutique here) and has continued to attract colorful crowds ever since. Pubs and restaurants abound, and the shops are quieter and generally more interesting than in central London. ♦ Sloane St and King's Rd. Tube: Sloane Sq

38 Chelsea Physic Garden A vast and unusual herb collection on three acres of grounds, this is one of Europe's oldest botanical gardens, founded by the Society of Apothecaries in 1673. The first cedars in England were planted here in 1683, and some curious seeds from its stocks changed the face of the American South when cotton was sent there in 1732. ♦ Admission. W 2-5PM; Su 2-6PM April-Oct. 66 Royal Hospital Rd (at Swan Walk and Chelsea Embankment). 3525646. Tube: Sloane Sq

39 Natural History Museum Within this twin-towered Byzantine beauty lies evidence that polar bears once called **Kew Gardens** home, and elephants and lions actually lived at **Trafalgar Square.** *Jurassic Park* fans will want ringside seats to watch the robotic dinosaurs devour each other. At press time the **Natural History Earth Galleries** were undergoing a £12-million redevelopment for a high-tech re-opening. The museum's **Leith's Restaurant** (9389123) features a changing menu with courses such as chicken Provençal and lamb curry. ♦ Admission; free after 4:30PM. Daily. Cromwell Rd (between Exhibition Rd and Queen's Gate). 9389123. Tube: South Kensington

Tate Gallery

London

40 Victoria and Albert Museum Admire alabaster carvings, textiles, modern glass, and antique tapestries at the **V&A**, as the largest decorative arts museum in the world is affectionately called. Queen Victoria laid the buildings' foundations in 1899, but the museum has its roots in the **Great Exhibition of 1851.** Since then the collection has outgrown its original 12 acres to include offbeat branches such as the **Theatre Museum** in **Covent Garden.** You can only "do" the whole museum in a day by going on a guided tour (free) of the museum's highlights. The **Dress Collection** has fashions from the 17th century to the present, and the **Toshiba Gallery of Japanese Art** displays enchanting *netsuke* (ornamental toggles). ♦ Free (donations requested). M afternoons; Tu-Sa. Exhibition and Cromwell Rds. 5896371. Tube: South Kensington

41 Science Museum From the oldest Rolls Royce (1905) to the actual *Apollo 10* capsule, this is a great place to find out the whys, hows, and wherefores of life. Founded in 1847 (though the building dates from 1913), the museum has exhibits on science, industry, technology, and medicine. Florence Nightingale's moccasins, dried human hands, and George Washington's ivory dentures are among the museum's more bizarre items. *Puffing Billy,* the world's oldest surviving locomotive, delights train buffs. The **Launch Pad** is the most popular gallery and features hands-on demonstrations of everyday technology; tickets are required on busy days so check at the gallery entrance before visiting the rest of the museum. ♦ Admission; free after 4:30PM M-Sa. Daily. Imperial College and Exhibition Rds. 9388000. Tube: South Kensington

42 Royal Albert Hall The excellent acoustics make this a favorite performance venue for opera singers and rock stars alike. Tickets are usually expensive. ♦ Kensington Rd (between Exhibition Rd and Queen's Gate). 9302377. Tube: South Kensington

43 Harrods Even though the district of Knightsbridge is a haunt of those with well-padded wallets, and royals do shop here, this department store—where the doormen turn away scruffily (or skimpily) dressed customers—merits a mention in a budget guidebook. In many departments, you can find small, affordable gifts; the green **Harrods** bags that come with a purchase provide a certain je ne sais quoi. ♦ M-Sa; W-F until 7PM. 87-135 Brompton Rd (at Hans Rd). 7301234. Tube: Knightsbridge

44 Hyde Park Henry VIII enclosed this park, which covers 390 acres today, for use as a hunting ground, but James I opened it to the public some 50 years later. **Rotten Row,** running along the south side, is thought to be a corruption of *Route du Roi* (Road of the King). At the northeast point near **Marble Arch** (see page 96), **Speakers' Corner** dates back to 1872 when, following mass demonstrations at the site, right of assembly was granted (for the audience, that is). It's at its liveliest late on Sunday morning, and hecklers are always welcome. ♦ Bounded by Knightsbridge and Bayswater Rds, and Park La and the Serpentine. Tube: Hyde Park Corner, Marble Arch, Lancaster Gate

45 Kensington Gardens This was part of **Hyde Park** until William III enclosed his palace garden. The **Serpentine** streams through both greenswards, though here it's known as the **Long Water.** First opened by George II "for respectably dressed people" on Saturdays only, the gardens welcomed all in 1841, thanks to Queen Victoria. Today, illicit skateboarders and roller skaters fly along the **Broad Walk** trying to outwit the keepers, and young skippers bring their boats to the **Round Pond.** The gardens' **Serpentine Gallery** (4026075) has free exhibitions. ♦ Bounded by Kensington and Bayswater Rds, and the Serpentine and Kensington Palace Gardens. Tube: Queensway, Lancaster Gate, High St Kensington

46 Kensington Palace In 1689, this was a country home (pictured above) for William and Mary because the air here suited the asthmatic king better than the soot-laden atmosphere of central London. Queen Victoria was born within these walls 130 years later, and was proclaimed queen here in 1837. Half of the palace still provides private apartments for modern royals such as Princess Diana and the queen's sister, Princess Margaret. The grandly bedecked and furnished **State Rooms** are open to the public but scheduled to be closed for renovation from autumn 1995 to spring 1997. Early in the 18th century, Queen Anne added the **Orangery,** now the site of a restaurant in summer months. ♦ Admission. Daily. Kensington Palace Gardens (near Palace Ave). 9379561. Tube: Notting Hill Gate, High St Kensington

Restaurants/Clubs: Red **Hotels:** Blue
Shops/ ♥ Outdoors: Green **Sights/Culture:** Black

London

Buckingham Palace

47 Portobello Road Market West London's colorful open-air market is a mile long and packed with ethnic panache. There's loads of junk, but some dedicated rummaging might just turn up a genuine heirloom. ♦ Sa 7AM-5PM. Portobello Rd (between Chepstow Villas and Golborne Rd. Tube: Notting Hill Gate

48 Marble Arch Built in 1827, the Arch, a version of Rome's Arch of Constantine was not meant to stand at the end of Oxford Street. It was originally the gate to **Buckingham Palace** until the facade was redesigned. As a result, the arch was moved close to the former site of the Tyburn Gallows, London's main spot for public executions. Only the royal family and the King's Troop Royal Horse Artillery are allowed to pass through it. ♦ Oxford St and Park La. Tube: Marble Arch

49 Oxford Street The busiest shopping street in London can be a headache if you're not prepared to go elbow to elbow with the crowds. A slew of clothing and department stores (notably **Debenhams** and **John Lewis**) loom large while street vendors at makeshift stalls sell cheap socks and watches until the police shoo them away. Perhaps the most worthwhile stop is **Selfridges** (6291234), at No. 400, which boasts the biggest perfume counter in Europe and a ground-floor food hall to rival London's finest. ♦ Between Charing Cross Rd and Park La. Tube: Marble Arch, Bond St, Oxford Circus, Tottenham Court Rd

---

Mark Twain on family hotels: "They are a London specialty. God has not permitted them to exist elsewhere. The once spacious rooms are split into coops which afford as much discomfort as can be had anywhere out of jail for any money. All the modern inconveniences are furnished, and some that have been obsolete for a century. The prices are astonishingly high for what you get. . . . The rooms are as interesting as the Tower of London, but older I think. Older and dearer, the lift was a gift from William the Conqueror, some of the beds are prehistoric. They represent geologic periods. Mine is the oldest."

---

50 Shepherd Market At the southeastern edge of **Hyde Park,** just northeast of Hyde Park Corner, is a small maze of streets crammed with cafes, restaurants, and boutiques. This area was once the site of the vice-ridden annual May Fair. In 1735, Edward Shepherd obtained a grant from George II to establish a marketplace in its place. To this day the area is known as a red-light district, albeit of a classy persuasion. ♦ Bounded by Piccadilly and Curzon St, and Half Moon St and Park La. Tube: Green Park, Hyde Park Corner

50 Hard Rock Cafe ★★$$ Oddly located at the quieter end of Piccadilly and jammed with pop star memorabilia, this is the original in the chain and a magnet for young people. The menu lists burgers, BLTs, and ribs. Specialty cocktails with names such as Lost Weekend and Ether Bunny keep everyone hopping. ♦ American ♦ Daily lunch and dinner. 150 Old Park La (at Piccadilly). 6290382. Tube: Hyde Park Corner

50 L'Artiste Musclé ★★$ This bistro is like a Left Bank wine bar, complete with sullen French waitresses. A tiny dining room upstairs and a wonderfully bohemian cellar both fill up quickly after 8PM. Try the *boeuf bourguignon* or the salmon steak. ♦ French ♦ M-Sa lunch and dinner; Su dinner. 1 Shepherd Market (off Curzon St). 4936150. Tube: Green Park

51 Green Park Living up to the name, these 60 acres are an oasis in an often gray city. Henry VIII enclosed the park; Charles II built the **Snow House** in the center (now marked by a mound) for cooling royal wine. Rent a deck chair in the spring and watch the daffodils grow. ♦ Bounded by Constitution Hill, Piccadilly, and the Mall. Tube: Green Park

London

52 Buckingham Palace Although most Royals live elsewhere, the queen's London home is "Buck House." In order to subsidize repairs to charred **Windsor Castle** (located outside London), Her Majesty now opens the 19 **State Rooms** in August and September, when visitors can see the inner courtyard of the original building, begun by **John Nash** in 1820 and finished by **Edward Blore**. The famous exterior with the balcony for royal family photo-ops was designed in 1913 by **Sir Aston Webb**. When Queen Victoria took up residence here in 1837, the drains didn't work, the bathrooms weren't ventilated, and many of the 600 doors and 1,000 windows wouldn't open and shut. But six years and countless repairs later, the queen wrote in her diary about how happy she was there (though, to look at her face on the **Queen Victoria Memorial** out front, you would never know it). The Changing of the Guard takes place in the front court (illustrated on page 96), and when the Queen is in residence, the Royal Standard flies overhead. Besides the foot soldiers, there are soldiers on horseback. Their changing of the guard takes place along the street called Horseguards Parade on Monday through Saturday at 11AM, and on Sunday at 10AM.
♦ Palace: admission; Changing of the Guard: free. Palace: daily Aug-Sept; changing of the Guard: 11:30AM, alternate days throughout the year. Buckingham Palace Rd (at Victoria Memorial). Tube: Charing Cross, Westminster

Within Buckingham Palace:

Queen's Gallery To the left of the gates is the only part of the palace that's open all year. Once the site of a conservatory and then a palace chapel (later bombed), this treasure-filled gallery was built in 1962. Changing exhibitions display the many works of art by the old masters from the queen's collection.
♦ Admission. Daily. Buckingham Palace Rd and Buckingham Gate. 7992331. Tube: Victoria

Royal Mews A sumptuous array of harnesses and other royal trappings are on show at the stables and coach house here, built by **John Nash** in about 1826. The ornate State Coach, acquired in 1762 by George III, carried Queen Elizabeth to **St. Paul's** during the **1977 Silver Jubilee**. ♦ Admission. Daily afternoons Apr-Aug; M-W, Th afternoons Sept; W afternoons Oct-Mar. Lower Grosvenor Pl and Buckingham Palace Rd. Tube: Victoria

53 St. James's Park Despite an ignominious beginning—this was a marshland where female lepers from St. James Hospice kept pigs in the 1200s—these lawns are now one of the prettiest parks in London, complete with a lake, fountains, ducks, and swans. Henry VIII turned the hospice into a hunting lodge and drained the marsh to create a bowling green and jousting field; the flamboyant Charles II turned it into London's first royal park. A century and a half later, **John Nash** softened the park's French formality. ♦ Bounded by Birdcage Walk and the Mall, and Horse Guards and Buckingham Palace Rds. Tube: St. James's Park

54 Whitehall Now the governmental thoroughfare, **Whitehall** once formed a vital link between Westminster and the City of London. At its heart stands the **Cenotaph**, where poppies are placed in remembrance of the war dead every November. Facing **Trafalgar Square**, keep an eye on Downing Street for important personages coming in and out of **Number 10**, the home of prime ministers since 1732. Farther along to the right is the 1622 **Banqueting House** (9304179) built by **Inigo Jones**. Rubens painted the ceiling frescoes in 1630 to honor the House of Stuart; Charles I, alas, was beheaded here in 1649. Behind the **Horse Guards Building** is where the Trooping the Colour ceremony takes place, marking the queen's official birthday in June.
♦ Banqueting House: admission. Banqueting House: M-Sa. Between Parliament and Trafalgar Sqs. Tube: Charing Cross, Westminster

55 Trafalgar Square The 185-foot-high **Nelson's Column** (illustrated below) dominates the square, which was leveled in 1830 to erect this tribute to Admiral Horatio Nelson, the hero of the Battle of Trafalgar against Napoleon in 1805, in which Nelson was killed. Sir Edwin Henry Landseer's serene lions were added to the base of the column in 1868. A statue of Charles I looks down **Whitehall** toward the **Old Admiralty**, headquarters of the Royal Navy; the best view of the square is from the **National Gallery**'s front balcony.
♦ Pall Mall East and Whitehall. Tube: Charing Cross, Embankment

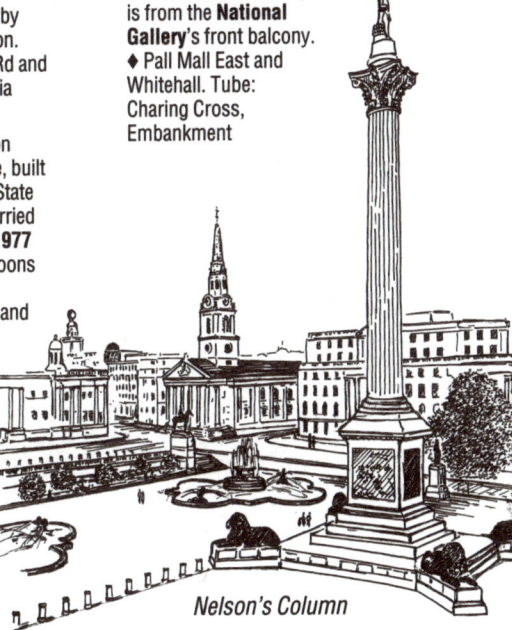

Nelson's Column

London

THE NATIONAL GALLERY

56 National Gallery This sterling art collection began in 1824, when Parliament bought 38 pictures from one of the City of London's merchant bankers. Today, though the number of works remains relatively small (about 2,200), the museum contains many of the world's best-known paintings from the 13th through the early 20th centuries. On view are Rembrandt's *Self-Portrait at 63* and Monet's *Bathers at Grenouillère*, as well as lesser-known pieces, such as Paul de la Roche's *Execution of Lady Jane Grey in the Tower of London, 1554*. Some of the rooms are in the process of being restored. ♦ Free. M-Sa; Su afternoons. Pall Mall E (Trafalgar Sq). 3891785, 8393526. Tube: Charing Cross

56 National Portrait Gallery Founded in 1856 "with the aim of collecting likenesses of famous British men and women," the gallery displays portraits from the Middle Ages to the present day. Here are the Brontë sisters painted by brother Branwell and feisty old Oliver Cromwell by Samuel Cooper. ♦ Free; admission for temporary exhibits. M-Sa; Su afternoons. 2 St. Martin's Pl (at Trafalgar Sq). 3060055. Tube: Charing Cross

57 St. Martin-in-the-Fields In 1726, **Sir Christopher Wren**'s disciple, **James Gibb**, finished re-creating this church from an earlier one on the site; the steeple was added in 1824. The interior is light and airy, with a lovely ceiling of Italian plasterwork; the exterior inspired numerous imitations in the American colonies. Lunchtime concerts are a respite from the city's hustle and bustle.

♦ Lunchtime concerts: M-W, F 1:05-2:00 PM; evening concerts: Th-Sa 7:30-9:30PM. Trafalgar Sq and Duncannon St. 9300089. Tube: Charing Cross

Within St. Martin-in-the-Fields:

Cafe in the Crypt ★★$ In this warm, dark haven, classical music and the smell of wholesome food fill the air. Try the spinach and cheese pancakes or the celery soup. Nell Gwynne, the mistress of Charles II, is buried "somewhere near the freezer." ♦ Cafe ♦ Daily lunch, dinner, and snacks. 8394342

Brass Rubbing Center Rub out a knight or two from facsimile medieval brasses or buy one ready-made. ♦ M-Sa; Su afternoons. 9309306

58 Cranks ★★$ Hungry vegetarians swarm into this place—one of seven sites—for the Combination Savoury Platter: two of the day's hot dishes plus salad and dessert for a very reasonable price. The take-out menu includes baked potatoes and other meatless treats. ♦ Vegetarian ♦ M-Sa breakfast, lunch, and dinner; Su lunch and early dinner. 8 Adelaide St (off the Strand). 8360660. Tube: Charing Cross. Also at: Unit 11, the Piazza. 3796508. Tube: Covent Garden. 17-19 Great Newport St. 8365226. Tube: Leicester Sq

THE STOCKPOT

59 The Stockpot ★★$ Some call the atmosphere animated, others call it loud, but for years this chain of restaurants has been the salvation of hungry students and anyone looking for a generous, flavorful, and cheap meal. Choose spaghetti bolognese, chicken casserole, or a zesty Spanish omelette. ♦ Continental ♦ M-Sa breakfast, lunch, and dinner; Su lunch and dinner. No credit cards accepted. 40 Panton St (off Charing Cross Rd). 8395142. Tube: Leicester Sq

National Gallery

London

60 Prince Charles Cinema A bargain for moviegoers, this theater usually sells tickets for less than two pounds. ♦ Daily. Leicester Pl (off Leicester Sq). 4378181. Tube: Leicester Sq

61 Piccadilly Circus The London counterpart of New York City's Times Square has more neon but much fewer New Year's Eve crowds (they gather in **Trafalgar Square**). The centerpiece here is the 1893 statue of Eros, designed and constructed by **Alfred Gilbert** to commemorate the philanthropic seventh Earl of Shaftesbury. ♦ Intersection of Shaftesbury Ave, Regent St, and Piccadilly. Tube: Piccadilly Circus

62 St. James's, Piccadilly Consecrated in 1684, this small church was designed by **Sir Christopher Wren.** Poet/artist William Blake was baptized here. Although severely damaged during World War II, its modern, vaulted interior illuminates the elaborate wooden carving around the altar. ♦ 197 Piccadilly (at Church Pl). 7344511. Tube: Piccadilly Circus

Within St. James's Church:

Piccadilly Market An assemblage of crafts, old maps, and tourist junk is on sale twice a week in the church's courtyard. Woolens and jewelry are plentiful and a stamp block stall features an amazing array of designs. ♦ F-Sa. Piccadilly (at Jermyn St). Tube: Piccadilly Circus

62 The Wren Wholefood Vegetarian Cafe ★$ Owned and run by **St. James's Church,** this bright cafe offers quiche, baked potatoes, chili, and bean casseroles. An attitude of environmental concern prevails among those sipping the herbal and specialty teas. ♦ Vegetarian ♦ M-Sa breakfast, lunch, and dinner; Su lunch and tea. 35 Jermyn St (at Church Pl). 4379419. Tube: Piccadilly Circus

FORTNUM & MASON

63 Fortnum & Mason Food glorious food. Food shops do not get more upscale than this. If you can afford nothing else, buy the tea so you can display the label on your kitchen shelf. Be sure to stop in at its **Fountain Restaurant** for afternoon tea. ♦ M-Sa. 181 Piccadilly (at Duke St). 7348040. Tube: Green Park

64 Museum of Mankind One of the least-known museums in London, this is the place to explore world cultures. Riveting artifacts include everything from a Zulu warrior's shield to a New Guinea magical mask. Ask about video shows, workshops, and changing exhibitions. ♦ Free. M-Sa; Su afternoons. 6 Burlington Gardens (at Burlington Arcade). 4372224. Tube: Green Park, Piccadilly Circus

65 Regent Street Pleasant for walking and lacking the crowds of neighboring Oxford Street, Regent Street was designed by **John Nash** and completed in 1820. "The most famous shopping street in the world" was also the first London street ever to be planned and then actually built. However, the modern-day version differs significantly from **Nash**'s original design. ♦ Between Piccadilly and Oxford Circuses. Tube: Piccadilly Circus, Oxford Circus

66 Liberty Though expensive, this respected store sometimes offers bargain-priced designer fabrics. In any case, it is worth going to the top-floor gallery of the Tudor building to see the carved balustrades, linenfold paneling, and oak staircases. ♦ M-Sa; Th until 7:30PM. 210-220 Regent St (at Great Marlborough St). 7341234. Tube: Oxford Circus

66 Hamley's Several floors of delightful children's toys attract such throngs during the Christmas season that one-way lanes are established in the store's narrow aisles. ♦ M-W; Th until 8PM; F-Sa until 7PM; Su afternoons. 188 Regent St (at Great Marlborough St). 7343161. Tube: Oxford Circus

67 Carnaby Street During the 1960s, Carnaby's shops were Hippie Central, with bell-bottoms and psychedelic patterns by the score. Today the adjoining "West Soho" streets have funky fashions and the street itself is laden with tourist kitsch and horrendously expensive leather goods. ♦ Between Foubert's Pl and Beak St. Tube: Oxford Circus

68 Wallace Collection A charming late–19th-century town house displays a permanent collection of paintings by Canaletto, Gainsborough, and Reynolds. ♦ Free. M-Sa; Su afternoons. Manchester Sq (north of Wigmore St, between Marylebone and Baker Sts). 9350687. Tube: Marble Arch, Bond St

---

An everyday reminder of the Great Plague of 1665 is the children's singing game "ring-around-the-rosy," which refers to the inflamed roselike blotches on the skin caused by the disease, while "a pocket full of posies" were bouquets carried to smother the stench of the dead and dying. Another legacy of the Black Death is the phrase "in the dead of night"—the only time it was permissible to bury victims.

Clink Street is named after a squalid prison in Southwark owned by the bishops of Winchester. Destroyed in 1780, its name has been immortalized by the word *clink*, slang for jail.

London

69 Madame Tussaud's You'll either love it or hate it, and if you don't want to spend half a day in line, forget it. The latest themed areas to show off the famous waxed figures include Hollywood legends and a time-taxi ride which re-creates 400 years of London's historical milestones. The adjoining **Planetarium** has been revamped. ♦ Admission. Daily. Marylebone Rd and Allsop Pl. 9356861. Tube: Baker St

70 Regent's Park In the early 19th century, an environmentally aware Prince Regent refrained from putting houses on the 500 acres here. Instead, beautiful stuccoed and columned terraces, designed by **John Nash,** surround the park and make it look like a gigantic wedding cake. It is home to the romantic **Queen Mary's Garden** (best seen between June and September), a small lake, and the **Open Air Theatre,** a splendid summer venue for Shakespeare. ♦ Bounded by Outer Circle (just north of Marylebone Rd). Tube: Regent's Park, Baker St, Camden Town, Great Portland St

71 London Zoo Spread over 36 acres, this is the world's oldest and most celebrated zoological garden, created in 1828. Most of the 8,000 animals roam in settings similar to their natural habitats—separated from the public by moats. Take in the *Meet the Animals* shows. The canal to the north is great for boat rides to **Little Venice** or **Camden Lock** (see below). ♦ Admission. Daily. Outer Circle (near Avenue Rd). 7223333. Tube: Camden Town, Regent's Park, Mornington Crescent

72 Hampstead Heath Cobbled lanes thread the stylish borough of Hampstead, dotted with bakeries, bistros, and antiquarian bookstores. Grand Georgian homes stand beside the modern digs of the rich and famous, who are drawn here as were their predecessors, such as Lord Byron, John Constable, Anna Pavlova, and George Orwell. Come to soak in the arty ambience and to walk or jog in the **Heath,** which consists of 802 preserved acres of grassland and woodland containing 100 species of birds as well as bathing ponds and the 319-foot **Parliament Hill.** ♦ Bounded by E Heath Rd and Hampstead La, and Highgate West Hill and Spaniards Rd. Tube: Hampstead

72 Hampstead Heath Youth Hostel $ Seekers of tranquillity find a sanctuary in this 200-bed **YHA** lodge, located just northwest of **Hampstead Heath.** The interior of the timber-framed hostel has been completely refurbished and modernized; it has a full cafeteria along with the usual amenities. All accommodations are dorm-style, all bathrooms are communal. ♦ 4 Wellgarth Rd (at North End Rd). 0181/4589054 and 4587196; fax 0181/2090546. Tube: Golders Green.

72 Keats' House The house where John Keats lived from 1818 to 1820 is lined with his letters, manuscripts, books, and other memorabilia. In the garden, he composed "Ode to a Nightingale." ♦ Free. M-F; Sa-Su afternoons Apr-Oct; daily afternoons Nov-Mar. Keats Grove (off South End Rd). 4352062. Tube: Hampstead

72 Sandringham $$ An American couple runs this lovely bed-and-breakfast establishment in the heart of trendy Hampstead. Some of the 15 rooms have private baths. Ask for a room with a view—either of the city or the adjacent greenery of **Hampstead Heath.** ♦ 3 Holford Rd (at East Heath Road). 4351569; fax 4315932. Tube: Hampstead

73 Camden Lock Market During the week, this market has some shops with crafts—handmade furniture, baskets, rugs, pottery, an abundance of small gift items, and the occasional New Age crystal. On weekends, when the tourists stream in, the market adds lots of stalls and vendors shift into high kitsch gear. ♦ Daily. Camden Lock Pl (at Camden High St). 2842084. Tube: Camden Town

74 International Students House (ISH) $ The **ISH**'s three residence halls, used mainly by students at the nearby **University College of London** and the **Polytechnic of Central London,** are basic accommodations enhanced by a licensed bar, restaurant, pool, launderette, currency-exchange facilities, and theater-booking service. There are more than 400 accommodations, including singles, twins, and dorms; no private baths, however. It's a short walk to **Regent's Park** and around 10 minutes to Oxford Street. Book early; beds are most often available during the Easter break or summer vacation. ♦ 229 Great Portland St (at Park Crescent). 6318300; fax 6318315. Tube: Great Portland St, Regent's Park, Warren St

---

Restaurants/Clubs: Red **Hotels:** Blue
Shops/ ♦ Outdoors: Green **Sights/Culture:** Black

London

75 London School of Economics Halls $ During summer vacation and the five-week Easter break, the four residence halls here become convenient, inexpensive lodging for travelers. The 148 rooms at **Passfield Hall,** for instance, are simple, with 28 communal bathrooms but the location—a few minutes' walk from **Euston Station**—is terrific. The price includes breakfast, but you can cook for yourself. Reserve well ahead of time. For information on the three other residences, call 3877743. ♦ 1 Endlseigh Pl (at Gordon St). 3873584; fax 3870419. Tube: Euston

76 Mabledon Court $$ Once a college dormitory, this charming hotel has 32 comfortable (but small) rooms, all with private baths. There's no restaurant, but a lounge is available to guests, and complimentary English breakfast is served in the dining room. ♦ 10 Mabledon Pl (off Euston Rd). 3883866; fax 3875686. Tube: Euston, King's Cross, Russell Sq

77 Jenkins Hotel $$ Guests feel as though they've wandered into a country inn at this cozy little bed-and-breakfast spot, but one with all the modern conveniences. Each of the 15 guest rooms has its own mini-refrigerator, and seven have private baths. The rooms don't, however, have TVs. And there's no restaurant, but breakfast is included. ♦ 45 Cartwright Gardens (at Mabledon Pl). 3872067; fax 3833139. Tube: Euston, King's Cross, Russell Sq

77 Central Club Hotel (YWCA) $ Clean and well located, the newly refurbished lodgings here are economical, particularly if you stay in a multibed or twin-bed room. Most of the 106 rooms have a TV, radio, and telephone; none has a private bath. You can opt for room only, room and breakfast, or half board. There are family rooms available, and discounts for students. Amenities include a launderette and a coffee shop. ♦ 16-22 Great Russell St (at Adeline Pl). Tube: Tottenham Court Rd. 6367512; fax 6365278

78 British Museum Established in 1753, the largest museum in Britain is without doubt one of the greatest museums in the world. Housed in a building designed by **Robert Smirke** in 1823 (illustrated below), its permanent collection comprises some four million objects from around the globe, ranging from flint axes to the Elgin Marbles—and that's not including the manuscripts and maps of the **British Library.** Everyone finds a favorite display, whether it's the majestic stone-sculpted pharaohs of Egypt or the beautiful golden torques in the Celtic collection. The library's treasures are innumerable: a *Gutenberg Bible,* the intricate, illuminated manuscripts of the *Lindisfarne Gospels,* a 15th-century *Canterbury Tales,* a first folio by William Shakespeare, and a collection of the original scrawl of Charles Dickens. Ask about free lectures and gallery talks at the main information desk. The museum's cafeteria is expensive, but the two gift shops are definitely worth your while. ♦ Free. M-Sa; Su afternoons. Great Russell St (between Montague and Gower Sts). 5801788. Tube: Tottenham Court Rd, Holborn, Russell Sq

79 Astor Museum Inn Hostel $ Stay here for access to the **British Museum, Covent Garden,** Oxford Circus, and Camden, but be prepared to part with your privacy. Most rooms have between five and 11 beds, though one triple and two double rooms are available at a slightly higher rate (book in advance). Prices depend on the room size and include breakfast and linens. Although all rooms have sinks, a mere four showers and baths must suffice for up to 60 guests. This place is definitely not quiet, but the staff is young and friendly. ♦ 27 Montague St (at Great Russell St). 5805360. Tube: Tottenham Court Rd, Russell Sq.

British Museum

London

79 St. Margaret's Hotel $$ Friendly and quiet for central London, this small hotel is owned by the Duke of Bedford and has been managed by the same Italian family for 40 years. Although some of the 64 rooms are cramped, they are pristine and come with TVs and phones. Rates include a full English breakfast, and the best value is when two people share a room. If you want one of the 10 rooms with private bath, book in advance and be prepared to pay extra. No credit cards accepted. ♦ 26 Bedford Pl (at Great Russell St). 6364277; fax 6363200. Tube: Russell Sq

80 Rock and Sole Plaice ★★$ Considered one of London's finest fish-and-chips joints, this place is clean, inexpensive, and rather small. Eat outside when the weather is fine. ♦ Fish and chips ♦ M-Sa lunch and dinner. 47 Endell St (at Shorts Gardens). 8363785. Tube: Covent Garden

80 Food for Thought ★$ This health-food restaurant caters to gourmands on a budget. The changing menu always has soup, three salads, a stir-fry, casserole, or hot bake. Look for the Scrunch dessert—a thick, oaty base that's topped with fruit, yogurt, and honey. ♦ Vegetarian ♦ M-Sa breakfast, lunch, and dinner; Su lunch and dinner. 31 Neal St (at Shorts Gardens). 8360239. Tube: Covent Garden

At least six big, black—and usually temperamental—ravens have called the Tower of London home since the 17th century. Legend has it that if the ravens leave the Tower, England will fall. To ensure against this eventuality, the ravens' wings get clipped. Understandably frustrated, the birds have been known to let a peck or two fly at unsuspecting tourists. The oldest Tower Raven, James Crow, lived to the age of 44.

The word "cockney" is derived from *cokeney*, the Old English word for a cock's egg—that is, a misshapen egg. It also meant an effeminate or simple person.

81 The Tea House Here you'll find everything for teatime, from bobby-shaped teapots to the drink itself in a wealth of fine flavors and styles. ♦ M-Sa; Su afternoons. 15 Neal St (at Long Acre). 2407539. Tube: Covent Garden, Tottenham Court Rd

81 Flip You won't find clothes in mint condition, but there are endless racks of secondhand shirts, trousers, and coats. This is the place to look for a bargain-priced leather jacket or coat. American style, country casual, cowboy chic, and fashion fun, including some evening wear—you'll find it all here. ♦ M-W, F; Th until 8PM; Su afternoons. 125 Long Acre (at Neal St). 8364688. Tube: Covent Garden

82 Bunjies This roots/folk/country music venue has a solid repertoire of singer/songwriters. Performances usually start at 8PM and the door charge is affordable. ♦ Admission. M-Sa from 8PM. 27 Litchfield St (at Charing Cross Rd). Tube: Leicester Sq. 2401796

ROYAL OPERA HOUSE

83 Royal Opera House Home to both the world-famous **Royal Opera** and the **Royal Ballet**, this has been London's main venue for international opera for more than a century. Students and senior citizens can buy low-price standbys from the foyer box office 1.5 hours before curtain time, and students may attend the popular discounted Saturday specials. Otherwise, cheap restricted-view seats are available, albeit in the vertigo-producing balconies. ♦ Box office: M-Sa 10AM-8PM. 48 Floral St (at Bow St). 3044000. Standby tickets: 8366903. Tube: Covent Garden

83 Covent Garden A 13th-century abbey in Westminster grew fruits and vegetables in the garden here, and a market was established in the 1700s. But in 1974, the garden moved south of the Thames because of overcrowding. Now high-quality, expensive crafts are sold in the covered market and adjacent streets, so come to look even if you can't afford to shop. Street performers are licensed to set up here, so there's always something going on—it could be a steel band, a puppet show, or a classical violin concert. There are numerous restaurants surrounding the market. Be forewarned: Things get extremely crowded on Friday nights and summer weekends. ♦ Daily. Long Acre and Drury La. Tube: Covent Garden

102

London

Within Covent Garden:

Market Cafe ★$$ At the west end of the square, the terrace and outside tables of this little cafe afford a fine view and great people watching. The fare consists of stone-baked pizzas, affordable crepes, and the like.
♦ French/Italian ♦ Daily lunch and dinner. 8362137

84 Museum of London This collection gives first-time visitors a helpful overview of the metropolis, from the prehistoric to the present. Permanent exhibits include the lord mayor's gilt coach, as it looked in 1757, and an 18th-century prison cell. ♦ Admission. Tu-Sa; Su afternoons. Aldersgate St and London Wall. 6003699. Tube: Barbican, St. Paul's, Moorgate

85 Barbican Centre The 1960s-designed/1980s-built **Barbican** serves as a cultural oasis in the workaday City of London. Both the main theater and the more intimate "Pit" are the London venues of the **Royal Shakespeare Company,** and the **London Symphony Orchestra** performs regularly in the wood-paneled concert hall. Good standby and student tickets are sold: for the theater, from 9AM on the day of the performance; for concerts, shortly before performances. There are also two cinemas, two art galleries, free foyer exhibitions, and free live music ranging from Bach to the Basin Street Blues. Two sandwich bars open before performances, and there are several cafes. ♦ Daily until 11PM. Box office: daily until 8PM. Silk St (near London Wall). Box office 6388891, general inquiries 6384141. Tube: Barbican

86 Petticoat Lane Clothes dealers traded petticoats and other apparel here in the 17th century. In Victorian times, when Jewish traders joined the Spanish, Italian, French, and Portuguese immigrants already working here, the market became London's largest, covering three miles with shops and stalls, over half of which sold clothes. Christians who were opposed to trading on Sundays drove through the market in fire engines to proclaim their discontent, but Parliament legalized the operation in 1936. Today, fame has upped the prices, but the East End traders still put on an amusing show. An adjoining market in Wentworth Street market sells food and clothes. ♦ Petticoat Lane: Su 9AM-2PM. Wentworth St: M-F 10AM-2PM. Bounded by Whitechapel High St, Bishopsgate, and Aldgate High St. Tube: Aldgate, Liverpool St

> "On rare days at home, the Queen is still surrounded at all times—by the famous corgis . . . and servants invariably know the royal whereabouts by the noise of at least nine sets of paws pattering along the palace floors."
>
> *The Western Mail*, 9 August 1993

Bests

Elaine Robertson
Travel Editor, *Cosmopolitan*

Bus for sightseeing: No. 12 runs from **Notting Hill Gate** to **Dulwich.** Get a top deck view of **Piccadilly Circus, Trafalgar Square, Whitehall, Houses of Parliament, Westminster Bridge.**

Cinema: Warner West End. Twelve screens in the heart of theaterland. Late shows on weekends. Lots of fun places to eat before or after.

Fish and chips: Best eaten from a newspaper (the traditional wrapping) with lots of vinegar on a cold night. A real taste of England.

Free entertainment: The Changing of the Guard, **Buckingham Palace.**

Listings magazine: *Time Out*. Every Wednesday. Packed with info on art, clubs, comedy, the gay scene, dance, film, music, theater. If it's not in *Time Out*, it's not happening.

Raincoats: If you've arrived in rainy England raincoat-less, splash out on a classic **Burberry.**

Store: Has to be **Harrods**. If it's good enough for our dear queen. . . . If money's tight, just go and stare—the food hall is fabulous.

Victoria Coleman
Tourist Guide

Shepherd Market in **Mayfair.**

Riding the top deck of the red buses for a different viewpoint.

Royal Festival Hall (in the **South Bank Centre**) at lunchtime. Take your own food and listen to the foyer concerts.

The bench outside the **Wallace Collection.**

The top of Primrose Hill in **Regent's Park:** great view across the **London Zoo** aviary to the **West End.**

Lucinda Boyle
Manager, Travellers Bookstore

Notting Hill Carnival in August.

Swimming in the **Serpentine.**

Kenwood House at **Hampstead Heath** for open-air concerts in the summer.

Richmond Park for a walk in the autumn.

Highgate Cemetery. Fascinating history.

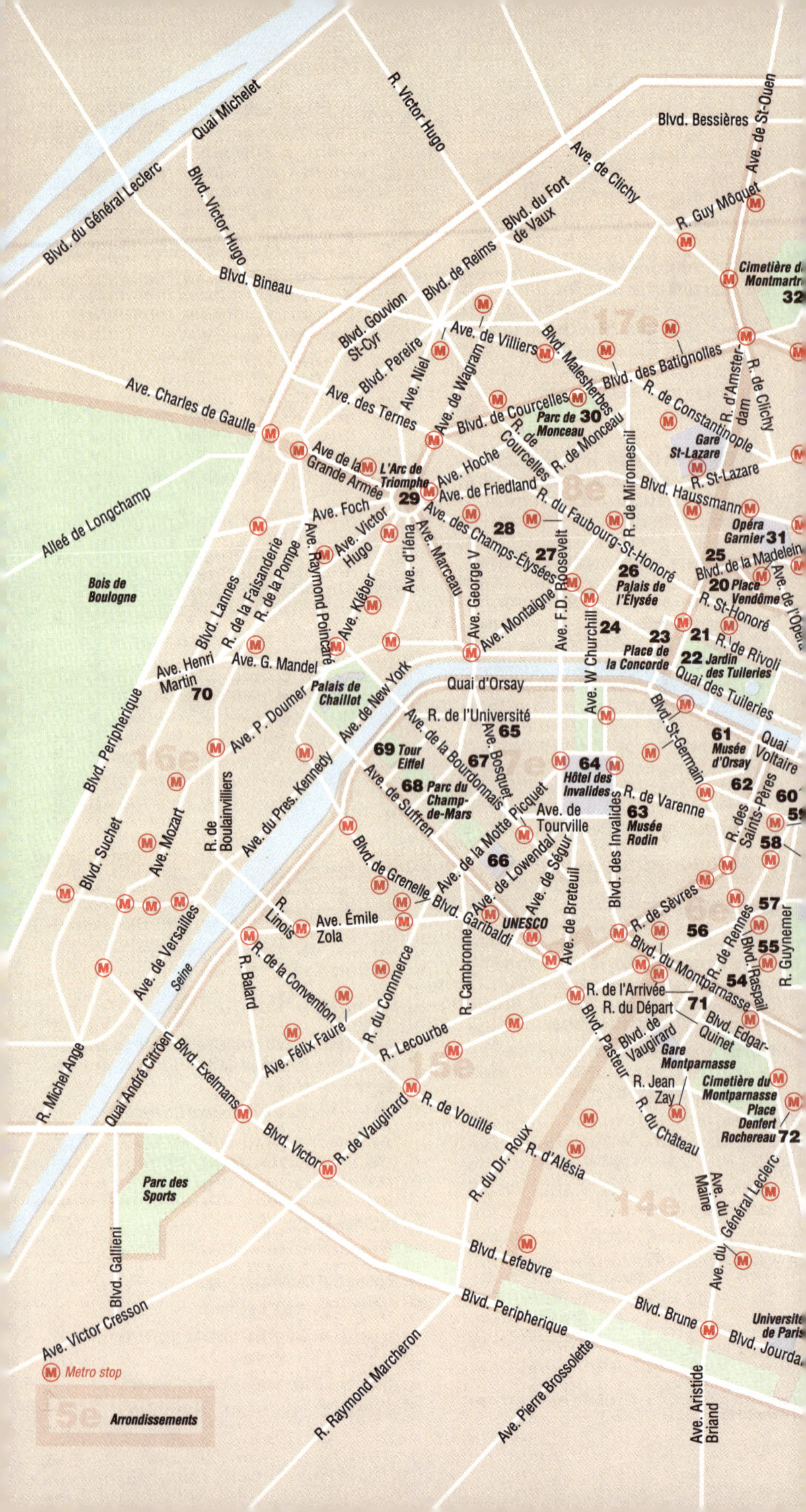
R. Victor Hugo
Quai Michelet
Blvd. du Général Leclerc
Blvd. Victor Hugo
Blvd. Bineau
Blvd. Bessières
Ave. de St-Ouen
Ave. de Clichy
R. Guy Môquet
Blvd. du Fort de Vaux
Blvd. de Reims
Cimetière de Montmartre
32
Blvd. Gouvion St-Cyr
Ave. de Villiers
Blvd. Malesherbes
17e
Blvd. des Batignolles
R. d'Amsterdam
R. de Clichy
Blvd. Pereire
Ave. Niel
Ave. de Wagram
Ave. des Ternes
Blvd. de Courcelles
Parc de Monceau
30
R. de Constantinople
Ave. Charles de Gaulle
R. de Courcelles
R. de Monceau
Gare St-Lazare
R. St-Lazare
Ave de la Grande Armée
L'Arc de Triomphe
29
Ave. Hoche
Ave. de Friedland
8e
R. de Miromesnil
Blvd. Haussmann
Allée de Longchamp
Ave. Foch
Ave. Victor Hugo
Ave. d'Iéna
Ave. Marceau
Ave. des Champs-Élysées
28
R. du Faubourg-St-Honoré
Opéra Garnier
31
27
R. F.D. Roosevelt
25
Blvd. de la Madeleine
Ave. de l'Opéra
Bois de Boulogne
Blvd. Lannes
R. de la Faisanderie
R. de la Pompe
Ave. Raymond Poincaré
Ave. Kléber
Ave. George V
26
Palais de l'Élysée
20
Place Vendôme
R. St-Honoré
Ave. Montaigne
Ave. F.D. Roosevelt
24
23
Place de la Concorde
21
R. de Rivoli
22
Jardin des Tuileries
Ave. Henri Martin
70
Ave. G. Mandel
Palais de Chaillot
Ave. de New York
Quai d'Orsay
Ave. W Churchill
Quai des Tuileries
Blvd. Periphérique
Ave. P. Doumer
R. de l'Université
Ave. de la Bourdonnais
Ave. Bosquet
65
Blvd. St-Germain
61
Musée d'Orsay
Quai Voltaire
16e
69
Tour Eiffel
67
7e
64
Hôtel des Invalides
Ave. du Pres. Kennedy
68
Parc du Champ-de-Mars
Ave. de Suffren
R. de Varenne
62
60
R. de Boulainvilliers
Ave. de la Motte Picquet
Ave. de Tourville
63
Musée Rodin
R. des Saints-Pères
58
59
Blvd. Suchet
Ave. Mozart
Blvd. de Grenelle
Ave. de Lowendal
Ave. de Ségur
66
Blvd. des Invalides
R. de Sèvres
6e
57
Blvd. Garibaldi
UNESCO
Ave. de Breteuil
R. Linois
Ave. Émile Zola
56
R. de Rennes
Blvd. Raspail
55
R. Guynemer
Ave. de Versailles
Seine
R. Balard
R. de la Convention
R. du Commerce
R. Cambronne
Blvd. du Montparnasse
54
R. de l'Arrivée
R. du Départ
71
Blvd. Edgar-Quinet
Blvd. Pasteur
Blvd. de Vaugirard
Gare Montparnasse
Ave. Félix Faure
R. Lecourbe
R. Michel Ange
Quai André Citroën
Blvd. Exelmans
15e
R. Jean Zay
Cimetière du Montparnasse
Place Denfert Rochereau
72
R. de Vaugirard
R. de Vouillé
R. du Château
Blvd. Victor
R. d'Alésia
R. du Dr. Roux
Ave. du Maine
Ave. du Général Leclerc
Parc des Sports
14e
Blvd. Gallieni
Blvd. Lefebvre
Blvd. Periphérique
Blvd. Brune
Université de Paris
Blvd. Jourda.
Ave. Victor Cresson
R. Raymond Marcheron
Ave. Pierre Brossolette
Ave. Aristide Briand
Metro stop
5e Arrondissements

Paris Map

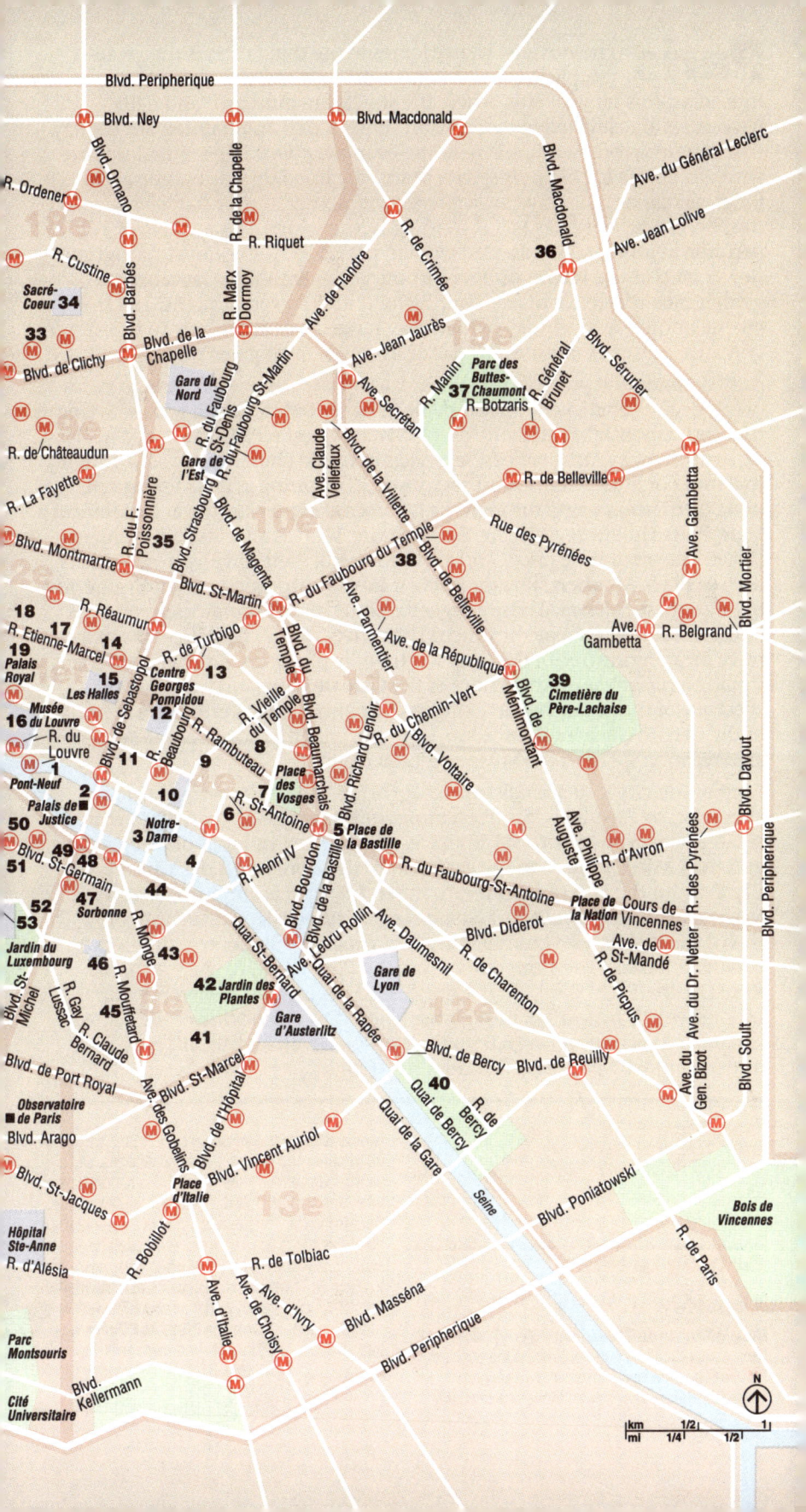

Boulevards and Streets:

- Blvd. Peripherique
- Blvd. Ney
- Blvd. Macdonald
- Ave. du Général Leclerc
- R. Ordener
- Blvd. Ornano
- R. de la Chapelle
- Ave. Jean Lolive
- R. Custine
- R. Riquet
- R. de Crimée
- Sacré-Coeur 34
- R. Marx Dormoy
- Ave. de Flandre
- Blvd. Barbès
- Blvd. de la Chapelle
- Ave. Jean Jaurès
- Blvd. Sérurier
- Blvd. de Clichy
- Gare du Nord
- R. du Faubourg St-Denis
- R. du Faubourg St-Martin
- Ave. Secrétan
- R. Manin
- Parc des Buttes-Chaumont
- R. Botzaris
- Blvd. Général Brunet
- R. de Châteaudun
- Gare de l'Est
- Ave. Claude Vellefaux
- Blvd. de la Villette
- R. de Belleville
- Ave. Gambetta
- R. La Fayette
- Blvd. de Strasbourg
- Blvd. de Magenta
- Rue des Pyrénées
- Blvd. Montmartre
- R. du F. Poissonnière
- Blvd. St-Martin
- R. du Faubourg du Temple
- Blvd. de Belleville
- Blvd. Mortier
- R. Réaumur
- Blvd. du Temple
- Ave. Parmentier
- Ave. de la République
- Ave. Gambetta
- R. Belgrand
- R. Etienne-Marcel
- R. de Turbigo
- Palais Royal
- Les Halles
- Centre Georges Pompidou
- R. Vieille du Temple
- Blvd. Beaumarchais
- Blvd. Richard Lenoir
- R. du Chemin-Vert
- Blvd. de Ménilmontant
- Cimetière du Père-Lachaise
- Musée du Louvre
- R. Rambuteau
- R. du Louvre
- Blvd. de Sébastopol
- R. Beaubourg
- Place des Vosges
- Blvd. Voltaire
- Pont-Neuf
- R. St-Antoine
- Place de la Bastille
- Palais de Justice
- Notre-Dame
- R. Henri IV
- R. du Faubourg St-Antoine
- Ave. Philippe Auguste
- R. d'Avron
- Ave. des Pyrénées
- Blvd. Davout
- Blvd. St-Germain
- Blvd. Bourdon
- Blvd. de la Bastille
- Ave. Ledru Rollin
- Ave. Daumesnil
- Place de la Nation
- Cours de Vincennes
- Sorbonne
- R. Monge
- Quai St-Bernard
- Quai de la Rapée
- Blvd. Diderot
- Ave. de St-Mandé
- Jardin du Luxembourg
- R. Mouffetard
- Jardin des Plantes
- Gare de Lyon
- R. de Charenton
- Ave. du Dr. Netter
- Ave. de Picpus
- Blvd. St-Michel
- R. Gay Lussac
- R. Claude Bernard
- Gare d'Austerlitz
- Blvd. de Bercy
- Blvd. de Reuilly
- Ave. du Gen. Bizot
- Blvd. Soult
- Blvd. de Port Royal
- Ave. des Gobelins
- Blvd. St-Marcel
- Blvd. de l'Hôpital
- Observatoire de Paris
- Blvd. Arago
- Blvd. Vincent Auriol
- Quai de Bercy
- Quai de la Gare
- Hôpital Ste-Anne
- R. d'Alésia
- Blvd. St-Jacques
- Place d'Italie
- Blvd. Poniatowski
- Bois de Vincennes
- R. Bobillot
- R. de Tolbiac
- R. de Paris
- Parc Montsouris
- Ave. d'Italie
- Ave. d'Ivry
- Ave. de Choisy
- Blvd. Masséna
- Blvd. Peripherique
- Cité Universitaire
- Blvd. Kellermann

Arrondissements: 18e, 19e, 9e, 10e, 20e, 2e, 3e, 11e, 1e, 4e, 5e, 12e, 6e, 13e

N ↑

km 1/2 1
mi 1/4 1/2

Paris

The novelist Henry James wrote that "Paris is the greatest temple ever built to material joys and the lust of the eyes." Indeed, in this sensual city, where the streets are museums and daily necessities are elevated to works of art, life is a rich and flamboyant display that can be savored without spending even a *centime:* The meticulous care with which the *haricot verts* (green beans) are lined up side by side at the produce market; the way the *boulanger* wraps your *tarte de framboise* (raspberry tart) in paper as if it were a gift; the whiff of Chanel No. 5 perfume as an elegantly dressed woman passes by; the colorful springtime flower beds at the **Jardin du Luxembourg** (Luxembourg Gardens); the golden incandescence of the **Tour Eiffel** (Eiffel Tower) at night; and the chameleonlike autumn sky, which may range from azure blue to threatening gray in a matter of minutes, all dazzle even the most jaded observer.

And, despite what you may have heard, a trip to Paris doesn't have to mean over-priced opera tickets, unaffordable designer fashions, and restaurant meals that cost a month's rent; many of the city's greatest pleasures are also her least expensive. An evening concert in a neighborhood church, such as **St-Julien-le-Pauvre** or **St-Germain-des-Prés**, can be as inspiring as it is inexpensive. An hour spent rummaging through the discount designer clothes at **Le Mouton à Cinq Pattes** might reveal a big-time treasure, such as an Yves Saint Laurent jacket, at a small-time price. And a visit to one of Paris's lively street markets, such as **Place Maubert, Rue du Buci**, or **Rue Montorgueil**, might inspire you to buy a roast chicken, a crispy baguette, some plump tomatoes, and a cool bottle of Saumur for a picnic lunch. The variety of the city's street life makes mere meandering one of the most worthwhile pleasures. An afternoon spent sipping a *café crème* on the terrace of the **Café de Flore** and watching the spectacle of the passersby, or taking in the myriad street performers in front of the **Centre Georges Pompidou**, can be as enlightening (well, almost) as an afternoon spent in the **Musée du Louvre**.

Each of the city's 20 *arrondissements* (quarters) boasts its own distinct character, so Paris feels less like a monstrous metropolis than like a score of small towns. You may travel from the villagey atmospheres of **Montmartre** and the **Latin Quarter**, to the grandeur of the **Boulevard des Champs-Elysées** and the **Opéra Garnier**, to the trendy area around the **Bastille**, to the classical panoramas of **Notre-Dame** cathedral. And cutting across the whole map is a seven-mile stretch of the **River Seine**, where a nighttime promenade, with the storied **Rive Gauche** (Left Bank) to the south, the **Rive Droite** (Right Bank) to the north, and the bridges and architectural monuments transformed into glowing beacons, can be one of life's most romantic experiences (even if you're alone!). Given all this, it's easy to understand why Paris is called the City of Light.

To call from the US, dial 011 (international access code), 33 (country code), 1 (city code), and the local number. When calling from inside France, dial 16-1, and the local number. After October 1996, dial 01, and the local number.

Getting to Paris

Airports

Roissy–Charles de Gaulle (48.62.12.12), located 19 kilometers (12 miles) north of town, is the busier of Paris's two airfields. It consists of two separate terminals: **Roissy I** handles all foreign carriers, and **Roissy II** services **Air France** only. Both have tourist information and money-exchange facilities, and a shuttle bus connects the two terminals. Connections into Paris are available daily, at 15-minute intervals, from **Roissy II**. The **Réseau Express Régional (RER)** train runs to the **Gare du Nord** and **Les Halles** métro stations in Paris. An **Air France** bus takes passengers to **L'Arc de Triomphe** and **Place de la Porte Maillot**, both of which connect with the métro. The **Roissy** bus runs from the airport to the **Place de l'Opéra**. A taxi into town is a good idea for late-night arrivals.

Orly Airport (49.75.52.52), about 14 kilometers (9 miles) south of central Paris, consists of two terminals: **Orly Sud** (south) handles both trans-Atlantic and European flights, and **Orly Ouest** (west) handles domestic flights. Both terminals have tourist information and money-exchange facilities, and there is frequent transportation service into the city. **Orly Rail** runs from the airport to the **St-Michel** and **Gare du Nord** métro stations in Paris. The **Orly** bus will whisk you directly to the **Place Denfert-Rochereau** in the 14th *arrondissement*. The **Air France** bus makes stops at the airline's **Montparnasse** and **Invalides** offices, both located in the city center. From there you can hop the métro or a bus to your final destination.

For car rentals at either airport, call **Avis** (49.75.44.90), **Europcar** (49.75.47.47), or **Hertz** (49.75.84.84).

Bus Station (Long-Distance)

Coaches arriving from other European cities arrive at the **Gare Routière Internationale** (Avenue General de Gaulle), in the eastern suburb of Bagnolet. The métro connection to the city center is via the **Galliéni** station. For bus information, call Eurolines (49.72.51.51).

Train Station (Long-Distance)

In Paris you can't simply jump into a taxi and cry *"A la gare!"* (To the station!). Paris boasts *six* train stations, each one of them serving and being served by different regions of France. For general train information and reservations, call 45.82.50.50.

Getting around Paris

Addresses Parisian addresses include a street name and a number, *plus* which of the 20 *arrondissements* it is in. For instance, an address in the Latin Quarter or fifth *arrondissement* might be "23 Quai St-Bernard, 5e" (the small "e" is the French equivalent of an English "th"), while an address in the Ile Saint-Louis or first *arrondissement* would read "25 Place Dauphine, 1er" ("er" standing in for the English "st").

Bicycles Unlike some other Eurocapitals, this is not a bicycle-friendly town—especially for tourists, who must concentrate so hard just to stay alive that they see nothing of the sights, and then must be wary of bike thieves. Masochists, however, can rent bicycles from **Paris Vélo** (2 Rue du Fer-à-Moulin, at Rue Geoffrey St-Hilaire, 5e, 43.37.59.22) or **La Maison du Vélo** (11 Rue Fénelon, between Pl Franz-Liszt and Rue de Belzunce, 10e, 42.81.24.72). For cycling information, contact **Fédération Française de Cyclotourisme** (8 Rue Jean-Marie-Jégo, between Pl Paul Verlaine and Rue des Cinq Diamants, 13e, 44.16.88.88, fax 44.16.88.99). If you write ahead they will send you a free list of practical information and scenic cycling routes.

Buses Riding the métro (see below) may be the quickest and easiest way to get around town, but buses are far more pleasant. Buses *24, 30, 48, 82,* and *95* execute marvelous circuits around Paris, all for the cheap price of a métro ticket. Single tickets are sold on board and multitrip tickets are available at all métro stations. Most buses run Monday through Saturday from 6AM until 8:30PM, but service sometimes varies so check individual schedules.

Driving The most civilized Parisian becomes a homicidal maniac on the road, where stoplights are ignored, and one-way streets simply imply a challenge. Rush hour is from 8 to 10AM, and 5 to 7PM on weekdays. Conditions are also rough on Sunday nights, between 5 and 9PM, when weekend travelers are heading back into the city. If you think driving is tough, wait until you try to park your car. *Bonne chance.*

Métro Nearly 120 miles of rail snake beneath the streets of Paris, connecting about 300 stations. Aboveground, you're never too far away from a métro stop, and stations are well-plastered with route maps. The system operates between 5AM and about 12:45AM (each train pulls into its final destination at 1:15AM). When purchasing tickets, your best bet is to buy a *carnet* (book of tickets) of 10, which cuts the price of a single ticket almost in half. Also available are three- and five-day tourists passes valid for both the métro and city buses. A *Formule 1* pass is valid for one day. A *carte orange*, good for an entire month, requires a photograph.

Taxis Hailing a cab is not an acceptable practice in Paris and most taxis will not stop in the middle of the street to pick up passengers. Look for the blue-and-white sign indicating a taxi station and wait for the next available cab. Taxis aren't expensive, but rates increase at night (between 10PM and 6:30AM), on Sunday, and for pick-ups at train stations, hotels, or outside the city. To arrange a pick-up call 49.36.10.10, 07.55.90.70, 47.39.47.39, or 46.85.85.85. Keep in mind that the meter starts the moment the cab driver receives the call.

Tours If observing the city through the windows of a climate-controlled, double-decker tour bus is your idea of an ultimate sight-seeing experience, climb aboard at **Cityrama** (4 Pl des Pyramides, 1e, 44.55.61.00) or **Paris Vision** (214 Rue de Rivoli, at Pl des Pyramides, 1e, 42.60.31.25). Both companies offer tours (in several languages) past all the main attractions, as well as separate tours to Versailles, Malmaison, Chantilly, Chartres, Fontainebleau, Mont St-Michel, the Loire Valley, and Barbizon. Within Paris, there are night tours to the **Moulin Rouge, Lido,** and **Folies Bergère.**

On a late summer afternoon, nothing surpasses an hour touring the Seine in a *bateau mouche* (a small passenger steamer), especially if you take along some creamy goat cheese, a fresh baguette, and a bottle of cool St-Joseph. Take a seat at the rear of the boat, out of range of the irritating recorded commentary. Rides are available from **Bateaux Mouches** (Embarcadére du Pont de l'Alma, near the Tour Eiffel, 42.25.96.10); **Bateaux Parisiens** (Port de La Bourdonnais, opposite the Tour Eiffel, 44.11.33.44); and **Vedettes du Pont-Neuf** (Sq du Vert-Galant, Ile de la Cité at the Pont Neuf, 46.33.98.38). The boats operated by **Vedettes du Pont-Neuf** tend to be smaller and have live guides (French speaking) rather than recorded commentary. From May through September, the large **Batobus** runs a commuter boat service up and down the Seine. The circuit covers five stops: **Port de la Bourdonnais** (near the Tour Eiffel); **Porte de Solferino** (near the Musée d'Orsay); **Quai Malaquais** (opposite the Louvre); **Quai de Montebello** (near Notre-Dame); and **Quai de Hôtel-de-Ville** (near Hôtel-de-Ville).

Paris

Tours of the **Canal St-Martin** are offered from April through November by **Paris Canal** (reservations required; 42.40.96.97) and run between the **Musée d'Orsay** and the **Parc de la Villette**. This offbeat three-hour cruise also passes through a mile and a half of subterranean tunnel under the **Place de la Bastille,** encountering nine locks and two turning bridges en route.

Walking Walking yields the grace notes, embellishments, and architectural details that define the feel and texture of Paris. But it can be a somewhat perilous proposition: On the street you're fair game for distracted drivers, and on the sidewalk you're likely to tread on what dogs have left behind. Every third Parisian owns a dog, and someone in **City Hall** (Hôtel-de-Ville) has calculated that the average pedestrian sets foot in canine droppings every 286th step.

FYI

Accommodations Finding a hotel room in high season may be difficult, so it's advisable to book in advance. Many hotels require a credit card to hold a reservation, but some of the smaller budget hotels do not accept credit cards at all. Hotel rates rise regularly, so it's always wise to call in advance to check rates. If you do arrive without accommodations, check at the **Office du Tourisme de Paris** (see "Visitors' Information," below).

The **Accueil des Jeunes en France (AJF)** maintains over 700 clean, safe, cheap beds in youth centers throughout Paris. Reservations must be made in person and those under 35 years of age have priority. Rooms generally sleep one to eight people and bathrooms are shared. The hostels in the **Marais** quarter, housed in seventeenth-century mansions, are the most desirable (**Maubuisson, Fauconnier, François Miron,** and **Fourcy**). To secure a room you should get to one of their offices at 9AM. (AJF Beaubourg: 119 Rue St-Martin, at Pl Georges Pompidou, 4e, 42.77.87.80; AJF St-Michel: 139 Blvd St-Michel, at Rue Val-de-Grace, 5e, 43.54.95.86; AJF Marais: 16 Rue Pont Louis-Philippe, between Quai de l'Hôtel-de-Ville and Rue François-Miron, 4e, 42.72.72.09).

Business Hours Banks are open Monday through Friday from 9AM until 4:30PM. Shops are usually open from 10AM until 7PM Monday through Saturday, but many stick to the tradition of closing on Monday or during the lunch hour (noon-2PM). Some larger department stores stay open late one night a week, usually on Thursday until 9PM. Museum hours vary: some are open daily, some close Monday, and some Tuesday.

Climate No matter what you've heard, chances are that Paris in the springtime will be soggy. The city logs more rainy days each year than London, so umbrellas or trench coats are in order. Winters are cold and damp, and summers can be as cool and dry as a martini. The average temperature ranges from 38 degrees in January to 75 degrees in July. May and September boast the best weather and the fewest tourists. August, when locals know to flee the city, can be quite hot.

Consulates and Embassies
Canada ....35 Ave Montaigne,
................................between Pl de l'Alma and
.....................Rond-Point des Champs-Elysées,
....8e. 44.43.29.00
U.K........................35 Rue du Faubourg-St.-Honoré,
....between Rue Royale and
...........................Ave de Marigny, 8e. 42.66.91.42
U.S. ....2 Rue St.-Florentin,
..................at Rue de Rivoli, 1er. 42.96.12.02

Discount Tickets Two kiosks in town sell half-price, day-of-performance tickets to about 120 events, including plays, concerts, ballets, and operas. They're located at the **Châtelet–Les Halles** métro station and at the **Place de la Madeleine**. For a daily recording (in English) of exhibitions and concerts, call 49.52.53.56. If you're planning on some serious museum-hopping, buy a *carte* pass (good for one, three, or five days), which gains you reduced admission to more than 60 Parisian museums and monuments. Passes are sold in major métro stations and at most of the participating attractions. Finally, if you have an International Student Identity Card (ISIC) you will qualify for a discount in many Paris museums.

Drinking The legal drinking age is 18. Drunk driving has become a problem, so police often stop erratic drivers for breath tests and fine them on the spot.

Emergencies The emergency number for Paris police is 17. For the fire department, it's 18. An English-language crisis line (operated 3PM-11PM) can be reached by dialing 47.23.80.80. For 24-hour medical house calls, dial 43.37.77.77. Most physicians at the **American Hospital**, just outside Paris (63 Blvd Victor-Hugo, Neuilly-sur-Seine, 46.41.25.25), speak English. For legal problems, call your consulate.

Laundry Self-serve *laveries* are peppered throughout the city. Try the **Dorvag** (25 Rue de Rosiers, between Rue Parée and Rue Vielle-du-Temple, 4e, 48.87.37.33); **Laverie Self-Service Monge** (113 Rue Monge, between Rue Censier and Rue du Fer-à-Moulin, 5e, 47.07.68.44); or **Louise Delpuech** (24 Pl du Marché-St-Honoré, 1er, 42.61.04.49). Most laundromats are open Monday through Saturday from 8AM until 8PM.

Money The basic unit of French currency is the *franc* (F). To exchange currency, look for those banks displaying a sign that reads "CHANGE." For the best exchange rates, try **American Express** (11 Rue Scribe, at Rue Auber, 9e, 47.77.77.07), which is open Monday through Friday, 9AM-6:30PM, and on Saturday (for money exchanges only) from 9:30AM-5:30PM. You can also change money at these train stations: **Gare d'Austerlitz** (until 8PM), **Gare de l'Est** (until 7PM), **Gare St-Lazare** (until 7PM), **Gare du Nord** (until 10:30PM), and **Gare de Lyon** (until 11PM). Credit cards are in wider use here than elsewhere in Europe.

Personal Safety Pickpockets flock to tourists, and busy métro lines are their natural habitat. Beware of bands of children—sometimes they possess a

Paris

sleight of hand Fagin would have envied. Don't leave possessions unattended anywhere.

Postal Services Post offices (marked **PTT**) are open from 8AM to 7PM on weekdays and from 8AM to noon on Saturday. The city's main post office (52 Rue du Louvre, at Rue Etienne-Marcel, 1er) is open 24 hours a day. Stamps can also be purchased at *tabacs* (tobacco shops), hotels, and some newsstands.

Publications The *International Herald Tribune* will keep you abreast of world events and Parisian happenings. It appears at newsstands every morning except Sunday. The French dailies in Paris are *Le Monde*, *Le Figaro*, and *Libération*.

Public Holidays New Year's Day, Easter Sunday and Easter Monday, Labor Day (1 May), Ascension Day (12 May), Bastille Day (14 July), Feast of the Assumption (15 August), All Saints' Day (1 November), Armstice Day (11 November), and Christmas Day.

Public Rest Rooms You can usually waltz right into a cafe to use the toilet, though in some instances you must tip the *gardienne* (keeper). The alternative is to use the beige automatic toilets in the streets. For two francs, these clever commodes automatically let you in and out and disinfect themselves between visits.

Restaurants The French generally lunch between noon and 2PM, and dine between 7:30 and 10PM. In less expensive restaurants, reservations are not usually necessary. At lunch, ordering the plat du jour, or daily special, is a good money-saving strategy. Dinner items may be ordered à la carte, although a prix-fixe menu is often a better bargain.

Smoking Despite their nostalgia for smoking, the French are seeing the first signs of nonsmoking consciousness. There's now a law that requires all restaurants in Paris to provide separate smoking and nonsmoking areas. However, most smokers and many restaurateurs still consider it only a politeness, certainly not a mandate, to refrain from smoking.

Street Plan At first glance, Paris's broad expanse looks like one great tangle of medieval streets. But don't be dismayed, for there's logic in the layout that makes the city surprisingly easy to navigate. Paris is subdivided into 20 *arrondissements*, or quarters. Starting from the first *arrondissement*, the area around the **Louvre**, they spiral outward like a snail's shell. The reference points provided by the major monuments and the Seine river make locating yourself reassuringly easy. While this overall understanding of Paris is helpful, however, it won't change the fact that the streets are labyrinthine. The basic tool for finding your way is the *Paris par Arrondissement*, a pocket-size book of maps sold at newsstands and bookstores throughout Paris and at travel bookstores throughout the world.

Taxes All prices you see posted—hotel, restaurant, and shops—are inclusive of a 15- to 18-percent tax.

Telephones Phone booths can be found on half the street corners in Paris. Most operate only with *télécartes* (phone cards), which are sold at post offices and *tabacs*. Many post offices have facilities for placing long-distance calls.

Tipping A 15-percent surcharge is already included in restaurant bills, but it's common to leave an additional five percent tip for extraordinary service. For taxis, tip 10 to 15 percent.

Visas A valid passport is all that's required to visit France.

Visitors' Information The **Office du Tourisme de Paris** (127 Ave des Champs-Elysées, between Pl Charles-de-Gaulle and Rue Gailiée, 8e, 49.52.53.54) is the home of the city's official tourist bureau, where you can find free maps and sight-seeing information; it's open daily. Four smaller *Bureaux d'Accueil* operate daily in the train stations of **Gare du Nord**, **Gare de L'Est**, **Gare de Lyon**, and **Gare d'Austerlitz**.

1 Pont-Neuf Despite its name (which means "New Bridge"), this span was completed way back in 1607, under Henri IV (the king remembered for promising his poor subjects "a chicken in every pot"). With its grand turrets and arches, all designed by **Androuet du Cerceau**, this is easily Paris's oldest and most famous river overpass. ♦ Between Quais de Conti and de la Mégisserie, 1er. Métro: Pont-Neuf

1 Taverne Henri IV ★★$ This bistro serves delicious charcuterie, regional cheeses, and goose rillettes and is well stocked with Bordeaux and Burgundy wines. ♦ French ♦ M-F, lunch and dinner; Sa dinner; closed 15 August-15 September. No credit cards accepted. 13 Pl du Pont-Neuf (at Pl Dauphine), 1er. 43.54.27.90. Métro: Pont-Neuf

1 Hôtel Henri IV $ The wallpaper is peeling, the 22 rooms are tiny, and the showers and bathrooms are down the hall. But those minor inconveniences are more than offset if you can score a room with a view of the **Place Dauphine**, that tranquil triangle of stone and redbrick town houses built in 1607 that takes its name from Henri IV's son, the princely dauphin who became Louis XIII. No credit cards accepted. Reserve at least one month in advance. ♦ 25 Pl Dauphine (near Pont-Neuf), 1er. 43.54.44.53. Métro: Pont-Neuf

2 La Conciergerie Best remembered as the dungeon for condemned revolutionaries during the Reign of Terror (January 1793-July 1794), this formidable structure—part of the sprawling **Palais de la Cité**—still preserves the cells of Marie Antoinette, Danton, and Robespierre. Guided tours are offered daily. ♦ Admission. Daily. 1 Quai de l'Horloge (at Blvd du Palais), 1er. 43.54.30.06. Métro: Cité

Restaurants/Clubs: Red
Shops/ ♀ Outdoors: Green
Hotels: Blue
Sights/Culture: Black

109

Paris

2 Ste-Chapelle This is the city's most important medieval monument after **Notre-Dame.** Saint Louis (Louis IX) built the chapel in 1248 to enshrine relics he had bought during his first crusade. The windows, illustrating 1,134 scenes from the Bible, form the largest expanse of stained glass in the world. Supposedly designed by **Pierre de Montreuil,** this Gothic gem was damaged severely during the Revolution (when it was used as a flour warehouse) and had to be made over during the 19th century by architect **Eugène-Emmanuel Viollet-le-Duc.** Classical concerts are now held here on several evenings a week between March and November. ♦ Admission. 2 Blvd du Palais (between Quais des Orfèvres and de l'Horloge), 1er. 43.54.30.09. Métro: Cité

3 Place Louis-Lépine One of the largest flower markets in Paris blooms here year-round, offering everything from chrysanthemums to lemon trees. On Sundays, the flower market is transformed into a bird market selling a broad palette of colorful canaries, finches, parrots, and other winged creatures. The nearby **Cité** métro station sports one of the original 141 Art Nouveau "dragonfly" entrances designed by **Hector Guimard** at the turn of the century. ♦ Rue de la Cité and Quai de la Corse, 4e. Métro: Cité

Notre-Dame

3 Notre-Dame For more than six centuries, this world-famous masterpiece (illustrated below) of the Middle Ages has endured as a sonnet in stone, harmonizing mass and elegance, asymmetry, and perfection. In 1163, Pope Alexander III laid the foundation stone on a site where the ancient Romans had built a temple to the god Jupiter, but the final touches were not completed until 1345. It was here, in 1804, that Napoléon Bonaparte, after his anointing by Pope Pius VII, defiantly snatched his crown from the pontiff and proclaimed himself emperor. Today the most frequent visitors are architecture students and tourists, all craning their necks for a look up at this cathedral's many statues, gargoyles, and other fine details. Every Sunday afternoon some of Europe's greatest organists offer free concerts on Notre-Dame's massive pipe organ. ♦ Rue d'Arcole (at Rue du Cloître-Notre-Dame), 4e. Métro: Cité, Maubert-Mutualité

3 Mémorial de la Déportation (Deportation Memorial) Designed by **G.H. Pingusson** in 1962, this stark and simple monument—a tunnel lined with quartz pebbles and small tombs of earth taken from European concentration camps—commemorates the 200,000 French, most of them Jewish, who died during the Holocaust. ♦ Daily. Quai de l'Archevêché (between Ponts de l'Archevêché and St-Louis), 4e. Métro: Cité

4 Brasserie d'Ile St-Louis ★★$$ This noisy Alsatian tavern is full of neighborhood habitués who sit elbow-to-elbow dining on sausage, sauerkraut, and *chopes* (steins) of Mutzig beer served by gruff waiters. Look for the 1913 silver-plated espresso machine. ♦ Alsatian ♦ M-Tu, Th-Su lunch and dinner until 1:30AM; closed in August. No credit cards accepted. 55 Quai de Bourbon (at Rue Jean-du-Bellay), 4e. 43.54.02.59. Métro: Pont-Marie

4 Nos Ancêtres les Gaulois ★$$ A cavernous 240-person all-you-can-eat establishment tackily decorated with sheepskins, battered shields, and wild boars' heads (in sunglasses) loosely evokes the Middle Ages. Earthy salads, greasy sausage platters, chocolate mousse, and barely digestible red wine are perennial hits with the students who wind up here. ♦ French ♦ M-Sa dinner until 1:30AM; Su lunch. Reservations required. 39 Rue St-Louis-en-l'Ile (between Rues des Deux-Ponts and Budé), 4e. 46.33.66.12. Métro: Pont-Marie

4 Berthillon ★★$ This landmark serves 50 flavors of the best ice cream and sorbet in Paris—with no artificial ingredients. Don't miss the black currant or hazelnut varieties. ♦ Ice cream ♦ W-Su; closed the last half of July-August and all school holidays. 31 Rue St-Louis-en-l'Ile (between Rues Poulletier and des Deux-Ponts), 4e. 43.54.31.61. Métro: Pont-Marie

Paris

4 Les Fous de l'Ile ★★★$ At Ile Saint-Louis's most relaxing and hip restaurant/tea salon, order the warm goat cheese salad or cheesecake, and survey the walls adorned with the work of local artists. ◆ French ◆ Tu-Su lunch and dinner to midnight. 33 Rue des Deux-Ponts (between Rue St-Louis-en-l'Ile and Quai de Bourbon), 4e. 43.25.76.67. Métro: Pont-Marie

5 Place de la Bastille On 14 July 1789, a mob stormed the **Bastille,** released its prisoners, lynched its governor, and demolished the fortress, thus sparking the French Revolution. The eight-towered structure, built in 1370 as a fortified palace for Charles V, was later transformed into a holding tank where political prisoners were detained without trial. The paving stones, laid where Rue du Faubourg-St-Antoine intersects the square, mark the site of the original towers. ◆ Blvd Beaumarchais and Rue du Faubourg-St-Antoine, 11e. Métro: Bastille

5 Chez Paul ★★$$ Authentic, old-fashioned bistro fare, such as lamb with rosemary and rabbit stuffed with goat cheese and mint, is served to the **Bastille** crowd in this unpretentious, well-worn restaurant. ◆ French ◆ Daily lunch and dinner. Reservations recommended. 13 Rue de Charonne (at Rue de Lappe), 11e. 47.00.34.57. Métro: Ledru-Rollin

5 Balajo At this old-style music hall, with extravagant decor from the 1930s, the balcony for the orchestra hovers right over over the steamy dance floor. Music ranges from mazurka and tango to waltz, cha-cha, and twist. Modern tunes and disco are played on Monday nights. ◆ M, F-Sa 10PM-4:30AM. 9 Rue de Lappe (between Rues de Charonne and de la Roquette), 11e. 47.00.07.87. Métro: Bastille

5 Opéra Bastille Opened in 1992, this facility is billed as the "people's opera house," and entertains more than 700,000 ticket-holders each year. It includes an amphitheater and a studio stage for smaller performances. Opera performances are now staged here, and the **Opéra Garnier** (see below) is reserved for dance spectacles. ◆ 120 Rue de Lyon (at Rue de Charenton), 12e. 44.73.13.99. Métro: Bastille

5 China Club ★★$$ Shanghai-chic meets Paris with an exotic Chinese-Deco air. The bourgeoisie from Paris's conservative west side like to come here, eat dim sum, and think they're living dangerously. ◆ Chinese ◆ Restaurant: daily dinner. Bar: 7PM-2AM. Reservations recommended for dinner. 50 Rue de Charenton (between Ave Ledru-Rollin and Pl de la Bastille), 12e. 43.43.82.02. Métro: Bastille, Ledru-Rollin, Gare-de-Lyon

5 Au Limonaire ★★$ This charming turn-of-the-century-style restaurant serves chicken livers with blueberries, veal with lemon and herbs, and excellent Côtes du Rhône wines. ◆ French ◆ M, Su dinner; Tu-Sa lunch and dinner; closed in August. Reservations recommended. 88 Rue de Charenton (at Rue Abel), 12e. 43.43.49.14. Métro: Bastille, Ledru-Rollin, Gare-de-Lyon

6 Thanksgiving ★$ Homesick Americans may find comfort in the tangy barbecued ribs and creamy cheesecake served at this food boutique and restaurant. If you're really desperate, get some Oreos to go. ◆ American ◆ Shop: daily. Restaurant: Tu-Su brunch and lunch. 20 Rue St-Paul (at Rue Charles-V), 4e. 42.77.68.29. Métro: St-Paul, Sully-Morland, Pont-Marie

6 Hôtel St-Louis Marais $$ This rustic 15-room (all with private baths) hotel is the successor to an 18th-century Celestins convent on this site. Around the corner on the Rue Beautrellis is the original entrance to the convent; all that remains is a stone portal with a weathered wooden door. ◆ 1 Rue Charles-V (at Rue du Petit-Musc), 4e. 48.87.87.04; fax 48.87.33.26. Métro: St-Paul, Sully-Morland

7 Place des Vosges Welcome to the oldest and perhaps most beautiful square in Paris. This symmetrical ensemble of 36 matching pavilions, with red-and-gold brick and stone facades, steep slate roofs, and dormer windows, was designed in 1612 by **Clément Metezeau.** The area fell into decline after Louis XIV (along with the rest of the French aristocracy) moved to Versailles in 1686, but was rescued in the 1960s, when it was rejuvenated as a historic district. ◆ Off Rue des Francs Bourgeois, 4e. Métro: Bastille, Chemin-Vert, St-Paul

Within Place des Vosges:

Musée Victor Hugo This museum was the French writer's home from 1833 until 1848, when Napoléon III's rise to power sent the author of *The Hunchback of Notre-Dame* and *Les Misérables* into voluntary exile on the Channel Islands. The museum's eclectic assortment includes the cap Hugo wore during the 1871 Siege of Paris and his bust sculpted by Rodin, along with macabre sketches of witches, demons, and the hanging of American abolitionist John Brown. ◆ Admission. Tu-Su. 6 Pl des Vosges, 4e. 42.72.10.16. Métros: Bastille, Chemin-Vert, St-Paul

Paris

MA BOURGOGNE

Ma Bourgogne ★★$$ This arcade-sheltered cafe is especially popular as a local hangout for Sunday breakfast. Specialties include sausages from Beaujolais and steak tartare. ♦ French ♦ Daily breakfast, lunch, and dinner; closed in February and one week in March. No credit cards accepted. 19 Pl des Vosges, 4e. 42.78.44.64. Métro: Bastille, Chemin-Vert, St-Paul

7 A l'Impasse ★★$$ This old neighborhood bistro serves delightful meals, including terrines of rabbit and *girolle* mushrooms, filet of duck in blueberry sauce, and rich chocolate profiteroles. ♦ French ♦ M, Sa dinner; Tu-F lunch and dinner; closed two weeks in August. Reservations recommended. 4 Impasse Guémenée (off Rue St-Antoine), 4e. 42.72.08.45. Métro: Bastille, St-Paul

7 Grand Hôtel Jeanne d'Arc $ Reserve at least one month in advance to secure a room at this charming hotel on a peaceful and pretty street in the heart of the popular Marais district. Some of the 36 guest rooms have their own bathrooms; some share. ♦ 3 Rue de Jarente (between Rues de Turenne and de Sévigné), 4e. 48.87.62.11; fax 48.87.37.31. Métro: St-Paul

7 Grand Hôtel Mahler $$ It remains a mystery how this lovely, well-located hotel keeps such astoundingly low prices. All 36 guest rooms have private baths. ♦ 5 Rue Mahler (between Rues St-Antoine and des Francs-Bourgeois), 4e. 42.72.60.92; fax 42.72.25.37. Métro: St-Paul

---

Watch for announcements during the second half of June for the *garçons de café*, when waiters and waitresses, beginning at the Place de l'Hôtel-de-Ville, race around the city balancing glasses and a bottle of water on a tray. Any spillage or breakage during the five-mile race disqualifies the entrant. You'll never see them moving this fast on the job.

In order to encourage the playing and enjoyment of music in all its forms, the much-loved former minister of culture, Jack Lang, founded the Fête de Musique. On 21 June, the longest day of the year, Paris is full of music, sometimes all night. Check schedules in newspapers for the locations of everything from rock to chamber music concerts.

Restaurants/Clubs: Red **Hotels:** Blue
Shops/ Outdoors: Green **Sights/Culture:** Black

8 Musée Picasso "Give me a museum and I'll fill it up," proclaimed painter Pablo Picasso, whose wish was granted posthumously. Today the 17th-century **Hôtel Salé** enshrines the artist's collection of his own works, the largest in the world, as well as his collection of pieces by other artists, from Matisse to Renoir to Cézanne and Rousseau. ♦ Admission. Daily. 5 Rue de Thorigny (between Rues de la Perle and des Coutures-St-Gervais), 3e. 42.71.25.21. Métro: St-Sébastien-Froissart

MUSÉE CARNAVALET

8 Musée Carnavalet In 1880, the 16th-century **Carnavalet Hôtel** mansion was put into service as the historical museum of the city of Paris. Today its displays reveal four centuries (1500-1900) of Parisian life quite vividly—in documents, shop signs, furniture, and portraits. ♦ Admission. Tu-Su. 23 Rue de Sévigné (between Rues des Francs-Bourgeois and du Parc-Royal), 3e. 42.72.21.13. Métro: Chemin-Vert, St-Paul

8 Marais Plus This two-story bazaarlike *boutique en mouvement* features an ever-changing stock of postcards, globes, dolls, stuffed animals, children's books, and Christmas decorations. The tea salon downstairs serves delicious tarts, salads, and desserts, as well as brunch on Sunday and plum pudding at Christmas. ♦ Daily. 20 Rue des Francs-Bourgeois (at Rue Payenne), 3e. 48.87.01.40. Métro: Chemin-Vert, St-Paul

8 Chez Janou ★★$$ When you're in the mood for a friendly family atmosphere, drop in here for the home-cooked wild mushroom pasta, the venison terrine, or the pheasant-and-chestnut soup. The owner's garden outside of Paris supplies the restaurant with its Jerusalem artichokes, flowers, and herbs. ♦ French ♦ M-F lunch and dinner. Reservations recommended. 2 Rue Roger-Verlomme (at Rue des Tournelles), 3e. 42.72.28.41. Métro: Chemin-Vert

9 Rue des Rosiers The *rosiers* (rosebushes) in the name once bloomed nearby, within the city's medieval wall. But the fragrances wafting along this crooked street today are anything but floral. Scents of hot pastrami and fresh matzos emanate from the kosher butcher shops, delis, and bakeries that line this little street, the *Platzel* of the Jewish quarter since the Middle Ages. ♦ Between Rues Mahler and Vielle du Temple, 4e. Métro: St-Paul

9 Le Loir dans la Théière ★★$ With its flea-market furniture and raffish air, this comfortable tea salon could just as well be in

112

Seattle or Berkeley. ♦ French ♦ Daily brunch, lunch, and tea. No credit cards accepted. 3 Rue des Rosiers (between Rues Pavée and Ferdinand-Duval), 4e. 42.72.90.61. Métro: St-Paul

Jo Goldenberg

9 Jo Goldenberg ★★$$ The sweet aroma of spiced meat, the clatter of dishes, and, particularly on Sunday afternoon, the babble of strong, animated voices fill this Jewish delicatessen. Try the *foie haché* (chopped liver), *poisson farci* (gefilte fish), and strudel, all washed down with a cold Pilsen. ♦ Jewish ♦ Daily breakfast, lunch, and dinner. 7 Rue des Rosiers (at Rue Ferdinand-Duval), 4e. 48.87.70.39. Métro: St-Paul

9 La Tartine ★★★$ The oldest wine bar in Paris features 60 different vintages from Bourgogne, Bordeaux, and the Loire Valley. The menu consists mostly of snacks to accompany the wine—sausages, sandwiches, cheese, and similar items. ♦ French ♦ M, Th-Su breakfast, lunch, and snacks; W lunch and snacks. No credit cards accepted. 24 Rue de Rivoli (between Rues Ferdinand-Duval and des Ecouffes), 4e. 42.72.76.85. Métro: St-Paul

10 Le Troumilou ★$ Generous helpings of home-cooked fare are served in this old-time bistro. Try the *canard aux pruneaux* (duck with prunes) or the ever-popular *poulet provençal* (chicken in tomato sauce with *herbes de Provence*). ♦ French ♦ Daily lunch and dinner. Reservations recommended. 84 Quai de l'Hôtel-de-Ville (between Ponts Louis-Philippe and d'Arcole), 4e. 42.77.63.98. Métro: Hôtel-de-Ville

10 Hôtel-de-Ville The **City Hall** is an example of late 19th-century architectural eclecticism. Part Renaissance palace, part Belle Epoque fantasy, its exterior is lavished with 146 statues. Visitors on guided tours of the state rooms are shown the splendid staircase by **Philibert Delorme** and a Rodin sculpture, *La République*. ♦ Tours: M 10:30AM, starting from the information desk at 29 Rue de Rivoli; call ahead the previous Friday to confirm. Pl de l'Hôtel-de-Ville, 4e. 42.76.50.49. Métro: Hôtel-de-Ville

11 Tour St-Jacques This 1522 architectural anomaly was once the Gothic belfry of **St-Jacques**, a church that met its end back in 1802. Cast your eyes up and you will see meteorological equipment lurking among the gargoyles—the tower is now used as a weather station. ♦ Sq de la Tour St-Jacques (on Rue de Rivoli), 4e. Métro: Châtelet

12 Centre Georges Pompidou/Centre National d'Art et Culture This surrealistic Tinker Toy of modern culture is the most-visited attraction in Paris. Built at the behest of former President Georges Pompidou and designed by Italian **Renzo Piano** and Englishman **Richard Rogers,** the revolutionary structure houses a modern art museum, the city's largest public library, one of the world's most advanced computer-music centers, a language library, a children's theater and dance workshop, and a fifth-floor restaurant with a four-star view. ♦ Free. M, W-Su until 10PM. Rue Rambuteau (at Rue Beaubourg), 4e. 44.78.12.33. Métro: Châtelet, Hôtel-de-Ville, Rambuteau

Within Centre Georges Pompidou:

Musée d'Art Moderne One of the world's largest collections of modern and contemporary art, this museum showcases works by Picasso, Matisse, Moore, and Bacon. ♦ Admission; free 10-2PM and all day Sunday. M, W-Su until 10PM. Third and fourth floors. 44.78.12.33

Salle de Cinéma This film archive and cinema presents three international classics every day but Tuesday. ♦ Admission. M, W-Su until 10PM. Ground floor. 44.78.12.33

12 Dame Tartine ★★$ Every delicious dish in this restaurant, from the salmon with orange hollandaise sauce to the grilled beef with mushrooms, is served with a *tartine* (toasted bread with butter). The outdoor terrace is an ideal point from which to observe the nearby **Rites of Spring Fountain,** a kinetic ballet of animals, serpents, and musical notes. ♦ French ♦ Daily lunch and dinner. 2 Rue Brisemiche (between Cloître St-Merri and Rue St-Merri), 4e. 42.77.32.22. Métro: Rambuteau

12 Hôtel St-Merri $$ Attached to the medieval church of **St-Merri,** this little hotel is delightfully quirky, as evidenced by its use of communion rails as banisters. One room (number nine) is cut through with a flying buttress from the church. There are 11 guest rooms here, all with their own bathrooms. No credit cards accepted. ♦ 78 Rue de la Verrerie (at Rue St-Martin), 4e. 42.78.14.15; fax 40.29.06.82. Métro: Hôtel-de-Ville, Châtelet

12 Les Briochères de Saint-Merry ★$ What a treat to find an authentic old-fashioned bakery complete with a rosy-cheeked baker proudly displaying his oven-fresh brioches on the white marble counters. ♦ Bakery ♦ M, W-Su. 81 Rue St-Martin (between Rues des Lombards and de la Reynie), 4e. 42.72.04.96. Métro: Hôtel-de-Ville, Châtelet

---

"Paris is a city which has France for a suburb."

Victor Hugo

Paris

Safety Tips for the Street Smart

Unseasoned travelers tend to have one of two extreme reactions to their new surroundings: either the strong suspicion that whatever is foreign is dangerous, or the naive assumption they've landed in the protected environs of a theme park. Well, Europe is not Disneyland, but it isn't crime central either. Prudence, common sense, and an awareness of your surroundings virtually guarantee a safe passage throughout Europe.

If you live in an urban area in the US, you're probably already street smart and crowd conscious. Europe will generally seem tame by comparison; the most common crimes are pickpocketing, bag snatching, petty thievery, and other forms of nonviolent robbery. The key is prevention. Leave attention-getting valuables such as expensive watches and jewelry at home, along with any items of sentimental worth. Make photocopies of your passport, visa, airline tickets, credit cards, and other official documents, and record airline and credit card company notification numbers, as well as the numbers of your traveler's checks; keep these copies with you but separate from the real McCoy. (It's also smart to leave a version with friends or relatives.) The State Department suggests you carry two additional passport photos in case a new passport has to be issued. Invest in a combination lock for your luggage (better than a key lock that can be easily picked); it will also prove handy for youth hostel lockers. Note also fire escapes and ledges near windows, from which entry would be possible, and check the condition of the locks on the door and windows.

The most secure way to carry your valuables—passport, visas, ID cards, money, credit cards, traveler's checks, airplane ticket—is in a neck or waist pouch that fits underneath your clothing. For extra insurance, divide money, credit cards, and traveler's checks into separate caches—a hidden pouch and a day pack, for instance—so that if one gets stolen you won't be caught pence-less. Carry your camera in a day pack or shoulder bag, instead of an identifiable camera bag. And if you're traveling by car, never leave your luggage unattended in the back seat; lock it in the trunk during the day and bring it inside at night. Keep your valuables with you and in sight at all times: on a plane or train when you get up to use the bathroom; in youth hostels, where petty thievery is known to occur; or at an outdoor cafe (when you're tempted to sling a bag across the back of your chair—don't). The only exception to this rule is if you are using your hotel or hostel's safe to store valuables.

When you're on the street, it helps to act like a native rather than a bewildered and befuddled tourist. Thieves pick up on the nuances of body language, so project confidence and don't fiddle with your possessions. The unfamiliarity of foreign currency makes the most rudimentary transaction less than automatic—but don't tarry on street corners counting your *lire*. Don't be embarrassed about counting change at the register. Stash away all currency and traveler's checks before you leave the bank.

Extra vigilance is especially required in crowded spots—rush-hour metro trains, pedestrian tunnels and walkways, cathedrals, and other tourist haunts—where people routinely bump up against one another. Keep a tight grip on your purse (shoulder straps bandolier-style across the chest are best) and consider slinging your day pack and fanny pack across your chest, or wear a money belt so that unseen hands can't go exploring. And to guard against snatch-and-ride thieves on motorbikes—a common variety in Europe—carry your shoulder bag on the side of your body not facing the street.

Transportation terminals pose their own particular concerns, so it pays to be especially alert when in transit. You're more vulnerable when you're hurrying to catch a flight or getting oriented after arriving by train in a strange city. Recently, overnight trains have become a common site for robberies, with bold thieves taking advantage of darkened cars and sleeping passengers to steal everything from unsuspecting travelers. Be wary of anyone who gets too close to you without your permission, and avoid any non—uniformed "railroad personnel" who offer to carry luggage. A typical ploy, in stations as well as on the street, is for a group of chattering children to surround a mark, and by the time the person realizes what's happening, his pockets have been picked. Another scam (legal but nonetheless annoying) is getting approached by a person who offers to guide you to inexpensive lodging. When you reach the hotel, which usually necessitates

ART BY ROLANDO CORUJO

Paris

a march clear across town, the great deal that was promised has suffered hyperinflation. These too-good-to-be-true offers usually are just that—avoid them.

Women travelers must still sometimes contend with aggressive men who assume that all women traveling alone—particularly Americans—are promiscuous. Unwanted overtures are to be expected, but not to be tolerated. If hassled by a man on the street, keep walking, avoid eye contact, say nothing—in other words, ignore him—and most likely he will get the message and go away. If he's incredibly dense and you're forced to say something, try "no," and don't smile when you say it. Be firm but not insulting. If he's a persistent devil, you may need to resort to a few sharp epithets in any language; threatening to call the police is much less effective.

Women can also avoid attention by only asking women or mixed couples for directions; and dressing modestly, particularly in southern European countries.

Even with all the proper precautions taken, crimes can and do occur. If you unfortunately wind up the victim of one, go to the police immediately, or contact the nearest US consulate or embassy. While embassies are not a panacea, they can help facilitate matters if you need a new passport, need to have money wired, or if you get arrested or wind up in serious trouble. They can also generally provide names of local attorneys or advise other legal recourse, if necessary. If you are robbed, obtain a copy of the police report for insurance purposes before you leave the country. The same holds true if you get involved in an automobile accident. Wait until the police arrive before moving the car (unless it's blocking traffic), and don't feel obligated to sign any form presented by the police if it's in a language you can't read and there's no one present to translate for you. On the form, write in English that you don't understand it.

Staying safe while you travel should not be such an overwhelming concern that it distracts you from all the pleasures of your trip. Constant fretting and over-caution can immobilize you as surely as any actual crisis. Take a "steady-as-she-goes" approach, but try to minimize the opportunities for bad fortune to befall you. Don't leave home without an alert attitude and a dose of common sense.

13 **404** ★★★$$ Exotic spices, delicate pastries, and simple cooking techniques displayed from the small open kitchen infuse this North African restaurant with an artful ambience and heavenly aromas. Don't miss the succulent stews. ♦ North African ♦ Daily lunch and dinner; closed last two weeks of August. Reservations required. 69 Rue des Gravilliers (between Rues du Temple and Beaubourg), 3e. 42.74.57.81. Métro: Arts-et-Métiers

14 **Rue Montorgueil** The last remaining survivor of *le ventre de Paris* (the belly of Paris) celebrated by 19th century French writer Emile Zola in his novel of the same name, this bustling street resounds with echoes of the old **Les Halles** markets. The nonstop hubbub of greengrocers, butchers, and fishmongers calling out to passersby can be enjoyed from the terrace of one of the street's several cafés. ♦ Between Rues Etienne Marcel and Reaumur, 2e. Métro: Les Halles, Sentier, Etienne-Marcel.

14 **Kurde Dilan** ★★$ One of the few Kurdish restaurants in the Western World serves delicious *tarator* (spinach with garlic and yogurt) and superb unleavened bread. ♦ Kurdish ♦ M-F lunch and dinner; Sa-Su dinner. 13 Rue Mandar (between Rues Montorgueil and Montmartre), 2e. 42.21.46.38. Métro: Sentier, Etienne-Marcel

14 **Bellevue et Charlot d'Or** $$ This attractive hotel is located conveniently near the **Place des Victoires** shopping area. There are 59 guest rooms, all with private baths. The rooms that sleep four offer the best deal for the money. ♦ 39 Rue de Turbigo (at Blvd de Sebastopol), 2e. 48.87.45.60; fax 48.87.95.04. Métro: Etienne-Marcel

14 **Duthilleul et Minart** For more than a century, this store has sold uniforms and work clothes—from waiters' aprons to chefs' toques—plus an array of uniquely French occupational garb. It's a great spot for unusual gifts, such as the popular French watchmakers' smocks. ♦ M-Sa. 14 Rue de

115

Paris

Turbigo (at Rue Etienne-Marcel), 1er. 42.33.44.36. Métro: Etienne-Marcel

15 St-Eustache Built in 1640 to rival **Notre-Dame,** this massive Gothic church is better known for its musical legacy than for its architectural grandeur. The Christmas midnight Mass is the most impressive in the city. A 45-minute tour is available Sunday at 3PM. ♦ 2 Rue du Jour (between Rues Coquillière and Montmartre), 1er. Métro: Les Halles

15 La Fauvette ★$ Executives, meat packers, and paint-spattered workers lunch on steak with *frites* (french fries) and coarse red wine in this small restaurant, characteristic of the days (between 1100 and the mid-1970s) when **Les Halles** marketplace dominated this neighborhood. ♦ French ♦ M-F lunch; closed in August. No credit cards accepted. 46 Rue St-Honoré (between Rues du Pont-Neuf and des Prouvaires), 1er. 42.36.75.85. Métro: Louvre, Les Halles, Châtelet

16 Musée du Louvre The single largest building in Paris and the largest palace in Europe took seven centuries to build and is the largest museum in the western world. Its history stretches back to 1190, when King Philippe Auguste surrounded Paris with a 30-foot-high city wall that included the fortified palace. More than three centuries later, François I tore down most of the old structure, and by 1546 he had constructed the **Cour Carrée** (Square Court). In 1578, Catherine de Médicis built a new palace, the **Tuileries,** at the far end of the present building. The two palaces were joined by Henri IV, who, in 1608, created a number of apartments in the **Long Gallery** for use by court painters and their families. Louis XIV established an art colony here, but when he moved to Versailles in 1678 this palace fell into disrepair. Louis XVI was only narrowly dissuaded from tearing the whole complex down, and shortly before he and Marie Antoinette were beheaded in 1793, he magnanimously put some of the royal art collection on display. Following his rise to power, Napoléon moved into the **Tuileries.** During the Second Empire, Napoléon's nephew Napoléon III and Baron Haussmann built the **North Wing** and the **Flore** and **Marsan** pavilions. The final touch came more than a century later, when architect **I.M. Pei** topped the **Cour Napoléon** (Napoléon Court) with a 70-foot-tall glass pyramid, which serves as the central entrance to the museum and as an enormous skylight over an underground foyer.

The museum's collection includes more than 400,000 works of art from all over the globe. It takes plenty of time to see even just the highlights: *Venus de Milo, Winged Victory of Samothrace, Mona Lisa,* the Crown Jewels, the **David Galleries,** *Eagle of Sugeríus,* the Law Code of Hammurabi, the **Rubens' Gallery,** Michelangelo's *Slaves,* and the *Seated Scribe.* ♦ Admission; half-price after 3PM and on Sunday. M, Th-Su; W until 10PM. Pl du Carrousel, 1er. 40.20.51.51. Métro: Louvre

Within Musée du Louvre:

Carrousel du Louvre Housed under the **Louvre** and skylit by a 150-ton inverted glass pyramid, this French version of a shopping mall features over 35 boutiques proffering goods and services that range from Lalique Crystal and châteaux rentals to tacky souvenirs and one-hour photo service. **Restagora,** an international food hall with seating for 700 people, offers fast food from around the world—Mexican, Lebanese, Asian, and, of course, French. During the shopping center's construction, architects **I.M. Pei** and **Michel Macary** uncovered a 14th-century moat built by Charles V, which has been incorporated into the structure and named the **Fossé Charles V.** ♦ Daily. Enter at 99 Rue de Rivoli or from the Louvre Museum foyer. Métro: Louvre

16 L'Arc du Carrousel Napoléon built this marble arch in 1808 to celebrate French military victories. It can be used like a gunsight to line up the grand alley of the **Tuileries'** fountains, the Egyptian **Obelisk of Luxor** in the **Place de la Concorde,** the **Champs-Elysées,** and the **Arc de Triomphe,** more than two miles away. ♦ Pl du Carrousel, 1er. Métro: Louvre

17 Lina's ★★$ This airy Americanized sandwich bar is the perfect vantage point for spying on the chic fashion show that promenades in the vicinity of the **Place des Victoires,** the 17th-century square that has become the *Rive Droit*'s hub of high fashion. ♦ Sandwiches ♦ M-Sa breakfast and lunch until 6PM; closed Saturdays in August. 50 Rue Etienne-Marcel (at Rue d'Argout), 2e. 42.21.16.14. Métro: Louvre, Sentier

17 Au Panetier ★$ In a Belle Epoque setting, this bakery sells hundreds of crispy sourdough baguettes daily, all fresh from a wood-fired oven. ♦ Bakery ♦ M-F. 10 Pl des Petits-Pères (between Rues Notre-Dame-des-Victoires and de la Banque), 2e. 42.60.90.23. Métro: Bourse, Pyramides

---

Had Emperor Napoléon not changed his mind in the nick of time, visitors to the Place Charles-de-Gaulle would be staring not at L'Arc de Triomphe but at a 160-foot-high elephant squirting water from its trunk. The decision was so close that a model of the pachyderm was made and stood for a while at the Place de la Bastille.

Window-shopping is a common pastime everywhere, but in France it's known as *lèche-vitrine,* which translates literally as "lick the window."

18 Bibliothèque Nationale (National Library) Four centuries worth of books and documents is now kept in one of the world's greatest national libraries. The 68 miles of shelves bend under the weight of more than nine million volumes, including two Gutenberg bibles and manuscripts by Marcel Proust and Victor Hugo. The library's most dramatic space dates back to 1854, when architect **Henri Labrouste** designed the magnificent top-lit **Salle des Imprimés,** a reading room that consists of nine square vaulted bays supported by 16 cast-iron columns and a network of perforated semi-circular iron arches. Although admittance to this room is for members only (and sometimes architects, if they can show their credentials), you can still peek in through the glass doors.

At press time, the library's vast collection was slated to be moved to a new ultramodern location along the Seine in Paris's 13th *arrondissement*. There the controversial new **Bibliothèque Nationale de France,** designed by architect **Dominique Perrault,** will house the precious volumes in four glass towers connected by an immense public esplanade the size of the **Place de la Concorde.** ♦ Galleries Mazarin and Mansart: open for temporary exhibitions. Musée des Médailles et Antiques: daily. Photo Gallery (4 Rue Vivienne): M-Sa. 58 Rue de Richelieu (between Rues des Petits-Champs and Colbert), 2e. 47.03.81.26. Métro: Bourse, Palais-Royal

18 Cafe San José ★$ This tiny stand-up coffee bar serves the best cappuccino in town. ♦ Cafe ♦ M-F. 30 Rue des Petits-Champs (between Rues de Richelieu and Ste-Anne), 2e. 42.96.69.09. Métro: Pyramides, Bourse

19 Palais Royal This six-acre enclave of flowering serenity, designed in 1642, got its name when Anne of Austria lived here with her son, young Louis XIV. In 1780, the property fell into the hands of Philippe, Duke of Orléans, who transformed the square into fancy apartments and shopping arcades. But the elegance soon frayed when he began renting out galleries to magicians, wax museums, circuses, and brothels. Today, the arcades are occupied by small shops. The larger court was transformed in 1987 by sculptor Daniel Buren, who planted 252 black-and-white-striped columns, deep pools, and airport lights in the courtyard floor. ♦ Pl du Palais Royal, 1er. Métro: Palais-Royal

19 Le Palet ★★$$ Hidden in a small street behind the **Palais Royal,** this restaurant features prix-fixe menus, including specialties such as *salade de gésiers* (with chicken gizzards), crème brûlée, and fresh fruit tarts. ♦ French ♦ M-F lunch and dinner; Sa dinner. Reservations recommended. 8 Rue de Beaujolais (between Rues de Valois and de Montpensier), 1er. 42.60.99.59. Métro: Pyramides, Bourse

19 L'Incroyable Restaurant ★★$ What's so incredible about this seven-table establishment, hidden on a cobblestone passage? How about bargain prices and generous portions? Try the homestyle pâtés, the crudités, or *boeuf bourguignon*. ♦ French ♦ M, Sa lunch; Tu-F lunch and dinner. No credit cards accepted. Entrances at 26 Rue de Richelieu and 23 Rue Montpensier (at Passage Potier), 1er. 42.96.24.64. Métro: Palais-Royal, Pyramides

20 Place Vendôme Designed in 1685 by **Jules Hardouin-Mansart,** this opulent octagonal square once held the impaled heads of Revolutionaries and a statue of Louis XIV (the latter toppled in 1792). It's now home to the **Hôtel Ritz,** Paris's ritziest stopover for almost a century now, and one of the world's greatest concentrations of jewelers, perfumeries, and banks. ♦ Rue de la Paix (between Rues St-Honoré and des Petits-Champs), 1er. Métro: Madeleine, Opéra, Tuileries

20 Hôtel du Lion d'Or $ Here is a small, quiet hotel, with 20 recently renovated rooms, all with private baths. It's superbly located near the **Louvre,** the **Tuileries,** and the **Palais Royal.** ♦ 5 Rue de La Sourdière (between Rues St-Honoré and Gomboust), 1er. 42.60.79.04; fax 42.60.09.14. Métro: Tuileries, Pyramides

21 Angelina ★★$$ This Rolls-Royce of Parisian tea salons (founded in 1903 as **Rumplemayer's,** on the former site of the king's stables) is filled with overworked waitresses delivering justly celebrated pastries, sumptuous hot chocolate, and *Mont Blanc*, a concoction of chestnut cream purée that was a favorite of the Aga Khan. ♦ French ♦ Daily breakfast, lunch, and tea; closed for three weeks in August. Reservations recommended for lunch. 226 Rue de Rivoli (between Rues d'Alger and de Castiglione), 1er. 42.60.82.00. Métro: Tuileries, Concorde

Paris

21 W.H. Smith and Son A bonanza of English paperbacks and magazines are stocked here. ♦ M-Sa. 248 Rue de Rivoli (at Rue Cambon), 1er. 42.60.37.97. Métro: Concorde

22 Jardin des Tuileries (Tuileries Gardens) These formal gardens, which were undergoing a $50-million face-lift at press time, were designed in 1649 for Louis XIV by André Le Nôtre, the king's gardener who also designed the gardens at Versailles, Chantilly, and the Château Vaux-le-Vicomte. ♦ Bounded by Quai des Tuileries and Rue de Rivoli, and Pl du Carrousel and Pl de la Concord, 1er. Métro: Tuileries

Within Jardin des Tuileries:

Musée de L'Orangerie This former citrus nursery in the northeastern corner of the **Tuileries Gardens** is the permanent home of an impressive collection of paintings, including 144 masterworks by such artists as Renoir, Cézanne, Picasso, and Matisse, as well as Monet's eight giant water lily murals, *Les Nymphéas*. ♦ Admission. M, W-Su. 42.97.48.16. Métro: Concorde

Galerie National du Jeu de Paume No, it's not a tennis museum, although that's how you would translate its name, which comes from its location: that of a royal tennis court (*jeu de paume*) in the southeastern corner of the **Tuileries**. Once home to France's chief collection of Impressionist masterpieces (now located across the river in the **Musée d'Orsay**; see below), this museum now features changing exhibits by contemporary artists. ♦ Admission. Tu-Su; Tu until 9:30PM. 47.03.12.50. Métro: Concorde

23 Place de la Concorde On Sunday, 21 January 1793, the guillotine was set up on the west side of this square; Louis XVI was beheaded and the 13-month Reign of Terror began. During the Revolution, no fewer than 1,343 people were executed here, including Marie Antoinette, Danton, and Robespierre. During this time, the square reeked so horribly of gore that herds of oxen balked at crossing it. In the center of the square is the **Obelisk of Luxor**, which was taken from the ruins of Egypt's famed Temple of Luxor. At 3,300 years old, it is unquestionably the oldest monument in Paris. ♦ Rue Royale and Ave des Champs-Elysées, 8e. Métro: Concorde

24 Petit Palais This little turn-of-the-century palace houses the city's fine arts collection, and specializes in 19th-century French painters such as Delacroix, Cézanne, and Bonnard. ♦ Admission. Tu-Su. Ave Winston-Churchill (at Pl Clemenceau), 8e. 42.65.12.73. Métro: Champs-Elysées-Clemenceau

24 Grand Palais Along with the **Petit Palais**, this exuberant stone, steel, and glass structure is Art Nouveau at its excessive zenith. Both structures went up for the **1889 Universal Exhibition of Paris**. It's now used for book fairs, car shows, and blockbuster art exhibitions. ♦ Admission. Open only for special exhibitions and salons. Check hours in *Pariscope*. Ave Winston-Churchill (at Pl Clemenceau), 8e. 44.13.17.17. Métro: Champs-Elysées-Clemenceau

25 La Madeleine This monumental building has always been an architectural orphan. Begun as a church in 1764 under the reign of Louis XV and modeled after a Greek temple, it has, at various times in its turbulent past, been slated to become a bank, parliament building, theater, stock exchange, and yet another temple to glorify Napoléon's army. In 1837, the windowless structure almost became a railway station, but five years later it was instead consecrated as a church dedicated to Saint Mary Magdalene. ♦ Pl de la Madeleine, 8e. Métro: Madeleine

25 Hôtel Opal $$ Here's a renovated hotel with 36 doll-sized chambers and private, modern bathrooms. It's located behind **La Madeleine**. ♦ 19 Rue Tronchet (between Rues de Castellane and des Mathurins), 8e. 42.65.77.97; fax 49.24.06.58. Métro: Madeleine

25 Le Roi du Pot-au-Feu ★★$$ For some warm consolation on a frigid evening, visit this offbeat little bistro. The specialty is its namesake, *pot-au-feu*, a marrow-rich beef broth served with meat and vegetables. ♦ French ♦ M-Sa lunch and dinner. 34 Rue Vignon (between Rues de Sèze and des Mathurins), 8e. 47.42.37.10. Métro: Madeleine

25 Ladurée ★★★$ Though posh and ultra-Parisian, this tea salon manages to avoid being snobbish. Habitués recommend its *financiers* (almond cakes), *royals* (almond biscuits with a dash of chocolate or mocha), and heavenly croissants. ♦ French ♦ M-Sa breakfast, lunch, and tea. 16 Rue Royale (between Rue St-Honoré and Pl de la Madeleine), 8e. 42.60.21.79. Métro: Concorde

25 Hôtel de Marigny $$ This modern, sparkling-clean hotel has 26 small guest rooms, all with their own baths. It's located near **La Madeleine** and a short walk from the **Place de la Concorde** and the **Gare St-Lazare**. ♦ 11 Rue de l'Arcade (between Rues Chauveau-Lagarde and des Mathurins), 8e. 42.66.42.71; fax 47.42.06.76. Métro: St-Lazare

26 Palais de l'Elysée The most famous address on the Rue du Faubourg-St-Honoré, if not in all of France, is this country's counterpart to America's White House. The

Paris

public is not admitted, but you can glimpse the dignified facade through the gateway. ♦ 55 Rue du Faubourg-St-Honoré (at Ave de Marigny), 8e. Métro: St-Philippe-du-Roule

27 La Place Boisterous Parisian university students dance to very loud music until the very wee hours at this popular nightclub. ♦ Daily midnight-4AM. 12 Rue de Ponthieu (between Rue Jean-Mermoz and Ave Franklin-D.-Roosevelt), 8e. 42.25.51.70. Métro: Franklin-D.-Roosevelt

27 La Boutique à Sandwiches ★★$$ Stop at this crowded two-story restaurant/snack bar for sandwiches or the perfect late-night snack: all-you-can-eat Swiss raclette, an all-you-can-stomach combination of cheeses served warm with baked potatoes, pickles, and ham. ♦ French ♦ Daily lunch and dinner until 1AM. 12 Rue Colisée (between Ave des Champs-Elysées and Rue de Ponthieu), 8e. 43.59.56.69. Métro: Franklin-D.-Roosevelt

27 Le Val d'Or ★★★$ On the ground floor of the area's most popular wine bar you'll find quiche, charcuterie, what are perhaps the best sandwiches in Paris, and, of course, an admirably selected list of wines. Under the house rules, wine must be ordered by the bottle, but you pay only for what you drink. ♦ French ♦ M-Sa breakfast, lunch, and snacks until 9PM. 28 Ave Franklin-D.-Roosevelt (between Rues du Colisée and de Faubourg-St-Honoré), 8e. 43.59.95.81. Métro: St-Philippe-du-Roule

28 Chicago Pizza Pie Factory ★$ Deep-dish pizza with traditional toppings (pepperoni, mushrooms, and olives) is served in a cavernous brick basement filled with the musical reverberations of Chuck Berry. Happy Hour, complete with half-price cocktails, is from 6 until 8PM daily. ♦ Pizza ♦ Daily lunch and dinner until 1AM. 5 Rue de Berri (between Ave des Champs-Elysées and Rue de Ponthieu), 8e. 45.62.50.23. Métro: George-V

29 Drugstore des Champs-Elysées This place sells not only aspirin and Band-Aids, but gourmet groceries, quick brasserie meals, wristwatches, banana splits, and Cuban cigars (yes, you read that right). ♦ Daily until 2AM. 133 Ave des Champs-Elysées (at Rue de Presbourg), 8e. Métro: Charles-de-Gaulle-Etoile. 44.43.79.00

29 Place Charles-de-Gaulle/L'Arc de Triomphe This square sprang to life in 1854 when **Baron Haussmann**, in order to create a 12-pointed star, added another seven avenues to the five that already spoked out from **L'Arc de Triomphe** (illustrated at right). The area is a total snarl of traffic, rotating around the triumphal arch, which Napoléon commissioned to honor his army's victory at the Battle of Austerlitz, but which wasn't completed until 1836, well after his downfall. From the arch's top is a magnificent panoramic view of Paris. ♦ Aves des Champs-Elysées and Kléber, 8e. Métro: Charles-de-Gaulle-Etoile

30 Parc de Monceau Dating back to 1778, this park features a whimsical landscape full of architectural follies: a pyramid, a pagoda, a Roman temple, windmills, and artfully placed ruins. Of particular interest is the round **Pavillon de Chartres**, one of four extant *barriéres* (tollhouses) built by **Claude-Nicholas Ledoux** along the old city wall in 1784. ♦ Between Blvd de Courcelles and Pl de Rio de Janeiro, and Velasquez and Van Dyck, 8e. Métro: Monceau

31 Opéra Garnier (Paris Opéra) This grand cultural palace now confines itself to the best of classical ballet and modern dance (opera performances are presented exclusively in the **Opéra Bastille**; see above). Architect **Charles Garnier**'s design frosted the facade with ornate friezes, winged horses, golden garlands, busts of famous composers, and a copper-green cupola topped by a statue of Apollo holding a lyre above his head. Inside, the splendid Baroque **Grand Staircase** and the gilt-encrusted **Grand Foyer** are by themselves worth a visit. In addition, the theater is famous for its six-ton chandelier, five tiers of loges bedecked in red velvet and gold, and Marc Chagall's 1964 painted ceiling depicting Parisian scenes and images from operas. Classic-movie fans will be interested to know that the underground grotto where Gaston Leroux's Phantom of the Opéra lurked actually exists, well beneath this building's cellars, where an artificial lake provides water for Paris's fire brigade. ♦ Admission. Box office:

L'Arc de Triomphe

Paris

M-Sa. Pl de l'Opéra (at Blvd des Capucines and Rue Auber), 9e. 40.17.35.35. Métro: Opéra

31 Cafe de la Paix ★★$$ Looking like a scene painted by Renoir, with green-and-white striped umbrellas, a dance of light, and brightly clothed patrons, this lovely old cafe is classified as a historic landmark, once popular with characters as diverse as Salvador Dalí, Harry Truman, and Maria Callas. ♦ French ♦ Daily breakfast, lunch, and dinner until 1:30AM. 3 Pl de l'Opéra (at Blvd des Capucines and Rue Auber), 9e. 40.07.30.20. Métro: Opéra

32 Cimetière de Montmartre The **Montmartre Cemetery** is a veritable academy of writers, composers, and painters. Among its permanent population are Zola, Alexander Dumas, Jacques Offenbach, and Edgar Degas. ♦ Daily. 20 Ave Rachel (et Rue Caulaincourt), 18e. Métro: Blanche

33 Moulin de la Galette Painted by Renoir and many others, this windmill (with its former dance hall) is the best known of the scores of mills that once crowned Montmartre. ♦ 79 Rue Lepic (between Rues Girardon and Caulaincourt), 18e. Métro: Lamarck-Caulaincourt, Blanche

33 Tim Hôtel $$ Had this hotel been here 80 years ago, you might have asked your neighbors Pablo Picasso or Georges Braque over for coffee and croissants. It has 60 guest rooms, all with private baths. ♦ 11 Rue Ravignan (off Pl Emile-Goudeau), 18e. 42.55.74.79; fax 42.55.71.01. Métro: Abbesses

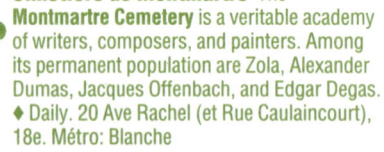

Parisian Delicacies

Eating out in Paris should be a pleasant experience, yet foreign menus can be minefields for the picky diner. Here are some of the more unusual French specialties that the sensitive eater might want to avoid:

Andouillette: sausage made with large chunks of pig intestines

Boudin: sausage or pudding made with blood

Cervelles: brains

Foie: liver

Gesiers: gizzards

Grenouille: frog

Ris de veau: veal sweetbreads

Rognons: kidneys

Tripe: stomach tissue

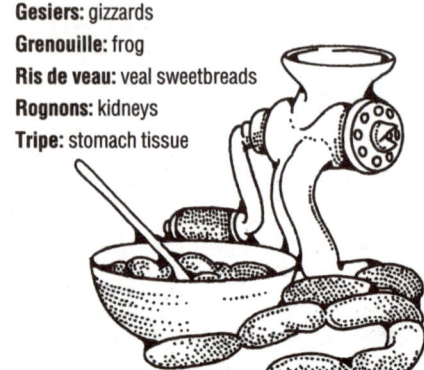

33 Résidence Charles-Dullin $$ These 76 kitchen-equipped apartments, located on the southeastern corner of a tranquil square, are rented by the night or by the week. ♦ 10 Pl Charles-Dullin (off Rue des Trois Frères), 18e. 42.57.14.55; fax 42.54.48.87. Métro: Anvers

33 A l'Angélus Try the *Alesien* coffee pralines and the *orangettes* in this neighborhood candy store-cum-tea shop. On a drizzly winter afternoon, nothing beats the hot cocoa made from melted chocolate bars. ♦ M-Tu, Th-Su. 1 Rue Tardieu (across from the Funicular), 18e. 46.06.03.75. Métro: Anvers

33 Wanouchka ★$$ Eastern European immigrants swarm here for classic pierogi, blintzes, Baltic herring, and borscht. Forget the wine list and order the plum-and-lemon vodka. ♦ Polish ♦ M-Tu, Th-Sa dinner; Su lunch and dinner. No credit cards accepted. 28 Rue la Vieuville (between Rue des Martyrs and Pl des Abbesse), 18e. 42.57.36.15. Métro: Abbesses

34 Sacré-Coeur Universally panned when it was conceived by architect **Paul Abadie** in the mid-19th century, this Roman-Byzantine basilica has nonetheless become enshrined in the Tourists' Top Ten. The highlight is not the church itself, but the view from its steps—or even better, from the dome—especially at dawn or dusk. ♦ Basilica: free. Dome: admission. Daily; basilica until 11PM. Pl du Parvis du Sacré-Coeur (between Rues Chappe and Lamarck), 18e. Métro: Abbesses, Anvers

34 St-Pierre-de-Montmartre An important example of early Gothic architecture, this modest, three-aisled structure was begun 16 years before **Notre-Dame** and claims to be the oldest sanctuary in Paris (of course, two other churches, **St-Germain-des-Prés** and **St-Julien-le-Pauvre,** make similar claims). ♦ 2 Rue du Mont-Cenis (between Rues Azaïs and du Chevalier), 18e. 46.06.57.63. Métro: Abbesses, Anvers

34 L'Eté en Pente Douce ★★$ The outdoor terrace of this cafe/tea salon is a quiet and peaceful haven in a lively neighborhood. In season, try the *filet mignon Sylvestre aux champignons* (wild boar steak with mushrooms). ♦ French ♦ Daily lunch and dinner until 11PM. 23 Rue Muller (at Rue Charles-Nodier), 18e. 42.64.02.67. Métro: Abbesses, Anvers

34 L'Ermitage Hôtel $$ Being greeted by this delightful hotel's smiling hostess, Maggie Canipel, feels like coming home. Housed in a three-story 1860 residence, the 12 breezy *chambres* and private baths have been lovingly decorated. Breakfast, served in your room, is included in the reasonable price. Reserve well in advance, and try for rooms 11 or 12 which open onto a bewitching terraced garden full of chirping birds. No credit cards accepted. ♦ 24 Rue Lamarck (between Rues Chevalier-de-la-Barre and Becquerel), 18e. 42.64.79.22; fax 42.64.79.22. Métro: Lamarck-Caulaincourt

35 Passage Brady Along this curry- and saffron-infused covered street known as Paris's "Little India," you will find inexpensive restaurants, exotic food and spice markets, and even an authentic Indian barbershop. ♦ Between Blvd de Strasbourg and Rue St-Denis, 10e. Métro: Château-d'Eau

35 Le Réveil du Xe ★★$ This honest brasserie specializes in cuisine from the Auvergne region, including sausages, country pâtés, and a combination of both called *assiettes de charcuterie*. Excellent Beaujolais wines are selected and bottled by proprietor Daniel Vidalenc. At lunchtime, the hearty plat du jour (daily special) keeps this place perpetually crowded. ♦ French ♦ M-F breakfast, lunch, dinner. 35 Rue du Château d'Eau (at Rue Bouchardon), 10e. 42.41.77.59. Métro: Château-d'Eau

36 Porte de la Villette The old 75-acre slaughterhouse district (bounded by Avenue Jean-Jaurès, Boulevards Sérurier and Macdonald, and Canal St-Denis) now boasts a huge complex of buildings and parks devoted to science and technology. The centerpiece is the huge **Cité des Sciences et de l'Industrie,** a research and exhibition building offering thematic science exhibitions. Adjacent is **La Géode,** a polished steel sphere that houses a movie theater projecting films 180 degrees above and around the audience. ♦ Admission. Cité des Sciences: Tu-Su. 211 Ave Jean-Jaurès (at Blvd Sérurier), 19e. 40.03.75.00. Métro: Porte-de-Pantin

37 Parc des Buttes-Chaumont This taste of urban wilderness was erected in 1867 on the site of a city dump. In an inspired use of landfill, a then-new material—concrete—was used to form cliffs, ravines, rivers, and an artifical lake. A classical colonnaded temple commands one of the city's most striking views of Montmartre and **Sacré-Coeur.** ♦ Bounded by Rues Botzaris and Manin, and Rue Crimée and Ave Simon-Bolivar, 19e. Métro: Buttes-Chaumont

38 La Nioullaville ★★★$$ An immense Asian restaurant, the kitchen staff here creates dishes from five countries. Such unusual selections as braised crab and abalone, salt-and-pepper quail, and seafood fondue are offered, as well as a tempting choice of dim sum. ♦ Southeast Asian ♦ Daily lunch and dinner. 32-34 Rue de l'Orillon (between Blvd de Belleville and Rue du Moulin-Joly), 11e. 43.38.30.44. Métro: Belleville

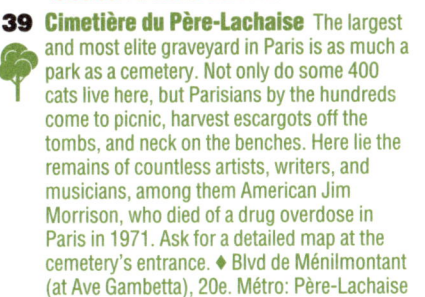

39 Cimetière du Père-Lachaise The largest and most elite graveyard in Paris is as much a park as a cemetery. Not only do some 400 cats live here, but Parisians by the hundreds come to picnic, harvest escargots off the tombs, and neck on the benches. Here lie the remains of countless artists, writers, and musicians, among them American Jim Morrison, who died of a drug overdose in Paris in 1971. Ask for a detailed map at the cemetery's entrance. ♦ Blvd de Ménilmontant (at Ave Gambetta), 20e. Métro: Père-Lachaise

40 American Center Founded by the American expatriate community in Paris in the 1930s, this center boasts an exuberant new building designed by bad-boy American architect **Frank Gehry**. The complex presents artistic works, including dance, theater, music, visual arts, electronic art, cinema, and literature. Call for information about hours and activities. ♦ 51 Rue de Bercy (between Rue de Dijon and Blvd de Bercy), 12e. 44.73.77.77. Métro: Bercy

41 Mosquée de Paris (Paris Mosque) This Moorish ensemble of soaring minarets, pink marble fountains, and crescent moons is the oldest mosque in France. It was constructed in 1926 by Arab artisans and French architects. A guided tour of the building, central courtyard, and Moorish garden offers an excellent introduction to the Islamic religion. ♦ Admission. M-Th, Sa-Su. Pl du Puits-de-l'Ermite (at Rue Quatrefages), 5e. 45.35.97.33. Métro: Place-Monge

41 Cafe de la Mosquée ★★$ Flaky Moroccan pastries, sweet mint tea, and Turkish coffee are served during the summer on a white patio shaded by leafy fig trees. In winter, tea is available in a quiet lounge adjoining the *hammam* (steam bath). ♦ Middle Eastern ♦ Cafe: daily breakfast, lunch, and dinner until 10PM; closed in August. Baths (for women): M, W-Th, Sa; (for men): F, Su. No credit cards accepted. 2 Rue Daubenton (at Rue Geoffroy-St-Hilaire), 5e. 43.31.18.14. Métro: Censier-Daubenton

---

The term *hôtel* in Paris often refers not to that overnight institution with room service, but rather to a *hôtel particulier,* meaning a town house or mansion.

"The customers of this cafe are regulars whom I've watched, year after year, come in and sit down at the same place. There is absolutely nothing to distinguish them from the rest of mankind. What draws them here? . . . For me, they are such natural phantoms that I scarcely notice them."

Louis Aragon, *Paris Peasant*

Paris

42 Jardin des Plantes Begun in 1626 by Louis XIII as a royal medicinal herb garden planted on an old rubbish heap, this 74-acre botanical garden now hosts a floral orgy of peonies, irises, roses, geraniums, and dahlias. Within the park is France's oldest public zoo, a rather shabby menagerie (animals are still jailed in Second Empire pavilions and rumors of stray cats being fed to snakes and reptiles run rampant). The park's **Musée National d'Historie Naturelle** (Museum of Natural History) possesses one of the world's richest mineral collections and some of the oldest fossilized insects on earth The newly renovated Grande Galerie, reopened in 1994 after 30 years, houses a superb collection on the evolution of life. ♦ Admission for zoo and museums. Garden and zoo: daily. Greenho uses and museum: M, W-Su. Bounded by Rues Buffon and Cuvier, Rue Geoffroy St-Hilaire, and the Seine. 40.79.30.00. Métro: Gare d'Austerlitz, Jussieu, Place-Monge

43 Le Baptiste ★$ This noisy, friendly restaurant is always crowded with locals who come for the *chèvre* (goat cheese) on green salad, the sirloin steak au poivre, and apple tart. ♦ French ♦ M-F lunch and dinner; Sa-Su dinner. Reservations recommended. 11 Rue des Boulangers (between Rues Linné and Monge), 5e. 43.25.57.24. Métro: Cardinal-Lemoine, Jussieu

43 Arènes de Lutèce (Roman Arena) After the **Roman Baths,** this enormous first-century amphitheater is the city's most important Roman ruin. Its 325-by-425-foot oval shape once seated 15,000 spectators. ♦ Rues de Navarre and des Arènes, 5e. Métro: Cardinal-Lemoine, Jussieu, Place-Monge

44 Le Rallye ★★$ Filled with smoke and people who look as if they've worked hard to make their hair a mess, this joint is more like one of Amsterdam's funky "brown cafes" than a typical Paris stop. The owner plays music that ranges from Jimi Hendrix guitar extravaganzas to opera. The dog, always in evidence, is named Figaro. Avoid the toilets. ♦ French ♦ Daily breakfast, lunch, and snacks until 2AM. No credit cards accepted. 11 Quai de la Tournelle (between Blvd St-Germain and Rue du Cardinal-Lemoine), 5e. 43.54.29.65. Métro: Cardinal-Lemoine, Maubert-Mutualité

Although classy restaurants do not take kindly to babies or young children (and Parisians know better than to bring them), a warm welcome is almost always extended to man's best friend, *le chien*.

44 Boulangerie Beauvallet Julien Come here for the best baguettes in Paris. ♦ M-Tu, Th-Su; closed in August. Baking times: 7AM, 11AM, 1PM. 6 Rue de Poissy (at Rue Cochin), 5e. 43.26.94.24. Métro: Maubert-Mutualité

44 Place Maubert Market This bustling local market is especially busy on Saturday. Don't miss Madame Pouppeville's fresh herb and wild mushroom stand, displaying earthy cèpes, girolles, and morels, or the lavender, honey, Savon de Marseille, and other Provençal products peddled by Monsieur Brockers. ♦ Tu, Th, Sa 7AM-1PM. Blvd St-Germain (at Rue Monge), 5e. Métro: Maubert-Mutualité

45 Hôtel le Central $ Located right in the heart of the Latin Quarter, this hotel certainly lives up to its name. Accommodations are nothing fancy, but the 16 guest rooms (some with bath) are clean and comfortable. ♦ 6 Rue Descartes (between Rues Clovis and St-Etienne-du-Mont), 5e. 46.33.57.93. Métro: Cardinal-Lemoine, Place-Monge.

45 Rue Mouffetard Leading out of the **Place de la Contrescarpe** is this 13th-century street, at one time the main Roman road to the southeast, Lyon, and Italy. A bustling pedestrian street market has convened at the bottom of the hill ever since 1350. Among the gastronomical items purveyed there are mangoes, horse meat, wild boar, sea urchins, and hundreds of marvelously smelly cheeses. ♦ Market: Tu-Su. Between Sq St-Medard and Pl de le Contrescarpe, 5e. Métro: Censier-Daubenton, Place-Monge

45 Brasserie Mouffetard ★★$ This is the best cafe on the street. The croissants, brioches, and fruit tarts are, of course, made fresh daily. ♦ French ♦ Tu-Sa breakfast, lunch, and dinner; Su breakfast and lunch; closed in July. No credit cards accepted. 116 Rue Mouffetard (at Rue de l'Arbalète), 5e. 43.31.42.50. Métro: Censier-Daubenton, Place-Monge

46 Panthéon When Louis XV recovered from gout in 1744, he vowed, in gratitude, to build a great temple honoring Sainte Geneviéve. This is the result, a classical, many-pillared edifice based on the form of a Greek cross. Finished in 1850, the building (illustrated on page 123) was secularized into a virtual temple of fame, serving as a necropolis for the distinguished atheists of France. In its rather depressing crypt rest Voltaire, Rousseau, Victor Hugo,

122

Emile Zola, Louis Braille, and the World War II Resistance leader Jean Moulin. ♦ Admission. Daily. Pl du Panthéon (at Rue Soufflot), 5e. 43.54.34.51. Métro: Cardinal-Lemoine

46 St-Etienne-du-Mont Completed in 1626 and dedicated to St. Stephen, this church's mélange of triple classical pediments, Gothic rose window, medieval-style belfry, and Renaissance dome defy the laws of architectural purity. The low-hanging chandeliers are a menace to anyone over six feet tall. But *mon Dieu!* it's beautiful. Don't miss the two graceful spiral staircases and the extraordinary wood pulpit from 1650. ♦ Pl Ste-Geneviéve (next to the Panthéon), 5e. 43.54.11.79. Métro: Cardinal-Lemoine

46 Tashi Delek ★★$ At this Tibetan restaurant run by refugees, you can sample regional dishes such as *momok* (beef ravioli) and *baktsa markou* (balls of pastry with melted butter and goat cheese). ♦ Tibetan ♦ M dinner; Tu-Sa lunch and dinner. 4 Rue des Fossés-St-Jacques (between Rues Clotaire and St-Jacques), 5e. 43.26.55.55. Métro: Luxembourg

46 Bistro de la Sorbonne ★$ This reasonably priced restaurant serves generous portions of chicken in cream sauce, warm goat-cheese salad, and steak with potatoes in an attractive and crowded student ambience. ♦ French ♦ M-Sa lunch and dinner. 4 Rue Toullier (between Rues Soufflot and Cujas), 5e. 43.54.41.49. Métro: Luxembourg, Cluny-La Sorbonne

47 Hôtel de Cluny, Museum, and Palais des Thermes (Roman Baths) This magnificent mansion, built by the abbots of Cluny in 1330 and rebuilt in 1510, is one of the oldest private residences in Paris. It straddles the exquisite ruins of second-century Roman baths and houses one of the world's finest collections of French medieval art, including the mysterious and beautiful *Lady and the Unicorn* tapestries. ♦ Admission. M, W-Su. 6 Pl Paul-Painlevé (between Rue de Cluny and Blvd St-Michel), 5e. 43.25.62.00. Métro: Cluny-La Sorbonne, St-Michel

47 Brasserie Balzar ★★$$ Albert Camus and Jean-Paul Sartre had their last argument at this spot. James Thurber, Elliot Paul, William Shirer, and the old *Chicago Tribune* crowd all gathered here for the beer and *choucroute garni* (sauerkraut). The literary clientele, cheery lighting and mirrors, and waiters in long white aprons combine to create an ambience that makes this one of Paris's finest brasseries. ♦ French ♦ Daily breakfast, lunch, and dinner until midnight. Reservations recommended. 49 Rue des Ecoles (between Rues de la Sorbonne and Champollion), 5e. 43.54.13.67. Métro: Maubert-Mutualité

47 Sorbonne France's most famous university began in 1253 as humble lodgings for 16 theology students. By the end of the 13th century, when it became the administrative headquarters for the **University of Paris,** there were 15,000 undergraduates studying in the city. Saint Thomas Aquinas and Roger Bacon were among its great teachers; Saint Ignatius Loyola, Dante, Erasmus, and John Calvin were students here, and Cardinal Richelieu was elected grand master in 1642. Don't be shy about wandering down the long stone corridors and visiting the impressive lecture halls, such as the **Amphithéâtre Descartes.** In the event that you enroll (as hundreds of Americans do every year) for a four-month crash course in French, you may come to know the dusty domed ceiling and stiff wooden benches of the shabbier **Richelieu Amphithéâtre** intimately. For an admission application, contact the Cours de Civilisation Française de la Sorbonne. ♦ 45-47 Rue des Ecoles (between Rues St-Jacques and de la Sorbonne), 5e. 40.46.26.64. Métro: Cluny-La-Sorbonne

47 Perraudin ★★★$ Popular among students and their profs, this bargain canteen offers a panoply of *cuisine bourgeoise:* lamb and kidney beans, beef stew, au gratin potatoes, and rough red wines. ♦ French ♦ M, Sa dinner; Tu-F lunch and dinner; closed the last two weeks in August. No credit cards accepted. 157 Rue St-Jacques (between Rues des Fossés-St-Jacques and Soufflot), 5e. 46.33.15.75. Métro: Luxembourg

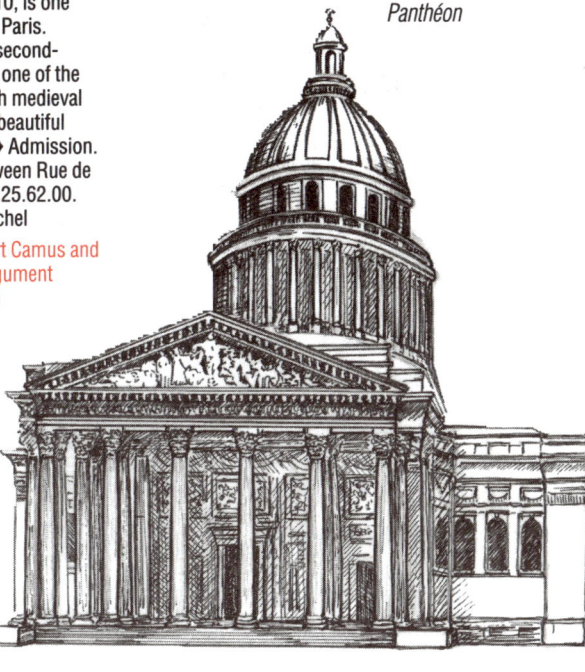

Panthéon

Paris

47 Hôtel Médicis $ This shabby but clean hotel has rented its 28 small rooms to young travelers for more than 30 years. Bathroom facilities are shared, but what do you expect in one of the city's best bargain hotels? ♦ 214 Rue St-Jacques (between Rues Gay Lussac and Royer-Collard), 5e. 43.54.14.66. Métro: Luxembourg

48 St-Julien-le-Pauvre An odd amalgam of Romanesque and Gothic church architecture squats on a small square lined with acacia trees, and looks more like a humble country church than a Parisian monument. Started in 1165 and named after St. Julian, a martyred third-century bishop who gave all his money to the poor, this church claims to be the oldest in Paris. Although its construction began two years after **Notre-Dame**'s, this church was finished first. It's been home to a Greek Orthodox congregation since 1889. It often hosts enjoyable evening concerts. ♦ 1 Rue St-Julien-le-Pauvre (at Rue St-Jacques), 5e. Métro: St-Michel

48 Esmeralda $$ This hotel is a favorite among struggling actors and artists. There are 19 guest rooms, some with private baths, and the hotel has become a bit run-down in recent years. Rooms with views of **Notre-Dame** are also, unfortunately, subjected to the noise of *The Rocky Horror Picture Show* crowds exiting the nearby **Studio Galande** cinema. ♦ 4 Rue St-Julien-le-Pauvre (at Rue de la Bûcherie), 5e. 43.54.19.20; fax 40.51.00.68. Métro: Maubert-Mutualité, St-Michel

48 Shakespeare and Company Proprietor George Bates Whitman—who claims poet Walt as a distant forebear—has spent 45 years running this charitable bookstore and inn for authors, vagabond intellectuals, and literature professors. Whitman's chaotic stacks, which defy the Dewey decimal or any other system of categorization, have been frequented by the likes of Henry Miller and beat poet Lawrence Ferlinghetti. ♦ Daily until midnight. 37 Rue de la Bûcherie (between Rues du Petit-Pont and St-Julien-le-Pauvre), 5e. 43.26.96.50. Métro: Maubert-Mutualité, St-Michel

48 Rue de la Huchette In medieval times, this ancient thoroughfare was called "Street of Roasters," because it offered a plethora of barbecue pits. Couscous and shish kebab joints continue the carnivorous tradition by roasting whole lambs and pigs in their front windows. ♦ Between Blvd St-Michel and Rue St-Jacques, 5e. Métro: St-Michel

48 Le Caveau de la Huchette All jazz buffs must pay a visit to this crowded, dingy cellar on a street which once rang with the sounds of bebop. This club still does its part to keep the music happening. ♦ Cover. M-Th, Su 9:30PM-2:30AM; F-Sa until 3AM. 5 Rue de la Huchette (between Rue Xavier-Privas and Pl St-Michel), 5e. 43.26.38.99. Métro: St-Michel

48 St-Séverin Constructed around 1220 on the burial site of a sixth-century hermit named Séverin, this relatively obscure edifice (illustrated below) is recognized as the city's richest example of Flamboyant Gothic architecture. ♦ Rue des Prêtres-St-Séverin (at Rue St-Séverin), 5e. Métro: St-Michel, Cluny-La-Sorbonne

St-Séverin

Paris

49 Fontaine St-Michel (Fountain of St. Michael) In 1860, **Gabriel Davioud** designed this 75-foot-high and 15-foot-wide spouting monster (illustrated above). The bronze of Saint Michael fighting the dragon is by Duret. On hot Saturday nights, a relatively nonviolent crowd of students, bikers, and drug pushers gather here. The **St-Michel** métro station boasts another of the Art Nouveau entrances designed by **Hector Guimard** in 1900. ◆ Rue Danton (at Rue St-André-des-Arts), 6e. Métro: St-Michel

49 Delhy's Hôtel $ This 21-room hotel off of the noisy **Place St-Michel** is clean and quiet. Some guest rooms have their own bathrooms, some share. ◆ 22 Rue de l'Hirondelle (6 Pl St-Michel), 6e. 43.26.58.25. Métro: St-Michel

49 Restauration Viennoise ★★$ In this *Rive Gauche* institution you can eavesdrop on the conversations of **Sorbonne** students while you snack on delicious tarts, cakes, strudels, tea, and hot chocolate. ◆ French ◆ M-F breakfast, lunch, and tea. No credit cards accepted. 8 Rue de l'Ecole de Médicine (between Rue Hautefeuil and Blvd St-Michel), 6e. 43.26.60.48. Métro: Odéon, St-Michel

50 Hôtel de Nesle $ This small 20-room hotel looks like a cross between grandmother's attic and a Berkeley dive. None of the accommodations have their own baths, but the place is still so popular that they can get away with refusing to take reservations over the phone—guests must register in person before noon. No credit cards accepted.
◆ 7 Rue de Nesle (between Rue Dauphine and Impasse de Nevers), 6e. 43.54.62.41. Métro: Odéon

50 Le Mouton à Cinq Pattes Fashion-minded bargain hunters can rummage through racks of Gaultier, Ferre, and Chanel for half-price designer duds with the labels cut out. ◆ M-Sa. 19 Rue Grégoire de Tours (between Blvd St-Germain and Rue de Buci), 6e. 43.29.73.56. Métro: Odéon, Mabillon. Also at: 8 Rue St-Placide (between Rues de Sèvres and Cherche-Midi), 6e. 45.48.20.49. Métro: Rennes

50 Buci Market One of the prettiest street markets in Paris. The intersection of Rues de Buci and de Seine is thronged with operatic hawkers hustling endives, homemade fettuccine, wild strawberries, hot baguettes, and pink tulips. ◆ Tu-Su. Rues de Buci and de Seine, 6e. Métro: Odéon, Mabillon

50 Le Chai de l'Abbaye ★★$$ Amazing! Here's a good wine bar in Paris that isn't crawling with yuppies. ◆ French ◆ Daily breakfast, lunch, and dinner until 2AM. 26 Rue de Buci (at Rue du Bourbon le Château), 6e. 43.26.68.26. Métro: Odéon, Mabillon

50 La Palette ★★$ Look out for the bearded waiter at this bohemian cafe, complete with artists' palettes strung about the walls. His name is Jean-François, and though he's kind-hearted, he can also be grouchy. You must order quickly and without indecision, or he'll ignore you until you've learned your lesson. Ask for the gruyère omelette, or maybe the country ham served on Pôilane country bread, with a delicious *tarte tatin* (apple tart) to finish. ◆ French ◆ M-Sa breakfast, lunch, and snacks until 1:30AM; closed in August. No credit cards accepted. 43 Rue de Seine (at Rue Jacques-Callot), 6e. 43.26.68.15. Métro: Odéon, Mabillon

51 Whiskey-a-Gogo A cellar bar playing dance music to French youths, this is the site of the original **Rock 'n' Roll Circus,** where American rocker Jim Morrison made his final professional appearance. ◆ Daily 11:15PM-6AM. 57 Rue de Seine (between Rue Sulpice and Blvd St-Germain), 6e. 43.29.60.01. Métro: Odéon, Mabillon

51 La Bolée ★$ *Une bolée* is a bowl of real Breton cider, the correct accompaniment for the delicious crepes on the menu here. ◆ French/Breton ◆ M-Sa lunch and dinner; Su lunch; closed last two weeks of August. 25 Rue Servandoni (between Rues de Vaugirard and Palatine), 6e. 46.34.17.68. Métro: Odéon, Luxembourg

52 Polidor ★★$ For more than a century, this restaurant's home-cooking has lured writers such as Hemingway, James Joyce, and Paul Verlaine out of their garrets for its earthy consolations of pumpkin soup, chicken in cream sauce, and rabbit in mustard sauce. ◆ French ◆ Daily lunch and dinner. No credit cards accepted. 41 Rue Monsieur-le-Prince (between Rues de Vaugirard and Racine), 6e. 43.26.95.34. Métro: Luxembourg, Odéon

Restaurants/Clubs: Red **Hotels:** Blue
Shops/ ♀ Outdoors: Green **Sights/Culture:** Black

125

Paris

53 Jardin du Luxembourg (Luxembourg Gardens) In 1610, tired of the **Louvre**, the widow of murdered Henri IV, Queen Mother Marie de Médici, decided that she would build an alcazar recalling those of her native Italy. Her **Palais du Luxembourg** is now home to the French Senate. Free guided tours are offered to the public on the first Sunday of every month (call 44.61.20.89 for reservations two weeks in advance). The surrounding 60-acre gardens are graced with fountains, sculptures, ponds, flowerbeds, tennis courts, pony rides, a marionette theater, and periodic outdoor band concerts. ♦ Bounded by Blvd de Montparnasse and Rue de Vaugirard, and Blvd St-Michel and Rue d'Assas, 6e. Métro: Luxembourg, Notre-Dame-des-Champs, St-Sulpice, Rennes

54 La Coupole ★★$$$ Talk about a cafe with a history; Josephine Baker, Man Ray, Matisse, Hemingway, Sartre, Fitzgerald, and Joyce all dined at this popular place. The capacious dining room contains a dozen columns painted by members of Montparnasse's artistic community in the 1920s, including Gris, Chagall, and Brancusi, and is now classified as a historic monument. The basement holds an enormous ballroom which has live music and dancing on Friday and Saturday nights, and tea dances on Sunday afternoons. ♦ French ♦ Daily breakfast, lunch, and dinner until 2AM. Ballroom: F-Sa 9:30PM-4AM. Tea dances: Su 3-7PM. 102 Blvd du Montparnasse (at Rue Delambre), 6e. 43.20.14.20. Métro: Vavin

55 Hôtel de l'Avenir $$ This medium-sized hostelry near the **Jardin du Luxembourg** is tremendously popular with students. All 35 guest rooms have their own baths. ♦ 65 Rue Madame (at Rue de Fleurus), 6e. 45.48.84.54; fax 45.49.26.80. Métro: St-Placide

56 Restaurant B.E.P. of the Ecole Ferrandi ★★$$ One of the best-kept culinary secrets in Paris is this training school for chefs, waiters, and waitresses run by the Paris Chamber of Commerce. The menu is prix-fixe and the meals are sumptuous. ♦ French ♦ M, W-F lunch; Tu lunch and dinner. Reservations required 10 days in advance. 11 Rue Jean Ferrandi (between Rues de Vaugirard and du Cherche-Midi), 6e. 49.54.28.00. Métro: St-Placide

57 Cafe Parisien ★★★$ This modest cafe has garnered a large following for its weekend brunches, pot-au-feu, hearty plats du jour (daily specials), and *tarte tatin*. ♦ French ♦ M-F lunch and dinner; Sa-Su brunch, lunch, and dinner. Reservations recommended. No credit cards accepted. 15 Rue d'Assas (between Rues de Vaugirard and de Rennes), 6e. 45.44.41.44. Métro: Rennes

58 St-Sulpice Interrupted by insurrection, insolvency, and even bolts of lightning, the construction of this church (illustrated at left) required the services of architects over a span of 134 years. In a side chapel, unknown to even most Parisians, are three magnificent biblical frescoes by Eugene Delacroix. ♦ Pl St-Sulpice (at Rue St-Sulpice), 6e. 46.33.21.78. Métro: St-Sulpice

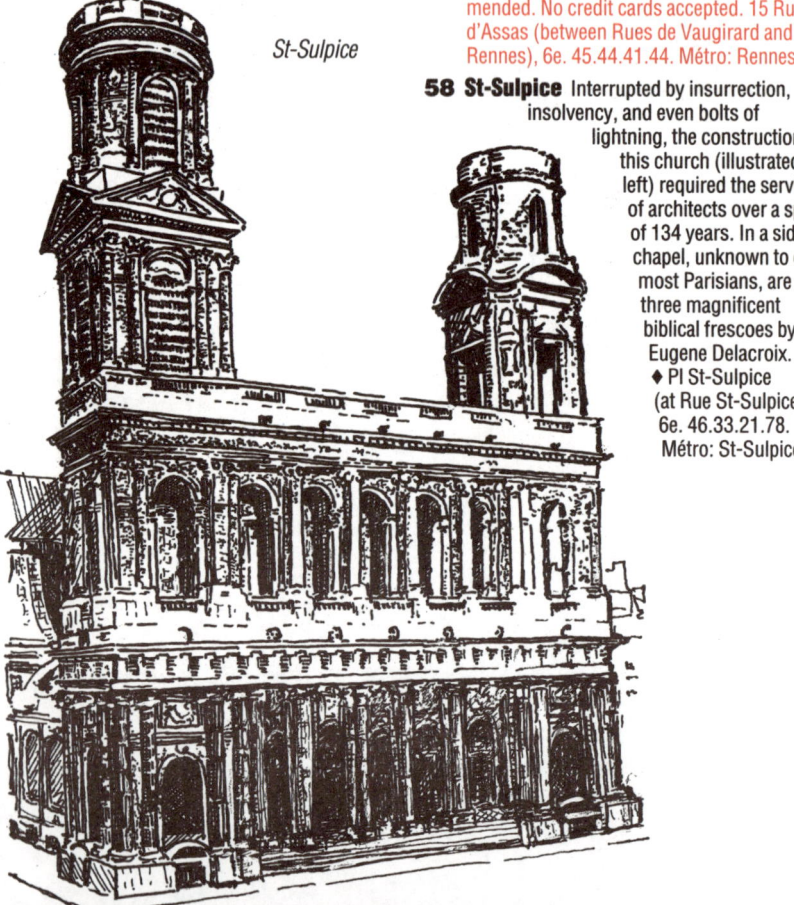

St-Sulpice

Paris

58 Café de la Mairie ★★$ Enjoy a *café crème* or a *citron pressé* (lemonade) on the terrace of this very French, very untouristy café overlooking the **Place St-Sulpice**. ♦ French ♦ M-Sa breakfast, lunch, and dinner. 8 Pl St-Sulpice (at Rue des Canettes), 6e. 43.26.67.82. Métro: St-Sulpice

58 Chez Georges This classic French bar is wallpapered with mug shots of the singers who have performed in the old cabaret downstairs. ♦ Tu-Sa until 2AM. No credit cards accepted. 11 Rue des Canettes (between Rues Guisarde and du Four), 6e. 43.26.79.15. Métro: Mabillon

58 Bistro Henri ★★$ This first-rate neighborhood joint is known for its delicious *magret de canard* (duck cutlet), green bean vinaigrette, *foie de veau* (veal liver), and homemade tarts. ♦ French ♦ M-Sa lunch and dinner. Reservations required. No credit cards accepted. 16 Rue Princesse (between Rues Guisarde and du Four), 6e. 46.33.51.12. Métro: Mabillon

58 Le Petit Vatel ★★$ One of Paris's smallest and cheapest restaurants is filled with famished students and artists. Tasty daily specials include Brazilian red beans, poached fish, and chocolate cake. ♦ French ♦ M-Sa lunch and dinner; Su dinner. 5 Rue Lobineau (between Rues de Seine and Mabillon), 6e. 43.54.28.49. Métro: Mabillon

59 St-Germain-des-Prés For more than 15 centuries a church has stood on this corner, which was *prés* (open pasture) in Roman times. The first church, built in 452 by Merovingian King Childebert, was repeatedly attacked by invading Normans and finally rebuilt, to last, in 1163. Today, the edifice is best known for its evening concerts of classical music. ♦ Guided tours: Tu, Th 1-5PM. Place St-Germain-des-Prés (at Blvd St-Germain), 6e. 43.25.41.71. Métro: St-Germain-des-Prés

59 Aux Deux Magots ★★★$$ This is where Hemingway and his cronies met to drink away the sting of rejection slips—a pastime he later reminisced about in *A Moveable Feast*. The menu offers 25 kinds of whiskey and little pots of strong espresso. From May through August, the sidewalk entertainment on the terrace opposite the **St-Germain-des-Prés** bell tower is always amusing and occasionally brilliant. ♦ French ♦ Daily breakfast, lunch, and dinner until 1:30AM. 6 Pl St-Germain-des-Prés (at Blvd St-Germain), 6e. 45.48.55.25. Métro: St-Germain-des-Prés

> You can do almost anything in Paris parks except have a picnic on the lawn. French grass is sacred, and a guard will appear to order you off before you've even had time to unwrap your salami and uncork the Bordeaux.

59 La Hune Pay a visit to one of the liveliest bookstores in Paris. ♦ M-Sa until midnight. 170 Blvd St-Germain (at Rue St-Benoît), 6e. 45.48.35.85. Métro: St-Germain-des-Prés

Café de Flore

59 Café de Flore ★★★$$ Jean-Paul Sartre and Simone de Beauvoir both hung out in this great cafe during World War II, more or less setting up house, working in the mornings, and meeting people by appointment in the afternoon. Today it's an excellent spot to have a real breakfast of *oeufs au plat* (fried eggs), bacon, and croissants. ♦ French ♦ Daily breakfast, lunch, and dinner until 1:30AM. No credit cards accepted. 172 Blvd St-Germain (at Rue St-Benoît), 6e. Métro: St-Germain-des-Prés. 45.48.55.26

59 Korean Barbecue ★$$ The fare here includes marinated beef and vegetables that you grill yourself over a gas stove at your table. ♦ Korean ♦ Daily lunch and dinner. 1 Rue du Dragon (at Blvd St-Germain), 6e. 42.22.26.63. Métro: St-Germain-des-Prés

59 Le Petit St-Benoît ★★$ Offering indigent Rive Gauche intellectuals the same menu for the last 125 years (including a respectable roast veal with mashed potatoes), this popular coach house bistro is hard to beat for low prices. ♦ French ♦ M-F lunch and dinner. 4 Rue St-Benoît (between Blvd St-Germain and Rue Jacob), 6e. 42.60.27.92. Métro: St-Germain-des-Prés

59 Place de Furstemberg Named after Egon de Furstemberg, a 17th-century abbot of the church of **St-Germain-des-Prés,** this hidden treasure attracts French filmmakers, flamenco guitar players, and harpists who like to play in the acoustically extraordinary courtyard. In spring the four trees at the center of the square burst into fragrant lavender bloom. ♦ Between Rues de l'Abbaye and Jacob, 6e. Métro: St-Germain-des-Prés

59 Musée Eugène Delacroix The old atelier of Eugène Delacroix, where he lived, worked, and, in 1863, died, is now a museum displaying his paintings, sketches, and letters. A quick tour will give you some idea of why Baudelaire described Delacroix as a "volcanic crater artistically concealed beneath bouquets of flowers." ♦ Admission. M, W-Su. 6 Rue de Furstemberg (Pl de Furstemberg), 6e. 43.54.04.87. Métro: St-Germain-des-Prés

Paris

60 Ecole des Beaux-Arts Established by Louis XIV, the city's **School of Fine Arts** has trained many of the architects and artists who have designed and decorated Paris over the centuries. Stop in to see the exhibitions of student work from January through March. ♦ 14 Rue Bonaparte (between Rue Jacob and Quai Malaquais), 6e. 47.03.50.00. Métro: St-Germain-des-Prés

60 Restaurant des Beaux-Arts ★★$ This bargain canteen is usually packed to the rafters with art students. Go early to avoid the lines, but don't miss the *coq au vin, boeuf bourguignon,* and rabbit in mustard sauce. Wine is included in the prix-fixe menu. ♦ French ♦ Daily lunch and dinner. No credit cards accepted. 11 Rue Bonaparte (between Rue des Beaux-Arts and Quai Malaquais), 6e. 43.26.92.64. Métro: St-Germain-des-Prés

60 Pont des Arts Providing a pedestrian crossing between the **Institut de France** and the **Louvre** (see above), this wooden-planked structure is a favorite of easel-toting artists who come here to sketch and daub that familiar view encompassing the Ile de la Cité, the **Place Dauphine,** the dignified form of the **Pont-Neuf,** and the spires of **Notre-Dame** and **Ste-Chapelle** in the distance. ♦ Between Quais du Louvre and Voltaire, 6e. Métro: Odéon

61 Musée d'Orsay Formerly a railway station and hotel, this magnificent museum houses the art that provides the chronological link between the **Louvre** and the **Centre Georges Pompidou,** bridging the end of Romanticism and the origins of Modern Art. The collection includes all the glorious Impressionist paintings formerly in the **Galerie National du Jeu de Paume** (see above) as well as selected works by Delacroix, Corot, Ingres, and the Barbizon landscape painters. ♦ Admission. Tu-W, F-Su; Th until 9:30PM. 1 Rue de Bellechasse (at Quai d'Orsay), 7e. 40.49.48.14. Métro: Musée d'Orsay, Solférino

61 Le Roupeyrac ★$ This simple restaurant in an elegant neighborhood offers crudités, grilled pork chops, and a better-than-average chocolate mousse. ♦ French ♦ M-F lunch and dinner; Sa lunch; closed in August. 62 Rue de Bellechasse (between Rues de Varenne and de Grenelle), 7e. 45.51.33.42. Métro: Solférino

62 Coffee Parisien ★$ An American brunch is served all day, with specialties such as pancakes with maple syrup, hash browns, bagels and cream cheese, and bacon cheeseburgers. ♦ American ♦ Daily brunch, lunch, and dinner until 11:30PM. 5 Rue Perronet (between Rues des Sts-Pères and St-Guillaume), 7e. 40.49.08.08. Métro: St-Germain-des-Prés

62 Than ★★$$ For 26 years the affable owner of this place has served delicious and affordable Cantonese and Vietnamese specialties. Try the lacquered duck or the caramelized spareribs. ♦ Asian ♦ Tu-Sa lunch and dinner. 42 Rue des Sts-Pères (between Blvd St-Germain and Rue Perronet), 7e. 45.48.36.97. Métro: St-Germain-des-Prés

63 Musée Rodin The **Hôtel de Biron,** which houses the **Rodin Museum,** is a 1730 Regency masterpiece. In 1908, after the building was subdivided into a cluster of artists' studios, Auguste Rodin moved in and stayed until his death in 1917. The works displayed here are arranged in order so visitors can follow Rodin's career chronologically, beginning with his academic paintings and his sketches in both classic and modern modes. The room containing *Sculptor with his Muse* also offers several works by Camille Claudel, the talented sculptor who, at the age of 17, became Rodin's muse, model, and lover. ♦ Admission. Tu-Su. 77 Rue de Varenne (at Blvd des Invalides), 7e. 47.05.01.34. Métro: Varenne

64 Hôtel des Invalides This monumental group of buildings went up in 1676 on the orders of Louis XIV to house the Sun King's old soldiers, many of them invalids who had been reduced to begging or seeking shelter in monasteries. The **Dôme des Invalides** is one of the most magnificent Baroque churches of the *grand siècle,* and France's greatest warriors, including Napoléon, are buried within its walls. ♦ Admission. Daily. Pl des Invalides, 7e. 44.42.30.11. Métro: Latour-Maubourg, Varenne

---

For the French, *la politesse* is a way of life, so it is best to respect their custom and address them formally. For example, say *"Bonjour Monsieur," "Pardon Madame,"* and *"S'il vous plaît Madame,"* rather than simply *"Bonjour," "Pardon,"* or *"S'il vous plaît."*

Restaurants/Clubs: Red **Hotels:** Blue
Shops/ Outdoors: Green **Sights/Culture:** Black

Reach Out and Touch

As the world keeps shrinking, thanks to the wonders of telecommunications, the concept of long distance is not quite what it used to be. Today, you're as reachable in Vienna as you are in Dubuque (assuming you want to be). The only difference is in the extra expense (always) and the time (usually) it takes to stay in touch from Europe. But here are some tips and shortcuts for connecting across the continents.

Granted, the mail between Europe and North America is not as slow as the Pony Express, but it will try your patience. Cross-Atlantic mail can take anywhere from five days to two weeks. If you would like to receive mail while traveling, have correspondents write to you *c/o Poste Restante* (the international phrase for "General Delivery"), *Central Post Office, City, Country,* and mark the envelope HOLD. It will be delivered to the central post office in the appointed city and be held there until you pick it up. In most cities it's clear which post office is the central one, but not always, so research names and addresses beforehand, especially if your itinerary includes larger cities. When you retrieve your mail you will probably need to show the postal clerk your passport or other picture ID. (The process will run smoothly if all mail is addressed to you in the same name that appears on your ID.)

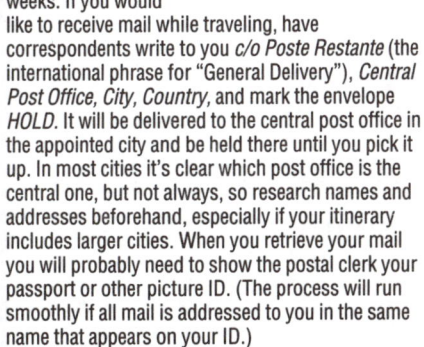

Another option is to have mail delivered directly to your hotel or hostel if your itinerary is set. Or, if you are an American Express cardholder (or are using their traveler's checks), your mail can be sent care of an American Express office, which will hold it at no charge. This service is available to the general public as well for a small fee. Correspondents should mark "Client Letter Service" on the envelope. For a free directory of American Express offices, call 800/528.4800.

To send or receive letters, aerograms, as they're known in the US, are cheaper than the conventional letter-inside-the-envelope because they weigh less. Parcel post regulations are intricate, so check with the post office in Europe when sending packages home. Or do your homework on the European postal system before you leave the states by consulting the *International Mail Manual,* available for perusal at most US post offices.

Phoning with a Sprint, MCI, or AT&T calling card saves you the hassle of rummaging for handfuls of coins to complete calls from pay phones. You also will be connected with the carrier's English-speaking operator—a blessing for those too embarrassed to try out their language skills on the host country's operator (who may be equally bad at English!). The cost of the call won't be much more expensive than dialing direct, since European telephone companies have lowered their costs due to increasing global competition and more standardization across Europe. But if you're calling from your hotel room, you'll at least be spared the hotel's international calling surcharge, although you'll probably still have to pay a local calling fee. Before you lift the phone from its cradle in any hotel room—even to call the brasserie down the street—check with the front desk about its telephone charge policy; otherwise, you can quickly rack up a small fortune in assorted surcharges.

To reach the US directly, first dial the international access code, which is usually listed on or near the phone; then the US country code, which is 1; then the area code and number. (Be aware that most toll-free numbers in the US and Canada are not reachable from abroad.)

A good way to avoid the surcharge situation and the loose change dilemma is to make calls from pay phones using a phone card—available from most newsstands and post offices. After purchasing a card in a set monetary increment—say 20 *deutsche marks*—you can talk as long as the card's value holds out. These cards are not yet transferable from country to country, and unfortunately, you can't get reimbursed for any money remaining on them.

For those who go into separation anxiety over their answering machines, there's Overseas Access, a service available through **EurAide**. You can pick up or leave messages by calling a number in Munich. This answering service may well make the most sense as a way of staying in contact with individuals throughout Europe; US callers, alas, must incur the expense of dialing Germany. Contact: **EurAide** at PO Box 2375, Naperville, IL 60567; 708/420.2343.

Fax machines aren't always available to guests in budget hotels; try post offices and neighborhood stationery/copy stores that advertise fax service in their windows. If your laptop will keep you company on the trip, check with your long-distance carrier before you leave. Services like **MCI Mail Global Access** (contact MCI at 800/444.MAIL) and **AT&T Mail** (contact AT&T at 800/MAIL.672) let you send or receive E-mail, faxes, and telexes using your computer.

Paris

65 Hôtel Malar $ The price of a room for four people in this peaceful hotel may be the best value in the attractive Invalides quarter. There are 18 guest rooms, most with private baths. ♦ 29 Rue Malar (between Rues St-Dominique and de l'Université), 7e. 45.51.38.46; fax 45.55.20.19. Métro: Latour-Maubourg.

66 Ecole Militaire (Military School) In an attempt to rival the nearby **Hôtel des Invalides,** Louis XV commissioned this military school, with its Corinthian columns, statues, dome, double-columned colonnade, and elegant wrought-iron fence. Its most famous cadet was Napoléon Bonaparte. Open by appointment only. ♦ Write to: Général Direction, Ecole Militaire, 1 Pl Joffre, 75007 Paris. Bounded by Aves de Lowendal and de la Motte-Piquet and Aves de Suffren and de la Bourdonnais, 7e. No phone. Métro: Ecole-Militaire

Eiffel Tower

67 Cafe de Mars ★★$$ Here's a California-cool restaurant frequented by students of the nearby **American University.** It offers chicken marinated with ginger and lemon, buffalo wings, and cheesecake. ♦ American ♦ M-F lunch and dinner; Sa brunch and dinner; Su brunch. 11 Rue Augereau (between Rues de Grenelle and St-Dominique), 7e. 47.05.05.91. Métro: Ecole-Militaire

68 Parc du Champ-de-Mars Named for the Roman god of war, this large rectangular greensward, stretching from the **Ecole Militaire** to the **Tour Eiffel,** has long been a site of battles, both actual and prospective. Here, in 52 BC, Roman legions defeated the Parisii. In 886, the Parisians beat back the invading Vikings, and in the early 18th century, when the Champs-de-Mars served as the parade ground for the **Ecole Militaire,** Napoléon drilled with his fellow cadets here. ♦ Bounded by Aves de la Motte Picquet and Gustav Eiffel, and Aves de Suffren and de la Bourdonnais, 7e. Métro: Bir-Hakeim, Champ-de-Mars, Ecole-Militaire

69 Tour Eiffel (Eiffel Tower) First dubbed a monstrosity and later considered the definitive symbol of Paris, this 984-foot tower (illustrated at left) was built to commemorate the centennial of the storming of the **Bastille** prison and to stand as the centerpiece of the **1889 International Exhibition of Paris.** The now-classic design by **Gustave Eiffel** won over 700 other entries in the design competition. (Among the losers, for obvious reasons, were a giant guillotine and a mammoth lighthouse.) The tower was the tallest structure in the world until 1930, when New York's Chrysler Building usurped that title. ♦ Admission varies for each level. Daily until 11PM; July-Aug until midnight. Ave Gustave Eiffel (between Aves de Suffren and de la Bourdonnais), 7e. 44.11.23.11. Métro: Bir-Hakeim, Champ-de-Mars

70 Musée Marmottan One of the best-kept secrets in Paris is this 19th-century town house containing more than a hundred original paintings, pastels, and drawings by Claude Monet. While tour buses full of noisy London schoolchildren and itinerant backpackers elbow past each other in the **Musée d'Orsay** (see above) to glimpse Monet's *Wild Poppies,* this treasure trove of the artist's work is relatively deserted. ♦ Admission. Tu-Su. 2 Rue Louis-Boilly (between Ave Raphaël and Blvd Suchet), 16e. 42.24.07.02. Métro: La Muette

Paris

71 Aux Produits du Sud-Ouest ★★$$ The attraction here is authentic southwestern French cuisine at pre-war prices. Don't skip the apple tart with Armagnac for dessert. ♦ French ♦ Tu-Sa lunch and dinner. No credit cards accepted. 21-23 Rue d'Odessa (between Rue du Depart and Blvd Edgar-Quinet), 14e. 43.20.34.07. Métro: Edgar-Quinet, Montparnasse

71 Crêperie de St-Malo ★★$ The Montparnasse district is rich in Breton restaurants, and this simple *crêperie* is one of the best. Try the crepes with smoked salmon or the dessert crepe filled with chocolate and honey. ♦ Crêperie/Breton ♦ Daily lunch and dinner until 1AM. No credit cards accepted. 53 Rue du Montparnasse (between Blvds Edgar-Quinet and du Montparnasse), 14e. 43.20.87.19. Métro: Edgar-Quinet, Montparnasse

---

Never say *"je suis pleine"* after enjoying one of those enormous Parisian meals, especially if you are a woman. Literally translated, the words mean "I am full," but idiomatically it is a rather vulgar way of declaring that you are pregnant.

"If you are lucky enough to have lived in Paris as a young man, then wherever you go for the rest of your life, it stays with you, for Paris is a moveable feast."

Ernest Hemingway, *A Moveable Feast*

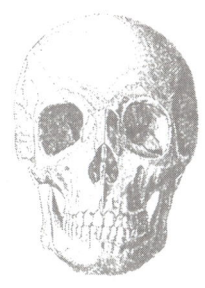

---

72 Catacombs In 1785, several million skeletons were transported from the overcrowded and unsanitary **Cimetière des Innocents** near **Les Halles** to these catacombs, which extend for miles beneath Paris. Here the bones were stacked in a neat but rather macabre fashion, with a warning carved near the entrance: "Stop. Beyond Here Is the Empire of Death." In the 20th century, these eerie passageways served as the headquarters of the French Resistance during the Nazi occupation. ♦ Admission. Tu-F 2-4PM; Sa-Su 9-11AM, 2-4PM. 1 Pl Denfert-Rochereau (at Ave du Général-Leclerc), 14e. 43.22.47.63. Métro: Denfert-Rochereau

72 Hôtel Floridor $ Right across from the entrance to the **Catacombs** is a comfortable hotel featuring private, renovated bathrooms and 48 recently wallpapered rooms. Ask for a room overlooking the **Place Denfert-Rochereau.** No credit cards accepted. ♦ 28 Pl Denfert-Rochereau (at Ave du Général-Leclerc), 14e. 43.21.35.53; fax 43.27.65.81. Métro: Denfert-Rochereau

Bests

Hélène Prevost
Professor/Lecturer, Association Civilisation et Culture Françaises

François Mauriac, a 20th century French writer, once said "the streets in Paris are the best museums." When the weekend comes around I like to stroll in the streets of Paris. Each area has its own smell, sounds, history.

In the 6th *arrondissement* I wander between **Rue de Rennes** and **Rue St-Placide,** window shopping. I stop for a few moments in the church of **St-Sulpice** to look at the Delacroix frescos and the Virgin sculpted by Jean-Baptiste Pigalle (18th century). Nearby, I sit on the terrace of the **Café de la Mairie** to drink a hot chocolate and watch the passersby. A short time later I find myself in **Place de Furstemberg** close to the church of **St-Germain-des-Prés.** This little square is enclosed by 17th century buildings, one of which was Delacroix's studio.

I continue my walk toward the **Louvre,** crossing the **Pont des Arts.** The **Louvre** is so beautiful at night when its architecture, stretching over four centuries from Henri II to François Mitterand, is lit up and all its history appears.

My promenade is finished in the **Passages** in the First and Second *arrondissments:* the **Passage Véro-Dodat,** the **Passage Colbert,** the **Galerie Vivienne.** These 19th-century, covered galleries are glass-roofed corridors lined with little boutiques.

Paris is best explored on foot—in each area a work of art leaps out, just as beautiful as Leonardo da Vinci's *Mona Lisa.*

Michel Aliani
Medical Student and Receptionist, Hôtel Deauville

Jardin du Luxembourg, a beautiful park situated in the center of Paris, with lovely flowers, is a great place to read a good book and sunbathe at the same time, or use the tennis courts if you want. There are fantastic statues, each with a little bird perched near the top, eager to welcome you. It's a place for all ages and all seasons. A little advice: If you go there with a sandwich, you'll have to share it with the birds that fly to you from all around the park.

HRADCANY

67 Prazsky Hrad (Prague Castle)

70 Belveder

66 Hradcanské nám.

65 Ke hradu — Zámecké Schody — Thunovská

68 Valdstejnská

69 M

62 Loretánská — U Kasaren

63 Jánsky vrsek — **64** Nerudova — **52 51** Malostranské nám. — Tomásská — Letenská

54 53 — Mostecká — U luz semináre

61 ← Úvoz — Pohorelec

Vlasská — Trziste — **55**

49 Karluv m. (Charles Bridge)

56 Karmelitská — Prokopská — **50** Na Kampe

MALÁ STRANA

Strahovská Zahr.

Lobkovicka Zahrada

Harantova — Pelclova

Hellichova

Ruzovy sad

Seminarská aZahrada

Újezd — Vsehrdova

57

Strahovská

Ríční

Petřínské sady

Vitezná

El. Peskové — Plaská

Malostranské nábrezi

most Legií

Olympijská

Melnická

Strelecky Ostrov

Chaloupeckého

Petrínská

58

Vanickova — Jezdecká

Vodní

Kinského Zahrada

Malátova

Detsky Ostrov

60 ←

Zubatého — Pavla Svandy ze Semcic

Na Hrebenkách

Korenského

Viktora Huga

V botanice

Jiráskův most

Svédská — Svédská — Zapova

Preslova

Matousova

Nábřezí

Holeckova — Kobrova

Drtinova

nám. 14 rijna

Holeckova — Grafická

Stefánikova

Zborovská

Palac. most

Plzenská

Kmchova — Kartouzaká — Plzenská

Lidická

Na belidle

Horejsí nábrezí

Duskova — **59** Mozartova

M

Prague City Map

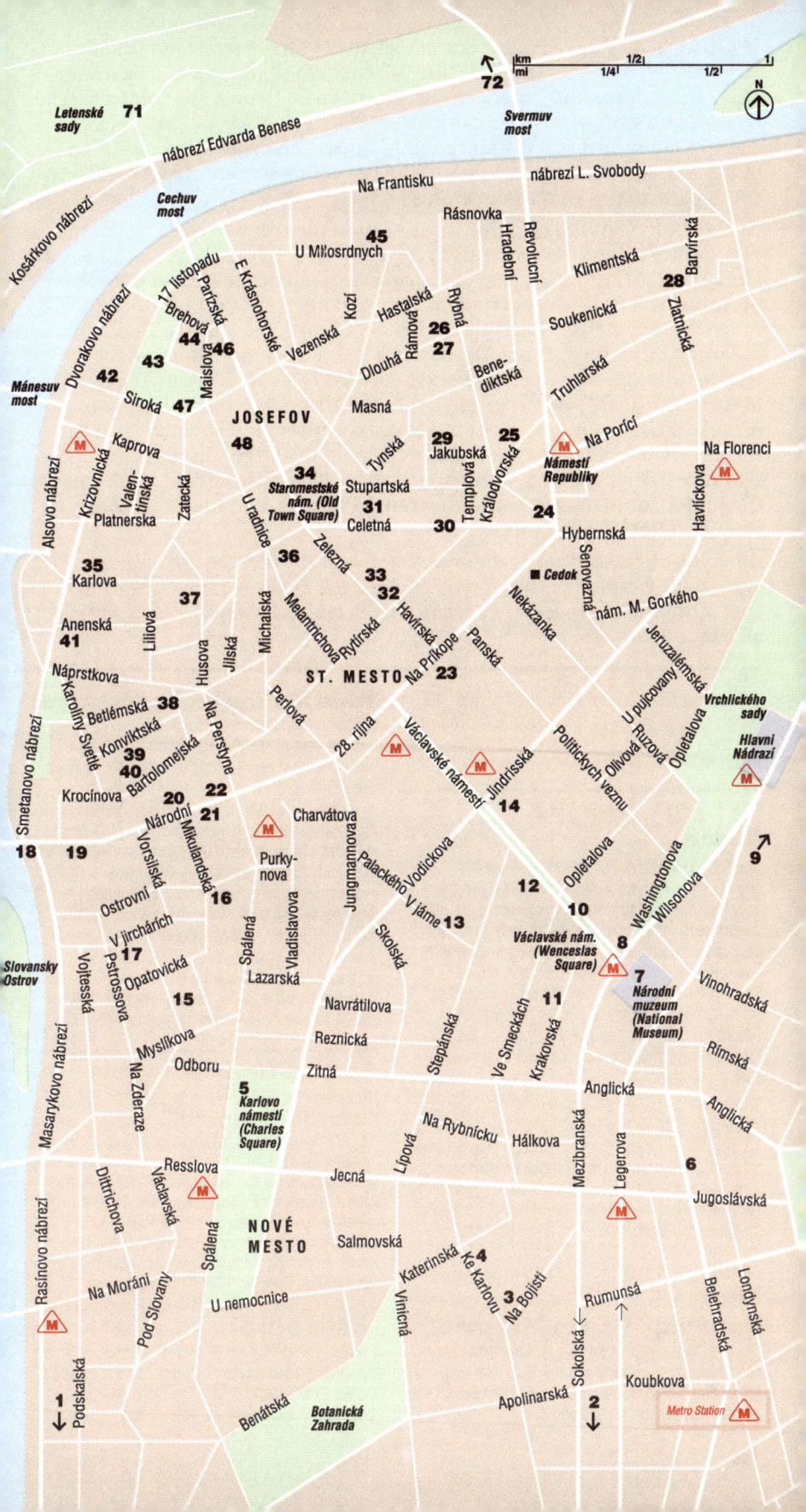

Letenské sady 71

72

Svermuv most

nábřeží Edvarda Beneše
Cechuv most

Kosárkovo nábřeží
Na Františku
nábřeží L. Svobody
U Milosrdných 45
Rásnovka

17 listopadu
Dvorakovo nábřeží
Brehová 44
Pařížská
E. Krásnohorské
Vezenská
Kozí
Hastalská
Rámová
Rybná 26 27
Revoluční
Hradební
Klimentská
Soukenická
Barvířská 28
Zlatnická

Mánesuv most
42 43
46
Široká 47
Maislova
Dlouhá
Masná
Benediktská
Truhlářská

Alšovo nábřeží
Křižovnická
Kaprova
Valentinská
Platnérská
Zatecká

JOSEFOV 48
34 Staroměstské nám. (Old Town Square)
U radnice
Tynská
Jakubská 29
25
Stupartská
Templová
Královodvorská
Náměstí Republiky
Na Poříčí
Na Florenci
Havlíčkova

31 Celetná 30 24
Hybernská
Cedok
Senovážná
nám. M. Gorkého

35 Karlova
36 Železná
33 32
Melantrichova
Rytířská
Havířská
Na Příkopě
Panská
Nekázanka
Jeruzalémská
Vrchlického sady
Hlavní Nádraží

37 Liliová
Anenská 41
Jilská
Husova
Michalská
ST. MESTO 23
U pujcovaný
Olivová
Ruzová
Opletalova

Náprstkova
Karoliny Světlé
Betlémská 38
Konviktská
Na Perštýně
Perlová
28. října
Václavské náměstí
Jindřišská
Politických veznu

39 40
Bartolomějská
Krocínova
20 22
21
Charvátova
Jungmannova
Palackého V jámě
14
Opletalova
9

Smetanovo nábřeží
Národní
Vorsilská
Mikulandská
16
Purkynova
Vodičkova
13
12
10
Washingtonova
Wilsonova

18 19
Ostrovní
V jirchářích
17
Pstrossova
Opatovická
15
Vladislavova
Školská
Václavské nám. (Wenceslas Square) 8
7 Národní muzeum (National Museum)
Vinohradská

Slovanský Ostrov
Voltěsská
Myslíkova
Odboru
Navrátilova
Řeznická
Stěpánská
Ve Smečkách
Krakovská
11
Rímská
Anglická
Anglická

Masarykovo nábřeží
Na Zderaze
Spálená
Lazarská
Zitná
Lipová
Na Rybníčku
Hálková
Meziřánská
Legerova
6
Jugoslávská

Rašínovo nábřeží
Dittrichova
Václavská
Resslova
5 Karlovo náměstí (Charles Square)
Jecná
Salmovská

Na Moráni
Pod Slovany
U nemocnice
Spálená
NOVÉ MESTO
Kateřinská
Ke Karlovu
4
Viničná
Na Bojišti 3
Sokolská
Rumunská
Belehradská
Londýnská
Koubková

1 Podskalská
Benátská
Botanická Zahrada
Apolinářská
2
Metro Station Ⓜ

Prague

"Prague doesn't let go of you...," wrote Franz Kafka. "This dear little mother has sharp claws." The nearly 40,000 Europeans and Americans who have taken to living in golden Prague (Praha in Czech) permanently since the 1989 "Velvet Revolution" put an end to Communist rule would certainly agree. This captivating city of "one hundred spires" (there are actually 500) has a little something for everyone, and is particularly kind to those on a budget.

History buffs can trace the city's origins from the crumbled remains of the 11th-century **Vyšehrad Fortress** to the Czech flag flying above **Pražský Hrad** (Prague Castle), the seat of the now democratically elected president. Art lovers will find "the heart of Europe" a living textbook of architecture, from the Romanesque **Bazilika sv. Jiří** (St. George's Basilica) to the Cubist **U černé Matky Boží** (House of the Black Mother of God). Romantics can wander through the cul-de-sacs and alleyways lit by lone street lamps in **Staré Město** (Old Town) and delight in a sunset walk on the Gothic **Karlův most** (Charles Bridge). Observers of economic transformation will marvel at the startling boom of entrepreneurship evident in the bright displays and neon signs nonexistent just a few years ago. And music fans can find Mozart in the **Rudolfinum**, jazz in the **Malostranská beseda**, and the latest European sounds in **Rock Club Bunkr**.

After you've trekked along the cobblestones of the contrasting, quirky, and exciting capital of the Czech Republic, the next time someone utters that oft-repeated phrase, "I've heard that Prague is beautiful . . . " you'll be able say, "I know."

To call from the US, dial 011 (international access code), 42 (country code), 2 (city code), and the local number. When calling from inside the Czech Republic, dial 02 and the local number.

Getting to Prague
Airport
About 20 kilometers (12 miles) northwest of the city center is **Ruzyně Airport** (367814), Prague's only international airport. Although there are plans for future reconstruction, at press time there was only one terminal, one currency-exchange booth, and one gate each for departures and arrivals. Consequently, when several planes land at once, there can be long lines at passport control. Departing flights to popular destinations also tend to crowd the terminal; it's best to arrive early.

There are several ways to get into the city. The very convenient **ČSA** shuttle bus (24210132) runs every 30 minutes daily; you pay your fare on board. Drop-off points in Prague are the **Dejvická** metro stop (*A* line) and the **ČSA Vltava Terminal** (25 Revoluční ulice, between Hradební and Nové mlýny ulice). For the ultra–low-budget scheme, buy a ticket for one of the local buses. *Nos. 254, 119,* or *108* run to the **Dejvická** metro stop; bus *179* terminates at the **Nové Butovice** metro stop (*B* Line).

Bus Station (Long-Distance)
The main bus terminal for international and cross-country travel is **Florenc** station (Křižíkova ulice, off Na Florenci ulice, 24211060). The station is connected to metro lines *B* and *C*.

Train Station (Long-Distance)
The main train station is **Hlavní nádraží** (2 Wilsonova třída, pedestrian entrance through Vrchlického sady). It has the most connections to international cities and is accessible from metro line *C*. Tickets can be purchased at the station but English skills at the counter vary, so consider purchasing tickets at **Čedok** (18 Na příkopě ulice, between Nekázanka ulice and náměstí Republiky). Other train stations with national and international connections are **Smíchovské nádraží** (Smichov Station; Nádražní ulice, metro line *B*); **Masarykovo nádraží** (Masaryk Station; Hybernská ulice, off Opletalova, metro line B); and **Nádraží Holešovice** (Holešovice Station, Vrbenského ulice, metro line *C*). The information phone number for all train stations is 24224200.

Getting around Prague
Bicycles The pedestrian zones of Staré město, **Hradčany** (The Castle District), and **Strahov** are good for bike riders, but negotiating the heavy traffic and inhaling exhaust fumes in the rest of the city can be hazardous. Bikes can be rented from **Cyclotramp** (02 Hrudičkova, off Gregorova ulice, 7953352), which is open Monday through Friday. The best cycling experience is to be had outside the city limits: From May through September the **Prague Information Service** (**PIS**; 544444) organizes one-day bicycle tours to **Karlštejn**, a castle about 28 kilometers (17 miles) outside of Prague.

Buses Tickets for buses, trams, and the metro are interchangeable and can be purchased at tobacco kiosks, newsstands, and in the metro stations. Riding illegally is discouraged by badge-flashing *revizors*,

134

who collect a fine on the spot if you don't have a valid ticket. Buses run daily between 5AM and midnight. You board at the back of the bus and validate your ticket in the hole-puncher near the doorway (pull the black tab toward you). Bus stops go unannounced, so memorize the number of stops or ask a fellow passenger about your final destination.

Driving Due to irregular streets and the free-for-all attitude of Prague's drivers, being behind the wheel is pretty hair-raising for the uninitiated; it's best to park and take public transportation. But, if you're going to drive, steer clear of the weekday rush hours (6-8AM and 3-5PM) and obey the in-city speed limit of 50 kph (37 mph). Covered, attended garages are located near Náměstí Jana Palacha (between Kaprova and Široká ulice); the **Národní divadlo** (National Theater) off Ostrovní ulice; and **Hlavní nádraží** (main train station) off Wilsonova ulice.

Metro The efficient Soviet-built metro operates daily, between the hours of 5AM and midnight. Tickets for the metro, buses, and trams are interchangeable and can be purchased at tobacco kiosks, newsstands, and from inside the metro stations. The system is divided into three lines designated by the letters A, B, and C and distinguished by the colors green, yellow, and red, respectively. Passengers can transfer as many times as necessary within a 50-minute period, and can transfer between lines at the **Muzeum, Můstek,** and **Florenc** stops. A metro station is indicated by an M symbol on a triangular signpost. Some useful words: *přestup* (transfer), *výstup* (exit). For metro information, call 294682.

Taxis Cabs can be hailed on the street or from taxi stands in front of hotels, on **Václavské náměstí** (Wenceslas Square) and in front of the **Obecní dům** (Municipal House) near náměstí Republiky. Despite meters, drivers are notorious for overcharging; ask for the approximate price before entering the cab. The least expensive radio taxi is **Profi Taxi** (61045555); other reputable companies are **DMV Taxi** (434918), **AAA Radio Taxi** (322444), and **Microlux** (350320).

Tours Half-day walking tours can be arranged through the **Prague Information Service (PIS)** (20 Na příkopě, between Nekázanka ulice and náměstí Republiky; 544444). **Čedok** (18 Na příkopě ulice, between Nekázanka ulice and náměstí Republiky; 24197111), a privately run tourist information agency, offers a three-hour bus and walking tour, "Historical Prague." **Wittmann Tours** (7 Uruguayská ulice, between Belgická and Americká ulice; 251235 or 4296293) specializes in topics of Jewish interest—walking tours of the **Židovská čtvrt** (Jewish Quarter), bus and walking tours of "Franz Kafka's City," and a bus tour of nearby **Theresienstadt** (Terezín) set up by the Nazis as a "model" concentration camp with its own orchestra and children's school.

Another inexpensive option is a cruise down the **Vltava River** by steamship with **Pražská Paroplavební Společnost** (Prague Passenger Lines; 24913882). There are several types of tours, but the introductory tour of historic Prague provides a splendid view of the city's landmarks. Board at Rašínovo nábřeží (between the Jiráskův and Palackého bridges).

Trams Often decorated with bright advertising schemes, trams crisscross the city and take you where the metro doesn't. Tram number *22*, in particular, is an inexpensive way to see the best of the city; board at the **Národní třída** stop and disembark at **Hradčany** (the Castle District). All trams run daily between 5AM and midnight; after midnight, trams *51-59* run approximately every 45 minutes. Timetables are posted at all stops. Tickets must be purchased in advance and are validated in the hole-puncher near the doorway.

Walking Prague is especially kind to walkers, mostly because its major sight-seeing areas—**Staroměstské náměstí** (Old Town Square), parts of **Malá Strana** (Lesser Quarter), and **Hradčany**—are pedestrian zones. The most famous and well-beaten track is called the **Coronation Route,** the trek of Bohemian kings to the castle: First, head down the broad avenue of **Václavské náměstí** (Wenceslas Square), continue through Staroměstské náměstí, follow Karlova ulice across the **Karlův most**, wander up through **Malostranské náměstí** (Lesser Quarter Square), and take Nerudova ulice up to **Hradčany**.

FYI

Accommodations Hotels, especially during the tourist season of May through September, fill up fast, so it's best to make reservations in advance. If you hit town without a bed, try one of the following agencies: **Ave Travel** (24223226), which is conveniently located in **Hlavní nádraží** and is open daily until 11PM; **Čedok** (6-8 Pařížská ulice, between Jáchymova ulice and Staroměstské náměstí; 2316978), which is open Monday through Friday until 7PM, and on Saturday and Sunday until 2PM; **Youth Travel Club** (12 Žitná ulice, between Štěpánská and Vodičkova ulice; 291240), which is open Monday through Friday 6PM, Saturday until 1PM.

Business Hours Most banks are open Monday through Friday from 8AM until noon; some reopen from 1:30 to 3:30PM. Shops and businesses may stay open until 6PM or 7PM, but it's best to use 9AM to 5PM from Monday through Friday as the guideline. Weekend shopping ends Saturday at 2PM, although some shops in tourist areas stay open until 5PM on Saturday. Sunday hours are rare but increasing. Classic Czech pubs and restaurants are usually open from 11AM until 11PM. (Very few restaurants, except those in hotels, offer breakfast.) Monday is the traditional closing day for museums.

Climate Prague's weather is temperate with an average annual temperature of 48 degrees. Spring and autumn are mild, and winters cold, with infrequent snowfall. July and August are the hottest months (58 to 78 degrees). Pack a sweater and at least an umbrella no matter what the season.

Consulates and Embassies

Canada ....6 Mickiewiczova (off Badeniho ulice); 24311108

UK ....14 Thunovská ulice (off Zámecká ulice); 24510439

US ....15 Tržiště ulice (between Karmelitská ....and Janský vršek); 24510847

135

Prague

Discount Tickets Not only are discounted admissions difficult to get, but many museums charge foreigners twice as much as residents. Try your luck.

Drinking The legal drinking age is 18. It's illegal to drive with any amount of alcohol in your bloodstream. *Hospadas* (pubs) are open until 10PM or 11PM; bars and nightclubs generally stay open until 2AM or later.

Emergencies For an ambulance, dial 155. For a police emergency, dial 158. To report a fire, dial 150. The only medical clinic with English-speaking doctors is at the **Nemocnice na Homolce** (2 Roentgenova ulice, close to Sídliště Homolka; 52922146 or 52922191); it's open 24 hours daily. **First Medical Clinic of Prague** (35 Vyšehradská, between Na Slovanech and U nemocnice ulice; 292286) also has English speakers on staff and is open for appointments Monday through Friday until 7PM. There's an emergency dental service at 22 Vladislavova ulice (between Purkyňova and Charvátova ulice; 24227663). The 24-hour pharmacy is at 1 Ječná ulice (between Salmovská ulice and Karlovo náměstí; 292940). In the event of legal problems, call your country's consulate or embassy.

Laundry One of the few self-service laundromats in Prague is **Laundry Kings** (16 Dejvická ulice, between Mařákova and Eliášova ulice); it's open daily until 10PM, but the washers and dryers can be used only until 8PM. There's no phone, but there are English-language newspapers, magazines, books, and strong coffee for sale. **Laundryland** (71 Londýnská, between Bruselská and Rumunská ulice; 251124) offers self- and full-service laundering, as well as dry cleaning and a bar; it's open daily until 10PM.

Money The official currency is the *koruna česká (kč)* or Czech crown. The lowest commission on currency exchange is offered by **Komerční banka** (42 Václavské náměstí, between Václavské náměstí and Ve Smečkách ulice), and by **Živnostenská banka** (20 Na příkopě ulice, at Nekázanka ulice). In a departure from usual banking hours, both of these are open Monday through Friday until 5PM; **Komerční banka** is also open on Saturday until 2PM. On nights and weekends, there are numerous **Chequepoint** exhange bureaus around the city. The one at **Václavské náměstí** (41 Vodickova, corner of Vodičkova and Václavské náměstí) is open 24 hours daily.

Personal Safety Pickpockets tend to work trams, buses, and heavily populated tourist areas such as Václavské náměstí and Karlův most. Prostitutes and illegal money changers operate in Václavskaé náměstí in the evening hours; lone women should avoid it after midnight. If you opt to drive during your stay in Prague, be aware that car theft is on the rise here.

Postal Services The main post office, **Hlavní pošta** (14 Jindřišská ulice, just off Václavské náměstí), is open 24 hours daily.

Public Holidays New Year's Day, Easter, Labour Day (1 May), Saints Cyril and Methodius (5 July), Anniversary of the Burning at the Stake of Jan Hus (6 July), Liberation from German Occupation (5 August), and Christmas (25-26 December).

Public Rest Rooms Many restaurants charge a small fee for the privilege of using their rest rooms. Public facilities are available in metro stations.

Publications The most comprehensive English-language events listings are to be found in the weekly *Prague Post* and in the Czech magazine *Pro*.

Restaurants Expensive restaurants recommend reservations, especially during the height of the tourist season, but most places are happy to take walk-in guests. In pubs and local restaurants it is common to share tables. In a *hospoda* or a *vinárna* (wine bar), your order is written down on a chit that is left on the table, and meals and beverages are ticked off as you order them. When you are ready to leave, tell your server *"zaplatím"* and your bill will be tallied.

Shopping Most of the shops that cater to tourists (selling glass, ceramics, jewelry, and crafts) are located in the historic areas. These items are also sold at a number of outdoor stands, particularly in **Staroměstské náměstí** and its surrounding streets, and on **Karlův most**. Many of Prague's large department stores (including **Kotva**) have been bought out by **K-Mart**. Their flagship store, **K-Mart** (26 Národní třída, at Spálená; 262341) is, ironically, one of the most expensive in town.

Smoking You can't light up on public transportation or in banks and stores. Some restaurants, wine bars, and pubs ban smoking from noon to 2PM.

Street Plan Prague is divided by the Vltava River. On the west side of the river are **Malá Strana** (Lesser Quarter) and Hradčany; on the east side are the primary sight-seeing areas of **Staroměstské náměstí** and **Václavské náměstí**.

Taxes The sales tax is already included in quoted prices for hotels, restaurants, and stores.

Telephones Some public phones take coins, but most now accept telephone cards, which can be purchased at tobacco kiosks, newsstands, and the main post office. When you're placing a long-distance call, try to use a phone card at a public phone, as placing calls from hotels is prohibitively expensive.

Tipping In inexpensive restaurants, round up the bill to the nearest factor of five or 10; in pricier places, leave 10 to 15 percent. Taxi drivers expect passengers to round up the fare to the nearest 10 for the tip.

Visas American and British travelers need only a valid passport for visits of up to 90 days. Canadians must obtain a visa from the Czech embassy before leaving Canada.

Visitors' Information A visitor's first stop should be the **Prague Information Service** (20 Na příkopě ulice, off Nekázanka ulice; 644444) or the **American Hospitality Center** (8 Melantrichova, between Husova and Kožná ulice; 24229961); both are open daily. The **American Express** office (56 Václavské náměstí, between Ve Smečkách and Krakovská ulice; 24216863) also has good tourist information; it's open Monday through Friday, and Saturday until 2PM.

Prague

1 Vyšehrad Fortress After Bohemia's first king, Prince Vratislav II, moved here from **Pražský Hrad** (see page 148) in the 11th century, this became the seat of power for three generations of the Bohemian ruling family, the Přemyslovci (Premyslids). Today only a stone arch of a bridge remains from the original ninth-century palace, but the visit is still worthwhile for the panoramic views of Prague. In addition, there's a museum documenting the history of the fortress, and the **Rotunda sv. Martina** (St. Martin's Rotunda), a restored Romanesque chapel built by Prince Vratislav II in the second half of the 11th century, and the **Kostel sv. Petra a Pavla** (Church of Sts. Peter and Paul), constructed in the 11th century and subjected to seven major architectural renovations before it was finally resolved into Neo-Gothic style by **Josef Mocker** in 1885. Next door to the church is the **Vyšehradský hřbitov** (Vyšehrad cemetery), the burial place of more than 600 celebrated Czechs, including composers Antonín Dvořák and Bedřich Smetana, writers Karel Čapek and Jan Neruda, and artist Alfons Mucha. ♦ Nominal admission. Daily. 1 Soběslavova ulice (near Vyšehrad metro station). 296651

1 Monica Hotel $$ This charming cliffside stucco villa has 24 tastefully furnished rooms with private bathrooms and sunny balconies. The accommodating staff and lovely location on the Vltava River make it a popular choice of repeat visitors. An added attraction is a breakfast room which is converted to a snack bar at night and offers a choice of five or six light meals, such as chicken with mushrooms or with peaches. ♦ 31A Vlnitá ulice (at Branická ulice). 464465; fax 464120

OAZA

1 Sport Hotel Oáza $$ A white tower with wooden balconies houses 27 guest rooms with satellite TVs, phones, and private bathrooms. The sports-inclined traveler will appreciate the tennis courts, mini-golf, volleyball, sauna, and swimming pool. The hotel also boasts a Czech restaurant, room service, and a snack bar. It's expensive if you're on a tight budget, but a bargain if you plan to take advantage of all the athletic amenities. ♦ 106 Jeremenkova ulice (at Perlitová ulice). 61215071; fax 61215075

2 Pension Madona $$ The owner's wife has furnished this cheerful three-story family villa with eclectic aplomb, running the gamut from fur-covered bar stools to Victorian armoires. If you're into frills, powder blue, and great bathtubs, ask for room No. 5. All 10 guest rooms have private baths; there's also a garden to enjoy in the summer, a sauna, and a breakfast room. No credit cards accepted. ♦ 24 Pod vilami (between Vladimírova and Podluží ulice). 6925836

3 U Kalicha ★$$ This pub, mentioned in Jaroslav Hašek's novel *The Good Soldier Svejk,* is where the famed soldier arranged to meet his World War I buddies at "six o'clock after the war." It's a tourist trap. ♦ Czech ♦ Daily lunch and dinner. 2 Na Bojišti ulice (between Sokolská and Ke Karlovu ulice). 290701

4 Muzeum Antonína Dvořáka (Antonin Dvorak Museum) The first floor of the Vila Amerika building, designed by **Kilian Ignaz Dientzenhofer,** houses a museum documenting the composer's life, including exhibits of his quill pens, walking sticks, and souvenirs from his sojourn to America. His library occupies the second floor. The museum serves as a venue for classical and chamber music concerts; check newspaper listings for scheduled events. ♦ Nominal admission. Tu-Su. 20 Ke Karlovu (between Na Bojišti and Kateřinská ulice). 298214

5 Karlovo náměstí (Charles Square) The largest and oldest square in Prague was established in 1398 by King Charles IV as a trade center and used as a cattle market until the 19th century. From 1398 to 1784 city officials governed from the **Novoměstské radnice** (New Town Hall) at the northern end of the square, where in 1419 an angry mob, incited by the Hussite priest Father Želivský, tossed the town's councilmen out the window. On the south side, the Baroque building at **No. 40** is known as **Faustův Dům** (Faust's House). Legend has it that alchemists practiced turning lead into gold and other mysterious arts here. ♦ Bounded by U nemocnice and Žitna, and Vodičkova and Spálená ulice

6 Radost/FX Owned by a group of American expats, this club is frequented by the city's glamour crowd. Prague's answer to New York City's hot spots, it boasts two bars, lots of seating room, a dance floor, and a big-screen TV, as well as a cafe, gallery, and music shop. ♦ Cover. Daily 9PM-5AM. 120 Bělehradská ulice (between Jugoslávská and Anglická ulice). 251210; fax 251210

Within Radost/FX:

FX Cafe ★★★$ Decorated with pâpier-maché faces, this cafe serves some of the best of the scarce vegetarian fare in town. Try the veggie pocket with yogurt dressing, nachos, or spicy Thai noodles. Sunday brunch features real orange juice and pancakes swimming in syrup. ♦ Vegetarian ♦ Daily breakfast, lunch, and dinner. 258938

Prague

7 Národní muzeum (National Museum)
This imposing neo-Renaissance structure was built by architect **Josef Shulz** in the 19th century. The museum houses some 55,000 mineral specimens, 750,000 coins, and 2.5 million fossils. The statistics are more interesting than the exhibits themselves, although you might wander in to see the only complete dodo bird skeleton in the world, assembled from bones gathered from all over the globe. The exterior still shows the scars of the 1968 Soviet invasion; soldiers mistook the museum for the capitol building and opened fire on it.
♦ Nominal admission. M, W-Su. 68 Václavské náměstí (at Wilsonova třída). 24230485

8 Socha sv. Václava (Statue of St. Wenceslas) A popular meeting place in the city, this statue was completed in 1912 by famed Czech sculptor Josef Václav Myslbek to honor the first Prince Wenceslas (of *Good King Wenceslas* Christmas carol fame; he was king of Bohemia from 1378 to 1419). In 1914, Czechoslovakian independence was declared at its base, where you can see the likenesses of the four patron saints of Bohemia: Procopius, Adalbert, Ludmilla, and Agnes.
♦ Václavské náměstí (in front of the Národní muzeum)

9 Hotel Apollon $$ Standing out from its concrete-block context, this seven-floor, 50-room hotel offers simply furnished rooms with phones, satellite TV, and small private bathrooms. There's an elegant pastel dining room where carefully prepared Continental and Czech meals are served. ♦ 158 Koněvova ulice (between Za žižkovskou vozovnou and Laudova ulice). 6442414; fax 6442430

9 Hotel Garni Jarov $$ The 70 guest rooms with WCs, showers, and mini-bars are nothing fancy, but the staff of this yellow two-story hotel goes all out to make your stay pleasant. Breakfast is served in the second floor dining room, and the nearby **Junior Club** disco offers meals and a peek into the local nightlife scene.
♦ 204 Koněvova ulice (between V zahrádkách and Jeseniova ulice). 24910113; fax 24910113

9 Vila Garni $$ The five homey rooms on the second floor of this bed and breakfast (pictured above) share one bathroom, and each opens into a communal dining room with a hot plate, all of which makes it pretty easy to get acquainted with your fellow travelers. Owner Zuzana Jarošová provides a few English-language books for browsing.
♦ 69 V domově ulice (between Koněvova and Na vrcholu ulice). 6832006

10 Václavské náměstí (Wenceslas Square)
This square, which was a horse market during the reign of Charles IV, is the Champs-Elysées of Prague. Here you'll find the city's overpriced hotels, shops, discos, and restaurants, as well as six movie theaters and a very crowded **McDonald's**. In November 1989, the square was packed with protestors who eventually brought about the downfall of the Communist government. Now shoppers and tourists throng here in the summer months; at night, musicians, performers, and seedy elements come out to play. ♦ Between Wilsonova třída and Na příkopě ulice

11 AghaRTA Jazz Centrum According to jazz fans, this is the best place to catch current stars and up-and-coming jazz, rock, and R&B hopefuls. The club also has a cafe and a CD shop stocked with favorites.
♦ Cover. M-F 4PM-1AM; Sa-Su 7PM-1AM. Performances start at 9PM. 5 Krakovská ulice (between Žitná ulice and Václavské náměstí). 24212914

12 Hospůdka Václavka ★★$ This sparsely decorated little pub with five tables, a bar, and outdoor seating (overlooking a parking lot) is one of the few inexpensive places to eat in this tourist-heavy area. A number of vegetarian meals are offered, including *halušky se sýrem* (Slovak-style dumplings with cheese), fried *květák* (cauliflower), and spaghetti. ♦ Czech ♦ Daily lunch and dinner. No credit cards accepted. 148 Václavské náměstí (between Ve Smečkách and Štěpánská ulice). 24219428

13 Jáma ★★$ Here is a hybrid of a Czech *hospoda* and North American college bar. The often-crowded, ground-floor tavern offers good beer, and those snack foods particularly hard to find outside the US: potato skins, onion rings, and nachos, as well as other Mexican favorites such as quesadillas and burritos, Czech style. But avoid the refried beans. Late at night, the joint is loud and smoky. ♦ American/Mexican ♦ Daily lunch and dinner. 7 V jámě (between Štěpánská and Vodičkova ulice). 264127

14 Hotel Evropa Cafe ★$$ Though a room at this hotel, designed in 1904 by **Alois Dryák** and **Bedřich Bendlemayer** in pure *Jugendstil*

138

Prague

(Art Nouveau) style, is beyond the budget traveler's reach, do stop by to sip a rather pricey Viennese coffee in the cafe or to take in the asymmetrical construction, floral motifs, and ironwork in the upstairs gallery. On your way out, peek into the French restaurant next door—it's a replica of the dining room of the *Titanic*. ♦ Cafe ♦ Daily 7AM-midnight. 9 Václavské náměstí (between Opletalova and Jindřišská ulice). 24228117

15 U Fleků ★$ In existence since 1499, this is Prague's pre-eminent *pivnice* (beer hall) for out-of-towners. The special dark brew is truly excellent, but the place is usually overcrowded with yodeling Germans and Americans. ♦ Czech ♦ Daily breakfast, lunch, and dinner. 11 Křemencova ulice (between Myslíkova and Opatovická ulice). 24915118

16 Kavárna Velryba ★★★$ Patterned wallpaper, black marble tables, and newspaper-covered window ledges give this subterranean cafe its bohemian ambience. Read a book, chat with your arty neighbor, and fill up on the good-size salads and heaping portions of *čočka s párkem* (sausage and lentils). There's a back room that is open until 1AM for general hanging out. ♦ Czech ♦ Daily lunch and dinner. 24 Opatovická ulice (at Ostrovní ulice). 24912391

17 Kmotra ★★★$ Walk through the cafe to the pizzeria downstairs, where the stucco walls and oak tables and chairs set a casual stage for what may be the best pizza in town. See what the special is, or ask for your favorite combo of toppings. ♦ Italian ♦ Daily lunch and dinner. Reservations recommended. No credit cards accepted. 12 V jirchářích (between Křemencova and Pštrossova ulice). 24915809

18 Národní divadlo (National Theater) In the late 19th century at the height of the National Revival movement, citizens donated everything from gold teeth to gold coins to build this theater. Designed by **Josef Zítek**, the neo-Renaissance building was completed in 1881, only to be gutted by a fire started by metalworkers a short two months after opening night. It took two years to reconstruct the interior of the most famous of Prague's theaters, where Antonín Dvořák (an unknown at that time) played the viola in the orchestra conducted by Bedřich Smetana. The boxy glass **Nová scéna** (New Theater) was added in 1981. In addition to its own theatrical company, the **National Theater** hosts performances of ballet, opera, and drama. ♦ Box office: daily. Performances: M-F 7PM; Sa-Su 2PM, 7PM. Closed July-August. 2-4 Národní třída (between Masarykovo nábřeží and Divadelní ulice). 24914204

19 Laterna Magika A Prague classic, this unique combination of film, theater, and pantomime was first shown at the Brussels Expo in 1958. Czech film director Miloš Forman, whose *Amadeus* was filmed in Prague, once worked for the troupe. ♦ Admission. Box office: M-Sa. Performances: M-F 8PM; Sa 5PM, 8PM. 4 Národní třída (between Voršilská and Divadelní ulice). 24212991

20 Studio Gag Borise Hybnerna Well-known Czech mime Boris Hybner uses this theater as an outlet for his one-man or ensemble comedy mime shows. According to Hybner, "Pantomime suits Prague like Prague's history of alchemy: making something from nothing." ♦ Admission. Box office: M-Sa. Performances: daily 7PM, 9PM. 25 Národní třída (between Na Perštýně and Karolíny Světlé ulice). 24229095; fax 24225990

21 Reduta Jazz Club Musical notes decorate the walls, tables and benches crowd the room, and the best jazz bands in the city play to a full house in this club, which occasionally sponsors English-language theater or has theme nights. ♦ Cover. Bar: daily 10AM-6PM, 8PM-3AM. Box office: daily. Shows: daily beginning at 9PM. Reservations recommended. 20 Národní třída (between Spálená and Mikulandská ulice). 24912246

TRAVELLERS' HOSTEL
new, comfortable, famous

21 Travellers' Hostel $ Set up in a former language school, this hotel offers three floors of rooms (first floor for men, top two floors for women) with 10 to 15 people per room. The open-air atrium and a volleyball court provide outdoor fun, while a snack bar offers breakfast and munchies throughout the day. The reception desk is open 24 hours and English-speaking staff make arrangements convenient. Bedding rental is available; try to arrive before 11AM to secure a place. Closed January-June, September-December ♦ 5 Mikulandská (between Ostrovní ulice and Národní třída). 24910739

Restaurants/Clubs: Red   **Hotels:** Blue
Shops/ ❦ Outdoors: Green   **Sights/Culture:** Black

139

Prague

22 U medvídků ★★$$ This complex (whose name translates to "At the Little Bears"), bills itself as beer hall, wine bar, and restaurant. The *svíčková s houskovým knedlíkem* (beef and dumplings in cream sauce) is good, if slightly sweet, and the *jihočeská bašta* (pork, corned beef, and sausage with two kinds of dumplings) is even better. Top off your meal with a *palačinka* (jam-filled crepe topped with chocolate sauce and whipped cream). ♦ Czech ♦ Daily lunch and dinner. 7 Na Perštýně ulice (between Národní třída and Martinská ulice). 24220930

23 Moser Glass The exquisite glassware sold here has graced the tables of King Fuad of Egypt, Queen Elizabeth II, and the Maharajah of Baroda. The giant snifters with such names as "Stout Gentleman" and "Big Bertha" are the most affordable. ♦ Daily. 12 Na příkopě (between Panská ulice and Václavské náměstí). 24211293

24 Obecní dům (Municipal House) Built between 1905 and 1911 by architects **Antonín Balšánek** and **Osvald Polívka** on the site of the former royal court, this building (illustrated below) represents the best work of a generation of Czech Art Noveau artists which include Alfons Mucha, Josef Šaloun, and Jan Preisler. The **Smetanova sín** (Smetana Hall) seats 1,500 and boasts a magnificent stained-glass ceiling. In January of 1918 the demand for independence was signed here by Czech and Moravian MPs. On special occasions it's possible to see the mayoral room, painted in lavender splendor by Mucha. At press time, the building was closed for reconstruction and scheduled to reopen in January 1997. ♦ 5 náměstí Republiky (between U Obecního domu and U Prašné brány ulice). 2315605

24 Prašná brána (Powder Tower) This Gothic structure was built in 1475 by schoolteacher Matěj Rejsek for King Vladislav II Jagiello, to replace one of the original 13 gates of Staré Město (Old Town). In the 17th century, it was used to store gunpowder; hence the name. ♦ Náměstí Republiky (corner of U Prašné brány and Celetná ulice)

25 Kotva Acquired by **K-Mart**, this is the one-stop shop for everything from fur coats to pens and souvenirs, with lots of familiar brands on the shelves. The ground floor stocks alcohol, fresh coffee, and chocolate suitable as gifts for Czech friends. The subterranean *potraviny* (supermarket) is reached by the staircase outside the store that looks like a metro entrance. ♦ M-W, F; Th until 8PM; Sa-Su until 2PM. 8 náměstí Republiky (at Revoluční ulice). 24801111

26 Granát Turnov This store is part of the Turnov monopoly that controls the industry for the Czech Republic's native stone, the garnet; shop here for silver bracelets or rings set with the rich red stones. ♦ Daily. 28 Dlouhá ulice (between Rybná and Rámová ulice). 2315612

27 Roxy Billing itself as a club that supports alternative culture, this cavernous "experimental" space has gained a reputation for offering an eclectic mix of artists and art from the local as well as the international scene. Exhibitions run the gamut from Norwegian performance art to James Bond films, and bands play anything from hard core metal to acoustic guitar. This is *the* place to dance on Friday and Saturday nights. Check local listings for special events. Oddly enough, there's also a tearoom on the first level. ♦ Cover. Tearoom: daily 5PM-midnight. Club:

Obecní dům (Municipal House)

Tu-Sa 8PM-5AM. 33 Dlouhá (between Rybná and Rámová ulice). 24810951

BuNkR ROCK CLUB

28 Rock Club Bunkr Despite periodic complaints from neighbors about the noise, this club—one of the first to open after the 1989 revolution—is still open. It's a great place to hear local and international bands play live. Tuesday and Sunday are dedicated to disco and women are admitted free on these nights. Rockers, occasional punks, and Czech literati hang out at the **Bunkr Cafe** next door. ♦ Cover. Club: daily 8PM-6AM. Cafe: daily 9AM-3AM. 2 Lodecka ulice (corner of Petrske náměstí and Lodecka ulice). 24810661

29 Kostel sv. Jakuba (Church of St. James) The church was founded in 1372, although Baroque flourishes were added in the late 17th century. Inside are 21 separate altars and lavish stucco works by Italian artist Ottavio Mosto. One bizarre relic is the remains of a human forearm on a chain, torn off of a thief who tried to steal the Madonna from the High Altar. If you can, attend a high Mass sung by the church's choir—the organ and acoustics are superb. The voices of Placido Domingo and Luciano Pavorotti have echoed in this nave, which is the second longest in Prague (**Chrám sv. Víta**, St. Vitus Cathedral, has the longest; see below). ♦ Malá Štupartská ulice (between Štupartská and Masná ulice)

29 Red Hot and Blues ★★★$ New Orleans–style and some Mexican cookin' spices up this popular expat hang-out. The chef recommends the spicy, grilled chicken breast, shrimp Creole, or étouffée. Blackened tuna is a frequent special. Blues musicians (of varying quality) play at the low podium in the center of the room several times a week; check local listings. ♦ American/Mexican ♦ Daily lunch and dinner. 12 Jakubská (between Templová and Malá Štupartská ulice). 2314639

30 Celetná ulice (Celetná Street) Lined with Baroque and rococo town houses, most of which have Gothic undertones, is one of the oldest streets in Prague. The six-story house at **No. 19** is known as the **U černé Matky Boží** (House of the Black Mother of God), named after the Marian statue in the niche. The building, designed by **Josef Gočár** in 1911-12, is the best-known example of the short-lived Cubist period in Czech architecture. Don't miss the Baroque accents on house **No. 3, U tří králů** (At the Three Kings), where Herman Kafka, Franz's father, had his first shop. ♦ Between the Prašná brána and Staroměstské náměstí

31 Vinárna u Hynků ★★★$ In one room is a *hospoda* with wooden tables, a comfy couch, and an Andy Warhol poster, while across the courtyard is a stylish *vinárna* (wine bar). The service is somewhat indifferent, but the decor, price, and quality of the food make up for it. This is one of the few places left in Staré Město that doesn't cater exclusively to tourists. Famed Czech writer Bohumil Hrabal is rumored to drop by on occasion. Try the *Štupartská směs speciál*, including appetizer, beef and pork combo, and dessert. ♦ Czech ♦ Daily lunch and dinner. No credit cards accepted. 11 Celetná ulice (entrance on 6 Štupartská ulice, between Templová and Týnská ulice). 2323406

32 Stavovské divadlo (Estates Theater) This jewel box of tiered seating was formerly named for Josef Kajetán Tyl, a member of the National Revival movement and one of the first to write plays in Czech instead of German. In 1787, Mozart premiered *Don Giovanni* here, conducting the orchestra himself. *Činohry* (dramas) are translated into English via headphones. ♦ Box office: daily. Performances: M-F 7PM; Sa-Su 2PM. Closed July-August. 6 Ovocný trh (at Železná ulice). Box office on Rytířská ulice (between Havelská ulice and Ovocný trh). 24914202

33 Karolinum (Carolinum) A complex of buildings serves as the rectorate of **Karlova Universita** (Charles University), the first university in Central Europe, founded in 1348 by King Charles IV. Jan Hus served as a rector, and after his death it became the hotbed of the Hussite movement until the Jesuits took over. From the street you can see the oriel window, a remnant of the original Gothic building. Inside, take a look at the magnificent 17th-century assembly hall. ♦ Tu-Su 10AM-noon, 1-6PM. 3 Ovocný trh (at Železná ulice). 2288441

34 Staroměstské náměstí (Old Town Square) Once the site of 30 Gothic churches and a marketplace, Prague's historic center now contains 11,000 square yards of cobblestones and countless white plastic cafe tables. Weaving among the tables, hawkers, and stalls, you'll be walking on the site of seminal events that changed the course of the country's history. After the Battle of White Mountain, Bohemia's Protestant leaders were decapitated here in 1621, thinning the ranks of the native aristocracy; in May 1945, bullets ricocheted off Old Town Hall when Czechs rose up against the Nazi occupation. ♦ Enter via Celetná ulice

At Staroměstské náměstí:

Prague

Jan Hus Memorial Art Nouveau sculptor Ladislav Šaloun designed this memorial, which was erected in 1915, 500 years after the celebrated Czech reformer Jan Hus was burned at the stake for heresy. Hus and his followers supported many of the same ideas as Martin Luther. The inscription reads "Truth Will Prevail." ♦ Northeast corner of the square (across from Palác Kinských)

Palác Kinských (Kinsky Palace) Designed by **Kilian Ignaz Dientzenhofer** and built by **Anselm Largo** from 1755 to 1785, this 18th-century Baroque palace with rococo trimmings now houses a permanent collection of 19th- and 20th-century graphic art and many changing exhibitions of the **Národní Galerie** (National Gallery). The young Franz Kafka attended school here; earlier, his father Herman ran a dry goods store on the site. ♦ Nominal admission. Tu-Su. 12 Staroměstské náměstí (north side of the square, off Dlouhá ulice). 24818758

Dům U kamenného zvonu (Stone Bell House) Art exhibitions are held in this Gothic structure named for the stone bell preserved in the corner of the house. The oldest section of the house is the ground-floor chapel bearing faint traces of murals dating from 1310. On the second floor is a beautiful Renaissance beamed ceiling sporting stylized flora. Check listings for chamber concerts. ♦ Nominal admission. Tu-Su. 13 Staroměstské náměstí (east side of the square). 24810036

Chrám Matky Boží před Týnem (Cathedral of the Virgin Mary before Týn) The main church of Staré Město since the Hussite revolution, the cathedral was founded in 1380. The 260-foot towers are the most recognizable of this city's 500 spires. Facing the main altar is a relief of Tycho de Brahe (1546-1610), the medieval astronomer who is best known for rejecting Copernican theory, insisting that the sun circled the earth. ♦ Tu-Su afternoons. 15 Staroměstské náměstí (east side of square). 2314936

34 Staroměstská radnice (Old Town Hall) Since the 13th century, this hall has been a piecemeal project, as city fathers continually annex neighboring buildings to the original **Welfin House**. The building underwent a major renovation after sustaining damage from Nazi tanks when Czechs revolted against their occupiers on 5 May 1945. Particularly impressive are the 15th-century council chamber lined with the coats of arms of 60 guilds, the chapel designed by **Petr Parléř** with 14th-century frescoes, and the dungeon. As you head up to the tower, pause for a look at the **Kostel sv. Mikuláše** (St. Nikolas Church) (see page 145). Far below, the city resembles the Cubist layers of a Braque painting. ♦ Nominal admission. M-F. In the direction of Malé náměstí. 24228456

Within Staroměstská radnice:

Orloj (Astronomical Clock) If you wonder what all the neck-craning in front of the tower is about, wait until the stroke of the hour. Master Hanuš built his astronomical timepiece in 1490, a mechanical masterwork of gears and dials. It broke down, however, and a new mechanism was installed in 1592. Since then, the clock tracks the movements of the sun and moon, indicates the length of the day, the equinoxes, the rising and setting of stars, and the signs of the zodiac. The lower dial illustrates the seasons in pastoral vignettes by painter Josef Mánes. On the hour the 12 apostles circulate through open shutters, and the allegorical figures of Death, Vanity, and Greed commence movement. The ceremony ends with the crow of a cock and the chiming of the bells.

Dům U Minuty (House at the Minute) In 1905, this Renaissance sgraffito depicting biblical and mythological scenes was discovered and later restored by Jindřich Čapek. ♦ 2-3 Staroměstské náměstí (off Malé náměstí)

35 Klementinum (Clementinum) A whole city block was razed to construct this complex of buildings for the Jesuits in the 18th century. Unfortunately, the magnificent Baroque library, with its 17th-century globes, astronomical clocks, and historic manuscripts, is closed to the public (although there are ongoing negotiations to reopen it; check with the **Prague Information Service** at 544444). At least visitors can walk through the courtyards to experience the overwhelming environment. Occasional chamber music concerts held in the gilded Baroque **Zrcadlová sín** (Mirror Chapel) are a feast for the ears and eyes. ♦ Free. Concerts: admission. Tu-Su. 190 Křižovnická ulice (between Křižovnická náměstí and Platnéřská ulice). 24229500

36 Country Life Such healthy comestibles as Japanese seaweed, soy milk and cheeses, tofu, and whole-grain breads fill this store. The stand-up snack bar makes an excellent, albeit small, salad with yogurt dressing, as well as vegetarian pizza, veggie sandwiches, and a decent goulash made from soy "meat." ♦ M-Th 7:30AM-6:30PM; F 10AM-2:30PM; Su afternoons. 15 Melantrichova ulice (between Havelská ulička and Kožná ulice). 24213366

37 Pražský dům fotografie U zlaté ovce This small gallery with the big name (it means **Prague House of Photography at the Golden Sheep**) showcases rotating exhibits of classic and modern Czech, Slovak, and European photography. In addition to the original art on display, there's a gift shop offering books and posters for sale. ♦ Nominal admission. Daily. 23 Husova ulice (at Karlova ulice). 229349

37 Středoevropská Galerie Browse through the current show of modern Czech graphic

Prague

artists at the **Central European Gallery** and take home an original print or a terrific poster to remember your trip. ◆ Daily. 19 Husova ulice (between Retězová and Karlova ulice). 24222068

38 Betlémská Kaple (Bethlehem Chapel) Built in 1392, this reconstructed Gothic church is the birthplace of the Hussite movement. Jan Hus, its founder, sermonized here against the excesses of the Catholic church from 1402 until his execution in 1415. He lived in the adjoining **House of Preachers**, which now contains a small exhibit on Hussitism. A memorial with choral groups is held on 6 July, the anniversary of his death. ◆ Nominal admission. 5 Betlémské náměstí (at Konviktská ulice).

39 Konvikt ★★★$ This noisy, smoke-filled *hospoda* was previously a monastery, prison, and army training school. Today it's one of the few places where backpackers and Czech rockers mingle comfortably. Sometimes-surly waiters serve up tasty *lečo* (spicy mixed tomatoes and peppers) and venison in season. ◆ Czech ◆ M-Sa lunch and dinner; Su dinner. 22 Konviktská ulice (between Průchodní and Karolíny Světlé ulice). 24212881

40 Unitas Le Prison $$ Located across the street from the famed **Bartolomějská** police station, where many dissidents were once detained, this cozy pension has converted prison cells into 52 rooms and shares its space with the **Cloister of the Sisters of Mercy**. President Václav Havel was once held here for questioning. There is a small breakfast room; bathroom facilities are all shared. ◆ 9 Bartolomějská ulice (between Na Perštýně and Karolíny Světlé ulice). 2327700; fax 2327709

41 Divadlo Na zábradlí (Theater on the Balustrade) The young Václav Havel first worked as a stagehand in this theater, graduating to playwright under the tutelage of celebrated Czech director Jan Grossman. Czech pantomime performances are held throughout the year; consult newspaper listings. ◆ Box office: M-F 2-7PM; Sa-Su 5- 7:30PM on performance days. Performances: 7PM. 5 Anenská náměstí (between Náprstkova and Na Zábradlí ulice). 24221933, 24220920

42 Rudolfinum (House of Artists) Designed by **Josef Zítek** and **Josef Shulz**, this neo-Renaissance building was completed in 1874 as the first Bohemian concert hall and exhibition center. Housing Prague's most exquisite concert hall, the **Dvořákova sín** (Dvorak Hall), the building is also the home of the **Czech Philharmonic Orchestra.** During the German occupation, it was used as the base for Hitler's Nazi choir. Enter from the Vltava River side and walk through the **Velké dvorany** (Great Hall) for a look at Viennese artist Pietro Isella's grotesques, garlands, putti, and allegorical figures. After a 1992 restoration, the two floors of galleries have been reopened. If you arrive early for a show, have a decadent sundae in the elegant **Rudolfinum Cafe.** ◆ Nominal admission for exhibits. Box office: M-F; Sa-Su on performance days; Performances: 7:30PM. Box office located on corner of náměstí Jana Palacha and 17 listopadu ulice. 12 Alšovo nábreží (at Široká ulice). 24893111

43 Uměleckoprůmyslové muzeum (Museum of Decorative Arts) If you don't have time for castle hopping in the country, this museum (illustrated above) is the place to see the goods from their interiors, particularly the inlaid cabinets, tapestries, porcelain, and pewterware dating from the Renaissance to the mid-19th century. ◆ Nominal admission. Tu-Su. 2, 17 listopadu ulice (between široká and Břehová ulice). 24811241

44 Starý židovský hřbitov (Old Jewish Cemetery) Step into another world where sandstone and white and pink marble tombstones lean, slope, and tumble into one another. Some 12,000 headstones mark an estimated 100,000 graves several layers deep. You'll find wish notes anchored with pebbles on many of the stones, especially on that of Rabbi Judah Low, credited with creating the *golem,* a man modeled of Vltava clay that the rabbi brought to life. Symbols on the stones represent names and professions: hands in prayer (Kohn clan), pitcher (Levite clan), bear (Hebrew name Dov), scissors (tailor), mortar

143

Prague

(pharmacist), and book (printer, binder, or cantor). ♦ Admission. M-F, Su. U starého hřbitova (between Maiselova and 17 listopadu ulice). 24810099

Connected to the Starý židovský hřbitov:

44 Bývalá obřadní síň (Former Ceremonial Hall) The neo-Romanesque building houses an exhibit of children's drawings from the Terezin ghetto, where more than 80 percent of the 140,000 prisoners (including 11,000 children) died. ♦ Admission. M-F, Su. 24810099

45 Klášter sv. Anežky (St. Agnes Convent) The convent, built in 1233, forms part of the oldest early-Gothic complex in Bohemia. It was founded by Anežka (Agnes), sister to King Wenceslas I, who was canonized in 1989. Inside the complex, shared by the nuns with the Franciscan brothers, is the **Kostel sv. Salvátora** (Church of the Holy Savior), dating from 1240 (look for the columns with portraits of the Premyslid family carved in the capitals); and the **Kostel sv. Františka** (Church of St. Francis), where Wenceslas I is buried. The convent also houses the **Národní Galerie** (National Gallery) collection of 19th-century Czech paintings, including the romantic and stylized works of the Mánes family and Mikoláš Aleš. ♦ Nominal admission. Tu-Su. 17 U Milosrdných ulice (at Anežská). 24810628

46 Staronová synagoga (Old-New Synagogue) Built in 1270, this early-Gothic building (pictured above) is the oldest surviving synagogue in Europe. Legend has it that the foundation stones were brought to Prague by angels after the destruction of the second Jerusalem Temple in 70 BC. Records show that Prague Jews asked French builders, who had been called by King Otakar II to build the **Klášter sv. Anežky** (see above), to construct what was then called the *Nová* (New) synagogue. The oldest section is the southern wing, originally used as a prayer hall and later rebuilt as a vestibule to house tax collection boxes. ♦ Nominal admission. M-F, Su Apr-Oct. M-Th, Su; F mornings Nov-Mar. Červená ulice (between Pařížská and Maiselova ulice). 24810099

46 Vysoká synagoga (High Synagogue) Built with the backing of financier Mordechai Maisel in 1568 as part of a Jewish town hall to serve as a prayer house for the community, this synagogue is most likely named for the height of the main nave, with its delicate floral Renaissance decoration. A permanent textile exhibition features hand-embroidered temple curtains, valances, Torah mantles, and pulpit covers confiscated from temples and family residences during World War II by the Nazis. At press time, the synagogue was closed indefinitely for reconstruction; date of reopening unknown. ♦ Nominal admission. M-F, Su. Červená ulice (between Pařížská and Maiselova ulice). 24810099

47 Pinkasova synagoga (Pinkas Synagogue) In 1535 this synagogue, a late-Gothic construction with Renaissance elements, was built on the site of the prominent Horowitz family's home and private house of prayer. After World War II, it was chosen as a site for a Holocaust memorial, and the names of 77,297 Bohemian and Moravian Jews sent to the camps were inscribed on the walls. The synagogue was closed for reconstruction after Czechoslovakia severed relations with Israel in 1967; during the repair work the names were "accidentally" plastered over. At press time, approximately two-thirds of the names had been repainted. ♦ Nominal admission. M-F, Su. 3 Široká ulice (enter from the Starý židovský hřbitov). 24810099

When in Prague, be sure to observe public transportation etiquette. This includes giving up your seat to pregnant women and women with young children, as well as to senior citizens. To avoid the angry stares of the city's terrifying tribe of *babičky* (grandmothers), it's best, as one publication on the topic put it, "to leap out of your seat if someone who looks even 20 minutes older than you gets on the train/bus/metro."

The Orloj (Astronomical Clock) and Zlatá ulička (Golden Lane) are the most-visited attractions in Prague.

Prague

48 Maiselova synagoga (Maisel Synagogue) Built in 1592 by the mayor of the Židovská čtvrt (Jewish Quarter), Mordechai Maisel, for his family, the building was reconstructed in several styles, achieving its present neo-Gothic appearance in 1905. On display is a collection of silver and pewter seder plates, Torah scroll covers, and Torah pointers in the form of tiny hands with extending index fingers. At press time the synagogue was undergoing reconstruction, and its date of reopening was not yet known. ♦ Nominal admission. M-F, Su. 9 Maiselova ulice (between Jáchymova and Široká ulice). 24810099

49 Karlův most (Charles Bridge) Packed with peddlers, street musicians, and tourists, this is still one of the most impressive and, during off-peak hours (2AM to 5AM), most romantic places in Prague. Commissioned by King Charles IV on 9 July 1357, it connects Staré Město with the **Malá Strana** (Lesser Quarter). On the Old Town side is a tower built by architect **Petr Parléř** featuring the king's coat of arms; on the Lesser Quarter side, two towers flank the bridge gate. The 30 statues were sculpted by Matthias Braun and Johan Brokoff and his sons. According to Prague mythology, if you touch the cross with the five gold stars marking the spot where St. John of Nepomuk was drowned, you're fated to return to the golden city. ♦ Between Karlova and Mostecká ulice

50 Na Kampě No one knows for sure whether this park was christened for the pottery market, **Kaufplatz**, once held on the street named Na Kampě Street, or for the Spanish military encampment of 1620. Either way it's a lovely strolling spot, especially at night when the Karlův most and the **Národní divadlo** are dramatically illuminated. The island is defined by the Čertovka canal (Devil's Stream), supposedly named for a nasty-tempered washerwoman who lived along its banks. ♦ Accessible from the staircase on the west side of Karlův most, or via Velkopřevorské náměstí

51 Malostranská beseda Located next to the former **Malostranská radnice** (Town Hall of the Lesser Quarter), this dingy, smoke-filled second-floor club offers rollicking rock, blues, and jazz performances. ♦ Cover. Daily 2PM-1AM. Shows: M-F 8PM, Sa 9PM. 21 Malostranské náměstí (at Letenská ulice). 539024

52 Kostel sv. Mikuláše (St. Nikolas Church) With its dome dominating Malostranské náměstí (Lesser Quarter Square), this church is the city's finest example of Baroque architecture. The Jesuits struggled with the city administration for permission to build it, and even then, it took 50 years to complete. **Kristof Dientzenhofer** was responsible for the 1702 design, notable for the sweeping convex and concave planes of the facade. After **Dientzenhofer**'s death, his son, **Kilian Ignaz**, added the immense dome, which so awed the congregation that they hovered outside until a 1750 report declared the structure safe. The interior is decorated by celebrated artists of the time and includes a ceiling fresco by Jan Lukas Kracker that is nearly one-third of an acre in area. Check listings for concerts. ♦ Nominal admission. Tu-Su. Malostranské náměstí (enter through Mostecká or Letenská ulice). 2322589

53 Jo's Bar ★★★$ The best Mexican food in Prague is served at this cozy bar with restaurant seating in the back. Service is lackadaisical and at night the place is a crowded ex-pat hangout, but it's great for an afternoon quesadilla or tostada. There's outdoor seating in the summer. ♦ Mexican ♦ Daily lunch and dinner. No credit cards accepted. 7 Malostranské náměstí (across from Kostel sv. Mikuláše). No phone

54 A Studio Rubín Enjoy a pre-theater drink at this underground bar/performance space. The 70-seat theater is a venue for alternative works by Prague's young playwrights, occasionally in English. ♦ Cover. Bar: M-Th 9:30PM-1AM; F-Su 5PM-1AM. Box office: M-Th 4-7PM. Performances: daily 7:30PM. 9 Malostranské náměstí (across from Kostel sv. Mikuláše). 535015

55 Vinárna u maltézských rytířů ★★★★$$ Originally a hospice named for the Knights of Malta, then a dance hall between the two world wars, this structure is now home to an excellent restaurant. The main dining area in the stucco-and-brick cellar rates high on romantic atmosphere. Though the menu is limited, the entrées are delicately prepared and worth the wait, particularly the steak Procopius (smothered in a caper-and-almond sauce) and the homemade apple strudel. ♦ Czech/Continental ♦ Daily lunch and dinner. Reservations required. 10 Prokopská ulice (between Harantova ulice and Malostranské náměstí). 536357

Restaurants/Clubs: Red   **Hotels:** Blue
Shops/ ♦ Outdoors: Green   **Sights/Culture:** Black

145

Prague

Utopenci and Bramboráky and Other Czech Delights

Czech food is hearty, occasionally heavy, and frequently accompanied by dumplings, made from rolling pin–size lumps of flour, potato, or bread dough which are boiled and then sliced and served with a rich sauce and some meat, most often pork or beef. When faced with an all-Czech menu, try the following sauces: *svíčková* (cream-based), *rajská* (tomato-based), or *guláš* (paprika and beef-based). Another Czech classic is *vepřo-knedlo-zelo* (pork-cabbage dumpling). Soup *(polévka)* such as *bramborová* (potato), *dršťkova* (tripe), or *gulášová* (spicy beef), supplemented with a basket of bread, can make a meal on its own. Fresh vegetables are becoming popular, but don't be surprised if you get the canned variety. The best salads are *Šopský* (with Balkan cheese) and *michaný* (mixed). In pubs and wine bars, vegetarians may order either an omelette or another Czech favorite, *smažený sýr* (batter-dipped, fried cheese with tartar sauce), or *smažený hermelín* (a cheese known as the Czech camembert). Authentic pubs have their own unique cuisine: Try *utopenci* (which translates as "drowned sausages"); *tlačenka* (head cheese with vinegar and onions); *zavináče* (fish in vinegar with onions); or *slanečky* (salted fish). Beer (10 to 12 percent alcohol) on tap is ordered *světlé* (light), *tmavé* (dark), or *řezané* (half-and-half). The better Moravian wines are dry white Müller Thurgau and the rich burgundy Frankovka. From October through November, sample *burčák*, a young wine that tastes almost like lemonade.

In addition to restaurant fare, plenty of food is sold by street vendors. For inexpensive, tasty, and authentic Czech food try some of these street eats:

párek v rohlíku: the equivalent of a hot dog

smažený sýr or smažený hermelín: fried cheeses

bramboráky: potato pancake

palačinky: crepe with fixings

langoše: batter-fried dough with cheese, garlic, or ketchup

chlebíčky: open-face sandwiches

bramborový salát: potato salad

vlašský salát: mixed veggies and mayo

vaječný salát: egg salad.

---

56 Kostel Panny Marie Vítězné (Church of St. Mary the Victorious) Formerly the German Lutheran **Church of the Holy Trinity**, this church was given to the Order of Barefoot Carmelites, reconsecrated, and reconstructed with a new Baroque facade—all by 1644. Hispanic visitors flock to see the miracle-working **Bambino de Praga**, a wax effigy of the Infant Jesus, brought from Spain in the mid-16th century by Maria Manriques de Lara and donated to the nuns by her daughter Polyxena in 1628. ♦ M-Tu, Th-F, Su. 9 Karmelitská ulice (between Hellichova and Tržiště ulice). No phone

57 Petřín Hill Take the *lanovka* (funicular) to the top of this green, wooded hill for great views of the orange rooftops of the city. On the summit, climb the **Petřínská rozhledna** (Petrin Lookout Tower), a replica of the Eiffel Tower built for the 1891 **Prague Industrial Exhibition**, or wander through the *bludiště* (maze) in the neighboring faux castle filled with squealing children. The hike down is a real thigh-stretcher. ♦ Nominal admission. ♦ Daily; funicular until 8PM. U lanové dráhy (on Újezd ulice between Říční and Všehrdova ulice)

58 Island Hostel $ Located on Střelecký Ostrov (Sniper's Island), this 55-bed hostel is open only in the summer months, and it's usually filled to capacity. Its tranquil setting on the river is a big plus, as are the half-cotton, half-silk sheets purchased from the **Palace Hotel**, which can be rented (so can feather quilts and pillows) for a luxurious change from the usual backpacked sleeping bag. Accommodations are dorm-style; some rooms are for women only. Bathrooms are communal, and there are no kitchen facilities, but a riverside cafe next door offers breakfast. Owner Tony Deny advises arrival before 11AM to secure a room. Credit cards are accepted. Closed January-May, October_December ♦ Střelecký Ostrov (enter from the Legií most). 292532

59 Villa Bertramka/Memorial to W.A. Mozart After Mozart spent time in this mansion preparing for the premiere of *Don Giovanni* at the **Stavovské divadlo** (Estates Theater; see above), he composed an aria for his hostess, soprano Josefina Dušková, wife of composer František Dušek. The museum showcases his bedroom and study, along with scores, letters, and musical instruments. Check listings for concerts. ♦ Nominal admission. M, W-F; closed in March. 169 Mozartova ulice (at Duškova ulice). 543893

Prague

60 Estec Hostel $ The clean and spare dorm-style rooms, showers down the hall, laundry facilities, breakfast and bar service, and a beer garden make this an international student favorite. The hostel can accommodate up to 100 visitors, and takes credit cards. The information service and organized walking tours in July and August are perks. ♦ 5 Vaníčkova ulice, block 5 (across from the Strahov Stadium). 527344; fax 527343

61 Strahovský klášter (Strahov Monastery) Within this compound (ca. 1140) is the **National Literature Memorial,** exhibiting illuminated Czech books and manuscripts, psalters, and hymnals. The more than 40,000 volumes in the library of the majestic **Philosophical Hall** stack to the ceiling, and the barrel vault of the **Theological Hall** is alive with allegorical frescoes painted by an unknown monk. ♦ Nominal admission. Tu-Su. 1 Strahovské nádvoří (between Strahovská and Pohořelec ulice). 24511137

62 U černého vola ★★$ Besides the picturesque murals, sloping ceilings, and clatter of beer mugs, what makes this pub special is that it's owned by a consortium of local residents and all the profits go to the **School for the Blind** next door. Try the classic *hospoda* fare: *tlačenka* (head cheese with vinegar and onions) or *sekaná* (meat loaf). ♦ Czech ♦ Daily lunch and dinner. No credit cards accepted. 1 Loretánské náměstí (off Loretánská ulice). 538637

If you've had enough of Prague's cobblestones, you might consider taking a train or a tour to nearby castles. Karlštejn is the most visited castle in the Czech Republic. Located about 28 kilometers (17 miles) from Prague, this 14th-century castle was built by Charles IV as a repository for the coronation jewels and the monarch's holy relics. Křivoklát castle is about 3 kilometers (2 miles) from Karlejn. Formerly a hunting lodge for Bohemian royalty, it now houses art from the late Gothic period as well as 17th through 19th-century arms, carriages, and sleighs. Konopiště, a Renaissance chateau about 42 kilometers (26 miles) from Prague, contains the arms and art collections of Archduke Francis Ferdinand, whose assassination precipitated World War I in 1914. Trains for Křivoklát and Konopiště leave from Hlavní nádraží; for Karlštejn from Smíchovské nádraží.

62 Loreta **Kristof** and **Kilian Ignaz Dientzenhofer** designed the exuberant Baroque church in 1626, and **Giovanni B. Orsi** added the *Holy Stable,* a prismatic representation of the stable where Jesus was born. A 27-bell carillon chimes on the hour, and the **Treasury** features 16th- to 18th-century reliquaries, including a monstrance studded with 6,200 diamonds. ♦ Nominal admission. Tu-Su. 7 Loretánské náměstí (between Loretánská and Kapucínská ulice). 536228

63 U zeleného čaje ★★★$ A former 1500s inn, this potpourri-scented teahouse was seen in Miloš Forman's *Amadeus*. In addition to the soothing ambience, there are more than 50 varieties of tea (including Czech herbal teas for all sorts of ailments), delicious salads, frothy cappuccino, and veggie pizza to choose from. Tea sets made by local artists are for sale here as well. ♦ Continental ♦ Daily lunch and dinner. No credit cards accepted. 19 Nerudova ulice (between Malostranské náměstí and Ke hradu ulice). 532683

64 Nerudova ulice (Neruda Street) This sharp incline is named for Jan Neruda, a 19th-century Czech journalist and author of short stories documenting life in the Malá Strana. The shops and houses with Baroque and Renaissance facades are beautifully preserved, and the street boasts more symbolic street signs (numbered addresses were not introduced until 1770) than any other street in Prague. Imagine that you might have lived at the **Red Eagle** (No. 6), the **Three Fiddles** (No. 12), or the **Golden Key** (No. 27). Also on the way up is the **Morin Palace** (No. 5), now the **Romanian Embassy,** with the somber Moor atlantes, and **Thun Palace** (No. 20), the **Italian Embassy,** with eagles sculpted by Matthias Braun. ♦ Accessible from Malostranské náměstí

Restaurants/Clubs: Red   **Hotels:** Blue
Shops/ Outdoors: Green   **Sights/Culture:** Black

147

Prague

65 Schwarzenberský palác (Schwarzenberg Palace) Covered with rich sgraffito decoration, this Renaissance palace is the home of the **Vojenské historické muzeum** (Military History Museum) displaying pre-1918 Bohemian military paraphernalia. Particularly hypnotizing are the nasty-looking spears, flails, and other armaments used during the Hussite wars. ♦ Nominal admission; free on Tuesdays. Tu-Su. 2 Hradčanské náměstí (at Loretánská ulice). 536488

66 Šternberský palác (Sternberg Palace) A fine collection of European art beginning with the Renaissance and ending with Cubism is displayed in this Baroque building. Among the highlights are works by Brueghel, Cranach, and Holbein, as well as the *Madonna of the Rose Garlands* (1506) by Dürer, the first group portrait in the history of non-Italian art. Much is made of the fact that it was originally sold for 22 guldens to the Strahov religious order and that in 1930 an anonymous American offered $1.25 million for it. Rodin's *Balzac* graces the rotunda, and the eerie fluidity of Oscar Kokoschka's *Praha from Dr. Kramer's Villa* captures mystical Prague. ♦ Nominal admission. Tu-Su. 15 Hradčanské náměstí (at Nový Svět ulice). 24510594

67 Pražský Hrad (Prague Castle) Reflecting more than 1,000 years of Bohemian, Czechoslovakian, and Czech Republican development, this castle is a complex array of historic buildings and monuments. Built in the ninth century on the site of a ducal palace, it was the seat of Bohemian kings and still serves as the seat of the Czech president. Free guided tours can be arranged in the information building in the second courtyard. ♦ Grounds: free. Grounds: Daily from 5AM to 11PM. Hradčany (accessible from Ke Hradu ulice off Nerudova ulice). 33373368

In the first courtyard:

Matyášova brána (Matthias Gate) The first secular Baroque building in the country was built as a new entrance to the castle in 1614. The changing of the guard takes place daily at noon in front of the gate. ♦ Daily

In the second courtyard:

Kaple sv. Kříže (Chapel of the Holy Cross) Charles IV was a fanatical collector of relics, and this chapel contains many of the "sacred" objects once housed in **Chrám sv. Víta** (St. Vitus Cathedral, in the third courtyard). Among the collection are items which were once purported to be Mary's robe and veil, as well as the tablecloth from the Last Supper. ♦ Nominal admission. Tu-Su

In the third courtyard:

Chrám sv. Víta (St. Vitus Cathedral) Charles IV founded the largest of Prague's churches in 1344 as part of his plan to turn the city into a leading architectural and cultural center. He chose two leading architects for the job: the Frenchman **Matthias Arres**, who built the east end of the chancel before his death in 1352, and **Petr Parléř** and his sons, who completed the building over the next 60 years. The Hussite wars interrupted the construction, and the cathedral wasn't consecrated until May 1929. The best examples of **Parléř**'s neo-Gothic styling are found in the window tracery of the **Chapel of the Holy Cross**, in the **St. Wenceslas Chapel,** with its mosaics of semiprecious stones, and in the bullet-shaped arches of the **Golden Portal** opening into the castle courtyard. Art Nouveau is represented with Alfons Mucha's stained glass in the third chapel and the powerful crucifixion representation by František Bílek. For a small fee you can visit the **Royal Crypt** and see the foundations of an earlier Romanesque basilica and the tombs of Charles IV, his four wives, and King Rudolf, or walk up the 287 steps within the cathedral's steeple. ♦ Nominal admission. Tu-Su

Prašná věž Mihulka (Powder Tower) Once part of the castle's fortifications, this cylindrical tower is now the site of an eclectic museum explaining metal casting, the military uses of the tower, period alchemy, and astronomy. ♦ Nominal admission. Tu-Su

Starży královský palác (Royal Palace) The frequently rebuilt royal residence transcended the Romanesque, Gothic, and Renaissance periods in architecture, and the most impressive result is the incredible late-Gothic **Vladislavský sál** (Vladislav Hall), constructed for Wenceslas I by architect **Benedict Reid.** It was used regularly for jousting tournaments (banquets and bazaars under Rudolf II), and, since 1918, for presidential inaugurations. The main room, the **Česká kancelář** (Czech Chancellery), is where the governors were forcibly exited through the window in the uprising of the Bohemian Estates against the Hapsburgs in 1618. The **Stará sněmovna** (Hall of the Diet), with its Renaissance motifs and portraits of the Hapsburg kings, served as the medieval supreme court. ♦ Nominal admission. Tu-Su

Bazilika sv. Jiří (St. George's Basilica) This building was was commissioned in AD 920 by Prince Vratislav. A Benedictine order founded a convent here in 973 and enlarged the main church to its present state; the vaulted ceiling, tower, and chapel were added after a disastrous fire in 1142. Vratislav is buried in this Romanesque restoration along with Princess Ludmilla, grandmother of St. Wenceslas. ♦ Nominal admission. Tu-Su

---

The Strahov Library contains the smallest Bohemian book (6x6 mm), consisting of the Lord's Prayer in seven languages.

Prague

Jiřský klášter (St. George's Convent) Part of the **Národní Galerie** (National Gallery), this Benedictine convent, the first in Bohemia, features two floors of Gothic art and one of Mannerist and Baroque works, much of it gathered from churches around the country. Be sure to see the expressive portraits of saints by court painter to Charles IV, Master Theodoric. ♦ Nominal admission. Tu-Su. 532646

Zlatá ulička (Golden Lane) This cul-de-sac of tiny, brightly colored houses was built for the 24 archers who defended the castle in the 16th century and named for the goldsmiths who set up shop here in the 17th century. In 1917, Franz Kafka rented house **No. 22,** where he wrote most of his short stories. Disappointingly, the interiors are largely filled with tired souvenirs, so just take a walk along the lane and soak up the atmosphere.

67 Jízdárna Pražského Hradu (Prague Castle Riding School) Reliefs of horses decorate the cornice, revealing this building's original function. It's now a museum of 19th- and 20th-century paintings. ♦ Admission. Tu-Su. 33373232

68 Valdštejnské zahrady (Wallenstein Gardens) The grounds of the first and largest of Prague's Baroque palaces (which now belongs to the Ministry of Education) contain five courtyards, including flower-filled garden terraces built in 1623 by **Giovanni Battista Pieronni.** The garden statuary are copies of sculptures by Adrian de Vries (the original sculptures were hauled off by the Swedes in 1648 and installed in their royal gardens). This is a popular venue for spring and summer concerts. ♦ Free. Daily May-Sept. Valdštejnské náměstí (intersections of Valdštejnská and Tomášská ulice)

69 Valdštejnská jízdárna (Wallenstein Riding Academy) To the east of **Valdštejnské zahrady** this Baroque building, originally part of the neighboring palace, was converted to an exhibition hall after World War II. It displays the best of **Národní Galerie** works and sponsors important—often modern—art exhibits. ♦ Nominal admission. Tu-Su. 3 Valdštejnská ulice (at Klárov ulice). 536814

70 Belveder (Royal Summer Palace of Belvedere) Best reached through the **Královské zahrady** (Royal Gardens), this palace, also known as Queen Anne's summer house, was built by King Ferdinand for his queen in 1564. The most important Renaissance structure north of the Alps, the palace is surrounded by an arcade of 36 Tuscan columns. The garden also contains a "singing" fountain (the melody comes from the flowing waters). This is yet another venue used by the **Národní Galerie** (National Gallery) to exhibit its collections. ♦ Nominal admission. Tu-Su. Mariánské hradby (enter through the Pražský Hrad/, via U Prašného mostu ulice). 206780

71 Letná Park This grassy, tree-lined expanse is perfect for picnics. The statue of Stalin that once topped the massive concrete platform has been replaced by a giant metronome that you either love or hate. ♦ Letenské sady (enter by climbing the steps across from Čechův most)

72 Globe Bookstore and Coffee House ★★★$ The laid-back atmosphere encourages browsing through the 8,000-plus English-language used books while sipping a cappuccino in the neighboring cafe. The self-serve bar features salads, sandwiches, soups, and for desperate New Yorkers, bagels with a shmear. Hard-core coffee lovers should try the "bowl o' soul." ♦ American ♦ Daily breakfast, lunch, and dinner. No credit cards accepted. 14 Janovského ulice (between Strossmayerovo náměstí and pplk. Sochora ulice). 3579161

Bests

Kateřina Flemrová
Student of English at Charles University

Have a picnic on the northern end of **Střelecký Ostrov** (Sniper's Island)—a beautiful place with huge trees and a view of **Karlův most** (Charles Bridge) and **Pražský Hrad** (Prague Castle).

Rent a boat on the **Vltava River** and row around the islands and under the bridges. Don't forget to sing old sailor's songs.

Karlův most is best before Christmas Eve when there are amateur performances and sing-alongs.

Try to get inside the **Karolinum;** just walking through the corridors is unforgettable.

The view of the **Pražský Hrad** from the quay between the **Národní divadlo** (National Theater) is best just before dusk, before they light up the castle.

Prague's best jazz is played at the **AghaRTA Jazz Centrum.**

There are many words in Czech for a pub. While the most common are *hospoda* or *pivnice*, sometimes a musty-smelling, smoke-filled local pub is known as a *konečná,* or the last stop, presumably the last stop of the working day or the last stop of pensioners.

"My Praguers, they understand me."

Mozart, after *Don Giovanni* bombed in Vienna

149

Tiber River
81
V. F. Corridoni
L. d. Vittoria
L. Flaminio
V. Flaminia
V. Tiziano
V. L. Luciani
V. Gomenizza
Circonval. Clodia
V. Angelico
V. Timavo
L. G. Oberdan
V. Bruno Buozzi
V. Teulada
V. Carso
V. Muggia
V. Monte Zebio
Pte. del Risorgimento
V. d. Belle Arti
V. Monte Santo
V. Osiavia
V. d. Villa Giulia
8 Museo Nazionale di Villa Giulia
Dardanelli
V. Sabotino
L. d. Armi
L. d. Navi
Pza. Firdusi
V. G. Mazzini
Pza. G. Mazzini
V. Bernadotte
Circonval. Trionfale
V. d. Giuliana
V. Luigi Settembrini
V. G. Ferrari
Pte. Matteotti
L. A. d. Brescia
V. F. La Guardia
V. Washington
V. Rodi
V. G. Lante
V. S. Pellico
V. Damiata
V. Lepanto
L. Michelangelo
V. C. Beccaria
V. d. Muro Torto
V. Trionfale
Pte. Nenni
P. le Napoleone I
V. d. Milizie
V. Legnano
V. Dullio
V.M.A. Colonna
Pza. del Popolo 9
V. A. Doria
V. Leone IV
V. Barletta
V. F. Massimo
V. G. d'Annunzio
10
V. Tunisi
V. Giulio Cesare
V. Silla
Pza. d. Quiriti
Pte. Margherita
L. in Augusta
V. d. Ripetta
V. d. Corso
11
V. Margutta
V. Candia
V. Ottaviano
V. Germanico
7
V. Cola d. Rienzo
L. d. Mellini
12
V. d. Babuino
2
V. Vaticano
6
Terenzio
5
V. Virgilio
V. Cicerone
V. F. Cesi
13
V. Crescenzio
14
Piazza Spag
15
Galerie e Musei Vaticani
Pza. Cavour
V. Ulpiano
V. d. Croce
16
1 Città del Vaticano (Vatican City)
V. d. P. Angelica
B. Vittorio
Pte. Cavour
V. Tomacelli
V. Condotti
4 Castel Sant'Angelo
V. Trib.
L. Prati
V. F. Borghese
27
V. Frattina
Pte. Umberto
29
28
V. d. Conciliazione
L. Castello
L. Marzio
V. d. Prefetti
26
V. d. Mercede
Basilica San Pietro
Piazza San Pietro
Pte. S. Angelo
30
V. d'Orso
25
V. d. Tritone
L. Vaticano
Pte. Vitt. Eman. II
L. Tor d. Nona
V. Zanardelli
V. d. Scrofa
31
V. S. d. Crocifeti
43
42
V. d. Pta. Cavalleggeri
Pte. Pr. Am. Sav. Aosta
V. d. Coronari
24
L. Gianicolense
V. Giulia
Corso Vittorio Emanuele II
44
Piazza Navona
Pza. della Rotunda
32
V. d. Seminario
L. d. Sangallo
V. Governo Vecchio
Corso Rinascimento
41
40
V. d. Corso
3
V. d. Monte del Gallo
Monte Gianicolo
39
Pza. della Minerva
48
45
38
Pte. G. Mazzini
L. d. Tebaldi
V. d. Cappellari
46
47
Campo dei Fiori
V. d. Chiavari
37
V. d. Cestari
33
V. d. Plebiscita
36
6
P. Venez
50
V. d. Giubbonari
53
V. d. Lungara
L. d. Farnesina
Tiber River
49 Piazza Farnese
Pass. d. Gianicolo
V. Arenula
V. S. Maria del Pianto
51
35
34
Piazza del Campidoglio
Pte. Sisto
L. d. Vallati
L. d. Cenci
Teatro Marcello
V. d. Cava Aurelia
54
V. d. Moro
L. R. Sanzio
Pte. Garibaldi
Isola Tiberina
Pte. Fabricio
L. d. Pierleoni
V. G. Garibaldi
V. d. Scala
52
Pte. Cestio
55
V. A. Antica
V. d. Fornaci
56
V. d. Lungaretta
Pte. Palatino
V. G. Medici
58
V. L. Manara
57
V. S. F. a Ripa
V. d. Trastevere
V. d. Genovesi
L. Ripa
Villa Doria Pamphili
V. d. S. Pancrazio
V. G. Carini
V. N. Fabrizi
Vle. Glorioso
59
V. d. S. Michele
P. d. Ripa Grande
L. Aventino
N
km
1/4
1/2
mi
1/8
1/4

Villa Grazioli
Pza. Verbano
V. Topino
V. Chiana
V. Lisbona
V.d. Villa Grazioli
V. Clitunno
V. A. Bertoloni
V. F. Siacci
V. Liegi
V. d. Villa Ruffo
V. d. T. Madonne
V. G. Rossini
V. Ulisse Aldrovandi
Giardino Zoologico
V. V. Bellini
V. G. d'Arezzo
V. Salaria
V. Tagliamento
V. Gorizia
Corso Trieste
V. Corsica
V. Capodistria
V. d. Appennini
V. d. Giardino Zoologico
V. Mercadante
V. Giovanni Paisiello
V. Regina Margherita
V. Simeto
Vle. d' Uccelliera
V. d. Valle Giulia
Villa Borghese
V. Po
V. d. Fontana
V. A. Torlonia
V. Dalmazia
Villa Albani
V. P. Canonica
V.d.C. Marini
Pza. di Siena
V. d. Villa Albani
Villa Torlonia
V. L. Spallazani
Museo e Galleria Borghese
V. Isonzo
Vle. S.P.d. Brasile
V. R. Emilia
V. Nizza
V. Nomentana
Pza. Galeno
V. A. Musa
V. Siracusa
V. d. Villini
V. Pinciana
Corso d'Italia
V. Romagna
Galoppatoio
20
V. Piemonte
V. Calabria
Piazzale Porta Pia
V. d. Villa Patrizi
V. G. B. Morgagni
V. Piave
V. d. Policlinico
Vle. Regina Elena
V. Vittorio Veneto
V. Quintino Sella
V. Boncompagni
V. d. P. Pinciana
V. Palestro
Vle. Castro Pretorio
V. Ludovisi
V. A. Salandra
V. L. Bissolati
V. S. M. d. Batt.
V. F. Crispi
Piazza Barberini
21
V. Barberini
19
8
V. Sistina
V. Cernaia
Terme di Diocleziano/ Museo Nazionale Romano
70
Città Universitaria
Vle. d' Università
22
V. d. Quattro Fontane
Pza. della Repubblica
V. L. Einaudi
V. Marsala
V. d. Scienze
V. d. Panetteria
V. XX Settembre
V. Torino
Pza. dei Cinquecento
V. Castro Pretorio
V. Pretoriano
23
Fontana di Trevi
V. d. M. Lavatore
V. d. Quirinale
V. Nazionale
V. A. de Pretis
V. Viminale
V. Giovanni Giolitti
V.d. Marruccini
V. d. Marruccini
Stazione Termini
V.d. Ramni
71
72
Basilica di Santa Maria Maggiore
V. d. Serpenti
V. 24 Maggio
V. Panisperna
V. d. S. M. Maggiore
V. C. Alberto
V. C. Cattaneo
V. Tiburtina
V. Cavour
V. d. Sabelli
76
V. 4 Novembre
V. G. Lanza
V. d. Statuto
Pza. Vittorio Emanuele II
75
V. d. Fori Imperiali
68
V. Cavour
67
64
Foro Romano
69
V. d. Annibaldi
73
V.P. Eugenio
V.d.C. Verde
V.d.P. Maggiore
74
V. N. Salvi
Parco Traiano
V. Mecenate
V. Merulana
V. Emanuele Filiberto
V.d.S. Croce in Gerusalemme
V. R. Bonghi
66
Colosseo
65
Palatino
V. Labicana
78
77
Vle. Manzoni
V. Statilia
Villa Wolkonsky
V. d. San Giovanni in Laterano
V. Claudia
V. Celimontana
V. d. Fontana
V. C. Felice
V. d. Cerchi
V. d. Circo Massimo
V. d. S. Gregorio
Villa Celimontana
V. d. S. S. Rotando
V. dell'Amba Aradam
79
80
V. La Spezia

Rome

For millennia Rome has been an unrivaled travel destination for pilgrims and travelers, and the city continues to offer a wealth of excellent choices for the visitor with or without limited *lire*. In fact, the budget traveler in Rome often fares better than the tourist following a far costlier agenda. The independent visitor who avoids international restaurants to eat in small, authentic trattorie; bypasses the climate-controlled tour buses in favor of the No. *118* local to the **Catacombs**; and opts to spend a leisurely afternoon meandering through the marvels of the **Musei Vaticani** (Vatican Museums) while hordes of tourists heel behind a whirlwind tour guide, creates memories that are more personal, romantic, spontaneous, and, well, more *Roman,* than those of members of the neatly prepackaged groups.

Italy has always meant good food, and every neighborhood has at least one simple, honest trattoria where diners can eat marvelously and pay very little. Tasty pizza-by-the-slice for lunch or a picnic made with fresh ingredients from the colorful **Campo dei Fiori** outdoor market, alternated with the occasional splurge, can keep the cost-conscious visitor contentedly and effortlessly within budget.

Whether it is the timeless allure of ancient Rome, the beauty of old Rome (medieval to Baroque), or the excitement of modern Rome (a combination of all these, plus horrific traffic and pollution problems) that leaves you reeling, the city will surely boggle your 20th-century imagination. One big open-air museum, it offers enough cultural and historical sites to fill one day or a lifetime, depending on how long you can afford to experience this legendary metropolis. After even a few days' stay, you'll begin to understand the emotion that moved Italian author Silvio Negro to write *Roma, Non Basta una Vita* (Rome, A Lifetime is Not Enough).

And, finally, wherever you see a large number of locals eating, looking happy, and basking in *la dolce vita* (the sweet life), join them. After all, when in Rome. . . .

To call from the US, dial 011 (international access code), 39 (country code), 6 (city code), and the local number. When calling from inside Italy, dial 06 and the local number.

Getting to Rome
Airports

Leonardo da Vinci International Airport (65951), also frequently called **Fiumicino**, is 26 kilometers (16 miles) from Rome. The airport has a tourist-information desk and currency-exchange facilities; both are open daily. There is train service from the airport to the principal **Stazione Termini** or the secondary **Stazione Tiburtina** train stations, both in downtown Rome. Trains run frequently, from 8AM until 10:25PM, daily. Bus service to **Stazione Tiburtina** is provided at night, after the last train.

Most charter and many domestic flights arrive at **Ciampino Airport** (794921), 13 kilometers (8 miles) from downtown Rome. The blue **COTRAL** bus runs between the airport and the **Stazione Anagnina** subway station, where it is possible to transfer to the subway or get a taxi.

Rental cars are available at both airports from **Avis** (4701229), **Budget** (65010289), or **Hertz** (3216886).

Bus Station (Long-Distance)
The **Piazza dei Cinquecento** in front of the **Stazione Termini**, and the adjacent **Piazza della Repubblica** are the hub for long-distance buses. For schedules and information, call **COTRAL** (57531). At press time, city planners were reviewing a proposed move of long-distance bus arrivals and departures outside of the city to cut down on traffic problems.

Train Station (Long-Distance)
The **Stazione Termini** (Piazza dei Cinquecento, 4775), located in the center of town, is the arrival and departure point for most international and national trains. Lines for information and tickets are usually long, so plan accordingly. Never leave your bags unattended in the train stations and try not to linger.

Getting around Rome

Buses The orange city buses, called **ATAC,** run frequently and efficiently from early morning until about midnight. Tickets, valid for 1.5 hours of travel time, are available at newsstands, tobacconists, and *caffès* displaying the **ATAC** sign. Daily, weekly, and monthly passes are available at the **ATAC** booth in front of the **Stazione Termini**, at the post office in **Piazza San Silvestro,** and at larger bus stations. By the way, fare-dodging can result in a hefty fine.

Rome

Driving The only thing worse than driving in Rome is parking in Rome—and both are expensive enough to make it an improbable choice for the budget-minded traveler.

Subway Rome's dense street traffic is notorious; if appropriate to your destination (the two-line network is limited), save time by taking the **Metropolitana** for distances of any length. Hours of operation are from 5:30AM until 11:30PM daily; tickets are sold at newsstands, tobacconists, and vending machines. Keep your ticket—you need to show it when you reach your destination.

Taxis There are plenty of taxis, but they're expensive for solo travelers. Cabs do not cruise, but they can be picked up in the major piazzas, at hotels, and near the big tourist attractions. Call 3570, 3875, or 4994 for pickup. Additional fees are levied for service at night; on Sundays and holidays, for luggage; and for trips to and from the airport.

Tours Although it is relatively easy to navigate the city yourself, travelers with limited time may want to take a tour to see as many sites as possible. The following tour operators offer a variety of half- and full-day tours, narrated in English: **Appian Lines** (Piazza dell'Esquilino 6/7, 4818841); **American Express** (Piazza di Spagna, 67641); **Carrani Tours** (Via V E Orlando 95, off Piazza della Repubblica, 4742501); and **CIT** (Piazza della Repubblica 64, 47941). The cheapest tour in town is the local bus *110:* It leaves from the **Piazza dei Cinquecento,** takes approximately three hours, and passes more than 40 of the city's principal sites. The English-speaking Roman Catholic **Fathers of the Atonement** (Via di Santa Maria dell'Anima 30, 6879552) lead walking tours of the city and **Città del Vaticano** (Vatican City) on Friday mornings. There is no charge, but donations are appreciated.

Walking A map of Rome appears daunting, but even the most distant tourist destinations, such as the **Vatican** and the **Spanish Steps,** are only a 40-minute walk apart. Walking is definitely the best way to get a sense of the city, but be careful of reckless drivers, of which there are many. Always cross at the white-striped crosswalk.

FYI

Accommodations Rome is one of the better cities for inexpensive accommodations: There are small hotels, youth hostels, and, in the summer months, religious houses. It's best to reserve in advance, but if you hit town without a bed, try the booking agencies at **Leonardo da Vinci Airport** or the **CTS** or **Enjoy Rome** agencies (see "Discount Tickets," below). Tip: Always check on the often-included but rarely obligatory cost of breakfast; it most probably will be less expensive to enjoy it at some charming little *caffè* in a piazza down the street.

Business Hours In winter, businesses are generally open Monday from 3:30PM until 7:30PM; Tuesday through Saturday from 9AM until 1PM, and again from 3:30PM until 7:30PM. In summer, the Monday morning closure usually shifts to Saturday afternoons. Some shops in the *centro storico* (historic center) have dropped the customary midday closing. And merchants have recently been permitted to open on Sunday, though the practice varies according to season and neighborhood. Food markets are open Monday through Saturday from 8:30AM until 1:30PM, and again from 5PM until 7:30PM; they close Thursday afternoons in winter, and Saturday afternoons in summer.

With some exceptions, Rome's major basilicas are open Monday through Saturday with no midday break; smaller churches close midday from 1PM until 4PM. Museum hours are ever-changing, so it's wise to call ahead or check with the tourist offices (see "Visitors' Information," below).

Climate December through February is cold (but rarely below freezing) and often rainy; from March through June temperatures range from 50 to 75 degrees; summers are hot and sunny, with temperatures often reaching 90 degrees or more; from September through November the climate is a mild 55 to 70 degrees Fahrenheit, with occasional rainy days.

Consulates and Embassies

Canada .... Via Giovanni Battista de Rossi 27
 .... (at Via Antonio Nibby); 445981

UK .... Via XX Settembre 80 (at Porta Pia);
 4825441

US .... Via Veneto 199A (at Via Buoncompagni);
 46741

Discount Tickets Centro Turistico Studentesco e Giovanile (CTS, Via Genova 16, off Via Nazionale, 46791), provides travel, accommodations, and sightseeing discounts, as well as general information for students and young travelers; its offices are open Monday through Friday and on Saturday mornings. **Enjoy Rome** (Via Varese 39, near Stazione Termini, 4451843) is a relatively new agency that offers a host of discounts and services, with no student or age requirements. It's open Monday through Friday and on Saturday mornings. Check with the tourist offices (see "Visitors' Information," below) for updates on the ever-changing list of museums that waive admission fees one night a week or the first Sunday of the month.

Discounted tickets for international train trips are available from **Transalpino**'s two locations: Piazza dell'Esquilino 10-12 (4870870), which is open Monday through Friday and on Saturday mornings; and **Stazione Termini** (4880536), which is open Monday through Saturday.

Drinking Wine plays a key role in the life of Italians, yet there is very little drunkenness in private or in public. Italians may skip wine at lunch, but it is always served with dinner. Beer pubs have become increasingly popular but most youths seem to be just as happy with a soda.

Emergencies Dial 113 in an emergency situation; an English-speaking operator is available. For 24-hour medical service, call the **International Medical Center** (4882371, 4881129; nights 4884051); an English-speaking assistant will arrange an

Rome

appointment or have a doctor sent to your hotel. For legal emergencies, contact Italy's Foreign Department: **Questura Ufficio Stranieri** (Via Genova 2, off Via Nazionale, 46862987).

Laundry Italy hasn't yet discovered self-service laundromats. The following are inexpensive laundry services that charge by the kilo (2.2 pounds) or by the load (4.5 kilos), with ironing and sometimes drying costing extra: **Baccon** (Via del Leone 15, between Piazza San Lorenzo in Lucina and Piazza Fontenella Borghese; 6871397); and **Zampa** (Piazza Campo dei Fiori 38, 6879096). Both are open Monday through Friday.

Money The monetary unit of Italy is the *lira;* the plural is *lire,* and it's abbreviated as either "L." or "Lit." The best places to exchange currency are at banks displaying the "Cambio" sign, **American Express** (Piazza di Spagna 38, 67641), or **Thomas Cook** (Piazza Barberini 21A, 4828082). Currency exchange facilities at the airport, train station, and independent cambios charge high commissions.

Personal Safety Highly professional pickpockets operate on buses, on subways, at the train stations, and anywhere crowds and bustle are an integral part of the scene. At night, avoid the area around the **Stazione Termini** and the **Villa Borghese** park.

Postal Services The central post office is **Poste e Telecommunicazioni** (Piazza San Silvestro 19); it's open Monday through Friday and on Saturday mornings. If you plan to visit the **Città del Vaticano** (and who doesn't?), use their postal service, which is run independently of its Italian counterpart and is considerably quicker. Note: Vatican stamps are valid only if mailed within the **Città del Vaticano**.

Publications English-language newspapers and magazines are available at most newsstands. *Un Ospite a Roma* (A Guest in Rome) and the bilingual *Here's Rome* can be picked up at tourist offices and at some hotels. The daily newspaper *La Repubblica* publishes a weekly supplement every Thursday called *TrovaRoma,* which lists local events, as do the biweekly *Metropolitan* and *Wanted in Rome*.

Public Holidays New Year's Day, Epiphany (6 January), Easter Monday, Liberation Day (25 April), Labor Day (1 May), Saints Peter's and Paul's Day (29 June), Assumption (15 August), All Saints' Day (1 November), Immaculate Conception (8 December), Christmas, and St. Stephen's Day (26 December).

Public Rest Rooms There are very few public rest rooms in Rome apart from those at the train station or museums. However, the price of a drink entitles you to ask for the cafe's *toiletta,* though hygiene is sometimes less than stellar; always bring your own tissue.

Restaurants Most restaurants close one day a week (which varies for each establishment), part of August (often the entire month), and between Christmas and New Year's Eve. Lunch starts around 1PM and last orders are taken around 2:30PM. The peak dining hour is 8:30PM and kitchens close about 11PM.

Shopping The pedestrian **Via del Corso** that runs north to south between the **Piazza Venezia** and the **Piazza del Popolo** is lined with inexpensive shops geared toward a young market. There's good

Roman Forum

Rome

shopping, particularly for shoes, in the streets spiking off the **Fontana de Trevi** (Trevi Fountain). Interesting finds also abound along the picturesque side streets, such as **Via del Governo Vecchio**, surrounding the **Piazza Navona**, and in the **Campo dei Fiori** neighborhood. The shopping areas on the Vatican side of the **Tiber**, around **Via Cola di Rienzo**, are less geared to a tourist trade so their prices are lower.

Smoking Many Italians are smokers, but the practice is forbidden on public transportation and in public offices.

Street Plan Tourists will generally find themselves concentrating their time and energy in the area surrounding the **Colosseo** (Colosseum) and the ancient ruins of the **Foro Romano** (Roman Forum); the shopping district at the foot of the **Spanish Steps**; the old medieval quarter encompassing the **Pantheon**, the **Piazza Navona**, and the **Campo dei Fiori**; and the **Città del Vaticano**, with the artsy quarter of **Trastevere** on its fringes.

Taxes The tax rate on hotel rooms and purchased goods varies according to the hotel category and the price of an item, but it is always included in the quoted cost.

Telephones The Italian phone system has its quirks, among them the varying number of digits in telephone numbers (anywhere from four to eight). Avoid making calls from your hotel room; there's always a costly hotel surcharge. The cheapest ways to call the US are to buy a calling card (*scheda* or *carta*), or to call collect and have them call you back. A third option is to pay cash at the **SIP-Telecom** telephone office (Piazza San Silvestro 20) next to the post office; it's open daily from 8AM until 9:50PM.

Tipping Taxi drivers get 10 percent of the fare. Tip restaurant servers 10 percent if there is no service charge on your bill; if the bill includes a service charge, leave about two to three percent more.

Visas Travelers need only a valid passport to enter Italy.

Visitors' Information There are information offices at **Stazione Termini** (4824078) and at Via Parigi 5 (off Piazza S. Bernardo; 48899253). Both are open daily from 8:15AM until 7:15PM.

Piazza San Pietro

1 Città del Vaticano (Vatican City) The smallest European state comprises 107.8 acres, about the size of an average golf course. Created during Mussolini's tenure, it is ruled by one man: the Bishop of Rome, a.k.a. the Pope. About 1,000 men, women, and children live within its borders; it has its own passport, flag, anthem, license plates, newspaper, radio station, postal system, and coins. The basilica and the museums are the only places open to the general public; otherwise entrance is by permission only. For information, check with the **Ufficio Informazioni** (Vatican Tourist Information Office) on the south side of **Piazza San Pietro**.
♦ Guided tours: M-Tu, Th-Sa Mar-Oct. Vatican Tourist Information Office: daily. Bounded by Viale Vaticano. Information Office: 69884866

Within Città del Vaticano:

Piazza San Pietro (St. Peter's Square) Designed and built by **Gian Lorenzo Bernini**, 1656 to 1667, the square (illustrated above) is actually an ellipse 262 yards wide. The colonnade comprises 284 Doric columns, each 64 feet high, in four rows and topped with statues of 140 saints. Two stone markers designate the vantage points from which the two sets of columns visually line up one behind the other.

In the center of the piazza is a 135-foot-high, 312-ton Egyptian obelisk, moved here in 1586 with the help of 900 men and 140 horses. Flanking it are twin granite fountains, erected by different architects—one by **Carlo Maderno** in 1613, the other by **Bernini**.

Above the right colonnade, the tallest and broadest building is the **Palazzo Apostolico** (Apostolic Palace), where the Pope lives and works. He appears at his library window every Sunday at noon (when in residence) to bless the crowds in the square. For information about the Pope's Wednesday audiences, check with the **Ufficio Informazioni** (69884866) on the south side of the piazza. ♦ Bounded by Via di Porta Angelica, Via della Conciliazione, and Via Porta Cavalleggeri

Restaurants/Clubs: Red **Hotels:** Blue
Shops/ ♦ Outdoors: Green **Sights/Culture:** Black

155

Rome

Basilica San Pietro (St. Peter's Basilica) The first church on this site dedicated to St. Peter was begun in AD 315. It was built over the spot where the Fisherman (and first pope) is believed to be buried. "Modernization" began in 1506, but the facade was not completed until 1614. The nave measures 610 feet long, and the dome (designed by **Michelangelo,** who died before it was completed) is 448 feet high. Among the treasures in the basilica is Michelangelo's beautiful *Pietà,* finished in 1500 when the artist was only 25 years old; it has stood behind bulletproof glass since its mutilation in 1972 (careful restoration has removed any visible scars). Before the main altar (where only the Pope can celebrate Mass) is a 13th-century bronze statue of a seated St. Peter, whose right foot is shiny from millions of pilgrims' kisses. Across from this statue and to the left of the main altar is the entry to the crypt (or **Vatican Grottoes**) and the ruins of the original church, as well as a number of early popes' tombs. The **Tesoro** (Treasury) has been systemically raided throughout the centuries, but its nine small rooms hold gifts given to the popes from emperors, kings, and modern statesmen.

The basilica's centerpiece is **Bernini's** seven-story, 46-ton **Baldacchino,** the bronze swirling-columned canopy (pictured at right) erected in 1633 that crowns the pontifical altar. It stands over the **Tomb of the Fisherman** and was made from bronze that Pope Urban VIII ordered stripped from the **Pantheon** portico. The apse is dominated by **Bernini**'s throne (dating from 1665), a magnificent bronze altar encasing what is attributed to be St. Peter's chair. Finish with a visit to the dome, at 352 feet above ground level, the most breathtaking view of the Eternal City. ♦ Basilica and grottoes: free; dome and treasury: admission. Piazza San Pietro

Galerie e Musei Vaticani (Vatican Galleries and Museums) The single entrance for the museums is on Viale del Vaticano. To reach the museums from the **Piazza San Pietro,** the options are a brisk 15-minute walk or a ride on one of the shuttle buses (fee charged) which depart every 30 minutes. The bus route is through the **Giardini Vaticani** (Vatican Gardens) and offers a way to see this beautiful greensward. Inside the museums, color-coded maps direct the visitor to areas of interest; all routes include the extraordinary **Sistine Chapel,** but other highlights are the **Pio-Clementine Museum of Greco-Roman Antiquities,** the **Egyptian Museum,** the **Etruscan Museum,** the **Raphael Rooms,** the **Borgia Apartments,** and the 18 rooms of the

Baldacchino

Vatican Picture Gallery. The **Sistine Chapel** is everything you ever imagined, and more. Constructed toward the end of the 15th century, its paramount attraction is the 15,000-square-foot ceiling fresco of the *Creation* painted by Michelangelo. Behind the altar is the artist's *Last Judgment,* whose restoration was completed in 1994. The controversial, multimillion-dollar restoration of both these works was financed by Japan's Nippon Television Network in exchange for exclusive film and photographic coverage of the unprecedented effort. Among the restorers' discoveries was the revelation of unexpectedly vibrant colors—coral, pink, and Nile green—confirming that Michelangelo was a skilled colorist influenced by the bright tones used by the Venetian masters who were his contemporaries. ♦ Admission; free the last Sunday of every month. Daily July-Sept, and the week before and after Easter; daily mornings Oct-June. Last admission 45 minutes before closing. Viale Vaticano (at Via Tunisi). 6988333

Hotel Alimandi ☆☆

2 Hotel Alimandi $ One of the nicest of the inexpensive hotels in the area, the 30 guest rooms (with or without private bathrooms) are simple and clean. Ever-present owner Paolo Alimandi gets extra credit for the fourth-floor garden and rooftop terrace; and the location—across from the main entrance

Rome

to the **Galerie e Musei Vaticani** (see above)—is unbeatable. There is no restaurant. ◆ Via Tunisi 8 (at Viale Vaticano). 39723948; fax 39723943

3 Suore Francescane dell'Antonement (Franciscan Sisters of the Atonement) $ This small hostelry is run by an order of friendly Italian and American nuns in a neighborhood convenient to the Città del Vaticano. There are 26 guest rooms, about half of which have private baths. Breakfast is included and half- or full-board is available (though not obligatory) in a comfortable, family-style dining room. Guests can enjoy a spacious pine-shaded garden, and are asked to respect the 11PM curfew. Public transportation is not always convenient; it's best to arrive by taxi. ◆ Closed 22 December-7 January. Via di Monte del Gallo 105 (off Piazzale Gregorio VII). 6307820; fax 6386149

4 Castel Sant'Angelo The best illustration of how Rome was built layer upon layer, this monument was designed in AD 139 to house the tomb of Emperor Hadrian. Turned into a medieval fortress by the warrior popes, the museum has served variously as the Vatican's bank, a papal refuge (a secret underground tunnel connects to the Vatican), a prison, and an air-raid shelter. Opera buffs will recognize the upper terrace as the setting for the final scene in Puccini's *Tosca*. The dramatic Ponte Sant'Angelo crosses the Tiber at this point. Several of the bridge's statues came from **Bernini**'s workshop. ◆ Admission. M, W-Su. Lungotevere Castello (at Ponte Sant'Angelo). 6875036

5 Franchi One side is a delicatessenlike *salumeria*, the other side is take-out heaven, with salads, vegetables, pizza slices, the most fragrant spit-roasted chicken in Rome, and much, much more. The only missing ingredient is a spot to sit, but even so, it's an excellent place to pick up a heavenly post-Vatican snack. ◆ M-Sa. Via Cola di Rienzo 204 (at Via Terenzio). 6874651

6 Via Cola di Rienzo and Via Ottaviano Not as centrally located as the Via del Corso but much more popular with budget-minded Romans, this area is the stomping grounds for local shoppers-in-the-know. The fashion boutiques, costume jewelry and accessories shops, and grocery stores offer more variety, sometimes better quality, and, for the most part, better prices than Via del Corso. ◆ Between Città del Vaticano and the Tiber

7 Residence Guggioli $ The sociable owner of this small hotel offers five antiques-furnished rooms, one with private bath; breakfast only is served. This just might be the best value in the vicinity of Città del Vaticano. No credit cards accepted. ◆ Via Germanico 198 (near Via Fabbio Massimo). 3242113

8 Museo Nazionale di Villa Giulia (Villa Giulia National Museum) Located in the vast **Villa Borghese** park, and commonly referred to as the **Museo Etrusco**, this museum contains the largest and most important collection of art and artifacts of the mysterious Etruscans, the primary inhabitants of Rome between the sixth and fifth centuries BC. Housed in the country villa of Pope Julius III (1550-55), the building was designed by **Vignola** and **Amannati**, with some collaboration by **Michelangelo**. ◆ Admission. Tu-Su. Piazza Villa Giulia 9 (off Viale delle Belle Arti). 3601951

9 Piazza del Popolo Nineteenth-century pilgrims arriving from the north through the **Porta del Popolo** supposedly swooned at this first glimpse of the splendor that was Rome. Today, visitors swoon over the works of Caravaggio, Pinturicchio, and other important Renaissance and Baroque masters in the 11th-century **Chiesa di Santa Maria del Popolo**, tucked away on the north side of the piazza near the historic *porta*, or gateway. A 3,000-year-old Egyptian obelisk commands the square, and its east side offers entrance to the **Villa Borghese** park. The Via del Corso, a direct link to the **Piazza Venezia**, stretches south from the piazza; closed to traffic, this popular street is the stage for Rome's daily ritual, the pre-dinner *passeggiata*, or promenade. ◆ Between Via del Corso and Piazzale Falminio

9 Caffè Rosati ★★$$ Sit outdoors on the beautiful piazza, or indoors in the wood-paneled turn-of-the-century cafe. You'll pay less by standing at the bar or taking out any of the scrumptious *gelati* (ice cream) for a stroll with the rest of Rome down the nearby pedestrian-only Via del Corso. ◆ Cafe ◆ M, W-Su 7AM-midnight. Piazza del Popolo 5A. 3225859

10 Pensione Fiorella $ It's no-frills, no-thrills in Signora Albano's eight-room hotel. There's no restaurant, heat can be scant during the winter, rooms are without private baths, and there's a 1AM curfew, but the location is good—a half block from the lively **Piazza del Popolo**—and the price is rock bottom. No advance reservations are accepted; call upon arrival and hope for a vacancy. No credit cards accepted. ◆ Via del Babuino 196 (near Piazza del Popolo). 3610597

11 Residenza Brotsky $ The rooftop garden and the venerable appeal of the well-worn rooms in this centrally located 17th-century palazzo draw a constant stream of young international travelers. Some of the 24 rooms (with and without private baths) have undergone a much needed face-lift, and a few have private balconies. There is no restaurant, but breakfast can be requested for an additional cost. No credit cards accepted. ◆ Via del Corso 509 (off Piazza del Popolo). 3612339

157

Rome

12 Hotel Margutta $ On a quiet street a minute's stroll from the **Piazza di Spagna,** this small hotel could use an occasional decorating tip. But its 24 rooms all have baths, and the great location, good housekeeping, and English-speaking staff make it a comfortable haven. Two guest rooms on the top floor each boast a fireplace, terrace, and view. There is no restaurant. ♦ Via Laurina 34 (near Via Margutta). 6798440; fax 3200395

13 La Buca di Ripetta ★★★$$ If you're going to splurge, do it here at "The Hole in the Wall." This warm, family-run trattoria with delicious, no-nonsense fare is always full, mostly with local cognoscenti. The menu looks like others around town—variety in Rome's inexpensive to moderate eateries is pretty marginal—but the execution is exceptional. Southern Italian classics like *lasagna al forno* (baked lasagna) and *melanzane alla parmigiana* (eggplant parmigiana) don't get any better than here. ♦ Italian ♦ Tu-Sa lunch and dinner; Su lunch; closed in August. Via di Ripetta 36 (near Piazza del Popolo). 3219391

14 Ara Pacis Augustae and Mausoleo di Augusto (Augustus's Altar of Peace and Mausoleum) Dismantled over the course of centuries, the legendary **Ara Pacis,** dedicated in 13 BC, was reassembled only within the last 100 years. The magnificent friezes and bas-relief carvings are portraits of Augustus, his family, and his political allies, as well as a cast of mythological characters. The altar commemorates the peace created throughout the Mediterranean after the emperor's many victorious campaigns. To the east of this reconstructed monument is the 28 BC **Mausoleum of Augustus** (closed to the public). Set in what once was a pasture, it has been used as a medieval stronghold and a 19th-century concert hall. Mussolini excavated it in the 1930s, hoping to use it as his own burial place. He was hanged in Milan. ♦ Admission. Tu-Su. Via de Ripetta (at Via dell'Ara Pacis). No phone

15 Otello alla Concordia ★★$$ Despite its central location and longtime popularity with tourists, this smart trattoria guarantees good food for reasonable rates, served by waiters who never seem to lose their cool. Cozy inside and charming in the covered courtyard, it's a good place to try the city's specialty, *abbacchio al forno* (tender roast lamb). ♦ Italian ♦ M-Sa lunch and dinner; closed in August. Via della Croce 81 (off the Piazza di Spagna). 6791178

16 Vertecchi This shop is a Roman institution. It's possible to spend hours pawing through the displays of art supplies, designer housewares, office furniture, and accessories. ♦ M-Sa; no midday closing. Via della Croce 70 and 38 (off Via del Corso). 6783110

16 Pasticceria d'Angelo ★$ This popular bar makes a good stop for a breakfast *cornetto* (croissant), a lunchtime panini, and bountiful cakes and teatime sweets. ♦ Continental ♦ Tu-Su 7:30AM-8:30PM; closed 15-21 August. Via della Croce 30 (at Via Boca di Leone). 6782556

17 Scalinata della Trinità dei Monti (Spanish Steps) Few vistas compare with that from the top of the recently restored **Spanish Steps** out over the rooftops of Rome—except, maybe, for the reciprocal view at the foot of the 137-step staircase (illustrated below), where the elegant Via dei Condotti begins; it's particularly beautiful during the Easter season, when the stairs are covered with masses of hot-pink azaleas. Long before the steps were built in 1721

Scalinata della Trinità dei Monti

Rome

(thanks to the largesse of the French ambassador; the Spanish embassy had been located in the area since 1622, hence the name), the beloved 15th-century **Trinità dei Monti** church loomed above the city. The adjacent **Convent of the Sacre Coeur** is off-limits, unless your child happens to attend its affluent **French Kindergarten.** ♦ Piazza di Spagna (at Via Condotti)

17 Casina di Keats (Keats and Shelley Memorial Museum) English poet John Keats lived out the last few months of his young life here before dying of tuberculosis at the age of 27. The second-floor museum holds a number of mildly morbid mementos such as the poet's plaster death mask, an urn containing Percy Shelley's ashes, and a reliquary sheltering locks of John Milton's and Elizabeth Barrett Browning's hair. More scholarly is the collection of original manuscripts and a tiny library devoted to the Romantic poets Keats, Shelley, and Byron. ♦ Admission. M-F; closed in August. Piazza di Spagna 26 (at Via Condotti). 6784235

18 La Rampa ★★$$ Great food and unusually reasonable prices for this tony neighborhood are the draws here. Reservations aren't accepted, but it's worth the wait for the antipasto platters and homemade pasta such as the *penne alla Rampa*, served in a cheese sauce with *speck* (smoked ham). In summer try for one of the tables that spills out onto the vine-covered piazza. ♦ Italian ♦ M dinner; Tu-Sa lunch and dinner; closed in August. No credit cards accepted. Piazza Mignanelli 18 (off Via Due Macelli). 6782621

19 Hotel Pensione Suisse $ At the foot of the chic Via Gregoriana (Valentino's temple of haute couture reigns at the other end of the street), this hotel guarantees cleanliness, but not quite the stylish allure of its neighboring boutiques. The 13 guest rooms (some with private bath) have TVs, and those on the top floor (reached via elevator) enjoy a view. There is no restaurant. ♦ Via Gregoriana 54 (near Via Capo le Case). 6783649; fax 6781258

20 Hotel Pensione Merano $ Located on the fourth and fifth floors of a hundred-year old palazzo, this hotel is well-priced for this high-rent district of *La Dolce Vita* fame, but don't expect award-winning interiors and there is no restaurant. The management is helpful, and the 30 rooms all have nice, private baths. If quietude is a priority, ask for a room in the rear of the hotel. ♦ Via Vittorio Veneto 155 (at Via Sicilia). 4821796; fax 4821810

21 Piazza Barberini Until the middle of the 19th century, this was an open field of kitchen gardens and vineyards, much of which belonged to the prosperous Barberini family. When the main train station was built in the nearby Termini area (named after the **Baths of Diocletian**; see below), this piazza, adorned with two fountains by **Bernini**, became a city hub. The piazza is at the foot of the legendary Via Veneto, notorious in the 1950s and 1960s for its nocturnal parade of movie stars and the paparazzi who followed in their wake. That period, known as *La Dolce Vita*, was immortalized in Federico Fellini's 1959 movie of the same name. ♦ Bounded by Via Vittorio Veneto, Via Sistina, and Via Barberini

HOTEL DOGE

22 Hotel Doge $$ The decor of this friendly, family-run hotel is—at best—creative, with odd color and pattern schemes and tiny bathrooms; but the 11 guest rooms (all with private baths) are clean and comfortable and just two blocks away from the **Piazza di Spagna.** Quarters on the street side suffer from the abundant automobile traffic in the area. ♦ Via Macelli 106 (near Via Trinità dei Monti). 6780038; fax 6791633

22 Pensione Erdarelli $$ Though it's on the higher end of the budget category, this hotel is reliable, clean, and always full. Efficiently run by the same family since 1935, it's a classic old-fashioned pensione for those who appreciate the basics. There's no restaurant, and some of the 37 rooms share baths. ♦ Via Due Macelli 28 (near Via del Tritone). 6791265; fax 6790705

D.H. Lawrence observed that the modern Italian is much closer in temperament and social habits to the pleasure-loving Etruscans than to the orderly and righteous ancient Romans.

The classic Italian meal unfolds like this:

Antipasto — a selection of cold meats, vegetables, shellfish, and olives

Primo Piatto — pasta, risotto, polenta, or soup

Secondo Piatto — meat or fish

Insalata or *Contorno* — salad or vegetable

Dolce — dessert (fruit, ice cream, or sweets)

Caffè — espresso

Rome

23 Fontana di Trevi (Trevi Fountain) This grandiose late-Baroque monument (pictured below), built in 1762, is one of Rome's most celebrated sites. Dominating a tiny piazza, a towering Oceanus rides a chariot drawn by a host of straining seahorses and tugging tritons. If you don't remember it from *Roman Holiday* or *Three Coins in the Fountain,* you must recall it as the setting for Anita Ekberg's glorious midnight dip in *La Dolce Vita.* Yesterday's rite of drinking the sweet *acqua vergine* (spring water) to assure your return to Rome has today been hygienically modified to tossing a coin over your left shoulder into the water. The fountain was fully cleaned in an elaborate three-year restoration completed in 1990 to the tune of $2.6 million. ♦ Piazza di Trevi (Via delle Muratte and Via del Lavatore)

23 Piccolo Arancio ★★$$ Tuesday and Friday are Fish Nights: Try the excellent homemade *gnocchi al salmone,* just one of 15 special first courses prepared with fish on those evenings. Other days are equally exciting: Try the local specialties in season, like *fiori di zucca* (deep-fried zucchini blossoms stuffed with mozzarella) or *carciofo alla giudia* (deep-fried baby artichoke). ♦ Italian ♦ Tu-Su lunch and dinner; closed the last three weeks of August. Vicolo Scanderberg 112 (at Via del Lavatore). 6786139

24 Fellini Fellini's belts will cinch your waist but not your wallet. Slightly removed from the dense concentration of shops nearer the **Piazza del Popolo,** this is belt heaven, offering men's and women's styles from classics to the newest trends. ♦ M-Sa; no midday closing. Via del Corso 340 (near Piazza Colonna). 6785800

25 Via del Corso This long pedestrian strip connecting the **Piazza del Popolo** with the **Piazza Venezia** is a favorite path for the predinner *passeggiata,* or evening stroll. Check out Rome's golden youths and their funky fashions-of-the-minute, or window shop at the inexpensive clothing stores that line this street. It's intersected midway by the ultra-expensive, ultrachic Via Condotti and the grid of side streets encircling it that leads up to the **Piazza di Spagna.** This is the city's most exclusive enclave of fine jewelry and high-design clothing stores. ♦ Between Piazza Venezia and Piazza del Popolo

25 La Rinascente Great buys are to be had in the Roman version of Bloomingdale's, particularly during the annual August and January sales. You'll find some designer-wear, but most of the quality clothing is their house label. Only the **Piazza Fiume** branch has children's clothes and a housewares department. ♦ Daily; no midday closing. Largo Chigi (at Via del Corso). 6797691. Also at: Piazza Fiume. 8841231

26 Pensione Parlamento $ In the same building that houses a few extraneous Parliament offices, this 22-room/14-bath hotel offers a great location, a flowery rooftop terrace, and some rooms with views and private balconies. Ask for one of the 11 recently renovated rooms. A caveat: The hotel occupies the third to the fifth floors and doesn't have an elevator; there is no restaurant. No credit cards accepted. ♦ Via delle Convertite 5 (near Piazza San Silvestro). 69921010

Fontana di Trevi

Rome

26 Alemagna ★$ This cafe is a downtown institution. Come in for a drink and you'll probably wind up at the tempting *gelateria/pasticceria/panini* bar, if only to feast your eyes. ♦ Italian ♦ M-Sa 7AM-10PM. Via del Corso 653 (at Via delle Convertite). 6789135

27 Ramirez It's not just the neighborhood's costly context that makes the prices here look so reasonable. This shoe store is a tried and true resource for those who want to look well-heeled without spending a bundle. ♦ Tu-Sa; no midday closing. Via Frattina 85A (near Via del Corso). 6792467

28 Gran Caffè-Europeo ★★$ Outdoor tables on a picturesque piazza from a bar serving arguably the best Sicilian pastry north of Palermo—what more can a wide-eyed, hungry, and foot-sore traveler ask? A host of ice cream and hot or cold sandwich possibilities are available as well. ♦ Cafe ♦ Daily 7:30AM-7:30PM Oct-March; until 11:30PM April-Sept. No credit cards accepted. Piazza San Lorenzo in Lucina 33 (off Via del Corso). 6876300

28 Vini e Buffet ★★$ Humble paper tablecloths don't hint at the truly fine wines poured here (a request for beer or water raises no eyebrows, by the way). Salads, a most un-Italian entrée, are the specialty. There are also great soups and a delicious cornmeal polenta with cheese or sausage. You may have to wait for a table, but go just once and you'll understand why. ♦ Italian ♦ M-Sa lunch and dinner. No credit cards accepted. Piazza della Toretta 60 (off Via Leone). 6871445

29 Hotel Marcus $ A homey place in an 18th-century palazzo off the ultra-popular, pedestrian-only Via del Corso, the 10 rooms, all with bathrooms (small), are cheap—and even cheaper in the slow summer months. There is no restaurant. ♦ Via del Clementino 94 (off Via della Scrofa). 68300320; fax 68300312

30 Fraterna Domus $ This is one of the more centrally located of the city's religious hotels, with tariffs comparable to small hotels in the area. If you don't mind an 11PM curfew, you'll enjoy the hospitality of the laypeople who run this 13th-century palazzo adjacent to their church. Of the 10 simply furnished rooms, most are doubles and all have private baths. Lunch or dinner is available at reasonable rates. Discounts are given to students. No credit cards accepted. ♦ Via Monte Brianzo 62 (at Via del Cancello). 68802727; fax 6832691

31 Giolitti ★$ There are certain things just not to be missed in Rome, and this *gelateria* is one of them. You'll pay more for the pleasure of sitting at a table in this classic ice-cream parlor—but the Champagne and Grand Marnier flavors (house inventions) taste just as good standing up. ♦ Ice cream ♦ No credit cards accepted. Tu-Su 7AM-2AM. Via Uffici del Vicario 40 (at Via della Madalena). 6901243

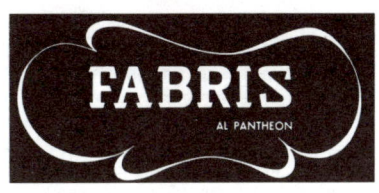

32 Fabris Despite its touristy location—or perhaps because of it—this handbag hot spot has maintained a reputation for good, moderately priced leather goods for more than 40 years. More than 1,000 handbag designs, plus attaché cases and luggage, make up the stock. ♦ M-Sa; no midday closing; closed one week in mid-August. Via degli Orfani 87 (off Piazza della Rotonda). 6795603

32 Caffé Tazza d'Oro Welcome to Coffee Heaven, just down the street from the **Pantheon** (see below). Alas, there's no place to sit, but hang out at the bar with the Romans who can't fathom a day without a caffeine fix (or two) here. If you, too, get hooked, you can arrange to have freshly ground coffee shipped home. Cognoscenti consider the *granita di caffè* (espresso-soaked shaved ice) the best in town. ♦ M-Sa 7AM-8:20PM. No credit cards accepted. Via degli Orfani 84 (off Piazza della Rotonda). 6797544

32 Albergo Abruzzi $ These 37 unadorned chambers offer neither breakfast nor private baths, and the somewhat jaded staff doesn't always extend itself, but if you're lucky enough to get a room facing the monumental **Pantheon,** you'll have great memories of this *albergo*. If you're a light sleeper, request a room in the back, away from the street noise. There is no restaurant. No credit cards accepted. ♦ Piazza della Rotonda 69 (at Via del Seminario). 6792021

33 Coronet Hotel $ Situated on the third floor of a 17th-century palazzo belonging to the aristocratic Doria Pamphili family, this small hotel offers travelers commodious quarters and relaxed management (who don't mind their guests' spontaneous congregations to compare notes on pizzerias or must-do side-trips). Nine of the 13 recently refurbished rooms have private baths; there is no restaurant. ♦ Piazza Grazioli 5 (off Via del Corso). 6792341; fax 69922705

161

Rome

Cheap Stays: The Ins and Outs of Hosteling

For any European traveler on a tight budget, staying at hostels is a lodging option that can't be beat. Where else can you find clean, affordable accommodations (averaging under $20 a night) that offer an incredibly wide range of selection? More than 3,000 hostels are scattered throughout Europe, in settings that range from cabins to castles. Hostels are also a great way to hook up with fellow budget-minded and flexible travelers.

Since its founding in 1932 for the purpose of offering lodging to young travelers, the **International Youth Hostel Federation**, as it was formerly called, has modeled its accommodations on group living, military style–dormitories, shared bathrooms, communal kitchens, curfews, and chores. Today, they're trying to soften their style: The number of beds per room is slowly approaching a civilized level, some offer prepared breakfasts, and very few require chores (although you are expected to clean up after yourself). Curfews, where they haven't been eliminated, have been extended. Separate dorms for men and women are still the norm, but some hostels provide rooms for couples, at somewhat higher rates for private rooms. Another sign of change is that hostels are no longer strictly for the younger generation: About 10 percent of guests are 55 or older, and families with children also take advantage of the inexpensive rates. The majority of lodgers, however, fall in the 18- to 30-year-old category.

In 1993, the federation changed its name to **Hostelling International (HI)** and adopted a blue triangle as its logo. Look for it when checking out properties in directories, on posters, and on the street—many establishments masquerade as official hostels. Most, but not all, hostels have switched to the new organization name and logo, so some confusion is possible. To stay in a hostel affiliated with Hostelling International (a good idea, since you'll be guaranteed a certain standard of accommodation), you must first join the organization. Memberships are available for an annual fee from your local hostel or the national office (see address and phone number below).

Hostels typically close midmorning and reopen in the late afternoon; the larger urban hostels, if they close at all, keep the dormitories off-limits, leaving public rooms open during the day. Hostels are relatively safe; just keep an eye out for petty thievery. Many provide secured lockers for stashing luggage in the daytime, and most offer self-service kitchens, equipped with cooking and eating utensils. Beds are equipped with blankets and pillows, but not linens or towels; hostels will rent or sell sleep sacks for a small fee. Veteran hostelers tote their own: a pillow case along with a bedsheet folded in half and sewn partly up the side. For sanitary reasons, the heavily trafficked urban hostels often prohibit the use of sleeping bags.

Other hostel rules a first timer should be aware of: In order to check in, your HI membership card and a picture ID may be required; no pets are allowed (except guide dogs for the disabled); alcoholic beverages are prohibited; smoking is prohibited or restricted to certain areas; guests under 18 may need a letter of permission from their parents or guardians.

Hostels used to operate on a first-come, first-served basis until all beds were taken. But in their efforts to modernize, many are making it easier to reserve space ahead of time. Procedures vary from hostel to hostel, as do deposit requirements, but generally you can reserve by mail, phone, or fax. If you're going the mail route, include an Advance Booking Postcard (available from local youth hostel organizations) or a note stating date of arrival, number of nights and beds required, and an international postal reply coupon with a self-addressed envelope. Include the same information if you are reserving by fax, along with your credit card number and date of expiration (also asked for when reserving by phone). Note that many hostels will not hold your bed reservation for you if you arrive more than a day late. During the height of the summer tourist season, reservations are essential. It's advisable to make them at least a few weeks in advance, especially for your first stop. But if you end up with the no-more-room-at-the-inn blues, remember that most hostel operators set aside a few beds for walk-ins.

Hostelling International has recently instituted a centralized **International Booking Network (IBN)** that currently includes properties in Amsterdam, Barcelona, London, Paris, Prague, Venice, Zurich, and many others; more cities are constantly being added. Beds can be reserved up to six months in advance and as late as six days beforehand for as many as nine people staying up to six nights on a single booking. A nominal, nonrefundable $5 fee is charged per booking. If you need to cancel, you must do so at least three days in advance and pay a processing fee. Bring the original **IBN** booking receipt to the reservations desk at any member hostel to receive an immediate refund. Contact **Hostelling International–American Youth Hostels**, 733 15th Street NW, Suite 840, Washington, DC 20005; 800/444.6111 for information; 202/783.6161; fax 202/783.6171.

Rome

33 Al Piedone ★$ This tiny restaurant is named after a nearby giant marble foot thought to be a fragment of Constantine's colossal fourth-century statue. A good wine list complements somewhat rustic Roman fare (fettuccine is prepared with either porcini mushrooms or salmon), which is rather delicious at far from monumental prices. If possible, ask for the upstairs seating area, which is particularly charming. ♦ Italian ♦ M-Sa lunch and dinner. Via del Piè di Marmo 28 (off Via del Corso). 6798628

34 Il Ghetto Jews lived freely in Rome for centuries prior to being confined behind walls here in the 16th through 19th centuries. The **Main Synagogue,** built in 1874, holds weekly services and houses the **Jewish Museum,** a permanent collection of 16th- to 19th-century ceremonial objects (admission; call 6875051 to verify the irregular hours). **Piazza Mattei**'s delightful 16th-century **Fontana delle Tortarughe** (Fountain of the Tortoises), whose bronze turtles were added by **Bernini** during a 1658 restoration, marks the heart of the Ghetto on the banks of the Tiber; the main street is Via del Portico d'Ottavia. Many Jewish families still live in this area, now rife with inexpensive restaurants and shops. ♦ Bounded by Via Portico d'Ottavia, Via Arenula, and Lungotevere dei Cenci

34 Leone Limentani Popping into this local landmark is not unlike shopping the off-price stores on Manhattan's Lower East Side. Choose from a huge hodgepodge of Italian and European housewares, fine china, stainless steel, and designer items, all at low prices. Don't worry, they'll ship. ♦ M-Sa; closed two weeks in mid-August. Via del Portico d'Ottavia 47/48 (off Lungotevere dei Cenci). 68806949

35 Uno al Portico d'Ottavia ★★$$ Complete a tour of the Ghetto with an Italian kosher meal that's light years away from the New York City delicatessen variety. The *carciofi alla giudea* make a nice nosh. If the restaurant is full, the dishes are just as delectable (although not kosher) at the well-known **Giggetto's** (6861105), a minute's walk south at Via del Portico d'Ottavia 21A. ♦ Italian ♦ M-Th lunch and dinner; F dinner; Sa lunch. Via del Portico d'Ottavia 1/E (off Via Arenula). 6547937

35 Hotel Arenula $ In the heart of Old Rome near the colorful **Campo dei Fiori** market (see below), this simple hotel has 50 rooms both with and without private baths. Those with heavy luggage take heed: the hotel has no elevator, the lobby is on the second floor, and rooms are found on the next floors. There is no restaurant. No credit cards accepted. ♦ Via di Santa Maria de' Calderai 47 (off Via Arenula). 6879454; fax 6896188

36 Area Sacra di Largo Argentina When Mussolini demolished a large corner of this medieval quarter to create a fascist parade ground, he happened upon these four Republican temples, the oldest relics (sixth and fifth centuries BC) ever excavated in urban Rome. They can only be observed from above (the view from the east side is optimal), as they sit four yards below street level (which rises approximately three feet every 500 years) and are otherwise closed to the public. Julius Caesar was supposedly assassinated here on the Ides of March in 44 BC. ♦ Largo di Torre Argentina (Via di Torre Argentina and Corso Vittorio Emanuele II)

37 Il Delfino ★$ *Tavola calda* (literally "hot table") is the Italian version of fast food. Italians pretend to disdain it, but you'll notice that the majority of customers at this popular pizzeria/cafeteria are locals. While not as good as cooked-to-order, a dish of *pasta alla puttanesca* (with tomatoes, black olives, chili peppers, and garlic), a bowl of *pasta e ceci* (pasta-and-chickpea soup), or any of the pizza selections do come quickly and cheaply. And the food is always fresh and the selection is good. Because of its convenient location, the place is usually full. ♦ Italian ♦ Daily lunch and dinner. Corso Vittorio Emanuele II 67 (at Largo di Torre Argentina). 6864053

37 Pascucci Gore Vidal described this haunt and its habitués, calling it a "hole in the wall: the most popular *frullateria* in town. Like swifts at sundown, motorcycled adolescents park on the sidewalk and swig fruit drinks. Efforts to get them on drugs or alcohol have so far failed: This is an Old City." Join those in the know for the frothy potions flavored with fresh fruit. ♦ M-Sa 6:30AM-midnight. No credit cards accepted. Via di Torre Argentina 20 (off Largo di Torre Argentina). 6864816

38 Hotel Navona $ A helpful Italo-Australian family runs this clean, popular 21-room hotel in a historic 15th-century palazzo named after Rome's fabled piazza a stone's throw away. They request payment by the day and ask that you leave your room by 10AM so it can be cleaned. But with the Eternal City awaiting, who'd want to linger? A dining area serves only breakfast, included in the cost of the room. No credit cards accepted. ♦ Via dei Sediari 8 (at Corso Rinascimento). 6864203; fax 68803802

In Italy, food is weighed by the *etto*, which is 100 grams (one-tenth of a kilo). So, 500 grams or 5 *etti* equal approximately one pound.

Restaurants/Clubs: Red **Hotels:** Blue
Shops/ ♟ Outdoors: Green **Sights/Culture:** Black

163

Rome

39 Chiesa di Santa Maria sopra Minerva (Church of St. Mary over Minerva) Founded in the eighth century on the remains of a temple dedicated to the goddess Minerva, the church was rebuilt in 1280 and is famed as the only church in Rome with a Gothic interior. It holds works by two great Renaissance artists who came to Rome from Florence: The superb frescoes (1489) in the south transept of the **Cappella Carafa** are by Filippino Lippi; to the left of the chancel is *The Risen Christ,* a statue begun by Michelangelo and finished by his pupils in 1521. The great 15th-century Dominican monk and painter Fra Angelico is entombed to the left of the altar. St. Catherine of Siena is also entombed in this church. ♦ Piazza della Minerva (near Piazza della Rotonda)

40 Pantheon The most perfectly preserved ancient building in Rome was begun in 27 BC by Consul Marco Agrippa as a temple to the planetary divinities, and rebuilt by Hadrian in AD 125. The essence of simplicity, its plan of pure geometry has rarely been equaled in ensuing millenia. Consecration as the Roman Catholic church of **Santa Maria ad Martyres** in 609 made it a mortal sin to remove so much as a stone from the site and probably insured its survival. The church's most remarkable architectural feature, the 143-foot-diameter dome, is constructed entirely out of poured concrete and has no supporting columns or buttresses. A number of historical luminaries are buried here: the Renaissance artist Raphael (Sanzio); Italy's first king, Vittorio Emanuele II; his son Umberto I; and Umberto's widow, Queen Margherita.
♦ Free. Daily. Piazza della Rotonda. 588951

41 Bar Sant'Eustachio ★★$ This small and elegant coffee bar wins accolades for the best brew in Rome—at least with those who don't argue on behalf of the nearby **Tazza d'Oro** (see above). Reached from the right rear corner of the **Pantheon,** try to procure a table on the small square and watch Rome stream by until well after midnight. ♦ Cafe ♦ Tu-Su 8AM-1AM. No credit cards accepted. Piazza Sant'Eustachio 82 (off Piazza della Rotonda). 6861309

41 Pensione Mimosa $ This 12-room place is a throwback to the cozy, threadbare, old-fashioned pensione (though this one has no restaurant), and it's governed by a kindly *signora* who's stern about her 1AM curfew and justifiably proud of her location in this vibrant Vecchia Roma neighborhood. No credit cards accepted. ♦ Via Santa Chiara 61 (off Piazza Sant'Eustachio). 68801753; fax 6833557

42 M&M Volpetti ★★$ An excellent, traditional *rosticceria* (take-out restaurant) and delicious *tavola calda* (cafeteria) are set up here under one roof. Spit-roasted chicken, sliced roasts, a variety of pasta, and sautéed greens satisfy the lunch crowds. ♦ Italian ♦ M-Sa 8AM-8PM; closed two weeks in mid-August. Via della Scrofa 31/32 (at Via della Stelletta). 6861940

43 Ai Monasteri This dark-paneled shop dispenses goodies and remedies made in more than 20 monasteries throughout the country. Elixirs, liqueurs, chocolates, honeys, beauty creams, and bath oils all make celestial gifts. ♦ M-Sa; closed in August. Piazza delle Cinque Lune 76 (at Corso Rinascimento). 68802783

44 Piazza Navona Built on the site of Emperor Domitian's first-century stadium, this popular piazza is a magnificent Baroque stage set of splashing fountains, imposing palazzi, outdoor cafes, and artists and hustlers hawking their wares. Pope Innocent X (whose secular name was Giovanni Pamphili) built the **Palazzo Pamphili** in the southwest corner (today the Brazilian embassy), later adding the church of **Sant'Agnese in Agone,** whose facade **Borromini** completed in 1657. But the square's centerpiece is by **Borromini**'s arch-rival, **Bernini:** the exuberant **Fontana dei Fiumi** (Fountain of the Rivers), with its imposing figures representing the Nile, Ganges, Danube, and Plata Rivers. ♦ Between Corso del Rinascimento and Via Santa Maria dell'Anima (north of Corso Vittorio Emanuele II)

44 Ai Tre Tartufi ★★$$ A table on this magnificent piazza may triple what you'd pay standing at the bar. But beauty has its price, and since a table offers the city's best people watching gratis, consider your costly cappuccino a bargain. This *gelateria* is famous for its own production of 30 flavors, and for having invented *tartufo,* a dense chocolate-covered ice-cream truffle. ♦ Ice cream ♦ M-Tu, Th-Su until midnight. Piazza Navona 28. 6541996

44 Al Sogno For the child at home or the child at heart, this is an extraordinary toy shop. A Noah's Ark of every conceivable stuffed animal, it also offers handcrafted dolls, wooden toys, and board games most of which are made in Italy. ♦ M-Sa. Piazza Navona 53 (at Via Agonale). 6864198

45 Cornici e Stampe (Frames and Prints) Look beyond the souvenirs and guidebooks—this place sells high-quality original prints of Rome and a selection of less expensive reproductions as well. ♦ M-Sa; no midday closing; closed in July. Via della Cuccagna 19 (off Piazza Navona). 6875822

Rome

45 Pensione Primavera $ Location is the draw here, not decor or charm. Three of the nine rooms have baths, and all are relatively quiet despite the hotel's location off a main thoroughfare (which makes catching public transport a breeze). And it's a mere minute's walk to **Piazza Navona,** one of the city's premier gathering spots. No credit cards accepted. ♦ Piazza San Pantaleo 3 (between Corso Vittorio Emanuele II and Piazza Navona). 68803109; fax 68803109

46 Albergo della Luneta $ These 30 rooms, half without private bath, are tidy if unimaginative and could use sprucing up. But the agreeable price and the setting amidst narrow cobblestoned streets, billowing laundry, and a wonderful mix of residents young and old, keep visitors coming back. There is no restaurant. No credit cards accepted. ♦ Piazza del Paradiso 68 (near Campo dei Fiori). 6861080; fax 6892028

46 Hostaria Farnese ★$$ Inexpensive, cheerful, and situated equidistant from the magnificent **Piazza Farnese** and the colorful **Campo dei Fiori,** this kitchen serves such favorites as spicy *penne alla arrabiata* (literally "angry," or spicy, macaroni), *faraone* (guineafowl), and zuppa inglese. Pizza has recently been added to an already ample menu. ♦ Italian ♦ M-W, F-Su lunch and dinner; closed in August. Via dei Baullari 109 (off Campo dei Fiori). 68801595

46 Il Fornaio This well-known bakery of the modest moniker (it means "the baker") sells out-of-this-world breads, pastries, pizza, and a bounty of almost-too-beautiful-to-eat fruit tarts. At Christmas, New York's Fifth Avenue windows don't have a thing on the edible mangers and marzipan villages here, their roofs frosted with sugary snow. ♦ M-W; Th mornings; F-Su. No credit cards accepted. Via dei Baullari 5/7 (at Corso Vittorio Emanuele II). 68803947

46 Grappolo d'Oro ★$$ Considering the splendid location, delicious antipasto buffet, and the kind service, the prices here are budget-friendly. A changing menu of local specialties often includes homemade pasta as well as *puntarelle* (a *friseé* salad with a distinctive anchovy dressing). This place has long been a favorite with not-necessarily-starving artists and the **Campo dei Fiori** market crowd from around the corner. ♦ Italian ♦ M-Sa lunch and dinner; closed in August. Piazza della Cancelleria 80 (at corner of Via dei Baullari). 6897080

47 Albergo del Sole $ What this hotel lacks in ambience it makes up for in price and in heritage: it sits on the remains of an ancient Roman theater dating to 55 BC. The 60-odd rooms run the gamut in quality: most of them (half with private baths) are more than adequate, if sometimes less than charming. There's no restaurant, not even a breakfast room, though a number of great coffee bars are in the area. Be careful not to confuse this hotel with the very expensive **Albergo del Sole al Pantheon.** No credit cards accepted. ♦ Via del Biscione 76 (off the Campo dei Fiori). 68806873; fax 6893787

47 Campo dei Fiori $$ Rustic rooms are small and simple, but hand-painted bathroom ceilings and the sixth floor roof garden—alas, there is no elevator—enhance this small hotel's appeal. All 27 rooms (most of which have recently been redone) now have private baths, and the location close to the **Campo dei Fiori** market and the handsome **Piazza Farnese** is a big plus. There is no restaurant. ♦ Via del Biscione 6 (off Campo dei Fiori). 68806865; fax 6876003

47 Campo dei Fiori Hardly a "field of flowers" any longer, this cobblestone piazza is in the middle of a dense medieval quarter best known for the open-air market held every morning but Sunday. Good-natured haggling is the rule as vendors tout a staggering stock of meat, fish, and produce in a cacophony of Roman dialect. Presiding over it all is the gloomy statue of Giordano Bruno, a philosopher/monk burned for heresy by the Counter Reformation papacy in this square in 1600. Like Brigadoon, all traces of the bustling market are gone by 2PM, when the piazza hosts another group of enthusiasts: the leisurely local and visiting crowd that comes to eat, drink, smoke, and debate. This is an incomparable spot for soaking up local color: Take the time to wander the alleyways that surround one of Rome's most picturesque neighborhoods. ♦ Between Lungotevere dei Tebaldi and Corso Vittorio Emanuele II

48 La Moretta ★$ A good value, especially for summer lunches of *farfalle* pasta with exquisite bell-pepper sauce or the typically Roman *buccatini* pasta served with a hearty *all'amatriciana* tomato sauce, enjoyed under outdoor umbrellas. ♦ Italian ♦ M-Sa lunch and dinner; closed two weeks in August. Via di Monserrato 158 (in Piazza della Moretta). 6861900

165

Rome

48 Laboratorio Pietro Simonelli If you can't make it to Venice, stop in this rare (for Rome) mask maker's shop. Choose from a wide selection of inventive disguises to wear or hang on the wall. Pietro keeps artisan's hours, and is open mid- to late morning through late afternoon. ◆ M-Sa. No credit cards accepted. Via Banchi Vecchi 125 (off Corso Vittorio Emanuele II). 6868912

49 Palazzo Farnese Considered the most beautiful of Rome's Renaissance palazzi, this building was begun in 1514 by **Sangallo**, continued by **Michelangelo** (who was responsible for the elaborate, extended cornice and the Farnese coat-of-arms), and finished by **della Porta**. When the Farnese family could no longer maintain the palazzo, the French Embassy agreed to rent it for the nominal fee of one lira per year in exchange for equally palatial digs for the Italian Embassy in Paris. It is not open to the public. ◆ Piazza Farnese (between Campo dei Fiori and Lungotevere dei Tebaldi)

49 Casa Religiosa di Santa Brigida $$ While it's not the bargain usually associated with religious accommodations, this unusual hostelry, the official Swedish parish in Rome, has the air of an aristocratic home. All 20 rooms have private baths and phones, and there's no curfew to curb night owls. Half board is encouraged—a pleasant way to meet the mix of interesting international guests. No credit cards accepted. ◆ Piazza Farnese 96 (between Lungotevere dei Tebaldi and Campo dei Fiori). 6865721; fax 68804780

50 Albergo Pomezia $ The *simpatico* Mariana family has run this tidy ship since 1932. Half of the 22 guest rooms have been recently restored and now have private bathrooms. The older section with shared baths is even less expensive; although nondescript it's just as clean and functional. Who needs a restaurant when the neighborhood market is the nearby **Campo dei Fiori**? ◆ Via dei Chiavari 12 (near Campo dei Fiori). 6861371

In ancient times, the Tiber was regarded as a god. River crossings were overseen by priests called *pontiffs*, meaning builders of bridges, or *ponti*.

The seven hills of Rome are: the Aventine, Celian, Capitoline, Esquiline, Palatine, Quirinal, and Viminal.

Restaurants/Clubs: Red **Hotels:** Blue
Shops/ ❢ Outdoors: Green **Sights/Culture:** Black

50 Hotel Piccolo $ This hotel's potential is enhanced by a great location and a helpful staff. Some of the 15 rooms share baths (six have private bathrooms); charm is at a minimum, and breakfast (not obligatory) is expensive, but all of this pales given the proximity to the **Campo dei Fiori** and **Piazza Navona**. There is no restaurant. ◆ Via dei Chiavari 32 (off Corso Vittorio Emanuele II). 68802560

50 Hotel Smeraldo $ The 35 rooms are on the small side, but recently refurbished: The less expensive quarters share baths. Rooms overlooking a back courtyard are especially quiet even though this is one of the liveliest neighborhoods at night. There is no restaurant, though a dining room offers breakfast at an additional cost. ◆ Vicolo dei Chiodaroli 9 (off Via dei Chiavari). 6875929; fax 6892121

50 Filettaro Santa Barbara ★★$ Try the excellent deep-fried strips of fresh codfish for which this easily overlooked eatery (otherwise known as **Filetti di Bacalà**) is renowned. There's not much else on the menu—the kitchen capitalizes on its strength. ◆ Fish ◆ M-Sa dinner. No credit cards accepted. Largo dei Librari 88 (near Campo dei Fiori). 6864018

51 Pica ★★$$ This popular *gelateria* offers all the classics, but also branches out with unusual flavors such as *mais* (corn). There's a good cafeteria-style *tavola calda* at lunchtime, and the outdoor tables shaded by umbrellas offer an island of serenity just off the raucous Via Arenula. ◆ Cafe/Ice cream ◆ M-Sa breakfast, lunch, and dinner. No credit cards accepted. Via della Seggiola 12 (off Via Arenula). 6875990

52 Corner Bookshop American Claire Hammond owns this friendly place, the most affordable of the English-language bookshops in town. Buying directly from publishers and not international distributors, she passes considerable savings on to appreciative customers. ◆ M-Sa. Via del Moro 48 (near Piazza Santa Maria in Trastevere). 5836942

52 La Galleria For those with an eye for colorful, hand-painted crockery, this shop sells ceramics and other crafts gathered from throughout Italy. Though not particularly convenient to carry, that big, bright Sicilian pasta bowl is worth all the trouble when you finally get it home. ◆ M-Sa; closed in August. Via della Pellicia 30 (near Piazza Santa Maria in Trastevere). 5816614

52 Cinema Pasquino Rome's only English-language movie house is a magnet for nostalgic expatriates and locals intent on polishing their English. The quality of films has improved as of late, and oh, *not* to hear Meryl or Arnold spouting Italian! In the summertime, the ceiling rolls open to let in the stars. An early flick here and an alfresco dinner in the Trastevere neighborhood make for a perfect Roman evening. ♦ Daily from 4PM; last show approximately 10PM; closed in August. Vicolo del Piede 19 (off Piazza Santa Maria in Trastevere). 5803622

L'ARTUSIANA

53 L'Artusiana ★★$$ Named for Artusi, the 19th-century food writer/gourmet, this restaurant's frequently changing menu would surely please his palate. Past highlights have included *tonnarelli* (a thin, flat noodle) with sage and saffron, duck sauce or mushrooms, and chicory; *ovoline fritte* (small, lightly fried mozzarella balls with mushroom sauce); and very fresh fish. ♦ Italian ♦ Tu-Sa dinner; closed in August. Via della Penitenza 7 (off Via della Lungara). 68307053

54 Pizzeria da Gildo ★★$ A roaring wooden oven keeps this place toasty, so you'll forgive Gildo if he closes for lunch during the hot summer months. Otherwise the three rooms are always full with contented diners who come for the antipasto and wide selection of delicious pizzas as well as a more extensive and expensive restaurant menu. ♦ Italian ♦ Daily dinner Apr-Sept; daily lunch and dinner Oct-Mar. Via della Scala 31A (at Via Garibaldi). 5800733

55 Da Lucia ★★$ Since 1938, a sign on the wall has advised patrons: "The kitchen cannot serve clients in a great hurry; all our food is freshly cooked to your order." Who can argue with this *mamma e papa* trattoria whose specialties include pasta *ai ceci* (with garbanzo beans), *e fagioli* (with white beans), and *ai broccoli*, and where the salamis dangling overhead aren't for decoration? This is authentic Roman peasant cooking, an excellent way to enjoy an alfresco evening in Trastevere. ♦ Italian ♦ Tu-Su lunch and dinner; closed three weeks in August. No credit cards accepted. Vicolo Mattonato 2 (near Via Garibaldi). 5803601

56 Santa Maria in Trastevere This is the oldest Christian structure in the city, its foundations dating back to AD 222. Twice rebuilt (in the fourth and 12th centuries), its lovely exterior mosaics are but a hint of the gems within; the apse is wrapped in a glittering 12th-century Byzantine mosaic, and the floor is magnificently paved with marble of many hues. Five popes are believed to be buried beneath the high altar. ♦ Piazza Santa Maria in Trastevere (at Via della Lungaretta)

57 Forno A. Bagagli Come in the early morning and ask for the *pane di grano* (bread made with a secret blend of wheat grain and whole meal flour). All baking is done on the premises nightly and when they're out of bread, you're out of luck. ♦ M-W, F; Th, Sa mornings. No credit cards accepted. Piazza San Cosimato 52 (off Via Luciano Manara). 5810720

58 Pensione Manara $ This five-room family-run hotel is an oasis of quiet in the thick of the lively Trastevere area. The quarters are comfortable, and if you don't mind sharing bathroom facilities, it's a real bargain. There is no restaurant. No credit cards accepted. ♦ Via Luciano Manara 25 (near Piazza San Cosimato). 5814713

59 Pensione Esty $ Don't come to this 10-room hotel for starched linens or private baths but for clean, serviceable rooms and sometimes friendly service. There's no restaurant. No credit cards accepted. ♦ Viale di Trastevere 108 (near Piazza San Cosimato). 5881202

60 Piazza Venezia This traffic-clogged square takes its name from the imposing 15th-century Renaissance building on the west side, which is infamous as the fascist headquarters. It was from the central balcony that Benito Mussolini declared war on France and the US as thousands cheered from the piazza below. The house where Michelangelo died in 1564 (at his request, he was buried in Florence) stood across the square. It was one of several structures demolished to make way for the monstrous white marble **Monumento a Vittorio Emanuele**, built in 1911 to immortalize the unification of Italy and the country's first and short-lived king, Vittorio Emanuele II. After World War I, the **Tomba del Milite Ignoto** (Tomb of the Unknown Soldier) was installed at the top of the stairs, and the two eternal flames were lit in the 1970s. ♦ End of Via del Corso

61 Confetteria Moriondo & Gariglio Follow the scent of simmering chocolate to its source and experience the legacy of this singular confectioner. Owner Marcello Proietti follows traditional recipes for his celebrated *marrons glacés* (candied chestnuts), candied violets, and good-as-gold ingots of bitter, semisweet, milk, and white chocolate. ♦ M-Sa. No credit cards accepted. Via della Pilotta 2 (off Via Quattro Novembre). 678662

62 Fori Imperiali (Imperial Forums) Much of Old Rome remains buried beneath the Via dei Fori Imperiali, the busy thoroughfare created by Mussolini in 1932. (He decreed that any structure obstructing his view of the **Colosseo** from the **Palazzo Venezia** be destroyed.) But, luckily, some of Julius Caesar's (and his successors') Imperial Fora escaped wholly or partially unscathed. Chief among them (illustrated on page 168) is the second-century **Foro di Traiano** (Trajan's Forum), highlighted by the recently restored **Colonna Traiana** (Trajan's Column), which stands at the eastern end of the **Piazza Venezia.** Erected in AD 112 and standing 131 feet tall, it consists of a

Rome

spiraling frieze of 2,500 historic figures. Down the street, the **Mercati di Traiano** (Trajan's Markets) provide another glimpse of ancient life. A three-story commercial center set into the hillside, its 150 *tabernae* (single-room specialty shops) originally sold Romans everything from pepper to custom-made sandals; the entrance is at Via IV Novembre.
♦ Trajan's Column and Forum: free; Trajan's Markets: admission. Tu-Sa; Su mornings Apr-Sept; Tu-Su mornings Oct-Mar. Between Via Alessandrina and Via dei Fori Imperiali

63 Piazza del Campidoglio (Capitoline Hill) This hill, originally the site of the capital of the ancient western world, was later crowned by **Michelangelo** with a spacious and elegant square reached by the **Cordonata**, a dramatic flight of stairs. The redesigned piazza turned its back on the old pagan city and redirected its view toward the then-new buildings of Renaissance Rome. Flanking the piazza are the **Palazzo Nuovo** and the **Palazzo dei Conservatori**, also designed by **Michelangelo**. Together these two buildings comprise the **Musei Capitolini** (Capitoline Museums), which contain masterpieces of Greco-Roman sculpture and a collection of paintings by 16th- and 17th-century Italian artists. The piazza's third building, the **Palazzo Senatorio** (Senator's Palace), has a tiny park just behind it that offers a postcard-perfect vantage point of the **Foro Romano**.
♦ Admission; free last Sunday of the month. Daily. Between Piazza d'Aracoeli and Via Campidoglio

64 Foro Romano (Roman Forum) The glory that once was Rome is hard to discern in these piles of stones. Enter from the gate on Via dei Fori Imperiali, where a passel of English-speaking tour guides promise to make sense of the ruins, an offer worth considering. (Illustrated guidebooks are available at the ticket office.) Still, this is an awe-inspiring place, if only as a kind of graveyard of past history. Turn right onto Via Sacra, the oldest street in Rome; triumphant generals trod its stones up to the **Tempio di Giove** (Temple of Jupiter). Worth seeking out are the **Basilica di Massenzio**; the **Tempio di Vesta** (Temple of Vesta, goddess of the hearth) and the nearby **Casa delle Vestali**, a sprawling complex of rooms for the six vestal virgins who presided over the rituals dedicated to the goddess; and the **Tempio di Saturno**. ♦ Joint admission with the Palatino (see below). Daily. Two entrances: Via dei Fori Imperiali (near Via Cavour); Via di San Gregorio (between the Arch of Constantine and the Colosseo)

65 Palatino (Palatine Hill) Rising 164 feet above sea level, this hill was said to have been home to Romulus and Remus, legendary founders of Rome in 753 BC. The paths through the pine trees, the cool breezes, and sweeping views make this a delightful place for a stroll and picnic. ♦ Joint admission with Foro Romano. Daily. Two entrances: Via dei Fori Imperiali (near Via Cavour); Via di San Gregorio (between the Arch of Constantine and the Colosseo)

Foro di Traiano

Rome

Colosseo

66 Colosseo (Colosseum) Built in AD 72-80 by Vespasian, the first of the Flavian emperors (hence its alternative name, **Flavian Amphitheater**), this structure (illustrated below) is composed of four stories exhibiting three orders of architectural columns: The first is Doric; the second, Ionic; the third and fourth are Corinthian in design. An unrivaled example of classical architecture, this oval covers an area of more than 7.5 acres and stands 135 feet tall. Its marble seats, shaded in summer by a moveable canvas roof, accommodated 50,000 spectators who arrived through 80 entrances. No historic proof exists that early Christians were martyred here, but there is documentation of all kinds of races and contests, including to-the-death gladiatorial combat. An eighth-century English historian proclaimed, "As long as the Colosseum stands, Rome shall stand; when the Colosseum falls, Rome shall fall; when Rome falls, the world shall end." Rome has been busily shoring up the building ever since.

Visible to the southwest (though closed to visitors) is the **Arco di Costantino** (Arch of Constantine), erected in AD 315 to commemorate the emperor's victory over his co-emperor Maxentius. Much of its ornamental low-reliefs were pillaged from pagan sources and have nothing to do with Constantine's achievements. ♦ Admission. Daily. Piazza del Colosseo (at the end of Via dei Fori Imperiali)

67 Hotel Romano $ Plain as a pikestaff but thoroughly renovated, this small hotel's main advantage is its convenient location at the foot of the Via Cavour. Eight of the 16 rooms have a private bath. There is no restaurant. ♦ Largo Corrado Ricci 32 (at Via del Colosseo). 6795851

68 Enoteca Cavour 313 ★$ After a hot day in ancient Rome or for a late night pick-me-up, refresh yourself at this wine bar where you'll share tables with a lively young crowd. A great selection of wines by the glass and a small but delicious menu of pâtés, polenta, finger foods, and sweets revives even the most fatigued sightseer. ♦ Wine bar ♦ M-Sa lunch and dinner. No credit cards accepted. Via Cavour 313 (at Via dei Fori Imperiali). 6785496

69 Hotel Perugia $ This simple, well-run hotel has 11 rooms, mostly without baths, at low, low rates. On a quiet side street just off the bustling Via Cavour, it's a stone's throw to all the major sites of ancient Rome. There is no restaurant. No credit cards accepted. ♦ Via del Colosseo 7 (near Largo Angesi). 6797220

70 Terme di Diocleziano (Baths of Diocletian) and the Museo Nazionale Romano (National Museum of Rome) During the reign of the Emperor Diocletian, 40,000 Christian slaves built this vast complex between AD 295 and 305. The baths accommodated the corporeal and cultural needs of 3,000 men and women daily with hot and cool pools, gymnasia, saunas, sculpture gardens, concert halls, art galleries, and libraries. An 86-year-old **Michelangelo** incorporated half of the 9,000-square-foot cold plunge into the foundations of the church of **Santa Maria degli Angeli.** The church's cloister has been converted into the **Museo Nazionale Romano,** an unrivaled collection of ancient sculpture, frescoes, and paintings dating to the sixth century BC. The baths and museum remain open to the public as an extensive multiple-year renovation is underway. ♦ Admission. Tu-Sa mornings. Viale E De Nicola 79 (in Piazza del Cinquecento). 4880530

Rome

71 YWCA $ Women traveling solo and wanting a room of their own should check out the Y (here also called *Foyer di Roma*); it's safe and it's clean. Fifty female students live here during the academic year, so if you're interested, you'll need to book far in advance. A separate guest floor accommodates an additional dozen rooms for married couples. Rooms accommodate from one to four women; they have sinks but share other bathroom facilities, and there's a midnight curfew. Special monthly rates include breakfast and lunch and require a deposit refunded upon departure. ♦ No credit cards accepted. Via Cesare Balbo 4 (off Via A De Pretis). 4883917; fax 4871028

72 Basilica di Santa Maria Maggiore (Basilica of St. Mary Major) One of Rome's four major basilicas, this church was erected atop the Equiline Hill (one of the famed seven hills of Rome) in AD 440, and was rebuilt four times over the centuries. Though the 18th-century facade is majestic, the real splendor lies in the perfectly proportioned plan, with the nave equal in width and height, as well as the remarkable fifth-century mosaics. The coffered ceiling is said to be gilded with gold from some of the first gold to arrive from the New World. ♦ Piazza Santa Maria Maggiore (off Via Cavour)

73 San Pietro in Vincoli (St. Peter in Chains) Best known as the church containing Michelangelo's statue of *Moses*, this is believed to be the site of the Roman court where Nero condemned Peter to his death. Nearly 400 years later, the empress Eudoxia acquired the two prison chains the saint allegedly wore in Rome, as well as those that shackled him in Jerusalem; they are now kept under the main altar. ♦ Piazza di San Pietro in Vincoli (near Via Cavour)

74 Hostaria da Nerone ★★$$ Midway between the **Colosseo** and **San Pietro in Vincoli** is this good and reasonably priced restaurant. Professors from the nearby university engineering school fill the place at lunch, but things are considerably calmer at dinner. There's a great antipasto buffet, grilled meats, and a daily fresh fish special. ♦ Italian ♦ M-Sa lunch and dinner. Via delle Terme di Tito 96 (near Via della Polveriera). 4745207

75 Fassi Palazzo del Freddo Some consider this century-old *gelateria* to be better than the venerable **Giolitti** (see page 161), but it's fun to conduct your own taste test. Table service helps you recuperate from shopping at the nearby **Mercato Piazza Vittorio Emanuele II**, in case you need an excuse to linger. ♦ Ice cream ♦ Daily 12PM-12AM April-Sept; Tu-Su 12PM-12AM Oct-March. No credit cards accepted. Via Principe Eugenio 65/67 (near Via Cairoli). 4464740

76 Il Dito e la Luna ★★$$ Classic Sicilian specialties are the draw at this handsome restaurant in the fashionably unfashionable San Lorenzo neighborhood near the university. ♦ Italian ♦ M-Sa dinner. No credit cards accepted. Via dei Sabelli 51 (off Via di Porta). 4940276

77 Chiesa di San Clemente The art and architecture of most of the Christian era is encapsulated at this church-cum–archaeological dig. Discoveries are ongoing, but the scenario so far is this: 18th-century Baroque additions were made to an 11th-century church, which in turn was based on a sixth-century church, it having been superimposed on a fourth-century temple to the Persian god Mithras. ♦ Lower basilica: admission. Via di San Giovanni in Laterano (at Piazza San Clemente)

Hotel Celio

78 Hotel Celio $$ Located just behind the **Colosseo** on a quiet residential street, this small, attractive 40-room hotel is named for Celian, one of the seven hills of Rome. Come here for a real big splurge: There's a nice, friendly atmosphere and such amenities as air-conditioning, color TV, small refrigerator, and breakfast served in your room (there is no restaurant) at no extra cost. ♦ Via dei S.S. Quattro 35 (corner of Via Ostilia). 70495333; fax 7096377

79 Basilica di San Giovanni in Laterano (Basilica of St. John Lateran) This church (pictured below), constructed circa AD 314, is the cathedral of the diocese of Rome, the pope's parish. It has been rebuilt time and again, withstanding vandalism, earthquakes, fires, and, in July 1993, a

Rome

terrorist's bomb that closed it temporarily to the public. It has since reopened but is still under repair. The church and the adjoining **Palazzo Lateranese** (Lateran Palace) were headquarters for the papacy until it relocated to Avignon in 1305. The older sections of the 13th-century **Cloisters,** the **Baptistry,** and the **Scala Santa** (believed to be the stairs climbed by Jesus in the Palace of Pontius Pilate) make up the complex, while Rome's oldest obelisk (fifth century BC) stands in the square.
♦ Basilica: free. Cloisters: admission. Daily. Piazza di San Giovanni in Laterano (Via dell'Amba Aradam and Merulana)

80 COIN Not as centrally located as **La Rinascente** (see above) and with fewer branches, this is Rome's "other" department store, where you can one-stop shop for everything from baby clothes to housewares. The better clothing and accessories are mostly from their moderately priced private label, and are somewhat more stylish than **La Rinascente**'s. ♦ M-Sa. Piazzale Appio 7 (at Via E Filiberto). 7080020

81 Via Appia (The Appian Way) and the Catacombs At the western end of the **Circus Maximus** (the fourth-century BC arena that once hosted 300,000 spectators), begins the ancient Via Appia. Built in 313 BC, it became the most important of all the consular roads and extended across the peninsula to the Adriatic Sea. Some stretches are still paved with the original basalt stones and pass through Roman countryside that remains virtually unchanged from imperial times. Bus No. *118* from Via Claudia near the **Colosseum** or No. *218* from **San Giovanni in Laterano** will take you to the **Catacombe di San Sebastiano,** one of the most impressive of the labyrinthine Christian burial grounds. From here it's a five-minute walk to the catacombs of **San Calisto.** An English guided tour is included in admission to each, but the catacombs are not recommended for the claustrophobic. Admission. San Sebastiano: M-W, F-Su. San Calisto: M-Tu, Th-Su. San Sebastiano: Via Appia Antica 136 (at Via di San Sebastiano). 7887035. San Calisto: Via Antica Appia 110 (at Largo Martiri delle Fosse Ardeatine). 5126725

81 Ostello del Foro Italico $ Rome's only youth hostel is located on the northern fringes of town: Take the metro line *A* to the **Ottaviano** stop and transfer to bus No. *32*. If the commute doesn't deter you, and you don't mind dormitory living that can accommodate over 330 guests in rooms of two to six beds or a midnight curfew, this is definitely the cheapest deal going. You can book a maximum of three days, which you can extend on arrival, depending on availability. A **HI (Hostelling International)** card is required. No credit cards accepted. ♦ Viale delle Olimpiadi 61 (near Olympic Stadium). Reception and general information 3236267, reservations 3242571; fax 32.42.613

Bests

Maureen Fant
Writer

Museum—The **Capitoline,** for its treasure trove of Greco-Roman sculpture.

Ancient monument—The **Pantheon,** the most beautiful building in the world.

Walk in Old Rome—The back streets between the **Piazza Navona** and the **Tiber River.**

Archaeological walk—the **Baths of Diocletian.**

Local food specialty—*fiori di zucca fritti* (deep-fried zucchini blossoms).

Ice Cream—**Giolitti, Giolitti, Giolitti!**

Moderately priced gourmet dinner—**Il Dito e la Luna.**

Coffee—**La Tazza d'Oro.**

Nancy Brown
Retired Nurse/History Buff/All-Around Romophile

Museum—**Museo Nazionale Romano.**

Best picnic spot—high atop the **Palatine Hill.**

Piazza—**Piazza Farnese.**

Outdoor cafe—**Caffè Rosati, Piazza del Popolo.**

Shop—**La Galleria** in **Trastevere** for ceramics.

Market—the incomparable **Campo dei Fiori** morning market.

Church—**Santa Maria sopra Minerva.**

Inexpensive hotel—the charming **Pensione Erdarelli.**

Francesco Filippi
Engineer

Most amusing public transportation line—the No. **30** tram.

Ancient monument—The **Colosseum** is unrivaled.

Archaeological walk—from **Via dei Fori Imperiali** up the **Capitoline Hill** and down the other side.

Local food—*rigatoni alla pagliata* (rigatoni pasta with a sauce made with diced veal intestine and stewed tomatoes—authentic Roman fare).

Moderately priced restaurant—**Hostaria da Nerone.**

Church—**San Clemente.**

Coffee—**Bar Sant'Eustachio.**

Walk in Old Rome—the **Celian Hill,** one of the Seven Hills of Rome, rising to the south of the **Colosseum.**

Map of Venice

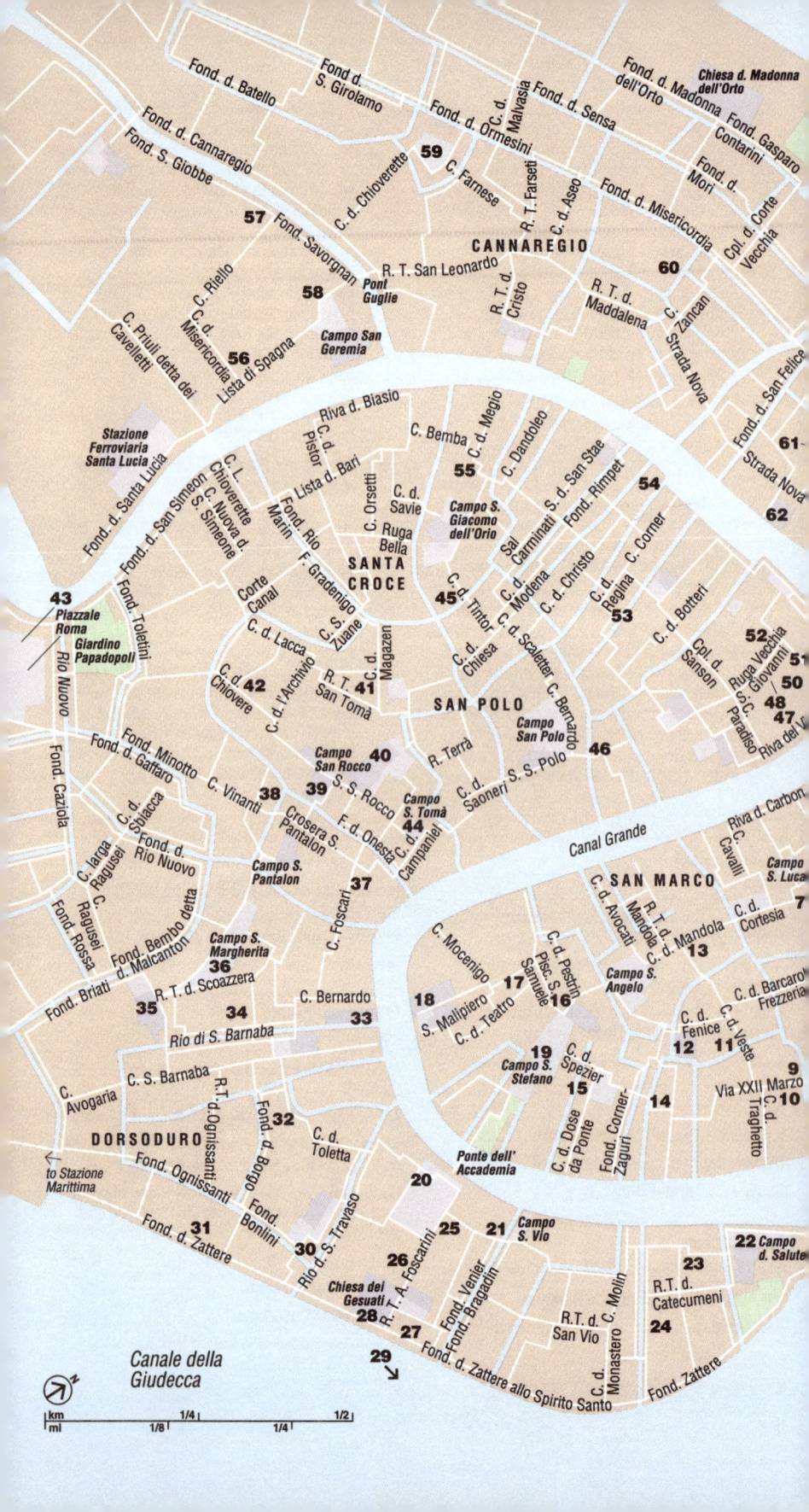

CANNAREGIO

- Fond. d. Batello
- Fond. d. S. Girolamo
- Fond. d. Ormesini
- C. d. Malvasia
- Fond. d. Sensa
- Fond. d. Madonna dell'Orto
- Chiesa d. Madonna dell'Orto
- Fond. Gasparo Contarini
- Fond. d. Cannaregio
- Fond. S. Giobbe
- C. d. Chioverette
- C. Farnese
- R. T. Farseti
- C. d. Aseo
- Fond. d. Misericordia
- Fond. d. Mori
- Cpl. d. Corte Vecchia
- C. Riello
- Fond. Savorgnan
- R. T. San Leonardo
- R. T. d. Cristo
- R. T. d. Maddalena
- C. d. Zancan
- C. Priuli detta dei Cavelletti
- C. d. Misericordia
- Pont Guglie
- Strada Nova
- Campo San Geremia
- Lista di Spagna
- Fond. d. San Felice
- Strada Nova

57, 59, 58, 56, 60, 61

SANTA CROCE

- Stazione Ferroviaria Santa Lucia
- Riva d. Biasio
- C. d. Pistor
- C. Bemba
- C. d. Meglio
- C. Dandoleo
- Fond. d. Santa Lucia
- Lista d. Bari
- C. d. Savie
- Sal. Carminati
- S. d. San Stae
- Fond. Rimpet
- Fond. d. San Simeon
- C. L. Chioverette
- C. Nuova d. Simeone
- Fond. Rio Marin
- C. d. Orsetti
- Ruga Bella
- Campo S. Giacomo dell'Orio
- C. d. Modena
- C. d. Christo
- C. Regina
- C. Corner
- F. Gradenigo
- C. d. Tintor
- C. d. Scaleter
- C. Bernardo
- C. d. Botteri
- Corte Canal
- S. Zuane
- Magazen
- Cpl. d. Sanson
- Ruga Vechia Giovanni
- Fond. Toletini
- C. d. Lacca
- C. d. l'Archivio
- R. T. d. San Tomà
- C. d. Chiesa
- S. C. Paradiso
- Riva d. Vin

43 Piazzale Roma, Giardino Papadopoli

55, 54, 45, 53, 52, 51, 50, 48, 47

SAN POLO

- Fond. Minotto
- Fond. d. Gaffaro
- C. Vinanti
- Campo San Rocco
- R. Terra
- Campo San Polo
- C. d. Saoneri S. S. Polo
- Rio Nuovo
- C. d. Chiovere
- S. S. Rocco
- Campo S. Tomà
- Campanici
- F. d. Onesta
- Crosera S. Pantalon
- Campo S. Pantalon
- C. Foscari
- Canal Grande

42, 40, 44, 46, 39, 38, 37

SAN MARCO

- Riva d. Carbon
- C. d. Cavalli
- Campo S. Luca
- C. Mocenigo
- C. d. Mandola
- R. T. d. Mandola
- C. d. Avocati
- C. d. Cortesia
- S. Malipiero
- C. d. Teatro
- C. d. Pestrin
- Pisc. S. Samuele
- Campo S. Angelo
- C. d. Barcaroli
- Frezzeria
- C. Fenice
- C. d. Veste
- Campo S. Stefano
- C. d. Spezier
- C. Larga Ragusei
- Fond. d. Rio Nuovo
- Fond. Briati
- Fond. Bembo detta d. Malcanton
- Fond. Rossa
- Campo S. Margherita
- R. T. d. Scoazzera
- C. Bernardo
- Via XXII Marzo
- C. d. Traghetto
- C. d. Dose da Ponte
- Fond. Corner-Zaguri

18, 17, 16, 19, 15, 14, 13, 12, 11, 10, 9, 7

35, 34, 36, 33

DORSODURO

- C. Avogaria
- C. S. Barnaba
- R. T. d. Ognissanti
- Fond. d. Borgo
- C. d. Toletta
- Fond. Ognissanti
- Fond. Bonlini
- Rio di S. Barnaba
- Fond. d. Zattere
- Rio d. S. Travaso
- Chiesa dei Gesuati
- R. T. A. Foscarini
- Fond. Venier
- Fond. Bragadin
- Campo S. Vio
- R. T. d. San Vio
- C. d. Molin
- C. d. Monastero
- Fond. Zattere
- Ponte dell' Accademia
- Campo d. Salute
- R. T. d. Catecumeni
- Fond. d. Zattere allo Spirito Santo

32, 31, 30, 20, 25, 21, 22, 23, 24, 28, 27, 26, 29

to Stazione Marittima

Canale della Giudecca

N ↑
km / mi   1/8   1/4   1/2

Map Labels

Water features:
- Canale delle Navi
- Canale di San Marco
- Rio Arsenale

Islands / areas:
- Isola di San Michele
- Cimitero San Michele
- Isola di S. Giorgio Maggiore
- Giardini Reali
- CASTELLO

Places (numbered):
- 1 Piazza San Marco
- 2 Palazzo Ducale
- 67 Campo San Giovanni e Paolo (San Zanipolo)
- 77 Campo San Zaccaria

Streets and landmarks:
- ca della ericordia
- C. lunga S. Caterina
- Fond. Nuove
- C. Marco Foscarini
- Fond. s. Caterina
- Chiesa d. Gesuiti
- C. Venier
- C. larga d. Botteri
- C. d. Pieta
- ruga due Pozzi
- R. T. d. Franceschi
- C. d. Fumo
- C. d. Testa
- R. T. d. Birri
- C. d. Squero
- Fond. Nuove
- Campo S. S. Apostoli
- S. S. Canciano
- C. Widmann
- C. Larga G. Gallina
- Fond. d. Mendicanti
- C. d. Miracoli
- S. S. Giov. Grisostomo
- C. d. Pont d. Erbe
- Barbaria d. Tole
- C. d. Cappucine
- C. d. Dose
- C. Bressan
- Ospedale
- C. Caffettier
- Fond. S. Giustina
- F. d. Preti
- C. d. Fava
- C. L. S. M. Formosa
- S. C. Cappello
- C. d. S. Francesco
- C. C. Sagredo
- C. d. Cimitero
- 63, 64, 65
- 66 C. d. Stagner
- C. Carminati
- 68 S. C. San Lio
- C. d. Paradiso
- 70
- C. Larga S. Lorenzo
- C. d. Fontego
- S. S. Giustina
- Fond. d. S. Severo
- C. d. Olio
- 81
- C. Merc S. Salvador
- C. d. Specchieri
- 71
- 72
- 73 Ruga Giuffa
- C. d. Bande
- F. d. S. Lorenzo
- C. d. Lion
- 80 C. d. Furlani
- S. S. d. Gatte
- C. Magno
- Campo d. Gorne
- 4 C. d. Fiubera
- C. Mercanti
- 75 Fond. d. Osmarin
- 74 S. d. Greci
- C. d. Arco
- 3
- C. d. Fabbri
- S. S. Provolo
- 76
- C. d. Greci
- S. d. Pignater
- 6 C. Cavalletto
- C. d. Albanesi
- 77 Campo San Zaccaria
- C. d. Pieta
- S. d. Forno
- C. d. Pestrin
- Fond. d. Piovan
- F. d. Madonna
- 5
- 78
- 79 Riva degli Schiavoni
- C. d. Dose
- C. d. Forni
- C. Vallaresso
- Molo Riva degli Schiavoni
- Riva Ca di Dio
- F. d. Arsenale
- Campo d. Tana
- Riva S. Biagio
- 82 V. Garibaldi
- 83 Riva dei Sette Martiri

Venice

A dazzling, fabled link between East and West, today's Venice unabashedly thrives on tourism, a realization best heeded early on by those watching their *lire*. Myriad masks and kitsch glass are displayed in every shop window, the odor of seafood (and of the sea itself) hangs in the air, and prices only occasionally correspond to quality. And yet, romantics and budgeteers alike can take heart. Through the centuries, Venice remains the world's most exciting—and, happily, not always the most expensive—city. The greatest tour in town is aboard a *vaporetto* (water bus), floating down the gently curving **Canal Grande** (Grand Canal), past ancient palaces and piazze, all for the price of a water-bus ticket. Wandering the city's intriguing maze of backstreets further enhances the experience.

The theatricality of the city's Gothic palazzi and the absence of automobiles give it an ageless quality reminiscent of its former epithet, *La Serenissima,* or Most Serene. Art and architecture from the likes of Titian, Tintoretto, Veronese, and Palladio abound. A priceless legacy, it's yours for the asking.

Not so with rooms, however: Venice hotels bear the dubious distinction of having some of Italy's priciest room rates. A number of good one- and two-star hotels do exist, however, and in central or convenient locations. It is also important to know that, with the exception of a handful of places, dining in the area surrounding the **Piazza San Marco** is guaranteed to strain your budget. Instead, search out the popular sandwich bars and the old-fashioned *bacari* (wine bars) that serve up a host of *cichetti,* or finger foods, for a light lunch. Those infamous budget-bending dinners needn't happen if you plan carefully; unless it's a special night out, stay away from fresh fish, the outrageously expensive staple of *la cucina veneziana* that will send your bill over the edge.

For a people who have seen it all, the Venetians somehow remain hospitable and enthusiastic, and will always be happy to direct you to your destination if you should get lost. And you *should* get lost—it just might be the best part of your Venetian experience.

To call from the US, dial 011 (international access code), 39 (country code), 41 (city code), and the local number. When calling from inside Italy, dial 041 and the local number.

Getting to Venice

Airports

Marco Polo Airport (661111) is 13 kilometers (eight miles) from Venice. The cheapest way into town is the local **ACTV** *5* bus that travels to the **Piazzale Roma;** from there, connect with the *vaporetto* to your hotel. A warning: During the peak season, some *vaporetto* lines charge extra for luggage. A slightly more expensive alternative is to take a *motoscafo* boat from the airport to either of its two scheduled stops at the **Lido** or **Piazza San Marco.** Both services are available daily, with schedules coordinated with flight times.

Train Station (Long-Distance)

The train station is **Santa Lucia** (Piazza Stazione, Cannaregio, 715555). When buying a ticket, make sure the train stops here, not in mainland **Mestre.** Should you make a mistake, don't despair; shuttles connect the two.

Getting around Venice

Gondolas These fabled boats hold up to six people (once the exorbitant fare is divided it's more affordable) and provide an unforgettable trip through the back canals. Less luxurious but highly functional are *traghetti,* gondolas that cross the Canal Grande at several places. Follow the yellow signs, pay a few hundred *lire,* and ride *alla veneziana*—standing up.

Motoscafi and Vaporetti *Motoscafi* are enclosed, express water buses that make limited stops; the partially open-air *vaporetti* make numerous stops. *Vaporetto* stops for each attraction below are noted at the end of the listing. Purchase a 24-hour, three-day, or seven-day *biglietto turistico* for unlimited travel on both at the **ACTV** office near **Piazza San Marco** (Calle dei Fuseri 1910, San Marco, 5287886).

Taxi Acqueo This private launch will take you anywhere in Venice for an exorbitant sum. There are taxi ranks all around town.

Walking Unquestionably the best way to get around Venice is a combination of walking and the water-transportation system. Once the *vaporetti* deposits you in a neigborhood, roam around at will. The entire city is about the size of New York City's Central Park.

Venice

FYI

Accommodations High season for hotels follows a calendar of its own. Maximum rates are in effect at *Carnevale* (the two weeks preceding Ash Wednesday); from 15 April to 1 July; in September and October; and for the Christmas/New Year's season. Reserve directly or through Venetian travel agencies, such as **C.I.T. Viaggi** (Via Mestrina 65, Mestre, 5040150; fax 5040174), or **Kele & Teo** (Ponte dei Bareteri 4930, San Marco, 5208722; fax 5208913). If you arrive without reservations, visit one of the **Azienda di Promozione Turistica (APT)** offices (see "Visitors' Information," below). During the summer months, many houses owned by religious orders open their doors to paying visitors. A tip: Save money by breakfasting standing up at a local bar, not in your hotel.

Business Hours Stores are open Monday through Saturday from 9AM to 1PM, and from 3:30 to 7:30PM. In winter, there are no Monday morning hours. Food markets are open Monday, Tuesday, and Thursday through Saturday from 9AM to 1PM, and from 5 to 8PM; on Wednesday they're open from 9AM until 1PM. Churches, with many exceptions, are open to sightseers Monday through Saturday, with a midday break from 12:30 until 3:30PM, and on Sunday afternoons. Most museums close on Tuesday, although that too varies.

Climate Good times to visit are May, when temperatures stay in the agreeable 60s, and September and October, when they don't drop below the mild 50s. Summers bring high heat and humidity; winter months are chillingly damp and the piazze sometimes flood. It rains often November through December and in March through April. That said, don't stay away on account of the weather—Venice enchants no matter the season.

Consulates and Embassies

UK .... Dorsoduro 1051, at Ponte dell'Accademia, ... 5227207

The nearest Australian, Canadian, and US consulates are in Milan.

Discount Tickets The Rolling Venice card is sold from June through September to visitors ages 14 to 29. It facilitates free or discounted access to most museums, exhibits, and concerts as well as offering reduced rates for transportation, hotels, restaurants, and shops. The card and copies of their discount guides are available from the **Ufficio Informativo Rolling Venice** office at **Santa Lucia** train station (open daily from 8AM to 8PM; 15 June to 30 September; 5244114, 5242851) and at the **Assessorato alla Gioventù** (off the Frezzeria, San Marco, 2707650). The Rolling Venice card provides the only student discounts for museums; there are no museum discounts for senior citizens. But a *biglietto cumulativo* (combination ticket; available to all visitors) allows entrance into nine museums, including the **Palazzo Ducale** (Doges' Palace) and the **Museo Correr**. Valid for one year,

it can be purchased only at the **Palazzo Ducale**. A good resource for students, the **Centro Turistico Studentesco e Giovanile (CTS)** has general information about what's free and what's cheap (Fondamenta del Tagliapietra 3252, Dorsoduro, 5205660).

Drinking There are plenty of wine bars throughout Venice. While these are popular gathering spots, they don't carry that frenzied party atmosphere of American bars or pubs.

Emergencies For medical emergencies call *Assistenza* at 5230000; for legal emergencies contact *Ufficio Stranieri* at 5203222 or 2703511.

Laundry Laundromats are not part of the Italian experience but the following laundries provide inexpensive service (ironing is extra) from Monday through Friday: **Centro Pulisecco** (Calle della Testa 6262/D, Cannaregio, 5225011); **Lavanderia SS. Apostoli** (Campo SS. Apostoli 4553a, Cannaregio; no phone).

Money The monetary unit of Italy is the *lira;* the plural is *lire,* and it's abbreviated as either "L." or "Lit." During business hours, exchange currency at the **American Express** office (Campo San Moisè 1471, San Marco, 5200844), **Guetta Viaggi** (Calle II dell'Ascenzione 1289, San Marco, 5208711), or any of the principal banks displaying a "Cambio" sign. Avoid the airport, train station, and the independent cambios around town as they charge high commissions.

Personal Safety You're safe strolling unpeopled alleyways, but watch your wallet on the crowded *motoscafi* and *vaporetti,* especially the lines servicing tourist stops.

Postal Services The main post office, **Poste e Telecommunicazioni (PTT),** is located near the **Ponte di Rialto** (Fontego dei Tedeschi 5554, San Marco, 5299111); it's open Monday through Saturday from 8:15AM until 6:45PM. There's a more centrally located branch at Calle Larga dell'Ascensione, just off **Piazza San Marco**; it's open Monday through Friday from 8:10AM until 1:40PM and Saturday from 8:10AM until noon.

Publications At the tourist office ask for a copy of the monthly *L'Agenda,* an exhaustive list of nightlife possibilities. (You'll also see posters plastered about town advertising concerts and the like.) *Un Ospite a Venezia* (A Guest in Venice) provides multilingual monthly listings of cultural events; pick up a copy at any of the tourist offices.

Public Holidays New Year's Day, Epiphany (6 January), Easter Monday, Liberation Day and St. Mark's Day (25 April), Labor Day (1 May), Assumption Day (15 August), All Saints' Day (1 November), Immaculate Conception (8 December), Christmas, and St. Stephen's Day (26 December).

Public Rest Rooms They're a rarity, but try the **Piazzale Roma,** the **Santa Lucia** train station, **Campo San Bartolomeo,** or the **Giardini Reali** behind **Piazza San Marco.** Otherwise, the price of a mineral water entitles you to ask for the *toletta*

175

Venice

in a bar or cafe. Helpful hint: Always carry a supply of tissues.

Restaurants Lunch is served between 12:30 and 2PM; dinner hours are usually from 7:30 until 9:30PM. Most bars and cafes open in the early morning and follow their own particular midday-break schedule; closing time varies from 8PM to midnight. Many eateries close for their vacation in January, February, before *Carnevale*, or in August, as well as between Christmas and New Year's.

Shopping The main shopping district is surrounding **Piazza San Marco** and the adjacent **Mercerie**'s zigzag maze of streets leading to the **Ponte di Rialto** (Rialto Bridge). Prices drop considerably when you venture off the main tourist drags and explore the hidden shops of Venice's backwater alleyways.

Smoking Don't even think of asking a smoker to put it out. Smoking is acceptable just about everywhere.

Street Plan Venice is divided into six *sestieri* (literally "sixths") or wards: **San Marco, Castello, Cannaregio, San Polo, Dorsoduro,** and **Santa Croce.** The central, downtown area is San Marco.

Taxes A 12-percent service charge is usually included in hotel and restaurant bills; look for the words *"servizio incluso."* Shop prices already include the tax.

Telephones For long distance calls, use an international phone card or pay cash at the phone company office, **SIP-TELECOM** (Fontego dei Tedeschi 5551, San Marco, 5333111), near the central post office and the **Ponte di Rialto;** it's open Monday through Saturday from 8AM until 7:45PM. Make local calls or calls throughout Italy from any orange pay phone; the phones take coins or telephone cards (which can be purchased at most bars).

Tipping If restaurant service is very good, add a small gratuity on top of the service charge included in the bill.

Visas A valid passport is needed for stays of up to 90 days.

Visitors' Information There are two locations of **Azienda di Promozione Turistica (APT): Palazzetto Selva** (5226356) near the famous **Harry's Bar** in the San Marco *sestiere;* and in the **Santa Lucia** train station (719078) in Cannaregio. **Assessorato al Turismo** (Ca' Giustinian, San Marco, 2707735) has information and tickets for all cultural events. All three offices are open Monday through Saturday from 8:30AM until 7PM.

Piazza San Marco

Venice

Basilica di San Marco

1 Piazza San Marco (St. Mark's Square) One of the most beautiful and harmonious spaces in the world, this piazza (illustrated on page 176) resonates with history. Most of what you see was built according to a plan devised by the Renaissance architect **Jacopo Sansovino**. Today, it remains the very hub of the city, best experienced while basking in the sun and listening to the music from any one of the adjacent cafes. (Enjoy their historic merit from a distance, as prices in these cafes are fit for a doge.) Make it a point to see the piazza in its many guises: in the mist of the early morning, in silence late at night, and even during the winter's frequent *acqua alta*, or "high water," when pedestrians must cross the piazza via a series of wooden planks. ♦ On Canale di San Marco, San Marco. Vaporetto: San Marco (1, 82, 52); San Zaccaria (1, 82, 52)

1 Basilica di San Marco (St. Mark's Basilica) Begun in the ninth century as the doges' private chapel, this basilica (illustrated above) is an architectural amalgam of medieval, classical, Byzantine, and Romanesque styles. It was built to house the body of Mark the Evangelist (Venice's patron saint), which was stolen from a tomb in Egypt—an event depicted in a 13th-century mosaic over the left arch on the exterior. Cresting the main entrance are copies of four gilded bronze horses; the originals, believed to be about 2,000 years old, were carted off by Napoleon, returned in 1815, and are now in the church museum, the **Museo Marciano.** The interior is a beautifully murky and mysterious space: The floor is paved in intricate patterns, and the walls are covered with mosaics dating from the 12th to the 18th centuries. Also in the basilica are the **Pala d'Oro,** a 12th-century golden altarpiece inlaid with precious stones; the **Tesoro** (Treasury), containing relics and booty from the Crusades; and the **Cappella dei Mascoli** in the left transept. Climb the stairs (or take the elevator) to the top of the 324-foot-high **Campanile** for the best vantage point over the city. In order to protect the basilica's status as a place of worship, the Italian government has instituted strict rules governing visits: Only 20 visitors are allowed inside each minute; tour groups of no more than 20 people are admitted every five minutes; no photographs may be taken; and no talking is allowed, except for tour guides speaking in moderate tones. ♦ Basilica: free. Pala d'Oro, Tesoro, Museum, Campanile: admission. Piazza San Marco (on Canale di San Marco), San Marco. Vaporetto: San Marco (1, 82, 52); San Zaccaria (1, 82, 52)

2 Palazzo Ducale (Doges' Palace) The doges' palatial apartments, assembly hall, and officers' headquarters were originally lodged in this ninth-century structure (shown on page 178). (The doges were the powerful leaders-for-life of The Most Serene Republic of Venice.) Enlarged and modified over the years, its present form dates to the 15th century. Sculptures adorn the pink-and-white palazzo's corners; column capitals are decorated with animals, warriors, and rather graphic representations of vices and virtues. The main entrance, the **Porta della Carta,** a Venetian Gothic masterwork by Giovanni and Bartolomeo Bon, shows Doge Francesco Foscari kneeling in front of St. Mark's lion. Mars and Neptune, symbols of Venice's dominion over land and sea, flank the **Scala dei Giganti** (Giants' Staircase). The palace interior was reconstructed after a 1574 fire, in which important paintings by Carpaccio, Giorgione, and Titian were destroyed. But there's plenty here to keep you in awe, in particular the elegant **Sala delle Quattro Porte,** with paintings by Tintoretto, and the small **Anticollegio** with a number of works by Tintoretto and Veronese. These same painters

177

Venice

are represented in the **Sala del Collegio,** the **Sala del Senato,** and the **Sala del Maggior Consiglio**. A door leads out to the early 17th-century Ponte dei Sospiri (Bridge of Sighs), said to be named for the suspirations of the prisoners who crossed over it on their way from the palazzo to jail. ♦ Admission. Daily. Piazza San Marco (on Canale di San Marco), San Marco. 5224951. Vaporetto: San Marco (1, 82, 52); San Zaccaria (1, 82, 52)

2 Caffè Chioggia ★★$$ Many cafes grace the magnificent square, but this is the only one that won't exhaust a week's budget in a single drink. Sit outdoors in the shadow of the **Palazzo Ducale,** with a flotilla of gondolas on the *laguna* to your right. A small orchestra plays everything from jazz to Vivaldi, and the waiters will let you nurse your drink for hours. ♦ Cafe ♦ M-Sa 9AM-1AM; Closed December-carnevale. Piazza San Marco 11 (on Canale di San Marco), San Marco. 5285011. Vaporetto: San Marco (1, 82, 52); San Zaccaria (1, 82, 52)

3 Torre dell'Orologio (Clock Tower) One of the fathers of the Venetian Renaissance, **Mauro Codussi** designed this tower at the conclusion of the 1400s. Its dual purpose was to hold a large clock (which still runs on a 15th-century mechanism) and to mark the entrance to Venice's main shopping area, **Le Mercerie**. At press time, the tower was closed indefinitely for repairs, but every hour on the hour two bronze Moors still chime the time with their hammers. ♦ Mercerie dell'Orologio 147 (at Piazza San Marco), San Marco. Vaporetto: San Marco (1, 82, 52); San Zaccaria (1, 82, 52)

4 Le Mercerie This series of narrow, zigzagging streets connecting the Ponte di Rialto with **Piazza San Marco** has long been the retail center of Venice. Most of the buildings date back to the 14th and 15th centuries. Shopping here mixes exclusive names, such as **Max Mara** and **Armani**, with trinkets shops where good souvenirs can be purchased. ♦ Between Piazza San Marco and Canal Grande, San Marco. Vaporetto: Rialto (1, 82); San Marco (1, 82)

5 Procuratie In the days of the Venetian Republic, erecting the procurators' headquarters next to the **Palazzo Ducale** established **Piazza San Marco** as the undisputed center of civic and religious life. Looking at it with your back to the basilica, the building on the right (**Procuratie Vecchie**) was reconstructed in the early 16th century by **Jacopo Sansovino**. Notice that its facade is lighter and less imposing than its counterpart on the opposite side of the square, **Procuratie Nuove**, also designed by **Sansovino** and completed 100 years later by **Baldassare Longhena**. ♦ Piazza San Marco, San Marco. Vaporetto: San Marco (1, 82, 52); San Zaccaria (1, 82, 52)

5 Museo Correr This museum comprises three sections: the **Collezioni Storiche** (Historical Collections), the **Museo del Risorgimento e dell'Ottocento Veneziano** (Museum of 19th-Century Venice), and the **Quadreria** (Paintings Collection). The most visited is the last of these, a large collection of minor painters who exemplify the evolution of Venetian art from the 13th to the 16th centuries. The talented Bellini family is well represented: Four paintings by Giovanni Bellini are exhibited next to works by Jacopo, his father, and Gentile, his brother. Also on view are two portraits by Vittorio Carpaccio: the well-known *Courtesans* (reputedly not courtesans at all, but members of the Venetian upper class), and the striking *Man in a Red Beret*. ♦ Admission. M, W-Su. Piazza San Marco 52, San Marco. 5225625. Vaporetto: San Marco (1, 82, 52); San Zaccaria (1, 82, 52)

Palazzo Ducale

Venice

6 Noemi $ If the idea of old-fashioned accommodations with old-fashioned rates appeals, book one of kindly Signora Noemi's 15 rooms. None has a private bath, but all are filled with an impressive mix and match of antiques. There's no restaurant, and no breakfast is served, which further discounts the cost of the room: a good choice for the shoestring traveler. No credit cards accepted. ♦ Calle dei Fabbri 909 (near Piazza San Marco), San Marco. 5238144. Vaporetto: San Marco (1, 82, 52)

7 Latteria Zorzi ★$ Billed as the city's only vegetarian restaurant, this is a *latteria* (dairy store) in the front with dining rooms in the back and upstairs. Pair hot or cold pasta dishes with fresh salads or grilled vegetables in this tranquil and charming spot that's perfect for light eaters and light budgets. ♦ Italian ♦ Tu-Sa 8AM-8PM. No credit cards accepted. Calle dei Fuseri 4359 (near Campo San Luca), San Marco. 5225350. Vaporetto: San Marco (1, 82, 52)

8 Murano Art Shop A group of young artisans dedicated to preserving traditional craft-making methods (and often putting a modern spin on their work) have opened a number of stores selling exquisite masks, dolls, music boxes, and mouth blown glassware. This store has the best stock and is centrally located in San Marco. Be ready to pay handsomely for a quintessential Venetian memento you'll keep for a lifetime. ♦ M-Sa. Frezzeria 1232 (near Piazza San Marco), San Marco. 5233851. Vaporetto: San Marco (1, 82, 52)

9 Libreria Sangiorgio One of the best bookstores for English-language literature, this shop carries a large selection of books on Venice in addition to a limited number of general fiction and nonfiction titles. ♦ M-Sa. Calle Larga XXII Marzo 2087 (near Campo San Moisè), San Marco. 5238451. Vaporetto: San Marco (1, 82, 52)

10 Flora $$ This is a budget-bender in high season, but if you're looking for a charming, intimate hotel in a perfect location, consider investing your savings here. Snuggled among some seriously sumptuous hotels, this 44-room jewel is best remembered for its flowering courtyard oasis where guests can have breakfast or early evening drinks. The nicest rooms overlook the courtyard. Caveat: some of the rooms are very small. ♦ Calle Larga XXII Marzo 2283-A (near Campo San Moisè), San Marco. 5205844; fax 5228217. Vaporetto: San Marco (1, 82, 52)

11 Vino Vino ★★$ Operated by the management of the elegant **Antico Martini**, this is a hip, casual, and definitely cheaper alternative to that culinary grande dame. It maintains an upscale atmosphere without upscale prices, and beckons with good food (especially the veggies and simple pasta dishes) and good times. Offering informal dining with an extensive selection of wines by the glass, it's one of the few places in Venice—certainly in this area—to stay open late, although the kitchen tends to run out of food as the evening wears on. ♦ Wine bar ♦ M, W-Su 10:30AM-midnight. Ponte delle Veste 2007/A (near Campo San Fantin), San Marco. 5237027. Vaporetto: Santa Maria del Giglio (1)

12 Teatro La Fenice (La Fenice Theater) A somber Neo-Classical facade (pictured above) is all that remains of this over-two-hundred-year-old theater after an electrical fire destroyed its elegant interior in January 1996. (Although at press time ther were doubts about the integrity of the walls.) This was the second fire in "The Phoenix's" history—the first occurred in 1836 and the house reopened a year later. At press time, officials were unsure when this historic building would rise again from the ashes, but architects will be guided by the plans of the 1836 restoration that were kept in a bank. ♦ Campo San Fantin 1365, San Marco. Vaporetto: Santa Maria del Giglio (1)

13 Gallini $$ The gregarious Gallini brothers, Adriano and Gabriele, have run this word-of-mouth favorite for close to 40 years; many of their repeat guests seem like family. With 50 rooms (seven without private baths), availability is somewhat greater than in smaller hotels. Rooms are unadorned and functional and there's no restaurant, but housekeeping and service are top-of-the-line. ♦ Closed 15 November to Carnevale. Calle della Verona 3673 (near Campo Sant'Angelo), San Marco. 5204515; fax 5209103. Vaporetto: Sant'Angelo (1)

Venetians swear they invented marzipan, insisting that the Latin root of *pane di Marco* (Mark's bread) refers to a sweet made in honor of the Republic's patron saint.

Restaurants/Clubs: Red   **Hotels:** Blue
Shops/ ♀ Outdoors: Green   **Sights/Culture:** Black

Venice

14 F.G.B. A treasure trove of all things Venetian, this small store sells hand-crafted mementos that, although not cheap, are one-of-a-kind beauties. Gifts from the owners' local glass factories include Christmas ornaments and "Venetian pearls" (multicolored glass beads). The store's workshop produces classical and contemporary *Carnevale* masks in leather, wood, and papier-mâché. ♦ Daily; no midday closing. Campo Santa Maria del Giglio 2459, San Marco. 5236556. Vaporetto: Santa Maria del Giglio (1)

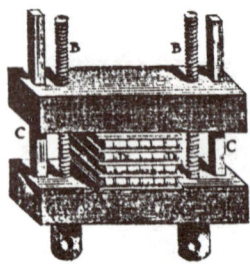

15 Legatoria Piazzesi Originally a bookbindery, this shop is now the most elegant of the many purveyors of marbleized paper goods in the city. Notebooks, desk accessories, and much more make this a great, albeit expensive, spot for visitors to pick up souvenirs. ♦ M-Sa. Santa Maria del Giglio 2511-C (near Campo Santa Maria del Giglio), San Marco. 5221202. Vaporetto: Santa Maria del Giglio (1)

16 Locanda Fiorita $ In a vine-covered villa, set back on its own raised *campiello* (small piazza) just off the handsome and popular **Campo Santo Stefano,** this 10-room inn is well-priced and charming—a find indeed. There is no restaurant and the rooms are plain, but recent work has been done to freshen up the place and there's a pleasant family atmosphere. ♦ Closed for three weeks in January. Campiello Nova 3457 (near Campo Santo Stefano), San Marco. 5234754; fax 5228043. Vaporetto: Sant'Angelo (1); San Samuele (82)

17 Al Bacareto ★$$ Perhaps because of its growing popularity with neighborhood artisans and tourists who come for the fresh pastas and fried calamari, this place is not as cheap as it used to be—but then again what is? It's rustic and informal, with a prized table or two outside usually grabbed by the denizens of the nearby **Palazzo Grassi** exhibition center (see below). ♦ Italian ♦ M-F lunch and dinner; Sa lunch; closed in August. Salizzada San Samuele 3447 (near Campo Santo Stefano), San Marco. 5289336. Vaporetto: San Samuele (82); Santa Maria del Giglio or Sant'Angelo (1)

17 Osteria alle Botteghe ★$$ This neighborhood eatery specializes in fresh panini (Italian-style sandwiches). Ogle the fillings at the counter and choose those that suit your fancy: eggplant, salami, or a variety of cheeses. There are also a number of main dishes, seasonal vegetables, and pizzas. Eat here or take away. ♦ Italian ♦ M-Sa lunch and dinner. No credit cards accepted. Calle delle Botteghe 3454 (near Campo Santo Stefano), San Marco. 5228181. Vaporetto: San Samuele (82); Santa Maria del Giglio or Sant'Angelo (1)

18 Palazzo Grassi Begun in 1718 by **Giorgio Massari,** this classical palazzo was acquired by the Fiat Corporation in the 1980s and restored by **Gae Aulenti** (designer of Paris's Musée d'Orsay) as a center for international exhibitions. The second most popular sight in Venice (after the **Palazzo Ducale**), the building alone is worth a visit. Art aficionados in the know come early or late to avoid interminable lines. ♦ Admission. Open only during special exhibitions. Salizzada San Samuele 3231 (off Campo San Samuele), San Marco. 5235133/5221375. Vaporetto: San Samuele (82); Santa Maria del Giglio or Sant'Angelo (1)

19 Campo Santo Stefano (St. Stephen's Square) One of the largest and loveliest squares in Venice (called **Campo Francesco Morosini** on some maps), this is the crossroads for the streets leading from the Ponte dell'Accademia to the Ponte di Rialto (north side) and **Piazza San Marco** (east side). Locals meet at the ever popular **Gelateria Paolin** (northwest corner) for creamy gelato, afternoon drinks, and cappuccino on Sunday morning. ♦ Between Chiesa di Santo Stefano and Ponte dell'Accademia, San Marco. Vaporetto: Accademia (1, 82); Santa Maria del Giglio (1)

20 Galleria dell'Accademia (Accademia Museum) This unrivaled catalog of 14th- to 18th-century Venetian art is housed in the 15th-century school, church, and convent of **Santa Maria della Carità** (St. Mary of Charity). Trace the Byzantine influence in works by Venetian Primitives, notably Paolo and Lorenzo Veneziano, and the explosive creativity of the Renaissance in the masterpieces by Giovanni and Gentile Bellini, Carpaccio, Giorgione, Veronese, Tintoretto, and Titian. The 17th and 18th centuries are represented by Tiepolo, Piazzetta, Canaletto, Longhi, and Guardi, whose views of Venice testify to how little the city has changed. Don't try to digest the full wealth of this 24-room collection in a single visit, and to avoid the high season's long lines, get here when it opens or go late in the day. ♦ Admission. Daily. Campo della Carità (at the Ponte dell'Accademia), Dorsoduro. 5222247. Vaporetto: Accademia (1, 82)

Venice

21 Collezione Peggy Guggenheim (Peggy Guggenheim Museum) In 1949 American millionaire Peggy Guggenheim chose this odd, unfinished one-story palazzo as a home for her extraordinary collection of 20th-century art. The 18th-century galleries contain seminal works of Cubism, Surrealism, and Abstract Impressionism. The museum is run by the Solomon R. Guggenheim Foundation which, at press time, had announced plans to open three additional museum sites in Venice by 1997. ♦ Admission; free Saturday after 6PM. M, W-Su. Calle Cristoforo 701 (near Campo San Vio), Dorsoduro. 5206288. Vaporetto: La Salute (1); Accademia (1, 82)

22 Santa Maria della Salute (St. Mary of Good Health) In 1630, to honor a vow for deliverance from the plague, the city dedicated this grandiose church to the Virgin of Good Health. Architect **Baldassare Longhena** was chosen over 11 competitors and for the next 50 years supervised a project that remains an outstanding example of large-scale Baroque urban planning. Using a circular scheme, **Longhena** set the church aboveground on a huge embankment supported by a million wood pilings. In contrast to the exuberant exterior, the interior is subdued and reverential, housing 12 paintings by Titian, and Tintoretto's *Marriage at Cana* (1551), considered one of his best. ♦ Campo della Salute, Dorsoduro. Vaporetto: La Salute (1)

23 Hotel Messner $$ Clean, pleasant, and unpretentious, this hotel's 11 guest rooms (all with private baths) have big windows overlooking a canal. A nearby annex houses 20 additional rooms (15 with private baths). There is no restaurant. ♦ Calle Madonna della Salute 216 (near Santa Maria della Salute), Dorsoduro. 5227443; fax 5227266. Vaporetto: La Salute (1)

24 Alla Salute da Cici $ It's only a short walk to Dorsoduro's major sites from this comfortable, efficiently run ex-*pensione*. (The national tourist board did away with the *"pensione"* category when most establishments, such as this one, did away with their restaurants.) Located along a charming canal, more than half of the 50 rooms here contain a private bath. No credit cards accepted. ♦ Fondamenta de Ca'Bala 222-28 (near Santa Maria della Salute), Dorsoduro. 5235404; fax 5222271. Vaporetto: La Salute (1)

25 Trattoria ai Cugnai ★$$ Still relatively inexpensive despite its surging popularity, this neighborhood favorite is run by two tireless sisters and their husbands *(cugnai* means brothers-in-law) whose homemade menu includes *spaghetti con vongole* (with clams), light gnocchi, and a good *prosecco* (sparkling) wine. ♦ Italian ♦ Tu-Su lunch and dinner. Piscina del Forner 857 (near Ponte dell'Accademia), Dorsoduro. 5289238. Vaporetto: Accademia (1, 82)

25 Agli Alboretti $$ Given its proximity to the **Galleria dell'Accademia** (and its easy access to the vaporetto stop), this well-run hotel is in demand. Its 22 guest rooms are comfortable and have private baths, although some rooms are on the smallish side and can be dark. ♦ Rio Terrà A. Foscarini 882-84 (near Ponte dell'Accademia), Dorsoduro. 5230058; fax 5210158. Vaporetto: Accademia (1, 82)

Adjoining Agli Alboretti:

Agli Alboretti ★$$ This spot is particularly convenient if you're staying at the neighboring hotel of the same name, or if you've just spent an exhilarating day at the **Accademia**. Caution when ordering—go for the pastas instead of expensive seafood—keeps this charming and well-known restaurant within budget. ♦ Italian ♦ M, Tu, Th-Su dinner; closed in January and August. Rio Terrà A. Foscarini 882-84 (near Ponte dell'Accademia), Dorsoduro. 5230058. Vaporetto: Accademia (1, 82)

26 Domus Cavanis $ Operated by Catholic priests, this religious institution is hoping for hostel status—that'll mean prices even lower than their already cheap rates. Fifteen simply furnished double and single rooms (all with shared bathrooms) are located in the theological center, and are popular enough to require deposits for peak-season reservations. This is the most central of the religious hostelries listed, and its midnight curfew is as late as you'll find. There is no restaurant. ♦ Closed January-May, October-December. No credit cards accepted. Calle Antonio Foscarini 896 (near Ponte dell'Accademia), Dorsoduro. 5287374; fax 5287374. Vaporetto: Accademia (1, 82)

"Your visit to Venice becomes a perpetual love affair."

Henry James

Venice

27 Pensione Seguso $$ An old-fashioned hotel still run by the Seguso family, this is one of very few places in town where half-board—breakfast plus one meal per day—is still required of its guests during high season, which may make it too pricey for some budgets. (If you know you'll be out for dinner and want to avoid a trip back to the hotel for the noon repast, ask the management if they wouldn't mind preparing a box lunch.) But regulars, many with young children, return again and again for the threadbare charm and comfort and a room with a view over the open Canale della Giudecca. Of the 38 rooms, 28 have private baths. ♦ Closed December-Carnevale. Fondamenta delle Zattere 779 (near Chiesa dei Gesuati), Dorsoduro. 5286858; fax 5222340. Vaporetto: Zattere (82, 52, 16)

27 La Calcina $$ Home to 19th-century British author John Ruskin while he wrote *The Stones of Venice*, this 40-room hotel has benefited from a much needed restoration. Request one of the renovated rooms with a view of the canal—it's worth the slight additional cost. There's no restaurant, but you'll find a number of neighboring outdoor pizzerias along the Zattere. ♦ Closed mid-January to mid-February. Fondamenta delle Zattere 780 (near Chiesa dei Gesuati), Dorsoduro. 5206466; fax 5227045. Vaporetto: Zattere (82, 52, 16)

28 Da Gianni ★★$$ Signor Gianni has been running this place for 30 years, sharing this prime location on the Canale della Giudecca with neighbor **Alle Zattere.** Avoid costly fresh-fish entrées in favor of such equally delicious specialties as *risotto nero di sepie* (rice blackened by squid ink) or *spaghetti alla busara* (with shrimp). If the tables are full, stroll a few doors down to **Alle Zattere** for a good pizza—you won't be disappointed there either. ♦ Italian ♦ M-Tu, Th-Su lunch and dinner; closed in January. Fondamenta Zattere 918 (near Chiesa dei Gesuati), Dorsoduro. 5237210. Vaporetto: Accademia (1, 82); Zattere (82, 52, 16)

There is only one piazza in Venice—Piazza San Marco. What are called piazze elsewhere in Italy are known in Venice as *campi,* and usually have a covered well in the center.

29 Ostello Venezia $ This is the only Hostelling International (HI) facility in Venice that stays open year-round (except for a two-week shutdown in January). Situated on Isola della Giudecca in an old granary warehouse and boasting a view of the distant **Palazzo Ducale,** the hostel sleeps over 250 people in dormitory-style rooms that accommodate four to six people; each room has an adjacent bathroom. The inexpensive restaurant and bar are relaxed and convenient spots to meet and greet fellow adventurers. Despite its size, the hostel recommends making reservations for summer stays as early as April. Don't forget your HI membership card, and mind the 11:30PM curfew. ♦ Closed last two weeks in January. No credit cards accepted. Fondamenta delle Zitelle 86 (near Chiesa delle Zitelle), Isola della Giudecca. 5238211; fax 5235689. Vaporetto: Zitelle (82)

30 Squero di San Trovaso (San Trovaso Boatyard) One of three boatyards in Venice that make new gondolas and restore old ones, this national landmark is one of the city's most photogenic sites. Visible from across the canal (visits inside the boatyard are not encouraged), the curious wooden buildings are typical 17th-century boat builders' workshops. They look like Dolomite mountain chalets, and in fact both the wood for the gondolas and the master carpenters often come from that region. Boats are built in strict accordance with the traditional, centuries-old methods. ♦ Campo San Trovaso 1092, Dorsoduro. Vaporetto: Accademia (1, 82); Zattere (82, 52, 16)

RISTORANTE

RIVIERA

31 Ristorante Riviera ★$$ This restaurant's chef/owner learned to keep the customers satisfied during his years at **Harry's Bar.** Relax at tables lining the canal, and stay under budget by keeping away from the fish entrées. An alluring alternative is the homemade gnocchi or *ravioli con zucca* (with pumpkin) or *di pesce* (fish). ♦ Italian ♦ Tu-F lunch and dinner; Sa dinner; Su lunch; closed 15-22 August. Fondamenta delle Zattere 1473 (near Chiesa dei Gesuati), Dorsoduro. 5227621. Vaporetto: San Basilio (82)

Venice

32 Locanda Montin $ *Trattoria Montin* rents seven upstairs rooms, whose only inconvenience is the lack of private bathrooms (there are four communal bathrooms with showers). Four rooms have small geranium-laden terraces and charming views over the canal. The restaurant downstairs is well-known though expensive. No credit cards accepted. ♦ Fondamenta di Borgo 1147 (near Chiesa di San Barnaba), Dorsoduro. 5227151. Vaporetto: Accademia (1, 82); Ca'Rezzonico (1)

33 Ca'Rezzonico—Museo del Settecento Veneziano (Museum of 18th-Century Venice) This imposing building, with its facade facing the Canal Grande, was begun by **Baldassare Longhena** in the 17th century and completed by **Giorgio Massari** in the 18th century. Poet Robert Browning died here in 1889. The palazzo is now a museum of 18th-century decorative arts, showcasing furniture, textiles, and other objects found in a patrician home of that period. Giambattista Tiepolo painted the ceilings in **Rooms 2, 6, 8,** and **14,** the latter called the **Sala dei Longhi** because it contains some 30 canvases by the popular 17th-century Venetian painter of everyday life, Pietro Longhi. **Room 29** holds a familiar work by Francesco Guardi, *Il Ridotto*. ♦ Admission. Daily. Fondamenta Rezzonico 3136 (on the Canal Grande), Dorsoduro. 5224542. Vaporetto: Ca'Rezzonico (1)

34 Mondonovo Home of Venice's master *mascheraio*—mask maker par excellence—this small shop has an international reputation. Upholding the highest artistic standards, owners Giano Lovato and Giorgio Spiller design masks and other papier-mâché objects for the theatre and movies. ♦ Daily; no midday closing. Rio Terrà Canal 3126 (near Campo Santa Margherita), Dorsoduro. 5287344. Vaporetto: Ca'Rezzonico (1)

34 Ristorante L'Incontro ★$ This spot has authentic atmosphere, an excellent wine list, and a consistently delicious *pasta del giorno* . . . and maybe you'll even catch Paolo, the headwaiter, in a good mood. ♦ Italian ♦ Tu-Su lunch and dinner. No credit cards accepted. Rio Terrà Canal 3062 (near Campo Santa Margherita), Dorsoduro. 5222404. Vaporetto: Ca'Rezzonico (1)

35 Chiesa and Scuola Grande dei Carmini (Church and School of the Carmelites) Built in the 1300s, this Gothic church is best known for its rich 17th-century wood carvings and two masterworks by Cima Da Conegliano and Lorenzo Lotto. During its heyday in the 17th century, the *scuola* (charitable fraternity or guild) of Santa Maria del Carmelo had a following of 75,000 people. Today it is noted for its collection of works by Giambattista Tiepolo; nine of his paintings adorn the ceiling of the main hall. Of particular note is the *Virgin Mary with the Blessed Simon Stock*, considered one of his greatest creations. ♦ Church: free. Scuola: admission. Scuola: M-F; Sa morning. Church: Campo dei Carmini, Dorsoduro. Scuola: Rio Terrà Santa Margherita 2616, Dorsoduro. Vaporetto: Ca'Rezzonico (1)

36 Pizzeria al Sole di Napoli ★$ Friendly and informal, this place draws crowds on summer evenings not just for its food but because its alfresco tables sit on one of Venice's most colorful *campi*. The simple *pizza margherita* (topped with tomatoes, mozzarella, and basil) is a classic, but first check out the daily homemade pasta special. Locals gather here when they don't feel like cooking and stay for hours. ♦ Italian ♦ No credit cards accepted. M-W, F-Su lunch and dinner. Campo Santa Margherita 3023, Dorsoduro. 5285686. Vaporetto: Ca'Rezzonico (1)

36 Campo Santa Margherita Neighborhood life is centered around this *campo*, one of the liveliest and largest in town. It's lined with food shops, cafes, and wide-open spaces where mothers watch their *bambini* cavort. Some of the adjacent homes are among the oldest and most charming in Venice: **No. 2931** (west side) is a 13th-century Gothic building still showing its original Byzantine elements. ♦ Between Campo dei Carmini and Campo San Pantalon, Dorsoduro. Vaporetto: Ca'Rezzonico (1)

36 Antico Capon $ Location, location, location. Three of the seven rooms (two without private bath) overlook the colorful *campo*. Rooms and baths are old, simple, and clean. There is no restaurant, which is perfectly fine for travelers content with the basics. ♦ Campo Santa Margherita 3004B, Dorsoduro. 5285292; fax 5285292. Vaporetto: San Tomà (1, 82); Ca'Rezzonico (1)

In the 18th century, 14,000 colorful gondolas—each a one-of-a-kind artwork—sailed Venice's canals. Today the boats number fewer than 500; by law they're all painted black.

183

Venice

37 Hotel Tivoli $ Attention to detail is apparent at this popular 24-room hotel. Handsome mahogany furniture, sheer white curtains, color TV, and chenille bedspreads outfit most of the newly refurbished rooms, of which only two lack private baths. There's no restaurant. ♦ Ca'Foscari 3838 (near Campo San Pantalon), Dorsoduro. 5222656; fax 5222656. Vaporetto: San Tomà (1, 82)

38 Hotel Falier $$ This stylish hotel is situated on a quiet street near the **Campo San Rocco** and **Scuola Grande di San Rocco** and a 15-minute walk from the **Piazzale Roma**. Its 20 rooms are small but tastefully decorated with lace curtains and flowery bedspreads; all have well-lit, modern bathrooms. The restaurant serves breakfast only. ♦ Salizzada San Pantalon 130 (near Campo San Rocco), Santa Croce. 5228882; fax 5206554. Vaporetto: San Tomà (1, 82)

39 Scuola Grande di San Rocco (School of St. Roch) This recently restored, 16th-century Renaissance building (illustrated above) was the seat of the powerful school or confraternity of St. Roch, the association of merchants, storekeepers, and other members of the Venetian bourgeoisie whose missions ranged from assisting the poor to redeeming sinners. The *scuola* commissioned Jacopo Tintoretto to decorate the interior, a job that took 18 years and resulted in an extraordinary cycle of 56 paintings. Brochures in English, available at the ticket booth, will guide you through the overwhelming collection; don't overlook the works by Titian and Tiepolo. ♦ Admission. Daily. Campo San Rocco 3054, San Polo. 5234864. Vaporetto: San Tomà (1, 82); Piazzale Roma (1, 82, 52)

When all of medieval Europe was competing in jousts and tourneys, Venice—lacking piazze to accommodate these recreations—held regattas on the Canal Grande and in the *laguna*. Today, more than 100 regattas take place annually, the most important being the Regata Storica, held on the first Sunday in September.

Gondoliers row *alla veneziana* (standing in the stern with one foot forward and using a single oar), a style that is unique in the world, as is the gondola, the only asymmetrical boat ever designed.

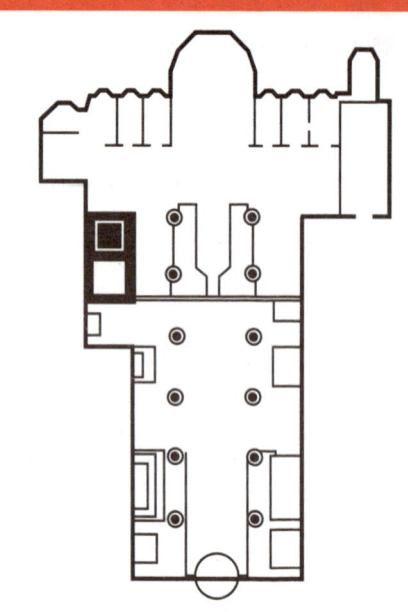

40 Chiesa dei Frari (Church of the Friars) The Franciscans' emphasis on prayer and poverty is appropriately represented by this church's somber Gothic exterior; inside (floor plan above), it has a quiet atmosphere, with tombs of doges and prominent citizens and masterworks by Titian and Giovanni Bellini, whose *Madonna and Child with Four Saints* hangs in the sacristy. ♦ Admission; free Sunday and holidays. Campo dei Frari, San Polo. 5222637. Vaporetto: San Tomà (1, 82); San Silvestro (1)

41 Mensa Universitaria $ Offering good food at rock-bottom prices, this eatery is a favorite among the city's lively student population. At least half the allure is mingling with the city's lively student population. ♦ Italian ♦ M-Sa lunch and dinner; Su lunch; closed late July-early September, Easter weekend, and 23 Dec-12 January. No credit cards accepted. Calle del Magazen 2840 (near Chiesa dei Frari), San Polo. 718069. Vaporetto: San Tomà (1, 82)

42 Domus Civica $ In the winter this former hotel operates as a residence for women, but in the summer months it's open to all travelers. Run by the lay branch of the Association Catholique Internationale Jeunesse Feminine, it offers 70 single and double rooms with shared baths. Advance bookings can be held by sending an international money-order deposit. The 11:30PM curfew lasts until 7:30AM, so if you have to catch an early train, you're out of luck. Prepare for the 15-minute trek to the train station by packing light and wearing your walking shoes. There is no restaurant. ♦ Closed January-June, October-December. No credit cards accepted. Calle Campazzo 3082 (near Calle delle Secchere), San Polo. 721103. Vaporetto: San Tomà (1, 82)

Venice

43 Piazzale Roma The closest cars can come to Venice is this piazza, built in the 1930s. It's a chaotic traffic hub where tour buses load and unload, gondoliers offer their services, and general tourist information can be gathered. ♦ On the Canal Grande (at Rio Nuovo), Santa Croce. Vaporetto: Piazzale Roma (1, 82, 52)

44 Trattoria San Tomà ★★$$ Set in the middle of the small **Campo San Tomà**, this neighborhood restaurant is known for its pizza, but don't overlook the homemade pastas, such as the tagliatelle prepared *al pomodoro e basilico* (with fresh tomato and basil). The most popular pizza is the simple *margherita*. Named after Italy's most beloved queen, the patriotic pie features the colors of the Italian flag. ♦ Italian ♦ Daily lunch and dinner; closed Tuesdays in winter. Campo San Tomà 2864-A, San Polo. 5238819. Vaporetto: San Tomà (1, 82)

45 Pizzeria alle Oche ★★$ Word is out on what used to be a well-kept secret: This is one of the best pizza places in Venice, boasting more than 70 varieties of pie and 10 interesting combination salads. You'll probably have to wait for a table inside or out (besides the small space in front, there's a rear garden); a choice of 30 beers will make it worth your while. ♦ Pizzeria ♦ Tu-Su lunch and dinner. Calle del Tintor 1552-B (near Campo San Giacomo dell'Orio), Santa Croce. 5241161. Vaporetto: San Stae (1)

46 Da Sandro $ Savor good pizza at reasonable prices at somewhat crowded tables along the busy *calle* leading to **Campo San Polo.** The place is especially nice in low season, when a less-harried Sandro has time to prepare yummy pasta dishes. ♦ Italian ♦ M-Th, Sa-Su 11:30AM-11:30PM; closed in January. Campiello di Meloni 1473 (near Campo San Polo), San Polo. 5234894. Vaporetto: San Silvestro (1)

47 Alla Madonna ★★$$ A 50-year-old favorite, this is one of the few restaurants in the center of Venice serving really fresh fish at decent prices. The eclectic clientele—from market vendors to the better-heeled—savors the *granseola* appetizer (a variety of local crab) and the risottos. ♦ Italian ♦ M-Tu, Th-Su lunch and dinner. Sotoportego della Madonna 594 (near Ponte di Rialto), San Polo. 5223824. Vaporetto: Rialto (1, 82); San Silvestro (1)

47 Locanda Sturion $$ One of the rare hotels that has Canal Grande views without grand rates. A recent refurbishing of this smart, 11-room establishment added heated towel racks and air-conditioning. There's no elevator, so steady yourself for the three-flight climb. If you're not lucky enough to procure one of two rooms on the canal, take solace in a breakfast in the pretty canal-side dining room. ♦ Calle del Sturione 679 (near Ponte di Rialto), San Polo. 5236243; fax 5228378. Vaporetto: Rialto (1, 82); San Silvestro (1)

48 L'Antico Dolo $ At this old-fashioned *osteria* or wine bar, the owner serves *pasta e fagioli* (bean soup) and a handful of other popular dishes that complement the carefully selected house wines. If you're eagle-eyed and fast, grab one of the small tables. Otherwise, join the throng standing three-deep at the counter. ♦ Wine bar ♦ M-Sa 10:30AM-3PM; 7PM-10PM. No credit cards accepted. Ruga Vecchia San Giovanni 778 (near Ponte di Rialto). 5226546. Vaporetto: San Silvestro (1)

49 Ponte di Rialto (Rialto Bridge) This simply-designed stone bridge, decorated with reliefs of the Annunciation, was built at the end of the 16th century to replace a wooden span too low to accommodate passing ships. Until the 1800s, the bridge (whose architect was the appropriately named **Antonio Da Ponte**) was the only Canal Grande crossing; it is joined today by the Accademia and the Scalzi bridges. ♦ Connecting the sestieri of San Marco and San Polo. Vaporetto: Rialto (1, 82)

50 Rialta In the sea of kitsch ebbing around the Ponte di Rialto, there is an island of good taste. Quality and variety set these souvenirs—dolls, glassware, masks—apart. There's also an opulent collection of costume jewelry, so stop here first. ♦ Daily; no midday closing. Sottoportici di Rialto 56 (at Ponte di Rialto), San Polo. 5285710. Vaporetto: Rialto (1, 82); San Silvestro (1)

51 Mercato della Frutta and Pescheria (Fruit and Fish Market) Despite the rapid decline of the rest of the market into a tourist trap, the sprawling produce section and fishmongers are still authentic. Before the days of industrial pollution, this *pescheria* was a heavyweight among fresh fish markets in the Adriatic. Today the majority of its sea creatures are flown in daily from Holland, Ireland, and Norway, but local fishermen still bring in their limited supplies snatched up early by the local restaurants. This is a scene not to be missed: Its sounds and smells will transport you to the bustling docks of Venice's past. ♦ Mercato della Frutta: M-Sa morning. Pescheria: Tu-Sa mornings. Ruga degli Orefici (at Ponte di Rialto), San Polo. Vaporetto: Rialto (1, 82); San Silvestro (1)

Restaurants/Clubs: Red **Hotels:** Blue
Shops/ ♦ Outdoors: Green **Sights/Culture:** Black

Venice

52 A Le Do Spade/Trattoria ★★$ The *cichetti* (finger foods) and bonhomie at this local *bacaro*—a small, homey wine bar—make for an ultra-Venetian experience. Sample the *prosciutto d'oca* (goose ham) or dabble with the excellent wine list. The regulars—workers from the market and savvy visitors—always stand at the counter, though tables have been added where both light and full-course meals can be enjoyed. The menu is typically Venetian with fish playing an important role. When Casanova was a regular here, this tavern was already 300 years old. ♦ Wine bar/Italian ♦ M-W, F-Sa 9AM-3PM, 5PM-midnight; Th 9AM-3PM; closed in August. Sottoportego Do Spade 860 (near Campo della Pescheria), San Polo. 5210574. Vaporetto: San Silvestro (1)

52 Ai Do Mori ★★$ Another *bacaro* pouring good wines and serving bar food that includes marinated calimari, savory deep-fried octopus meatballs, and platters of salami and prosciutto. There's no place to sit, so blend into the counter crowd and partake of the local color. ♦ Wine bar ♦ M-Tu, Th-Sa 8:30AM-1:30PM, 5:30PM-8:30PM; W 8:30AM-1:30PM. No credit cards accepted. Calle Do Mori 429 (near Campo della Pescheria), San Polo. 5225401. Vaporetto: San Silvestro (1)

53 Osteria al Non Risorto ★$ In keeping with its origins, this remodeled wine bar cultures a slightly bohemian ambience. A new order is evident, however, in the quality of both the food—try the slightly spicy *gnocchi alla busera* (with scampi in a tomato sauce)—and the service. The side garden is heavenly in the summer, scented with the perfume of a large wisteria tree. ♦ Italian ♦ M-Tu, Th-Su lunch and dinner. Sottoportego de Sora Betina (near Campo di San Cassiano), Santa Croce. 5241169. Vaporetto: San Stae (1)

54 Ca'Pesaro—Museo d'Arte Moderna and Museo d'Arte Orientale Early in the 17th century, the wealthy Pesaro family acquired three adjacent buildings on the Canal Grande and commissioned the fashionable architect **Baldassare Longhena** to create an imposing palazzo. The result is distinct in its Baroque grandeur and elegance. The **Museo d'Arte Moderna,** occupying the first two floors, was at press time undergoing extensive restoration and was only partially open; its collection is culled from exhibitions at the Venice Biennale and includes works by De Chirico, Morandi, Chagall, Kandinsky, and Klimt to name but a few. The same building houses the **Museo d'Arte Orientale.** ♦ Admission. Tu-Su. Fondamenta Ca'Pesaro 2076 (on the Canal Grande), Santa Croce. Modern Art: 5240695; Oriental Art: 5241174. Vaporetto: San Stae (1)

55 La Zucca ★$$ "The Pumpkin," opened by a group of women in the early 1970s, when Venice's feminist movement was in its nascence, is an informal eatery that has maintained something of its original nonconformist atmosphere. The emphasis is still on good vegetarian cooking, as can be witnessed by the *minestra di zucca e porri* (pumpkin and leek soup) and the lasagna made with radicchio. ♦ Italian ♦ M-Sa lunch and dinner. Ponte del Megio 1762 (near Campo San Giacomo dell'Orio), Santa Croce. 5241570. Vaporetto: San Stae (1)

56 Hotel Santa Lucia $ Signora Emilia is the gracious hostess of this 15-room hotel where snow-white sheer curtains and the clean smell of scrubbed tiled floors are appreciated by both backpacking students and professors on sabbatical. Some of the large, sunny rooms overlook a patio where breakfast (only) is served in warm weather. Her son, Giangelo, speaks English. ♦ Closed 10 January to 10 February. Calle della Misericordia 358 (near Campo San Geremia), Cannaregio. 715180; fax 715180. Vaporetto: Ferrovia (1, 82, 52)

56 Union $ Echoes of its glory days are evident in the stately lobby and trellised garden of this rambling, old, three-star hotel. If budget is paramount, request a back room—some of the 30 rooms lack views, direct sun, and private baths, but these cost less than half the tariff of the standard accommodations. No restaurant. ♦ Lista di Spagna 127 (near the train station), Cannaregio. 715055; fax 715621. Vaporetto: Ferrovia (1, 82, 52)

57 Hotel Hesperia $$ This romantic 20-room hotel would cost far more if it were closer to the city's hub; but its location on a lazy little canal only enhances its charm. Rooms are of average size but the decor is thoughtfully done and private, spacious baths are a plus. The hotel's **Il Melograno** restaurant has a few tables outside where breakfast is offered in warm weather. ♦ Calle Riello 459 (near Campo San Geremia), Cannaregio. 715251; fax 715112. Vaporetto: Guglie (52)

58 Hotel San Geremia $ Lack of an elevator has kept this 20-room hotel with two- and three-star amenities (phones and TVs in every room, and hairdryers and heated towel racks in the nicely tiled bathrooms) in the one-star price category. Niceties include bright, new bathrooms in 16 of the 20 rooms, as well as small terraces (Rooms 419 and 420) and windows overlooking the *campo*. Fresh linens

Venice

and dried flowers grace the breakfast room. There's no restaurant, though a few tables are set up outside for lemonade sipping and people watching. ♦ Campo San Geremia 290A, Cannaregio. 716245; fax 5242342. Vaporetto: Ferrovia (1, 82, 52)

58 Hotel al Gobbo $ English-speaking Signora Maria runs her hotel with uncommon care and pride: Walls are hung with paintings of Venice, and guest rooms with comfortable furnishings overlook either the small *campo* or the picturesque garden. Of the 10 rooms, three have private baths; the others have their own sink and shower but share large, clean WCs. There is no restaurant. ♦ Closed mid-December to 1 February. No credit cards accepted. Campo San Geremia 312, Cannaregio. 715001. Vaporetto: Ferrovia (1, 82, 52)

59 Campo del Ghetto (The Ghetto) In the 16th century, Jews of many nationalities were isolated on this island and subjected to harsh conditions. Tenements wrapped around this small square, and as new families arrived, additional floors (some only 6.5 feet high) were constructed—hence the centuries-old elevatorless "skyscrapers" that stand up to eight stories high. Jews could work and circulate around town but a severely imposed nighttime curfew was enforced by Christian guards. It was not until Napoleon conquered the Republic that Jews were allowed to move out of the ghetto. Only a handful of Jewish families still live here or in Venice, but the museum and community center keep their poignant heritage alive. Of the five synagogues in the ghetto, three are located on the square; tours are arranged only through the **Museo Ebraico**. ♦ Campo del Ghetto Nuovo, Cannaregio. Vaporetto: San Marcuola (1, 82); Guglie (52)

59 Museo Ebraico (Jewish Museum) A legacy of four centuries of Jewish life in the Venice ghetto—precious books, tapestries, jewels, and sacred articles—are gathered in this small museum run by a young and helpful staff. A small kosher cafeteria was scheduled to open at press time. The entrance fee includes a guided tour, in English, to three synagogues otherwise closed to the public. ♦ Admission. M-F, Su; closed Saturday and Jewish holidays; no synagogue visits on Friday. Campo del Ghetto Nuovo 2902/b, Cannaregio. 715359. Vaporetto: San Marcuola (1, 82); Guglie (52)

60 Ostello Santa Fosca $ A 15-minute walk from the train station, this hostel is convenient to **Campo del Ghetto.** Male and female guests, accommodated in 27 separate dormitory-like rooms, needn't supply the usual HI membership card, aren't subjected to maximum stays, and even have communal use of a kitchen. Boasting its own volleyball court and a young staff of friendly students who live here when the university is in session, the hostel's only drawback is the 11:30PM curfew—but Venice goes to sleep early anyway. ♦ Closed January-June, October-December. No credit cards accepted. Fondamenta Canal 2372 (near Campo San Fosca), Cannaregio. 715775; fax 715775. Vaporetto: San Marcuola (1, 82)

61 Trattoria dalla Vedova ★★$ The sign over the door reads **Trattoria Ca'd'Oro,** but everyone calls this spot **dalla Vedova.** The owners have retained the original atmosphere of this working-class wine shop, though it has been "discovered" and now caters to both sides of the tracks. Finger food is available at the bar, but ask what's cooking as well—it may be worth sipping your vino for a few minutes while the risottos, spaghetti, or *pasta e fagioli* receive their final touches. ♦ Italian ♦ M-W, F-Su lunch and dinner. Rame Ca'd'Oro 3912 (near Ca'd'Oro), Cannaregio. 5285324. Vaporetto: Ca'd'Oro (1)

62 Ca'd'Oro/Galleria Franchetti The beautiful pink-and-white marble facade of this splendid 15th-century Venetian Gothic masterpiece was recently unshrouded after a lengthy restoration. The gallery holds an impressive array of early Venetian and Byzantine sculptures, Mantegna's *St. Sebastian,* and works by Tintoretto, Titian, Guardi, and Van Dyck. ♦ Admission. Calle Ca'd'Oro 3932 (on the Canal Grande), Cannaregio. 5238790. Vaporetto: Ca'd' Oro (1).

"Wonderful city, streets full of water, please advise," humorist Robert Benchley allegedly cabled home on his first visit to Venice. A canal here is called a *rio,* and you'll need advice about the streets that aren't full of water, too. Here are translations for some common Venetian terms:

Calle—street

Campo—piazza

Campiello—small piazza

Stretto—narrow passageway

Sottoportego—passageway or covered street

Ruga—also street, from the French "rue"

Fondamenta—street alongside a canal

Riva—principal *fondamenta*

Salizadda—one of the original paved streets

Rio terrà—filled-in canal, now a street

Lista—street fronting a former (as in Republican days) embassy, once a place of diplomatic immunity

Piscina—filled-in cul-de-sacs

Venice

62 Trattoria all'Antica Adelaide ★$$ In the summer, diners move outdoors under capacious umbrellas, giving this trattoria a shady advantage over its rival **Trattoria dalla Vedova** (see above). The aroma of the grilled *mazzancolle* (jumbo shrimp) promises a pricey meal, so consider any of the classic first courses, such as the *spaghetti con vongole* (with clams). ♦ Italian ♦ Tu-Su lunch and dinner. Calle Racchetta 3728 (near Ca'd'Oro), Cannaregio. 5203451. Vaporetto: Ca'd'Oro (1)

63 COIN Fashionable visitors should experience the Italian version of one-stop shopping for middle- to high-end apparel and accessories. Costume jewelry, cosmetics, and handbags are more reasonably priced than the clothing, particularly during the July/August and January/February sales. ♦ M-Sa. Salizzada de San Giovanni Grisostomo 5787 (near Ponte di Rialto), Cannaregio. 703581. Vaporetto: Rialto (1, 82)

64 Osteria al Milion ★$$ Still informal, still well-run, and still as popular as ever, this traditional eatery has raised its prices from rock-bottom to moderate. Try the risotto with arugula and shrimp. ♦ Italian ♦ M-Tu, Th-Su lunch and dinner; closed in August. No credit cards accepted. Corte Prima al Milion 5841 (near Chiesa San Giovanni Grisostomo), Cannaregio. 5229302. Vaporetto: Rialto (1, 82)

65 Osteria Ai Rusteghi ★★$ Congenial owners Manuela and Roberto handle the constant flow of back-slapping locals and neighboring merchants who drop in to sample the freshly made panini sandwiches, or to meet and exchange news. It's standing room only, and dozens of combinations are offered: Grilled vegetables with smoked ricotta cheese, and fresh arugula with locally made salami are the favorites. Join in and order an *ombra* (a glass of red house wine), or stock up on panini to go if you're leaving town by train. ♦ Italian ♦ M-Sa lunch and snacks. No credit cards accepted. Campo San Bartolomeo 5529 (near Ponte di Rialto), San Marco. 5232205. Vaporetto: Rialto (1, 82)

The word *vaporetto* (water bus) is derived from *vapore* (steam). Propelled by steam in the 19th century, the boats now use diesel oil. Environmentalists have long touted the benefits of electrical power, but change comes slowly to this retired Queen of the Adriatic.

Yes, Virginia, there *are* Venetian blinds in Venice. Whether or not they originated here depends upon whom you ask. They are called *veneziane* and are often used together with exterior wooden shutters (called *persiane*).

66 Rosticceria San Bartolomeo ★★$ This is one of the better places in Venice for both counter service or food *da portare via* (take-out). The excellent kitchen proffers tempting pastas, risottos, lasagna, roast chicken, and grilled fish. Chances are you'll dine better here than at some of the neighborhood's more conventional restaurants; opting for the seating area upstairs will increase your tab slightly. ♦ Italian ♦ Tu-Sa lunch and snacks. Calle della Bissa 5424 (near Campo San Bartolomeo), San Marco. 5223569. Vaporetto: Rialto (1, 82)

67 Chiesa di Santissimi Giovanni e Paolo Native dialect has unofficially rechristened this Dominican church **San Zanipolo**, a contraction of the two saints' names. Filled with tombs, chapels, monuments, and artworks, this place provides a quick education in the history of Venetian art and politics. Don't miss the recently restored *Polyptych of St. Vincent Ferreri*, attributed to Giovanni Bellini, or the three paintings by Paolo Veronese on the ceiling of the reconstructed **Rosary Chapel**. The spacious *campo* where the church stands is still an anchor of local life; a constant flow of pedestrians crosses in all directions, and old men while away the afternoon in cafes, playing cards and arguing over yesterday's soccer scores. ♦ Campo San Giovanni e Paolo, Castello. Vaporetto: Rialto (1, 82)

68 Osteria da Alberto ★$ This venerable wine bar has remained a well-kept secret to non-Venetians, mostly because it's hard to find—though it's well worth the search. At **Campo Santa Maria Formosa** ask someone for directions to **Campo Santa Marina**; once there, ask for the bar by name. Elegant it's not, delicious it is, with a varied array of *cichetti* and a hot pasta special each day. ♦ Italian ♦ M-Sa 9AM-3PM; 5:30PM-9PM; closed in January and August. Calle Malvasia 6015 (near Chiesa di San Lio), Castello. 5229038. Vaporetto: Rialto (1, 82)

68 Canada $ If you don't mind the hike to the third-story lobby, ask for one of the two top-floor rooms with wood-beamed ceilings and small terraces. Sitting on a quiet, charac-teristic *campiello* (small square), the hotel has 25 guest rooms; private, modern baths; and an attentive, capable management. There is no restaurant. ♦ Campo San Lio 5659, Castello. 5229912; fax 5235852. Vaporetto: Rialto (1, 82)

69 Foresteria Valdese $ A hostel for grownups since 1925, this church-run 18th-century palazzo is open year-round—an unusual advantage for an institution of this type. The Waldesian Church offers dormitory lodging here, although there are three apartments for five to six people, which are usually booked far in advance. Baths are shared, and a deposit is required for peak-

188

season reservations. No restaurant. ♦ Closed last two weeks in November. No credit cards accepted. Calle Lunga Santa Maria Formosa 5170 (near Campo Santa Maria Formosa), Castello. 5286797; fax 5286797. Vaporetto: Rialto (1, 82)

69 Osteria al Mascaron ★★$$ Friendly, trendy and forever crowded, this wine bar serves excellent snacks as well as a roster of daily changing pastas and entrées. It's patronized by students, intellectuals, and a growing number of tourists in the know. At press time, the owners were preparing to open another wine bar just down the street, called **La Mascheretta**. ♦ Italian ♦ Daily lunch and dinner. Calle Lunga Santa Maria Formosa 5225 (near Campo Santa Maria Formosa), Castello. 5225995. Vaporetto: Rialto (1, 82)

70 Chiesa di Santa Maria Formosa Neither saints nor prophets populate the facade of this early Renaissance church, designed by **Mauro Codussi**; in their stead stand members of the powerful Cappello family, who financed the building. Adorning churches with portraits of patrons was a common practice in Venice and accounts for the puzzling mix of sacred and profane elements all over town. ♦ Campo Santa Maria Formosa, Castello. Vaporetto: Rialto (1, 82)

"CIP CIAP"

70 Cip Ciap Slabs of luscious pizza fill the windows at this take-out shop. Buy any combination of hot slices (they're priced by weight), and pull up a bench in nearby **Campo Santa Maria Formosa**. ♦Daily. No credit cards accepted. Calle del Mondo Novo 5799, (near Campo Santa Maria Formosa), Castello. 5236621. Vaporetto: Rialto (1, 82)

71 Riva $ This 12-room hotel (10 with private bath) is owned by an amiable doctor-turned-innkeeper who points with pride to such tasteful details as the marble-tiled bathrooms and Richard Ginori china in the breakfast room (no other meals are served). Some rooms overlook the narrow Canale dei Sospiri, a favorite route for singing gondoliers who pass under the legendary Ponte dei Sospiri (Bridge of Sighs) not far away. ♦ Closed January-December. No credit cards accepted. Ponte dell'Angelo 5310 (near Piazza San Marco), San Marco. 5227034. Vaporetto: San Marco (1, 82)

72 Locanda Remedio $ A great value, this 14-room hotel in a 16th-century palazzo was renovated in 1992. Airy and comfortable, the 10 doubles (five with air-conditioning) have formal-style furniture and handsome baths; some even have frescoed ceilings. The spacious, sunny sitting room invites lingering, though you'll need to look elsewhere for a restaurant. ♦ Calle del Remedio 4412 (near Piazza San Marco), Castello. 5206232; fax 5210485. Vaporetto: San Zaccaria (1, 82, 52)

73 Gianni & Luciana Pitacco In Venice there is no shortage of objects covered in marbleized paper. Reasonable prices, however, aren't so abundant, making a visit to this shop a priority. The congenial couple who own the store do fine work. ♦ M-Sa. No credit cards accepted. Ruga Giuffa 4758 (near Campo Santa Maria Formosa), Castello. 5208687. Vaporetto: San Zaccaria (1, 82, 52)

74 Renzo Marega Since *Carnevale* was revived in 1980, the city has been awash in mask stores, many selling mediocre products at very inflated prices. Spare yourself some *lire* and go to Renzo Marega's shop for substantial savings, a variety of masks, and the generous hospitality of this talented young artisan. ♦ Daily; closed Sunday in January. No credit cards accepted. Fondamenta dell'Osmarin 4968 (near Campo San Provolo), Castello. 5223036. Vaporetto: San Zaccaria (1, 82, 52)

74 Bar Ai Do Moro ★$ The canalside tables with blue umbrellas and yellow and red tablecloths attract passersby to this typical *bacaro* (pub). Low prices, friendly service by young owners Daniele and Massimo, and simple but good food (fresh sandwiches and small pizzas) keep them coming back for more. Be prepared to stand: There are very few seats. ♦ Italian ♦ M-Sa lunch and snacks. Fondamenta dell'Osmarin (near Chiesa San Giorgio degli Schiavoni), Castello. No phone. Vaporetto: San Zaccaria (1, 82, 52)

Addresses in Venice are based on a byzantine system that confuses even the locals. Places have both a street address and a somewhat different mailing address (both use the same building number). The latter uses the *sestiere* (postal district) of the building—no reference to a street is made. (When asked directions, Venetians typically cite *campi* and churches, not addresses.)

Restaurants/Clubs: Red   **Hotels:** Blue
Shops/ ♀ Outdoors: Green   **Sights/Culture:** Black

Venice

75 Anticlea Antiquariato In a city awash with "Venetian pearls"—colorful glass beads of all sizes, colors, shapes, and costs—Gianna and her daughter Elena have the best collection of antique beads in their tiny shop, with drawers arranged according to color and value. Pick and choose and string them yourself, or have the owners do it for you. Some of the 18th-century beads were used for trade as far away as Turkey and Africa and have found their way back home. ♦ M-Sa, no midday closing. Campo San Provolo 4719 (near Piazza San Marco), Castello. 5286946. Vaporetto: San Zaccaria (1, 82, 52)

76 Casa Fontana $$ A family atmosphere prevails in this unpretentious small hotel, a two-minute stroll from **Piazza San Marco**. The 14 tidy guest rooms have private baths; a few have terraces or views of the church of **San Zaccaria**. There is no restaurant. ♦ Campo San Provolo 4701 (near Piazza San Marco), Castello. 5210533; fax 5231040. Vaporetto: San Zaccaria (1, 82, 52)

77 Campiello $$ This family-run hotel sits in a tiny piazza off the prestigious Riva degli Schiavoni. Its 15 rooms are always in demand—air-conditioning, tasteful furnishings, private baths, and an English-speaking staff explain why. Only breakfast is served in the restaurant. ♦ Calle del Vin 4647 (near Campo San Zaccaria), Castello. 505764; fax 5205798. Vaporetto: San Zaccaria (1, 82, 52)

77 Doni $ This is a central, no-frills, family-run lodging. A little outmoded and without a restaurant, but well-maintained and spotless, the 11 large, airy bedrooms overlook either docked gondolas or the courtyard garden. All rooms have sinks but share baths. ♦ Closed January-Carnevale. No credit cards accepted. Calle del Vin 4656 (off Riva degli Schiavoni), Castello. 5224267. Vaporetto: San Zaccaria (1, 82, 52)

Pensione Wildner

78 Wildner $$ The *simpatica* Signora Lidia runs this 19-room hotel whose vistas of the island of San Giorgio and the *laguna* match those of its five-star neighbors. Book ahead and request a room with a view. ♦ Riva degli Schiavoni 4161 (near Chiesa di San Zaccaria), Castello. 5227463; fax 5227463. Vaporetto: San Zaccaria (1, 82, 52)

Within Wildner:

Ristorante Wildner ★$ You can't beat the scenery or the value at this convenient lagoon-side restaurant. Three tasty *menù turistici* whet the appetite without whipping the budget. ♦ Italian ♦ Daily lunch and dinner; closed Wednesday mid-November to mid-January. 5227463

79 Chiesa della Pietà Known to locals as Vivaldi's church, **La Pietà** was designed by architect **Giorgio Massari** in the mid-18th century for a local orphanage. The children received musical training, and their concerts were renowned throughout Europe. (The word *conservatorio* originally meant "place where abandoned children are kept.") Composer Antonio Vivaldi taught at the orphanage until his death. The interior, conceived more as a concert hall than a church, was restored in 1988. Baroque music performances (most importantly of works by Vivaldi) are held regularly; the tourism office has the schedule (see "Visitors' Information"). ♦ Riva degli Schiavoni 4150 (at Calle della Pietà), Castello. Vaporetto: San Zaccaria (1, 82, 52)

80 Scuola di San Giorgio degli Schiavoni (School of St. George of the Dalmatians) The building shelters nine early 16th-century works by Vittorio Carpaccio. By depicting sacred subjects in a mortal manner, the painter took a daring step toward freeing art from the grip of religion. ♦ Admission. Tu-Sa; Su mornings. Calle dei Furlani (near Campo San Lorenzo), Castello. 5228828. Vaporetto: Arsenale (1); San Zaccaria (1, 82, 52)

81 Arsenale The Arsenale's notoriety was assured when Dante made reference to it in his *Inferno*. The vast 12th-century compound (comprising one-fifth of the city's area) embodies the maritime might of the "Most Serene Republic." Its 16,000 workers could construct a mighty galley in a single day. Enclosed by crenellated walls, it's currently off-limits military turf. (Sneak a peak inside from the No. *52 vaporetto* that cuts through here on its route to Murano). The four lions that guard the entrance are spoils of war; the second from the right is believed to be from the Greek island of Delos, circa sixth century BC. Naval history buffs must visit the nearby **Museo Storico Navale** where exhibits trace the annals of Venetian seafarers to the present day. ♦ Campo dell'Arsenale, Castello. Vaporetto: Arsenale (1)

Around 1750, Venice experienced its first *acqua alta*: The canals and lagoons flooded the city. Over time, these floods have become more frequent; they now occur as often as 50 times a year. The worst flooding on record was in 1966, when the tide rose nearly 6.5 feet above normal sea level.

Venice

81 Ristorante da Paolo ★$$ Sited near the **Arsenale** portal, next to a quiet canal, this restaurant offers great alfresco dining. The regular clientele returns for the spaghetti with clams or the variety of great pizzas. ♦ Italian ♦ Tu-Su breakfast, lunch, and dinner until midnight. No credit cards accepted. Campo dell'Arsenale 2389, Castello. 5210660. Vaporetto: Arsenale (1)

82 Hotel Bucintoro $$ This hotel has an unparalleled location on the Riva di San Biagio just past the **Arsenale:** Most of its 28 rooms enjoy a view over the lagoon, with the **Public Gardens** and the **Lido** to the east, and the **Basilica di San Marco** to the west. There's no restaurant and no elevator, but the stairs are not too steep. Book in advance for a corner room. ♦ Closed January, December. No credit cards accepted. Riva di San Biagio 2135 (near Museo Storico Navale), Castello. 5223240; fax 5235224. Vaporetto: Arsenale (1)

83 Patronato Salesiano $ This modern building was created as student housing, but in the summer the Salesian order offers accommodations to everyone. Thirty-five small double rooms have sinks (but share bathrooms) and—a major plus for night owls—there is no curfew. Half- or full-board is available for a modest fee. Reservations required in writing; advance notice is greatly appreciated. Heavy packers rejoice: the hotel is just a three-minute walk from the nearest *vaporetto* stop. ♦ Closed January–mid-June, October-December. No credit cards accepted. Calle San Domenico 1281 (off Via Garibaldi), Castello. 5285586; fax 5285189. Vaporetto: Giardini (1, 52)

Bests

Samantha Durell
Owner, Venice Travel Advisory Service

Circle the city in the wee hours in an outdoor seat on the No. *1 vaporetto*—it's the top tour in town.

Prime people-watching at any neighborhood square, where bicycles, skateboarders, and rollerskaters whirl through clusters of chatting mothers. If you're passing through **Campo San Luca** or **Campo San Bartolomeo** in the early evening, you'll find them packed with young people who meet here to exchange news before wandering off to dinner or an *aperitivo*.

If you're canal-side when a gondola carrying an accordion player and a singer of traditional Venetian songs passes, sit yourself down for a treat: more sonorous skiffs are likely to glide by. The strains of their music resonating across the water is nothing short of magical.

Late evenings at the **Caffè Chioggia** in **Piazza San Marco** you'll hear the coolest jazz east of Manhattan. It's worth every *lira*. You can sit forever without being rushed.

Try to get tickets for any of the baroque concerts around town, particularly those at the **Chiesa della Pietà** that feature the music of Vivaldi.

Vespers at the **Basilica San Marco** will transport you to the far-away times of *La Serenissima*.

An unforgettable moment is spying a bride and groom exiting a church or passing in their wedding gondola. The boats are decked out for the occasion with special furnishings, flowers, and *gondolieri* attired in elegant livery.

Laundry day—Monday morning—provides some terrific photo ops. Use high-speed color film to catch the Kodachrome shows billowing in the breeze.

A picnic at the **Punta della Dogana** just beyond the church of **Santa Maria della Salute.** There are no chairs, but pull up a piece of the quay and feast your eyes on the **Palazzo Ducale (Doge's Palace)** and the **Piazza San Marco** across the *laguna*.

Ringside seats for the annual Regata Storica (first Sunday in September) are free, if you can find a spot on either side of the **Ponte di Rialto.**

Dodging *vaporetti* and riding the wake of water taxis on the *traghetto* north of the Ponte di Rialto is an adventure to remember on one of the most beautiful stretches of the gently winding canal.

The absolute best snack is fresh, creamy, delicate ricotta cheese. Stop by a well-stocked *salumeria*, buy an *etto* and some crusty bread, and nibble away to your heart's content.

Umberto Montagnaro
Gondolier

It is with great pride that I have chosen to follow the waves made by my father, taking up the oars of the gondola. I am the fourth generation of *gondoliere* in my family. Our work days are intense, particularly during the high season. So when we want to enjoy ourselves, we usually have to do so late at night. We often head out to the beach and find ourselves the only ones there.

On our days off, my friends and I turn not to the waterways but to *terra firma*, hopping in a car and heading to the mountains where we bask in a day of peace and quiet. When looking for less serenity, we head for the discotheques on the **Lido**, such as **Rouge e Noir.**

But generally we just meet at a number of local bars, such as **Bar Ai Do Moro** (not far from **Piazza San Marco**), **and Sotto Sopra** near **Campo Santa Margherita.**

88
1
2
3
Hauptbahnhof (Main Train Station)
89
For nos. 4-71, see pg. 196
Bahnhofbrücke
Lagerstr.
Militärstr.
Gessnerbrücke
Kasernenstr.
Gessnerallee
Löwenstr.
Uraniastr.
Linth-Eschergasse
Bahnhofquai
Seilergraben
Künstlergasse
Rämistr.
Schmelbergstr.
Universitätsspital Zürich
Voltastr.
Hochstr.
Gladbachstr.
Gloriastr.
Mousson
Nägelistr.
Bergstr.
74
75
Uraniastr.
Sihlstr.
Rennweg
Limmat
Limmatquai
Niederdorfstr.
Pestalozzistr.
Attenhoferstr.
Zürichbergstr.
Freiestr.
Eleonorenstr.
90
Augustinergasse
Pelikanstr.
Bahnhofstr.
Talacker
Hirschengraben
Heimplatz
Kirchg.
Hottingerstr.
Steinwiesstr.
Plattenstr.
Hofstr.
Dolderstr.
Treichlerstr.
Selnaustr.
91
Poststr.
Fraumünsterstr.
73
Zeltweg
Gemeindestr.
Talstr.
Rämistr.
Gartenstr.
Freigutstr.
Bleicherweg
Stockerstr.
92
Glärnischstr.
Brückequai
72
Theaterstr.
76
Merkurstr.
Dreikönigstr.
Genferstr.
Gotthardstr.
77
Kreuzbühlstr.
Klosbachstr.
Minervastr.
Eidmattstr.
Falkenstr.
78
80
79
Utoquai
Gen. Guisanquai
Gen. Willestr.
Arboretum
Mühlebachstr.
Signaustr.
Kreuzstr.
Ferry
Ferry
81
Florastr.
Neumünsterstr.
Lavaterstr.
Alfred Escherstr.
Mythenquai
Grütlistr.
Gablerstr.
Feldeggstr.
Seefeldstr.
Dufourstr.
Hammerstr.
Bellerivestr.
Neuer Botanischer Garten
Zollikerstr.
93
Seestr.
Belvoir Park
Seefeldquai
Höschgasse
82
83
84
Wildbachstr.
Hornbachstr.
86
Fröhlichstr.
Münchhaldenstr.
87
Ferry
85
Banhof Tiefenbrunnen
Kappelistr.
Ferry
Lake Zurich
94
Staubstr.
Seestr.
Mythenquai
Ferry
Ferry
95
Albisstr.
96
N
km
1/2
1
mi
1/4
1/2

Zurich

Prosperous, sophisticated, and eminently livable, Zurich is the largest city in Switzerland and one of the most beautiful in Europe. Nestled alongside the **Limmat River** where it flows out of **Lake Zurich**, it is surrounded by forested hills, with magnificent views of the nearby **Swiss Alps**.

The popular image of Zurich as a city of banks run by highly efficient "gnomes" is quite misleading. Though international banking makes the city's wheels turn, Zurich is also rich in cultural resources, with more than 30 museums, an opera house, historic buildings, lovely parks, great food, and an electric night scene.

Zurich's small and compact size is one of its principal attractions: Most of the major sites are found in the area that includes both sides of the Limmat River from the **Hauptbahnhof** (**HBF**; Main Train Station), to Lake Zurich, a distance of little more than a kilometer (.6 miles). Only 370,000 people live within the city limits. From the **Hauptbahnhof**, visitors emerge onto **Bahnhofplatz**, which looks down **Bahnhofstrasse**, a famous shopping street and the heart of Zurich's financial center. To the left, between Bahnhofstrasse and the river is the upscale neighborhood of **Altstadt** (Old Zurich), and across the Limmat is the **Niederdorf**, the colorful neighborhood of tiny streets, historic buildings, shops, bars, and restaurants where all of Zurich goes for round-the-clock fun.

While it's true that Zurich is an expensive city, it is also very intertwined with nature, so a great many of its finest pleasures are free—such as walking along the quais, swimming in the lake, or hiking in the woods. And in a country known for its clocks and watches, no one pays attention to the time when relaxing over coffee or a drink in the city's numerous—and relatively inexpensive—cafes and bars.

To call from the US, dial 011(international access code), 41 (country code), 1 (city code), and the local number. When calling from inside Switzerland, dial 01 and the local number.

Getting to Zurich

Airports
Served by 110 different airlines, **Kloten Airport** (8127111) is Switzerland's largest and one of Europe's most convenient. It's located about 12 kilometers (7.5 miles) from Zurich. Trains from the airport to Zurich's main train station **(Hauptbahnhof)** run daily, at 15-minute intervals, from 6AM until midnight. Rental cars are available from **Avis** (1550403), **Budget** (8133131), **Europcar/Inter Rent** (1554040), and **Hertz** (1551234). The journey into the city takes about 10 minutes by train or 20 minutes by car.

Bus Station (Long-Distance)
The long-distance bus terminal is just north of the **Hauptbahnhof** at the corner of **Sihlquai** and **Limmatstrasse** (exit the **HBF** on the **Platform 18-19** side, turn left, then right after crossing the **River Sihl** onto Sihlquai; the station will be on your left). For schedules and information, contact Eurobus (4441212).

Train Station (Long-Distance)
Zurich's main train station, **Hauptbahnhof**, is located at the intersection of **Bahnhofplatz** and **Bahnhofquai**.

The general information number for **Swiss National Railways (SBB)** is 1573333.

Getting around Zurich

Bicycles Switzerland is a cyclist-friendly country. Bikes can be rented at every train station, taken aboard the trains for a small fee, and returned at any station.

Driving A car is more of a hindrance than a help in Zurich, where parking and speeding tickets are readily handed out. Street parking is metered and restricted to two hours or less. A brochure on parking in the city is available from the tourist information office, **Verkehrsverein Zürich** (Hauptbahnhof, 2114000; fax 2120141).

Public Transportation Trains, trams, buses, and even boats and cable cars are all connected in one system, allowing riders to switch from one to another with relative ease. Tickets are purchased from a machine (which gives change) before boarding, and prices are based on the number of zones of travel. Multilingual brochures—available at train stations and tourist offices—help visitors through the process. The **VPZ** public transportation system runs daily from 5:30AM until midnight; for general information, call 2111110.

Taxis Zurich taxis are among the most expensive in the world. But, if you've got the bucks, cabs can be hailed all over the city; a light on top indicates availability. For pick up, call **Taxi Central** (2724444; toll free: 1555551).

Zurich

Tours An hour-long city tour on the "Old Timer" tram is offered on Wednesday, Friday, and Saturday from May through October. Information and tickets are available at the **Hauptbahnhof**. Another fun way to get an overview of the city is aboard the Limmatschiff (Limmat boat). The boat runs daily; board at Bahnhofquai (4821033).

Walking Zurich is a walker's city, with plenty of cobblestone streets, green parks, and riverside promenades to explore. It's relatively compact: Most of the main attractions for visitors are located within a two-mile radius of the **Hauptbahnhof**.

FYI

Accommodations True to its reputation, Zurich is very expensive, and accommodations on the cheaper end of the scale are somewhat limited. It's best to make hotel or youth hostel reservations in advance. If you do arrive without confirmed reservations, head for the **Hauptbahnhof**'s tourist office: **Verkehrsverein Zürich** (2114000; fax 2120141); open daily.

Business Hours Banks are open from 8:30AM until 4:30PM, Monday through Friday. In general, stores are open Monday through Friday from 9AM to 6:30PM, and until 9PM on Thursday nights. Stores close at 4PM on Saturday and nearly all are closed on Sunday, except some newsstands and bakeries. Some stores close from noon until 2PM for a lunch break. Shops at the airport, the **Stadelhofen** station (Stadelhoferst, at Gottfried Kellerstr, 2516644), and the **Hauptbahnhof** are open until 8PM on Sunday. The closing day for museums varies; almost all museums close from noon until 2PM.

Climate Zurich's average temperature ranges from around 60 degrees during the summer, to around 30 degrees during the winter. It can rain any time of year, and even in summer nights can be cool, especially at higher altitudes, so pack a sweater and a waterproof jacket.

Consulates and Embassies

UK ....Dufourstr 56, between Bellerivestrasse ....and Seefeldstrasse, 2611520

The nearest American and Canadian embassies are in Bern.

Drinking Beer, wine, and hard liquor are available in most restaurants, bars, and grocery stores. In theory you need to be 18 to enter a bar, but in practice no one pays any attention to your age when you go to buy drinks.

Emergencies For an ambulance, dial 144; for police, 117; for fire, 118. To find an English-speaking physician, call 2616100, or the **University Hospital**, 2551111.

Language Swiss Germans don't speak German; they speak *Schwyzerdütsch*, a dialect that exists in nearly as many versions as there are valleys in this mountainous land. But a great many people, especially the young, speak English, many surprisingly well. As elsewhere, any effort you make to learn a few phrases will be appreciated by the locals.

Laundry MM Speed Wash (Müllerstr 55, at Kanonengasse, 2429914), a coin-operated laundry, is open Monday through Saturday.

Money The official currency is the Swiss franc (Sfr). Money can be exchanged daily at every train station in the country, or at any bank during general business hours. Hotels and tourist shops accept foreign currency, but the convenience comes at a price—their exchange rates are higher. Some establishments don't accept credit cards, so ask first if you plan to use one.

Personal Safety Watch out for pickpockets, particularly around the main tourist hangouts. If you need to go through your wallet, don't do it in public. Though the violent-crime rate is low, it's best to avoid empty cars on trams or trains late at night.

Postal Services Many post offices have telefax machines, called Publifax, and phone booths where you can place international calls and pay when you're done. The central post office, **Sihlpost** (Kasernenstrasse 95, between Lagerstrasse and Post Brücke; 2962111), adjacent to the **Hauptbahnhof,** is open Monday through Saturday.

Publications The two main Zurich dailies are the *Neue Zürcher Zeitung (NZZ)* and the *Tages Anzeiger*, both in German. On Friday, the *Tages Anzeiger* has a very useful English and German insert, "Züri Tips," on everything going on in Zurich. English and other-language publications are widely available at newsstands throughout the city. For timely local information, the weekly *Zurich News* is quite useful.

Public Holidays New Year's Day and the day after, Good Friday, Easter Sunday and Monday, Ascension Day (12 May), Independence Day (1 August), and Christmas Day and the day after.

Public Rest Rooms Many public rest rooms have been closed because of ongoing problems with drug addicts, but all restaurants have clean facilities. Some of them are quite high tech: If you can't find a flush lever, look for a button to step on or just leave the stall and the toilet will flush automatically. Also, many basins turn on the water only after you put your hands under the spigot. There are showers and hair dryers at the public rest rooms in the **Hauptbahnhof;** they're open daily from 6AM until midnight.

Restaurants A good strategy for the penny-pinching visitor to Zurich is to eat at street stands and in department stores. It's good food, and the price is right. The **Hauptbahnhof** even has a coin-operated automat. In restaurants, the traditional lunchtime is from noon until 2PM, with dinner from 7 until 9PM. It is not generally necessary to make reservations at budget-priced restaurants. A service charge is included in the bill.

Shopping Langstrasse, a funky—by Swiss standards—working-class area, offers cheaper shopping than does Bahnhofstrasse; there are lots of good shops along **Limmatquai;** and **Seefeldstrasse** is great for inexpensive "pre-worn" designer wear.

Zurich

As for department stores, **EPA** and **ABM** offer the best value for the money. The **Migros** chain is tops all around for food and clothes. For alcohol or tobacco, try the **Denner** markets. **Migros, Coop,** and **Interdiscount** are the best places to buy film. Don't throw old batteries in the trash. Every store in Switzerland that sells them is required to have a box to collect them for recycling.

Smoking Smokers are widely tolerated. However, there is no smoking aboard trams, buses, or new suburban trains (main line trains have clearly marked smoking and nonsmoking compartments), and some restaurants have non-smoking areas.

Street Plan Zurich spreads out on either side of the Limmat River until it reaches the shores of the large Lake Zurich. On the west side of the river is the **Altstat,** the Old City, whose main thoroughfare is Bahnhofstrasse. The east bank is home to the popular Niederdorf neighborhood.

Taxes All prices you see listed—whether in hotels, restaurants, or shops—already include the appropriate taxes.

Telephones Orange call boxes for information or emergencies are located throughout the city. Push the black lever down for a moment, release it, and then wait for a voice from the loudspeaker before depositing money. The *stadt* (city) phone book lists information in English and common phrases in five languages. Avoid high phone surcharges by making all long-distance calls from outside your hotel room; make international calls from the post office or from the special phone center in the **Hauptbahnhof.** A private company called **Anglo-Phone** (1575014) operates 24 hours a day and gives travel and general information about Switzerland in English. There is a surcharge for the service.

Tipping A 15-percent service charge is automatically added to all hotel, restaurant, and taxi charges in Switzerland. If your service was particularly good, however, you can offer an additional small tip.

Visas Citizens of Canada, Great Britain, and the US need only a valid passport to enter Switzerland for a three-month visit for tourist or business purposes.

Visitors' Information The Zurich tourist information office, **Verkehrsverein Zürich,** is located on the Bahnhofplatz side of the **Hauptbahnhof.** The office (2114000; fax 2120141) is open daily from 8:30AM until 8:30PM April through October, and until 6:30PM November through March. In addition to hotel and tour reservations, they have brochures galore for Zurich and the rest of the country. An automatic hotel reservation board is also located on the ground floor of the **Hauptbahnhof,** between main line train **Platforms 9** and **10.**

1 Hauptbahnhof (Main Train Station) In operation since 1871 and now a historical monument, Zurich's main train station was a significant architectural and engineering achievement when it was built. Located in the heart of the city, it has main line trains to all of Switzerland and Europe, suburban Zurich, and the **Kloten Airport,** plus offers a wide variety of services and shops. On the ground level, under a huge Japanese clock, is the **Treffpunkt** (meeting place), where marked signs show arrows converging on a point. Adjacent is **Les Arcades** cafe, a more comfortable place to meet friends. Nearby is the automatic hotel reservation board, train and airline ticket counters, luggage storage, and a post office. A few steps away is the tourist office, where you can get information, pick up maps and brochures, or arrange guided tours. The telephone center, luggage lockers, and good, clean bathrooms and showers are located on the first basement level. The next level down is **Shopville,** which has a wide variety of shops and restaurants. Highlights include **Pannini** for sandwiches, **Marinello** for wine and picnic supplies, **Reform** for health-food products, and **Silberkugel,** a good fast-food place with salads and burgers. On the lowest level are the **S-Bahn** (Zurich's regional trains) platforms. ♦ Bahnhofpl 15 (at Bahnhofquai). 1573333

2 Landesmuseum (Swiss National Museum) Architect **Gustav Gull** designed this delightful Neo-Gothic building, which opened in 1898. It houses a fabulous collection of historical material on Switzerland from the stone age to the present, including works of art, china, and military memorabilia. ♦ Free. Tu-Su. Museumstr 2 (between Sihlquai and the Limmat River). 2186511

3 Limmatschiff A small relative of the Parisian *bateau mouche,* the Limmat boat is a fun way to get a panoramic view of the city. Take it to **Bürkliplatz** (see below). Zurich public transport tickets are valid. ♦ Left bank of the Limmat on Bahnhofquai, adjacent to the Landesmuseum and just downstream of Walchebrücke. 4821033

195

Map of Old Zurich

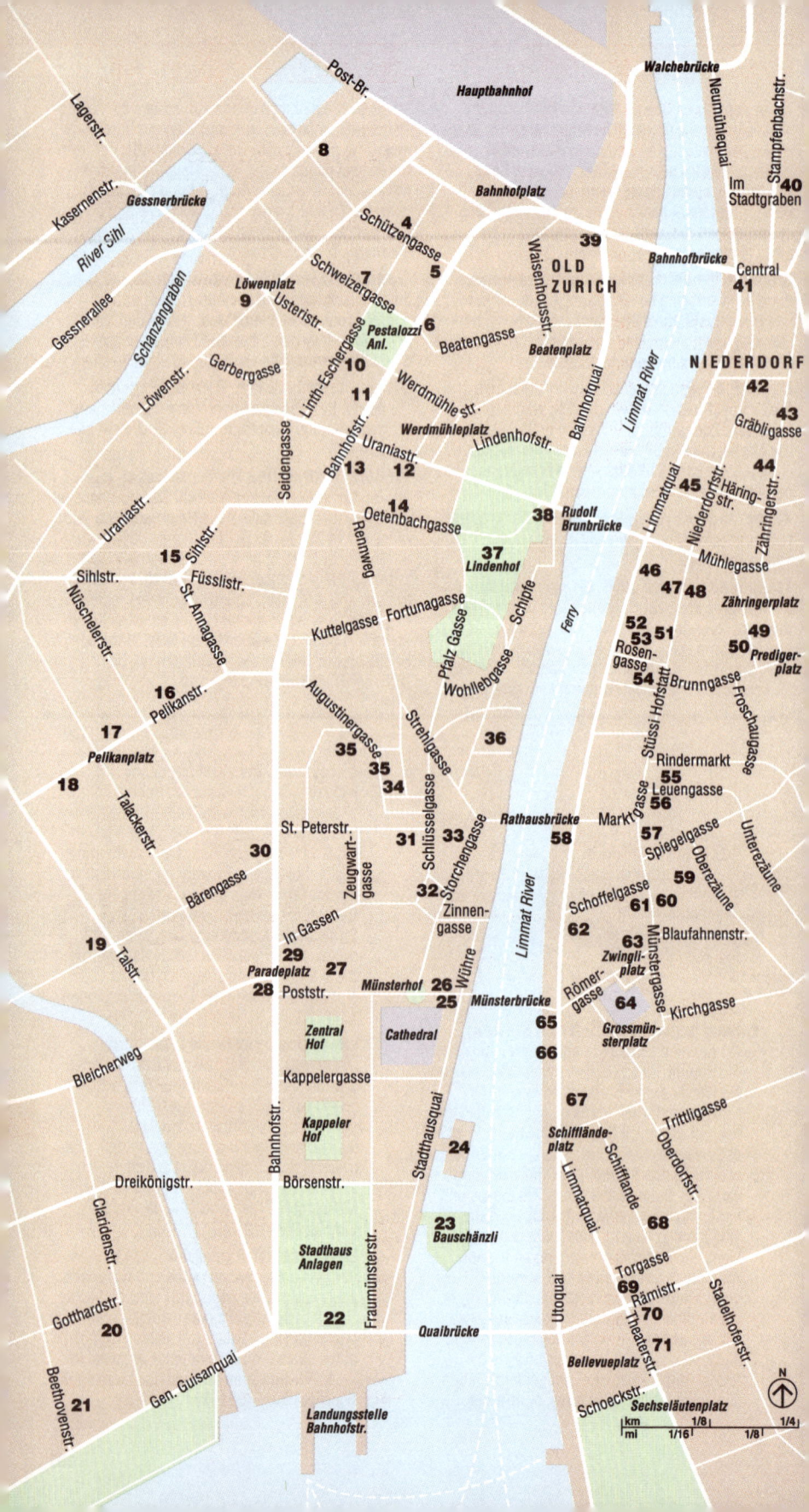

Streets and Places:

- Lagerstr.
- Kasernenstr.
- Post-Br.
- Hauptbahnhof
- Walchebrücke
- Neumühlequai
- Stampfenbachstr.
- Gessnerbrücke
- River Sihl
- Gessnerallee
- Schanzengraben
- Schützengasse
- Bahnhofplatz
- Waisenhousstr.
- Bahnhofbrücke
- Im Stadtgraben
- Löwenplatz
- Schweizergasse
- OLD ZURICH
- Central
- Löwenstr.
- Usteristr.
- Pestalozzi Anl.
- Beatengasse
- Beatenplatz
- NIEDERDORF
- Gerbergasse
- Linth-Eschergasse
- Werdmühle str.
- Bahnhofquai
- Gräbligasse
- Seidengasse
- Bahnhofstr.
- Uraniastr.
- Werdmühleplatz
- Lindenhofstr.
- Limmat River
- Limmatquai
- Niederdorfstr.
- Häringstr.
- Zähringerstr.
- Uraniastr.
- Oetenbachgasse
- Rudolf Brunbrücke
- Mühlegasse
- Sihlstr.
- Rennweg
- Lindenhof
- Zähringerplatz
- Sihlstr.
- Füsslistr.
- Kuttelgasse
- Fortunagasse
- Pfalz Gasse
- Schipfe
- Rosengasse
- Predigerplatz
- Nüschelerstr.
- St. Annagasse
- Wohllebgasse
- Ferry
- Brunngasse
- Froschaugasse
- Pelikanstr.
- Augustinergasse
- Strehlgasse
- Stüssi Hofstatt
- Rindermarkt
- Pelikanplatz
- Leuengasse
- Marktgasse
- Untere Zäune
- Taleckerstr.
- St. Peterstr.
- Schlüsselgasse
- Rathausbrücke
- Spiegelgasse
- Oberezäune
- Bärengasse
- Zeugwartgasse
- Storchengasse
- Schoffelgasse
- Talstr.
- In Gassen
- Zinnengasse
- Blaufahnenstr.
- Paradeplatz
- Münsterhof
- Wühre
- Römergasse
- Zwingliplatz
- Münstergasse
- Poststr.
- Münsterbrücke
- Grossmünsterplatz
- Kirchgasse
- Zentral Hof
- Cathedral
- Kappelergasse
- Schifflände-platz
- Trittligasse
- Stadthausquai
- Schifflände
- Oberdorfstr.
- Bahnhofstr.
- Kappeler Hof
- Limmatquai
- Dreikönigstr.
- Börsenstr.
- Bleicherweg
- Stadthaus Anlagen
- Bauschänzli
- Utoquai
- Torgasse
- Rämistr.
- Fraumünsterstr.
- Quaibrücke
- Theaterstr.
- Stadelhoferstr.
- Claridenstr.
- Gotthardstr.
- Gen. Guisanquai
- Landungsstelle Bahnhofstr.
- Bellevueplatz
- Beethovenstr.
- Schoeckstr.
- Sechseläutenplatz

N

km 1/8 1/4
mi 1/16 1/8

Zurich

4 Walliser Kanne ★★★$$ Excellent fondue—prepared according to recipes from the high valleys of western Switzerland—is served in this restaurant with rustic decor. The bottled wines are expensive, but you can have a taste by ordering them by the deciliter (1/10 liter, the size of a small glass). ♦ Swiss ♦ M-Sa lunch and dinner. Linth-Eschergasse 21 (at Schützengasse). 2113133; fax 2123586

5 Le Café St. Gotthard ★★★$$ An elegant Swiss landmark, this is a fine spot to meet a friend for a drink or indulge in a moderate splurge for lunch. The terrace makes a great perch for people watching in the summer. ♦ Continental ♦ Daily lunch and dinner. Bahnhofstr 87 (between Schweizergasse and Schützengasse). 2115500

6 Dolmetsch Cutlery Swiss Army knives and every other imaginable sort of fine cutlery is sold in this shop. The prices are no higher than elsewhere and the quality is top-notch. ♦ M-W, F-Sa; Th until 9PM. Bahnhofstr 92 (between Beatengasse and Schützengasse). 2112060. Also at: Hauptbahnhof, 2116132; Kloten Airport, 8162919

7 Bistretto ★$ Pizza and pasta are on order in this tastefully decorated fast-food franchise that's popular with students. All the furniture comes from Swiss churches around the country. No alcohol is served. ♦ Italian ♦ Daily lunch and dinner. Schweizergasse 6 (at Linth-Eschergasse). 2111630

8 Gessnerallee ★★★$$ Once strewn with hay, these old military stables were turned into a restaurant in 1989. The reasonable prices and good traditional food make it well worth a visit. Try the veal with *knöpfli* (egg noodles). Dine on the terrace in the summer. ♦ Swiss/International ♦ Daily lunch and dinner. Schützengasse 32 (at Gessnerallee). 2212833

9 Migros City Excellent quality and good prices are the hallmark of Switzerland's largest chain store, whose stock includes everything from groceries to television sets. The restaurant serves simple, well-prepared food for lunch and dinner. ♦ M-Sa. Löwenstr 33-35 (near Löwenpl). 2115981

10 McDonald's ★$ Feeling homesick? Standard McD fare is served here at twice the price you would pay in the US. Another difference from the American franchises: Beer is sold. The place is a hangout for the younger crowd on Friday and Saturday nights. ♦ Fast food ♦ Daily breakfast, lunch, and dinner. Behind Bahnhofstr 79 (corner of Linth-Eschergasse and Usteristr). 2210919

11 Vilan After perusing the upscale merchandise in this tony department store, grab a quick lunch or dinner in the restaurant, which serves decent fare at reasonable prices. ♦ M-Sa. Bahnhofstr 75 (between Uraniastr and Usteristr). 2295111

12 Jules Verne Bar/Observatory Spectacular panoramic views of Zurich, including the Alps when weather permits, are the main attraction at this expensive bar, reached via the elevator through **Brasserie Lipp** (excellent French food) on Uraniastrasse 9. You can stargaze through a telescope in the **Observatory.** ♦ Admission to observatory. M-Sa 9-11PM (no entry after 10PM) May-Aug; M-Sa 8-10PM (no entry after 9PM) Sept-Apr. Open only during clear weather. Uraniastr 9 (between Lindenhofstr and Bahnhofstr). 2111155; fax 2121726

13 Stäheli Bookshop Pick up a paperback for the next leg of your trip at this nifty little English-language bookshop. Prices are high by American standards, but it's still a nice place to browse. ♦ M-W, F-Sa; Th until 9PM. Bahnhofstr 70 (between Oetenbachgasse and Uraniastr). 2013302; fax 2025552

14 Lion's Pub ★★$ English-speaking expatriates frequent this British-style pub that serves good sandwiches and 30 types of beer from all over the world. ♦ British ♦ Daily lunch. Oetengbachgasse 24 (between Lindenhofstr and Rennweg). 2111155

As Switzerland is the home of permanent armed neutrality, it's only logical that one of Zurich's major events is the annual Knabenschiessen (the second weekend in September), a shooting contest traditionally for males but now open to females as well. The event also serves as the rationale for a three-day fair encompassing all of Zurich.

Restaurants/Clubs: Red   **Hotels:** Blue
Shops/ ♀ Outdoors: Green   **Sights/Culture:** Black

197

Zurich

15 Hiltl Restaurant ★★★$ Owned by the same family since 1898, this not-to-be-missed vegetarian restaurant offers a tasty selection of vegetarian plates at inexpensive prices. The modern Italian decor is beautiful. Wine is also served. ♦ Vegetarian ♦ Daily breakfast, lunch, and dinner. Sihlstr 28 (between St. Annagasse and Füsslistr). 2213870

16 James Joyce Pub ★$$ Brought over in pieces from Ireland and reassembled in Zurich, this authentic Irish pub is a nice place for a beer while recovering from window shopping. ♦ Swiss ♦ M-Sa lunch and snacks. Pelikanstr 8 (between St. Annagasse and Nüschelerstr). 2211828

17 Kaufleuten One of the most popular spots in Zurich, this combination bar, restaurant, concert hall, and disco is offbeat in both decor and ambience. "The artist formerly known as Prince" played an after-hours concert here during his most recent European tour. ♦ M-Th, Su 9AM-2AM; F-Sa 9AM-4AM. Pelikanstr 18 (near Pelikanpl). 2211506

18 Pitta-Inn ★★$ Great take-out meat or vegetarian pitas are prepared using fresh, kosher ingredients. There are a few tables, too. ♦ Middle Eastern ♦ M-F lunch. Pelikanstr 37 (between Pelikanpl and Talstr). 2123340

19 Wohnmuseum Bärengasses (Museum of Habitation) Visit these 16th- and 17th-century houses for a peek at how Zurich's upper crust lived centuries ago, with period furniture, ceramic-tile ovens, a music room with old instruments, and a small puppet museum in the basement. ♦ Admission. M afternoons; Tu-Su. Bärengasse 20-22 (at Talstr). 2111716

20 Tonhalle Johannes Brahms conducted his own works at the inaugural concert here in 1895. World-renowned for its acoustics, the hall features regular concerts by international virtuosos. Last-minute tickets are frequently available at very reasonable prices. Inquire at the box office for schedules and prices. ♦ Box office: daily. Claridenstr 7 (between General Guisanquai and Gotthardstr). 2063434; fax 2063436

21 Le Bal One of Zurich's up-and-coming discos, this club features live blues and rock. ♦ Cover. W-Th, Su 10PM-2AM; F-Sa 10PM-4AM. Beethovenstr 8 (between General Guisanquai and Gotthardstr). 2063640

22 Bürkliplatz Zurich's main "port" is the launching point for boats to Wollishofen and Zurichhorn or tours of Lake Zurich. The port is the locale for fruit and vegetable markets on Tuesday and Friday mornings and a flea market on Saturday from March until October. ♦ Quaibrücke and Stadthausquai

23 Bauschänzli ★★$$ This open-air restaurant is situated on an island where the Limmat flows out of Lake Zurich. It's a great place to have a glass of wine and a plate of schnitzel, feed the swans, and watch the world float by on a summer day. ♦ Swiss ♦ Daily lunch and dinner Apr-Oct. Stadthausquai 13 (off of Bürklipl). 2124919

24 Stadthausquai Frauenbad Elegant, old-fashioned, relaxing, and immaculate, this summer bathhouse is the only one in Zurich that's exclusively for women. ♦ Admission. Daily until 8PM mid-May to mid-Sept. Opposite Stadthausquai 13 (between Börsenstr and Kappelergasse). 2119592

25 Fraumünster Founded in 853 by Charlemagne's grandson, King Ludwig, this cathedral was once the **Convent of Saints Felix and Regula** for noblewomen. Construction of the current building began around 1170. The stained-glass windows Marc Chagall added in 1970 are an absolute must-see. ♦ Stadthausquai and Münsterhof. 2114100

26 Zunfthaus zur Meisen Originally a guildhall for wine merchants, the building now holds the 18th-century porcelain collection of the **Landesmuseum** (see page 195). The unusual portraits by stuccoist Franz Ludwig Wind are said to be his revenge on guild members for slow payment of his bills. ♦ Free. Tu-Su. Münsterhof 20 (corner of Stadthausquai and Münsterbrücke). 2212807

Chässtube

27 Chässtube ★★$$ Good, unpretentious, old-fashioned food is served here, including fondue and raclette (all you can eat). Make reservations for the first floor or arrive early to get a table. ♦ Swiss ♦ M-Sa lunch and dinner. Waaggasse 4 (between Münsterhof and In Gassen). 2111660

28 Sprüngli Chocolate and coffee addicts head straight to this shop adjacent to the architecturally noteworthy Paradeplatz (a cattle market in the 18th century), which floats above the gold reserves of Swiss banks. Try their famous *luxemburgerli* (macaroons with buttercream), made fresh every day. ♦ M-F from 7:30AM; Sa from 8AM. Bahnhofstrasse 21 (at Paradeplatz). 2211722. Also at: Kloten Airport, 8163657

Zurich

28 Restaurant Mövenpick ★★$$ A Swiss chain of restaurants and hotels featuring good international cuisine and famous for their fantastic ice cream. ♦ Swiss ♦ Daily breakfast, lunch, and dinner. Paradepl 4 (off Bahnhofstr). 2213252

29 Zeughaus Keller ★★$$ Zurich's main armory for 500 years, this huge hall has been a restaurant since 1927. The traditional dishes—especially the *kalbsbratwurst* (veal sausage)—are very good and the atmosphere is lively. ♦ Swiss ♦ Daily lunch and dinner. Bahnhofstr 28a (between Waaggasse and In Gassen). 2112690

30 Museum der Zeitmessung Beyer (Beyer's Museum of Time Measurement) Highlights of this charming little watch museum located above a clock and jewelry store are the rare time-measuring instruments, including wooden cogwheel, sand, water, oil, and sun clocks. ♦ Free. M-F. Bahnhofstr 31 (between Bärengasse and St. Peterstr). 2211080

31 St. Peter's The earliest Protestant parish church in the city dates from the 13th century. The clockface, 8.7 meters (28.5 feet) in diameter and built in 1537, is the largest in Europe. ♦ St. Peter-Hofstatt (at Schlüsselgasse). 2112588

teuscher
teuscher
teuscher
teuscher
teuscher
teuscher
teuscher

32 Teuscher Some of the world's most luscious chocolates are made here. This is a good place to pick up gifts for friends back home. ♦ M-Sa. Storchengasse 9 (between In Gassen and Stegengasse). 2115153

33 Römischer Bad (Roman Baths) Two-thousand-year-old remnants of the days when Zurich was a Roman province called **Turicum** can still be seen in this little easy-to-miss alley. At either end look for a black button that illuminates the display of the ruins, which are mostly underneath the metal-grid walkway. ♦ Thermengasse (between Storchengasse and Schlüsselgasse).

34 Churrasco Steakhouse ★$$ This is one of Zurich's best places for steaks, which are grilled at tableside. ♦ Steak house ♦ Daily lunch and dinner. Glockengasse 9 (at Rennweg). 2211144

35 Augustinergasse Lining this quaint street, which curves gently down toward Bahnhofstrasse, are 17th- and 18th-century houses decorated with lovely bay windows. ♦ Between St. Peter-Hofstatt and Bahnhofstr

36 Pedestrian Gallery The picturesque scenery along this walkway bordering the Limmat River below the Lindenhof is reminiscent of Venice. ♦ Between Rollengasse and Schipfe

37 Lindenhof Great views of the Limmat and the old town can be had from this spacious cobblestoned park at the site of the original Roman customs fort. The giant chess sets are for public use. ♦ Above the intersection of Fortunagasse and Pfalz Gasse

38 Heimatwerk Expensive Swiss crafts by local artists and a terrific selection of minerals are showcased in this shop. Those on a budget can stop in and soak up ideas before visiting the flea markets. ♦ M-W, F-Sa; Th until 8PM. Rudolf Brunbrücke (at Uraniastr). 2115780. Also at: Hauptbahnhof, 2122797; Kloten Airport, 8163488

39 The Pub ★★$$ Au pairs and the young international set favor this British-style establishment with good club sandwiches. Arrive around 5PM or be prepared to wait for a table; it gets crowded here in the evening. ♦ British ♦ Daily lunch and dinner. Bahnhofquai 15 (at Bahnhofbrücke). 2210308; fax 2123488

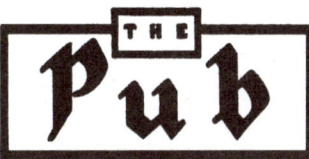

40 Commihalle ★★★$$ Excellent, reasonably priced Italian food is served in this friendly restaurant. The *tavolata* buffet—an all-you-can-eat antipasto, salad, ravioli, and wine affair—will satisfy the hungriest of travelers. ♦ Italian ♦ Daily lunch and dinner. Stampfenbachstr 8 (near Im Stadtgraben). 2624610

41 Polybahn Funicular For just a few cents and in less than three minutes, this little funicular owned by Switzerland's largest bank takes you up to a terrace overlooking the city. The funicular is over 100 years old. ♦ Admission. Daily. Limmatquai (just off Central)

41 Hotel Limmathof $$ Though this hotel's rates straddle the budget category, the prime location and excellent facilities make it worth the stretch. Continental breakfast, served in the hotel's restaurant, is included in the price. ♦ Limmatquai 142 (below Central). 2614220; fax 2620217

The word Zurich comes from Turicum, the name of the settlement the Romans built in 15 BC. Today, the site is a pleasant park known for its chess players and the view of Old Zurich and the Limmat River.

Zurich

42 Rheinfelder Bierhalle ★$ Known for centuries as the "bloody thumb" by locals (no one knows why), this restaurant attracts a diverse crowd of intellectual students and beer guzzlers reminiscing over the last Oktoberfest. The cuisine is cheap and heavy blue-collar European food. ♦ Swiss ♦ Daily lunch and dinner. Niederdorfstr 76 (between Gräbligasse and Central). 2515464

43 Martahaus $ It may look like a concrete bunker, but this very clean hotel, popular with students, is the cheapest option in the central area of the city. Those really strapped for cash can opt for one of the 87 beds here. Accommodations are dormitory-style, with cubicles separated by curtains. Bathrooms are shared; facilities include a communal TV lounge and a 24-hour front desk.
♦ Zähringerstr 36 (between Gräbligasse and Central). 2514550; fax 2514540

BASILEA

44 Hotel Basilea $$ The 1970s decor may be outdated, but the 64 guest rooms have TVs and private baths. In addition, there's a restaurant, bar, and discotheque. Added bonus: Breakfast is included in the price.
♦ Zähringerstr 25 (between Häringstr and Gräbligasse). 2614250; fax 2517411

45 Gitano ★★★$$ Very good Mexican food is served in this popular restaurant with a friendly staff. Start with a flavor-of-the-day margarita and a platter of nachos; proceed to enchiladas, tacos, and burritos. ♦ Mexican ♦ M-F lunch and dinner; Sa dinner. Schmidgasse 3 (between Niederdorfstr and Limmatquai). 2622462

45 Babalu Pink stucco walls, soft lighting, gaudy chandeliers, and good drinks attract a young crowd to this small bar with a Spanish flavor. ♦ M-F 4PM-midnight; Sa 2PM-midnight; Su 5PM-midnight. Schmidgasse 6 (between Niederdorfstr and Limmatquai). 2519732

46 Hotel Krone $$
This small, nicely decorated hotel has a special electronic key system that allows you to come and go as you please. The 40 guest rooms are clean and come with minibars and sinks. Shared bathrooms are located on each floor. Breakfast is included, and the hotel's restaurant serves lunch and dinner.
♦ Limmatquai 88 (between Köngengasse and Badergasse). 2514222; fax 2514763

47 Hotel Schäfli $$ A favorite with backpackers, this old, slightly run-down building is in the heart of the popular Niederdorf district. The 50 guest rooms are simple, with shared bathrooms on each floor. There's no restaurant, but the disco/bar on the ground floor serves cocktails and foreign beers. ♦ Badergasse 6 (between Niederdorfstr and Limmatquai). 2514144; fax 2513476

48 Kon-tiki/Züri Bar These two connected bars are a focal point of the Niederdorf scene, and the prices are surprisingly reasonable. The **Kon-tiki** has imitation bits of Thor Heyerdahl's ship hanging on the walls.
♦ M-Sa noon-midnight; Su 6PM-midnight. Niederdorfstr 24 (between and Hirschenplatz and Preyergasse). 2513577

49 Predigerkirche (Preachers' Church) This church was originally a Dominican monastery established around 1230; its nave was completed in the 13th century and remodeled in 1609. The Neo-Gothic tower, the tallest in Zurich, dates from 1900.
♦ Zähringerpl 6 (between Predigerpl and Mühlegasse). 2611219

50 Kollektiv Cafe Zähringer ★★$$ Founded by young left-wing "Zürchers," this cooperative serves inventive food from organic farms. Try the raclette. ♦ Cafe ♦ Daily breakfast, lunch, and dinner. Zähringerpl 11 (at Spitalgasse). 2520500

51 Malatesta This small bar has prime tables for people watching on the **Hirschenplatz** in the summer. ♦ Daily 11AM-11:30PM. Niederdorfstr 15 (between Grauegasse and Hirschengasse). 2513205

52 Limmatbar Live DJs, loud music, and good drinks, including nonalcoholic ones, help make this one of the hottest spots in Zurich.
♦ M-Th, Su 7PM-2AM; F-Sa 7PM-4AM. Limmatquai 82 (between Rosengasse and Grauegasse). 2616530

53 Hotel Splendid $$ Reasonably priced by Zurich standards, this 43-bed hotel has communal bathrooms on each floor. There's no restaurant, but the intimate piano bar is a relaxing place to have a drink. ♦ Rosengasse 5 (between Niederdorfpl and Limmatquai). 2525850; fax 2612559

54 Spaghetti Factory ★★★$$ Italian food is served in a beautiful dining room with a carved wood ceiling and stained-glass windows. One dish, called "American Disaster," features spaghetti topped with fried

---

Restaurants/Clubs: Red **Hotels:** Blue
Shops/ ♦ Outdoors: Green **Sights/Culture:** Black

Zurich

eggs and bacon. But don't be put off—the pastas are very good and so are the prices. ♦ Italian ♦ Daily lunch and dinner. Niederdorfstr 5 (at Weingasse). 2519400

55 Oliver Twist Pub Popular with English-speaking students and expatriates, this friendly, smoky pub has a lively atmosphere and lots of good beer. Snacks are served to help soak it all up. ♦ M-F 11:30AM-midnight; Sa 3PM-midnight; Su 4PM-midnight. Rindermarkt 6 (between Neumarkt and Stüssi Hofstatt). 2524710

56 Pigalle Bar A highlight of this nightspot is a circular bar and the mosaic wall behind it. Created by a group of artists who were regulars here, the mosaic is an architectural landmark protected by the city. Appropriately, this bar draws an artistic crowd. ♦ M-Sa 6PM-2AM. Marktgasse 14 (between Spiegelgasse and Leuengasse). 2521530

57 Casa Bar Zurich's only remaining spot for jazz is small and very crowded during performances. Drinks are expensive, so you'll have to sip slowly to get through an entire evening with your budget intact. ♦ Daily 5PM-2AM. Münstergasse 30 (between Krebsgasse and Ankengasse). 2612002

58 Rathaus Zurich's town hall is located in this lovely Baroque building constructed in 1694 and rich in architectural detail. The banquet hall in the splendid original interior is a must-see. Across the street is the **Zunfthaus zur Saffran**, one of Zurich's famed guild houses, built for the guild of spice merchants in 1723. Neither building is open to the public. ♦ Limmatquai 55 (at Rathausbrücke)

59 Café Schober ★★$ This fine, old-fashioned European cafe would fit as perfectly in Vienna as it does in Zurich. The hot chocolate can't help but be excellent: **Teuscher** (see above) supplies the chocolate, and the milk comes from the owner's own cows. ♦ Cafe ♦ M-Sa breakfast, lunch, and snacks. Napfgasse 4 (between Oberezäune and Münstergasse). 2518060

60 Schlauch Upstairs from a restaurant named **Pfeffermühle** is Zurich's legendary hangout for billiards. Have a beer and shoot a few games in this old-style pool hall. ♦ W-Su 10AM-midnight. Münstergasse 20 (between Zwinglipl and Schoffelgasse). 2512304

61 Spanische Weinhalle ★★★$$ Spanish tapas and seafood are served in this ground-floor wine shop, which has a slightly run-down 1920s decor and waiters that can be rude. The place attracts a diverse crowd, including lots of students. Upstairs is the

Bodega, a fancy Spanish restaurant. Don't get them confused or your wallet may never recover. ♦ Spanish ♦ Daily lunch and dinner. Münstergasse 15 (between Zwinglipl and Schoffelgasse). 2512310

62 Haus Zum Rüden ★★$$$ The setting of this restaurant is its primary attraction. The historic building began life as the municipal mint and was used to receive visiting dignitaries from 1348; the Gothic interior is still intact, with interesting late-Gothic windows. If you dine here, have one of the delicious seafood dishes. ♦ Continental ♦ M-F lunch and dinner. Limmatquai 42 (between Römergasse and Schoffelgasse). 2619566

63 Mère Catherine and Le Philosophe ★★★$$ Excellent continental dishes are served in this delightful restaurant with a casual and friendly atmosphere. The small plaza is ideal for a summer lunch with friends. Have fresh pasta or a tasty salad. Adjoining the restaurant is **Le Philosophe,** a sophisticated Italian bar. ♦ Continental ♦ Restaurant: daily lunch and dinner. Bar: daily 9AM-midnight. Reservations recommended for restaurant. Nägelihof 3 (down a little dead-end passage off Rüden-Pl, between Römergasse and Schoffelgasse). 2622250

63 Dézaley, the Cave Vaudoise ★★★$$$ Excellent food from the Lake Geneva region, particularly fondue and raclette, is served in this pleasant restaurant. Try a glass of their St. Saphorin wine. ♦ Western Swiss ♦ M-Sa lunch and dinner. Römergasse 7 (between Nägelihof and Münstergasse). 2516129

64 Grossmünster Zurich's great Gothic cathedral is the city's principal landmark. Founded by Charlemagne on the site where Zurich's patron saints, Felix and Regula, were buried, the oldest parts of the present structure date to the 11th century. The stained-glass windows are by Giacometti and the bronze doors by Munch. ♦ Zwinglipl and Grossmünsterpl. 2615311

65 Helmhaus The original wooden structure on this site was first a court of law and then a cloth market. Today's building, an interesting example of late Baroque Classicism designed by **Bluntschi the Elder,** dates from 1794. ♦ Limmatquai 31 (at Münsterbrücke)

66 Wasserkirche (Water Church) The late-Gothic (1479-84) church was erected by Zurich's master builder of the time, **Felder the Elder,** on the spot where, legend has it, Zurich's patron saints Felix and Regula and their servant Exuperantis were beheaded in AD 300 because of their Christian faith. The three are not buried here, but at the **Grossmünster** (see above). ♦ Limmatquai and Helmhaus

67 Café Select The principal claim to fame of this cafe, popular with students and artsy types, is that Lenin hung out here and planned

Zurich

You Better Shop Around

Of all the ways to experience a foreign country, shopping ranks right up there with restaurant hopping, museum traipsing, and architectural touring. Shopping puts you in touch with neighborhoods, shopkeepers, and regional specialties. You'll notice that items that are highly prized the world over—like Italian leather goods, Scottish wool, and Belgian lace—can be treated with nonchalance on their home turf. Go to open-air markets for a sneak preview of what the locals will be cooking for dinner, and duck into record shops to hear a different beat (don't be surprised if tastes favor American and English imports). Shopping is just one more window into a country's soul, and one that's definitely worth opening.

But face it, shopping is also loads of fun, and you'll probably want to bring home souvenirs. Avoid the temptation to load up on Eiffel Tower paperweights and other knickknacks (they have a way of losing their charm by the time you get home). And don't waste money on entertainment industry "collectibles;" you'll find mostly the same items in Times Square. Instead, pop for a specialty handicraft, such as a piece of Murano glass from Venice.

Though there are still bargains, the days when US-dollar exchange rates were at their headiest and Americans brought empty suitcases abroad for the big haul home have sadly ended. If you're tempted to buy that buttery-soft leather jacket in Florence, do so because it's the jacket of your dreams, not because it seems like a great deal—it may not be. Such top-quality goods, which you'd expect to be cheaper in their country of origin, are often in line with US prices.

Shoppers abroad also will confront the Value Added Tax (VAT), which is tacked on to the price of most goods and services. Although everyone must pay the tax, if the purchase is made at a shop participating in the national rebate program (not every store takes part), visitors often are eligible for a refund. Usually the store will give you a form which you must complete and present, along with the receipt, to customs officials at an international airport. The rebate may arrive in the form of a check mailed to your home or, if the purchase was made with a credit card, as a credit to your account. If the store participates in the international Europe Tax-Free Shopping (ETFS) program, you should be able to get a cash refund at the airport. For customs and rebate information, contact each country's embassy, consulates, tourist offices, Europe Tax-Free Shopping offices, or customs agency.

You must declare to the US customs official at the point of entry everything you have acquired in Europe. The standard duty-free allowance for US citizens is $400. If your trip was shorter than 48 continuous hours, or if you were outside the US within 30 days of your current trip, the duty-free allowance is reduced to $25. Families traveling together may make a joint customs declaration. A duty of 10 percent is charged on the next $1,000, and additional items are taxed at a variety of rates. Some articles are duty-free only up to certain limits. If buying liquor, check your state's liquor and other importing laws; state restrictions prevail over federal allowances.

Everything you bring in must be for personal—not commercial—use, which means that returning from Switzerland with 30 Swatch watches may raise a few eyebrows. And US regulations prohibit the import of some goods sold abroad, such as fresh fruits and vegetables, and most meat and dairy products. Also prohibited are articles made from plants or animals on the endangered species list.

You might consider shipping purchases home, especially if you've caught shopping fever, or the items are fragile or bulky. For an extra charge, some shops will take care of packaging, insuring, and shipping. (It's always best to pay with a credit card so that you have recourse in case the Spode china arrives damaged or not at all.) Sending purchases by parcel post may be cheaper than having the store do it for you. You can ship up to $200 per day in gifts (excluding alcohol, perfume, and tobacco) to the US duty-free.

Contrary to popular belief, duty-free shops don't necessarily offer the cheapest prices—shop for regional souvenirs before you head for the airport. You *can* get a good deal on some items, but know what they cost elsewhere. And although these goods are free of the duty that European customs normally would assess, they will be subject to US import duty upon your return to the US.

For further information, consult the following publications, available from the **US Customs Service** (PO Box 7407, Washington, DC 20044): *Currency Reporting; International Mail Imports; Know Before You Go; Pets, Wildlife, US Customs;* and *Pocket Hints.* Another book, *Travelers' Tips on Bringing Food, Plant, and Animal Products into the United States,* is available from the **United States Department of Agriculture, Animal and Plant Health Inspection Service** (USDA-APHIS; 6505 Belcrest Rd, Room 613-FB, Hyattsville, MD 20782; 301/436.7799; fax 301/436.5211). For tape-recorded information on customs-related topics, call 202/927.2095 from any touch-tone phone.

the Russian Revolution. Join the eclectic crowd on the large terrace. ♦ M-Sa. Limmatquai 16 (at Schiffländepl). 2524372

HOTEL VILLETTE ★★
Pinte Vaudoise
The one with the wellknown Fondues!
Kruggasse 4 beim Bellevue

68 Hotel Villette $$ Tucked away in a quiet corner of the Niederdorf is this fine little hotel with a restaurant. The 25 guest rooms are available with private or shared baths. ♦ Kruggasse 4 (between Oberdorfstr and Schiffländepl). 2512335; fax 2512339

69 Odeon Zurich's most famous cafe/bar—and reputedly Einstein's favorite—opened its doors in 1911 and today attracts a diverse crowd who come for coffee, beer, and conversation. ♦ M-Th 7AM-2AM; F-Sa 7AM-4AM; Su 11AM-2AM. Limmatquai 2 (at Torgasse). 2511650

70 Kronenhalle ★★★★$$ The art on the walls in this first-class restaurant, which includes paintings by Miró, Chagall, and Picasso, was supposedly obtained in exchange for meals given to the then-starving artists. Full meals are expensive, but you can always order a beer at the bar or—between normal meal hours—sit at a table and indulge in the delectable chocolate mousse. If you're feeling flush, come for lunch and enjoy some of the best fondue in Zurich. ♦ Continental ♦ Daily lunch and dinner. Rämistr 4 (at Theaterstr). 2516669

71 Vorderer Sternen ★★$ Don't miss the best bratwurst (grilled sausage) in Zurich at this fast-food spot. Upstairs is a nicer (and more expensive) restaurant, with a few tables

Zurich

on the balcony overlooking Bellevue, that sometimes features reasonably priced specials in the evening. Also on the premises is a clean and simple—if a little noisy—hotel with rooms with shared bathrooms. ♦ Fast food ♦ Daily lunch and dinner. Theaterstr 22 (at Bellevuepl). 2514949

72 Mascotte One of Zurich's first discos, this spot is small, crowded, and popular with young singles. Sundays are for men only. ♦ Cover. M-Th, Su 9PM-2AM; F-Sa 9PM-4AM. Theaterstr 10 (between Gottfried Kellerstr and St. Urbangasse). 2524481

73 Zurich Kunsthaus (Zurich Art Museum) One of the major art institutes in Europe, this museum has a world-class collection of old masters, Swiss paintings, and modern art (most notably Monet, Munch, Picasso, Chagall, and Rodin), plus works by Expressionists and Surrealists (from Dadaism, which began in Zurich) to the present. ♦ Admission. Tu-Th until 9PM; F-Su. Heimpl 1 (between Rämistr and Hirschengraben). 2516755

74 Pension St. Josef $$ This pleasant and unpretentious hotel with 45 nicely furnished rooms is well located and reasonably priced. There are some doubles with private baths, but for the most part, bathrooms are shared. ♦ Hirschengraben 64 (at the intersection of Bahnhofbrücke, Limmatquai, and Hirschenbraben). 2512757; fax 2512808

75 Universität Zurich Einstein received poor grades here, but he later taught at this nononsense university. Students often go down to the Niederdorf below to play. ♦ Rämistr 71 (between Künstlergasse and Schenbergasse). 2571111

76 Stadelhofen Bahnhof (Train Station) This bold concrete structure designed by Spanish architect **Santiago Calatrava** is a key link in Zurich's suburban train system and has an underground shopping mall that's open on Saturday evenings and all day Sunday. Frequent trains to the **Hauptbahnhof** (see above) and other stops on the regional network pass through the station. If you're nearby and have the urge to hop on a train, consider one of the following excursions into the hills: Take *Tram 15* to Römerhof, then ride the **Dolderbahn**, a funicular railway just uphill from the tram stop, to **Bergstation** about five minutes away. Walking paths, as well as an ice-skating rink in winter, await you there. Or take the *S18 Forchbahn* (you'll need to add one zone to your central Zurich ticket) to **Zollikerberg**, a park/forest with walking paths and fine views. ♦ Stadelhoferstr (at Gottfreid Kellerstr). 2516644

In Zurich, as in most of Europe, floor numbers start with the ground floor *(Erdgeschoss)*, then first, second, and so on.

Zurich

77 Opern Haus Zürich (Opera House) Just 21 months after Zurich's first opera house burned in 1890, this Neo-Baroque building opened. The city donated the land, shareholders raised the capital, and the Viennese theater builders **Fellner and Helmer** used the plans they had prepared for a never-built theater in Cracow, Poland. Tickets are occasionally available at the last minute. ♦ Box office: daily. Theaterpl (at Utoquai). 2620909; fax 2515896

78 Gleich ★★$$ Vegetarian cuisine is the specialty of this elegant wood-paneled restaurant. Most of the ingredients are from organic farms, and nearly everything, including the pastries, is homemade. Offerings include crepes with mushroom ragout, carmelized apple or banana pancakes, and daily specials. The restaurant also sells its own brand of coffee, tea, and homemade jam. No alcohol is served. ♦ Vegetarian ♦ M-F lunch and dinner; Sa lunch. Seefeldstr 9 (between Seehofstr and Falkenstr) 2513203

79 Seefeldstrasse Shops selling "pre-worn" designer clothes make this pleasant shopping street worth a stroll. You might find an item with a fancy label at an affordable price to wear on that special evening out. ♦ Between Bahnhof Tiefenbrunnen and Falkenstr

80 Hotel Seefeld $$ The price and location of this 30-room hotel, which is near the lake and public transport, can't be beat. Guest rooms are available with and without baths. There is no restaurant. ♦ Seehofstr 11 (between Seefeldstr and Dufourstr). 2522570

The letters "CH" on the back of Swiss cars stand for *Confoederatio Helvetica* (Helvetia Confederation), the Latin name for Switzerland. In the same vein, the postage stamps say "Helvetia." In a country with four national languages, both practices make a lot of sense.

Restaurants/Clubs: Red
Shops/♦ Outdoors: Green
Hotels: Blue
Sights/Culture: Black

81 Utoquai Badanstalt On the lakeshore, this nice bathhouse has lockers, dressing rooms, and showers. Swim with the swans and lounge on the grass. Tops are optional for bathers. ♦ Admission. Daily mid-May to mid-Sept. Utoquai (at Faberstr). 2516151

82 Museum Bellerive Located in a former private mansion, this museum features frequently changing exhibitions from the largest collection of decorative arts in Switzerland. ♦ Free. Tu-Su; W until 9PM. Höschgasse 3 (by the lake promenade). 3834376; fax 3834468

83 Heidi Weber Haus A beautiful example of "total concept art," this was the last building designed by **Le Corbusier,** complete with furnishings to his specifications; it was constructed in 1966-67. ♦ Admission. W-Su afternoons June-Oct. Höschgasse 8 (by the lake promenade). 3836470

84 Chinese Garden Built by Chinese craftsmen from Kunming, a sister city of Zurich, this oasis features carved pagodas (no nails were used in the construction) and traditional Chinese landscaping. It is one of the most important examples of Chinese landscaping outside of China. ♦ Seefeldquai (between Zurichhorn and Museum Bellerive)

85 Zurichhorn For a respite with nature, walk along the lake in this beautiful park. Boat service from **Bürkliplatz** (see above) is available. In summer, there's an open-air cinema. ♦ Between Bellerivestr and Lake Zurich

86 Tres Kilos ★★★$$ Though the food at this popular Mexican restaurant doesn't really compare to the genuine article, the terrific margaritas make it a non-issue. ♦ Mexican ♦ M-F lunch and dinner; Sa-Su dinner. Reservations recommended. Dufourstr 175 (near Frölichstr). 4220233

87 Sammlung E.G. Bührle (E.G. Bührle Collection) A must for Impressionist art-lovers, this elegant museum housed in an old mansion has one of the finest collections of 19th- and 20th-century works by French and Dutch artists. Some very famous paintings by van Gogh and Matisse are on display here. ♦ Admission. Tu, Th-F afternoons; W until 8PM. Zollikerstr 172 (near Wildbachstr). 4220086; fax 4225696

KUNSTHALLE ZÜRICH

88 Kunsthalle Zürich (Zurich Modern Art Museum) Dedicated entirely to avant-garde art, this museum is located in a renovated factory. Many other galleries are in the area as

Zurich

well. ♦ Admission. Tu-Su afternoons. Hardturmstr 114 (at Förrlibuckstr). 2721515; fax 2721888

89 Langstrasse This is a working-class neighborhood with lots of Italian restaurants, strip joints, shops, and bars—including some good grunge and biker hangouts. Zurich's tragic hard drug scene starts to get serious at Limmatplatz. ♦ Between Helvetiapl and Limmatpl

90 EPA Practical needs for just about everything can be satisfied in this low-priced department store. A restaurant within the store serves cheap, hearty fare for lunch and dinner. ♦ M-Sa. Sihlstr 55 (between Talstr and Schanzengraben Moat). 2213215

91 St. George's Hotel $$ The 58 guest rooms in this friendly hotel are simple and clean, and bathrooms, showers, and telephones are located on each floor. The lobby has been tastefully renovated and has a TV lounge. There is no restaurant, but continental breakfast (included in the rate) is served in the breakfast room. ♦ Weberstr 11 (at Hallwylpl). 2411144

92 Le Petit Prince If you want to splurge a little, this elegant nightclub and bar has great DJs and Swiss Tech light and video shows. The dress code is almost as uppity as the prices, but jeans and a nice jacket are fine. ♦ Cover. M-F, Su 9PM-2AM; Sa 9PM-4AM. Bleicherweg 21 (between Beethovenstr and Stockerstr). 2011739

93 Museum Rietberg Set amid spacious, splendidly manicured gardens, this old Neo-Classical mansion hosts fine exhibitions of Asian, African, and other non-European art. Across the street is the **Villa Schönberg**, a mansion built on the ruins of the refuge where Richard Wagner composed large parts of *Tristan und Isolde* from 1857 to 1858. ♦ Admission. Tu-Su. Villa Wesendonck, Gablerstr 15 (between Grütlistr and Joachim Hefti-Weg). 2024528; fax 2025101

94 Uetliberg A favorite getaway for Zürichers, this mountain is just a 20-minute train ride southwest of the city (take the *S10 SZU Bahn* from the **Hauptbahnhof**). The **Berghaus Uto Kulm**, with wild sculptures and fantastic views of Zurich and the Swiss Alps, is a short trek from the last train stop. Walking trails wind

through the area, including the **Planet Path**, which will take you to Felsenegg in about two hours. After your hike, a cable car from the top will take you back down to **Adliswil**, where you can catch the *S4 SZU Bahn* back to Zurich.

94 Zurich Youth Hostel $ This uninspired concrete-block building is extremely clean, with impeccable facilities, a convenience store, a fax machine, and a foreign currency exchange. There are beds for about 80 people; all baths are shared. The inexpensive restaurant within the hostel serves decent meals at breakfast, lunch, and dinner. *Bus 66* stops in front, and it's a five-minute walk from **Bahnhof Wollishofen** and 10 minutes from the **Wollishofen Ship Station**. ♦ Mutschellenstr 114 (between Besenrainstr and Kürbsensteig). 4823544; fax 4819992.

95 Rote Fabrik An old factory the city gave to the younger generation after the student riots of 1980 has been converted into an alternative culture center. The restaurant is good and cheap, the gallery showcases avant-garde art, and there's a concert hall and a summer terrace. Nadine Gordimer, the 1991 Nobel Prize–winning author, has lectured here, and the American rock band Living Color has performed here. On Sunday afternoon in summer at a nearby lakeside park, "spontaneous" techno-dance parties take place. ♦ Special events: admission. Center: daily. Restaurant: daily breakfast, lunch, and dinner. Seestr 395 (adjacent to Wollishofen Ship Station). 4815950; fax 4829210

96 Camping Platz Seebucht Located on the lake's edge, this large parklike campground with full facilities is the cheapest place to stay in the city. Tents are mandatory, and reservations are highly recommended. From the **Rote Fabrik**, it's a 10-minute walk along the Seestrasse away from Zurich or two stops on *Bus 161* or *165* toward Stadtgrenze. ♦ Open May-Sept. Seestr 559 (near Rote Fabrik). 4821612

Bahnhofstrasse, now one of the world's most elegant and expensive shopping streets, was formerly known as Froschengraben (frog's ditch).

One of Zurich's two major festivals is the Sechselauten (third Monday in April), in which guild members dress up in traditional costumes. The event really gets underway when the Böög, a snowman, is set on fire to symbolize the end of winter.

205

Zurich

Bests

Raisa Seppänen
Waitress, The Pub

Zurich can be quite expensive, but there are ways around this and it's a great city for young people.

The Pub is a good spot for a before-dinner drink. If you're a man, a membership card might be asked for after 6:30PM, so come around 5PM. The crowd is young and international.

The **Commihalle** near Central for spaghetti. Even better is the "Spaghettiplausch" special for three or more people—all you can eat, with six sauces.

My favorite spot in the **Niederdorf** is the **Spanische Wein halle** downstairs at the **Bodega**. Just take a place at one of the long tables and make new friends.

Not far away is the **Oliver Twist Pub.** Look for special events like barbecues in the summer.

Beautiful architecture at the **Odeon,** where everyone is a "native."

Buy your Swiss chocolates in supermarkets. The specialty shops are only for gifts.

Lots of stores on expensive **Bahnhofstrasse** have a "tourist" corner where you can buy any souvenir, from Swiss-style hats to little wooden cows.

Zurich is pretty safe, but the drug scene is a problem, so be alert and keep to the crowded streets at night.

Summer in the city is great. Spend a lot of it with the locals on or in the lake. Feed the swans and ducks. Find a party and join in.

Emma Herbert
High School Student

An evening with friends at the zany **Tres Kilos** near **Tiefenbrunnen**—Tex-Mex, well, sort of, and all the margaritas you could want, only a stumble away from the nearest tram stop.

Time spent by the soothing edge of **Lake Zurich.** Create your own atmosphere with a bonfire and some bratwurst.

Mosey through **Niederdorf,** the old part of town, on a Saturday night, when the air is filled with live music.

Visit the **Rheinfelder Bierhalle** to learn what it really means to drink (cheaply), or **Kon-tiki,** where the music is loud and the customers spill out of the windows onto the street.

Lion's Pub, behind the **Brasserie Lipp,** is reminiscent of an English pub, red call box and all.

Like to dance? Then hit the **Limmatbar** with your buddies by your side for an evening of frolicking on the dance floor.

Hungry but don't fancy **McDonalds?** Take time out to visit downtown **Stadelhofen Station's Sandwich Bar** for the best and cheapest sandwich concoctions

and the fabulous **Mövenpick** ice cream (you gotta try it!).

If you do hunger for a taste of home, Zurich has a **Häagen-Dazs,** but be prepared for a price as well as a flavor shock.

For women only: Dump the males that you're with and visit **The Pub.**

Running barefoot in the rain down the famous **Bahnhofstrasse** to the horror of all!

In the market for new clothes? **Migros City** has the best quality for the money if you are in need of bare necessities.

Craving a shower after hours spent on a train? Use the luxurious facilities at the **Hauptbahnhof** or just jump off the nearest bridge!

For a dose of culture, check out the **Kunsthaus** with its weird, wacky, and ever-changing Giacometti sculptures.

Skate freaks should head out to the lake and join the young at heart.

You're in luck if you're here in winter when the wine boats are in town. Need I say there is plenty of wine to taste?

Jump on a train and head for **Uetliberg** mountain to experience the feeling of sitting at the top of the world.

If you're just out for a good time and want to experience Zurich life, then grab a bench and watch the world go by. People-watching is primo—and no, you're not in a time warp, hippies are still a major part of the Zurich scene.

Rosmarie Leuthold
Ground Hostess, Kuoni Travel

Zeughaus Keller restaurant. Medieval steeting, great traditional food at cheap prices.

Bauschänzli terrace and restaurant on the **Limmat.** Fun to watch passersby while eating an ice cream.

Sechse-Laüten festival at the end of April marks the end of winter. At 6PM the Böög (winter-man) is set on fire and horses gallop around the bonfire. A corso, wearing the traditional costumes of every trade, goes through the city. Great atmosphere. The whole city's there!

Migros City supermarkets. A national institution. Everything is cheaper than elsewhere. You can find anything except alcohol and cigarettes. The founder was a teetotaler.

Index

Budget Europe Orientation
Map key **6**
Orientation **2**

Features
Cheap Stays: The Ins and Outs of Hosteling **162**
Expand Your Horizons: Work or Study Abroad **90**
Packin' It **70**
Parisian Delicacies **120**
Reach Out and Touch **129**
Safety Tips for the Street Smart **114**
Trains, Buses, & Automobiles **4**
Utopenci and Bramboráky and Other Czech Delights **146**
You Better Shop Around **202**
Your Student ID: Don't Leave Home Without It **59**

Bests
Aliani, Michel (Medical Student and Receptionist, Hôtel Deauville, Paris) **131**
Boyle, Lucinda (Manager, Travellers Bookstore, London) **103**
Brown, Nancy (Retired Nurse/History Buff/All-Around Romophile) **171**
Coleman, Victoria (Tourist Guide, London) **103**
Courtney, Martin (Distribution and Sales, *Checkpoint*, Berlin) **61**
Durell, Samantha (Owner, Venice Travel Advisory Service) **191**
Fant, Maureen (Writer, Rome) **171**
Filippi, Francesco (Engineer, Rome) **171**
Flemrová, Kateřina (Student of English at Charles University, Prague) **149**
Herbert, Emma (High School Student, Zurich) **206**
Leuthold, Rosmarie (Ground Hostess, Kuoni Travel, Zurich) **206**
Martin, Ilaria (Interpreter and Translator, Florence) **81**
Martinez, Carmen (Assistant Professor, Universidad Autónoma de Barcelona) **41**
Montagnaro, Umberto (Gondolier, Venice) **191**
Ortega, Maria Jesus Morte (Student, Jean D'Estrées Center of Aesthetics, Barcelona) **41**
Prevost, Hélène (Professor and Lecturer for the Association Civilisation et Culture Françaises, Paris) **131**
Queralt, Joan Marc (Student, Center of Tourism Studies, Barcelona) **41**
Rainero, Enrico (Photographer, Florence) **81**
Robertson, Elaine (Travel Editor, *Cosmopolitan*, London) **103**
Seppänen, Raisa (Waitress, The Pub, Zurich) **206**
Sterk, Raul (Freelance Journalist, Berlin) **61**
Taminiau, Odette (Public Relations and Protocol, City Hall, Amsterdam) **23**
Wamsteeker, Els (Public Relations Manager, VVV Amsterdam Tourist Office) **23**
Ward, Ed (Associate Editor, *Checkpoint*/Contributor, National Public Radio's *Fresh Air*, Berlin) **61**

Maps
Amsterdam **6**
Barcelona **24**
Berlin **42**
Europe *see inside front cover*
Florence **62**
London **82**
Map key **4**
Paris **104**
Prague **132**
Rome **150**
Venice **172**
Zurich **192**
Zurich detail **196**

Restaurant Ratings
Only restaurants with star ratings are listed in the Restaurants indexes. All restaurants are listed alphabetically in the main (preceding) index for each city. Always call in advance to ensure a restaurant has not closed, changed its hours, or booked its tables for a private party. The restaurant price ratings are based on the average cost of an entrée for one person, excluding tax and tip.

★★★★ An Extraordinary Experience
★★★ Excellent
★★ Very Good
★ Good
$$ The Price is Right
$ On a Shoestring Budget

Hotel Ratings
The hotels listed in the Hotels indexes are grouped according to their price ratings; they are also listed in the main index for each city. The hotel price ratings reflect the base price of a standard room for two people for one night during the peak season.

$$ The Price is Right
$ On a Shoestring Budget

Amsterdam

A
Accommodations **10**
Agora $$ **16**
Airports **9**
Albert Cuyp Markt **19**
Albert Heijn **16**
Allard Pierson Museum **15**
Alto **22**
Americain, Cafe **21**
American Book Center **15**
Amstelkring Museum (Our Lord in the Attic) **12**
Amsterdam Diamond Center **13**
Amsterdam Historisch (Historical) Museum **14**
Anne Frankhuis (Anne Frank House) **22**
ARENA Sleep In $ **19**
Artis **19**
Athenaeum News Centrum **14**
Atrium, The **15**

B
Begijnhof **14**
Belga, Hotel **22**
Berlage, Hendrik Petrus **12**
Beurs van Berlage (Berlage's Stock Exchange) **12**
Bicycles **9, 12**
Bimhuis **18**
Bloemenmarkt (Flower Market) **16**
Bob's Youth Hostel $ **14**
Bojo ★$ **21**
Bridge of the 15 Bridges **17**
Broekmans & Van Poppel, Muziekhandel **20**
Broodje van Kootje ★$ **15**
Buses **9**
Business hours **10**

C
Cafe Americain $$ **21**
Cafe Dantzig ★★$$ **18**
Cafe Descartes ★★$$ **19**
Cafe Panini ★★$$ **19**
Cafe Vertigo ★★$$ **21**
Caffè Esprit ★$$ **15**
Canal boats **9**
Casa di David ★$$ **22**
Centraal Station **9, 11**
China Corner ★$$ **13**
Christian Youth Hostel (Eben Haezer) **22**
Climate **10**
Concertgebouw (Concert Building) **20**
Condomerie Het Gulden Vlies **12**
Consulates **10**
Cuypers, P.J.H. **11, 19**

D
Dam Square **13**
Dansen bij Jansen **15**
Dantzig, Cafe **18**
David & Goliath Cafe ★$$ **14**
David, Casa di **22**
De Drie Fleschjes **13**
De Jaren ★★$$ **16**
De Keuken van 1870 ★$ **13**
de la Poste, Hotel **17**
De Looier Art and Antique Center (Kunst & Antiekcentrum De Looier) **22**
De Melkweg (The Milky Way) **21**
De Nieuwe Kerk (New Church) **13**
De Prins ★★$ **22**
Descartes, Cafe **19**
De Stadsschouwburg **21**
De Waag (Weigh House) **12**
Discount tickets **10**
Drie Fleschjes, De **13**
Drinking **10**
Driving **9**
Drugs **10**

E
Eben Haezer (Christian Youth Hostel) $ **22**
Eetsalon Van Dobben B.V. ★$ **17**
Embassies **10**
Emergencies **10**
Engelsekerk (English Church) **14**
Escape **17**
Esprit, Caffè **15**

F
Ferry **9**
Flower Market (Bloemenmarkt) **16**
Frascati Cafe ★★$$ **15**
Friday Book Market/Sunday Art Market on the Spui **14**

G
Gambling **10, 21**

207

Index

Gary's Muffins ★$ 21
Getting around Amsterdam 9
Getting to Amsterdam 9
Gollem 14

H
Haesje Claes ★★$$ 14
Hajenius, P.G.C. 15
Heineken Brewery 19
Hema 16
Het Muziektheater (Music Theater) 17
Historisch (Historical) Museum, Amsterdam 14
Hoksbergen, Hotel 22
Holidays, public 11
Holland Casino Amsterdam 21
Holland Rent-A-Bike 12
Hollandsche Schouwburg 18
Homomonument 22
Hortus Botanicus 18
Hostel, Bob's Youth 14
Hostel, Christian Youth 22
Hostel, Stadsdoelen Youth 16
Hotel Belga $$ 22
Hotel de la Poste $$ 17
Hotel Hoksbergen $$ 22
Hotel Keizershof $$ 19
Hotel Piet Hein $$ 21
Hotel Prinsenhof $$ 19
Hotel Seven Bridges $$ 17
Hotel Verdi $$ 20

I
Intertaal 20
iT 17

J
Jacob Hooy & Co. 12
Jaren, De 16
Joods Historisch Museum (Jewish Historical Museum) 18

K
Keizershof, Hotel 19
Keuken van 1870, De 13
Keyser, Hendryk de 16, 22
Koninklijk Paleis (Royal Palace) 13
Koophandel 22
Kunst & Antiekcentrum De Looier (De Looier Art and Antique Center) 22
Kwekkeboom ★$ 17

L
Langedoksbrug (Long Dock's Bridge) 12
Laundry 10

M
Madame Tussaud's Scenerama 13
Magizijn de Bijenkorf 13
Magna Plaza 14
Map 6
Maritime Museum (Nederlands Scheepvaart Museum) 12
Medieval Torture Museum 22
Melkweg, De 21
Meneer Pannekoek ★$$ 14
Mint Square (Muntplein) 16
Mister Coco's ★$ 17
Money 10
Municipal (Stedelijk) Museum 20
Muntplein (Mint Square) 16
Music Theater (Het Muziektheater) 17
Muziekcafe Kapitein Zeppo's ★$$ 15

Muziekhandel Broekmans & Van Poppel 20

N
Nederlands Filmmuseum (Netherlands Film Museum) 20
Nederlands Scheepvaartmuseum (Maritime Museum) 12
New Church (De Nieuwe Kerk) 13
NJHC Vondelpark $ 21
Noorderkerk (North Church) 23
Noordermarkt 23

O
Odeon 16
Oudemanhuispoort (Old Men's House Gate) Bookmarket 16
Our Lord in the Attic (Amstelkring Museum) 12
Outmayer ★$ 12

P
Panini, Cafe 19
Paradiso 21
Personal safety 10
P.G.C. Hajenius 15
Piet Hein, Hotel 21
Pompadour ★★$$ 22
Portuguese Israeli Synagogue 18
Postal services 10
Poste, Hotel de la 17
Prins, De 22
Prinsenhof, Hotel 19
Publications 10
Public holidays 11
Public rest rooms 11

R
Rembrandthuis (Rembrandt House) 18
Restaurants 11
Rest rooms, public 11
Rietveld, Gerrit 20
Rijksmuseum 19
Rokin Hotel $$ 15
Roxy 16
Royal Palace (Koninklijk Paleis) 13

S
Safety, personal 10
Schiphol Airport 9
Schrierstoren (Tower of Tears) 11
Seven Bridges, Hotel 17
Shelter, The 12
Shopping 11
Sisters ★★$$ 15
Smoking 11
Stadsdoelen Youth Hostel $ 16
Stadsschouwburg, De 21
Stedelijk (Municipal) Museum 20
Stock Exchange, Berlage's 12
Street plan 11
String, The 15
Subway 9
Sunday Art Market on the Spui/Friday Book Market 14

T
Taminiau, Odette 23 (bests)
Taxes 11
Taxis 9
Telephones 11
The Atrium ★$ 15
The Milky Way (De Melkweg) 21
The Shelter $ 12

The String 15
Tickets 11
Tickets, discount 10
Tipping 11
Tours 9
Tower of Tears (Schrierstoren) 11
Trains 9
Trams 9
Transportation, local 9
Tropenmuseum (Tropical Museum) 19
Tuschinski Theater 16

V
van Campen, Jacob 13
Van Dobben, B.V., Eetsalon 17
Van Gogh Museum 20
Van Onna Hotel $$ 23
Verdi, Hotel 20
Vertigo, Cafe 21
Visas 11
Visitors' information 11
Vondelpark 20

W
Waag, De 12
Walking 9
Walletjes 12
Wamsteeker, Els 23 (bests)
Waterlooplein 18
Weigh House (De Waag) 12
Weissmann, A.W. 20
Wertheim Park 18
Westerkerk 22

Y
Youth Hostel, Bob's 14
Youth Hostel, Christian 22
Youth Hostel, Stadsdoelen 16

Amsterdam Restaurants

★★
Cafe Dantzig $$ 18
Cafe Descartes $$ 19
Cafe Panini $$ 19
Cafe Vertigo $$ 21
De Jaren $$ 16
De Prins $ 22
Frascati Cafe $$ 15
Haesje Claes $$ 14
Pompadour $$ 22
Sisters $$ 15

★
Bojo $ 21
Broodje van Kootje $ 15
Caffè Esprit $$ 15
Casa di David $$ 22
China Corner $$ 13
David & Goliath Cafe $$ 14
De Keuken van 1870 $ 13
Eetsalon Van Dobben B.V. $ 17
Gary's Muffins $ 21
Kwekkeboom $ 17
Meneer Pannekoek $$ 14
Mister Coco's $ 17
Muziekcafe Kapitein Zeppo's $$ 15
Outmayer $ 12
The Atrium $ 15

Amsterdam Hotels

$$
Agora 16

Index

Hotel Belga **22**
Hotel de la Poste **17**
Hotel Hoksbergen **22**
Hotel Keizershof **19**
Hotel Piet Hein **21**
Hotel Prinsenhof **19**
Hotel Seven Bridges **17**
Hotel Verdi **20**
Rokin Hotel **15**
Van Onna Hotel **23**

$

ARENA Sleep In **19**
Bob's Youth Hostel **14**
Eben Haezer (Christian Youth Hostel) **22**
NJHC Vondelpark **21**
Stadsdoelen Youth Hostel **16**
The Shelter **12**

Barcelona

A
Accommodations **27**
Airports **26**
Alberg Juvenil Palau $ **33**
Alberg Mare Déu de Montserrat $ **39**
Alberg Pere Tarrés $ **39**
Albergue Juvenil Kabul $ **33**
Altaïr **36**
Anella Olímpica (Olympic Ring) **40**
Antic Hospital de la Santa Creu **31**
Antoni Tàpies Foundation (Fundació Antoni Tàpies) **36**
Arribas, Alfredo **37**
Ausich, Josep **31**
Australia Residencial $ **29**

B
Barcelona Brewing Company **37**
Barcelona, Catedral de **30**
Barcelona Pipa Club **33**
Barceloneta **34**
Bar Mirablau **39**
Battló, Casa **36**
Berenguer, Francesc **38**
Bicycles **27**
Biocenter ★★$ **31**
Boqueria, La **31**
Buigas, Carles **40**
Buses **26, 27**
Business hours **27**

C
Cafè de L'Opera ★★$ **32**
Capitol, Hotel **29**
Casa Batlló **36**
Casa Huéspedes Mari-Luz $ **33**
Casa Martí Els Quattro Gats **30**
Casa Milà (La Pedrera) **37**
Casa-Museu Gaudí **38**
Casa Vicens **36**
Castell de Montjuïc **41**
Catalan Concert Hall (Palau de la Música Catalana) **35**
Catalunya, Plaça de **29**
Catedral de Barcelona **30**
Ceramic Museum (Museu de Ceràmica) **39**
Church of St. Mary of the Sea (Església de Santa Maria del Mar) **35**
Church of the Holy Family (Templo Expiatorio de la Sagrada Família) **37**
Churreria San Ramon **31**
Ciutadella, Parc de la **35**

Climate **27**
Consulates **28**

D
Diaz, Carlos **35**
Discount tickets **28**
Domènech i Montaner, Lluís **35, 36, 38**
Drassanes Reials (Royal Shipyards) **34**
Drinking **28**
Driving **27**

E
Egipte, Restaurant **32**
El Encants **32**
El Gallo Kiriko ★★$ **33**
El Pi Antic ★★$$ **31**
El Prat Airport **26**
Els Tres Bots ★★$ **32**
El Tastavins ★★$$ **38**
El Xampanyet ★★$ **35**
Embassies **28**
Emergencies **28**
Encants, El **37**
Església de Santa Maria del Mar (Church of St. Mary of the Sea) **35**
Estació de França **26**
Estació del Nord **26**
Estació de Sants **26**
Estació Marítima **26**

F
Felipe II, Hostal **37**
Ferries **26**
Fonda, La **34**
Fontserè, Treball de **35**
Forn de Sant Jaume ★★$$ **36**
Foster, Norman **39**
França, Estació de **26**
Francesca, Llibreria **37**
Fuentes de Montjuïc **40**
Fundació Antoni Tàpies (Antoni Tàpies Foundation) **36**
Fundació Miró **41**
Funiculars **27**

G
Gallo Kiriko, El **33**
Ganiveteria Roca, S.A. **31**
Gaudí, Casa-Museu **38**
Gaudí i Cornet, Antoni **32, 35, 36, 37, 38, 39**
Gelateria Italiana Pagliotta **30**
Getting around Barcelona **27**
Getting to Barcelona **26**
Govinda ★★$$ **30**
Gran Bodega ★★$$ **36**
Gran Teatro del Liceu **32**
Güel, Palau **32**
Güell, Park **38**

H
Harlem Jazz Club **33**
Holidays, public **28**
Hospital de la Santa Creu i Sant Pau **38**
Hostal de Joves Internacional Colon III $ **33**
Hostal Felipe II $$ **37**
Hostal Levante $ **33**
Hostal Marítima $ **34**
Hostal Nuevo Colón $ **34**
Hostal Oliva $$ **36**
Hostal Palacios $$ **36**
Hotel Capitol $$ **29**
Hotel Inglés $$ **32**

Hotel Lloret $$ **29**
Hotel Peninsular $ **32**
Hotel Rey Don Jaime I $$ **30**
Huéspedes Mari-Luz, Casa **33**
Huespedes Colmenero $$ **31**

I
Indigo **37**
Inglés, Hotel **32**
Isard, Pension L' **29**
Itaca **33**

J
Jazz Club, Harlem **33**
Joves Internacional Colon III, Hostal de **33**
Jugolandia ★★$$ **38**
Juvenil Kabul, Albergue **33**
Juvenil Palau, Alberg **33**

L
La Boqueria (Mercat de Sant Josep) **31**
La Fonda ★★$$ **34**
Laie ★$$ **36**
La Manual Alpargatera **33**
Language **28**
La Pallaresa ★★$ **31**
La Palmera ★★$$ **36**
La Pedrera (Casa Milà) **37**
La Rambla **29**
Laundry **28**
Levante, Hostal **33**
Liceu, Gran Teatro del **32**
L'Isard, Pension **29**
Llibreria Francesa **37**
Lloret, Hotel **29**
Lluna Plena ★★$$ **35**
London Bar **32**
L'Opera, Cafè de **32**
Los Toreros ★$ **31**
Lourdes, Pensión-Residencia **35**
L'Ovella Negra **29**

M
Manual Alpargatera, La **33**
Map **24**
Mare Déu de Montserrat, Alberg **39**
Marítima, Estació de **26**
Marítima, Hostal **34**
Maritime Museum (Museu Marítim) **34**
Martí Els Quattro Gats, Casa **30**
Martinez, Carmen **41** (bests)
Mas i Vila, Josep **31**
Mercat de Sant Josep (La Boqueria) **31**
Metro (subway) **27**
Mies van der Rohe, Ludwig **40**
Mies van der Rohe, Pavelló **40**
Milà, Casa **37**
Mirablau, Bar **39**
Miró, Fundació **41**
Moll de la Fusta **34**
Monestir de Pedralbes **39**
Money **28**
Montjuïc **39**
Montjuïc, Castell de **41**
Montserrat, Residencia **37**
Mont Tibidabo **39**
Museu d'Art Contemporani **29**
Museu d'Art Modern **35**
Museu de Ceràmica (Ceramic Museum) **39**
Museu de Zoologia (Zoo) **35**
Museu d'Història de la Ciutat (Museum of City History) **30**

209

Index

Museu Marítim (Maritime Museum) **34**
Museu Nacional d'Art de Catalunya (National Art Museum of Catalonia) **40**
Museu Picasso **35**

N

Nacional, Palau **40**
National Art Museum of Catalonia (Museu Nacional d'Art de Catalunya) **40**
Nord, Estació del **26**
Nou Camp F.C. Barcelona **39**
Nova Icària, Platja de la **34**
Nuevo Colón, Hostal **34**

O

Oliva, Hostal **36**
Olympic Ring (Anella Olímpica) **40**
Opera, Cafè de L' **32**
Ortega, Maria Jesus Morte **41** (bests)
Otto Zutz **38**
Ovella Negra, L' **29**

P

Palacios, Hostal **36**
Palau de la Música Catalana (Catalan Concert Hall) **35**
Palau de la Virreina **31**
Palau de Pedralbes **39**
Palau Güel **32**
Palau Nacional **40**
Pallaressa, La **31**
Palmera, La **36**
Parc de la Ciutadella **35**
Park Güell **38**
Pastís **34**
Pavelló Mies van der Rohe **40**
Pedralbes, Monestir de **39**
Pedralbes, Palau de **39**
Pedrera, La **37**
Pelayo **14 29**
Peninsular, Hotel **32**
Pension L'Isard $ **29**
Pensión-Residencia Lourdes $ **35**
Pension San Medín $$ **38**
Pere Tarrés, Alberg **39**
Personal safety **28**
Pi Antic, El **31**
Picasso, Museu **35**
Pi, Plaça del **31**
Pitarra Restaurant ★★$$ **34**
Plaça de Catalunya **29**
Plaça del Pi **31**
Plaça del Rei **30**
Plaça del Sol **38**
Plaça de Sant Jaume **30**
Plaça de Sant Josep Oriol **31**
Plaça Reial **32**
Platja de la Nova Icària **34**
Poble Espanyol (Spanish Village) **40**
Pollo Rico ★$ **32**
Postal services **28**
Prat Airport, El **26**
Publications **28**
Public holidays **28**
Public rest rooms **28**
Puig i Cadafalch, Josep **36**

Q

Quatro Gats ★★$$ **30**
Queralt, Joan Marc **41** (bests)

R

Rambla, La **29**

Reial, Plaça **32**
Rei, Plaça del **30**
Residencia Montserrat $$ **37**
Restaurant Egipte ★$$ **32**
Restaurants **28**
Rest rooms, public **28**
Rey Don Jaime I, Hotel **30**
Royal Shipyards (Drassanes Reials) **34**

S

Safety, personal **28**
Sagnier, Enric **36**
Sagrada Família, Templo Expiatorio de la **37**
San Medín, Pension **38**
Santa Creu i Sant Pau, Hospital de la **38**
Santa Maria del Mar, Església de **35**
Sant Jaume, Plaça de **30**
Sant Josep Oriol, Plaça de **31**
Sants, Estació de **26**
Satanassa Antro Bar **36**
Shopping **28**
Smoking **28**
Sol, Plaça del **38**
Spanish Village (Poble Espanyol) **40**
Street plan **28**
Subway (metro) **27**

T

Tasca El Corral ★★$ **34**
Tastavins, El **38**
Taxes **28**
Taxis **27**
Telefèrics **27**
Telephones **29**
Templo Expiatorio de la Sagrada Família (Church of the Holy Family) **37**
Tibidabo, Mont **39**
Tickets, discount **28**
Tijuana ★$ **37**
Tipping **29**
Toreros, Los **31**
Tours **27**
Trains **26, 27**
Transportation, local **27**
Tres Boots, Els **32**
Tusquets, Oscar **35**

V

Vaso de Oro ★★$ **34**
Velvet **37**
Verboom, Prospère **34**
Vicens, Casa **36**
Virreina, Palau de la **31**
Visas **29**
Visitors' information **29**

W

Walking **27**

X

Xampanyet, El **35**

Z

Zebra **34**
Zoo (Museu de Zoologia) **35**

Barcelona Restaurants

★★

Biocenter $ **31**
Cafè de L'Opera $ **32**
El Gallo Kiriko $ **33**

El Pi Antic $$ **31**
Els Tres Bots $ **32**
El Tastavins $$ **38**
El Xampanyet $ **35**
Forn de Sant Jaume $$ **36**
Govinda $$ **30**
Gran Bodega $$ **36**
Jugolandia $$ **38**
La Fonda $$ **34**
La Pallaresa $ **31**
La Palmera $$ **36**
Lluna Plena $$ **35**
Pitarra Restaurant $$ **34**
Quatro Gats $$ **30**
Tasca El Corral $ **34**
Vaso de Oro $ **34**

★

Laie $$ **36**
Los Toreros $ **31**
Pollo Rico $ **32**
Restaurant Egipte $$ **32**
Tijuana $ **37**

Barcelona Hotels

$$

Hostal Felipe II **37**
Hostal Oliva **36**
Hostal Palacios **36**
Hotel Capitol **29**
Hotel Inglés **32**
Hotel Lloret **29**
Hotel Rey Don Jaime I **30**
Huespedes Colmenero **31**
Pension San Medín **38**
Residencia Montserrat **37**

$

Alberg Juvenil Palau **33**
Alberg Mare Déu de Montserrat **39**
Alberg Pere Tarrés **39**
Albergue Juvenil Kabul **33**
Australia Residencial **29**
Casa Huéspedes Mari-Luz **33**
Hostal de Joves Internacional Colon III **33**
Hostal Levante **33**
Hostal Marítima **34**
Hostal Nuevo Colón **34**
Hotel Peninsular **32**
Pension L'Isard **29**
Pensión-Residencia Lourdes **35**

Berlin

A

Accommodations **45**
Adler, Café **60**
Aedes, Cafe **50**
Ägyptisches Museum (Egyptian Museum) **47**
Airports **44**
Alexanderplatz **55**
Alte Nationalgalerie (Old National Gallery) **56**
Altes Museum (Old Museum) **56**
Anhalter Rail Station (Bahnhof Anhalter) **60**
Arsenal (Zeughaus) **54**
Ashoka $ **49**
A Trane **49**

B

Bahnhof Anhalter (Anhalter Rail Station) **60**

Index

Bahnhof Friedrichstrasse (Friedrichstrasse Rail Station) **56**
Bahnhof Zoologischer Garten (Zoo Station) **44**
Bauhaus-Archiv **52**
Bayou ★$$ **51**
Belvedere **47**
Berio, Cafe **51**
Berliner Arbeiterleben um 1900, Museum **58**
Berliner Dom (Berlin Cathedral) **55**
Berlin-Schönefeld Airport **44**
Berlin-Tegel Airport **44**
Berlin Zinnfiguren Kabinet **49**
Bethanien Artists' House (Künstlerhaus Bethanien) **58**
Beth, Cafe **57**
Bicycles **44**
Bierhimmel **59**
Bodemuseum **56**
Bogota, Hotel **50**
Botanischer Garten und Botanisches Museum (Botanical Garden and Museum Berlin-Dahlem) **49**
Brandenburger Tor (Brandenburg Gate) **53**
Brücke Museum **48**
Buses **44**
Business hours **45**

C
Café Adler ★$$ **60**
Cafe Aedes ★$$ **50**
Cafe Bar Morena ★★$$ **60**
Cafe Bar Tiago ★★$$ **49**
Cafe Berio ★$$ **51**
Cafe Beth ★$ **57**
Café • Bistro Zeughaus ★★$$ **54**
Cafe Einstein ★★$$ **51**
Cafe Hardenberg ★$ **49**
Cafe M $ **51**
Cafe Orange ★$$ **57**
Café Oren & Restaurant ★★$$ **57**
Cafe Restaurant Milagro ★$ **60**
Cafe Silberstein ★$ **57**
Central Bus Station (Zentralen Omnibus-Bahnhof) **44**
Chamäleon Variete **57**
Charlottenburg Public Pool (Stadtbad Charlottenburg) **47**
Checkpoint **60**
Checkpoint Charlie Museum **60**
Climate **45**
Condomi **49**
Consulates **45**
Courtney, Martin **61** (bests)

D
Dahlem Museums **48**
Deutsches Historisches Museum (German Historical Museum) **54**
Discount tickets **45**
Diyar ★★$$ **59**
Dralle's ★$ **49**
Drinking **45**
Driving **45**
Drugs **45**

E
East Side Gallerie **58**
Egyptian Museum (Ägyptisches Museum) **47**
Einstein, Cafe **51**

Embassies **45**
Emergencies **45**
Ethnological Museum (Museum für Volkskunde) **48**

F
Fernsehturm (TV Tower) **55**
Filmbühne am Steinplatz, Restaurant **49**
Franz Club **58**
Friedrichstrasse Rail Station (Bahnhof Friedrichstrasse) **56**
Funk, Hotel Pension **50**

G
Galerie der Romantik **47**
Garage **51**
Gemäldegalerie (Picture Gallery) **48**
Gendarmenmarkt (Gendarmes Market) **54**
German Historical Museum (Deutsches Historisches Museum) **54**
Getting around Berlin **44**
Getting to Berlin **44**
Görs $$ **48**
Grisebach, Villa **50**
Gropius, Martin **61**
Gropius, Walter **52, 61**
Grossbeerenkeller ★★$$$ **60**

H
Habibi ★$ **51**
Hackbarth's ★$$ **57**
Hardenberg, Cafe **49**
Harry Lehmann **48**
Haus der Kulturen der Welt (House of World Cultures) **53**
Henne Alt-Berliner Wirtshaus ★★★$ **58**
Holidays, public **46**
Hotel Bogota $$ **50**
Hotel Pension Funk $$ **50**
Hotel-Pension Imperator $$ **50**
Hotel Pension Majesty $$ **49**
Hotel Pension Modena $$ **49**
Hotel-Pension Nürnberger Eck $$ **51**
Hotel-Pension Pariser-Eck $$ **50**
Hotel Transit $ **60**
House of World Cultures (Haus der Kulturen der Welt) **53**
Husemannstrasse **58**

I
Imperator, Hotel-Pension **50**
Indische Kunst, Museum für **48**
Insel, Museum **55**
Islamische Kunst, Museum für **48**

J
Jüdischer Friedhof in Weissensee (Jewish Cemetery in Weissensee) **58**
Jugendgästehaus am Zoo $ **49**

K
KaDeWe **51**
Kaiser-Wilhelm-Gedächtniskirche (Kaiser Wilhelm Memorial Church) **50**
Kammermusiksaal **52**
Karl Friedrich Schinkel Pavilion **47**
Käthe Kollwitz Museum **50**
Keller-Restaurant ★$$ **56**
Knesebeck, Pension **49**
Knobelsdorff, Georg Wenzeslaus von **54**
Knoblauch, Eduard **57**
Krähe ★$$ **58**
Kumpelnest 3000 **52**

Künstlerhaus Bethanien (Bethanien Artists' House) **58**

L
Langhans, Carl Gotthard **47, 53**
Laundry **45**
Leysieffer ★★★$$$ **50**
Loft, The **51**
Luise ★$ **48**

M
Majesty, Hotel Pension **49**
Map **42**
Marché, Restaurant **50**
Martin Gropius Bau **61**
Marx-Engels Forum **55**
M, Cafe **51**
Mendelsohn, Erich **48**
Metropol **51**
Mies van der Rohe, Ludwig **52**
Milagro, Cafe Restaurant **60**
Modena, Hotel Pension **49**
Money **45**
Morena, Cafe Bar **60**
Museum Berlin-Dahlem **49**
Museum Berliner Arbeiterleben um 1900 (Museum of Berlin Working-Class Life Around 1900) **58**
Museum für Indische Kunst (Museum of Indian Art) **48**
Museum für Islamische Kunst (Museum of Islamic Art) **48**
Museum für Naturkunde (Museum of Natural History) **56**
Museum für Volkskunde (Ethnological Museum) **48**
Museum Insel (Museum Island) **55**
Museum of Berlin Working-Class Life Around 1900 (Museum Berliner Arbeiterleben um 1900) **58**
Museum of Indian Art (Museum für Indische Kunst) **48**
Museum of Islamic Art (Museum für Islamische Kunst) **48**
Museum of Natural History (Museum für Naturkunde) **56**

N
Neue Nationalgalerie (New National Gallery) **52**
Neues Museum (New Museum) **56**
Neue Synagoge (New Synagogue) **57**
Neue Wache (New Guardhouse) **54**
Neunzig Grad **52**
New Museum (Neues Museum) **56**
New National Gallery (Neue Nationalgalerie) **52**
New Synagoge (Neue Synagoge) **57**
Nürnberger Eck, Hotel-Pension **51**

O
Old Museum (Altes Museum) **56**
Old National Gallery (Alte Nationalgalerie) **56**
Operncafe ★$$ **54**
Orange, Cafe **57**
Oren, Café, & Restaurant **57**
Original Times, The **58**
Osteria No. 1 ★★$$ **60**

P
Palast der Republik (Palace of the Republic) **54**
Pariser-Eck, Hotel-Pension **50**

211

Index

Pension Knesebeck $$ **49**
Pergamonmuseum **56**
Personal safety **45**
Philharmonie **52**
Picture Gallery (Gemäldegalerie) **48**
Pinguin Club **52**
Podewil **55**
Postal services **46**
Potsdamer Platz **61**
Publications **46**
Public holidays **46**
Public rest rooms **46**
Public transportation **45**

Q

Quasimodo **49**

R

Reichstag **53**
Restaurant Filmbühne am Steinplatz $ **49**
Restaurant Marché ★★$ **50**
Restaurants **46**
Restauration 1900 ★★$$ **58**
Rest rooms, public **46**
Romantik, Galerie der **47**

S

Safety, personal **45**
Savarin ★$ **52**
Scharoun, Hans **52**
Schaubühne am Lehniner Platz **48**
Schinkel, Karl Friedrich **47, 54, 56, 61**
Schloss Charlottenburg **47**
Schloss Park **47**
Schlüter, Andreas **54**
Schwarzes Cafe $$ **50**
Shopping **46**
Siegessäule (Victory Column) **52**
Silberstein, Cafe **57**
Smoking **46**
Sophienclub **57**
Sowjetisches Ehrenmal (Soviet War Memorial) **58**
Speer, Albert **58**
Staatsoper (State Opera) **54**
Stadtbad Charlottenburg (Charlottenburg Public Pool) **47**
Sterk, Paul **61** (bests)
Street plan **46**
Stubbin, Hugh A. **53**
Stüler, Friedrich August **56, 57**
Subways **45**

T

Tacheles **57**
Taxes **46**
Taxis **45**
Telephones **46**
The Loft **51**
The Original Times ★$$ **58**
Tiago, Cafe Bar **49**
Tickets, discount **45**
Tiergarten **52**
Tipping **46**
Topography of Terror **61**
Tours **45**
Trains **44**
Trams **45**
Transit, Hotel **60**
Transportation, local **44**
Transportation, public **45**
TV Tower (Fernsehturm) **55**
TY BREIZh ★$$ **48**

V

van Loon ★★★$$ **60**
VEB Oz **57**
Victory Column (Siegessäule) **52**
Villa Grisebach **50**
Visas **46**
Visitors' information **46**
Volkskunde, Museum für **48**

W

Walking **45**
Wallot, Paul **53**
Ward, Ed **61** (bests)
Winterfeldt Markt **51**

Z

Zentralen Omnibus-Bahnhof (Central Bus Station) **44**
Zeughaus (Arsenal) **54**
Zeughaus, Café • Bistro **54**
Zille Hof **50**
Zoologischer Garten (Zoo) **50**
Zoo Station (Bahnhof Zoologischer Garten) **44**
Zur kleinen Markthalle ★★$ **59**

Berlin Restaurants

★★★
Henne Alt-Berliner Wirtshaus $ **58**
Leysieffer $$$ **50**
van Loon $$ **60**

★★
Cafe Bar Morena $$ **60**
Cafe Bar Tiago $$ **49**
Café • Bistro Zeughaus $$ **54**
Cafe Einstein $$ **51**
Café Oren & Restaurant $$ **57**
Diyar $$ **59**
Grossbeerenkeller $$$ **60**
Osteria No. 1 $$ **60**
Restaurant Marché $ **50**
Restauration 1900 $$ **58**
Zur kleinen Markthalle $ **59**

★
Bayou $$ **51**
Café Adler $$ **60**
Cafe Aedes $$ **50**
Cafe Berio $$ **51**
Cafe Beth $ **57**
Cafe Hardenberg $ **49**
Cafe Orange $$ **57**
Cafe Restaurant Milagro $$ **60**
Cafe Silberstein $ **57**
Dralle's $ **49**
Habibi $ **51**
Hackbarth's $$ **57**
Keller-Restaurant $$ **56**
Krähe $$ **58**
Luise $ **48**
Operncafe $$ **54**
Savarin $ **52**
The Original Times $$ **58**
TY BREIZh $$ **48**

Berlin Hotels

$$
Hotel Bogota **50**
Hotel Pension Funk **50**
Hotel-Pension Imperator **50**
Hotel Pension Majesty **49**
Hotel Pension Modena **49**
Hotel-Pension Nürnberger Eck **51**
Hotel-Pension Pariser-Eck **50**
Pension Knesebeck **49**

$
Hotel Transit **60**
Jugendgästehaus am Zoo **49**

Florence

A

Accademia Museum (Galleria dell'Accademia) **75**
Accommodations **65**
Acqua al Due ★$ **78**
a al Due ★$ **78**
Addresses **65**
Airports **64**
Albergo Firenze $ **67**
Alberti, Leon Battista **72**
Aldini $$ **67**
Alessi Paride **67**
Alimentari Orizi ★$ **71**
Alle Murate (Vineria) ★$$ **77**
Amannati **80**
Amerigo Vespucci Airport **64**
Anna $ **73**
Annalena $$ **80**
Antica Casa Fiorentina, Museo dell' **71**
Antico Ristoro di' Cambi ★$$ **79**
Aprile $$ **71**
Archibusieri $$ **69**

B

Baccus ★$ **71**
Bargello **78**
Bar Perseo **68**
Battistero di San Giovanni (Baptistry of St. John) **66**
Belle Donne ★★$$ **72**
Bellettini $ **73**
Biblioteca Mediceo-Laurenziana (Medici Library) **74**
Bicycles **64**
Boboli $ **80**
Boboli Gardens (Giardino di Boboli) **80**
Bordino ★$ **80**
Brunelleschi, Filippo **66, 75, 76, 78**
Brunori $ **77**
Buses **64**
Business hours **65**

C

Cafe Rivoire **68**
Campanile **66**
Cantinetta dei Verrazzano ★★$$ **67**
Cappelle Medicee (Medici Chapels) **73**
Carmine ★★$$ **79**
Casci $ **75**
Cathedral and Bell Tower (Duomo and Campanile) **66**
Centro Vegetariano $ **74**
Chiesa di Santa Croce **77**
Chiesa di Santa Maria del Carmine **79**
Chiesa di Santo Spirito **78**
Chiesa e Chiostri di San Lorenzo (Church and Cloisters of San Lorenzo) **74**
Chiesa e Chiostri di Santa Maria Novella (Church and Cloister of Santa Maria Novella) **72**
Chiostro Verde **73**
Cibreino, Il **76**
Climate **65**
C.O.I. (Commercio Oreficerie Italiane) **69**

212

Index

COIN **67**
Colomba $ **75**
Commercio Oreficerie Italiane (C.O.I.) **69**
Consulates **65**
Cravatte & Dintorni **68**

D
Danny Rock $ **77**
Dante $$ **77**
Da Rocco $ **76**
Davanzati Museum (Museo dell'Antica Casa Fiorentina) **71**
Dino Bartolini **75**
Discount tickets **65**
Drinking **65**
Driving **64**
Duomo and Campanile (Cathedral and Bell Tower) **66**

E
Embassies **65**
Emergencies **65**
Enza $ **74**
Erboristeria Palazzo Vecchio **69**

F
Fiaschetteria Torrini ★$ **67**
Fiorino $ **78**
Firenza, Albergo **67**
Friggitoria Luisa ★$ **73**

G
Galileo Galilei Airport **64**
Galleria degli Uffizi (Uffizi Gallery) **69**
Galleria dell'Accademia (Accademia Museum) **75**
Gelateria dei Neri ★$ **78**
Gelateria delle Carrozze **69**
Getting around Florence **64**
Getting to Florence **64**
Ghiberti, Lorenzo **67**
Giardino di Boboli (Boboli Gardens) **80**
Giotto **66**
Giotto $ **73**
Gioventù, Ostello della **81**
Gould Institute $ **79**
Guardaroba **77**
Guelfo Bianco, Il **75**

H
Hermitage $$ **69**
Holidays, public **65**

I
I Ghibellini ★$ **77**
Il Cibreino ★★$ **76**
Il Guelfo Bianco $$ **75**
Il Latini ★★$$ **71**
Il Palottino ★★$ **78**
Il Torchio **80**
Il Triangolo delle Bermude **73**
I Mascherari **68**

L
La Loggia **81**
La Ménagère **74**
La Residenza $$ **71**
La Scaletta $ **80**
Latini, Il **71**
Laundry **65**
Laurentian Library **74**
Le Mossacce ★$$ **77**
Liana $ **76**

Loggia dei Lanzi **69**
Loggia, La **81**
Loggiata dei Serviti **76**

M
Madova **80**
Map **62**
Mario $$ **73**
Martin, Ilaria **81** (bests)
Medici Chapels (Cappelle Medicee) **73**
Medici Library (Biblioteca Mediceo-Laurenziana) **74**
Ménagère, La **74**
Mensa Universitaria $ **74**
Mercato Centrale **73**
Mercato di San Lorenzo (San Lorenzo Market) **74**
Mercato Nuovo **68**
Michelangelo **74**
Michelangiolo, Piazzale **81**
Michelozzo **75**
Money **65**
Mopeds **64**
Morandi Alla Crocetta $$ **76**
Mossacce, Le **77**
Museo dell'Antica Casa Fiorentina (Davanzati Museum) **71**
Museo dell'Opera del Duomo **75**
Museo di San Marco **75**

N
Nerbone ★$ **74**
Norma $ **71**

O
Officina Profumo-Farmaceutica di Santa Maria Novella **71**
Opera del Duomo, Museo dell' **75**
Orsanmichele **68**
Ostello della Gioventù $ **81**
Ostello Santa Monaca $ **79**
Ottaviani $ **72**

P
Palazzo Pitti **80**
Palazzo Riccardi-Medici **75**
Palazzo Vecchio **68**
Palottino, Il **78**
Paperback Exchange **77**
Passamaneria Toscana **74**
Pendini $$ **67**
Perché No!... **68**
Perseo, Bar **68**
Personal safety **65**
Piazza della Repubblica **67**
Piazza della Signoria **68**
Piazzale Michelangiolo **81**
Piazza Santissima Annunziata **76**
Pitti, Palazzo **80**
Ponte Vecchio **78**
Postal services **65**
Publications **65**
Public holidays **65**
Public rest rooms **65**

R
Rainero, Enrico **81** (bests)
Repubblica, Piazza della **67**
Residenza, La **71**
Restaurants **66**
Rest rooms, public **65**
Riccardi-Medici, Palazzo **75**
Rivoire, Cafe **68**
Rocco, Da **76**

S
Safety, personal **65**
St. James Anglican Church $ **71**
San Lorenzo, Chiesa e Chiostri di **74**
San Lorenzo Market (Mercato di San Lorenzo) **74**
San Marco, Museo di **75**
San Miniato al Monte **81**
Santa Croce, Chiesa di **77**
Santa Maria del Carmine, Chiesa di **79**
Santa Maria Novella, Chiesa e Chiostri di **72**
Santa Monaca, Ostello **79**
Santissima Annunziata, Piazza **76**
Santo Spirito, Chiesa di **78**
Sbigoli Terrecotte **77**
Scaletta, La **80**
Scoti $ **72**
Sergio $ **74**
Shopping **66**
Signoria, Piazza della **68**
Smoking **66**
Sorelle Bandini $ **79**
Sostanza ★★$$ **71**
Standa **73**
Street plan **66**

T
Taxes **66**
Taxis **64**
Telephones **66**
Tickets, discount **65**
Tipping **66**
Torchio, Il **80**
Tours **64**
Trains **64**
Transportation, local **64**
Triangolo delle Bermude, Il **73**

U
Uffizi Gallery (Galleria degli Uffizi) **69**
Universo $ **72**
UPIM **67**

V
Vasari, Giorgio **69, 72, 78**
Vecchio, Palazzo **68**
Verde, Chiostro **73**
Viceversa **75**
Vineria (Alle Murate) **77**
Vini del Chianti ★$ **68**
Visas **66**
Visconti $ **72**
Visitors' information **66**
Vivoli ★★$ **78**

W
Walking **64**

Y
Yellow Bar $ **77**

Z
Zà Zà ★$$ **74**

Florence Restaurants
★★
Belle Donne $$ **72**
Cantinetta dei Verrazzano $$ **67**
Carmine $$ **79**
Il Cibreino $ **76**
Il Latini $$ **71**
Il Palottino $ **78**

Index

Sostanza $$ **71**
Vivoli $ **78**

★
Acqua al Due $ **78**
Alimentari Orizi $ **71**
Alle Murate (Vineria) $$ **77**
Antico Ristoro di' Cambi $$ **79**
Baccus $ **71**
Bordino $ **80**
Fiaschetteria Torrini $ **67**
Friggitoria Luisa $ **73**
Gelateria dei Neri $ **78**
I Ghibellini $ **77**
Le Mossacce $$ **77**
Nerbone $ **74**
Vini del Chianti $ **68**
Zà Zà $$ **74**

Florence Hotels
$$
Aldini **67**
Annalena **80**
Aprile **71**
Archibusieri **69**
Dante **77**
Hermitage **69**
Il Guelfo Bianco **75**
La Residenza **71**
Mario **73**
Morandi Alla Crocetta **76**
Pendini **67**

$
Albergo Firenze **67**
Anna **73**
Bellettini **73**
Boboli **80**
Brunori **77**
Casci **75**
Colomba **75**
Enza **74**
Fiorino **78**
Giotto **73**
Gould Institute **79**
La Scaletta **80**
Liana **76**
Norma **71**
Ostello della Gioventù **81**
Ostello Santa Monaca **79**
Ottaviani **72**
Scoti **72**
Sorelle Bandini **79**
Universo **72**
Visconti **72**

London

A
Accommodations **85**
Airbus **84**
Airports **84**
Albert Hall, Royal **95**
Alison House Hotel $$ **94**
Artiste Musclé, L' **96**
Astor Museum Inn Hostel $ **101**

B
Baker, Herbert **89**
Ballet, Royal **102**
Bank of England/Museum **89**
Banqueting House **97**
Barbican Centre **103**
Bermondsey (New Caledonian) Market **88**
Bicycles **85**
Blore, Edward **97**
Boyle, Lucinda **103** (bests)
Brass Rubbing Center **98**
Bridge, London **88**
British Museum **101**
Buckingham Palace **97**
Bunjies **102**
Buses **84, 85**
Business hours **85**

C
Cafe in the Crypt ★★$ **98**
Camden Lock Market **100**
Carnaby Street **99**
Central Club Hotel (YWCA) $ **101**
Central Criminal Court **91**
Chambers, William **91**
Changing of the Guard **97**
Chelsea/Sloane Square **94**
Chelsea Physic Garden **94**
City of London Youth Hostel $ **91**
Cleopatra's Needle **92**
Climate **85**
Clock Museum, Guildhall, Worshipful Company of Clockmakers' **89**
Coffee Shop, Tate Gallery ★★$ **94**
Coleman, Victoria **103** (bests)
Consulates **85**
Courtauld Institute Galleries/Somerset House **91**
Covent Garden **102**
Cranks ★★$ **98**
Crypt, Cafe in the **98**

D
Discount tickets **85**
Drinking **85**
Driving **84, 85**
Dungeon, London **88**

E
Economics Halls, London School of **101**
Elizabeth Hotel $$ **94**
Embankment Gardens **92**
Embassies **85**
Emergencies **86**
Exchange, Royal **89**
Exchange, Stock **89**

F
Festival Buffet **92**
Festival Hall, Royal **92**
Film Theatre, National **92**
Fleet Street **91**
Flip **102**
Food for Thought ★$ **102**
Fortnum & Mason **99**
Fountain Restaurant **99**

G
Gatwick Airport **84**
George Inn, The **88**
Getting around London **85**
Getting to London **84**
Gibb, James **98**
Gilbert, Alfred **99**
Globe Centre, The International Shakespeare **88**
Green Park **96**
Guildhall **89**
Guildhall Clock Museum, Worshipful Company of Clockmakers' **89**
Guildhall Library **89**

H
Hamley's **99**
Hampstead Heath **100**
Hampstead Heath Youth Hostel $ **100**
Hard Rock Cafe ★★$$ **96**
Harrods **95**
Hayward Gallery **92**
Heathrow Airport **84**
Holidays, public **86**
Hostel, Astor Museum Inn **101**
Hostel, City of London Youth **91**
Hostel, Hampstead Heath Youth **100**
Hostel, Rotherhithe Youth **88**
Houses of Parliament **93**
Hyde Park **95**

I
Imperial War Museum **93**
Inner Temple **91**
Inns of Court—Middle Temple **91**
International Shakespeare Globe Centre, The **88**
International Students House (ISH) $ **100**

J
Jenkins Hotel $$ **101**
Jones, Horace **91**
Jones, Inigo **97**

K
Keats' House **100**
Kensington Gardens **95**
Kensington Palace **95**

L
L'Artiste Musclé ★★$ **96**
Laundry **86**
Leith's Restaurant **94**
Liberty **99**
London Bridge **88**
London Dungeon **88**
London, Museum of **103**
London National Postal Museum **91**
London School of Economics Halls $ **101**
London Symphony Orchestra **103**
London Tourist Board **84**
London, Tower of **87**
London Zoo **100**

M
Mabledon Court $$ **101**
Madame Tussaud's **100**
Mankind, Museum of **99**
Mansion House **89**
Map **82**
Marble Arch **96**
Market Cafe ★$$ **103**
Mews, Royal **97**
Middle Temple—Inns of Court **91**
MOMI (Museum of the Moving Image) **92**
Money **86**
Monument **88**
Museum of London **103**
Museum of Mankind **99**
Museum of the Moving Image (MOMI) **92**

N
Nash, John **97, 99, 100**
National Film Theatre **92**

214

Index

National Gallery **98**
National Portrait Gallery **98**
National Postal Museum, London **91**
National Theatre, Royal **92**
Natural History Museum **94**
New Caledonian (Bermondsey) Market **88**

O
Old Bailey **91**
Olde Cheshire Cheese, Ye **91**
Opera House, Royal **102**
Oxford Street **96**

P
Palace of Westminster **93**
Parliament, Houses of **93**
Parliament Square **93**
Personal safety **86**
Petticoat Lane **103**
Piccadilly Circus **99**
Piccadilly Market **99**
Portobello Road Market **96**
Postal Museum, London National **91**
Postal services **86**
Prince Charles Cinema **99**
Publications **86**
Public holidays **86**
Public Record Office Museum **91**
Public rest rooms **86**
Pugin, Augustus **93**

Q
Queen's Gallery **97**

R
Regent's Park **100**
Regent Street **99**
Restaurants **87**
Rest rooms, public **86**
Robertson, Elaine **103** (bests)
Rock and Sole Plaice ★★$ **102**
Rotherhithe Youth Hostel $ **88**
Royal Albert Hall **95**
Royal Ballet **102**
Royal Exchange **89**
Royal Festival Hall **92**
Royal Mews **97**
Royal National Theatre **92**
Royal Opera House **102**
Royal Shakespeare Company **103**

S
Safety, personal **86**
St. James's Park **97**
St. James's, Piccadilly **99**
St. Margaret's Hotel $$ **102**
St. Martin-in-the-Fields **98**
St. Paul's Cathedral **89**
Sandringham $$ **100**
Science Museum **95**
Shakespeare Company, Royal **103**
Shepherd Market **96**
Shopping **87**
Sloane Square/Chelsea **94**
Smirke, Robert **101**
Smoking **87**
Soane, John **89**
Somerset House/Courtauld Institute Galleries **91**
South Bank Brasserie ★★★$$ **93**
South Bank Centre **92**
Southwark Cathedral **88**
Stock Exchange **89**
Stockpot, The **98**

Street plan **87**
Studio Six ★★$ **93**
Subway (Underground) **84, 85**
Symphony Orchestra, London **103**

T
Tate Gallery **94**
Tate Gallery, Coffee Shop **94**
Tate Gallery Shop **94**
Taxes **87**
Taxis **85**
Tea House, The **102**
Telephones **87**
Temple Bar Monument and The Temple **91**
Theatre Museum **95**
The George Inn $ **88**
The International Shakespeare Globe Centre **88**
The Stockpot ★★$ **98**
The Tea House **102**
The Temple, Temple Bar Monument and **91**
The Wren Wholefood Vegetarian Cafe ★$ **99**
Tickets, discount **85**
Tipping **87**
Tourist Board, London **84**
Tours **85**
Tower Bridge/Museum **87**
Tower of London **87**
Trafalgar Square **97**
Trains **84**
Transportation, local **85**

U
Underground **84, 85**

V
Victoria and Albert Museum **95**
Victoria Coach Station **84**
Victoria Embankment **91**
Visas **87**
Visitors' information **87**

W
Walking **85**
Wallace Collection **99**
War Museum, Imperial **93**
Webb, Aston **97**
Westminster Abbey **93**
Westminster Bridge **93**
Westminster, Palace of **93**
Whitehall **91**
Wig and Pen Club **91**
Windermere $$ **94**
Worshipful Company of Clockmakers' Guildhall Clock Museum **89**
Wren, Christopher **89, 91, 98, 99**
Wren Wholefood Vegetarian Cafe, The **99**

Y
Ye Olde Cheshire Cheese ★★$$ **91**
Youth Hostel, City of London **91**
Youth Hostel, Hampstead Heath **100**
Youth Hostel, Rotherhithe **88**
YWCA (Central Club Hotel) **101**

Z
Zoo, London **100**

London Restaurants

★★★
South Bank Brasserie $$ **93**

★★
Cafe in the Crypt $ **98**
Coffee Shop, Tate Gallery $ **94**
Cranks $ **98**
Hard Rock Cafe $$ **96**
L'Artiste Musclé $ **96**
Rock and Sole Plaice $ **102**
Studio Six $ **93**
The Stockpot $ **98**
Ye Olde Cheshire Cheese $$ **91**

★
Food for Thought ★$ **102**
Market Cafe ★$$ **103**
The Wren Wholefood Vegetarian Cafe ★$ **99**

London Hotels

$$
Alison House Hotel **94**
Elizabeth Hotel **94**
Jenkins Hotel **101**
Mabledon Court **101**
St. Margaret's Hotel **102**
Sandringham **100**
Windermere **94**

$
Astor Museum Inn Hostel **101**
Central Club Hotel (YWCA) **101**
City of London Youth Hostel **91**
Hampstead Heath Youth Hostel **100**
International Students House (ISH) **100**
London School of Economics Halls **101**
Rotherhithe Youth Hostel **88**

Paris

A
Abadie, Paul **120**
Accommodations **108**
Accueil des Jeunes en France (AJF), youth hostels **108**
Addresses **107**
Airports **106**
A l'Angélus **120**
Aliani, Michel **131** (bests)
A l'Impasse ★★★$$ **112**
American Center **121**
Angelina ★★$$ **117**
Arc de Triomphe, L' **119**
Arc du Carrousel, L' **116**
Arènes de Lutèce (Roman Arena) **122**
Art Moderne, Musée d' **113**
Au Limonaire ★★$ **111**
Au Panetier ★$ **116**
Aux Deux Magots ★★★$$ **127**
Aux Produits du Sud-Ouest ★★$$ **131**
Avenir, Hôtel de l' **126**

B
Balajo **111**
Baptiste, Le **122**
Bastille, Opéra **111**
Bastille, Place de la **111**
Beaux-Arts, Ecole des **128**
Beaux-Arts, Restaurant des **128**
Bellevue et Charlot d'Or $$ **115**
B.E.P. of the Ecole Ferrandi, Restaurant **126**
Berthillon ★★$ **110**
Bibliothèque Nationale (National Library) **117**

215

Index

Bicycles **107**
Bistro de la Sorbonne ★$ **123**
Bistro Henri ★★$ **127**
Bolée, La **125**
Boulangerie Beauvallet Julien **122**
Boutique à Sandwiches, La **119**
Brasserie Balzar ★★$$ **123**
Brasserie d'Ile St-Louis ★★$$ **110**
Brasserie Mouffetard ★★$ **122**
Briochères de Saint-Merry, Les **113**
Buci Market **125**
Buses **107**
Business hours **108**
Buttes-Chaumont, Parc des **121**

C

Café de Flore ★★★$$ **127**
Café de la Mairie ★★$ **127**
Cafe de la Mosquée ★★$ **121**
Cafe de la Paix ★★$$ **120**
Cafe de Mars ★★$ **130**
Cafe Parisien ★★★$ **126**
Cafe San José ★$ **117**
Carrousel du Louvre **116**
Catacombs **131**
Caveau de la Huchette, Le **124**
Central, Hôtel le **122**
Centre Georges Pompidou/Centre National d'Art et Culture **113**
Chai de l'Abbaye, Le **125**
Champ-de-Mars, Parc du **130**
Champs-Elysées, Drugstore des **119**
Charles-Dullin, Résidence **120**
Chez Georges **127**
Chez Janou ★★$$ **112**
Chez Paul ★★$$ **111**
Chicago Pizza Pie Factory ★$ **119**
China Club ★★$$ **111**
Cimetière de Montmartre **120**
Cimetière du Père-Lachaise **121**
Cinéma, Salle de **113**
Cité des Sciences et de l'Industrie **121**
City Hall (Hôtel-de-Ville) **113**
Climate **108**
Cluny, Hôtel de **123**
Coffee Parisien ★$ **128**
Conciergerie, La **109**
Concorde, Place de la **118**
Consulates **108**
Coupole, La **126**
Crêperie de St-Malo ★★$ **131**

D

Dame Tartine ★★$ **113**
Davioud, Gabriel **125**
Delacroix, Eugène, Musée **127**
Delhy's Hôtel $ **125**
Delorme, Philibert **113**
Deportation Memorial (Mémorial de la Déportation) **110**
Discount tickets **108**
Drinking **108**
Driving **107**
Drugstore des Champs-Elysées **119**
du Cerceau, Androuet **109**
Duthilleul et Minart **115**

E

Ecole des Beaux-Arts (School of Fine Arts) **128**
Ecole Militaire (Military School) **130**
Eiffel, Gustave **130**
Eiffel Tower (Tour Eiffel) **130**
Elysée, Palais de l' **118**

Embassies **108**
Emergencies **108**
Ermitage Hôtel, L' **120**
Esmeralda $$ **124**
Eté en Pente Douce, L' **120**

F

Fauvette, La **116**
Flore, Café de **127**
Floridor, Hôtel **131**
Fontaine St-Michel (Fountain of St. Michael) **125**
404 ★★★$$ **115**
Fous de l'Ile, Les **111**
Furstemberg, Place de **127**

G

Galerie National du Jeu de Paume **118**
Garnier, Charles **119**
Gehry, Frank **121**
Géode, La **121**
Getting around Paris **107**
Getting to Paris **106**
Grand Hôtel Jeanne d'Arc $ **112**
Grand Hôtel Mahler $$ **112**
Grand Palais **118**
Guimard, Hector **110**, **125**

H

Hardouin-Marsart, Jules **117**
Haussmann, Baron **119**
Henri, Bistro **127**
Henri IV, Hôtel **109**
Henri IV, Taverne **109**
Holidays, public **109**
Hôtel de Cluny, Museum, and Palais des Thermes (Roman Baths) **123**
Hôtel de l'Avenir $$ **126**
Hôtel de Marigny $$ **118**
Hôtel de Nesle $ **125**
Hôtel des Invalides **128**
Hôtel-de-Ville **113**
Hôtel du Lion d'Or $ **117**
Hôtel Floridor $ **131**
Hôtel Henri IV $ **109**
Hôtel le Central $ **122**
Hôtel Malar $ **130**
Hôtel Médicis $ **124**
Hôtel Opal $$ **118**
Hôtel St-Louis Marais $$ **111**
Hôtel St-Merri $$ **113**
Huchette, Rue de la **124**
Hune, La **127**

I

Incroyable Restaurant, L' **117**
Invalides, Hôtel des **128**

J

Jardin des Plantes **122**
Jardin des Tuileries (Tuileries Gardens) **118**
Jardin du Luxembourg (Luxembourg Gardens) **126**
Jeanne d'Arc, Grand Hôtel **112**
Jeu de Paume, Galerie National du **118**
Jo Goldenberg ★★$$ **113**

K

Korean Barbecue ★$$ **127**
Kurde Dilan ★★$ **115**

L

La Bolée ★$ **125**

La Boutique à Sandwiches ★★$$ **119**
Labrouste, Henri **117**
La Conciergerie **109**
La Coupole ★★$$$ **126**
Ladurée ★★★$ **118**
La Fauvette ★$ **116**
La Géode **121**
La Hune **127**
La Madeleine **118**
La Nioullaville ★★★$$ **121**
La Palette ★★$ **125**
La Place **119**
L'Arc de Triomphe/Place Charles-de-Gaulle **119**
L'Arc du Carrousel **116**
La Tartine ★★★$ **113**
Laundry **108**
Le Baptiste ★$ **122**
Le Caveau de la Huchette **124**
Le Chai de l'Abbaye ★★$$ **125**
Ledoux, Claude-Nicholas **119**
Le Loir dans la Théière ★★$ **112**
Le Mouton à Cinq Pattes **125**
Le Palet ★★$$ **127**
Le Petit St-Benoît ★★$ **127**
Le Petit Vatel ★★$ **127**
Le Rallye ★★$ **122**
Le Réveil du Xe ★★$ **121**
L'Ermitage Hôtel $$ **120**
Le Roi du Pot-au-Feu ★★$$ **118**
Le Roupeyrac ★$ **128**
Les Briochères de Saint-Merry ★$ **113**
Les Fous de l'Ile ★★★$ **111**
L'Eté en Pente Douce ★★$ **120**
Le Troumilou ★$ **113**
Le Val d'Or ★★★$ **119**
Lina's ★★$ **116**
L'Incroyable Restaurant ★★$ **117**
Lion d'Or, Hôtel du **117**
Loir dans la Théière, Le **112**
Louis-Lépine, Place **110**
Louvre, Carrousel du **116**
Louvre, Musée du **116**
Luxembourg Gardens (Jardin du Luxembourg) **126**
Luxor, Obelisk of **118**

M

Ma Bourgogne ★★$$ **112**
Macary, Michel **116**
Madeleine, La **118**
Mahler, Grand Hôtel **112**
Mairie, Café de la **127**
Malar, Hôtel **130**
Map **104**
Marais Plus **112**
Marigny, Hôtel de **118**
Marmottan, Musée **130**
Mars, Cafe de **130**
Maubert Market, Place **122**
Médicis, Hôtel **124**
Mémorial de la Déportation (Deportation Memorial) **110**
Metezeau, Clément **111**
Métro (subway) **107**
Military School (Ecole Militaire) **130**
Monceau, Parc de **119**
Money **108**
Montorgueil, Rue **115**
Montreuil, Pierre de **110**
Mosquée, Cafe de la **121**
Mosquée de Paris (Paris Mosque) **121**
Mouffetard, Rue **122**

216

Index

Moulin de la Galette **120**
Mouton à Cinq Pattes, Le **125**
Musée Carnavalet **112**
Musée d'Art Moderne **113**
Musée de L'Orangerie **118**
Musée d'Orsay **128**
Musée du Louvre **116**
Musée Eugène Delacroix **127**
Musée Marmottan **130**
Musée Picasso **112**
Musée Rodin **128**
Musée Victor Hugo **111**
Musée National d'Historie Naturelle (Museum of Natural History) **122**

N

National Library (Bibliothèque Nationale) **117**
Nesle, Hôtel de **125**
Nioullaville, La **121**
Nos Ancêtres les Gaulois ★$$ **110**
Notre-Dame **110**

O

Obelisk of Luxor **118**
Opal, Hôtel **118**
Opéra Bastille **111**
Opéra Garnier (Paris Opéra) **119**
Orangerie, L' **118**
Orly Airport **106**
Orsay, Musée d' **128**

P

Paix, Cafe de la **120**
Palais de l'Elysée **118**
Palais des Thermes (Roman Baths) **123**
Palais du Luxembourg **126**
Palais Royal **117**
Palet, Le **117**
Palette, La **125**
Panthéon **122**
Parc de Monceau **119**
Parc des Buttes-Chaumont **121**
Parc du Champ-de-Mars **130**
Parisien, Cafe **126**
Paris Mosque (Mosquée de Paris) **121**
Paris Opéra (Opéra Garnier) **119**
Passage Brady **121**
Pei, I.M. **116**
Perraudin ★★★$ **123**
Perrault, Dominique **117**
Personal safety **108**
Petit Palais **118**
Petit St-Benoît, Le **127**
Petit Vatel, Le **127**
Piano, Renzo **113**
Picasso, Musée **112**
Pingusson, G.H. **110**
Place Charles-de-Gaulle/L'Arc de Triomphe **119**
Place de Furstemberg **127**
Place de la Bastille **111**
Place de la Concorde **118**
Place des Vosges **111**
Place, La **119**
Place Louis-Lépine **110**
Place Maubert Market **122**
Place Vendôme **117**
Plantes, Jardin des **122**
Polidor ★★$ **125**
Pompidou Center (Centre Georges Pompidou/Centre National d'Art et Culture) **113**
Pont des Arts **128**
Pont-Neuf **109**
Porte de la Villette **121**
Postal services **109**
Prevost, Hélène **131** (bests)
Publications **109**
Public holidays **109**
Public rest rooms **109**

R

Rallye, Le **122**
Résidence Charles-Dullin $$ **120**
Restaurant B.E.P. of the Ecole Ferrandi ★★$$ **126**
Restaurant des Beaux-Arts ★★$ **128**
Restaurants **109**
Restauration Viennoise ★★$ **125**
Rest rooms, public **109**
Réveil du Xe, Le **121**
Rodin, Musée **128**
Rogers, Richard **113**
Roi du Pot-au-Feu, Le **118**
Roissy-Charles de Gaulle Airport **106**
Roman Arena (Arènes de Lutèce) **122**
Roman Baths (Palais des Thermes) **123**
Rosiers, Rue des **112**
Roupeyrac, Le **128**
Royal, Palais **117**
Rue de la Huchette **124**
Rue des Rosiers **112**
Rue Montorgueil **115**
Rue Mouffetard **122**

S

Sacré-Coeur **120**
Safety, personal **108**
St-Benoît, Le Petit **127**
Ste-Chapelle **110**
St-Etienne-du-Mont **123**
St-Eustache **116**
St-Germain-des-Prés **127**
St-Jacques, Tour **113**
St-Julien-le-Pauvre **124**
St-Louis Marais, Hôtel **111**
St-Merri, Hôtel **113**
St-Pierre-de-Montmartre **120**
St-Séverin **124**
St-Sulpice **126**
Salle de Cinéma **113**
San José, Cafe **117**
School of Fine Arts (Ecole des Beaux-Arts) **128**
Shakespeare and Company **124**
Smith and Son, W.H. **118**
Smoking **109**
Sorbonne **123**
Sorbonne, Bistro de la **123**
Street plan **109**
Subway (Métro) **107**

T

Tartine, La **113**
Tashi Delek ★★$ **123**
Taverne Henri IV ★★$ **109**
Taxes **109**
Taxis **107**
Telephones **109**
Than ★★$$ **128**
Thanksgiving ★$ **111**
Tickets, discount **108**
Tim Hôtel $$ **120**
Tipping **109**
Tour Eiffel (Eiffel Tower) **130**
Tours **107**
Tour St-Jacques **113**
Trains **107**
Transportation, local **107**
Troumilou, Le **113**
Tuileries Gardens (Jardin des Tuileries) **118**

V

Val d'Or, Le **119**
Vendôme, Place **117**
Victor Hugo, Musée **111**
Viennoise, Restauration **125**
Viollet-le-Duc, Eugène-Emmanuel **110**
Visas **109**
Visitors' Information Centers **109**
Vosges, Place des **111**

W

Walking **108**
Wanouchka ★$$ **120**
Whiskey-a-Gogo **125**
W.H. Smith and Son **118**

Y

Youth hostels, Accueil des Jeunes en France (AJF) **108**

Paris Restaurants

★★★
A l'Impasse $$ **112**
Aux Deux Magots $$ **127**
Café de Flore $$ **127**
Cafe Parisien $ **126**
404 $$ **115**
Ladurée $ **118**
La Nioullaville $$ **121**
La Tartine $ **113**
Les Fous de l'Ile $ **111**
Le Val d'Or $ **119**
Perraudin $ **123**

★★
Angelina $$ **117**
Au Limonaire $ **111**
Aux Produits du Sud-Ouest $$ **131**
Berthillon $ **110**
Bistro Henri $ **127**
Brasserie Balzar $$ **123**
Brasserie d'Ile St-Louis $$ **110**
Brasserie Mouffetard $$ **122**
Café de la Mairie $ **127**
Cafe de la Mosquée $ **121**
Cafe de la Paix $$ **120**
Cafe de Mars $$ **130**
Chez Janou $$ **112**
Chez Paul $$ **111**
China Club $$ **111**
Crêperie de St-Malo $ **131**
Dame Tartine $ **113**
Jo Goldenberg $$ **113**
Kurde Dilan $ **115**
La Boutique à Sandwiches $$ **119**
La Coupole $$$ **126**
La Palette $ **125**
Le Chai de l'Abbaye $$ **125**
Le Loir dans la Théière $ **112**
Le Palet $$ **117**
Le Petit St-Benoît $ **127**
Le Petit Vatel $ **127**
Le Rallye $ **122**
Le Réveil du Xe $ **121**
Le Roi du Pot-au-Feu $$ **118**
L'Eté en Pente Douce $ **120**
Lina's $ **116**
L'Incroyable Restaurant $ **117**

217

Index

Ma Bourgogne $$ **112**
Polidor $ **125**
Restaurant B.E.P. of the Ecole Ferrandi $$ **126**
Restaurant des Beaux-Arts $ **128**
Restauration Viennoise $ **125**
Tashi Delek $ **123**
Taverne Henri IV $ **109**
Than $$ **128**

★

Au Panetier $ **116**
Bistro de la Sorbonne $ **123**
Cafe San José $ **117**
Chicago Pizza Pie Factory $ **119**
Coffee Parisien $ **128**
Korean Barbecue $$ **127**
La Bolée $ **125**
La Fauvette $ **116**
Le Baptiste $ **122**
Le Roupeyrac $ **128**
Les Briochères de Saint-Merry $ **113**
Le Troumilou $ **113**
Nos Ancêtres les Gaulois $$ **110**
Thanksgiving $ **111**
Wanouchka $$ **120**

Paris Hotels
$$

Bellevue et Charlot d'Or **115**
Esmeralda **124**
Grand Hôtel Mahler **112**
Hôtel de l'Avenir **126**
Hôtel de Marigny **118**
Hôtel Opal **118**
Hôtel St-Louis Marais **111**
Hôtel St-Merri **113**
L'Ermitage Hôtel **120**
Résidence Charles-Dullin **120**
Tim Hôtel **120**

$

Delhy's Hôtel **125**
Grand Hôtel Jeanne d'Arc **112**
Hôtel de Nesle **125**
Hôtel du Lion d'Or **117**
Hôtel Floridor **131**
Hôtel Henri IV **109**
Hôtel le Central **122**
Hôtel Malar **130**
Hôtel Médicis **124**

Prague

A
Accommodations **135**
AghaRTA Jazz Centrum **138**
Airport **134**
Antonin Dvorak Museum (Muzeum Antonína Dvořáka) **137**
Apollon, Hotel **138**
Arres, Matthias **148**
Astronomical Clock (Orloj) **142**
A Studio Rubín **145**

B
Balšánek, Antonín **140**
Bazilika sv. Jiří (St. George's Basilica) **148**
Belveder (Royal Summer Palace of Belvedere) **149**
Bendlmayer, Bedřich **138**
Betlémská Kaple (Bethlehem Chapel) **143**

Bicycles **134**
Buses **134**
Business hours **135**
Bývalá obřadní sín (Former Ceremonial Hall) **144**

C
Cafe, Hotel Evropa **138**
Carolinum (Karolinum) **141**
Cathedral of the Virgin Mary before Tyn (Chrám Matky Boží před Týnem) **142**
Celetná ulice (Celetná Street) **141**
Central European Gallery (Středoevropská Galerie) **142**
Chapel of the Holy Cross (Kaple sv.Kříže) **148**
Charles Bridge (Karlův most) **145**
Charles Square (Karlovo náměstí) **137**
Chrám Matky Boží před Týnem (Cathedral of the Virgin Mary before Tyn) **142**
Chrám sv. Víta (St. Vitus Cathedral) **148**
Church of St. James (Kostel sv. Jakuba) **141**
Church of St. Mary the Victorious (Kostel Panny Marie Vítězné) **146**
Clementinum (Klementinum) **142**
Climate **135**
Consulates **135**
Country Life **142**

D
Dientzenhofer, Kilian Ignaz **137, 142, 145, 147**
Dientzenhofer, Kristof **145, 147**
Discount tickets **136**
Divadlo Na zábradlí (Theater on the Balustrade) **143**
Drinking **136**
Driving **135**
Dryák, Alois **138**
Dům U kamenného zvonu (Stone Bell House) **142**
Dům U Minuty (House at the Minute) **142**
Dvorak Museum (Muzeum Antonína Dvořáka) **137**
Dvořákova sín (Dvorak Hall) **143**

E
Embassies **135**
Emergencies **136**
Estates Theater (Stavovské divadlo) **141**
Estec Hostel $ **147**

F
Flemrová, Kateřina **149** (bests)
Former Ceremonial Hall (Bývalá obřadní sín) **144**
FX Cafe ★★★$ **137**

G
Garni Jarov, Hotel **138**
Garni, Vila **138**
Getting around Prague **134**
Getting to Prague **134**
Globe Bookstore and Coffee House ★★★$ **149**
Gočár, Josef **141**
Golden Lane (Zlatá ulička) **149**
Granát Turnov **140**

H
High Synagogue (Vysoká synagoga) **144**
Holidays, public **136**
Hospůdka Václavka ★★$ **138**
Hostel, Estec **147**
Hostel, Island **146**
Hostel, Travellers' **139**
Hotel Apollon $$ **138**
Hotel Evropa Cafe ★$$ **138**
Hotel Garni Jarov $$ **138**
House at the Minute (Dům U Minuty) **142**
House of Artists (Rudolfinum) **143**
House of the Black Mother of God (U černé Matky Boží) **141**

I
Island Hostel $ **146**

J
Jáma ★★$ **138**
Jan Hus Memorial **142**
Jiřský klášter (St. George's Convent) **149**
Jízdárna Pražského Hradu (Prague Castle Riding School) **149**
Jo's Bar ★★★$ **145**

K
Kaple sv. Kříže (Chapel of the Holy Cross) **148**
Karlovo náměstí (Charles Square) **137**
Karlův most (Charles Bridge) **145**
Karolinum (Carolinum) **141**
Kavárna Velryba ★★★$ **139**
Kinsky Palace (Palác Kinských) **142**
Klášter sv. Anežky (St. Agnes Convent) **144**
Klementinum (Clementinum) **142**
Kmotra ★★★$ **139**
Konvikt ★★★$ **143**
Kostel Panny Marie Vítězné (Church of St. Mary the Victorious) **146**
Kostel sv. Jakuba (Church of St. James) **141**
Kostel sv. Mikuláše (St. Nikolas Church) **145**
Kotva **140**

L
Largo, Anselm **142**
Laterna Magika **139**
Laundry **136**
Letná Park **149**
Loreta **147**

M
Madona, Pension **137**
Maiselova synagoga (Maisel Synagogue) **145**
Malostranská beseda **145**
Map **132**
Matyášova brána (Matthias Gate) **148**
Memorial to W.A. Mozart/Villa Bertramka **146**
Metro (subway) **135**
Military History Museum (Vojenské historické muzeum) **148**
Mocker, Josef **137**
Money **136**
Monica Hotel $$ **137**
Moser Glass **140**
Municipal House (Obecní dům) **140**
Museum of Decorative Arts (Uměleckoprůmyslové muzeum) **143**

218

Index

Muzeum Antonína Dvořáka (Antonin Dvorak Museum) **137**

N
Na Kampě **145**
Národní divadlo (National Theater) **139**
Národní muzeum (National Museum) **138**
Nerudova ulice (Neruda Street) **147**
Nová scéna (New Theater) **139**

O
Oáza, Sport Hotel **137**
Obecní dům (Municipal House) **140**
Old Jewish Cemetery (Starý židovský hřbitov) **143**
Old-New Synagogue (Staranová synagogue) **144**
Old Town Hall (Staroměstská radnice) **142**
Old Town Square (Staroměstské náměstí) **141**
Orloj (Astronomical Clock) **142**
Orsi, Giovanni B. **147**

P
Palác Kinských (Kinsky Palace) **142**
Parléř, Petr **142, 145, 148**
Pension Madona $$ **137**
Personal safety **136**
Petřín Hill **146**
Pieronni, Giovanni Battista **149**
Pinkasova synagoga (Pinkas Synagogue) **144**
Polívka, Osvald **140**
Postal services **136**
Prague Castle (Pražský Hrad) **148**
Prague Castle Riding School (Jízdárna Pražského Hradu) **149**
Prašná brána (Powder Tower) **140**
Prašná věž Mihulka (Powder Tower) **148**
Pražský dům fotografie U zlaté ovce (Prague House of Photography at the Golden Sheep) **142**
Pražský Hrad (Prague Castle) **148**
Publications **136**
Public holidays **136**
Public rest rooms **136**

R
Radost/FX **137**
Red Hot and Blues ★★★$ **141**
Reduta Jazz Club **139**
Reid, Benedict **148**
Restaurants **136**
Rest rooms, public **136**
Rock Club Bunkr **141**
Roxy **140**
Royal Palace (Starý královský palác) **148**
Royal Summer Palace of Belvedere (Belveder) **149**
Rudolfinum (House of Artists) **143**
Ruzyně Airport **134**

S
Safety, personal **136**
St. Agnes Convent (Klášter sv. Anežky) **144**
St. George's Basilica (Bazilika sv. Jiří) **148**
St. George's Convent (Jiřský klášter) **149**
St. Mary the Victorius, Church of **146**
St. Nikolas Church (Kostel sv. Mikuláše) **145**
St. Vitus Cathedral (Chrám sv. Víta) **148**
Schwarzenberský palác (Schwartzenberg Palace) **148**
Shopping **136**
Shulz, Josef **138, 143**
Smetanova síň (Smetana Hall) **140**
Smoking **136**
Socha sv. Václava (Statue of St. Wenceslas) **138**
Sport Hotel Oáza $$ **137**
Staroměstská radnice (Old Town Hall) **142**
Staroměstské náměstí (Old Town Square) **141**
Staronová synagoga (Old-New Synagogue) **144**
Starý židovský hřbitov (Old Jewish Cemetery) **143**
Starzy královský palác (Royal Palace) **148**
Statue of St. Wenceslas (Socha sv. Václava) **138**
Stavovské divadlo (Estates Theater) **141**
Šternberský palác (Sternberg Palace) **148**
Stone Bell House (Dům U kamenného zvonu) **142**
Strahovský klášter (Strahov Monastery) **147**
Středoevropská Galerie (Central European Gallery) **142**
Street plan **136**
Studio Gag Borise Hybnerna **139**
Subway (metro) **135**

T
Taxes **136**
Taxis **135**
Telephones **136**
Theater on the Balustrade (Divadlo Na zábradlí) **143**
Tickets, discount **136**
Tipping **136**
Tours **135**
Trains **134**
Trams **135**
Transportation, local **134**
Travellers' Hostel $ **139**

U
U černého vola ★★$ **147**
U černé Matky Boží (House of the Black Mother of God) **141**
U Fleků ★$ **139**
U Kalicha ★$$ **137**
U medvídků ★★$$ **140**
Uměleckoprůmyslové muzeum (Museum of Decorative Arts) **143**
Unitas Le Prison $$ **143**
U zeleného čaje ★★★$ **147**

V
Václavské náměstí (Wenceslas Square) **138**
Valdštejnská jízdárna (Wallenstein Riding Academy) **149**
Valdštejnské zahrady (Wallenstein Gardens) **149**
Vila Garni $$ **138**
Villa Bertramka/Memorial to W.A. Mozart **146**
Vinárna u Hynků ★★★$ **141**
Vinárna u maltézských rytířů ★★★★$$ **145**
Virgin Mary before Tyn, Cathedral of the **142**
Visas **136**
Visitors' Information Centers **136**
Vojenské historické muzeum (Military History Museum) **148**
Vyšehrad Fortress **137**
Vysoká synagoga (High Synagogue) **144**

W
Walking **135**
Wallenstein Gardens (Valdštejnské zahrady) **149**
Wallenstein Riding Academy (Valdštejnská jízdárna) **149**
Wenceslas Square (Václavské náměstí) **138**

Z
Zítek, Josef **139, 143**
Zlatá ulička (Golden Lane) **149**

Prague Restaurants

★★★★
Vinárna u maltézských rytířů $$ **145**

★★★
FX Cafe $ **137**
Globe Bookstore and Coffee House $
Jo's Bar $ **145**
Kavárna Velryba $ **139**
Kmotra $ **139**
Konvikt $ **143**
Red Hot and Blues $ **141**
U zeleného čaje $ **147**
Vinárna u Hynků $ **141**

★★
Hospůdka Václavka $ **138**
Jáma $ **138**
U černého vola $ **147**
U medvídků $$ **140**

★
Hotel Evropa Cafe $$ **138**
U Fleků $ **139**
U Kalicha $$ **137**

Prague Hotels

$$
Hotel Apollon **138**
Hotel Garni Jarov **138**
Monica Hotel **137**
Pension Madona **137**
Sport Hotel Oáza **137**
Unitas Le Prison **143**
Vila Garni **138**

$
Estec Hostel **147**
Island Hostel **146**
Travellers' Hostel **139**

Rome

A
Abruzzi, Albergo **161**
Accommodations **153**
Ai Monasteri **164**
Airports **152**

Index

A

Ai Tre Tartufi ★★★$$ **164**
Albergo Abruzzi $ **161**
Albergo della Luneta $ **165**
Albergo del Sole $ **165**
Albergo Pomezia $ **166**
Alemagna ★$ **161**
Alimandi, Hotel **156**
Al Piedone ★$ **163**
Al Sogno **164**
Amannati **157**
Appian Way, The **171**
Ara Pacis Augustae and Mausoleo di Augusto (Augustus's Altar of Peace and Mausoleum) **158**
Area Sacra di Largo Argentina **163**
Arenula, Hotel **163**
Artusiana, L' **167**
Augustus's Altar of Peace and Mausoleum (Ara Pacis Augustae and Mausoleo di Augusto) **158**

B

Barberini, Piazza **159**
Bar Sant'Eustachio ★★$ **164**
Basilica di San Giovanni in Laterano (Basilica of St. John Lateran) **170**
Basilica di Santa Maria Maggiore (Basilica of St. Mary Major) **170**
Basilica San Pietro (St. Peter's Basilica) **156**
Baths of Diocletian (Terme di Diocleziano) **169**
Bernini, Gian Lorenzo **155, 156, 157, 159, 163, 164**
Borghese, Villa **157**
Borromini, Francesco **164**
Brotsky, Residenza **157**
Brown, Nancy **171** (bests)
Buca di Ripetta, La **158**
Buses **152**
Business hours **153**

C

Caffè Rosati ★★$$ **157**
Caffè Tazza d'Oro **161**
Campo dei Fiori **165**
Campo dei Fiori $$ **165**
Capitoline Hill (Piazza del Campidoglio) **168**
Capitoline Museums (Musei Capitolini) **168**
Casa Religiosa di Santa Brigida $$ **166**
Casina di Keats (Keats and Shelley Memorial Museum) **159**
Castel Sant'Angelo **157**
Catacombs **171**
Celio, Hotel **170**
Chiesa di San Clemente **170**
Chiesa di Santa Maria sopra Minerva (Church of St. Mary over Minerva) **164**
Ciampino Airport **152**
Cinema Pasquino **166**
Città del Vaticano (Vatican City) **155**
Climate **153**
COIN **171**
Cola di Rienzo, Via **157**
Colosseo (Colosseum) **169**
Confetteria Moriondo & Gariglio **167**
Consulates **153**
Corner Bookshop **166**
Cornici e Stampe (Frames and Prints) **164**
Coronet Hotel $ **161**
Corso, Via del **160**

D

Da Lucia ★★$ **167**
Delfino, Il **163**
della Porta, Giacomo **166**
Discount tickets **153**
Dito e la Luna, Il **170**
Doge, Hotel **159**
Drinking **153**
Driving **152, 153**

E

Ebraico, Museo **187**
Embassies **153**
Emergencies **153**
Enoteca Cavour 313 *$ **169**
Erdarelli, Pensione **159**
Esty, Pensione **167**
Etruscan Museum (Museo Etrusco) **157**

F

Fabris **161**
Fant, Maureen **171** (bests)
Farnese, Hostaria **165**
Farnese Palace (Palazzo Farnese) **166**
Fassi Palazzo del Freddo **170**
Fellini **160**
Filettaro Santa Barbara ★★$ **166**
Filippi, Francesco **171** (bests)
Fiorella, Pensione **157**
Fiumicino Airport **152**
Fontana di Trevi (Trevi Fountain) **160**
Fori Imperiali (Imperial Forums) **167**
Fornaio, Il **165**
Forno A. Bagagli **167**
Foro Italico, Ostello del **171**
Foro Romano (Roman Forum) **168**
Frames and Prints (Cornici e Stampe) **164**
Franchi **157**
Franciscan Sisters of the Atonement (Suore Francescane dell'Antonement) **157**
Fraterna Domus $ **161**

G

Galerie e Musei Vaticani (Vatican Galleries and Museums) **156**
Galleria, La **166**
Getting around Rome **152**
Getting to Rome **152**
Ghetto, Il **163**
Giolitti ★$ **161**
Gran Caffè-Europeo ★★$ **161**
Grappolo d'Oro ★$$ **165**

H

Holidays, public **154**
Hostaria da Nerone ★★$$ **170**
Hostaria Farnese ★$$ **165**
Hotel Alimandi $ **156**
Hotel Arenula $ **163**
Hotel Celio $$ **170**
Hotel Doge $$ **159**
Hotel Marcus $ **161**
Hotel Margutta $ **158**
Hotel Navona $ **163**
Hotel Pensione Merano $ **159**
Hotel Pensione Suisse $ **159**
Hotel Perugia $ **169**
Hotel Piccolo $ **166**
Hotel Romano $ **169**
Hotel Smeraldo $ **166**

I

Il Delfino ★$ **163**
Il Dito e la Luna ★★$$ **170**
Il Fornaio **165**
Il Ghetto **163**
Imperial Forums (Fori Imperiali) **167**

J

Jewish Museum **163**

K

Keats and Shelley Memorial Museum (Casina di Keats) **159**

L

Laboratorio Pietro Simonelli **166**
La Buca di Ripetta ★★★$$ **158**
La Galleria **166**
La Moretta ★$ **165**
La Rampa ★★$$ **159**
La Rinascente **160**
L'Artusiana ★★$$ **167**
Laundry **154**
Leonardo da Vinci International Airport **152**
Leone Limentani **163**
Luneta, Albergo della **165**

M

Maderno, Carlo **155**
Manara, Pensione **167**
M&M Volpetti ★★$ **164**
Map **150**
Marcus, Hotel **161**
Margutta, Hotel **158**
Merano, Hotel Pensione **159**
Michelangelo **156, 157, 166, 168, 169**
Mimosa, Pensione **164**
Money **154**
Moretta, La **165**
Musei Capitolini (Capitoline Museums) **168**
Museo Etrusco (Etruscan Museum) **157**
Museo Nazionale di Villa Giulia (Villa Giulia National Museum) **157**
Museo Nazionale Romano (National Museum of Rome) **169**

N

National Museum of Rome (Museo Nazionale Romano) **169**
Navona, Hotel **163**
Navona, Piazza **164**
Nerone, Hostaria da **170**

O

Ostello del Foro Italico $ **171**
Otello alla Concordia ★★$$ **158**
Ottaviano, Via **157**

P

Palatino (Palatine Hill) **168**
Palazzo Farnese **166**
Pantheon **164**
Parlamento, Pensione **160**
Pascucci **163**
Pasticceria d'Angelo ★$ **158**
Pensione Erdarelli $$ **159**
Pensione Esty $ **167**
Pensione Fiorella $ **157**
Pensione Manara $ **167**
Pensione Mimosa $ **164**
Pensione Parlamento $ **160**
Pensione Primavera $ **165**

220

Index

Personal safety **154**
Perugia, Hotel **169**
Piazza Barberini **159**
Piazza del Campidoglio (Capitoline Hill) **168**
Piazza del Popolo **157**
Piazza Navona **164**
Piazza San Pietro (St. Peter's Square) **155**
Piazza Venezia **167**
Pica ★★$$ **166**
Piccolo Arancio ★★$$ **160**
Piccolo, Hotel **166**
Pizzeria da Gildo ★★$ **167**
Pomezia, Albergo **166**
Popolo, Piazza del **157**
Postal services **154**
Primavera, Pensione **165**
Publications **154**
Public holidays **154**
Public rest rooms **154**

R
Ramirez **161**
Rampa, La **159**
Residence Guggioli $ **157**
Residenza Brotsky $ **157**
Restaurants **154**
Rest rooms, public **154**
Rinascente, La **160**
Roman Forum (Foro Romano) **168**
Romano, Hotel **169**
Rosati, Caffè **157**

S
Safety, personal **154**
St. Peter in Chains (San Pietro in Vincoli) **170**
St. Peter's Basilica (Basilica San Pietro) **156**
St. Peter's Square (Piazza San Pietro) **155**
San Clemente, Chiesa di **170**
Sangello **166**
San Giovanni in Laterno, Basilica di **170**
San Pietro in Vincoli (St. Peter in Chains) **170**
San Pietro, Piazza **155**
Santa Brigida, Casa Religiosa di **166**
Santa Maria in Trastevere **167**
Santa Maria Maggiore, Basilica di **170**
Santa Maria sopra Minerva, Chiesa di **164**
Sant'Angelo, Castel **157**
Sant'Eustachio, Bar **164**
Scalinata della Trinità dei Monti (Spanish Steps) **158**
Shopping **154**
Sistine Chapel **156**
Smeraldo, Hotel **166**
Smoking **155**
Sole, Albergo del **165**
Spanish Steps (Scalinata della Trinità dei Monti) **158**
Street plan **155**
Subway **153**
Suisse, Hotel Pensione **159**
Suore Francescane dell'Antonement (Franciscan Sisters of the Atonement) $ **157**

T
Taxes **155**
Taxis **153**
Tazza d'Oro, Caffè **161**

Telephones **155**
Terme di Diocleziano (Baths of Diocletian) and the Museo Nazionale Romano (National Museum of Rome) **169**
The Appian Way (Via Appia) **171**
Tickets, discount **153**
Tipping **155**
Tours **153**
Trains **152**
Transportation, local **152**
Trevi Fountain (Fontana di Trevi) **160**
Trinità dei Monti **158**

U
Uno al Portico d'Ottavia ★★$$ **163**

V
Vatican City (Città del Vaticano) **155**
Vatican Galleries and Museums (Galerie e Musei Vaticani) **156**
Venezia, Piazza **167**
Vertecchi **158**
Via Appia (The Appian Way) and the Catacombs **171**
Via Cola di Rienzo **157**
Via del Corso **160**
Via Ottaviano **157**
Vignola **157**
Villa Borghese **157**
Villia Giulia National Museum (Museo Nazionale di Villa Giulia) **157**
Vini e Buffet ★★$ **161**
Visas **155**
Visitors' Information Centers **155**

W
Walking **153**

Y
YWCA $ **170**

Rome Restaurants

★★★
Ai Tre Tartufi $$ **164**
La Buca di Ripetta $$ **158**

★★
Bar Sant'Eustachio $ **164**
Caffè Rosati $$ **157**
Da Lucia $ **167**
Filettaro Santa Barbara $ **166**
Gran Caffè-Europeo $ **161**
Hostaria da Nerone $$ **170**
Il Dito e la Luna $$ **170**
La Rampa $$ **159**
L'Artusiana $$ **167**
M&M Volpetti $ **164**
Otello alla Concordia $$ **158**
Pica $$ **166**
Piccolo Arancio $$ **160**
Pizzeria da Gildo $ **167**
Uno al Portico d'Ottavia $$ **163**
Vini e Buffet $ **161**

★
Alemagna $ **161**
Al Piedone $ **163**
Enoteca Cavour 313 $ **169**
Giolitti $ **161**
Grappolo d'Oro $$ **165**
Hostaria Farnese $$ **165**
Il Delfino $ **163**

La Moretta $ **165**
Pasticceria d'Angelo $ **158**

Rome Hotels

$$
Campo dei Fiori **165**
Casa Religiosa di Santa Brigida **166**
Hotel Celio **170**
Hotel Doge **159**
Pensione Erdarelli **19**

$
Albergo Abruzzi **161**
Albergo della Luneta **165**
Albergo del Sole **165**
Albergo Pomezia **166**
Coronet Hotel **161**
Fraterna Domus **161**
Hotel Alimandi **156**
Hotel Arenula **163**
Hotel Marcus **161**
Hotel Margutta **158**
Hotel Navona **163**
Hotel Pensione Merano **159**
Hotel Pensione Suisse **159**
Hotel Perugia **169**
Hotel Piccolo **166**
Hotel Romano **169**
Hotel Smeraldo **166**
Ostello del Foro Italico **171**
Pensione Esty **167**
Pensione Fiorella **157**
Pensione Manara **167**
Pensione Mimosa **164**
Pensione Parlamento **160**
Pensione Primavera **165**
Residence Guggioli **157**
Residenza Brotsky **157**
Suore Francescane dell'Antonement **157**
YWCA **170**

Venice

A
Accademia Museum (Galleria dell'Accademia) **180**
Accommodations **175**
Agli Alboretti $$ **181**
Agli Alboretti ★$$ **181**
Ai Do Mori ★★$ **186**
Ai Do Moro, Bar **189**
Airports **174**
Ai Rusteghi, Osteria **188**
Antica Adelaide, Trattoria all' **188**
Al Bacareto ★$$ **180**
Alberto, Osteria da **188**
A Le Do Spade/Trattoria ★★$ **186**
Alla Madonna ★★$$ **185**
Alla Salute da Cici $ **181**
Anticlea Antiquariato **190**
Antico Capon $ **183**
Antico Dolo, L' **185**
Arsenale **190**
Aulenti, Gae **180**

B
Bar Ai Do Moro ★$ **189**
Basilica di San Marco (St. Mark's Basilica) **177**
Botteghe, Osteria alle **180**
Bucintoro, Hotel **191**
Business hours **175**

Index

C
Ca'd'Oro/Galleria Franchetti **187**
Caffè Chioggia ★★$$ **178**
Calcina, La **182**
Campiello $$ **190**
Campo del Ghetto (The Ghetto) **187**
Campo Santa Margherita **183**
Campo Santo Stefano (St. Stephen's Square) **180**
Canada $ **188**
Ca'Pesaro—Museo d'Arte Moderna and Museo d'Arte Orientale (Museum of Modern Art and Museum of Oriental Art) **186**
Ca'Rezzonico—Museo del Settecento Veneziano (Museum of 18th-Century Venice) **183**
Casa Fontana $$ **190**
Chiesa and Scuola Grande dei Carmini (Church and Great School of the Carmelites) **183**
Chiesa dei Frari (Church of the Friars) **184**
Chiesa della Pietà (Church of the Pieta) **190**
Chiesa di Santa Maria Formosa (Church of St. Mary of Formosa) **189**
Chiesa di Santissimi Giovanni e Paolo (Church of Sts. John and Paul) **188**
Chioggia, Caffè **178**
Church and Great School of the Carmelites (Chiesa and Scuola Grande dei Carmini) **183**
Church of St. Mary of Formosa (Chiesa di Santa Maria Formosa) **189**
Church of Sts. John and Paul (Chiesa di Santissimi Giovanni e Paolo) **188**
Church of the Friars (Chiesa dei Frari) **184**
Church of the Pieta (Chiesa della Pietà) **190**
Cip Ciap **189**
Climate **175**
Clock Tower (Torre dell'Orologio) **178**
Codussi, Mauro **178, 189**
COIN **188**
Collezione Peggy Guggenheim (Peggy Guggenheim Museum) **181**
Consulates **175**
Correr Museum (Museo Correr) **178**
Cugnai, Trattoria ai **181**

D
Da Gianni ★★$$ **182**
Da Ponte, Antonio **185**
Da Sandro $ **185**
Discount tickets **175**
Doges' Palace (Palazzo Ducale) **177**
Domus Cavanis $ **181**
Domus Civica $ **184**
Doni $ **190**
Drinking **175**
Durell, Samantha **191** (bests)

E
Embassies **175**
Emergencies **175**

F
Falier, Hotel **184**
F.G.B. **180**
Fiorita, Locanda **180**
Flora $$ **179**

Fontana, Casa **190**
Foresteria Valdese $ **188**
Frari, Chiesa dei **184**
Fruit and Fish Market (Mercato della Frutta and Pescheria) **185**

G
Galleria dell'Accademia (Accademia Museum) **180**
Galleria Franchetti/Ca'd'Oro **187**
Gallini $$ **179**
Getting around Venice **174**
Getting to Venice **174**
Ghetto, Campo del **187**
Gianni & Luciana Pitacco **189**
Gobbo, Hotel al **187**
Gondolas **174**
Grassi, Palazzo **180**
Great School of St. Roch (Scuola Grande di San Rocco) **184**

H
Hesperia, Hotel **186**
Holidays, public **175**
Hotel al Gobbo $ **187**
Hotel Bucintoro $$ **191**
Hotel Falier $$ **184**
Hotel Hesperia $$ **186**
Hotel Messner $$ **181**
Hotel San Geremia $ **186**
Hotel Santa Lucia $ **186**
Hotel Tivoli $ **184**

I
Incontro, Ristorante L' **183**

J
Jewish Museum (Museo Ebraico) **187**

L
La Calcina $$ **182**
La Fenice Theater (Teatro La Fenice) **179**
L'Antico Dolo $ **185**
Latteria Zorzi ★$ **179**
Laundry **175**
La Zucca ★$$ **186**
Legatoria Piazzesi **180**
Le Mercerie **178**
Libreria Sangiorgio **179**
L'Incontro, Ristorante **183**
Locanda Fiorita $ **180**
Locanda Montin $ **183**
Locanda Remedio $ **189**
Locanda Sturion $$ **185**
Longhena, Baldassare **178, 181, 183, 186**

M
Map **172**
Marco Polo Airport **174**
Mascaron, Osteria al **189**
Massari, Giorgio **180, 183, 190**
Mensa Universitaria $ **184**
Mercato della Frutta and Pescheria (Fruit and Fish Market) **185**
Mercerie, Le **178**
Messner, Hotel **181**
Milion, Osteria al **188**
Mondonovo **183**
Money **175**
Montagnaro, Umberto **191** (bests)
Montin, Locanda **183**
Motoscafi **174**

Murano Art Shop **179**
Museo Correr (Correr Museum) **178**
Museo Ebraico (Jewish Museum) **187**
Museum of 18th-Century Venice (Ca'Rezzonico—Museo del Settecento Veneziano) **183**
Museum of Modern Art and Museum of Oriental Art (Ca'Pesaro—Museo d'Arte Moderna and Museo d'Arte Orientale) **186**

N
Noemi $ **179**
Non Risorto, Osteria al **186**

O
Ostello Santa Fosca $ **187**
Ostello Venezia $ **182**
Osteria Ai Rusteghi ★$ **188**
Osteria alle Botteghe ★$$ **180**
Osteria al Mascaron ★★$$ **189**
Osteria al Milion ★$$ **188**
Osteria al Non Risorto ★$ **186**
Osteria da Alberto ★$ **188**

P
Palazzo Ducale (Doges' Palace) **177**
Palazzo Grassi **180**
Paolo, Ristorante da **191**
Patronato Salesiano $ **191**
Peggy Guggenheim Museum (Collezione Peggy Guggenheim) **181**
Pensione Seguso $$ **182**
Personal safety **175**
Piazzale Roma **185**
Piazza San Marco (St. Mark's Square) **177**
Pietà, Chiesa della **190**
Pizzeria alle Oche ★★$ **185**
Pizzeria al Sole di Napoli ★$ **183**
Ponte di Rialto (Rialto Bridge) **185**
Postal services **175**
Procuratie **178**
Publications **175**
Public holidays **175**
Public rest rooms **175**

R
Remedio, Locanda **189**
Renzo Marega **189**
Restaurants **176**
Rest rooms, public **175**
Rialta **185**
Rialto Bridge (Ponte di Rialto) **185**
Ristorante da Paolo ★$$ **191**
Ristorante L'Incontro ★$ **183**
Ristorante Riviera ★$$ **182**
Ristorante Wildner ★$ **190**
Riva $ **189**
Roma, Piazzale **185**
Rosticceria San Bartolomeo ★★$ **188**

S
Safety, personal **175**
St. Mark's Basilica (Basilica di San Marco) **177**
St. Mark's Square (Piazza San Marco) **177**
St. Mary of Good Health (Santa Maria della Salute) **181**
St. Stephen's Square (Campo Santo Stefano) **180**
Sangiorgio, Libreria **179**
San Geremia, Hotel **186**

222

Index

Sansovino, Jacopo **177, 178**
Santa Fosca, Ostello **187**
Santa Lucia, Hotel **186**
Santa Margherita, Campo **183**
Santa Maria della Salute (St. Mary of Good Health) **181**
Santa Maria Formosa, Chiesa di **189**
Santissimi Giovanni e Paolo, Chiesa di **188**
San Tomà, Trattoria **185**
Santo Stefano, Campo **180**
San Trovaso Boatyard (Squero di San Trovaso) **182**
Scuola di San Giorgio degli Schiavoni (School of St. George of the Dalmatians) **190**
Scuola Grande dei Carmini, Chiesa and **183**
Scuola Grande di San Rocco (Great School of St. Roch) **184**
Seguso, Pensione **182**
Shopping **176**
Smoking **176**
Squero di San Trovaso (San Trovaso Boatyard) **182**
Street plan **176**
Sturion, Locanda **185**

T
Taxes **176**
Taxi Acqueo **174**
Teatro La Fenice (La Fenice Theater) **179**
Telephones **176**
The Ghetto (Campo del Ghetto) **187**
Tickets, discount **175**
Tipping **176**
Tivoli, Hotel **184**
Torre dell'Orologio (Clock Tower) **178**
Trains **174**
Transportation, local **174**
Trattoria ai Cugnai ★**$$ 181**
Trattoria all'Antica Adelaide ★**$$ 188**
Trattoria dalla Vedova ★★**$ 187**
Trattoria San Tomà ★★**$$ 185**

U
Union $ **186**

V
Vaporetti **174**
Vedova, Trattoria dalla **187**
Venezia, Ostello **182**
Vino Vino ★★$ **179**
Visas **176**
Visitors' Information Centers **176**

W
Walking **174**
Wildner $$ **190**
Wildner, Ristorante **190**

Z
Zucca, La **186**

Venice Restaurants
★★
Ai Do Mori $ **186**
A Le Do Spade/Trattoria $ **186**
Alla Madonna $$ **185**
Caffè Chioggia $$ **178**
Da Gianni $$ **182**
Osteria Ai Rusteghi $ **188**

Osteria al Mascaron $$ **189**
Pizzeria alle Oche $ **185**
Rosticceria San Bartolomeo $ **188**
Trattoria dalla Vedova $ **187**
Trattoria San Tomà $$ **185**
Vino Vino $ **179**

★
Agli Alboretti $$ **181**
Al Bacareto $$ **180**
Bar Ai Do Moro $ **189**
Latteria Zorzi $ **179**
La Zucca $$ **186**
Osteria alle Botteghe $$ **180**
Osteria al Milion $$ **188**
Osteria al Non Risorto $ **186**
Osteria da Alberto $ **188**
Pizzeria al Sole di Napoli $ **183**
Ristorante da Paolo $$ **191**
Ristorante L'Incontro $ **183**
Ristorante Riviera $$ **182**
Ristorante Wildner $ **190**
Trattoria ai Cugnai $$ **181**
Trattoria all'Antica Adelaide $$ **188**

Venice Hotels
$$
Agli Alboretti **181**
Campiello **190**
Casa Fontana **190**
Flora **179**
Gallini **179**
Hotel Bucintoro **191**
Hotel Falier **184**
Hotel Hesperia **186**
Hotel Messner **181**
La Calcina **182**
Locanda Sturion **185**
Pensione Seguso **182**
Wildner **190**

$
Alla Salute da Cici **181**
Antico Capon **183**
Canada **188**
Domus Cavanis **181**
Domus Civica **184**
Doni **190**
Foresteria Valdese **188**
Hotel al Gobbo **187**
Hotel San Geremia **186**
Hotel Santa Lucia **186**
Hotel Tivoli **184**
Locanda Fiorita **180**
Locanda Montin **183**
Locanda Remedio **189**
Noemi **179**
Ostello Santa Fosca **187**
Ostello Venezia **182**
Patronato Salesiano **191**
Riva **189**
Union **186**

Zurich
A
Accommodations **194**
Airports **193**
Augustinergasse **199**

B
Babalu **200**
Bal, Le **198**

Basilea, Hotel **200**
Bauschänzli ★★$$ **198**
Bellerive, Museum **204**
Beyer's Museum of Time Measurement (Museum der Zeitmessung Beyer) **199**
Bicycles **193**
Bistretto ★$ **197**
Bluntschi the Elder **201**
Bührle, Sammlung E.G. **204**
Bürkliplatz **198**
Buses **193**
Business hours **194**

C
Café St. Gotthard, Le **197**
Café Schober ★★$ **201**
Café Select **201**
Calatrava, Santiago **203**
Camping Platz Seebucht **205**
Casa Bar **201**
Chässtube ★★$$ **198**
Chinese Garden **204**
Churrasco Steakhouse ★$$ **199**
Climate **194**
Commihalle ★★★$$ **199**
Consulates **194**
Corbusier, Le **204**

D
Dézaley, the Cave Vaudoise ★★★$$$ **201**
Dolmetsch Cutlery **197**
Drinking **194**
Driving **193**

E
E.G. Bührle Collection (Sammlung E.G. Bührle) **204**
Embassies **194**
Emergencies **194**
EPA **205**

F
Felder the Elder **201**
Fellner and Helmer **204**
Fraumünster **198**
Funicular, Polybahn **199**

G
Gessnerallee ★★★$$ **197**
Getting around Zurich **193**
Getting to Zurich **193**
Gitano ★★$$ **200**
Gleich ★★$$ **204**
Grossmünster **201**
Gull, Gustav **195**

H
Hauptbahnhof (Main Train Station) **195**
Haus Zum Rüden ★★$$$ **201**
Heidi Weber Haus **204**
Heimatwerk **199**
Helmhaus **201**
Herbert, Emma **206** (bests)
Hilti Restaurant ★★★$ **198**
Holidays, public **194**
Hotel Basilea $$ **200**
Hotel Krone $$ **200**
Hotel Limmathof $$ **199**
Hotel Schäfli $$ **200**
Hotel Seefeld $$ **204**
Hotel Splendid $$ **200**
Hotel Villette $$ **203**

223

Index

J
James Joyce Pub ★$$ **198**
Jules Verne Bar/Observatory **197**

K
Kaufleuten **198**
Kloten Airport **193**
Kollektiv Cafe Zähringer ★★$$ **200**
Kon-tiki **200**
Krone, Hotel **200**
Kronenhalle ★★★★$$ **203**
Kunsthalle Zürich (Zurich Modern Art Museum) **204**

L
Landesmuseum (Swiss National Museum) **195**
Langstrasse **205**
Language **194**
Laundry **194**
Le Bal **198**
Le Café St. Gotthard ★★★$$ **197**
Le Corbusier **204**
Le Petit Prince **205**
Le Philosophe **201**
Leuthold, Rosmarie **206** (bests)
Limmatbar **200**
Limmathof, Hotel **199**
Limmatschiff **195**
Lindenhof **199**
Lion's Pub ★★$ **197**

M
Malatesta **200**
Maps **192, 196**
Martahaus $ **200**
Mascotte **203**
McDonald's ★$ **197**
Mère Catherine and Le Philosophe ★★★$$ **201**
Migros City **197**
Money **194**
Mövenpick, Restaurant **199**
Museum Bellerive **204**
Museum der Zeitmessung Beyer (Beyer's Museum of Time Measurement) **199**
Museum of Habitation (Wohnmuseum Bärengasses) **198**
Museum Rietberg **205**

O
Odeon **203**
Oliver Twist Pub **201**
Opern Haus Zürich (Opera House) **204**

P
Pedestrian Gallery **199**
Pension St. Josef $$ **203**
Personal safety **194**
Petit Prince, Le **205**
Philosophe, Le **201**
Pigalle Bar **201**
Pitta-Inn ★★$ **198**
Platz Seebucht, Camping **205**
Polybahn Funicular **199**
Postal services **194**
Predigerkirche (Preachers' Church) **200**
Pub, The **199**
Publications **194**
Public holidays **194**
Public rest rooms **194**
Public transportation **193**

R
Rathaus **201**
Restaurant Mövenpick ★★$$ **199**
Restaurants **194**
Rest rooms, public **194**
Rheinfelder Bierhalle ★$ **200**
Rietberg, Museum **205**
Römischer Bad (Roman Baths) **199**
Rote Fabrik **205**

S
Safety, personal **194**
St. George's Hotel $$ **205**
St. Gotthard, Le Café **197**
St. Josef, Pension **203**
St. Peter's **199**
Sammlung E.G. Bührle (E.G. Bührle Collection) **204**
Schäfli, Hotel **200**
Schlauch **201**
Schober, Café **201**
Schönberg, Villa **205**
Seefeld, Hotel **204**
Seefeldstrasse **204**
Select, Café **201**
Seppänen, Raisa **206** (bests)
Shopping **194**
Smoking **195**
Spaghetti Factory ★★★$$ **200**
Spanische Weinhalle ★★★$$ **201**
Splendid, Hotel **200**
Sprüngli **198**
Stadelhofen Bahnhof (Train Station) **203**
Stadthausquai Frauenbad **198**
Stäheli Bookshop **197**
Street plan **195, 196** (map)
Swiss National Museum (Landesmuseum) **195**

T
Taxes **195**
Taxis **193**
Telephones **195**
Teuscher **199**
The Pub ★★$$ **199**
Tipping **195**
Tonhalle **198**
Tours **194**
Trains **193, 195, 203**
Train Station, Main (Hauptbahnhof) **195**
Train Station (Stadelhofen Bahnhof) **203**
Transportation, local **193**
Transportation, public **193**
Tres Kilos ★★★$$ **204**

U
Uetliberg **205**
Universität Zurich **203**
Utoquai Badanstalt **204**

V
Vilan **197**
Villa Schönberg **205**
Villette, Hotel **203**
Visas **195**
Visitors' Information Centers **195**
Vorderer Sternen ★★$ **203**

W
Walking **194**
Walliser Kanne ★★★$$ **197**
Wasserkirche (Water Church) **201**
Wohnmuseum Bärengasses (Museum of Habitation) **198**

Y
Youth Hostel, Zurich **205**

Z
Zähringer, Kollektiv Cafe **200**
Zeitmessung Beyer, Museum der **199**
Zeughaus Keller ★★$$ **199**
Zunfthaus zur Meisen **198**
Züri Bar **200**
Zurichhorn **204**
Zurich Kunsthaus (Zurich Art Museum) **203**
Zurich Modern Art Museum (Kunsthalle Zürich) **204**
Zurich Youth Hostel $ **205**

Zurich Restaurants

★★★★
Kronenhalle $$ **203**

★★★
Commihalle $$ **199**
Dézaley, the Cave Vaudoise $$$ **201**
Gessnerallee $$ **197**
Gitano $$ **200**
Hilti Restaurant $ **198**
Le Café St. Gotthard $$ **197**
Mère Catherine and Le Philosophe $$ **201**
Spaghetti Factory $$ **200**
Spanische Weinhalle $$ **201**
Tres Kilos $$ **204**
Walliser Kanne $$ **197**

★★
Bauschänzli $$ **198**
Café Schober $ **201**
Chässtube $$ **198**
Gleich $$ **204**
Haus Zum Rüden $$$ **201**
Kollektiv Cafe Zähringer $$ **200**
Lion's Pub $ **197**
Pitta-Inn $ **198**
Restaurant Mövenpick $$ **199**
The Pub $$ **199**
Vorderer Sternen $ **203**
Zeughaus Keller $$ **199**

★
Bistretto $ **197**
Churrasco Steakhouse $$ **199**
James Joyce Pub $$ **198**
McDonald's $ **197**
Rheinfelder Bierhalle $ **200**

Zurich Hotels

$$
Hotel Basilea **200**
Hotel Krone **200**
Hotel Limmathof **199**
Hotel Schäfli **200**
Hotel Seefeld **204**
Hotel Splendid **200**
Hotel Villette **203**
Pension St. Josef **203**
St. George's Hotel **205**

$
Martahaus **200**
Zurich Youth Hostel **205**